Statistical Indicators of Cyclical Revivals and Recessions

GEOFFREY H. MOORE

OCCASIONAL PAPER 31

NATIONAL BUREAU OF ECONOMIC RESEARCH, INC.

Statistical Indicators of Cyclical Revivals and Recessions

GEOFFREY H. MOORE

Occasional Paper 31
NATIONAL BUREAU OF ECONOMIC RESEARCH, INC.
1950

PRICE: $1.50

COPYRIGHT, 1950, BY
NATIONAL BUREAU OF ECONOMIC RESEARCH, INC.
1819 BROADWAY, NEW YORK 23, N. Y.

ALL RIGHTS RESERVED

DESIGNER: EUGENE M. ETTENBERG
MANUFACTURED IN THE U. S. A. BY
THE GALLERY PRESS, NEW YORK

OFFICERS

Boris Shishkin, *Chairman*
Harry Scherman, *President*
C. C. Balderston, *Vice-President*
George B. Roberts, *Treasurer*
W. J. Carson, *Executive Director*
Martha Anderson, *Editor*

DIRECTORS AT LARGE

D. R. Belcher, *American Telephone & Telegraph Co.*
Oswald W. Knauth, *New York City*
Simon Kuznets, *University of Pennsylvania*
H. W. Laidler, *Executive Director, League for Industrial Democracy*
Shepard Morgan, *New York City*
C. Reinold Noyes, *New York City*
George B. Roberts, *Vice-President, National City Bank*
Beardsley Ruml, *New York City*
Harry Scherman, *President, Book-of-the-Month Club*
George Soule, *Bennington College*
N. I. Stone, *Consulting Economist*
J. Raymond Walsh, *WMCA Broadcasting Co.*
Leo Wolman, *Columbia University*
Theodore O. Yntema, *Vice President-Finance, Ford Motor Company*

DIRECTORS BY UNIVERSITY APPOINTMENT

E. Wight Bakke, *Yale*
C. C. Balderston, *Pennsylvania*
Arthur F. Burns, *Columbia*
G. A. Elliott, *Toronto*
Frank W. Fetter, *Northwestern*
H. M. Groves, *Wisconsin*
Gottfried Haberler, *Harvard*
Clarence Heer, *North Carolina*
R. L. Kozelka, *Minnesota*
Paul M. O'Leary, *Cornell*
T. W. Schultz, *Chicago*

DIRECTORS APPOINTED BY OTHER ORGANIZATIONS

Percival F. Brundage, *American Institute of Accountants*
Thomas C. Cochran, *Economic History Association*
Frederick C. Mills, *American Statistical Association*
S. H. Ruttenberg, *Congress of Industrial Organizations*
Murray Shields, *American Management Association*
Boris Shishkin, *American Federation of Labor*
Warren C. Waite, *American Farm Economic Association*
Donald H. Wallace, *American Economic Association*

RESEARCH STAFF

Arthur F. Burns, *Director of Research*
Geoffrey H. Moore, *Associate Director of Research*

Moses Abramovitz
Harold Barger
Morris A. Copeland
Daniel Creamer
David Durand
Solomon Fabricant
Milton Friedman
Millard Hastay
W. Braddock Hickman
F. F. Hill
Thor Hultgren
Simon Kuznets
Clarence D. Long
Ruth P. Mack
Frederick C. Mills
Raymond J. Saulnier
Lawrence H. Seltzer
George J. Stigler
Leo Wolman

This paper is a product of the thought and labor of many individuals in the Business Cycle unit of the National Bureau, and of a number outside that group. Arthur F. Burns collaborated on the project when it began several years ago, and guided it over much of its course. The manuscript has benefited from his suggestions in innumerable ways. Much of the statistical work was directed by Millard Hastay, who also aided in developing the criteria described in Section 4. Florence Robinson, Sophie Sakowitz, and Johanna Stern were largely responsible for the compilations and calculations, and Milton Lipton assisted in constructing the methods illustrated in Appendix A. W. Braddock Hickman gave generously of his time in planning certain IBM tabulations used in Section 6, and commented upon the manuscript. I have benefited, too, from the comments of Moses Abramovitz, Martha Anderson, Elmer C. Bratt, Daniel Creamer, Thor Hultgren, Frederick C. Mills, George B. Roberts, and Leo Wolman. The charts were drawn by H. Irving Forman. It is a pleasure to record my indebtedness to all these individuals and to the late Wesley C. Mitchell, who laid the foundation for this and many future studies of business cycles.

G. H. M.

Contents

1	Aim of the Study and Summary of Findings	1
2	An Experiment with Indicators	3
3	Varieties of Cyclical Behavior and Their Consensus	8
4	Criteria for Selecting Indicators	20
5	Classification of Series According to Conformity and Timing	31
6	Behavior of Selected Groups of Indicators, 1885-1940	45
7	A Tentative List of Current Indicators	63

APPENDIX

A	A Technique for Summarizing the Current Behavior of Groups of Indicators	78
B	List of Series with Acceptable Conformity and Timing, in Three Timing Groups	92

TABLE

1	Reference Dates and Durations of Business Cycles, United States, 1854-1938	6
2	Cyclical Timing of 21 Statistical Indicators	7
3	Conformity Measures, Seven Series	27
4	Timing Measures, Five Series	29
5	Classification of All Series Examined for Acceptability as Indicators	34
6	Percentage of Series with Acceptable Conformity and Timing, by Economic Groups	36
7	Percentage of Series with Acceptable Conformity and Timing: Prices, Production, Employment, and Payrolls	37
8	Distribution of Acceptable Series by Timing Classifications Based upon the Full Period Covered and on 1919-1938	40
9	Timing Observations Before and After 1919, Two Groups of Series	42
10	Timing of Percentage of Series Expanding and Contracting in Successive Business Cycles, 1879-1938, Two Groups of Series	46
11	Timing of Medians of Corresponding Specific Cycle Turns, 1885-1938, Three Groups of Series	55

TABLE

12	Record of Timing of Selected Statistical Indicators at Business Cycle Turns	64
13	Chronology of Postwar Peaks in Selected Statistical Indicators	74
A1	Measures of Timing and Smoothness of Fifteen Statistical Indicators	80
A2	Distribution of Fifteen Indicators by Duration of Run in Moving Averages	82
A3	Duration of Run in Moving Averages, Seven Leading and Eight Roughly Coincident Indicators	86
A4	Timing of Cumulated Percentage Expanding and Cumulated Average Duration of Run, Two Groups of Indicators, 1920-1938	87

CHART

1	Behavior of Twenty-one Statistical Indicators, 1932-1939	4
2	Reference Cycle Patterns of Seven Series, 1919-1938	10
3	Percentage of Series Reaching Specific Cycle Peaks and Troughs and Percentage Expanding, All Series with 'Acceptable' Conformity	14
4	Number of Series Reaching Specific Cycle Peaks and Troughs, Three Groups of Series	50
5	Percentage of Series Expanding, Three Groups of Series	58
6	Behavior of Selected Statistical Indicators, 1936-1949	70
7	Percentage Expanding, All Series with 'Acceptable' Conformity; Average Duration of Run, 15 Series	84
8	Cumulated Percentage Expanding, All Series with 'Acceptable' Conformity; Cumulated Average Duration of Run, 15 Series; FRB Index of Industrial Production	85
9	Average Duration of Run, 7 Leading and 8 Roughly Coincident Series	88
10	Cumulated Average Duration of Run, 7 Leading and 8 Roughly Coincident Series	89

1
AIM OF THE STUDY AND SUMMARY OF FINDINGS

In December 1937, in response to a request by a public agency, the National Bureau undertook a brief study, based upon materials already at hand, of statistical indicators of cyclical revivals. At that time the economy was experiencing a sharp business contraction. For many years the Bureau had been analyzing time series—monthly, quarterly, and annual—on a wide variety of economic processes, in order to achieve a better understanding of how business cycles come about. Consequently, a considerable fund of information was available to answer the question, what statistical series are most likely to give some sign of the approaching end of a business contraction?

Wesley C. Mitchell and Arthur F. Burns proceeded to apply certain objective criteria to approximately 500 monthly or quarterly series, and selected 71 that on the basis of performance promised to be fairly reliable indicators of revival. A closer screening of the 71 yielded 21 series that were deemed the most trustworthy. In May 1938 the series were listed in 'Statistical Indicators of Cyclical Revivals' (*Bulletin 69*), together with an explanation of the criteria of selection and a record of the cyclical behavior of each series.

The measures of behavior upon which the selection was based were for different periods, depending upon when the particular series became available. The longest series went back to 1854 and covered 21 revivals; many began in 1919 and covered only 5 revivals. The measures ended with 1933, the last revival before the study was made. The National Bureau has since added many series to its collection, revised the measures of cyclical behavior, and extended them through the business cycle of 1933-38.[1] Because many series cover only a few cycles, the addition of even a single cycle materially increases our information on cyclical behavior. Also, the numerous political and economic changes after 1933 make it important that the experience of this period be considered. Hence it seems desirable now to revise the list of in-

[1] We have not as yet determined the turning points of any business cycle since 1938; see, however, Sec. 7.

dicators of revivals and to extend the analysis to recessions. That is the immediate aim of this study.

We have also a broader objective: to exhibit some of the differences among economic processes in respect of their role in business cycles. While we cannot undertake to account for the differences here, we can demonstrate their existence and indicate their nature. To know what are the leading and the lagging processes, and to have some measures of their performance in successive cycles, is fundamental to an understanding of business cycles.

This report is preliminary. We have not applied as many objective criteria to the selection of indicators as we plan to, and further work on problems connected with the use and interpretation of indicators is in progress. Nevertheless, the investigation points to certain general conclusions, with which we may acquaint the reader at the outset. These conclusions, and the sections of the report in which they are developed, are:

1) Economic processes, as represented by monthly and quarterly time series, differ widely in the timing of their fluctuations during business cycles. While there is a strong tendency for many processes to expand and contract at about the same time, in every cycle the cyclical turning points of different series are rather widely dispersed. For example, of 400 series especially selected for the regularity of their behavior during business cycles seldom more than 80 percent were undergoing cyclical expansion (or contraction) at any time between 1885 and 1940. Their peaks and troughs clustered around peaks and troughs in aggregate economic activity, but each cluster was spread over a year or two or three. Indeed, by the time the last few series in a cluster reached peaks, the first troughs in the next cluster had usually begun to appear. For examples and evidence see Sections 2 and 3.

2) By the application of objective criteria it is possible to select series whose timing in successive business cycles has been relatively systematic, and which therefore may be of value as indicators of revivals and recessions. That is, one can identify a group of series whose turning points have typically preceded the cyclical turns in aggregate economic activity; another group whose turns have typically coincided (roughly) with the turns in aggregate economic activity; and still another whose turns have typically followed those in aggregate economic activity. In many

cases the reasons for the differences in behavior of different series are apparent, though a thoroughgoing explanation may be lacking. In Section 4 we set forth the criteria so far adopted for selecting indicators, and in Section 5 describe the broad groups of series that appear to have useful indicator characteristics.

3) Series in all three timing groups (leaders, coinciders, and laggers), when interpreted in the light of their past behavior and economic significance, may prove useful in anticipating and identifying cyclical revivals and recessions. The evidence each type of series supplies serves to confirm or qualify that supplied by the others, and together they may be expected to provide helpful signs of an approaching recession or revival, and especially to facilitate prompt recognition of such a development once it occurs. These expectations are based upon study of the behavior of various groups of series in successive business cycles since 1885 (Sec. 2, 6, 7, and App. A). But this study also suggests that the interpretation of statistical indicators is subject to numerous difficulties and will often be attended by considerable uncertainty.

2

AN EXPERIMENT WITH INDICATORS

Our comprehension of, not to say interest in, the problem of selecting and using indicators can be advanced by performing a little experiment with the 21 indicators listed in *Bulletin 69*. As stated above, they were chosen on the basis of their behavior at revivals, the last revival considered being that of 1933. How did they behave at the next revival, in 1938? At the recession in 1937? Here we have a test of the validity of the selection.

One of the first steps in our analysis of a time series, once its seasonal variations have been removed, is to mark off what we call specific cycles. In a chart on which the entire series is plotted we look for broad swings in the data, of a duration (from peak to peak or trough to trough) roughly similar to that of business cycles, that is, two to ten or twelve years. Once we have identified the swings we date their turning points, aided in both processes by certain rules laid down in advance and applied uniformly to all series.[2] In Chart 1 the asterisks identify the specific cycle peaks and troughs of the 21 indicators in 1932-39.

At an early stage of the National Bureau's business cycle

[2] See Arthur F. Burns and Wesley C. Mitchell, *Measuring Business Cycles* (National Bureau of Economic Research, 1946), pp. 56-66.

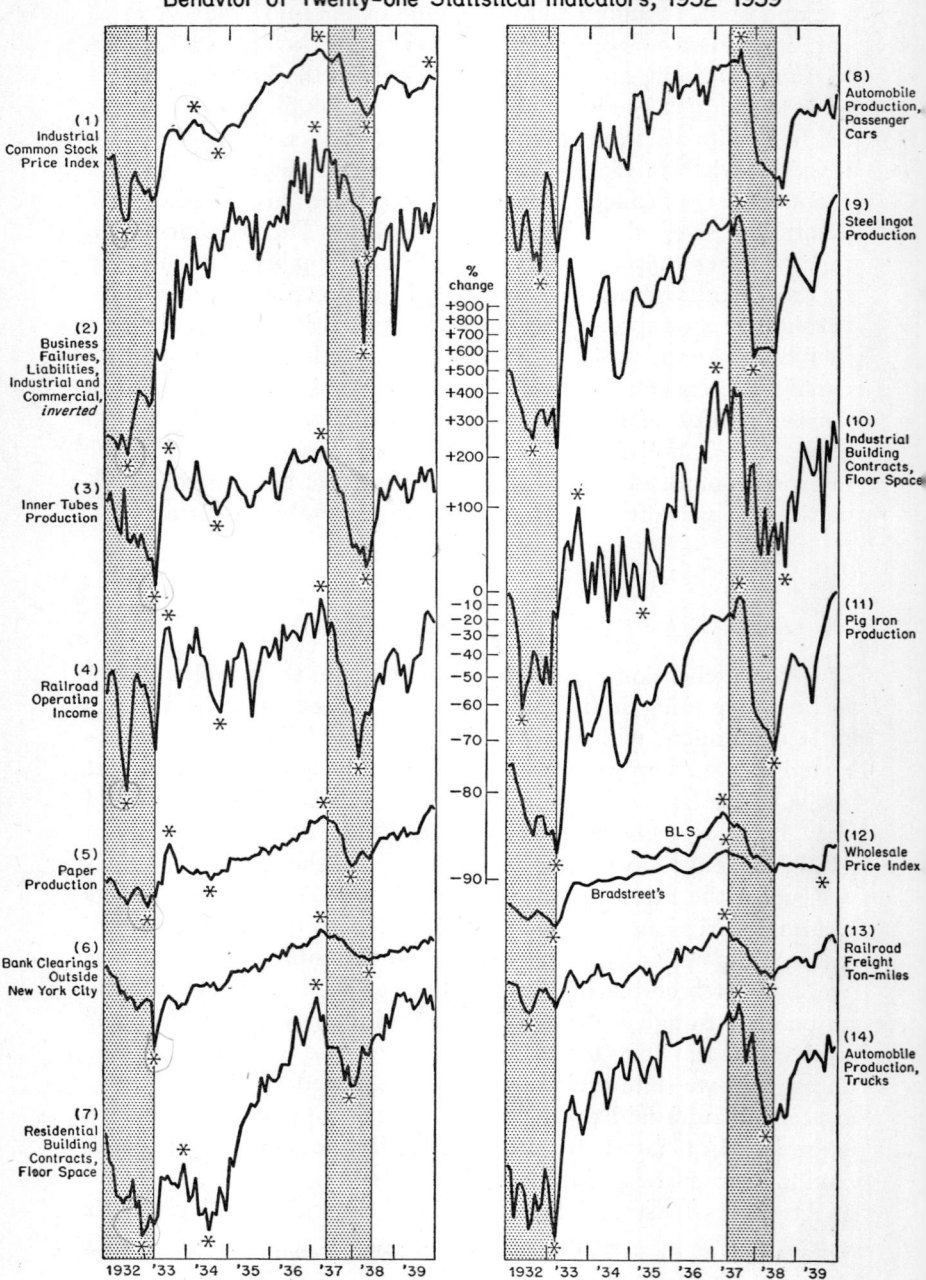

Chart 1
Behavior of Twenty-one Statistical Indicators, 1932–1939

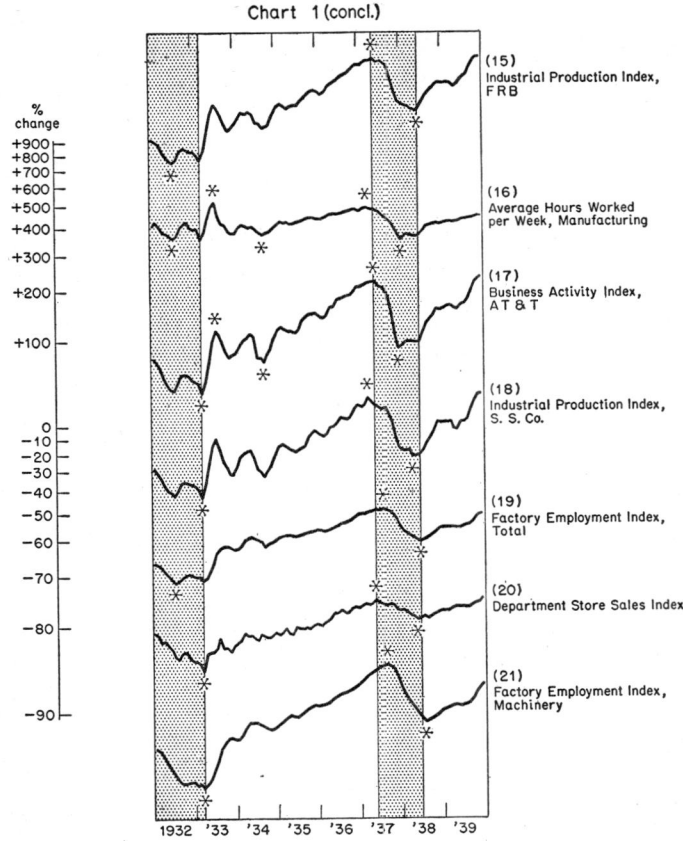

Chart 1 (concl.)

See note to Table 2. Series, except 1 and 12, are adjusted for seasonal variations. Shaded areas represent reference contractions; white areas, reference expansions. Asterisks identify peaks and troughs of specific cycles.

studies a need developed for a set of 'reference dates', or dates of peaks and troughs of business cycles—not merely to identify the object to be studied but more particularly to facilitate investigation of the interrelations among numerous time series. For example, rather than compare the dates of specific cycle peaks in each series of a group with those in every other series, it is ordinarily much simpler to compare each series' peaks with a standard set of dates, then compare the results for the different series. Also, the data for the period between any two successive reference troughs (or peaks) may be used to compute a cyclical pattern showing the movement of a given series, and since the period is the same for all series the patterns may be directly compared.

Consequently, after examining the movements of numerous economic time series and studying the contemporary reports of observers of the business scene, a set of reference dates was chosen which fairly represented the dates when expansions and contractions in general business activity culminated (Table 1). The reference dates occurring in 1932-39 bound the shaded areas in Chart 1.

The number of months by which the specific cycle peaks and troughs of the 21 indicators lead or lag behind the 1937-38 reference dates are entered in Table 2, together with the averages of similar entries for prior reference dates. Whether the results are considered favorable or unfavorable depends, of course, on one's expectations. Each of the indicators reached a peak that could be compared with the May 1937 reference peak and a

TABLE 1

Reference Dates and Durations of Business Cycles
United States, 1854-1938

MONTHLY REFERENCE DATES		DURATION IN MONTHS			QUARTERLY REFERENCE DATES	
Peak	Trough	Expansion[a]	Contraction[b]	Full Cycle	Peak	Trough
	Dec. 1854					4Q 1854
June 1857	Dec. 1858	30	18	48	2Q 1857	4Q 1858
Oct. 1860	June 1861	22	8	30	3Q 1860	3Q 1861
Apr. 1865	Dec. 1867	46	32	78	1Q 1865	1Q 1868
June 1869	Dec. 1870	18	18	36	2Q 1869	4Q 1870
Oct. 1873	Mar. 1879	34	65	99	3Q 1873	1Q 1879
Mar. 1882	May 1885	36	38	74	1Q 1882	2Q 1885
Mar. 1887	Apr. 1888	22	13	35	2Q 1887	1Q 1888
July 1890	May 1891	27	10	37	3Q 1890	2Q 1891
Jan. 1893	June 1894	20	17	37	1Q 1893	2Q 1894
Dec. 1895	June 1897	18	18	36	4Q 1895	2Q 1897
June 1899	Dec. 1900	24	18	42	3Q 1899	4Q 1900
Sep. 1902	Aug. 1904	21	23	44	4Q 1902	3Q 1904
May 1907	June 1908	33	13	46	2Q 1907	2Q 1908
Jan. 1910	Jan. 1912	19	24	43	1Q 1910	4Q 1911
Jan. 1913	Dec. 1914	12	23	35	1Q 1913	4Q 1914
Aug. 1918	Apr. 1919	44	8	52	3Q 1918	2Q 1919
Jan. 1920	July 1921	9	18	27	1Q 1920	3Q 1921
May 1923	July 1924	22	14	36	2Q 1923	3Q 1924
Oct. 1926	Nov. 1927	27	13	40	3Q 1926	4Q 1927
June 1929	Mar. 1933	19	45	64	2Q 1929	1Q 1933
May 1937	June 1938	50	13	63	2Q 1937	2Q 1938

Source: Arthur F. Burns and Wesley C. Mitchell, *Measuring Business Cycles*, Table 16. Three of the trough dates have been revised: from September to July 1921, from December to November 1927, and from May to June 1938.
[a] From trough on preceding line to peak.
[b] From peak to trough on same line.

6

trough that could be compared with the June 1938 reference trough. Series often fail in this respect, either by not having any corresponding cyclical movement or by having more than one in the same vicinity, though failures are less likely when the general contraction is sharp, as in 1937-38. Relatively few series, that is, exhibit one to one correspondence between their cycles and

TABLE 2

Cyclical Timing of Twenty-one Statistical Indicators

LEAD (—) OR LAG (+) IN MONTHS, AT BUSINESS CYCLE TURNS

SERIES AND REFERENCE PERIOD COVERED	Troughs before 1938 Range	Av.	June 1938 Trough	Peaks before 1937 Range	Av.	May 1937 Peak
1 Indus. stock price index, 1899-1938	—18 to +1	—8	—2	—21 to +3	—6	—3
2 Indus. & comm. failures, liab.,¹ 1882-1938w	—12 to +6	—7	—2	—23 to +2	—8	—4
3 Inner tube production, 1921-38	—12 to 0	—5	—2	—15 to —2	—9	—2
4 Railroad operating income, 1907-38w	—11 to +1	—5	—4	—7 to 0	—3	—2
5 Paper production, 1918-38	—10 to 0	—5	—6	—7 to 0	—3	—1
6 Bank clearings outside NYC, 1879-1938w	—10 to +6	—5	—1	—13 to +10	+1	—2
7 Resid. bldg. contracts, fl. space, 1919-38	—7 to 0	—4	—6	—16 to +8	—7	—3
8 Auto. production, passenger cars, 1914-38	—6 to 0	—4	+2	—10 to +7	—3	+3
9 Steel ingot production, 1899-1938	—13 to +1	—4	—6	—10 to +9	+1	+3
10 Indus. bldg. contracts, fl. space, 1919-38	—10 to 0	—3	+3	—4 to 0	—2	—4
11 Pig iron production, 1879-1938	—13 to +1	—3	0	—11 to +11	+2	+3
12 Wholesale price index, 1893-1938w	—11.5 to +5	—3	+14	—18 to +8	—3	—1
13 Railroad freight ton-miles, 1908-38	—10 to +1	—2	—1	—4 to +3	0	—1
14 Auto. production, trucks, 1913-38	—6 to 0	—2	—2	—13 to +8	—1	+3
15 Indus. production index, FRB, 1919-38	—8 to 0	—2	0	0 to +2	+1	0
16 Av. hours worked per week, mfg., 1921-38	—8 to +5	—2	—5	—11 to +4	—4	—2
17 Bus. activity index, AT&T, 1879-1938	—8 to +1	—2	—6	—15 to +9	—1	0
18 Indus. prod. index, S.S. Co., 1919-38	—4 to +1	—1	—2	—1 to +1	0	—2
19 Factory emp. index, total, 1914-38	—8 to +2	—1	0	—19 to +2	—5	+2
20 Department store sales index, 1919-38	0 to +5	+2	—1	+3 to +9	+5	0
21 Factory emp. index, machinery, 1919-38	0 to +3	+2	+1	0 to +2	+2	+3

SUMMARY

			NUMBER OF LEADS AND LAGS		
Leads		19	14		13	12
Coincidences			3		2	3
Lags		2	4		6	6

MEANS

Series 1– 7	—6	—3		—5	—2
Series 8–14	—3	+1		—1	+1
Series 15–21	—1	—2		0	0
Series 1–21	—3	—1		—2	0

MEDIANS

Series 1– 7	—5	—2		—6	—2
Series 8–14	—3	0		—1	+3
Series 15–21	—1	—1		0	0
Series 1–21	—3	—2		—2	—1

For sources and brief descriptions of the behavior of these series see *Bulletin 69*, pp. 8-10. The measures in this table, based on our latest analyses, differ slightly from those given in the bulletin. Series 2 (Bradstreet's) was discontinued in January 1933; the similar compilation by Dun is used thereafter. Series 12 (Bradstreet's index) was discontinued in November 1937; the BLS index of wholesale prices of 28 basic commodities, which begins in 1935, is used here to determine the 1938 trough (see Sec. 7).

[1] Inverted; see note 9.

w War cycle observations (timing comparisons at the 1918 peak, 1919 trough, and 1920 peak) are omitted.

business cycles. Eight of our 21, indeed, had an 'extra' contraction in 1933-35, as the chart reveals.

At the 1938 revival the turning points are fairly closely bunched a few months in advance of the reference trough; the leads are less numerous at the 1937 peak, but that is what one would expect from the averages. The sequences that might be inferred from the average timing at preceding peaks or troughs were, however, only roughly followed at the 1937 peak and the 1938 trough, and the fallibility of single series as indicators is evident. As will be shown more fully below, at every cyclical turn some of the series that typically lead are likely to lag. Moreover, while on the whole the series confirm one another in indicating a recession about May 1937 and a revival about June 1938, the chart exhibits many little puzzles that would have plagued, and no doubt did plague, contemporary observers of month by month developments.

3

VARIETIES OF CYCLICAL BEHAVIOR AND THEIR CONSENSUS

Chart 1 and Table 2 demonstrate, in some degree, the varieties of cyclical behavior to be found in economic processes. The 21 series differ in their amplitude of cyclical fluctuation, in their smoothness or freedom from erratic movements, in the general pattern of their movement during 1932-39, in the timing of their fluctuations relative to business cycles. The problem of selecting statistical indicators of business cycles is essentially to systematize this variety, so that it may be put to use.

The variety that actually exists in statistical records far exceeds that exhibited in the table and chart. A more extensive view will be provided by the materials presented in subsequent sections of this report.[3] Meanwhile it may be helpful to examine a small sample of series selected for the diversity of their behavior. Chart 2 shows 'reference cycle patterns' of 7 monthly series during 5 successive business cycles, 1919-38, together with their average patterns for this period. Two of the 7, residential building contracts and the industrial production index, are from the 21 indicators of Chart 1; the rest are different.

[3] A still more comprehensive analysis of varieties of cyclical behavior will be presented in Wesley C. Mitchell's forth-coming volume, *What Happens during Business Cycles*.

Since we shall have occasion later to use measures based upon reference cycle patterns, an understanding of how they are computed is essential. First, the monthly seasonally adjusted series is divided into so-called reference cycle segments—the intervals between successive reference troughs. Next we compute the average standing of the series during each segment, and express the monthly figures as percentages of this base. These percentages are called 'reference cycle relatives'. This step reduces the original data for every series to a common unit, so that series expressed in diverse units may be compared. The third step is to compute a 9-point pattern for each reference cycle segment by breaking the segment into 9 stages and computing the average of the relatives for each stage. Stage I covers the three months centered on the initial trough, stage V the three months centered on the peak, and stage IX the three months centered on the terminal trough. Stages II, III, and IV cover successive thirds of the length of the expansion, and stages VI, VII, and VIII successive thirds of the contraction. By averaging the reference cycle relatives for the months included in each stage we get the reference cycle patterns plotted in Chart 2.[4] Finally, the 9-point patterns for a series may be averaged over as many cycles as the series covers, or any subset. The averages in Chart 2 are confined to the five cycles of 1919-38, though some series cover earlier cycles.

Let us examine first these average patterns. The pattern for residential building contracts declines before the expansion in general business activity ends and rises in the later stages of the general contraction. The index of industrial production moves roughly synchronously with the ebb and flow of general business. Deliveries of railroad locomotives fluctuate widely and lag at both peaks and troughs. Failures of manufacturing enterprises, measured by their liabilities, decline as prosperity advances and rise in depression, but tend to lead. Their average pattern is almost an inverted replica of that of residential building contracts. Stocks of refined copper also are 'inverted', declining steadily as business expands and rising when it contracts, neither leading nor lagging perceptibly. Bond sales in the financial markets begin to

[4] The effect of this process may be visualized by comparing the patterns in Chart 2 for residential building contracts and the industrial production index, 1933-38, with the corresponding monthly data for these series in Chart 1. The reference patterns and conformity measures used in this report are based on reference dates as they stood *before* the revisions noted in Table 1; but the measures of timing of specific cycles are based on the revised dates.

Chart 2
Reference Cycle Patterns of Seven Series, 1919-1938

1 Residential Building Contracts, Floor Space
2 Industrial Production Index, FRB
3 Railroad Locomotive Shipments
4 Business Failures, Liabilities, Manufacturing Companies
5 Refined Copper Stocks
6 Bond Sales, New York Stock Exchange
7 Agricultural Marketings Index

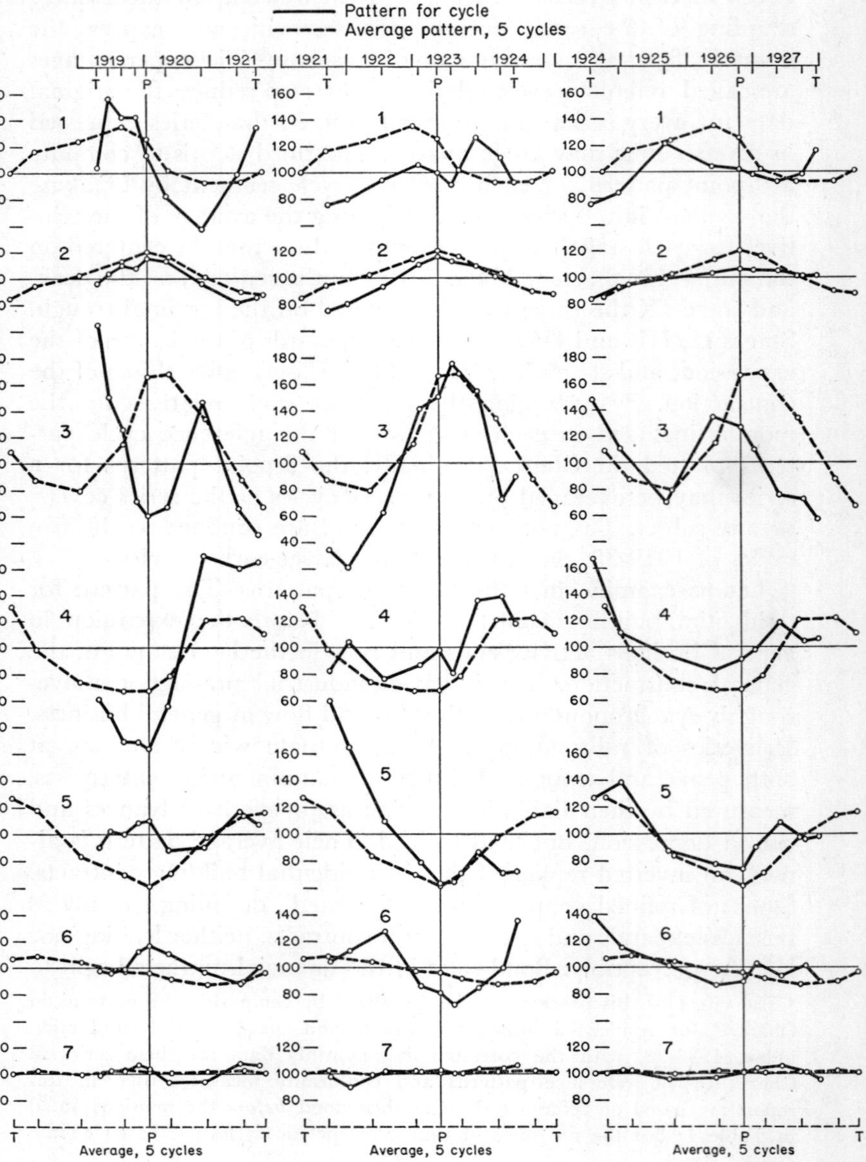

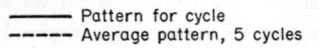
———— Pattern for cycle
-------- Average pattern, 5 cycles

Chart 2 (concl.)

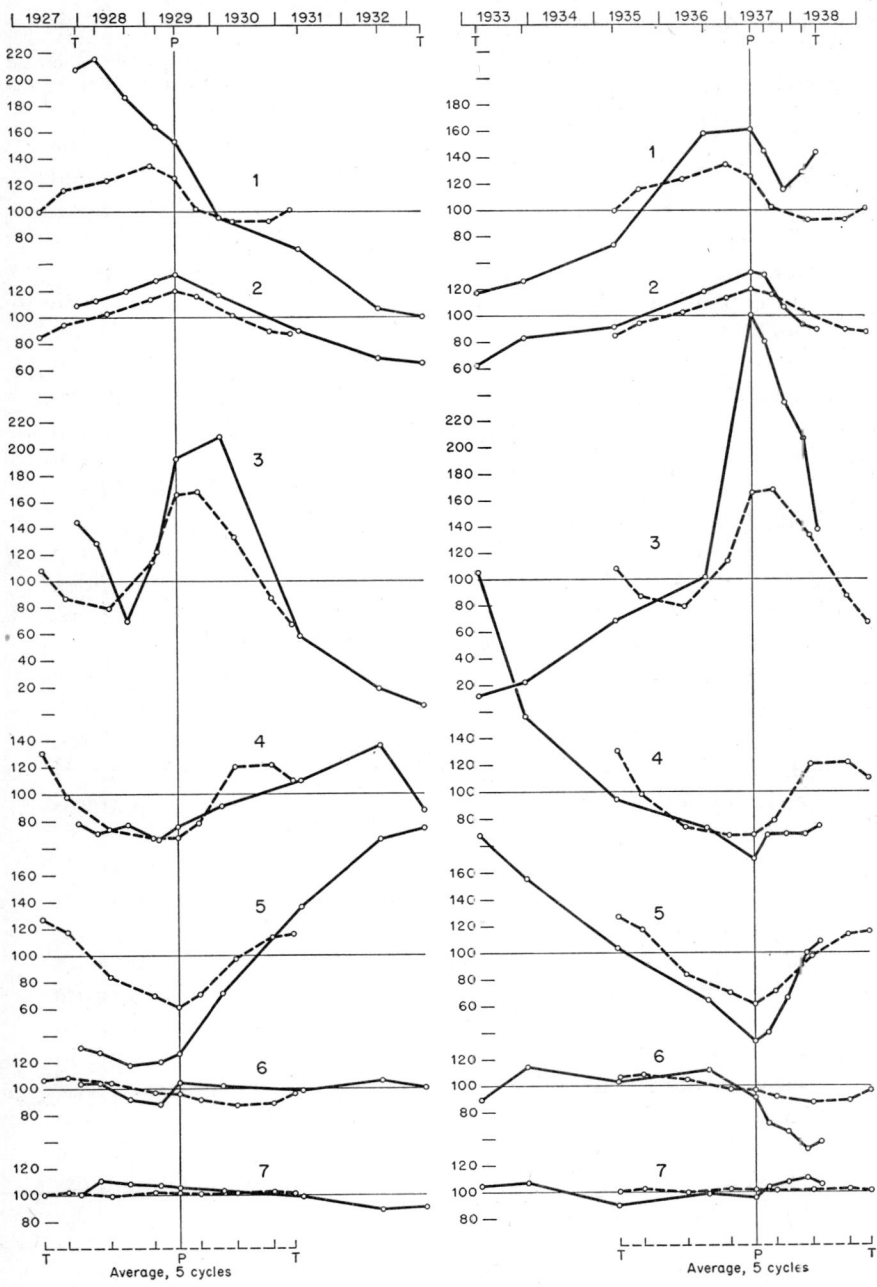

decline early in expansion and continue to decline until the business contraction is well advanced, when they begin to rise. Their timing is but one step removed from that of residential building contracts. The average pattern for marketings of agricultural products deviates little from a horizontal line.

Now if the average patterns were strictly representative of the individual cycle patterns, the variety of behavior depicted would be considerable. But clearly they understate the variety that actually exists. The set of patterns for each individual cycle differs from the average set in countless ways. Sometimes, as in 1919-20, the expansion is much shorter than average; sometimes, as in 1933-37, much longer. In the 1926-27 contraction the movements of most series were smaller than their average movement in contractions; in the 1937-38 contraction most of the movements were larger than average. In four contractions the upturn in residential building contracts preceded that in the index of industrial production, as it did on the average; but this did not happen in the 1929-33 contraction.

The averages are far more representative for some series than for others. There is so little repetition in the behavior of the index of agricultural marketings in successive business cycles that the fluctuations largely cancel themselves out in the average; hence the latter approximates a straight line. At the opposite extreme is the index of industrial production, which matches almost perfectly the successive phases marked out by the reference dates. The behavior of the other series is moderately consistent in successive cycles; but the distinctive timing of their average patterns is not repeated in every cycle.

Chart 2 makes it plain that no two business cycles are exactly alike—amplitudes, durations, and timing sequences differ. Cycle forecasting is not simple. However, the sample of series in this chart is too small to represent well what happens during business cycles. Timing sequences there are, and they are a vital feature of every business cycle. But there is also a consensus: ". . . a cycle consists of expansions occurring at about the same time in many economic activities, followed by similarly general recessions, contractions, and revivals which merge into the expansion phase of the next cycle. . . ."[5] What Chart 2 fails to demonstrate is that most economic activities, on any reasonable definition, expand and contract roughly in unison.

[5] *Measuring Business Cycles*, p. 3.

This consensus can be demonstrated in various ways. One can examine the reference cycle patterns of various series of broad scope, such as production indexes, total employment, national income, bank debits, retail sales, railway traffic, price indexes. Or one can summate, in one way or another, the reference cycle patterns of the 800 odd individual monthly or quarterly series we have analyzed for the United States. The use of reference cycle patterns, of course, presupposes that the reference dates are at least roughly accurate; if no consensus were revealed, it might be due to inaccuracy in the dates. On the other hand, one can examine the concentration in time of specific cycle turning dates, either in the broad aggregates or in the mass of lesser series. These are determined independently of the reference dates and independently in the different series.[6]

We need not pursue this matter far, for it is treated at length, especially by use of reference cycle materials, in Mitchell's *What Happens during Business Cycles* (see note 3). Besides, here we are primarily interested in timing sequences. However, one product of this study is a chronology of specific cycle peaks and troughs in a large number of series, and this chronology is worth examining for the light it throws not only on the consensus of cyclical behavior but also on the nature of revivals and recessions.

From our full collection of more than 800 series we selected, by a process described in Sections 4 and 5, the 404 series whose fluctuations conformed most consistently to business cycles over the period each series covers, after allowance for systematic differences in timing. The number reaching a peak or a trough in a given month, taken as a percentage of the total number of series available in that month, is recorded in Chart 3.[7] The number available does not remain the same over the whole period, as the accompanying figures taken in January at ten year inter-

	1890	1900	1910	1920	1930	1940
No. of series	83	140	175	326	356	330

vals show. New series are incorporated whenever they begin (or rather, in order to simplify the procedure, they are treated as if they began one month before their initial specific cycle turning point), and some drop out, so that the total included at any one

---

[6] Exceptions in both respects are occasionally made; see ibid., pp. 58 and 138-9.

[7] In series that are considered to be inverted in relation to business cycles, troughs are counted as peaks and vice versa; see note 9.

Chart 3
Percentage of Series Reaching Specific Cycle Peaks and Troughs and Percentage Expanding
All Series with 'Acceptable' Conformity
(solid vertical lines indicate reference troughs; broken vertical lines, reference peaks)

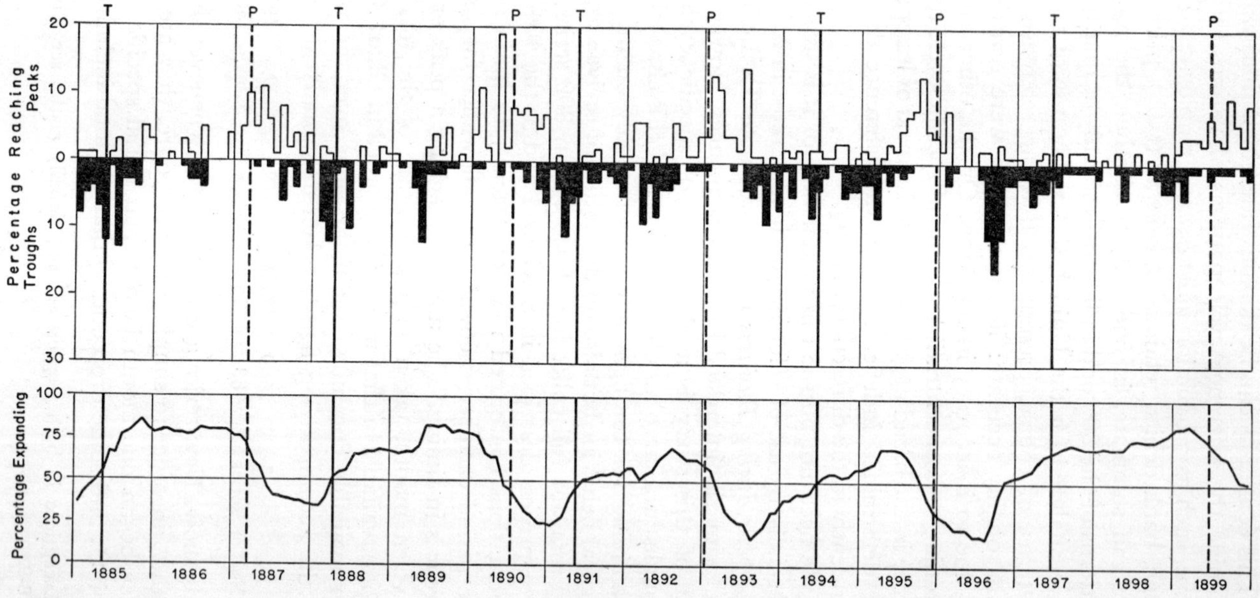

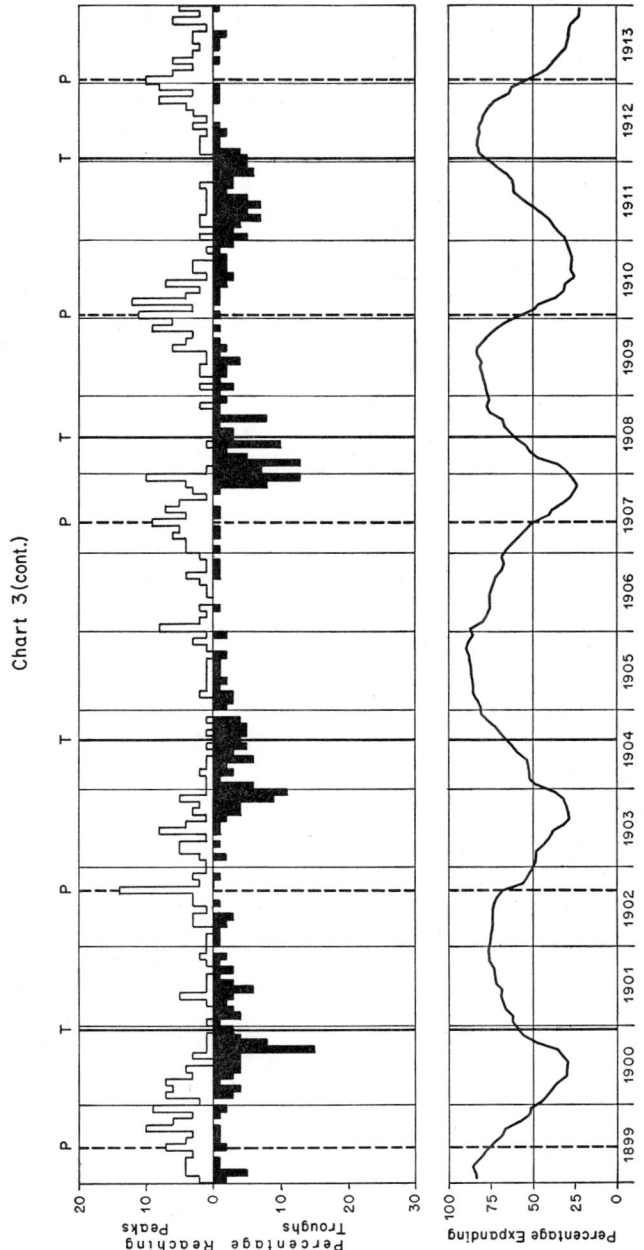

Chart 3 (cont.)

Chart 3 (cont.)

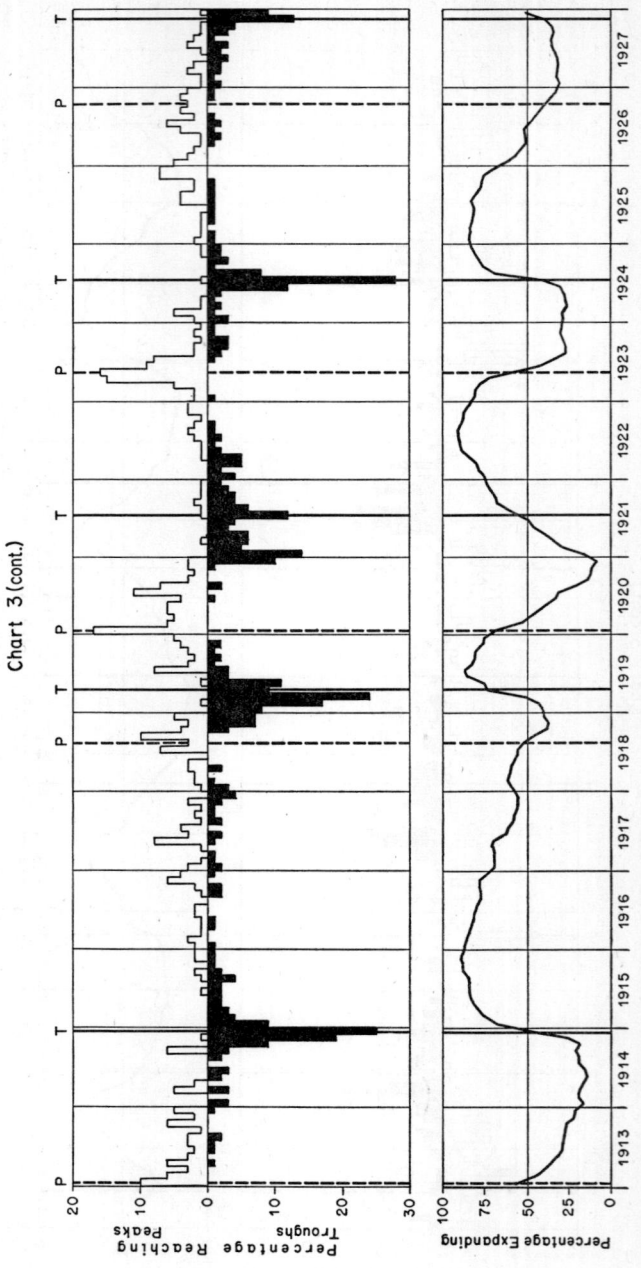

Chart 3 (concl.)

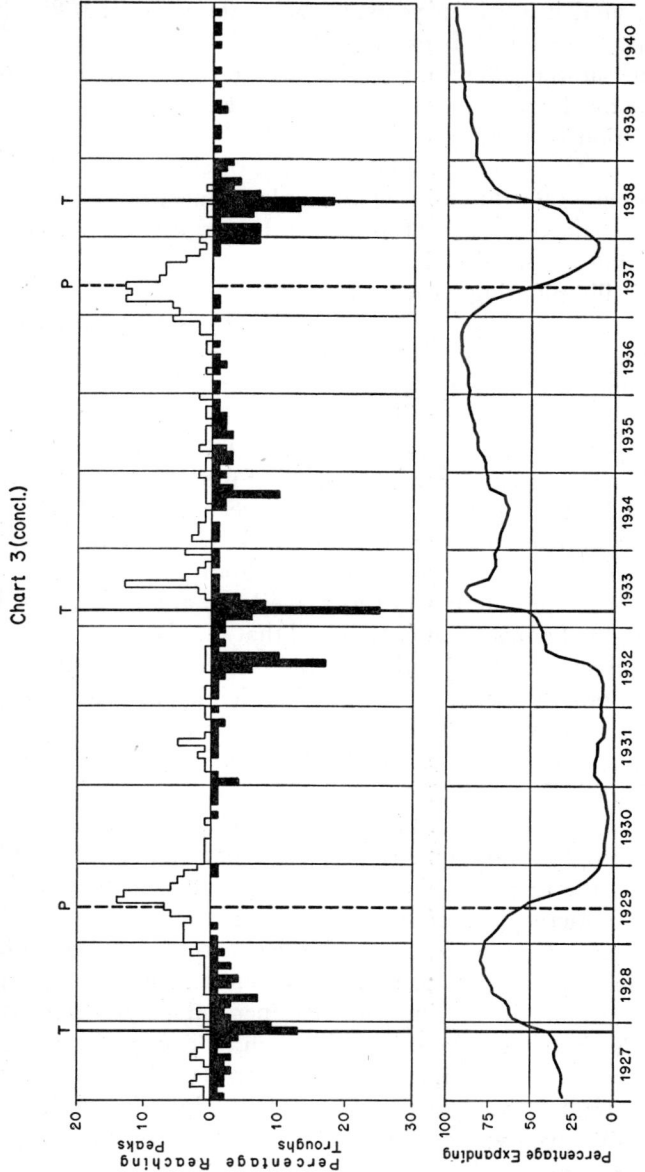

time never reaches 404. Since the number of series available is much smaller in earlier years, we begin the chart in 1885, though it could be extended back to 1854.

The sample, therefore, varies in size and content. Also it is biased by the way it was selected. Nevertheless it covers a large proportion of our full collection and a broad array of economic processes (see Sec. 5). The inclusion of similar information for the other 400 odd series would only reduce, not eliminate, the relative concentration of peaks and troughs around particular dates that appears in Chart 3.

It is illuminating to record the data also in terms of the percentage of series undergoing specific cycle expansion in each month. If in a given month 20 out of 100 series are contracting, including, say, 10 series that reach troughs in that month, while 80 are expanding, including 20 that reach peaks, then the number expanding the next month will be $80 + 10 - 20 = 70$. The number expanding in each succeeding month can be determined simply by adding the difference between the number reaching troughs and the number reaching peaks each month. The wavelike line in Chart 3 shows the result of this operation, when changes in the number of series available are allowed for by reducing the figures to percentages of that number.

Whereas the white and black bars in the chart reveal the concentrations of specific peaks in the vicinity of reference peaks, and of specific troughs in the vicinity of reference troughs, the continuous curve shows that the proportion of series expanding has invariably reached its highest point some time before the reference peak and its lowest point some time before the reference trough. The curve is, as stated above, mathematically related to the turning point distribution; but what they both show is not a mere piece of statistical arithmetic. The percentage of series expanding begins to decline when the percentage of series reaching peaks begins to exceed the percentage reaching troughs, and continues to decline until the percentage reaching troughs exceeds that reaching peaks. Its cyclical course has been fairly continuous because the first condition (peaks more prevalent than troughs) has persisted for a fairly long interval, and has gradually given way to a period in which the second condition is dominant, and so on.

Thus Chart 3 demonstrates a consensus: "expansions occurring at about the same time in many economic activities, followed by similarly general recessions, contractions, and revivals which merge into the expansion phase of the next cycle." The reference dates identify these general cycles with tolerable accuracy. No additional cycles of similar generality seem to appear, nor could any that are identified as reference cycles have well been omitted.[8]

But from Chart 3 we can draw a more complete picture of a business cycle. To be specific, let us trace the developments in 1921-24, a fairly typical cycle. The reference trough, July 1921, is roughly in the center of a period in which many series reached troughs, few reached peaks. Troughs apparently associated with this zone began to appear as early as June 1920, even while other series were reaching peaks apparently associated with the preceding peak zone. By July 1921 the percentage of series expanding had already been rising for seven months, and had reached approximately 50. It continued to grow until July 1922, when it was 90 percent. By this time most of the series had already reached troughs, and a few peaks were beginning to appear. A concentration of peaks occurred in the first half of 1923, neatly grouped around the May reference peak. The percentage of series expanding had by then receded from 90 to 60, while the percentage contracting had grown, of course, from 10 to 40. The contraction continued to spread until the autumn of 1923, when the percentage contracting reached 75, where it remained until the middle of 1924. During that interval approximately as many series were reaching troughs as were reaching peaks. In July 1924, the reference trough, nearly 30 percent of the sample reached troughs, and the percentage expanding shot up rapidly. While the concentration of troughs in June, July, and August 1924 was much denser than in the corresponding months of 1921, the zone of troughs apparently associated with the 1924 revival extended from the middle of 1923 until late in 1925. By that time the next expansion was well under way.

[8] In 1933-35 there is some concentration of peaks and troughs, but the percentage of series expanding never falls below 63, whereas in every other reference contraction it falls well below 50. See the discussion of this period in *Measuring Business Cycles,* pp. 87-90, and the analysis of the dependability of the reference dates, ibid., pp. 94-114. Although in Chart 3 reference dates often coincide with the month of highest concentration of peaks or troughs, this does not necessarily indicate their accuracy, or their failure to do so their inaccuracy. For one thing, Chart 3 does not take into account differences in the economic significance of the series; for another, it does not allow for differences in their typical behavior during business cycles. These considerations and others underlie the concept and procedures used in selecting reference dates (cf. ibid., pp. 71-81.)

Thus even the series in this sample, selected for the regularity with which they conform to business cycles, show wide differences in the timing of their cyclical fluctuations. The percentage of series expanding rarely exceeded 80 or fell below 20 in any month between 1885 and 1940. The zones in which the peaks (or troughs) concentrate extend over a year or two or three, and the peak zones often overlap the trough zones. In the words of Mitchell and Burns (*Bulletin 69,* p. 2), a business cycle revival or recession "is not an event that happens in a single month, but a complicated series of changes that occur cumulatively in various economic processes during a period that may last a year or more". This very fact spells some hope for the user of statistical indicators.

4

CRITERIA FOR SELECTING INDICATORS

Bulletin 69 described an ideal statistical indicator of cyclical revivals and recessions in the following terms:

1) It would cover half a century or longer, thus showing its relation to business cycles under a variety of conditions.
2) It would lead the month around which cyclical revival centers by an invariable interval—say three months, or better, six months. It would also lead the central month of every cyclical recession by an invariable interval, which might differ from the lead at revival.
3) It would show no erratic movements; that is, it would sweep smoothly up from each cyclical trough to the next cyclical peak and then sweep smoothly down to the next trough, so that every change in its direction would herald the coming of a revival or recession in general business.
4) Its cyclical movements would be pronounced enough to be readily recognized, and give some indication of the relative amplitude of the coming change.
5) It would be so related to general business activity as to establish as much confidence as the nature of such things allows that its future behavior in regard to business cycles will be like its past behavior.

As is, of course, obvious from Table 2 and Chart 1, no series possessing all these characteristics was found. Nor have we had better success in this investigation. The synthetic curve plotted in Chart 3 (the percentage of series expanding) comes perhaps as close as any to meeting the specifications, but even it does not lead the central months of cyclical revivals and recessions by an invariable interval nor is it free from erratic movements. Its merits will be discussed more fully in Section 6.

Realizing that the ideal indicator was not to be found in their collection, the authors of *Bulletin 69* looked for series that most nearly approached the ideal. The criterion for their initial selection of 71 indicators was what may be called the 'two-thirds rule'. That is, a series was considered an acceptable indicator of revivals if its specific cycle troughs led the corresponding reference troughs at two-thirds or more of the reference troughs it covered; or if it was 'roughly coincident' (turned within three months of the reference trough) at two-thirds or more of the troughs; or even if it lagged at two-thirds or more of the troughs.[9] Of course, if an ideal leading indicator could be found, the other types would be superfluous. As it is, both the roughly coincident and lagging series yield useful information on the course of a business cycle.

For the further screening given the 71 indicators selected by the two-thirds rule (which was relaxed slightly in a few cases), the five general criteria quoted above were spelled out into eleven specific characteristics. Other things being equal, a series was considered more useful as an early indicator of revivals

1) The longer its average lead at past revivals,
2) The more uniform these leads are in occurrence and length,
3) The closer its specific cycles come to having a one to one correspondence with business cycles,
4) The more clearly defined its specific cycles,
5) The less intense its erratic movements in comparison with the amplitude of its specific cycles,

---

[9] The peaks of a series taken to be inverted with respect to business cycles, such as business failures, are compared with reference troughs. Usually it is easy to decide whether a series should be treated positively or invertedly; but it is difficult when the series leads or lags by long intervals. Throughout this report we adhere to the objective rule we follow in our standard analyses (cf. *Measuring Business Cycles*, pp. 115-7, 188-9). For example, the series on bond sales (Chart 2) is treated invertedly under our rule; hence most of the timing observations are lags. If it were treated positively it would lead. Adherence to the rule does not, of course, necessarily lead to the most useful or sensible treatment.

6) The fewer the changes in the direction of its month to month movements,
7) The smaller and more regular the seasonal variations that have to be 'eliminated' before the specific cycles can be studied,
8) The larger the number of revivals covered,
9) The further back in time any irregularities in conformity to business cycle revivals occurred,
10) The broader the range of activities represented,
11) The more stable the economic significance of the process represented.

A sifting of the 71 series on the basis of these criteria gave the 21 listed in Table 2.

Clearly, many considerations enter into the selection of a series as an indicator of revival or recession. Some that have nothing to do with the behavior of the series might be added to the eleven noted. For example, a lag in the publication of a series is often sufficient to justify its rejection as a useful indicator. Again, whether or not the series is published in seasonally adjusted form is a consideration, for seasonal elimination is expensive and time-consuming.

In this study we have not yet carried the application of selective criteria as far as in *Bulletin 69*, though we plan to continue work along these lines. What we have done is to design and apply a method for rating series on the basis of two criteria: the consistency with which their movements have conformed to business cycles, and the consistency with which their turning points have led, lagged, or roughly coincided with the reference dates. A series' rating is based upon estimates of the probability that, for specified measures of its past performance, a result as good as or better than the one observed would occur in random sampling.

These measures of performance may be based on all the cycles covered by a series; then the computed probability takes into account differences in the lengths of series, i.e., differences in the amount of information on cyclical behavior available for each series. The two-thirds rule did not do this. On the other hand, to avoid ambiguities due to differences in time coverage and to possible changes in behavior, it is desirable to have measurements based upon a fixed and recent period for all series. Consequently, two sets of measures have been used: one based on all cycles covered by the series, the other on 1919-38, a period covered by most of the series.

The first criterion, conformity, is designed to spot series whose movements have paralleled business cycles consistently. If a series consistently expands during business expansions and contracts during business contractions, it has at least one of the qualities of a good indicator. However, allowance should be made for the fact that some series typically contract during business expansions and expand during contractions, and that others show characteristic differences in timing in relation to business cycles.

These differences are revealed, at least crudely, by the reference cycle patterns computed for each series (cf. Chart 2). Consequently, we examine the patterns to determine the set of 'stages', or interval, during which the series typically expands, and those during which it typically contracts.[10] For example, the expansion intervals for the first six series in Chart 2, taking into consideration all the cycles covered by each series, are: residential building contracts, VII-IV; industrial production index, I-V; locomotive shipments, III-VI; liabilities of business failures, IV-VII; refined copper stocks, V-IX; bond sales, VII-II. The seventh series in Chart 2, agricultural marketings, behaves so irregularly in successive reference cycles that a division into typical expansion and contraction intervals is not justified.

The expansion interval usually corresponds rather closely to the interval during which the average reference pattern rises, and the contraction interval to the interval during which the average pattern declines, as the reader can verify from Chart 2. The intervals, of course, imply a certain kind of timing. Thus the expansion interval, VII-IV, for residential building contracts implies that the series typically leads by one stage at business peaks and by two stages at business troughs. The typical sequences among the series can be traced by the arrangement that follows, which utilizes the expansion and contraction intervals.

Once the expansion and contraction intervals have been fixed, one can measure the consistency of performance in successive cycles by counting the number of cycles in which the series rises between the initial and terminal expansion stages and the number in which it falls; likewise one can count the number of cycles in which there is a decline and the number in which there is a rise between the initial and terminal contraction stages.

[10] For an account of how this is done the reader is referred to *Measuring Business Cycles,* pp. 185-97.

	TYPICAL DIRECTION OF CHANGE BETWEEN STAGES							
	I-II	II-III	III-IV	IV-V	V-VI	VI-VII	VII-VIII	VIII-IX
	BUSINESS EXPANSION				BUSINESS CONTRACTION			
	Trough to first third	First to middle third	Middle to last third	Last third to peak	Peak to first third	First to middle third	Middle to last third	Last third to trough
Resid. bldg. contracts	+	+	+	−	−	−	+	+
Indus. prod. index	+	+	+	+	−	−	−	−
Locomotive ship.	−	−	+	+	+	−	−	−
Failures, liab., mfg.	−	−	−	+	+	+	−	−
Ref. copper stocks	−	−	−	−	+	+	+	+
Bond sales, N. Y. S. E.	+	−	−	−	−	−	+	+

In Chart 2 the industrial production index has a perfect conformity score: it rises during its expansion interval in each of the five cycles (that is, the standing at stage V is higher than at stage I in five cycles); and it declines between V and IX in each cycle. Refined copper stocks rise in four out of five cycles during their expansion interval, V-IX, and decline in four cycles out of five during their contraction interval. Bond sales rise three times out of five during their expansion interval, VII-II,[11] and decline four times out of five during their contraction interval.

The expansion and contraction conformity scores, when combined, measure the parallelism between the movements of the series and business cycles. For this purpose, the number of rises in the series' typical expansion interval and declines in its contraction interval can be taken as a proportion of the total number of expansions and contractions covered. This measure would be $\frac{10}{10}$ or unity for the index of industrial production, $\frac{8}{10}$ for copper stocks, $\frac{7}{10}$ for bond sales. It could not exceed unity, nor could it fall much below one-half if the expansion interval was at all typical.

However, this simple measure is the same for a series lapsing once from perfectly consistent conformity in five phases as for a series lapsing twice out of ten. Should one not have more confidence in the excellence of the series in the second case than in the first? If some simplifying assumptions are made, it is easy to compute the probability that as few as, say, two lapses in conformity out of ten will occur by chance, and this may be compared with the

---

[11] In this case, to compare stage VII of one cycle with stage II of the next, the standing at stage II is recomputed on the base of the preceding cycle.

probability of obtaining as good a result as one lapse out of five by chance. Our method, then, is simply to compute these probabilities for each series' expansion and contraction scores, and to combine the expansion and contraction probabilities for a given series by multiplying them: the smallest product probabilities indicate the best series so far as conformity is concerned.[12]

A small product probability may, however, result from a strong secular trend in the series. An upward trend can help to produce a high expansion score, and the corresponding expansion probability may be so low as to offset a relatively high contraction probability and yield a relatively low product. Two procedures help to avoid this. First, we require that there be both an excess of rises over declines in expansion intervals *and* an excess of declines over rises in contraction intervals. This eliminates series in which the effect of trend is so strong as to produce more rises than declines in both phases (or vice versa). Such series cannot be said to parallel business cycles. Although they may reflect the influence of business cycles by alternately rising faster and slower, and hence not be entirely valueless as indicators, they may well be set aside at the start.

The second and more important procedure is to subject the expansion and contraction probabilities to a maximum acceptance level, .188. When either probability is above this level (or rather, above the nearest possible approximation to it in the given case), the series is rejected. The .188 level is the probability that one or fewer lapses in conformity will occur in five phases. Series that would get a low product probability merely because of an exceptionally low expansion (or contraction) probability are thereby eliminated. Reasonably good conformity to both ex-

---

[12] The underlying assumptions are that the probability that a series will rise (or fall) during its expansion interval in a given business cycle is one-half, and that the results in successive cycles are independent. Then the probability that no lapses will occur in, say, 5 phases is $(\frac{1}{2})^5 = .03125$; that 1 lapse will occur, $5(\frac{1}{2})^5 = .15625$; 2 lapses, $10(\frac{1}{2})^5 = .3125$; and so on according to the binomial expansion. Cumulating, one obtains the probability for as good a result as no lapses, .03125; one lapse, .1875; two lapses, .5; etc. Both underlying assumptions are open to question, and the computed probabilities cannot be interpreted in any strict sense. Several other procedures were tried but the above seemed adequate for rating series roughly, which is all that is possible since the conformity scores themselves contain a rather limited amount of information about the series' behavior. When a series does not change in its expansion (or contraction) interval in a given cycle the observation is counted as one-half rise, one-half fall.

pansions and contractions is an essential characteristic of a good indicator, whether revivals or recessions are of chief interest.

The general effect of the procedure, as the accompanying figures illustrate, is that for the same proportion of lapses in conformity the longer the series the lower the probability; and the longer the series the higher the maximum acceptable proportion of lapses in conformity. When the conformity probability cri-

Phases covered by series, no.	5	10	15	20
Lapses in conformity, no.	1	2	3	4
Probability	.188	.055	.018	.0058
Maximum acceptable no. of lapses	1	3	5½	7½
Probability	.188	.172	.214	.182

terion is applied to the full periods covered by the seven series of Chart 2, two series are rejected (Table 3).

Series with acceptable conformity are then subjected to the timing criterion. Timing is measured by comparing the dates of a series' specific cycle peaks and troughs with the reference dates, and the intervals, in months, are classified as leads, lags, or rough coincidences.[13] A consistent leader at peaks, then, is a series that leads at a large proportion of the reference peaks covered. What is a large proportion and what a small is determined by computing the probability that, when a series covers a certain number of reference peaks (or troughs), a specified number of timing comparisons of a given type will be equaled or exceeded by chance.[14] As with conformity, a maximum acceptance level is adopted, corresponding as nearly as may be to the probability (.223) that four or more timing comparisons will appear in a given group when the series covers six reference turns. The accompanying figures illustrate how the timing probabilities vary with the length of the

[13] For purposes of the probability criterion described below, an exact coincidence was counted as a half lead and a half lag. Rough coincidences include exact coincidences and leads or lags of one, two, or three months. Any timing comparison must be in one of the three timing groups, and some may be in two (leads and rough coincidences, or lags and rough coincidences). But at some reference turns there may not be any timing comparison, either because no specific cycle turn occurs in the vicinity or because several turns compete. Cf. *Measuring Business Cycles,* pp. 116-28.

[14] Since a tabulation of the total number of leads, lags, and rough coincidences for all series having acceptable conformity revealed that the number in each class was roughly the same—about 43 percent of the number of reference turns covered by the series, .43 was adopted as the probability that a series will produce a timing comparison of a given type at a reference turn.

TABLE 3
Conformity Measures, Seven Series

SERIES & REFERENCE PERIOD COVERED BY CONFORMITY MEASURES	Expansion Interval	NO. OF CYCLES IN WHICH THE SERIES DURING ITS				CONFORMITY PROBABILITY			Series Accepted or Rejected
		EXPANSION INTERVAL		CONTRACTION INTERVAL		Expansion	Contraction	Product	
		Rises	Falls	Rises	Falls				
Resid. bldg. contracts, fl. space, 1919-38	VII-IV	4	1	1	4	.188	.188	.035	Accepted
Indus. production index, FRB, 1919-38	I-V	5	0	0	5	.031	.031	.0010	Accepted
Railroad locomotive shipments, 1918-37	III-VI	4	1	1	4	.188	.188	.035	Accepted
Bus. failures, liab, mfg, 1894-1938[w]	IV-VII	9	1	1	9	.011	.011	.00012	Accepted
Refined copper stocks, 1910-38[a]	V-IX	5	2	2	4	.227	.344	.078	Rejected
Bond sales, N. Y. Stock Exchange, 1888-1938	VII-II	12	2	3	11	.0065	.029	.00019	Accepted
Agricultural marketings index, 1919-38	[b]	4	1	3	2	[b]	[b]	[b]	Rejected

[a] Data are not available for the 1914-19 cycle.
[b] Timing is irregular; stages I-V are used as the expansion interval but series is rejected (see text).
[w] War cycle observations (1914-21) are omitted.

series. A series leading at two-thirds of the reference peaks covered is assigned a much lower probability if it achieves this record in 21 cycles than in 6. A record of leads at 11 peaks in 21 cycles

No. of ref. peaks (or troughs) covered by series	6	12	18	21
Timing comparisons of one type, no.	4	8	12	14
Probability	.223	.087	.037	.025
Timing comparisons of one type, min. accept. no.	4	7	10	11
Probability	.223	.216	.210	.257

is roughly equivalent, on a probability basis, to a record of 4 in 6 cycles.[15] Table 4 shows the timing probabilities for the five series of Chart 2 that have acceptable conformity.

Since the conformity and timing probabilities just described are based on a series' behavior during all the business cycles it covers,[16] they do not take account of possible secular changes in cyclical behavior. For example, a series whose conformity has improved may get a lower rating than its recent performance would justify. Or a series may be classed as a leader at peaks, when recently it has lagged. While significant shifts of this sort do not appear to be widespread, our measures may be misleading when they do occur.

A few illustrations will suffice to reveal the nature of the problem. A series on railroad freight ton-miles is rejected on the basis of its conformity during all cycles covered (1867-1938), because in nearly half the reference contraction intervals it does not decline. But its failure is confined to its early years; since 1907 it has declined in every contraction except one, that of 1910-12, a rather mild depression. This shift in behavior is due to the de-

[15] A series that leads at 11 peaks out of 21 has not, it is true, achieved a good record as a leader if it lags at the other 10. Our method, in effect, gives some weight to the possibility that the series will not reach a corresponding peak at all 21 reference peaks. The difficulty could be avoided by computing two probabilities, one based on the number of corresponding turns relative to the number of reference turns, the other on the number of leads relative to the number of corresponding turns.

A simpler expedient would be to adopt a higher acceptance level. The probability (.057) corresponding to 5 leads out of 6 reference turns covered would be fairly satisfactory, since it would require a minimum of 13 leads in 21 turns (P = .064). The classification of series in Sec. 5 and 6 is based, however, on the procedure described in the text. A saving feature is that a well conforming series with, say, 11 leads and 10 lags is likely to have at least as many rough coincidences, in which case it will be classified also as a 'coincider'.

[16] An exception is made in price and certain value series, observations during war cycles being omitted.

TABLE 4

Timing Measures, Five Series

SERIES, REFERENCE PERIOD COVERED, & REFERENCE TURN	NO. OF REF. TURNS COV- ERED	NO. OF TIMING OBSERVA- TIONS THAT ARE				AV. LEAD (−) OR LAG (+) IN MONTHS	TIMING PROBABILITY[a]		
		Leads	Exact coin.	Lags	Rough coin.		Leads	Lags	Rough coin.
Resid. bldg. contracts, fl. sp., 1919-38									
Reference peaks	5	4		1	1	−6.2	.112		
Reference troughs	6	5	1		2	−4.5	.019		
Industrial production index, FRB, 1919-38									
Reference peaks	5		3	2	5	+0.6		.204	.015
Reference troughs	6	4	2		5	−2.2	.057		.057
Railroad locomotive shipments, 1918-38									
Reference peaks	6	1	1	3	2	+1.4			
Reference troughs	6			6	1	+10.0		.0063	
Business failures, liab, mfg.,[i] 1895-1938[w]									
Reference peaks	10	8	2		4	−6.5	.0031		
Reference troughs	11	8	1	2	2	−6.3	.022		
Bond sales, N. Y. Stock Exchange,[i] 1890-1937									
Reference peaks	14	3		10	2	+5.8		.030	
Reference troughs	13	2		11	2	+7.2		.0027	

[a] Only the accepted timing probabilities are recorded; see text.
[i] Inverted; see note 9.
[w] War cycle observations (1918-20) are omitted.

clining secular rate of growth of railroad freight traffic (the rate of growth in the early years being so rapid as to offset depressions) and perhaps also, in some degree, to the declining relative volume of agricultural traffic.

Shifts in conformity are often related to shifts in timing. An improved conformity may mean a more consistent timing relationship, i.e., the proportion of reference turns for which there are no corresponding specific turns may be smaller, and noncorresponding, or extra, specific turns may be less frequent. For example, in 1867-1919 total exports conformed irregularly, rising in 10 and falling in 3 expansions and rising in 9 and falling in 4 contractions; since 1919 exports have increased in each expansion and declined in each contraction. The pre-1919 period yields only 11 timing comparisons; 15 reference turns are skipped and there are 24 extra specific turns. After 1919 there are 7 comparisons; only 4 turns are skipped and there are only 5 'extras'.

Besides shifts in the degree of correspondence between specific and business cycles, shifts may occur in the kind of timing. Prior to 1913 railroad ton-miles lagged at each of the 8 reference peaks with which a specific peak could be matched, often by substantial intervals. Since then it has led at 4 peaks, and lagged only twice; none of these intervals exceeded four months. Orders for railway equipment illustrate another type of shift in timing. In the early years they led business revivals by much longer intervals than in recent cycles. Burns and Mitchell (*Measuring Business Cycles,* pp. 414-6) attribute this to a shift of the railroad industry from a dominant to a subordinate position as an object of investment.

The method we have chosen to meet the problem of shifts in conformity and timing is to rate all series on the basis of their performance after 1919, provided they cover at least the four cycles 1921-38. Comparison with results based on all cycles covered will bring to light changes in behavior. Furthermore, by rating all series on the basis of performance in 1919-38 we can test the performance of identical groups of series in earlier cycles; in other words, test whether secular or other changes in behavior have been so general as to make it impossible to discover stable behavior characteristics. Looking backward in time, we can make the same sort of test that was made in Table 2 looking forward. Another advantage of fixing the period (approximately) is that the arbitrary method of equating different historical periods by a probability scheme is avoided. In particular, since the dates of reference troughs seem to have a small bias in the early years, long series are in fact not treated on precisely the same basis as short, in respect of their behavior at troughs. The reference dates in 1919-38 are more firmly established and in any event fixing the period eliminates the difficulty.

The conformity and timing probabilities (for the full period covered by the series and for 1919-38) are the measures so far developed and applied in this study. Both types of measure contribute useful information about the quality of a series as an indicator. While they are not strictly independent in a statistical sense, they utilize the data in quite different ways, and the two together contribute more information than either alone. Nevertheless, by themselves they will not yield a wholly satisfactory set of indicators. For one thing, the acceptance levels we have set are met by very many series, and a long list of indicators is practically a serious inconvenience. But we did not wish to set the levels much higher (see, however, note 15), for that would mean giving disproportionate weight to what are, in and of themselves, rather rough measures of behavior. We plan, instead, to apply additional criteria to achieve a finer selection. Some consideration, for example, should be given to the length of the average lead or lag; this is done only indirectly and crudely by the timing probabilities (see Sec. 5). Again, a series may get a low conformity and a low timing probability, yet have such large erratic movements as to be of little value as an indicator. Moreover, account has not been taken directly of how closely the movements of a series match the variations in amplitude of successive business cycles. Consequently, the classifications of series based upon the probability measures, which we present and utilize in Sections 5 and 6, must be taken as provisional and subject to elaboration and revision.

5

CLASSIFICATION OF SERIES ACCORDING TO CONFORMITY AND TIMING

The 801 monthly and quarterly time series for the United States analyzed in connection with the National Bureau's general investigation of business cycles are the foundation of this study.[17] Assembled over a period of years for a variety of purposes, they

[17] Included are 57 series on the status of national banks at 5 irregularly spaced 'call dates' within the year; 61 'short' series are excluded (see text).

cover a wide range of economic activities. The measures of cyclical behavior computed for each series on a standard plan have been subjected to the techniques described in the preceding section. We now show how groups of series on different economic processes are classified by these techniques.

As our monthly and quarterly reference dates cover 1854-1938 the cyclical measures for an individual series do not go beyond these dates. Most series, of course, begin much later than 1854 and some end before 1938. Since the behavior of discontinued series may provide clues to useful series that are or might become currently available, we have included them in our tabulations. We have excluded, for the time being, some 61 series that cover less than four business cycle expansions and four contractions, on the ground that our simple procedures, devised to achieve a rough grading of the great mass of series, are inadequate to assess the value of very short series. These, together with other series that have come into being since 1938, should be considered as candidates in a final selection of indicators, and some attention is given them in Section 7.

In general, the highly uneven distribution of series according to the type of economic activity represented (Table 5, col. 2 and 3) is the result of variations in both the availability of data and the degree of intensity with which certain parts of the National Bureau's business cycles research program have been pursued. These exigencies, of course, affect the selection of indicators, for we cannot select indicators from types of activity for which we do not have any series. Some of these deficiencies, fortunately, can be made up from data that have become available in recent years and cover only a brief period.

Eighty-two of the 576 'rejected' series (col. 2), or about 10 percent of the collection, conform so irregularly to business cycles that no expansion or contraction interval seems typical; e.g., contracts for public construction, production of foodstuffs, railroad rates and fares, and certain classes of inventories. These series are not without significance for business cycle analysis, for processes that fluctuate more or less independently of business cycles are part of the economic environment and may exert sufficient force to alter substantially the course of a business cycle. Nevertheless, it is important to separate them from the more reliable indicators.

An additional 315 series in column 2 fail to meet our minimum standard for conformity, although they conform better than the 82 series just mentioned. All told 397, or nearly half, of the

801 series are rejected on grounds of irregular conformity, while 404 have 'acceptable' conformity when behavior during the entire period of the series is considered. Applying the test for consistency in timing to these 404 series we reject 179 series. That is, 179 series fail to meet the timing test at either reference peaks or troughs or both. These, added to the 397 series rejected for conformity, make up the 576 series in column 2. The remaining 225 series (col. 3) show acceptable, but not necessarily similar, timing at both turns.

The application of the conformity and timing criteria eliminates all the wholesale sales series, exports, contracts for public construction, production of foods, prices of farm products and foods, and Federal Reserve Bank and member bank series. In general, the percentage of acceptable indicators varies strikingly among different types of economic process (Table 5, col. 4, and Tables 6 and 7). This percentage is useful in pointing to areas in which a search for indicators is likely to be rewarded. But it is merely a guide. In the great majority of groups some series are 'acceptable' and others are not. The individual series must be examined to find out which is which. Moreover, the position of a group in the array is affected by the particular types of series that get into it. The timing and conformity of the wholesale sales group would undoubtedly be better were the series available for a longer period; most of the series in this group are too short to get included in the table, and the others are not representative of wholesale sales in general. The better showing of the national bank than of the member bank series must be interpreted in the light of the fact that all except one of our national bank series end in 1914, while our sample of member bank series not only covers a later period and a different banking system but also a narrower range of banking processes. The larger percentages of acceptable employment and payroll series than of production series (see Table 7) are probably partly accounted for by the wider coverage of the individual employment and payroll series. The percentages, therefore, require careful interpretation, but they are at least suggestive.

The various types of economic process distinguished in Table 5 differ not only in potency as sources of acceptable indicators but also in the kind of timing the acceptable series exhibit (col. 5-9). By separating series that have an acceptable number of both leads and rough coincidences from those that have an acceptable number of leads only we can get a crude indication of the size of the lead: series of the latter type are likely to lead by longer in-

Table 5

Classification of All Series Examined for Acceptability as Indicators

Group (1)	Number of series Rejected (2)	Number of series Accepted (3)	% Accepted (4)	Leads only (5)	Number of series[a] accepted for — Leads & rough coin. (6)	Rough coin. only (7)	Lags & rough coin. (8)	Lags only (9)
Retail sales	9	3	25	.. ..	.. ..	1 2	.. ..	2 1
Wholesale sales	6	..	0	.. ..	.. ..	.. ..	.. ..	.. ..
Imports	10	3	23	.. ..	1 ..	1 2	.. ..	1 1
Exports	7	..	0	.. ..	.. ..	.. ..	.. ..	.. ..
New orders	8	7	47	7 6	.. 1	.. ..	.. ..	.. ..
Const. contracts & permits Public & private	7	7	50	7 7	.. ..	.. ..	.. ..	.. ..
Private	12	15	56	12 10	1 2	1 3	.. ..	1 ..
Public	16	..	0	.. ..	.. ..	.. ..	.. ..	.. ..
Inventories	54	2	4	1 1	.. ..	.. ..	.. ..	1 1
Production General indexes	7	16	70	3 2	3 6	3 8	5 ..	2 ..
Foodstuffs	45	..	0	.. ..	.. ..	.. ..	.. ..	.. ..
Other perishables	21	5	19	1 2	.. 2	1 1	.. ..	3 ..
Semidurables	20	5	20	1 5	.. ..	3 ..	.. ..	1 ..
Durables	29	15	34	5 7	1 4	3 4	3 ..	3 ..
Trans. & commun. Traffic	10	1	9	.. ..	.. 1	1 ..	.. ..	.. ..
Rates & fares	7	1	12	1 ..	.. ..	.. ..	.. ..	.. 1
Other series	15	6	29	.. 1	6 5	.. ..	.. ..	.. ..
Employment General indexes	..	5	100	.. 3	1 ..	1 1	2 1	1 ..
Perish. goods indust.	8	2	20	.. ..	.. ..	.. 1	1 1	1 ..
Semidur. goods indust.	9	6	40	1 6	.. ..	3 ..	1 ..	1 ..
Dur. goods indust.	5	6	55	1 ..	.. 1	2 3	3 2	.. ..
Av. hours worked per week	3	6	67	4 5	.. ..	1 1	1 ..	.. ..
Earnings per employee	18	1	5	.. ..	.. 1	.. ..	.. ..	1 ..

Group (1)	NUMBER OF SERIES Rejected (2)	NUMBER OF SERIES Accepted (3)	% ACCEPTED (4)	NUMBER OF SERIES[a] ACCEPTED FOR				
				Leads only (5)	Leads & rough coin. (6)	Rough coin. only (7)	Lags & rough coin. (8)	Lags only (9)
Payrolls & other income payments								
General indexes	1	2	67	.. .	.. ..	.. 1	2 1	.. ..
Perish. goods indust.	5	4	44	.. ..	.. ..	.. 1	.. 2	4 1
Semidur. goods indust.	8	6	43	.. 5	.. ..	1 1	4 ..	1 ..
Dur. goods indust.	3	5	62	.. 1	.. ..	.. 1	2 3	3 ..
Prices of commodities								
General indexes	9	3	25	1 1	2 1	.. 1	.. ..	.. ..
Farm products & foods	51	..	0	.. ..	.. ..	.. ..	.. ..	.. ..
Other perishables	19	2	10	1 1	.. ..	.. ..	.. ..	1 1
Semidurables	14	4	22	.. 1	.. ..	2 ..	.. ..	2 3
Durables	34	10	23	4 2	2 1	2 1	1 2	1 4
Banking & money								
National Bank series	37	21	36	6 10	.. 1	1 2	.. ..	14 8
Fed. Reserve member bank series	16	..	0	.. ..	.. ..	.. ..	.. ..	.. ..
Fed. Reserve Bank series	9	..	0	.. ..	.. ..	.. ..	.. ..	.. ..
Other monetary series	3	1	25	.. ..	.. ..	.. ..	.. ..	1 1
Interest rates & bond yields	15	8	35	.. ..	.. ..	1 ..	.. ..	7 8
Stock exchange transactions	..	3	100	2 2	.. ..	.. ..	.. ..	1 1
Stock prices	..	6	100	6 6	.. ..	.. ..	.. ..	.. ..
Security issues, corporate	10	4	29	3 3	.. ..	.. ..	.. ..	1 1
Business profits	4	7	64	1 5	3 1	3 ..	.. 1	.. ..
Business failures	6	8	57	8 8	.. ..	.. ..	.. ..	.. ..
Bank clearings & debits	..	5	100	.. 4	2 1	.. ..	3 ..	.. ..
Bus. activity indexes	..	12	100	1 2	2 10	5 ..	4 ..	.. ..
Unclassified	6	2	25	1 1	.. ..	.. ..	.. ..	1 1
All series	576	225	28	78 107	24 38	36 34	32 13	55 33

[a] First line is the distribution of series according to their behavior at peaks; second line, the distribution at troughs.

The classification of series by type of activity was designed by Wesley C. Mitchell and used in his forthcoming volume, *What Happens during Business Cycles*. The term 'accepted' means accepted for conformity and for timing at both peaks and troughs (see text).

TABLE 6

Percentage of Series with Acceptable Conformity and Timing, by Economic Groups

Group	No. of Series in Group	% Accepted
Employment, general indexes	5	100
Stock exchange transactions	3	100
Stock prices	6	100
Bank clearings & debits	5	100
Business activity indexes	12	100
Production, general indexes	23	70
Average hours worked per week	9	67
Payrolls, general indexes	3	67
Business profits	11	64
Payrolls, durable goods industries	8	62
Business failures	14	57
Private construction contracts & permits	27	56
Employment, durable goods industries	11	55
Public & private construction contracts & permits	14	50
New orders	15	47
Payrolls, perishable goods industries	9	44
Payrolls, semidurable goods industries	14	43
Employment, semidurable goods industries	15	40
National bank series	58	36
Interest rates & bond yields	23	35
Production, durables	44	34
Transportation & communication, other series	21	29
Security issues, corporate	14	29
Retail sales	12	25
Commodity prices, general indexes	12	25
Other monetary series	4	25
Unclassified series	8	25
Imports	13	23
Commodity prices, durables	44	23
Commodity prices, semidurables	18	22
Production, semidurables	25	20
Employment, perishable goods industries	10	20
Production, other perishables	26	19
Transportation & communication, rates & fares	8	12
Commodity prices, other perishables	21	10
Transportation & communication, traffic	11	9
Earnings per employee	19	5
Inventories	56	4
Wholesale sales	6	0
Exports	7	0
Public construction contracts	16	0
Production, foodstuffs	45	0
Prices, farm products & foods	51	0
Federal Reserve member bank series	16	0
Federal Reserve Bank series	9	0
All series	801	28

Source: Table 5.

TABLE 7

Percentage of Series with Acceptable Conformity and Timing
Prices, Production, Employment, and Payrolls

Group	Commodity Prices	Production	Employment	Payrolls
Foodstuffs*	0	0	} 20	} 44
Other perishables	10	19		
Semidurables	22	20	40	43
Durables	23	34	55	62
General indexes	25	70	100	67

Source: Table 5.
* In the case of commodity prices this group includes farm products.

tervals. Hence the five timing groups in Table 5 indicate roughly series whose timing is characterized by 'long leads', 'short leads', 'short leads or lags', 'short lags', and 'long lags'.

Before we consider the differences among the economic groups we must note one peculiarity of the over-all totals—the rough symmetry in the distribution of series at peaks and the decided asymmetry at troughs. That is, while at peaks the leaders somewhat outnumber the laggards, at troughs nearly three times as many series lead as lag. It is evidently easier to find advance indicators of revivals than of recessions.

Why this should be we are not entirely sure. Several reference troughs may have been postdated a few months, whereas it seems that errors in reference peaks are more evenly distributed (cf. Sec. 6). But these errors occur before 1919; since then the reference dates are determined from better statistical materials, have been reviewed more carefully, and seem substantially correct. Yet the results of classifying series according to their timing in 1919-38 (see Table 8) are similar to those in Table 5, which utilize the entire period covered by the series. When the timing comparisons of all series with acceptable conformity are put together, leads outnumber lags at only 3 of the 5 reference peaks in 1919-38 but at 5 of the 6 troughs (the exception is November 1927). This difference between peaks and troughs seems to be characteristic, however, only of the series whose timing is acceptable. Among the rejected series leads outnumber lags at 3 of the 5 reference peaks and at 3 of the 6 reference troughs. The roughly symmetrical behavior of the rejected series seems to dispose of the question of a bias in the reference dates in this period (though not, of course, of errors in individual dates).

A plausible hypothesis is that our sample is biased, containing an undue proportion of series that turn up early in revival for economic reasons.[18] This can hardly be due to a concentration in the sample of a particular type of economic process, however, since the distribution of many groups of series at troughs in Table 5 is biased towards leads as compared with their distribution at peaks. The effect is noticeable in production, employment, payrolls, money and banking series, profits, bank clearings and debits, and business indexes. The only sizeable group that tends in the opposite direction is commodity prices.

Strong upward trends might produce such a widespread effect. But it must be remembered, first, that the reference dates also are influenced by trends—they are not determined exclusively from trend-adjusted data. Second, if upward trends produced leads at troughs they might well, though not necessarily, produce lags at peaks.[19] This, however, is not what we find. Upward trends, coupled with a tendency towards sharp cyclical declines after peaks and gradual declines before troughs, would have the required asymmetrical effect. Whether investigation will show this type of specific cycle pattern to be prevalent we do not know.

Whatever the explanation there can be no doubt that the distribution of turning points in many types of economic process in this country is on the average different for troughs and peaks. At revivals, the upturn in aggregate economic activity is typically preceded by upturns in a substantial majority of these processes. At recessions, on the other hand, there is no such rule.

Two other features of Table 5 are fundamental. First, the series within a given economic group frequently tend to have similar timing at peaks and at troughs. In some groups this is

[18] In the accepted group the preponderance of leads at both peaks and troughs is greater than in the rejected group, as the accompanying figures show. No doubt the explanation is that leading series tend to be more sensitive to business cycles than lagging series, hence larger proportions qualify under our tests.

TIMING COMPARISONS, 1919-1938

	Leads	NUMBER OF Exact coin.	Lags	Total	RATIO: LEADS TO LAGS
		At Five Reference Peaks			
Rejected group	314	68	319	701	.98
Accepted group	420	124	364	908	1.15
		At Six Reference Troughs			
Rejected group	374	105	328	807	1.14
Accepted group	521	256	297	1074	1.75

[19] See *Measuring Business Cycles*, pp. 276-8.

obvious from the entries in the table, even though the individual series are not identified. For example, 6 of the 7 accepted series in the new orders group are classified 'leads only' at both peaks and troughs, while one is classified 'leads only' at peaks and 'leads and rough coincidences' at troughs. For some other groups the situation is much less clear. In a cross-tabulation of all 225 acceptable series, however, 113 series are classified in precisely the same timing group at peaks and at troughs: 64 are 'leads only', 9 'leads and rough coincidences', 8 'rough coincidences only', 6 'lags and rough coincidences', and 26 'lags only'.[20] The result is similar in a simpler cross-tabulation, involving only 3 classes (leads, lags, and rough coincidences) instead of 5. Classifying each of the 225 acceptable series by its most common type of timing,[21] at peaks and troughs separately, we find that 75 series lead at peaks and at troughs, 29 roughly coincide, and 30 lag. On this basis 60 percent of the acceptable series have similar timing at revivals and recessions. Other things being equal, indicators of this sort have distinct advantages since one can use the same series continuously, instead of shifting from one set to another. We shall have occasion to examine these three groups of series in Sections 6 and 7; the individual series are listed in Appendix B.

The second fundamental fact revealed by Table 5 is that economic processes differ strikingly in timing. The differences among groups are more distinct at peaks than at troughs, because of the bias toward leads at troughs. Nevertheless, combining the classifications at the two turns, we can say that the acceptable series in the following groups tend to be classified mainly as leaders (col. 5): new orders, private construction contracts and permits, hours of work per week, stock exchange transactions and prices, security issues, and business failures. Groups in which the series are classified largely as leaders or rough coinciders (col. 5, 6, and 7) are: transportation, business profits, bank clearings and debits,

[20] If it were equally likely that a series would be in any one of the 5 classes and the results at peaks and troughs were independent, we would expect only 45 series to be classified identically at peaks and troughs. Allowing for the actually observed unequal distributions of series at peaks and at troughs raises the expected figure to 57. Both are far below the observed number, 113.

[21] When the number of leads and rough coincidences is the same, a series is classified as a leader; when the number of lags and rough coincidences is the same, a lagger.

TABLE 8
Distribution of Acceptable Series by Timing Classifications Based upon the Full Period Covered and on 1919-1938

	NUMBER OF SERIES ACCEPTED FOR					
	Leads only	Leads & rough coin.	Rough coin. only	Lags & rough coin.	Lags only	Total No. of Series
ALL SERIES						
Full period class. of timing at						
Peaks	78	24	36	32	55	225
Troughs	107	38	34	13	33	225
1919-38 class. of timing at						
Peaks	42	16	30	26	29	143
Troughs	57	26	36	16	8	143
SERIES THAT DO NOT COVER 1919-1938						
Full period class. of timing at						
Peaks	21	3	2	3	15	44
Troughs	27	5	3	..	9	44
SERIES THAT COVER 1919-1938 ONLY						
Full period & 1919-38 class. of timing at						
Peaks	27	9	16	19	18	89
Troughs	38	18	20	10	3	89
SERIES THAT COVER MORE THAN 1919-1938						
Accepted both full period and 1919-38						
Full period class. of timing at						
Peaks	11	7	10	6	9	43
Troughs	20	9	8	3	3	43
1919-38 class. of timing at						
Peaks	11	6	9	7	10	43
Troughs	16	6	14	4	3	43
Accepted full period, rejected 1919-38						
Full period class. of timing at						
Peaks	19	5	8	4	13	49
Troughs	22	6	3	..	18	49
Rejected full period, accepted 1919-38						
1919-38 class. of timing at						
Peaks	4	1	5	..	1	11
Troughs	3	2	2	2	2	11

Only series accepted for conformity and for timing at peaks and troughs are included. The 1919-38 classifications are based on cyclical measures ending with 1938 and beginning 1919, 1920, or 1921, depending upon when the series starts and whether the first cycle following World War I is omitted.

and indexes of business activity. In only one group do laggers (col. 9) plainly predominate: interest rates and bond yields. But payrolls are classified mainly as laggers or rough coinciders (col. 7, 8, 9), and retail sales might be put tentatively in this category, too. The production series do not concentrate heavily in any timing group, though leaders outnumber laggers. Employment and commodity price series also are fairly evenly scattered, while the national bank series tend either to lead or to lag by long intervals.

So much for a general view of the results obtained by applying our standards of conformity and timing to the full record of each series. Now let us consider briefly the results of applying these standards to 1919-38 alone.

Since a large proportion of our series begin in 1919 or shortly before, we should not expect these results, in the aggregate, to differ greatly from the previous ones. In 1919-38, 143 series have acceptable conformity and timing at peaks and troughs and of these 89 cover 1919-38 only (Table 8). As in the full period analysis leaders preponderate, and more at troughs than at peaks. However, the proportion of series that lead or lag by long intervals ('leads only' or 'lags only') is considerably smaller in 1919-38. This is clearly due to the prevalence of long leaders and laggers in two groups of series: the 44 acceptable series that do not cover 1919-38 and the 49 series that are accepted on the basis of the full period but rejected in 1919-38. In the other groups long leaders or laggers do not predominate so much.

The timing characteristics of the 44 series that end some time before 1938 are intriguing, but they must be reserved for later investigation. Nearly half are national bank series, which we have not compiled beyond 1914. On the other hand, the timing classification of the 49 series that are accepted for the full period but rejected for 1919-38 poses a question we cannot ignore. Did this substantial group of series behave in a significantly different way after 1919?

Table 9 is designed to answer the question. Section A shows the timing of this group before and after 1919. For comparative purposes Section B shows the timing before and after 1919 of the 54 series that were accepted in 1919-38 and extend back of 1919 (including 11 series rejected on the basis of their full period behavior). Since the latter series are classified solely on the basis of their timing in 1919-38, the pre-1919 data are strictly independent of the data used to classify the series.

TABLE 9
Timing Observations Before and After 1919, Two Groups of Series

A   Series Accepted for the Full Period, but Rejected 1919-1938[a]

	TIMING CLASSIFICATION, FULL PERIOD				
	Leads only	Leads & rough coin.	Rough coin. only	Lags & rough coin.	Lags only
TIMING AT PEAKS BEFORE 1919					
Number of series	19	4[b]	8	4	13
Total ref. turns covered	168	30	73	34	111
Total timing observations	161	30	70	34	101
Number of					
Leads exceeding 3 months	93	10	11	1	4
Leads of 3 months or less	31	11	16	4	2
Exact coincidences	8	4	10	3	2
Lags of 3 months or less	13	4	21	17	21
Lags exceeding 3 months	16	1	12	9	72
Av. lead (—) or lag (+), mo.	—6.7	—2.8	—0.1	+2.8	+6.7
TIMING AT PEAKS, 1919-1938					
Number of series	19	4[b]	8	4	13
Total ref. turns covered	88	16	37	18	61
Total timing observations	79	15	33	16	48
Number of					
Leads exceeding 3 months	41	4	8	..	6
Leads of 3 months or less	15	6	12	5	6
Exact coincidences	4	2	2	3	1
Lags of 3 months or less	6	1	6	4	8
Lags exceeding 3 months	13	2	5	4	27
Av. lead (—) or lag (+), mo.	—4.7	—3.2	—1.5	+1.1	+3.1
TIMING AT TROUGHS BEFORE 1919					
Number of series	22	6	3	..	17[c]
Total ref. turns covered	199	50	12	..	152
Total timing observations	192	50	12	..	141
Number of					
Leads exceeding 3 months	124	22	4	..	13
Leads of 3 months or less	42	26	3	..	10
Exact coincidences	10	2	1	..	7
Lags of 3 months or less	6	..	3	..	18
Lags exceeding 3 months	10	..	1	..	93
Av. lead (—) or lag (+), mo.	—6.6	—3.9	—1.7	..	+8.2
TIMING AT TROUGHS, 1919-1938					
Number of series	22	6	3	..	17[c]
Total ref. turns covered	124	33	16	..	89
Total timing observations	108	32	14	..	72
Number of					
Leads exceeding 3 months	55	2	..	..	13
Leads of 3 months or less	16	8	3	..	5
Exact coincidences	7	16	2	..	8
Lags of 3 months or less	12	5	5	..	13
Lags exceeding 3 months	18	1	4	..	33
Av. lead (—) or lag (+), mo.	—2.7	—0.5	+2.3	..	+5.8

B Series Accepted 1919-1938[a]

	Leads only	Leads & rough coin.	Rough coin. only	Lags & rough coin.	Lags only
TIMING AT PEAKS BEFORE 1919					
Number of series	15	7	13[b]	7	10[b]
Total ref. turns covered	69	51	62	45	52
Total timing observations	52	43	53	42	49
Number of					
Leads exceeding 3 months	17	11	12	11	10
Leads of 3 months or less	15	11	8	6	7
Exact coincidences	4	4	7	8	5
Lags of 3 months or less	5	9	15	7	6
Lags exceeding 3 months	11	8	11	10	21
Av. lead (—) or lag (+), mo.	—4.2	—1.2	—0.2	—0.4	+0.9
TIMING AT PEAKS, 1919-1938					
Number of series	15	7	13[b]	7	10[b]
Total ref. turns covered	69	30	64	35	50
Total timing observations	66	30	63	35	50
Number of					
Leads exceeding 3 months	39	7	6	1	5
Leads of 3 months or less	19	18	18	2	1
Exact coincidences	3	3	16	11	5
Lags of 3 months or less	2	2	18	17	22
Lags exceeding 3 months	3	..	5	4	17
Av. lead (—) or lag (+), mo.	—5.4	—3.9	—0.6	+1.2	+2.8
TIMING AT TROUGHS BEFORE 1919					
Number of series	14[d]	7[c]	15[c]	5[c]	5
Total ref. turns covered	49	64	73	35	44
Total timing observations	46	56	64	25	42
Number of					
Leads exceeding 3 months	23	20	25	12	6
Leads of 3 months or less	9	19	15	6	10
Exact coincidences	9	8	12	3	1
Lags of 3 months or less	3	7	4	2	8
Lags exceeding 3 months	2	2	8	2	17
Av. lead (—) or lag (+), mo.	—3.6	—3.7	—1.5	—1.9	+1.9
TIMING AT TROUGHS, 1919-1938					
Number of series	14[d]	7[c]	15[c]	5[c]	5
Total ref. turns covered	79	41	86	28	28
Total timing observations	76	41	86	27	28
Number of					
Leads exceeding 3 months	48	9	10	2	4
Leads of 3 months or less	13	14	14	3	1
Exact coincidences	5	15	35	1	3
Lags of 3 months or less	4	3	22	16	8
Lags exceeding 3 months	6	..	5	5	12
Av. lead (—) or lag (+), mo.	—4.4	—1.6	—0.2	+1.7	+4.8

[a] 'Accepted' means accepted for conformity and for timing at peaks and troughs. Only series that cover reference turns before 1919 and through 1938 are included. War cycle observations are omitted in certain series.

[b] One series beginning 1914 is omitted here since the war cycle (1918) peak is omitted; the series is included in the distributions for troughs.

[c] One series beginning 1918 is omitted here but included in the distributions for peaks.

[d] Five series beginning 1918 are omitted here but included in the distributions for peaks.

The 49 series of Section A plainly deteriorated somewhat in quality as indicators after 1919. Whereas before 1919 there was a corresponding specific turn at 95 percent of all the reference peaks covered by the entire group of series, after 1919 the percentage was only 87; similarly, the percentage at troughs declined from 96 to 86. Indeed, every timing group has fewer timing observations relative to the number of reference turns covered after 1919 than before. In other words, the cycles in these series did not match the reference cycles as well after 1919 as before. Moreover, the proportion of leads shown by the leading series and of lags by the lagging series declined considerably, though not sufficiently to obscure the broad differences in the timing of the different groups. The leaders tended to lead and the laggers to lag after as well as before 1919.

We may conclude, first, that classification of the 49 series on the basis of their full period behavior is not wholly misleading with respect to their recent behavior; second, that while our technique has identified series that have in general deteriorated in quality or altered their timing, we would do well to examine each series more closely before deciding that its behavior has altered significantly.[22] On the average, the 49 series covered nearly twice as many reference turns before 1919 as after, so that the full period test was based on about three times as much information as the 1919-38 test. As the table demonstrates, the pre-1919 information was definitely useful in determining the nature of the timing relationships among these series. Ignoring that information may make for errors in classification. By the same token it would seem particularly desirable in the case of short series to supplement our simple measures of conformity and timing by more information about the same series or by information about related series.

Even when the information utilized in classifying series is confined to 1919-38, however, the results are not without utility outside of this period. The pre-1919 behavior of the 54 series classified in Section B of Table 9 resembles their behavior during

---

[22] Of the 329 series that cover more than 1919-38 only 54, or 16 percent, are accepted on the basis of their behavior during 1919-38, whereas 92, or 28 percent, are accepted on the basis of their full period behavior. In itself, this does not necessarily mean that the series deteriorated after 1919. Even if each series behaved in exactly the same way after 1919 as before we should expect the percentage accepted for 1919-38 to be smaller than for the full period because the levels of acceptable conformity and timing are higher the shorter the period (see Sec. 4).

1919-38, though the differences among the groups are less sharp. The timing relationships among economic processes evidently have some degree of stability.

6

Behavior of Selected Groups of Indicators, 1885-1940

We have not found any single series that bears an invariant relation to business cycles as defined by our reference dates. The series classified in the timing group 'rough coincidences' have the smallest variations in timing. But even here variations do occur, and some series have extra cycles or 'skip' reference turns. Moreover, the more interesting indicators of revivals and recessions are the leaders or (as we shall see) the laggers, and for them the variations in timing are larger. Few long series that tend to lead have a perfect record of leads without lags, and none leads by a constant interval.

Evidently it would be unwise to place sole reliance upon a single indicator of revivals or recessions. Special circumstances can always arise that will cause it to fail. But what of the alternative —using several indicators? To answer this question let us examine the behavior in successive business cycles of the groups of series obtained by applying our conformity and timing criteria.

We have already presented in Chart 3 the percentage of the 404 series with 'acceptable' conformity reaching a specific cycle peak or trough in each month 1885-1940, together with the derived percentage expanding. And we have noted the clustering of specific cycle peaks around reference peaks and of specific troughs around reference troughs. No reference peaks or troughs are skipped by these concentrations, nor do appreciable concentrations appear outside the vicinity of the reference dates, except possibly in 1933-35 (cf. note 8). This is to be expected, of course, if the reference dates are accurate. The really noteworthy feature of Chart 3 is that these clusters are spread over a considerable period, usually a year or more, and in phases of moderate length the clusters of peaks begin at about the time the clusters of troughs end, and vice versa. Hence the intriguing possibility presents itself that we may be able to recognize the clusters well before the peak or trough in aggregate economic activity.[23]

[23] Some interesting experiments along this line were reported by C. Ashley Wright in a paper presented at the Conference on Business Cycles Research, National Bureau of Economic Research, November 25-27, 1949.

TABLE 10

Timing of Percentage of Series Expanding and Contracting in Successive Business Cycles, 1879-1938: Two Groups of Series

A   Business Expansions

HIGHEST PERCENTAGE OF SERIES EXPANDING

Monthly Reference Dates		All Series with Acceptable Conformity[a] No. of Months				Series That Lead at Peaks and Troughs[b] No. of Months			
Trough	Peak	Date[c]	After ref. trough	Before ref. peak	%	Date[c]	After ref. trough	Before ref. peak	%
(1)	(2)	(3)	(4)	(5)	(6)	(7)	(8)	(9)	(10)
3/79	3/82	1/80	10	26	85.7	2/80	11	25	100.0
5/85	3/87	11/85	6	16	85.9	7/85	2	20	100.0
4/88	7/90	9/89	17	10	82.9	6/89	14	13	82.6
5/91	1/93	8/92	15	5	70.0	11/91	6	14	92.0
6/94	12/95	6/95	12	6	70.1	5/95	11	7	64.5
6/97	6/99	3/99	21	3	85.8	7/97	1	23	97.1
12/00	9/02	12/01	12	9	76.0	4/01	4	17	83.3
8/04	5/07	10/05	14	19	89.8	11/04	3	30	100.0
6/08	1/10	8/09	14	5	83.1	11/08	5	14	100.0
1/12	1/13	3/12	2	10	83.1	2/12	1	11	83.3
12/14	8/18	11/15	11	33	90.4	6/15	6	38	100.0
4/19	1/20	7/19	3	6	87.9	5/19	1	8	90.0
7/21	5/23	8/22	13	9	90.7	4/22	9	13	100.0
7/24	10/26	1/25	6	21	84.2	7/25	12	15	96.7
11/27	6/29	10/28	11	8	79.7	1/28	2	17	91.7
3/33	5/37	9/36	42	8	92.0	11/36	44	6	94.3
Average 1879-1918			12.2	12.9			5.8	19.3	
Av. Dev. 1879-1918			3.7	7.7			3.4	7.2	
Average 1919-37			15.0	10.4			13.6	11.8	
Av. Dev. 1919-37			10.8	4.2			12.2	3.8	
Average 1879-1937			13.1	12.1			8.2	16.9	
Av. Dev. 1879-1937			5.6	6.8			6.4	6.4	

The curve representing the percentage of series **expanding**, based on the same data, suggests this possibility even more strongly. Its cycles are extraordinarily well defined, are in one to one correspondence with business cycles, and reach their maxima and minima long before the corresponding reference peaks and troughs. On the average in 1879-1938 the percentage of series expanding reached its highest level about a year after the expansion in general activity began and about a year before it ended (Table 10, A, col. 4 and 5). Similarly, the percentage expanding reached its lowest level (the percentage contracting its highest level) in mid-contraction, on the average (Table 10, B, col. 4 and 5). But the intervals between the peaks and troughs in the

TABLE 10 (CONCL.)

B Business Contractions
HIGHEST PERCENTAGE OF SERIES CONTRACTING

Monthly Reference Dates		All Series with Acceptable Conformity[a]				Series That Lead at Peaks and Troughs[b]			
			No. of Months				No. of Months		
Peak	Trough	Date[c]	After ref. peak	Before ref. trough	%	Date[c]	After ref. peak	Before ref. trough	%
(1)	(2)	(3)	(4)	(5)	(6)	(7)	(8)	(9)	(10)
3/82	5/85	5/84	26	12	88.7	5/84	26	12	95.2
3/87	4/88	2/88	11	2	65.0	8/87	5	8	73.9
7/90	5/91	1/91	6	4	76.3	11/90	4	6	82.6
1/93	6/94	8/93	7	10	83.9	7/93	6	11	96.3
12/95	6/97	8/96	8	10	83.3	2/96	2	16	90.9
6/99	12/00	7/00	13	5	71.4	11/99	5	13	86.1
9/02	8/04	8/03	11	12	72.4	6/03	9	14	89.7
5/07	6/08	11/07	6	7	76.5	10/07	5	8	90.0
1/10	1/12	7/10	6	18	75.0	3/10	2	22	95.7
1/13	12/14	5/14	16	7	85.2	3/13	2	21	93.9
8/18	4/19	11/18	3	5	63.1	6/17	—14[d]	22	72.7
1/20	7/21	12/20	11	7	90.6	8/20	7	11	91.8
5/23	7/24	3/24	10	4	74.2	8/23	3	11	78.3
10/26	11/27	1/27	3	10	69.4	11/26	1	12	81.7
6/29	3/33	8/30	14	31	96.3	10/31	28	17	100.0
5/37	6/38	11/37	6	7	90.1	11/37	6	7	92.6
Average 1882-1919			10.3	8.4			4.7	13.9	
Av. Dev. 1882-1919			4.7	3.7			5.0	4.6	
Average 1920-38			8.8	11.8			9.0	11.6	
Av. Dev. 1920-38			3.4	7.7			7.6	2.3	
Average 1882-1938			9.8	9.4			6.1	13.2	
Av. Dev. 1882-1938			4.2	4.6			5.7	4.1	

[a] 404 series; see Sec. 5.
[b] 75 series; see Sec. 5 and App. B.
[c] Dates are determined in accordance with rules for marking specific cycle turns. See *Measuring Business Cycles*, pp. 56-66.
[d] Highest percentage contracting precedes reference peak by 14 months.

curve and the preceding or following reference dates varied greatly from one cycle to another, ranging from two or three months to more than three years.

Two other characteristics of the curve in Chart 3 should be noted. First, particularly in recent cycles, the curve reaches the 50 percent level at or about the time of the reference peak or trough. Some of the discrepancies in earlier cycles (e.g., 1899) may be due to misdated reference turns. This feature of the curve, of course, enhances its value as an indicator, assuming it could be made available on something like a current basis (see App. A).

Second, the maximum or minimum levels reached during a

business cycle expansion or contraction are fairly closely associated with the amplitude of the phase. The lowest level reached during the relatively mild business contraction of 1926-27 (31 percent) was relatively high compared, say, with the lowest level reached during the Great Depression (4 percent, in 1930). In other words, in no month during the 1926-27 contraction were more than 69 percent of the series contracting, whereas in 1929-33 the figure reached 96 percent.

The fact is, as Burns and Mitchell have observed, that the diffusion of business cycle movements among economic processes is related to the amplitude of the cyclical phase.[24] Severe contractions are widely diffused, mild contractions moderately diffused. Similarly, expansions that attain large amplitudes are usually spread over many sectors of the economy, while mild expansions tend to be confined to fewer sectors. The Chart 3 curve is interesting, therefore, because it confirms Burns' and Mitchell's finding; it utilizes a much larger sample of series and it measures diffusion in a different way.[25] Again, this property of the curve enhances its potential value as an indicator.

Chart 3 is based upon all series with acceptable conformity, regardless of what kind of timing they exhibit. The general shape of the distributions of specific cycle turning points in Chart 3 might lead one to suspect that some sort of random process was at work: that the turning points in different series tend to cluster around certain points in time but that the position of an individual series in this cluster is a matter of chance.[26] No doubt there is a random element or 'error' in the selection of specific cycle turns in individual series, since these are determined from

[24] *Measuring Business Cycles,* p. 106.

[25] They used a sample of 46 long series (a smaller number before 1890) and measured diffusion by the number of series rising or falling in a given reference phase (i.e., using conformity measures). In five mild expansions during 1879-1933 they found (Table 26, p. 106) the average percentage of series that rose, when allowance is made for systematic leads and lags, was 81; in five moderate expansions, 90; in five vigorous expansions, 94. The average percentage of series that declined in five mild contractions was 75; in five moderate contractions, 82; in five severe contractions, 98. The corresponding average percentages based on the entries through 1933 in our Table 10, column 6, are, for expansions: 78, 84, and 87; and for contractions: 71, 76, and 87.

[26] The smaller size of the 'sample' in the early years contributes to the greater irregularity of the percentage distributions in those years.

the original data adjusted only for seasonal variations. But the series are not independent of one another. In the first place, there is a considerable amount of statistical duplication—we include not only indexes of production but also many component series, etc. Secondly, the series are interrelated economically. One result is that sequences in the turning dates of individual series and groups of series tend to be repeated in cycle after cycle, a fact demonstrated in Chart 4.

As described in Section 5, the three groups of series in Chart 4 are obtained by applying our conformity and timing criteria to the full period covered by each series and selecting the series that have similar timing at business cycle peaks and troughs. Appendix B lists the 75 series in the leading group, the 29 in the roughly coincident group, and the 30 in the lagging group. Not all are available at any one time, however; the numbers in January every tenth year are:

	1890	1900	1910	1920	1930
Leading group	23	36	47	61	60
Roughly coincident group	1	1	5	22	29
Lagging group	12	18	21	20	22

The significance of the chart may be grasped more easily if we trace the events recorded by it in the 1921-24 cycle, as we did in connection with Chart 3. Starting in the middle of the chart with the distribution of troughs in the leading group (which comprises such series as new orders for goods, construction contracts, hours of work per week, stock market activity), we see that some of these series began to turn up in the second half of 1920, (point a in the chart) and that more than half had reached bottom by the end of the first quarter in 1921 (b).[27] By that time a few series in the roughly coincident group (which includes several indexes of production, employment, railroad traffic, etc.) had begun to reverse their downward movement, but most of the upturns in this group occurred in the third quarter of 1921 (c),

---

[27] For clarity the distributions in Chart 4 are plotted by quarters instead of by months; nearly all the individual series, however, are monthly. The medians (shown by arrows) are computed and plotted on a monthly basis. They are derived, not from all the specific cycle turns recorded in the chart, but from the 'corresponding' turns, i.e., those that in the analysis of the individual series are compared with reference turns. This procedure defines the clusters of turns for which the medians are computed. Roughly 95 percent of the turns in these groups of series are 'corresponding'.

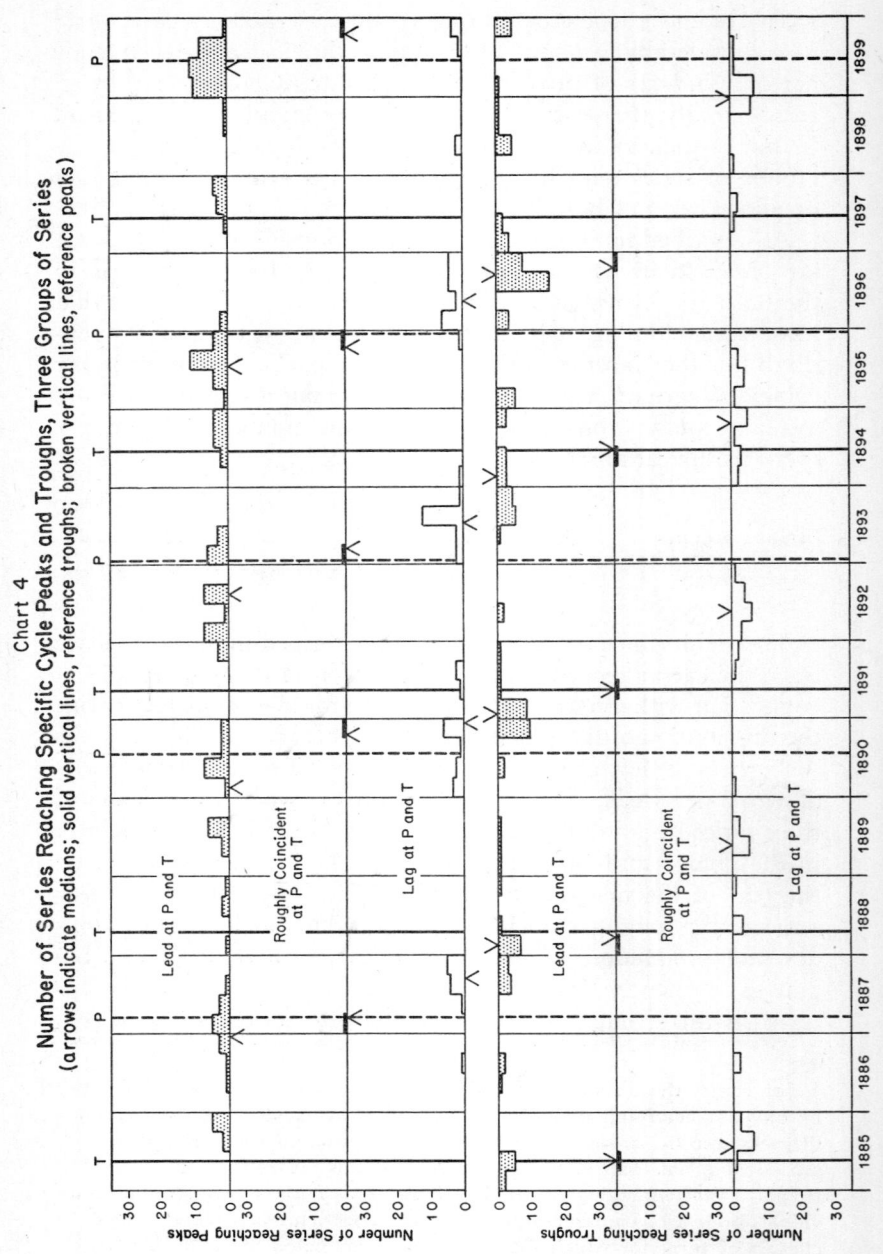

Chart 4
Number of Series Reaching Specific Cycle Peaks and Troughs, Three Groups of Series
(arrows indicate medians; solid vertical lines, reference troughs; broken vertical lines, reference peaks)

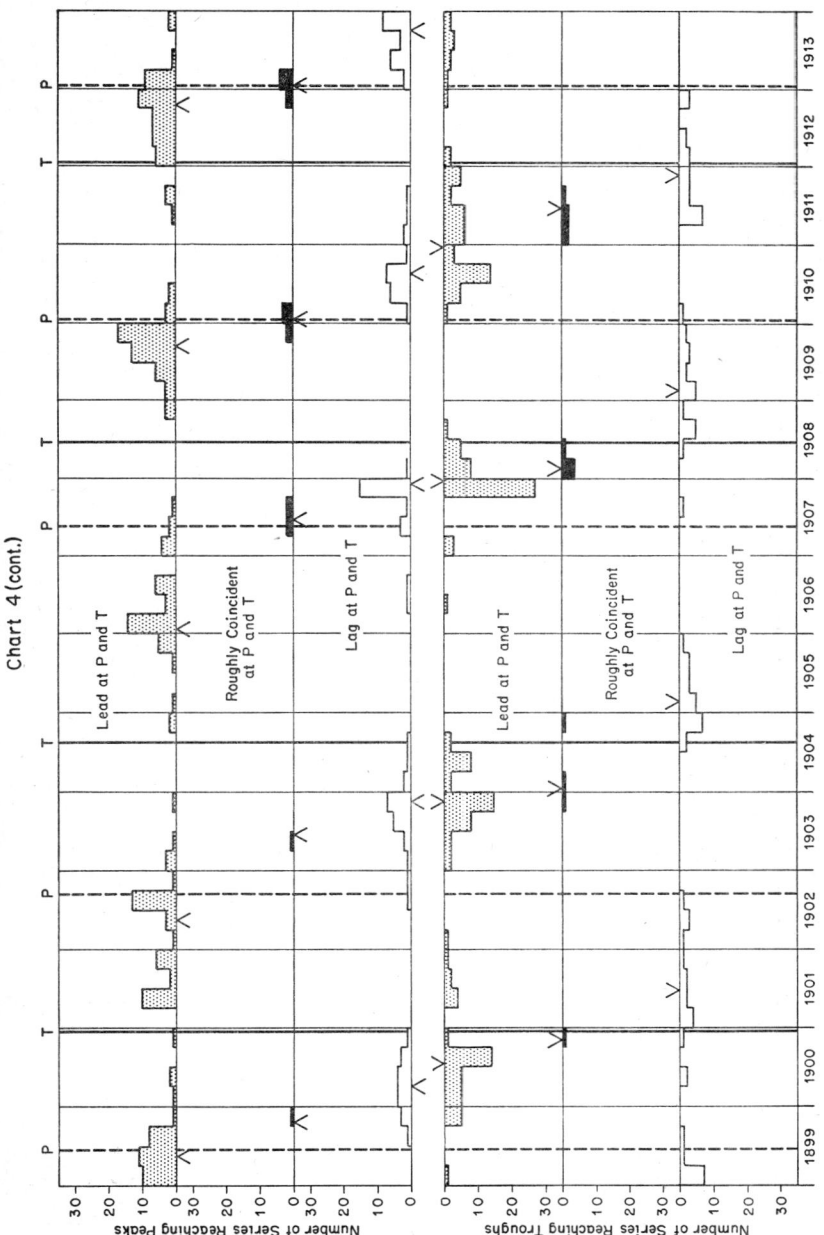

Chart 4 (cont.)

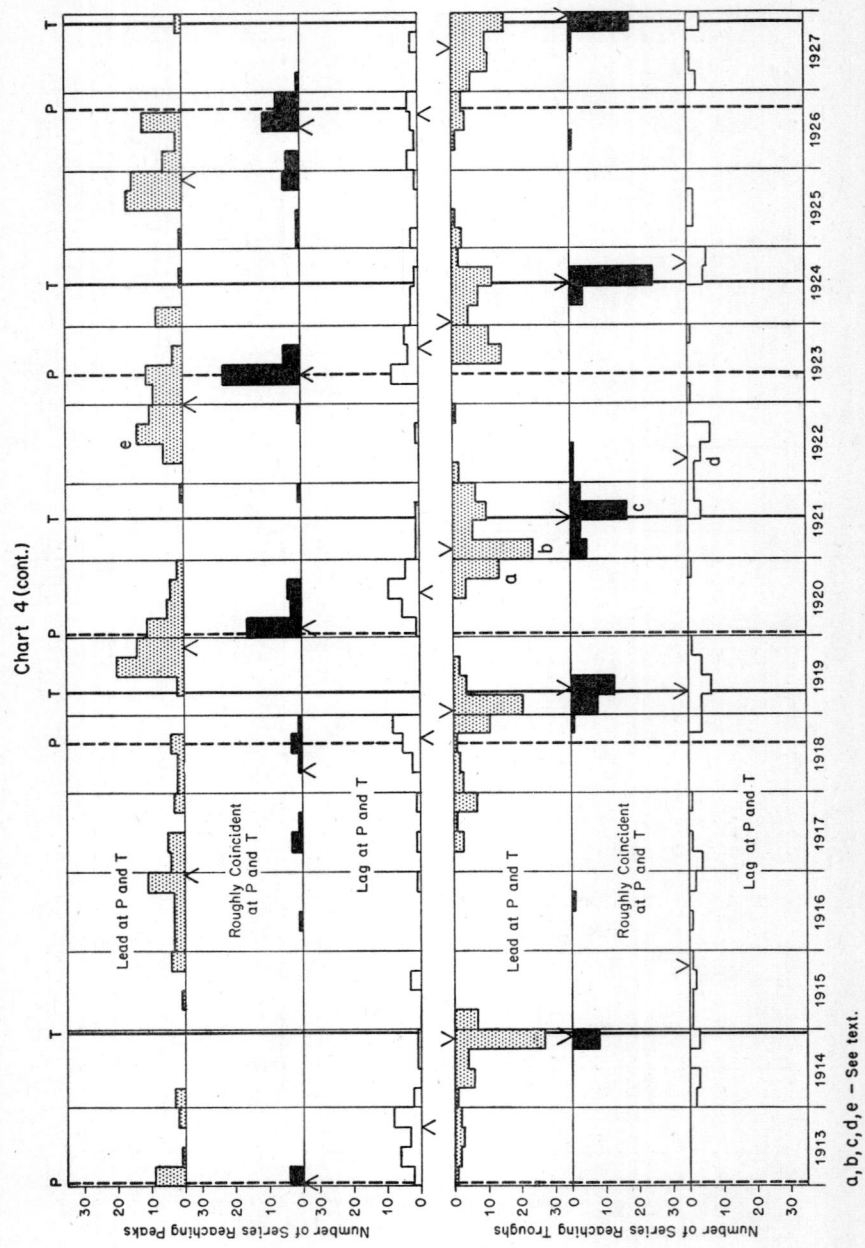

Chart 4 (cont.)

a, b, c, d, e — See text.

Chart 4 (concl.)

where the reference trough is placed (July). Nearly all the troughs in the lagging series (payrolls, certain price series, interest rates, etc.) came after the reference trough, their turns being scattered through the second half of 1921 and the first three quarters of 1922 (d). Thus more than a year elapsed between the median upturn in the leading group and that in the lagging group.

The second and third quarters of 1922 not only saw the last of the upturns in the lagging group but also the first of the downturns in the leading group (e, top of chart). By the beginning of 1923 half of the leading series had reached peaks, and in the second quarter most of the roughly coincident series began to decline. In May 1923 the reference expansion that began in July 1921 ended. The lagging group registered peaks throughout the ensuing contraction. Hardly had the contraction begun, however, when upturns in the leading series began to appear. They occurred in two waves: in the second half of 1923 and in mid-1924. Troughs in the roughly coincident series were concentrated in mid-1924, when the next reference expansion started. In the third and fourth quarters of 1924 many of the lagging series joined in this expansion.

By following the chart up and down in this manner one gets a lively impression of the continuity and the sequence of events in successive business cycles. It should be borne in mind that the sample of series in each of the three groups remains substantially the same from cycle to cycle, varying only because a series is discontinued or a new one becomes available. We would, of course, expect to find a difference in the timing of the three groups when results for the period as a whole are considered, for the series were selected on the basis of their timing during the period they covered. But what emerges from Chart 4 is that the expected sequence among the groups, as reflected, say, in the medians, appears at every single business cycle peak and at all except two troughs (1919 and 1933). Moreover, between peaks and troughs the sequence is highly consistent too. The median trough of the lagging group invariably precedes the median peak of the leading group; and with only one exception, 1903, the median peak of the lagging group precedes the median trough of the leading group (Table 11).

Not only is there a notable degree of consistency in the timing of the medians, but the average leads and lags are fairly long. In fact, the medians for the leading and lagging groups tend to

TABLE 11

Timing of Medians of Corresponding Specific Cycle Turns, 1885–1938 Three Groups of Series[a]

Reference Peak	LEAD (−) OR LAG (+) AT REFERENCE PEAKS (MONTHS)			PEAKS Median trough, leading group	Reference Trough	LEAD (−) OR LAG (+) AT REFERENCE TROUGHS (MONTHS)			TROUGHS Median peak, leading group
	Median trough, lagging group	Leading group	Roughly coin. group	Lagging group			Median peak, lagging group	Leading group	Roughly coin. group	Lagging group	
Mar. 1887	−20	−3	0[b]	+6	+11	May 1885	−7	−6	0[b]	+2	+19
July 1890	−14	−5	+3[b]	+5	+6	Apr. 1888	−5	−2	−1[b]	+13	+22
Jan. 1893	−8	−5	+2[b]	+6	+13	May 1891	−11	−4	0[b]	+12	+15
Dec. 1895	−14	−5	−2[b]	+5	+9	June 1894	−13	−4	0[b]	+4	+13
June 1899	−6	−1	+4[b]	+9.5	+13	June 1897	−9	−9	−8[b]	+18	+23
Sep. 1902	−15	−4	+9[b]	+14	+14	Dec. 1900	−8.5	−5	−2[b]	+6	+17
May 1907	−27	−16	+1	+6.5	+7	Aug. 1904	−9	−9	−7	+6	+17
Jan. 1910	−11	−4	0	+7	+11	June 1908	−6.5	−6	−4	+8	+15
Jan. 1913	−14	−3	0	+8.5	+22	Jan. 1912	−17	−13	−7	−2	+9
Aug. 1918	−34	−20	−4	+1	+5	Dec. 1914	−14.5	−1	−0.5	+10	+24
Jan. 1920	−9	−2	+1	+6.5	+13	Apr. 1919	−7	−3	+0.5	0	+7
May 1923	−13	−4.5	0	+4	+8	July 1921	−11.5	−5	0	+9	+17.5
Oct. 1926	−24	−11	−3	−1	+9	July 1924	−10	−6	0	+3	+16
June 1929	−15	−5	+1	+2	+40	Nov. 1927	−14	−4	+1	+4	+14
May 1937	−50	−2	0	+3	+9	Mar. 1933	−43	−5	0	0	+48
						June 1938	−10	−4	0	+10	
Average 1885–1918	−16.3	−6.6	+1.3	+6.8	+11.1		−9.8	−5.9	−3.0	+7.7	+16.5
Av. dev. 1885–1918	6.4	4.6	2.6	2.3	3.5		3.2	2.7	2.8	4.5	4.2
Average 1919–38	−22.2	−4.9	−0.1	+2.9	+15.8		−17.7	−4.5	+0.2	+4.3	+23.9
Av. dev. 1919–38	11.8	2.5	1.2	1.9	9.7		10.1	0.8	0.3	3.4	12.1
Average 1885–1938	−18.3	−6.0	+0.8	+5.5	+12.7		−12.5	−5.4	−1.8	+6.4	+18.4
Av. dev. 1885–1938	8.5	3.8	2.1	2.6	5.2		5.2	2.1	2.4	4.4	5.8

[a] For list of series in each group see App. B. [b] Based on one series only.

be almost uniformly distributed over the cycle, as the average intervals in the accompanying tabulation show. Even the average

Intervals between Median Turns
in Leading and Lagging Groups, 1887-1938

	Interval			Average interval, 15 observations	Average Deviation	Range	Range of middle 13 observations
				(m	o n	t h	s)
A)	Peak, leading	to	Peak, lagging	11.6	3.6	17.5 (5 to 22.5)	14 (7 to 21)
B)	Peak, lagging	to	Trough, leading	7.1	5.3	38 (0 to 38)	13 (0.5 to 13.5)
C)	Trough, leading	to	Trough, lagging	12.1	4.1	24 (3 to 27)	11 (5 to 16)
D)	Trough, lagging	to	Peak, leading	12.2	5.7	45 (3 to 48)	12 (5 to 17)

deviations of the intervals do not differ greatly, whether based on like or unlike turns.[28]

Chart 5 demonstrates the extraordinarily long leads of the leading series when their movements are expressed in terms of the percentage of series expanding (see also Table 10, col. 9), and confirms the striking differences in timing of all three groups. The maxima of the curve for the lagging group coincide roughly with the reference peaks, as indeed they must since the downturns in these series are usually clustered in the period immediately following the reference peak. Likewise the minima approximately coincide with the reference troughs since the upturns in the lagging series tend to come just after the reference trough. Much of the time this curve is moving in precisely the opposite direction to the curve for the leading group.[29]

[28] The larger average deviations in intervals B and D are caused by the extreme intervals that occurred in the 1929-37 cycle; excluding these, the average deviations would actually be smaller than in intervals A and C. But rough uniformity in variability is suggested by the ranges of the middle 13 items.

[29] The curve for the leading group also tends to lead the curve in Chart 3, based on series undifferentiated as to timing. The leading curve crosses the 50 percent line before the reference peak or trough in nearly every instance, and it almost invariably reaches a maximum level before the curve in Chart 3. Like the latter, the level reached by the leading curve during a reference phase tends to be correlated with the amplitude of the phase. The average percentages corresponding to those in note 25, computed from Table 10, col. 10, are, for expansions: 87, 90, 99; and for contractions: 85, 84, 95.

The sequences exhibited in cycle after cycle by the groups of series in Charts 4 and 5 are not mere statistical effects produced by our method of classification. First, as suggested above, the application of the method would not, by itself, be expected to produce similar sequences cycle by cycle. Secondly, and this is the clue to the real explanation, the processes that tend to lead and lag are not the same, as Section 5 makes clear. It is beyond the scope of this report to explain why certain processes lead and others lag, though the reasons are, in many cases, fairly obvious. New orders for goods and contracts for construction would be expected to lead the output of the products to which they give rise. Changes in hours of work would be expected to take precedence over changes in the work force (employment) when the work load shifts. But many significant timing differences are more subtle (e.g., the lead in liabilities of business failures, inverted; the lag in long-term interest rates, or their lead when taken invertedly; the lag in bond sales, inverted), and to develop a thoroughgoing explanation is one of the principal tasks of business cycle theory. In this connection the possibility of a causal connection between the turns in lagging series and the subsequent opposite turns in leading series should not be overlooked.

No doubt the charts idealize the situation somewhat. If the processes that lead and lag had been picked in advance (on the basis of experience) and tested over subsequent cycles, the sequences would likely have been blurred to some extent—though not entirely. Of that we have evidence in the experiment with 21 indicators reported in Section 2, and further evidence will emerge in Section 7. Moreover, the pre- and post-1919 tests in Table 9 also indicated a fairly high degree of continuity in timing relationships. Burns and Mitchell reached a similar conclusion in a series of tests on a small sample of series for several successive periods.[30]

Our brief examination of the cyclical behavior of groups of series is pertinent not only to the selection and use of indicators but also to an understanding of the nature of business cycles. Business cycles consist of "expansions occurring at about the same time in many economic activities, followed by similarly general recessions, contractions, and revivals. . ."[31] But the sequence of

---

[30] *Measuring Business Cycles*, pp. 393-400, 485-90.

[31] Ibid., p. 3.

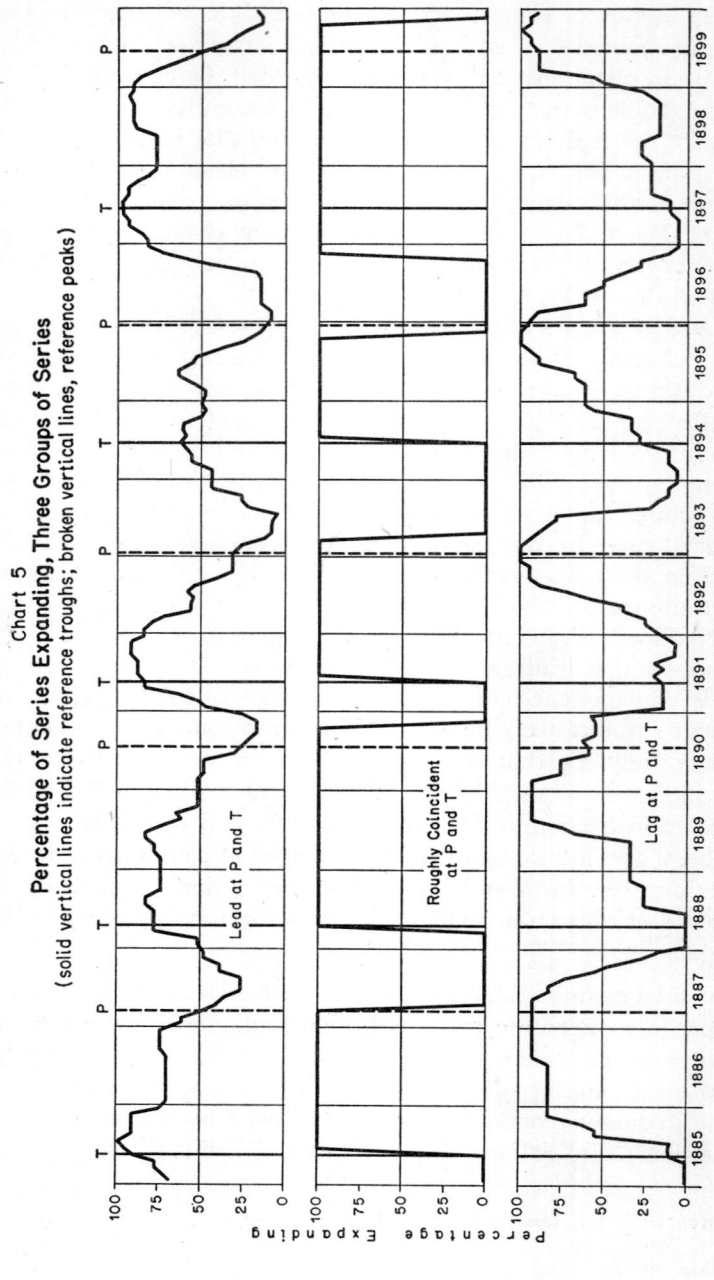

Chart 5
Percentage of Series Expanding, Three Groups of Series
(solid vertical lines indicate reference troughs; broken vertical lines, reference peaks)

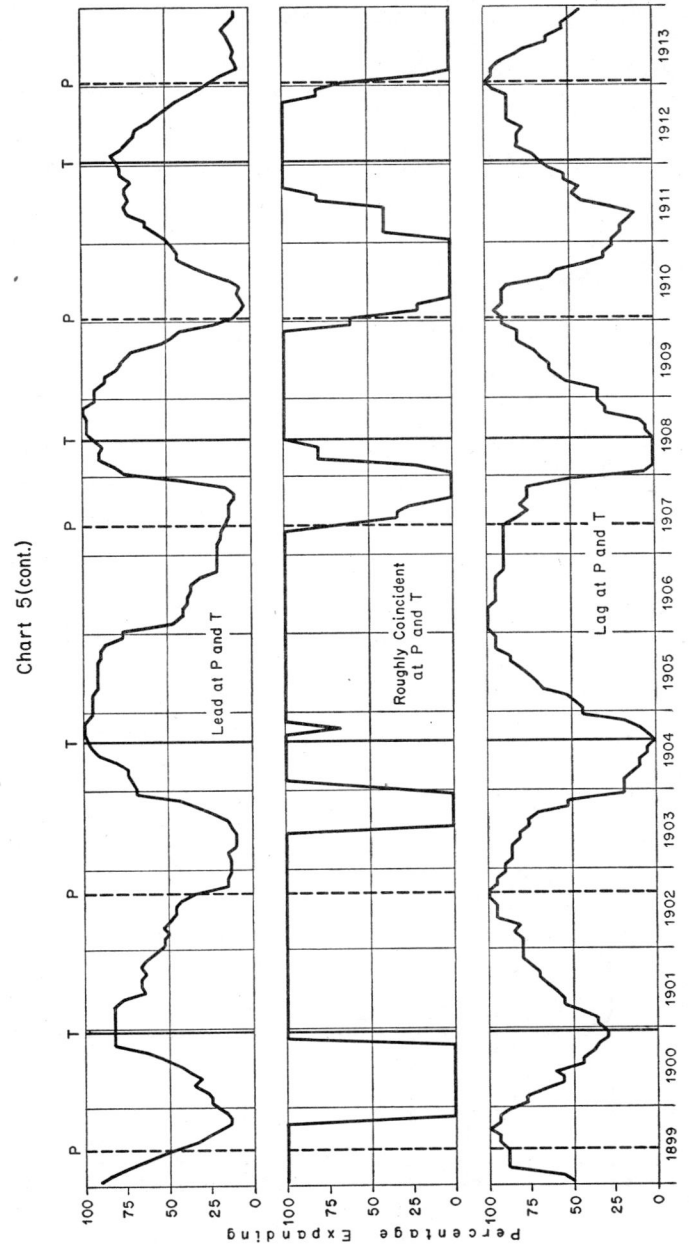

Chart 5(cont.)

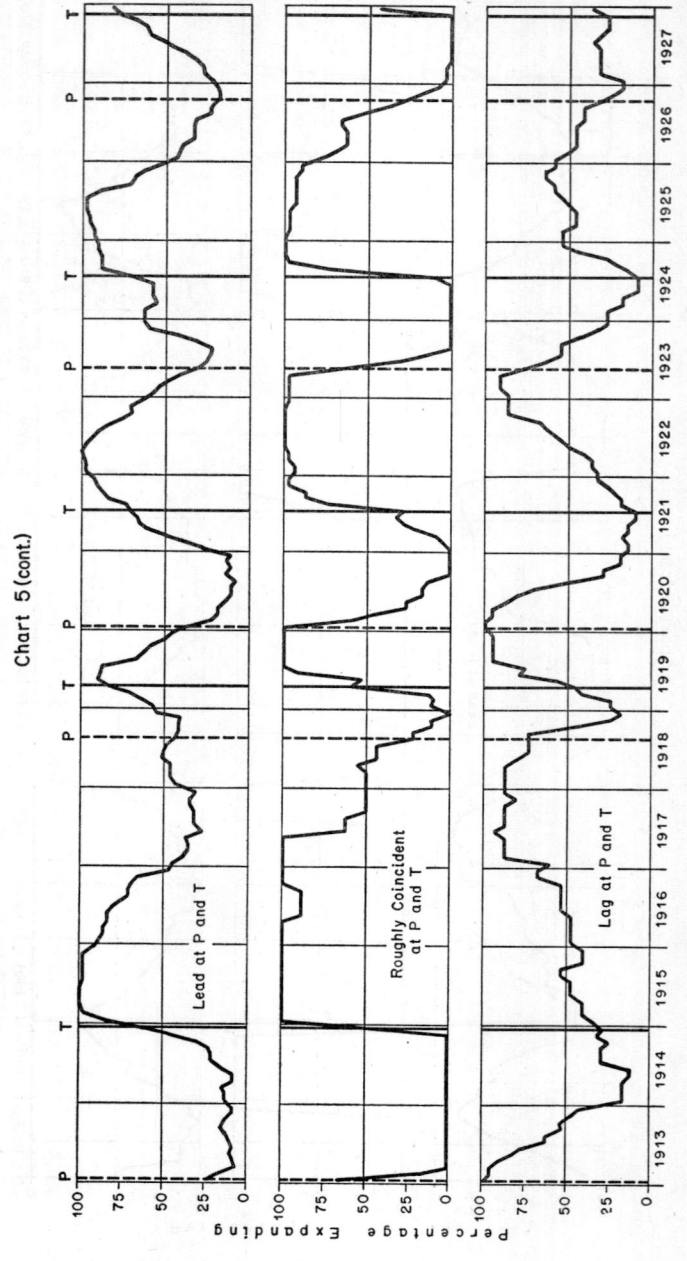

Chart 5 (cont.)

Chart 5 (concl.)

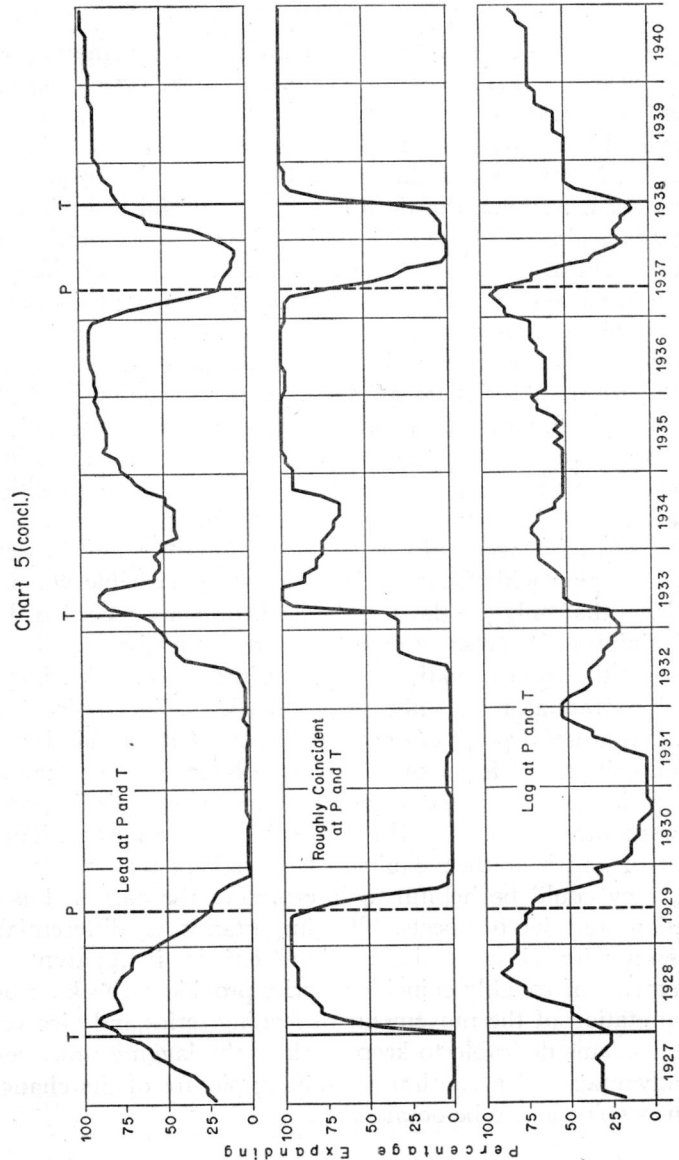

change in economic processes also plays a role. Leading and lagging processes, symptomatic of the influence of current changes on subsequent events, doubtless have a part in generating business cycles.[32]

From Chart 4 one might draw the following schematic picture of business cycles. A few months after a business cycle trough, the series that typically lag begin to rise; shortly after most of the laggards have started to rise the series that typically lead begin to fall; then the group that typically turns near business cycle peaks declines; once the decline has become fairly general, the laggards begin to fall; on their heels come the processes that lead, which begin to rise; they in turn are soon followed by the group whose turns tend to coincide with business troughs; then the laggards begin to show their heads again and the round of events is repeated.[33] This description is not very meaningful, of course, unless the groups of series are specified. One specification is provided in Appendix B. However, as we remarked above, significant processes whose timing is not recorded in Chart 4 participate in the cyclical procession. They too differ in their timing characteristics, though their behavior is less consistent from cycle to cycle.

The degree of continuity suggested by Charts 4 and 5, viewed in conjunction with Chart 3, is the more remarkable when one considers that only the dates of cyclical turns are recorded. Even this minimum of (discontinuous) information gives the impression that the transformation of one business cycle phase into the next is a gradual, not an abrupt process. If this impression is correct, it is a useful point of departure for current appraisals of the business situation; for it means that we have a better chance of recognizing at what stage of the cycle the economy is likely to be a few months hence than if the transition were abrupt. Thus if Charts 4 and 5 or their equivalents were kept reasonably up to date, they could be helpful in interpreting the current business situation and its prospects. The importance of differentiating processes with different timing characteristics is apparent. The movements of roughly coincident series provide a check on one's interpretation of the movements of leading series and vice versa. Also, it seems desirable to keep track of the lagging processes, if the advantages of a continuous moving picture of the changing business scene are to be obtained.

[32] Cf. ibid., p. 488.

[33] Cf. ibid., p. 70.

7

A Tentative List of Current Indicators

One goal of this investigation is a brief list of current statistical indicators, systematically selected and properly annotated. We have not reached this goal. But we have gone a considerable distance toward it, and it may be helpful to take a jump ahead and set forth the best brief list we can devise at present. No doubt it will be revised as the investigation proceeds, and criteria besides timing and conformity are systematically applied to the National Bureau's collection of series. The list we offer (Table 12 and Chart 6) is not based on any such systematic weeding; hence it is highly tentative. In making it we have not held strictly to the historical series actually analyzed in the investigation, even when they are currently available, but whenever possible have substituted essentially similar series of broader coverage.

Our best guides to a selection are the broad indications of Table 5 and the detailed list of series in Appendix B. Since our list is short, we confine it to series with similar timing at peaks and troughs, classifying them in three groups: leading, roughly coincident, and lagging. The series are arranged in Table 12 and Chart 6, however, according to the average timing they (or their nearest equivalents) exhibited at both peaks and troughs up to 1938. The averages present a more or less continuous array from long leads to long lags, rather than three sharply defined groups.

For leaders, Table 5 points to new orders, private construction contracts and permits, average hours worked per week, stock exchange transactions and prices, security issues, and business failures. That is to say, since in each of these groups leading series predominate, the chances are good that any particular series we select will have the indirect support of related series. Representatives of each of these groups as well as of others are in the Leading group, Appendix B.

New orders are represented in our short list by the current Department of Commerce series on the value of new orders for durable goods placed with manufacturers. This compilation begins in 1939, but the similar series by the National Industrial Conference Board beginning 1929, and several series on the physical volume of orders for certain types of durable goods, available for a longer period, give some indication of how it might have be-

TABLE 12 Record of Timing of Selected Statistical Indicators at Business Cycle Turns

SELECTED INDICATOR[a]	SERIES USED FOR RECORD OF TIMING	REF. PERIOD COVERED	NUMBER OF REF. TURNS COVERED[b]	NUMBER[b] Leads	NUMBER[b] Exact coin.	NUMBER[b] Lags	NUMBER OF Rough coin.	AVERAGE LEAD (−) OR LAG (+), MONTHS[b]
A LEADING GROUP								
1 Bus. failures, liab., indus. & comm., Dun's[i]	Same as prec. col.	1879-1938[w]	14 / 16	11 / 14	1	1 / 1	2 / 1	−10.5 / −7.5
2 Indus. common stock price index, Dow-Jones	Same as prec. col.	1899-1938	11 / 11	8 / 8	1	2 / 1	6 / 4	−6.0 / −7.2
3 New orders, dur. goods indus., value, D.ofC.	5 series, physical vol.[c]	1919-38	25 / 30	21 / 24	1 / 1	2 / 4	9 / 10	−6.9 / −4.7
4 Resid. bldg. contracts, fl. space, Dodge	Same as prec. col.	1919-38	5 / 6	4 / 5		1	1 / 2	−6.2 / −4.5
5 Comm. & indus. bldg. contracts, fl. space, Dodge	Same as prec. col.	1919-38	5 / 6	4 / 4	1	1 / 1	2 / 4	−5.2 / −1.7
6 Av. hours worked per week, mfg., BLS	Av. hours worked per week, mfg., NICB	1921-38	4 / 5	3 / 3	1	1 / 1	1 / 1	−3.8 / −2.6
7 New incorporations, no., Dun's	New incorp., no., Evans	1860-1938	20 / 20	12 / 15	1 / 1	4 / 3	8 / 4	−2.5 / −3.5
8 Whol. price index, 28 basic commod., BLS	Whol. price index, Bradstreet's	1893-1937[w]	11 / 11	7 / 8	1	2 / 1	5 / 5	−2.6 / −3.2
B ROUGHLY COINCIDENT GROUP								
9 Employ. in nonagric. establishments, BLS	Factory employ. index, Jerome (to 1914), BLS See text	1890-1938	14 / 14	3 / 7	1 / 4	−8 / 1	7 / 7	−0.2 / −3.3
10 Unemployment, D.ofC.[i]								
11 Corporate profits, quarterly, D.ofC.	Corp. profits, quarterly, Barger	1920-38[w]	4 / 5	2 / 3	1 / 1	1 / 1	3 / 4	−1.5 / −1.8
12 Bank debits outside NYC, FRB	Clearings outside NYC, C & FC (to 1919); debits outside NYC, FRB	1879-1938[w]	14 / 16	3 / 13	1 / 1	9 / 1	9 / 9	+2.0 / −4.3
13 Freight car loadings, AAR	Same as prec. col.	1918-38	6 / 6	1 / 2	3 / 4	2	5 / 5	−0.3 / −1.3
14 Industrial production index, FRB	Same as prec. col.	1919-38	5 / 6	4	3 / 3	2	5 / 5	+0.6 / −2.2

Table 12 (concl.)

Selected indicator[a]	Series used for record of timing	Ref. period covered	Number of ref. turns covered[b]	Number[b] of Leads	Exact coin.	Lags	Rough coin.	Average lead (—) or lag (+), months[b]
15 Gross national product, quarterly, D.ofC.	See text							
16 Whol. price index, excl. farm products & foods, BLS	Same as prec. col.	1914-38[w]	4	3			2	—3.5
			6	1	1	3	3	+3.7
C Lagging Group								
17 Personal income, D.ofC.	Income payments, Barger (to 1929), D.ofC.	1921-38	4			3	2	+4.0
			5	1	2	1	4	—0.2
18 Sales by retail stores, D.ofC.	Department store sales index, FRB	1919-38	5		1	4	3	+3.8
			6	1	1	3	4	+1.8
19 Consumer instalment debt, FRB	Same as prec. col.	1929-38	2			2		+5.0
			2			2	1	+3.5
20 Bank rates on bus. loans, quarterly, FRB	Same as prec. col.	1919-38	5		1	3	1	+5.5
			6			5	3	+4.8
21 Mfrs'. inventories, in current prices, D.ofC.	Mfrs'. inventories, in current prices, NICB	1929-38	2			2		+6.5
			2			2	1	+7.5

[a] Numbers and titles identify the series plotted in Chart 6, except as follows: The initial segments (in Chart 6) of series 3, 10, and 21 are compilations of the National Industrial Conference Board. The initial segment of series 7 (4 states) is compiled by the Corporation Trust Co. For series 11 the Department of Commerce series (beginning 1939) was extended back to 1936 by the use of data for 242 corporations compiled by Thor Hultgren. All series except 2, 8, 16, 20 are adjusted for seasonal variations. Series 1, 4, 5, 6, 7, 10, 12, 13, 19 were adjusted by the National Bureau.

[b] Entry on first line is for reference peaks, second line for reference troughs.

[c] The five series are new orders for southern pine lumber, oak flooring, architectural terra cotta, fabricated structural steel, and machine tools & forging machinery. The timing entries are totals for the 5 series; the averages are simple averages of the average timing of each series. See also note 34.

[i] Inverted; see note 9.

[w] War cycle observations are omitted.

AAR: Association of American Railroads
Barger: Harold Barger, *Outlay and Income in the United States, 1921-38* (NBER, 1942)
BLS: U.S. Bureau of Labor Statistics
Bradstreet's: The Bradstreet Co. (after 1933, Dun & Bradstreet, Inc.)
C & FC: *Commercial and Financial Chronicle* (1879-83, *The Public*)
D. of C.: U.S. Department of Commerce
Dodge: F. W. Dodge Corporation
Dow-Jones: Dow-Jones & Co., Inc.
Dun's: R. G. Dun & Co. (after 1933, Dun & Bradstreet, Inc.)
Evans: G. Heberton Evans, Jr., *Business Incorporations in the United States, 1800-1943* (NBER, 1948)
FRB: Board of Governors of the Federal Reserve System
Jerome: Harry Jerome, *Migration and Business Cycles* (NBER, 1926)
NICB: National Industrial Conference Board

haved earlier.[34] Two series on building contracts are included (residential, and commercial and industrial), each in terms of floor space rather than value since the physical dimension is of greater interest and more relevant to the physical volume of industrial activity such contracts call forth. For hours of work we use the Bureau of Labor Statistics series for manufacturing, which begins in 1932. Its prior behavior presumably resembled that of the similar compilation by the National Industrial Conference Board, which was discontinued after July 1948. We omit stock exchange transactions and security issues, because the erratic movements in such series make it difficult to judge their cyclical course currently. Stock prices are somewhat less erratic, and we include a stock price index. Liabilities of business failures, taken, of course, on an inverted basis, completes the list of leaders suggested by the timing classification of Table 5. We add two other series: number of new incorporations (see App. B) and the BLS index of wholesale prices of 28 basic commodities. The latter, which begins in 1935, seems to be roughly equivalent, in terms of composition and effective weighting, to Bradstreet's index (see App. B), which had an extraordinarily consistent cyclical record before it was discontinued in 1937.[35]

For roughly coincident series Table 5 defines four areas in which most of the series display roughly coincident timing with a tendency to lead (transportation, profits, bank clearings and debits, and indexes of business activity); three without marked leading or lagging tendency (production, employment, and commodity prices); and two in which the series display both roughly coincident and lagging tendencies (payrolls and retail sales), which we shall consider in connection with our lagging group. Our selections for transportation and profits are freight carloadings and total corporate profits, both being listed in the Roughly Coincident section of Appendix B. Bank debits outside New York City, our third selection, is not listed in Appendix B, though both New York City and total clearings and debits are. The reason is that the outside clearings and debits series is classed as a lagger at peaks and a leader at troughs. But in recent cycles this difference has practically disappeared, and in 1919-38 out-

[34] The NICB series leads the reference turns in 1937 and 1938 (see Chart 6), is coincident at the 1933 trough. Its timing at the 1929 peak is uncertain.

[35] Nevertheless, the two indexes are very differently constructed, Bradstreet's being the aggregate price per pound of some 96 commodities, the BLS' an unweighted geometric mean of relatives for 28 products.

side debits is classed as a rough coincider at both turns while neither the New York City component nor the total meet our acceptance levels for conformity and timing.

In the roughly coincident group we include gross national product, the most comprehensive value of output aggregate available on a quarterly basis since 1939, and the Federal Reserve Board index of industrial production. The timing of the former is probably fairly close to that of clearings and debits outside New York City. Employment is represented by the BLS series for non-agricultural establishments, which begins in 1935 and is seasonally adjusted by the Federal Reserve Board. The Bureau of the Census publishes the monthly unemployment estimates, beginning 1940, which we have adjusted for seasonal variations. The timing of both the employment and the unemployment series can be only roughly judged from factory employment, the most comprehensive historical employment series in monthly form, but there is no reason to doubt that they both belong in the roughly coincident category. The commodity price series that appears to be most suitable for this group is the BLS index of wholesale prices of all commodities other than farm products or foods.

As laggers, interest rates and bond yields, payrolls, and retail sales are the most promising groups, according to Table 5. In recent years both short- and long-term interest rates have conformed to business cycles less well than they did formerly; nevertheless, we include bank rates on business loans. This series did not quite meet our minimum standard of conformity in 1919-38, hence it is not listed in Appendix B; yet its timing was fairly consistent, as Table 12 reveals. Instead of an index of factory payrolls we use the more comprehensive, albeit less sensitive, Department of Commerce series on personal income. Wages are, of course, a large element in the latter, and many of the other components, such as salaries, rent, dividends, and interest payments may be expected to lag. For retail sales we select the comprehensive retail stores series which begins in 1935.

The two other lagging series in Table 12 were selected on the basis of other information than that in Table 5 or Appendix B. The tendency for manufacturers' total inventories to lag is demonstrated and analyzed in Abramovitz' forthcoming study, *Inventories and Business Cycles*.[36] Consumer instalment debt

[36] See also Moses Abramovitz, The Role of Inventories in Business Cycles, *Occasional Paper 26* (National Bureau of Economic Research, May 1948). Note, however, that this essay deals solely with the physical volume of inventories, whereas our monthly series is in terms of book value.

series are not covered in Table 5 because they are too short; nevertheless, their lagging tendency seems to be well established.[37]

Our tentative list of indicators (Table 12), then, consists of 8 leaders, 8 rough coinciders, and 5 laggers, 21 in all. Fourteen cover the processes represented by the 21 selected indicators of revivals in *Bulletin 69* (cf. Table 2). The other seven (new orders, incorporations, unemployment, incomes, inventories, bank rates, and instalment debt) are not represented in the earlier list, a circumstance that in part reflects the growth in the statistical material at our disposal in the last decade.

Obviously many other series compete for the analyst's attention, and it would have been easy to expand our list. In interpreting the behavior of the comprehensive series listed it will often be helpful to examine series of narrower scope. The recent study of manufacturers' inventories by Abramovitz, cited above, illustrates how enlightening this may be. On the other hand, more comprehensive aggregates than some of those we have selected have a bearing on the course of business; e.g., total construction contracts, or total consumer debt outstanding. Where value aggregates are listed the analyst may wish to compile physical volume series, and vice versa. Moreover, series that are similar in coverage may be needed for certain comparisons. For example, many of the series in our list that differ in coverage can be restricted to manufacturing industries alone. Finally, considerable interest attaches to series that are, at least to an approximation, first differences of the series on our list. Examples are the gross and net labor accession rate, inventory investment, and gross and net changes in consumer debt.

What sort of picture do our 21 indicators draw of business conditions in recent years? In Chart 6 we attempt to identify specific cycle peaks and troughs in each series since 1936, comparing each new possible specific cycle expansion or contraction with earlier phases in the same or equivalent series, following the procedure laid down in *Measuring Business Cycles* (pp. 56-66). Since the most recent phases are nearly always incomplete, this may result in an undercount of recent specific cycle turns, which must be allowed for in interpreting the series as a group.

In the 1937-38 contraction the three groups of series behaved in rather characteristic fashion. The leading group tended to lead, both at the May 1937 reference peak and the June 1938

[37] See Gottfried Haberler, *Consumer Instalment Credit and Economic Fluctuations* (National Bureau of Economic Research, 1942), pp. 54-69.

trough. The turns in the roughly coincident group are distributed within a narrow range on both sides of the reference dates. The lagging group tended to lag. With the advent of war, however, the fairly orderly sequence was violently disturbed. There is no need here to describe the course of events or to analyze the various factors that influenced the movement of each series. It is more important to consider whether, since the war, the prewar pattern of relationships has been restored.

We think the behavior of the series in the vicinity of the business contraction that began in the autumn of 1948 indicates there has been a substantial restoration. Considering first the roughly coincident group we find that most of these series expanded rather rapidly in 1946, made smaller gains in 1947, and reached peaks in 1948 (Table 13). The declines recorded during 1948-49, according to Chart 6, were not so large as in 1937-38, but the recent declines exceed those in some of the milder business contractions of the past.[38]

All the series in the leading group were contracting by June 1948. In sharp contrast to the concentration of peaks in this group in 1936 and 1937, the postwar peaks are scattered over several years, owing partly to special circumstances connected with the war. Business failures began to increase even before the postwar business expansion got under way, but leveled off in 1947. Stock prices, residential building contracts, new incorporations, and commercial and industrial building contracts began to decline early in 1946, fluctuated narrowly about a horizontal level through 1947 and part of 1948, then declined further. Average hours worked per week in manufacturing, after declining sharply from the wartime peak, did not rise sufficiently in 1946-47 for the movement to be considered a specific cycle expansion, but the high point was reached in December 1947.[39] The basic

[38] The percentage decline in the FRB industrial production index between 3-month averages centered on November 1948 and July 1949 was 14. In 1937-38 the percentage decline from peak to trough was 32; in 1929-33, 53; in 1926-27, 5; in 1923-24, 16; and in 1920-21, 32. A similar comparison based on the average relative change in three indexes of business activity (AT&T, Barron's, and Cleveland Trust Co.) that cover 16 business cycle contractions 1882-1938 shows that 6 of the contractions were smaller, 10 larger, than the 1948-49 decline.

[39] The series compiled by the National Industrial Conference Board on average hours in 25 manufacturing industries, discontinued after July 1948, shows a specific cycle expansion from February 1946 (39.0 hours) to December 1947 (41.2 hours).

Chart 6
Behavior of Selected Statistical Indicators, 1936-1949
A. Leading Series

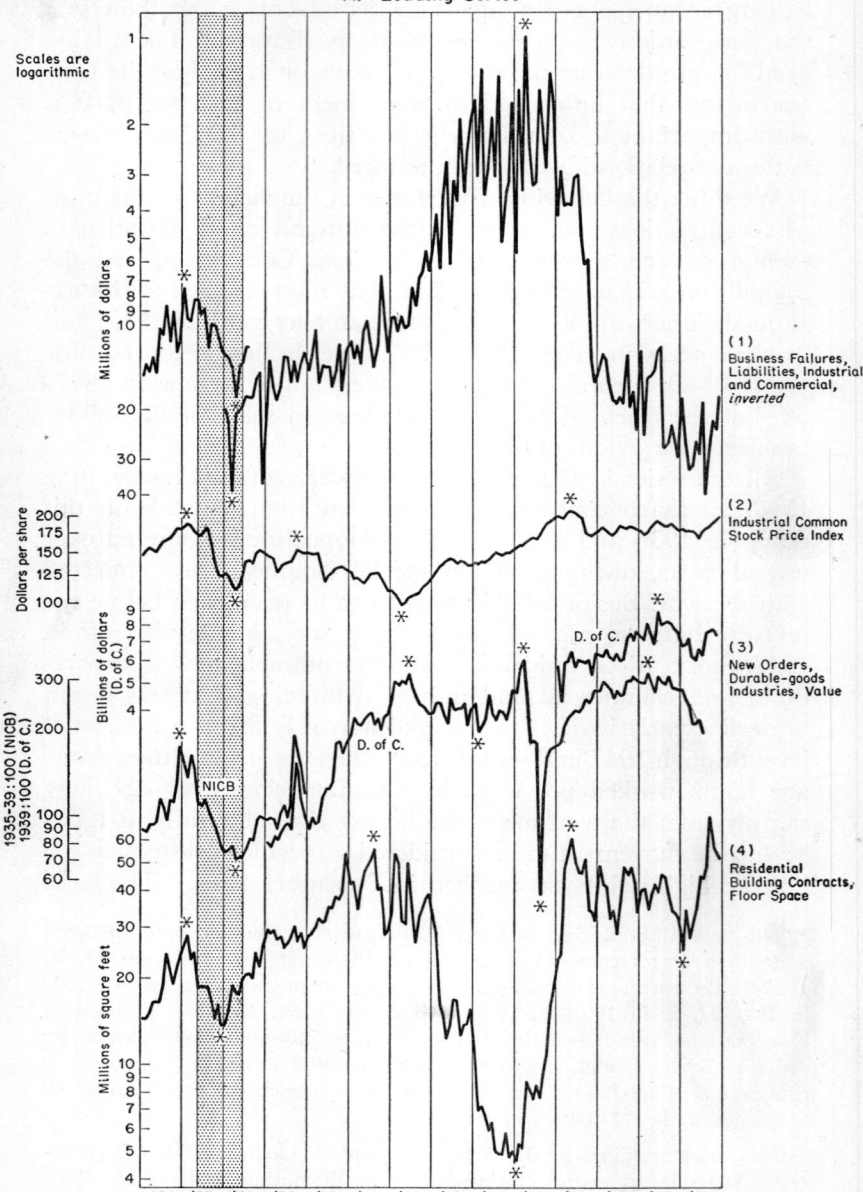

Note: Shaded area represents the 1937-38 reference contraction. Asterisks identify peaks and troughs of specific cycles. Series are adjusted for seasonal variations, except (2), (3) since 1939, (8), (16), and (20). For sources see Table 12.

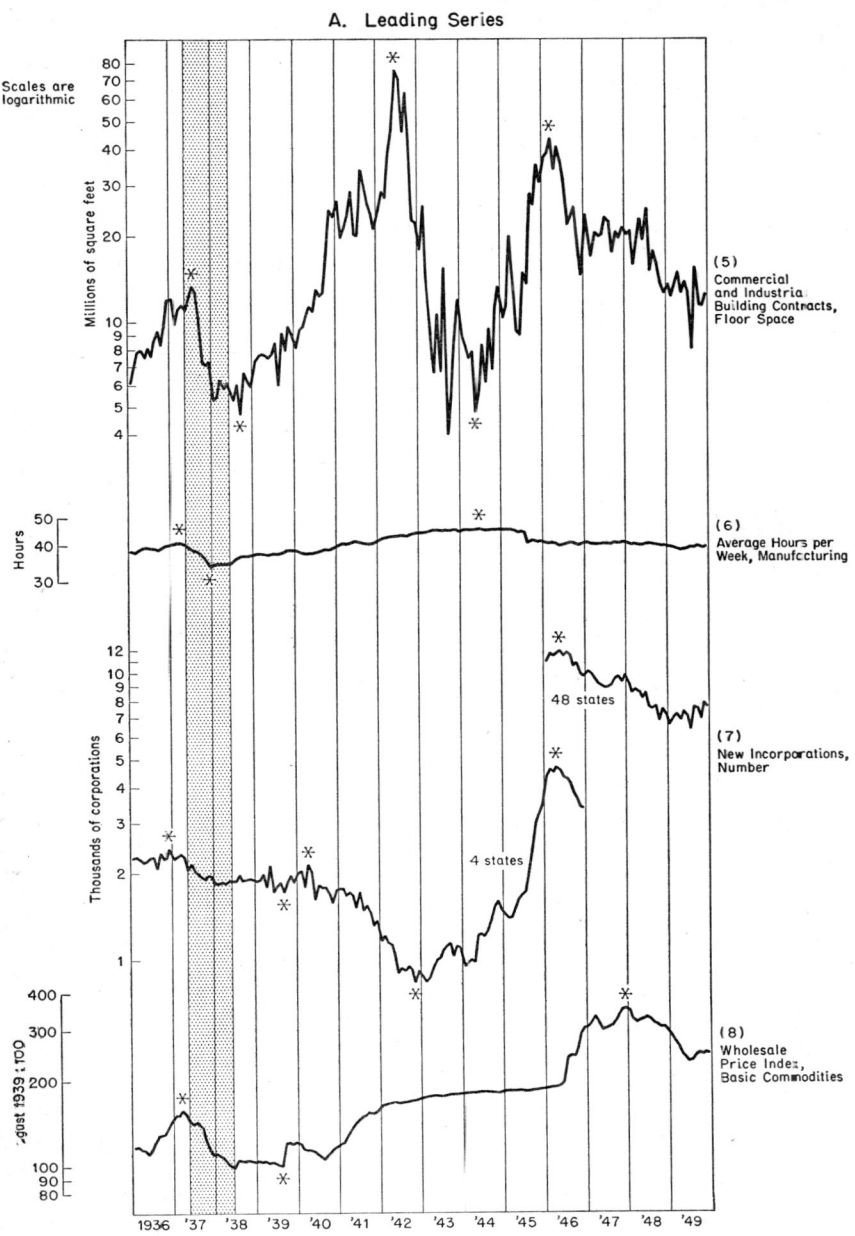

Chart 6 (cont.)
A. Leading Series

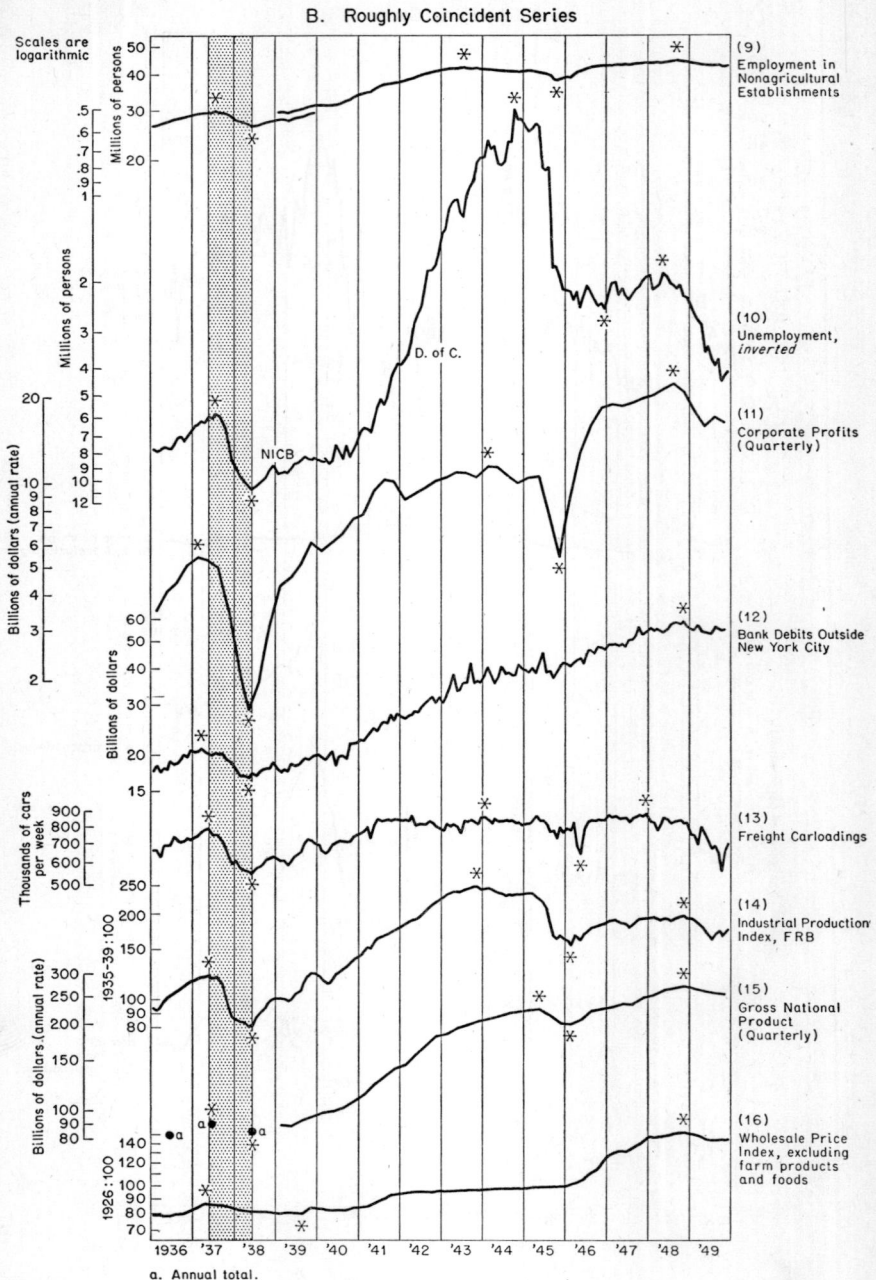

Chart 6 (cont.)
B. Roughly Coincident Series

Chart 6 (concl.)
C. Lagging Series

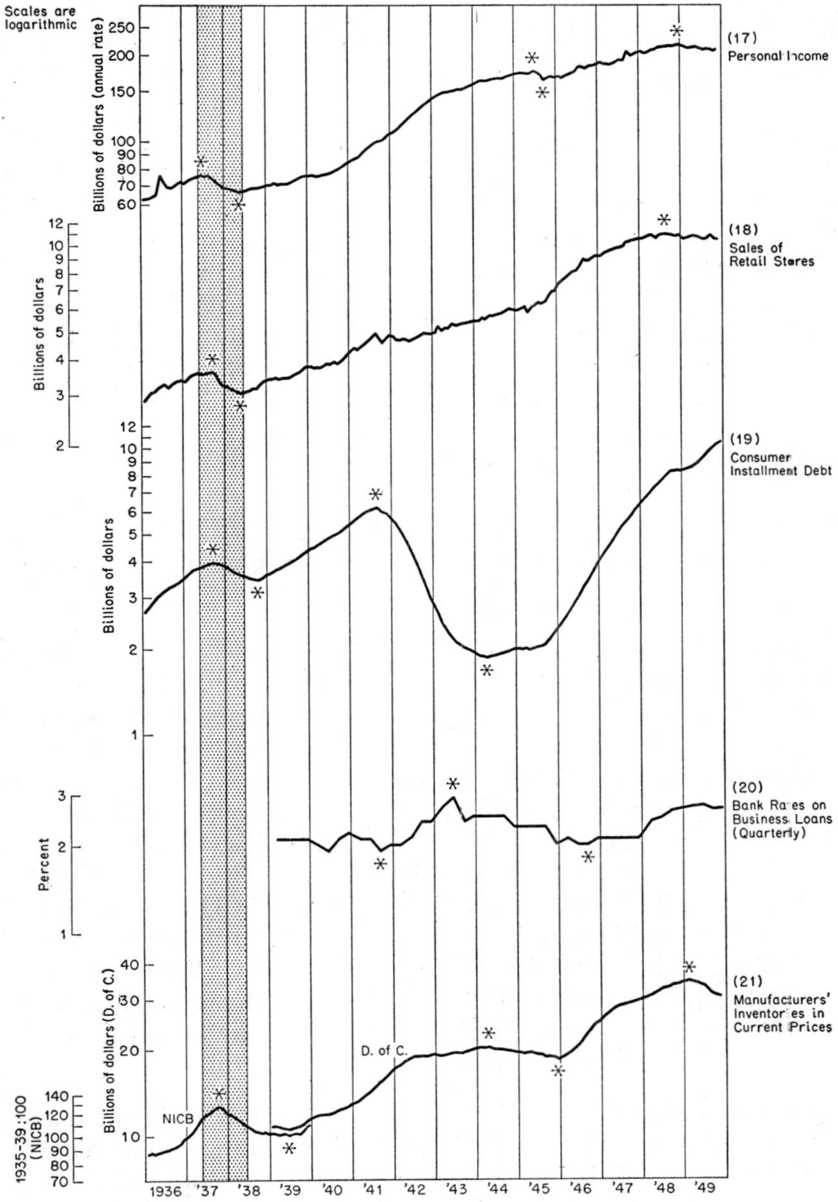

TABLE 13

Chronology of Postwar Peaks in Selected Statistical Indicators

		Leading Group[a]	Roughly Coincident Group	Lagging Group[b]
Mar.	1946	Comm. & indus. bldg. contracts		
May	1946	Resid. bldg. contracts New incorporations Industrial stock prices		
Dec.	1947	Basic commodity price index	Freight carloadings	
May	1948		Unemployment (inv.)	
June	1948	New orders, durables		
Aug.	1948		Corp. profits (quart.)	Retail Sales
Sep.	1948		Nonagric. employ.	
Nov.	1948		Indus. prod. index Gross nat. prod. (quart.) Debits outside NYC Wh. price index excl. farm & food prod.	
Dec.	1948			Pers. income
Feb.	1949			Mfrs'. invent.

[a] Average hours worked per week and liabilities of business failures (inverted) reached peaks in June 1944 and April 1945, respectively.

[b] Consumer instalment debt had not reached a peak by December 1949. Bank interest rates in September and December 1949 were only slightly below the peak figure reached in June 1949.

commodity price index began to fall in January 1948, and new orders for durable goods followed in June. There is hardly any question, then, that the prewar tendency for declines in the leading group of series to precede those in the roughly coincident group has reasserted itself.

Like the roughly coincident series, all the lagging series rose in 1946-48, some continuing an expansion that, by 1948, had lasted ten years with hardly an interruption. The peak in retail sales came in August 1948, personal income in December, and manufacturers' inventories in February 1949. Bank interest rates declined slightly after the second quarter of 1949, but consumer instalment debt continued to rise throughout the year. Thus the behavior of this group of series is somewhat mixed, but the lagging tendency clearly prevails.

In concluding this examination of the recent behavior of our tentatively selected list of indicators, it is well to underline some limitations on their use. It is perhaps unnecessary to point out that all of our analysis has been directed toward revivals and recessions in general business activity. This is not always the matter of chief interest; cyclical developments in a particular industry, line of activity, or area may properly claim the analyst's attention. Although he may find that some of our results can be adapted to such ends, obviously each such question requires careful examination and a fresh approach.

In attempting to judge the course of cyclical movements in the economy as a whole the user of statistical indicators will not find his task easy. The cautions Mitchell and Burns voiced in 1938 (*Bulletin 69*, pp. 10-12) bear repeating. Most of them are as applicable to recessions as to revivals.

"A person who attempts to determine by studying the series we have listed whether or not any trustworthy indications of a cyclical revival exist at a given time will find that he must equip himself with a great deal of additional information before he can reach a reasoned judgment.

"The first obstacle he will encounter is that monthly statistical records are never up to date. The monthly series may tell him what the status of business was a month or two ago; they cannot tell him what the status of business is today. The only way to meet the obstacle of tardy monthly reports is to use weekly or daily figures when available. Although data by such short time units are likely to be of little direct use in judging cyclical turns, they make it possible to estimate the standing of individual series in the current month.

"A second difficulty arises in treating seasonal components. When seasonal variations change from year to year, the problem of making satisfactory adjustments for current months is hard to solve. . . . A poor seasonal adjustment may produce an upturn that is readily misinterpreted as cyclical or may cancel for a month or more a genuine cyclical upturn. We know no protection against this danger other than a careful comparison of the original and seasonally-adjusted data, plotted on the same chart.

"Even when a series is free of seasonal variations, it is difficult to recognize a cyclical turn at the time it actually occurs. A series that has made cyclical upturns usually, if not consistently, some months before our reference dates for revival seems to have high prognostic value, but the chances are fair that it has merely historical value. The reason is that the cyclical movements of economic series are diversified by erratic fluctuations. . . .

"Another difficulty is that no sequence of average leads of time series in past cyclical revivals can tell what the exact sequence will be at the next revival. . . . The variations are at times irregular; at others they reflect secular or structural changes . . . . Such changes in cyclical timing are full of instruction to the student of business cycles. They are important also to the man of affairs; he must be alert to changes in the making, eschew simple formulas, test his judgments by study of numerous statistical series, and stand ready to revise his list of indicators as the economic environment changes.

"The chief hazard in forming judgments [about cyclical revivals] is that cyclical depressions not uncommonly end in a 'double bottom'. Several of the depressions of which we have fair statistical knowledge show two troughs about equally low separated by a mild upturn. The behavior of general business in 1932-33 is a notable example. . . . A large proportion of the most trustworthy indicators of business conditions participated in the abortive upturn of the autumn of 1932 and in the relapse that followed.

"So far as we know, there is no certain way of telling at the time it begins whether an incipient revival will suffer a relapse or develop into a cyclical expansion. Yet the occasions are frequent when speculation about the future course of business is demanded by pressing present needs. Those whose hard duty it is to make these guesses have the best chance of being substantially right if they combine analysis of current business data with some knowledge of the history of business cycles, such information as is available concerning important factors arising outside the realm of business, and a firm determination not to let their hopes and fears color their judgments more than is inevitable."

While this study has, we hope, contributed something to render guesses about the future course of business less hazardous, we find little to justify more optimism than Mitchell and Burns expressed. Our impression is that forecasts of revivals and recessions by means of the materials and approaches described in this paper will be subject to all the difficulties mentioned above. Nevertheless, there is some ground for confidence that objective use of these methods will at least reduce the usual lag in recognizing revivals or recessions *that have already begun*.[40] If, after an ex-

[40] Though difficult to measure, this lag is clearly not negligible. If the user of statistical indicators could do no better than recognize contemporaneously the turns in general economic activity denoted by our reference dates, he would have a better record than most of his fellows. For example, the reference peaks preceding the severe contractions of 1920-21, 1929-33, and 1937-38 come in January 1920, June 1929, and May 1937, respectively. But it was not until autumn in each of those years that economic difficulties received general notice. The contraction of 1948-49 began in the autumn of 1948; but it was not until the spring of 1949 that most observers were convinced that a recession was underway.

pansion in a group of roughly coincident series, several begin to decline, careful study of the recent behavior of a group of leading series may yield convincing evidence that the decline is or is not cyclical, and that a recession is or is not under way. True, this is forecasting of a sort. But it is forecasting with a highly important element of confirmation, which works in two directions. The behavior of the roughly coincident series confirms or fails to confirm that of the leading series, and vice versa. Some clue to the prospect that the emerging expansion or contraction will be comparable in magnitude to previous cyclical movements may be given by the extent to which it is already diffused among the processes being examined. Perhaps other aids to interpretation, such as those we describe in Appendix A, can be developed. In any case, if errors are to be minimized, painstaking study of the current and past behavior of the individual series, intelligent analysis of the factors that underlie their interrelationships, and judgment of the changing political and economic environment, will be required.

Appendix A

A Technique for Summarizing the Current Behavior of Groups of Indicators

The user of statistical indicators must, as a final step in his analysis, sum up what he believes they indicate. From one set of data he may make many different types of summary, depending upon what significance he attaches to each series and how he interprets its movements. Several types of summary are presented in this paper. Chart 3, based upon a large group of series selected for the consistency with which they conform to business cycles, illustrates two forms of summary: the distribution in time of peaks and troughs in the series and the percentage of series expanding. Series that have not conformed well to business cycles are ignored, all other series are given equal weight, and the magnitude of the cyclical expansions and contractions in the individual series is not taken into account (except in identifying their cycles). Despite their simplicity these forms of summary appear to have some merit in identifying business cycles.

In Charts 4 and 5 similar information is organized differently. Series that not only conform well to business cycles but exhibit consistently similar timing at revivals and recessions are classified in three groups, and summaries struck for each group separately. This threefold summary utilizes more information about the cyclical characteristics of the series, information that also should prove useful in identifying business cycles.

In all three charts the basic data are the dates of cyclical peaks and troughs in the individual series. Often there is some uncertainty about these dates when one seeks to determine them historically, and identifying them currently is much more difficult. Can curves analogous to the percentage expanding curves of Charts 3 and 5 be constructed without recognizing cyclical turning points explicitly?

One way would be simply to take the direction of change in each series from month to month as an observation on its cyclical phase and count how many series rise each month. Obviously, if series rose smoothly to their cyclical peaks and declined smoothly to their troughs this would give the same result as the method of Charts 3 and 5. But most series do not behave in this way, and during a cyclical expansion some go down almost as often as they go up, on a month to month basis. Moreover, differences among series in this respect are substantial, and the directions of change would provide a less reliable indication of cyclical phase in some series than in others. A simple count of directions of change would not, therefore, be satisfactory.

A modification of the plan can avoid this difficulty; namely, use different intervals for series that behave differently. That is, one might record month to month directions of change for very smooth series, and directions of change over longer intervals, say between the first and fifth months, for choppy series. This is equivalent to smoothing the series with moving averages of different periods and observing the month to month changes in the moving averages, or to smoothing the first differences of the series with moving averages of different periods and recording the signs of these moving averages.

By means of moving averages, then, it should be possible to reduce series to something like equivalent degrees of smoothness. But there are limitations. Very long-period moving averages must be avoided, for two reasons: when centered they will be much out of date; and they may seriously distort the timing of series at cyclical turns. It is common practice to use in effect a 12-month moving average by comparing, say, December of this year with December of last year. Though this obviates the need for seasonal adjustments the change in a moving average centered on a date 6 months ago not only is a crude device for recording cyclical developments then but also is obviously out of date with respect to cyclical developments *now*.

To offset the imperfect smoothness of relatively short-period moving averages we may adopt another device, and record both the direction of change in the given month and the number of months the series has been moving in that direction. That is, a rise of 1 month in the moving average (preceded by a decline) is counted as a run of $+1$, a continued rise the second month, $+2$, and so on. Declines are registered as -1, -2, etc. The reason for observing runs is that the longer the run the more likely is it to correspond in direction with the cyclical phase of the series.

To summarize the behavior of a group of series month by month frequency distributions of runs by direction and duration

TABLE A1

Measures of Timing and Smoothness of Fifteen Statistical Indicators

SERIES	AV. LEAD (—) OR LAG (+) AT REF. TURNS 1919-38	AV. DURATION OF RUN		PERIOD OF MOVING AVERAGE[b]
		Original data[a]	Smoothed data 1919-38	
	MONTHS			
1 Inner tube production	—5.7[c]	1.8	5.0[c]	6
2 Resid. bldg. contracts, fl. space	—5.4	1.9	6.1	5
3 Railroad operating income	—4.8[e]	1.8	4.3	6
4 Indus. common stock price index	—4.1	2.9	5.7	3
5 Bus. failures, liab., indus. & comm., inverted	—3.4[e]	1.6	3.2	7
6 Av. hours worked per week, mfg.	—3.2[d]	2.3	5.0[d]	4
7 Indus. bldg. contracts, fl. space	—2.2	1.5	3.6	7
Average, 7 leading series	—4.1	2.0	4.7	5.4
8 Railroad freight ton-miles	—1.2	2.4	4.3	4
9 Wholesale price index, BLS	—1.2[e]	3.4	3.9	2
10 Factory employ. index, total	—1.0	5.1	5.2	1
11 Steel ingot production	—0.8	2.7	4.2	4
12 Indus. production index, FRB	—0.8	3.3	5.5	2
13 Indus. production index, S.S. Co.	—0.6	4.4	4.1	1
14 Bank clearings outside NYC	—0.1[e]	1.7	5.8	6
15 Bus. activity index, AT&T	+0.9	3.4	5.0	2
Average, 8 roughly coincident series	—0.6	3.3	4.8	2.8
Average, 15 series	—2.2	2.7	4.7	4.0

[a] *Bulletin 69*, Table 2, col. 14. Based, for most series, on data for 1919-33; hence not strictly comparable with entries for smoothed data.
[b] Selected according to scale given in text.
[c] Data begin in 1921.
[d] Data begin in 1920.
[e] War cycle observations (1919-20) are omitted.

may be drawn up, an average for each month's distribution struck, and so on. In computing the average duration of the runs recorded for a group of series in a given month, weights might be applied to runs of different length, based perhaps on probability considerations. We have not, however, devised such a system of weights. In averaging we have found it expedient to group together all runs of 6 months or more, counting them as runs of 6. In effect, the observed direction of change in the moving average of a series in a given month is weighted by the number of months (from 1 to 6) that the moving average has been proceeding in the same direction. Of course, since we record only directions of change there is no need actually to compute the moving average; for a 5-month average the direction of change is obtained simply by comparing the first month with the sixth, the second with the seventh, and so on.

To test and illustrate this method we have applied it to 15 economic time series selected from the list of statistical indicators in *Bulletin 69* (Table A1). The first step was to determine the appropriate periods of the moving averages. After some experimentation the accompanying scale was adopted, whereby the period of moving average is selected according to the average duration of run in the original data.

AV. DURATION OF RUN, ORIGINAL DATA	PERIOD OF MOVING AVERAGE	AV. DURATION OF RUN, SMOOTHED DATA, 15 SERIES
MONTHS		
1.5–1.6	7	3.2; 3.6
1.7–1.8	6	4.3; 5.0; 5.8
1.9–2.2	5	6.1
2.3–2.7	4	4.2; 4.3; 5.0
2.8–3.2	3	5.7
3.3–3.9	2	3.9; 5.0; 5.5
4.0 or more	1	4.1; 5.2

This scale appears to yield an average duration of run in the smoothed data of about 5 months.[1]

The durations of run of the centered moving averages were recorded month by month for each of the 15 sample series, and frequency distributions drawn up. The striking shifts in these distributions in the 1948-49 recession are illustrated in Table A2. In June 1948 most of the series were rising, though the upward runs were relatively brief. By December all except one of the moving averages were declining and half had been declining 5 months or more. In the June 1949 distribution some series have still longer declines, others, brief rises. The September 1949 distribution is just about equally divided between rises and declines, and the whole distribution is widely dispersed.

To interpret these distributions (ignoring for the moment the identity and timing characteristics of the individual series), they must be viewed in an historical perspective. For this purpose averages are useful, and in Chart 7 the average durations of run

[1] The average duration of run in the original data for some of the series approaches the expected value for a random series, 1.5. Nevertheless, the average durations obtained in the smoothed data, using 7-month moving averages, considerably exceed the expected value, 2.0, for a moving average (of any period) of a random series. This is, of course, a manifestation of the fact that smoothing tends to expose the cyclical elements these series clearly contain.

TABLE A2

Distribution of Fifteen Indicators by Duration of
Run in Moving Averages

DURATION OF RUN, MONTHS	NUMBER OF SERIES			
	June 1948	Dec. 1948	June 1949	Sept. 1949
More than +6	1			1
+5 or +6	1	1		1
+3 or +4	5		1	2
+1 or +2	4		3	3
—1 or —2	4	3	3	5
—3 or —4		3	2	1
—5 or —6		7	1	1
More than —6		1	5	1
Total	15	15	15	15
AV. DURATION OF RUN, MONTHS[1]	+2.1	—3.5	—2.5	+0.1

[1] Runs of more than 6 months are counted as runs of 6 months.

for the 15 series 1919-49 are recorded and compared with the percentage expanding curve of Chart 3, which is based in 1919-39 on the specific cycle movements of about 350 series. The larger movements in the two curves are quite similar, but the average duration is more erratic than the percentage expanding. Probably it would be smoother if more series were used; but the difference is partly inherent in the methods of constructing the curves, since the moving averages used in the one method do not smooth out all the irregularities that are ignored in identifying the specific cycles upon which the other method is based.

In view of the irregularities in the average duration of run it is helpful to express it in cumulative form, and in Chart 8 both curves of Chart 7 are plotted in this fashion. The cumulated percentage expanding is derived by first taking the deviations of the percentage expanding in each month from 50 percent, then cumulating the deviations. The excess of the percentage expanding above 50 is a measure of the scope of the expansion in the economy; when this excess declines to zero the expansion can be said to have ceased—contraction balances expansion; and as the expansion percentage declines below 50 the scope of the contraction increases. A positive excess in a given month indicates that economic activity, in general, has attained a higher level than the month before, and the cumulative curve rises; a negative excess indicates that economic activity has receded to a lower level, and the cumulative curve falls. The cumulated average duration may be interpreted similarly, since in computing the average duration the falling series offset the rising series for a given duration of run (and all runs of 6 months or more are counted alike).

The peaks and troughs in the cumulative curves very nearly match the reference peaks and troughs, a result of the fact that the curves of Chart 7 cross their respective base lines on or near the reference dates; this in turn reflects the approximate centering of the alternate clusters of peaks and troughs in the series on the reference dates.[2] Moreover, the cyclical swings in the cumulative curves resemble the swings in various economic aggregates; for example, the FRB index of industrial production. As remarked in Section 6, the amplitude of a cyclical movement in the economy is associated with the extent to which it is diffused throughout the economy. In Chart 8 the FRB index records amplitude, while the slopes of the cumulative curves, into which no measure of the magnitude of a cyclical rise or fall enters, record diffusion. Obviously, the larger the percentage of series that expand during a given cyclical expansion the greater will be the rise in the cumulative curves.

In the noncumulative curves of Chart 7 diffusion is measured by the height reached by the curves during a cyclical expansion and their depth during a cyclical contraction. A rather critical average duration of run for the group of 15 series seems to be about 3 months. In all of the business contractions (the intervals between P and T on the chart) the curve reached the level -3 or lower, as it did at the end of 1948. Moreover, it reached the -3 level fairly early in each contraction. Similar statements might be made about the level $+3$ and business expansions. The implication is that from a curve of this type one should be able to tell, at a rather early stage, something about the strength or weakness of current cyclical movements in the economy, though the critical level would of course vary with the sample of series.

This potentiality will be enhanced if the processes covered by the sample are classified by their typical timing characteristics. We have divided the 15 series into two groups according to their average timing at business cycle peaks and troughs in 1919-38 (Table A1). One group consists of 7 series whose average timing

---

[2] The number of series expanding is itself a cumulation of the number of troughs minus the number of peaks (see Sec. 3). Hence the serial distribution of turning points (peaks counted negatively) is the second difference of the cumulated number expanding.

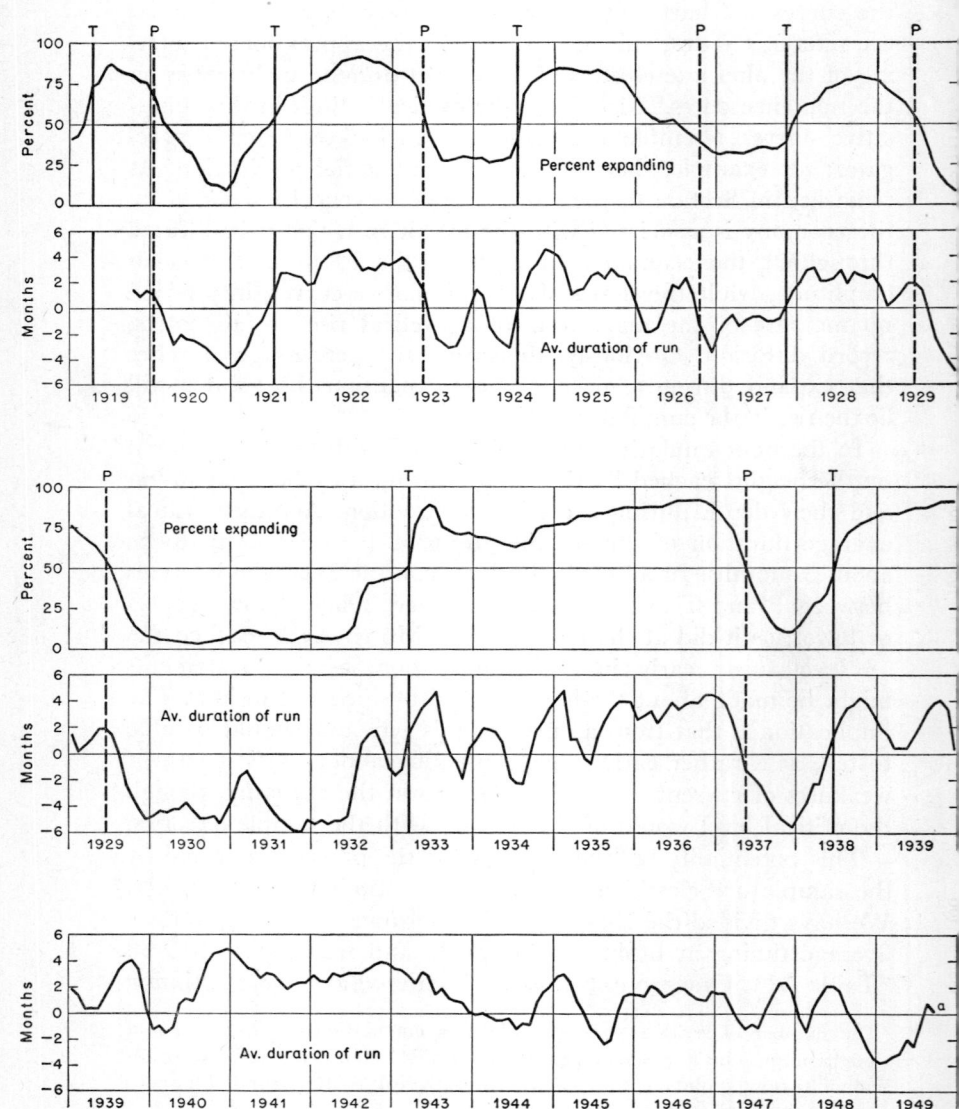

Chart 7
Percentage Expanding, All Series with 'Acceptable' Conformity
Average Duration of Run, 15 Series
(solid vertical lines indicate reference troughs; broken vertical lines, reference peaks)

a July-September 1949 partly extrapolated. See text.

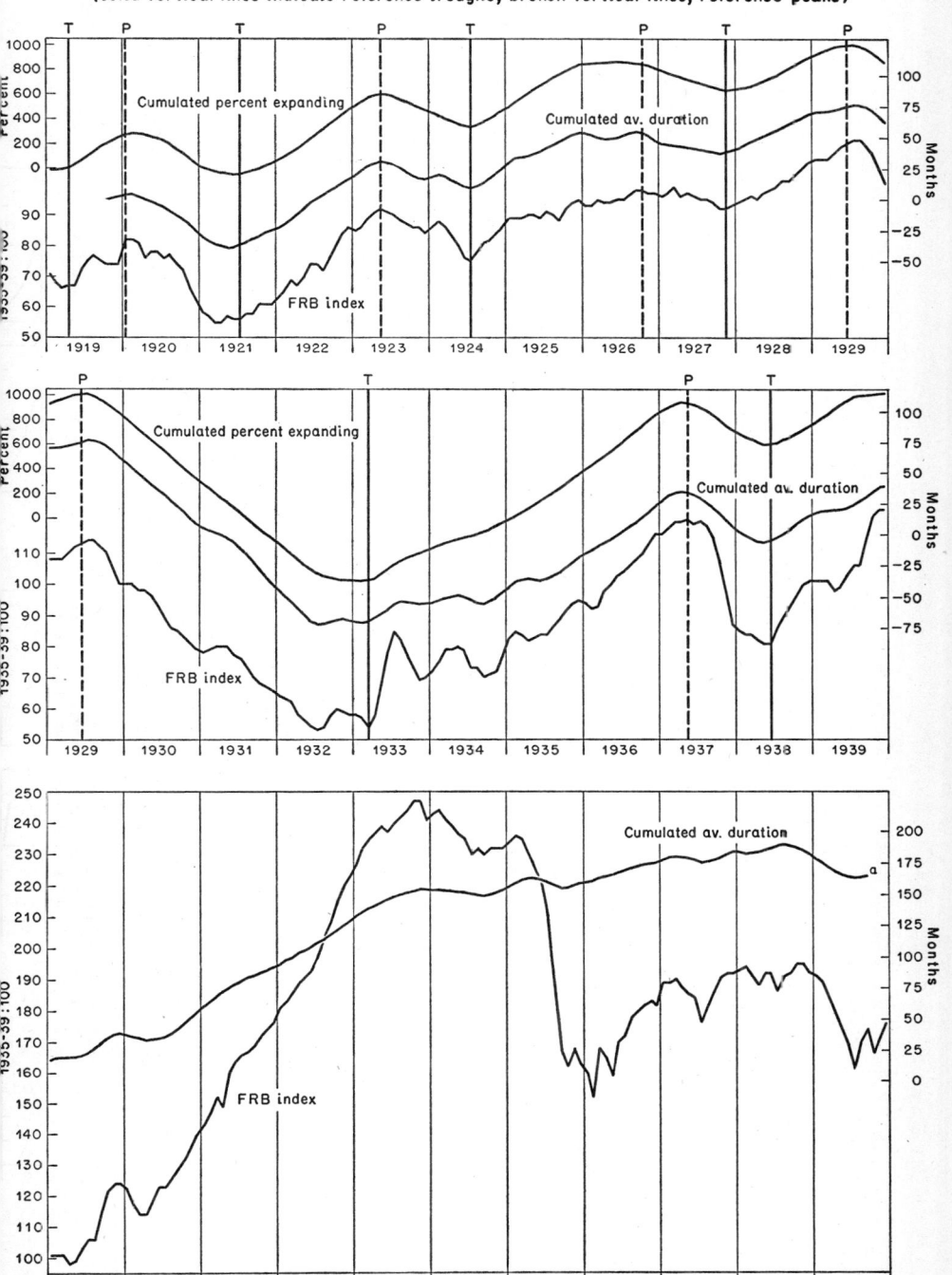

Chart 8
Cumulated Percentage Expanding, All Series with 'Acceptable' Conformity
Cumulated Average Duration of Run, 15 Series; FRB Index of Industrial Production
(solid vertical lines indicate reference troughs; broken vertical lines, reference peaks)

a July-September 1949 partly extrapolated. See text.

TABLE A3

Duration of Run in Moving Averages, Seven Leading and Eight Roughly Coincident Indicators

DURATION OF RUN, MONTHS	JUNE 1948 Leading	JUNE 1948 Roughly coincident	DECEMBER 1948 Leading	DECEMBER 1948 Roughly coincident	JUNE 1949 Leading	JUNE 1949 Roughly coincident	SEPTEMBER 1949 Leading	SEPTEMBER 1949 Roughly coincident
More than +6	Rr. income			Steel prod.			Resid. con.[1]	
+5 or +6		Clearings					Av. hours	
+3 or +4	Tube prod. Stock prices Av. hours	Ton-miles Wh. prices			Resid. con.		Stock prices Bus. fail.[2]	
+1 or +2	Resid. con.	Employment Steel prod. SS index			Rr. income Bus. fail. Av. hours		Rr. income[3]	Employment SS index
−1 or −2	Bus. fail. Indus. con.	FRB index AT&T index			Tube prod.	SS index Clearings	Indus. con.[2]	Wh. prices FRB index Clearings[3] AT&T index
−3 or −4				Ton-miles Wh. prices Clearings	Stock prices	Ton-miles	Tube prod.[3]	
−5 or −6			Tube prod. Resid. con. Rr. income Stock prices Av. hours Indus. con.	Employment		Steel prod.		Ton-miles
More than −6			Bus. fail.		Indus. con.	Wh. prices Employment FRB index AT&T index		Steel prod.[1]
Average[4]	+2.3	+2.0	−5.3	−2.0	−0.3	−4.4	+2.0	−1.5

See Table A1 for full titles of series.
[1,2,3] Moving average extrapolated by extending last month of original data 1, 2, or 3 months, as indicated.
[4] Runs longer than 6 months are counted as runs of 6 months.

ranges from a lead of 6 months to a lead of 2 months, averaging 4 months. The other group consists of 8 series whose average timing ranges from a lead of 1 month to a lag of 1 month, averaging about a half month lead. Thus there is a difference of about three and a half months in the average timing of the two groups.

When frequency distributions of runs are drawn up separately for leading and roughly coincident series (Table A3), some rather striking differences appear. In December 1948 all 7 series in the leading group had been declining 5 months or more, whereas most of the declines in the roughly coincident series were shorter. By June 1949 the position of the two groups was reversed: most of the roughly coincident series showed long declines, whereas some of the leading series exhibited brief rises. In September 1949 the rises in the leading group were further extended, and the long declines in most roughly coincident series had ceased. These shifts reflect differences in the timing of the movements of the two groups, as inspection of the average durations in Chart 9 and the cumulated average durations in Chart 10 makes clear.

During 1920-38 the cumulated average durations have almost precisely the average timing expected of them on the basis of the average (specific cycle) timing of the component series (compare Tables A1 and A4). Indeed, the peaks and troughs in the cumulated durations match rather closely the peaks and troughs in the cumulated percentage expanding, as derived from

TABLE A4

Timing of Cumulated Percentage Expanding and Cumulated Average Duration of Run, Two Groups of Indicators, 1920-1938

	LEAD (—) OR LAG (+) AT REFERENCE TURNS			
	7 LEADING SERIES		8 ROUGHLY COIN. SERIES	
REFERENCE TURN	Cum. % expanding	Cum. av. duration	Cum. % expanding	Cum. av. duration
		MONTHS		
Peak, Jan. 1920	—5	—2	+2	+2
Trough, July 1921	—5	—4	0	—1
Peak, May 1923	—1	—2	0	0
Trough, July 1924	—9	0	0	0
Peak, Oct. 1926	—7	—10	—1	—1
Trough, Nov. 1927	—1	—6	0	+1
Peak, June 1929	—4	—5	+2	+2
Trough, Mar. 1933	—8	—8	—1	—1
Peak, May 1937	—3	—2	0	—1
Trough, June 1938	—2	—2	—1	—1
Average	—4.5	—4.1	+0.1	0.0

87

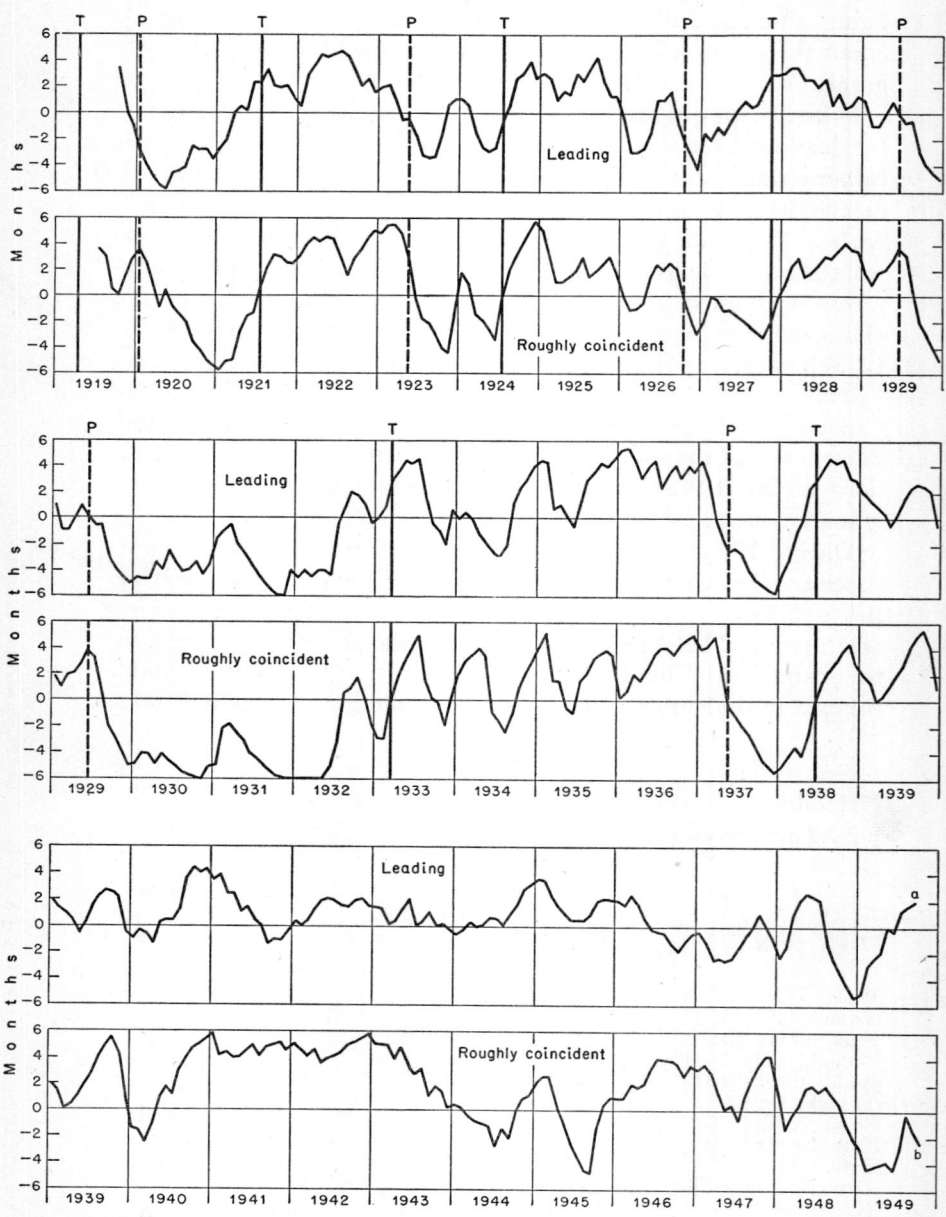

Chart 9
Average Duration of Run, 7 Leading and 8 Roughly Coincident Series
(solid vertical lines indicate reference troughs; broken vertical lines, reference peaks)

a July-September 1949 partly extrapolated. See text.
b August-October 1949 partly extrapolated. See text.

Chart 10
Cumulated Average Duration of Run, 7 Leading and 8 Roughly Coincident Series
(solid vertical lines indicate reference troughs; broken vertical lines, reference peaks)

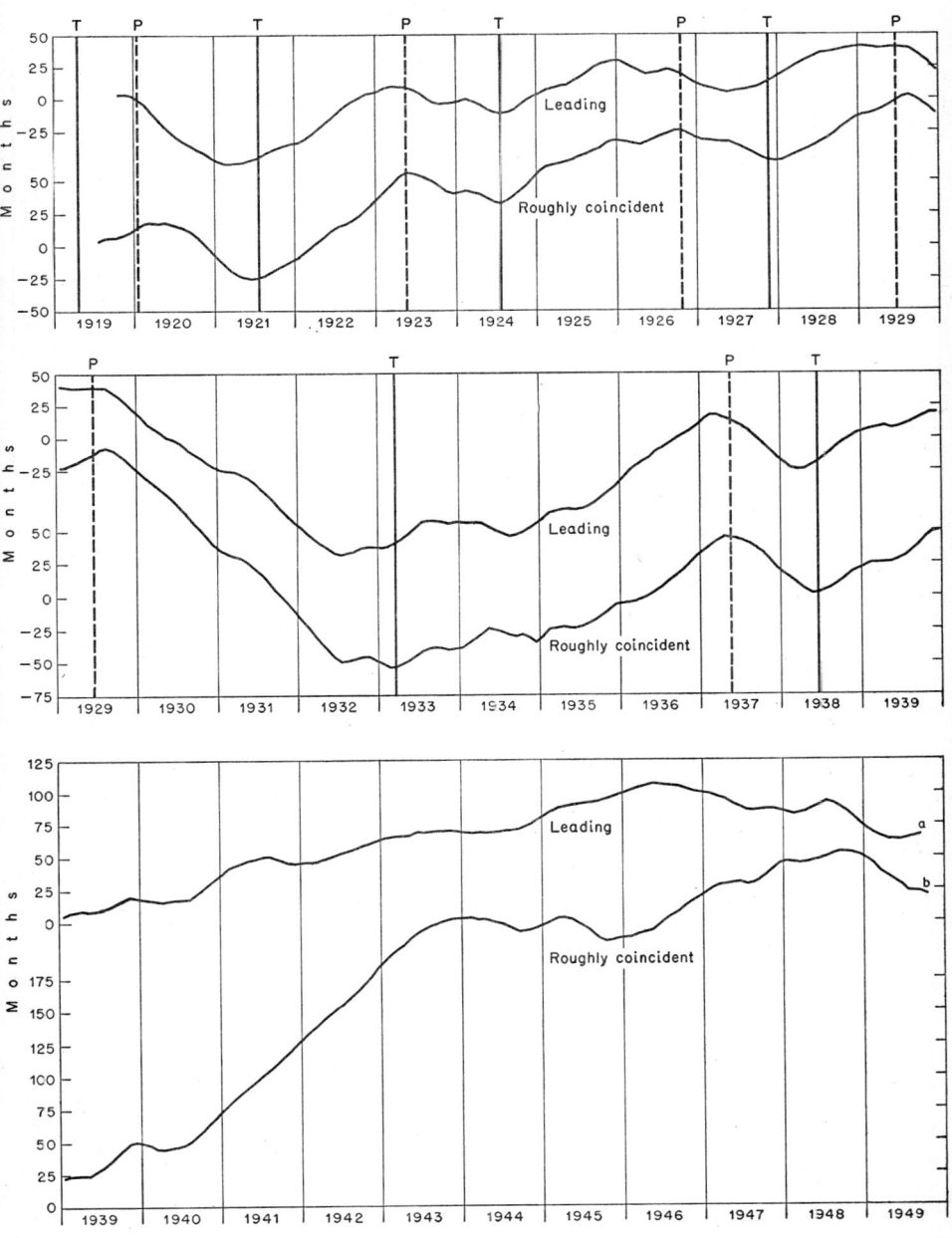

a   July-September 1949 partly extrapolated. See text.
b   August-October 1949 partly extrapolated. See text.

the specific cycle turns in the same groups of series. Clearly the moving averages reflect rather closely, at least for groups of series, the cyclical turns in the series.

The so-called critical level for the average durations of the smaller but more homogeneous samples of series in Chart 9 should be somewhat higher than when the samples are combined, as in Chart 7. In Chart 9 an average duration of $3\frac{1}{2}$ or 4 months, instead of 3 months, might be taken as a fairly critical level. In each contraction the leading group approached this level, -3.5, a few months after the reference peak, and the roughly coincident group usually approached it a month or two later.

The notion of critical levels is an aid in interpreting the average duration curves of Chart 9. Another point to bear in mind is that one curve may serve to confirm or qualify the indications of the other. In this way the chances of being misled by false indications in one curve or the other can be reduced. A case in point is 1947. The average duration for the leading group sagged through 1946, passing the zero level in June and reaching its lowest level, -2.7, the following May. Taken by itself this indicated that a recession was in the offing, though the figures still were not at a critical level. The roughly coincident curve, however, while it showed a sympathetic fluctuation in mid-1947, went below the zero line in only one month, July 1947, and then only slightly below. The price one pays for this sort of check is, of course, delay in the prognosis. But frequently the delay is not long, particularly in comparison with the usual lag in recognizing revivals or recessions after they have begun. In December 1948, for example, both curves seem to indicate rather clearly that a recession of some consequence was in the making, and even before that the curves indicate a weakening of the situation (cf. Sec. 7, note 40).

The use of runs in moving averages is subject to a special difficulty with respect to getting an up-to-date picture, however, since the centered moving averages will not cover the most recent months for which data are available. In the case of a 7-month moving average (the longest period used) the original data cover three months beyond the last moving average value. Nevertheless, since the only information required for measuring runs is the direction of change in the moving average, it should not be difficult to devise a reasonably accurate method of extrapolation. Perhaps a simple autoregressive scheme would be effective. An even simpler method is to extrapolate the last available month of original data (cf. Table A3). This is equivalent to reducing the period of the moving average and centering this average closer to the end of the data than it should be. The general effect, therefore, is to shorten the runs, so the distribution of runs in a group of series may be shifted toward the central values (short runs up or down). Some allowance for this, based on experience with the method under various conditions, can no doubt be made. Further experimentation on this and other features of the method of summarizing the behavior of statistical indicators suggested in this note may lead to improvements.

Appendix B

List of Series with Acceptable Conformity and Timing, in Three Timing Groups

For an explanation of the criteria met by series in this list, the types of series that did not qualify, and the timing classification see Sections 4 and 5. No attempt has been made to identify series completely, since the list itself can serve only as a rough guide to a choice of useful indicators. Series that in our analysis do not extend as far as the 1938 reference trough are marked with an asterisk. The parenthetic figure following the group title is the number of series in the group.

Series that Lead at Peaks and Troughs (75)

NEW ORDERS (6)
Locomotives; freight cars; railroad passenger cars; rails;* steel sheets;* oak flooring.

PUBLIC AND PRIVATE CONSTRUCTION CONTRACTS AND PERMITS (7)
Total contracts, value; total contracts, adjusted for changes in cost; total contracts, New England, value;* total building contracts, value; same, floor space; total building permits, value; building plans, Manhattan, value.

PRIVATE CONSTRUCTION CONTRACTS (10)
Total private, value; total residential, value; same, floor space; 1 and 2 family dwellings, value; commercial and industrial building, value; same, floor space; commercial building, number of projects; industrial building, value; same, floor space; food factories, value.

INVENTORIES (1)
Tin, visible supply.

PRODUCTION (6)
Paper; inner tubes; southern pine lumber; oak flooring (shipments); steel sheets; lead ore (shipments).

TRANSPORTATION AND COMMUNICATION (2)
Operating revenues of railroads, freight; railroad operating expense per traffic unit (inverted).

92

EMPLOYMENT (2)
Percentage employed, all trade union members, Massachusetts;*
same, textile industry.*

AVERAGE HOURS WORKED PER WEEK, MANUFACTURING (4)
All wage earners; all male; male skilled and semi-skilled; male
unskilled.

PRICES, WHOLESALE (4)
Bradstreet's index;* inedible tallow; common bricks; slab zinc.

NATIONAL BANK SERIES (6)
Individual deposits, New York City;* same, central reserve
cities;* bank deposits, New York City;* same, central reserve
cities;* ratio, loans and discounts to individual deposits, country
districts (inverted);* ratio, loans and discounts to net deposits,
country districts (inverted).*

STOCK EXCHANGE TRANSACTIONS (2)
Shares sold, New York Stock Exchange, number; same, value.*

STOCK PRICE INDEXES (6)
Common stocks, Cowles, S. & P.; same, Frickey;* preferred
stocks, Frickey;* industrial stocks, Dow-Jones; transportation
stocks, Mitchell;* railroad stocks, Macaulay.*

SECURITY ISSUES, CORPORATE (3)
Cash obtained thru new issues, Ayres;* stocks, all corporations;
stocks, American and Canadian corporations.

BUSINESS PROFITS (4)
Railroad operating income; net railroad operating income; net
revenue from railroad operations; same, per traffic unit.

BUSINESS FAILURES, NUMBER, INVERTED (2)
Large manufacturing companies; suspended banks.*

BUSINESS FAILURES, LIABILITIES, INVERTED (6)
Total;* industrial and commercial; all manufacturing companies; large manufacturing companies; trading companies;
suspended banks.*

BANK CLEARINGS AND DEBITS (2)
Clearings (to 1919) and debits, total; same, New York City.

BUSINESS ACTIVITY INDEXES (1)
Deposits activity, adjusted for trend.

UNCLASSIFIED (1)
New incorporations, number.

Series that Are Roughly Coincident at Peaks and Troughs (29)

RETAIL SALES (1)
Sales, 2 mail order houses, adjusted for trend and changes in prices.

IMPORTS (1)
Semi-manufactures, value.

PRODUCTION, GENERAL INDEXES (6)
Physical volume of business activity, Babson; industrial production, S. & P.; manufactures, FRB; producer goods, Leong; durable goods, FRBNY; producer durable goods, FRBNY.

PRODUCTION, OTHER (2)
Coke; merchant pig iron.

TRANSPORTATION AND COMMUNICATION (5)
Freight carloadings; ton-miles per freight car on line; ton-miles per serviceable freight car; ton-miles per freight locomotive; ton-miles per serviceable freight locomotive.

EMPLOYMENT, FACTORY (5)
Total, New York state; durable goods; cement, clay, and glass; iron and steel products; machinery.

AVERAGE HOURS WORKED PER WEEK (1)
Class I railroad employees, unskilled.

PAYROLLS, FACTORY (3)
Boots and shoes; lumber and products; iron and steel products.

PRICES, WHOLESALE (1)
Douglas fir lumber.

BUSINESS PROFITS (2)
All corporations; mining corporations.

BUSINESS ACTIVITY INDEXES (2)
Annalist; AT&T, adjusted for trend.

Series that Lag at Peaks and Troughs (30)

RETAIL SALES (1)
Sales per store, 3 restaurant chains.

IMPORTS (1)
Coffee (inverted).

INVENTORIES (1)
Cotton, at mills.

PAYROLLS, FACTORY (4)
Total; food products; baking; glass.

PRICES, WHOLESALE (4)
Fuel and lighting; bleached muslin; ginghams; building materials.

NATIONAL BANK SERIES (8)
Lawful money holdings, central reserve cities (inverted);* ratio, loans and discounts to individual deposits, total;* same, New York City;* same, reserve cities other than central;* ratio, loans and discounts to net deposits, total;* same, New York City;* same, central reserve cities;* same, reserve cities other than central.*

OTHER MONETARY SERIES (1)
Currency in public circulation.

INTEREST RATES AND BOND YIELDS (7)
Ninety-day time money rates; commercial paper rates; bond yields, 60 high grade; same, 15 industrial; same, 15 public utility; same, railroad; same, municipal.

STOCK EXCHANGE TRANSACTIONS (1)
Bond sales, New York Stock Exchange (inverted).

SECURITY ISSUES, CORPORATE (1)
Short term bonds and notes, American and Canadian corporations.

UNCLASSIFIED (1)
Magazine advertising, lineage.

Index to Principal Samples of Series

SAMPLE	DESCRIPTION, PAGE	TABLE	CHART
801 series, full collection	31-2	5, 6	
404 series with 'acceptable' conformity	13, 18, 33	10	3, 7, 8
225 series with 'acceptable' conformity and timing	33, 39	5, 6, 8	
75 series that lead at peaks and troughs	39, 49, 92-3	10, 11	4, 5
29 series that roughly coincide at peaks and troughs	39, 49, 94	11	4, 5
30 series that lag at peaks and troughs	39, 49, 95	11	4, 5
21 indicators, 1938 list	1, 21-2	2	1
15 indicators, 1938 list	81	A1, A2, A3	7, 8
7 leading indicators, 1938 list	83, 87	A3, A4	9, 10
8 roughly coincident indicators, 1938 list	83, 87	A3, A4	9, 10
21 indicators, present list	63, 66-8	12, 13	6
7 selected series	8	3, 4	2

NATIONAL BUREAU PUBLICATIONS ON BUSINESS CYCLES

I Books on Business Cycles

Business Cycles and Unemployment (1923)   448 pp., $4.10
Committee on Unemployment and Business Cycles of the President's Conference on Unemployment, and a Special Staff of the National Bureau

Employment, Hours and Earnings in Prosperity and Depression, United States, 1920-1922 (1923)   150 pp., 3.10
W. I. King

Business Annals (1926)   382 pp., 2.50
W. L. Thorp, with an introductory chapter, Business Cycles as Revealed by Business Annals, by Wesley C. Mitchell

Migration and Business Cycles (1926)   258 pp., 2.50
Harry Jerome

Business Cycles: The Problem and Its Setting (1927)   514 pp., 5.00
Wesley C. Mitchell

Planning and Control of Public Works (1930)   292 pp., 2.50
Leo Wolman

The Smoothing of Time Series (1931)   174 pp., 2.00
F. R. Macaulay

Strategic Factors in Business Cycles (1934)   256 pp., 1.50
J. M. Clark

German Business Cycles, 1924-1933 (1934)   308 pp., 2.50
C. T. Schmidt

Public Works in Prosperity and Depression (1935)   482 pp., 3.00
A. D. Gayer

Prices in Recession and Recovery (1936)   602 pp., 4.00
Frederick C. Mills

Some Theoretical Problems Suggested by the Movements of Interest Rates, Bond Yields and Stock Prices in the United States Since 1856 (1938)   612 pp., 5.00
F. R. Macaulay

Consumer Instalment Credit and Economic Fluctuations (1942)   262 pp., 2.50
Gottfried Haberler

Measuring Business Cycles (1946)   592 pp., 5.00
A. F. Burns and Wesley C. Mitchell

Price-Quantity Interactions in Business Cycles (1946)   158 pp., 1.50
Frederick C. Mills

Changes in Income Distribution During the Great Depression (1946)   192 pp., 2.50
Horst Mendershausen

American Transportation in Prosperity and Depression (1948)   432 pp., 5.00
Thor Hultgren

II Papers on Business Cycles

Testing Business Cycles (Bulletin 31, March 1, 1929)
Wesley C. Mitchell

The Depression as Depicted by Business Annals (Bulletin 43, September, 19, 1932)
Willard L. Thorp

Gross Capital Formation, 1919-1933 (Bulletin 52, November 15, 1934) .50
Simon Kuznets

The National Bureau's Measures of Cyclical Behavior (Bulletin 57, July 1, 1935) .50
Wesley C. Mitchell and Arthur F. Burns

Production during the American Business Cycle of 1927-1933 (Bulletin 61, November 9, 1936) .50
Wesley C. Mitchell and Arthur F. Burns

Technical Progress and Agricultural Depression (Bulletin 67, November 29, 1937) .50
Eugen Altschul and Frederick Strauss

Statistical Indicators of Cyclical Revivals (Bulletin 69, May 28, 1938) .25
Wesley C. Mitchell and Arthur F. Burns

Commodity Flow and Capital Formation in the Recent Recovery and Decline 1932-1938 (Bulletin 74, June 25, 1939) .25
Simon Kuznets

*A Significance Test for Time Series and Other Ordered Observations (Technical Paper 1, September 1941) .50
W. Allen Wallis and Geoffrey H. Moore

Railway Freight Traffic in Prosperity and Depression (Occasional Paper 5, February 1942) .25
Thor Hultgren

*Wartime 'Prosperity' and the Future (Occasional Paper 9, March 1943) .35
Wesley C. Mitchell

Railroad Travel and the State of Business (Occasional Paper 13, December 1943) .35
Thor Hultgren

Railway Traffic Expansion and Use of Resources in World War II (Occasional Paper 15, February 1944) .35
Thor Hultgren

Economic Research and the Keynesian Thinking of Our Times (Twenty-sixth Annual Report, June 1946)
Arthur F. Burns

The Role of Inventories in Business Cycles (Occasional Paper 26, May 1948) .50
Moses Abramovitz

The Structure of Postwar Prices (Occasional Paper 27, July 1948) .75
Frederick C. Mills

Cyclical Diversities in the Fortunes of Industrial Corporations (Occasional Paper 32, 1950) .50
Thor Hultgren

New Facts on Business Cycles (Thirtieth Annual Report, April 1950)
Arthur F. Burns

*Out of print.

Cyclical Diversities in the Fortunes of Industrial Corporations

THOR HULTGREN

OCCASIONAL PAPER 32

NATIONAL BUREAU OF ECONOMIC RESEARCH, INC.

Cyclical Diversities in the Fortunes of Industrial Corporations

THOR HULTGREN

OCCASIONAL PAPER 32
NATIONAL BUREAU OF ECONOMIC RESEARCH, INC.
1950

Price: fifty cents

Copyright, 1950, by National Bureau of Economic Research, Inc.
1819 Broadway, New York 23, N. Y. All Rights Reserved
Manufactured in the U.S.A. by John N. Jacobson & Son, Inc.

Contents

When Are Rising Profits Most Common?	1
Quarterly reports needed; more and more available	1
Seasonal adjustments needed and made	4
Fewer Companies with Rising Profits in Late Business Expansion, More in Late Contraction	4
Quarter by quarter changes	4
Broader movements	6
Turning Points in Profits of Individual Companies Clustered about Turns in Business	8
Always Some Exceptional Companies	11
No Consistent Lead or Lag in Aggregate Profits	12
Possible Explanations of Early Cyclical Changes	15
Encroachment of costs on prices	15
Scatter of turning points in production	16
Profits in Durables Did Not Lead Profits in Other Industries	17
Can Profits Forecast Business Cycles?	17
A possible forecasting procedure	18
Variable leads	21
Delayed availability	22
Profits one piece of evidence	23
A simplified approach to the seasonal problem	23
Recent Developments	26
Old sequence disturbed during war	26
Sequence reestablished?	28
Diversity and New Investment	29

TABLE

1	Characteristics of Samples of Quarterly Profits; Assets of Sample and Other Companies	3
2	Turning Points in Profits	14
3	Aggregate Profits: Change Per Quarter in Earlier and in Later Quarters of Each Business Phase	15
4	Date of Most Common Turning Point in Profits of Producers of Durables and of Nondurables	18
5	Frequency of Turning Points in Profits in Early, Median, and Late Quarters: Producers of Durables and of Nondurables	19
6	Peaks and Troughs in (A) the Number of Companies with Profits Higher than in Preceding Quarter, (B) the Number with Expanding or Peak Profits, 1921-38: Producers of Durables and of Nondurables	20
7	Hypothetical Forecasts of Business Turns	21

CHART

1	Percentage Ratio, Number of Companies with Profits Higher than in Preceding Quarter to Number in Sample	5
2	Profits of Phillips Petroleum Company	7
3	Percentage Ratio, Number of Companies with Profits in Expansion or at Peak to Number in Sample	7
4	Profits of Colonial Beacon Oil Company	9
5	Profits of American Safety Razor Corporation	9
6	Scattering of Turns in Profits	10
7	Profits of Frank G. Shattuck Company	12
8	Aggregate Profits of All Companies in Sample	13
9	Number of Companies (out of 244) with Profits Higher than in Preceding Quarter: Two Methods of Seasonal Adjustment Compared	24
10	Percentage Ratio, Number of Companies with Profits Higher than in Preceding Quarter to Number in Sample (Computed by Alternative Method)	25
11	Profits of All Corporations, Seasonally Adjusted Annual Rates (Department of Commerce Estimates)	27
12	Earnings of Large Industrial Corporations (Federal Reserve Data)	28

WILLIAM I. GREENWALD shared in every stage of the work underlying this paper. Elma Oliver helped to prepare and check the basic records. H. Irving Forman drew the charts. Martha Anderson, Arthur F. Burns, Benjamin Caplan, Daniel Creamer, Solomon Fabricant, Irwin Friend, Albert G. Hart, Geoffrey H. Moore, Wilson F. Payne, Warren C. Waite, and Leo Wolman read preliminary drafts and made valuable suggestions. I am indebted to George B. Roberts and D. R. Young for access to and aid in the use of statistical files in the National City Bank of New York.

T. H.

OFFICERS

Boris Shishkin, *Chairman*
Harry Scherman, *President*
C. C. Balderston, *Vice-President*
George B. Roberts, *Treasurer*
W. J. Carson, *Executive Director*
Martha Anderson, *Editor*

DIRECTORS AT LARGE

Donald R. Belcher, *American Telephone and Telegraph Co.*
Oswald W. Knauth, *New York City*
Simon Kuznets, *University of Pennsylvania*
H. W. Laidler, *Executive Director, League for Industrial Democracy*
Shepard Morgan, *New York City*
C. Reinold Noyes, *New York City*
George B. Roberts, *Vice-President, National City Bank*
Beardsley Ruml, *New York City*
Harry Scherman, *President, Book-of-the Month Club*
George Soule, *Bennington College*
N. I. Stone, *Consulting Economist*
J. Raymond Walsh, *WMCA Broadcasting Co.*
Leo Wolman, *Columbia University*
Theodore O. Yntema, *Vice President - Finance, Ford Motor Company*

DIRECTORS BY UNIVERSITY APPOINTMENT

E. Wight Bakke, *Yale*
C. C. Balderston, *Pennsylvania*
Arthur F. Burns, *Columbia*
G. A. Elliott, *Toronto*
Frank W. Fetter, *Northwestern*
H. M. GROVES, *Wisconsin*
Gottfried Haberler, *Harvard*
Clarence Heer, *North Carolina*
R. L. Kozelka, *Minnesota*
Paul M. O'Leary, *Cornell*
T. W. Schultz, *Chicago*

DIRECTORS APPOINTED BY OTHER ORGANIZATIONS

Percival F. Brundage, *American Institute of Accountants*
Thomas C. Cochran, *Economic History Association*
Frederick C. Mills, *American Statistical Association*
Stanley H. Ruttenberg, *Congress of Industrial Organizations*
Murray Shields, *American Management Association*
Boris Shishkin, *American Federation of Labor*
Warren C. Waite, *American Farm Economic Association*
Donald H. Wallace, *American Economic Association*

RESEARCH STAFF

Arthur F. Burns, *Director of Research*
Geoffrey H. Moore, *Associate Director of Research*

Moses Abramovitz
Harold Barger
Morris A. Copeland
Daniel Creamer
David Durand
Solomon Fabricant
Milton Friedman
Millard Hastay
W. Braddock Hickman
F. F. Hill
Thor Hultgren
Simon Kuznets
Clarence D. Long
Ruth P. Mack
Frederick C. Mills
Raymond J. Saulnier
Lawrence H. Seltzer
George J. Stigler
Leo Wolman

WHEN ARE RISING PROFITS MOST COMMON?

A modern private enterprise economy passes alternately through periods in which the general level of economic activity rises and periods in which it falls. We call these waves of activity business cycles. There are broadly similar waves in the profits of industrial corporations. Net earnings of all corporations combined rise in a business expansion and fall in a contraction. But not every corporation participates at every stage in these broad swings. Even when profits in the aggregate grow, those of some companies at times diminish. When aggregate profits decline, those of some companies meanwhile rise. At what point in a business cycle is the number of companies with rising profits largest? At what point smallest? In this paper we endeavor to answer these and cognate questions.

Quarterly reports needed; more and more available

To arrive at an answer, we ought to have profit data for a large number of corporations. In each instance, they should cover at least one full business cycle. They should be monthly or quarterly. Annual profit figures are not very helpful in dealing with the questions we have in mind. Suppose, for example, that a company's earnings in the year 1937 were very high and its earnings in the year 1938 very low in comparison with other nearby years. We may infer that the company suffered a contraction of profits more or less corresponding to the general decline in business activity from the second quarter of 1937 to the second quarter of 1938. But we cannot tell whether its profits began to decline before or after the second quarter of 1937; they may have been at their highest in the first quarter, for example, or in the fourth. Fortunately the National City Bank of New York has compiled extensive quarterly data on profits of individual companies, and has graciously made them available to us. We use them in conjunction with some additional data collected by Harold Barger.[1]

Thirty years ago very few corporations publicly reported their earnings as often as once every three months. Since 1920, however, the custom has been growing; at present hundreds of companies issue quarterly statements. If we compile a separate sample of companies for each business cycle, therefore, we can form larger samples for the more recent cycles and so gradually broaden the statistical basis of our investigation. Business cycles can be thought of as running either from trough to trough or from peak to peak; we have compiled samples on both conceptions (Table 1). While our earliest sample pertains to only 17 companies, our latest covers 244.[2]

---

[1]*The Commercial and Financial Chronicle* and *Moody's Investors' Service* reproduce the profit and loss statements of numerous companies. From these sources the bank, beginning with 1923, compiled the final net profit figures — net income available for dividends. From the same sources, Barger collected figures for some additional companies, and for 1920-22; see his *Outlay and Income in the United States, 1921-38* (NBER, 1942), Appendix B, pp. 235 ff. After editing the figures to some extent to make them more comparable with income tax returns (pp. 242-4), he used the bank's and his own supplementary data to estimate the aggregate profits of each industry, and hence of all industry. Aggregates for a large group of companies had been compiled and published by various authorities for railroads, the communications industry, and other public utilities. Consequently he had no occasion to collect data for individual companies in those industries, and the figures we use do not include such enterprises. The great majority of the companies we deal with were manufacturing or mining corporations. The others were engaged in water or other transportation, restaurant operations, the moving picture business, or miscellaneous activities.

In some instances our data on the profits of a company may show an increase merely because it absorbed another company. Suppose, for example, that company A had profits of $600,000 per quarter and B profits of $200,000 per quarter before A absorbed B, and that after absorbing B, A earned $700,000 per quarter. A would figure in our tabulations as having rising profits, although the profits after merger, excluding those derived from the business formerly conducted by B, might be less than $600,000. It did not seem feasible to eliminate such illusory growth from the figures. But mergers are sporadic and many would not alter the direction of change in profits.

[2]Our earliest samples are smaller than the National City Bank sample because we confine ourselves to companies whose profits are available for the full cycle.

TABLE 1

Characteristics of Samples of Quarterly Profits; Assets of Sample and Other Companies

CHARACTERISTICS	1	2	3	4	5	6	7	8
Period covered								
First quarter	1Q 1920	1Q 1921	1Q 1923	1Q 1924	1Q 1926	1Q 1927	1Q 1929	1Q 1933
Last quarter	4Q 1923	4Q 1924	4Q 1926	4Q 1927	4Q 1929	4Q 1933	4Q 1937	4Q 1938
Ref. turn to which sample corresponds[a]								
Level of business	Trough	Peak	Trough	Peak	Trough	Peak	Trough	Peak
Date	3Q 1921	2Q 1923	3Q 1924	3Q 1926	4Q 1927	2Q 1929	1Q 1933	2Q 1937
No. of cos. in sample								
Producers of durables	10	17	39	57	80	82	91	121
Other companies	7	14	32	44	73	73	94	123
All companies	17	31	71	101	153	155	185	244
Mining or mfg. cos.	17	30	65	91	135	137	165	219
Cos. in other industries	0	1	6	10	18	18	20	25
ASSETS (*millions of dollars*)[b]								
(1) All companies in sample	3867	4363	7399	8663	13412	12051	13621	14466
(2) Mfg. & mining cos. in sample	3867	4327	7268	8385	12579	11564	13017	13807
(3) Mfg. & mining cos. in U.S.[c]	d	d	76899	77147	82114	66760	64869	62337
(4) General Motors Corp.	593	593	921	1098	1325	1184	1567	1598
(5) U.S. Steel Corp.	2421	2414	2454	2434	2286	2103	1919	1711
(6) G.M. + U.S.S.C. (4) + (5)	3014	3007	3375	3532	3611	3287	3486	3309
(7) All others in sample (1) − (6)	853	1356	4024	5131	9801	8764	10135	11157
(8) Third largest company[e]	137	136	646	652	802	658	804	811
RATIOS								
(9) (2) ÷ (3)	d	d	.095	.109	.153	.173	.201	.221
(10) (6) ÷ (1)	.779	.689	.456	.408	.269	.273	.256	.229
(11) (8) ÷ (7)	.161	.100	.161	.127	.082	.075	.079	.073

Notes are at bottom of page 4.

Seasonal adjustments needed and made

The earnings of most of our companies were obviously affected by seasonal influences. From quarter to quarter they often followed a marked pattern of rise and fall, recurring year after year. As reported, such figures tell us little about the relation between profits and business cycles. Adjusted for seasonal variation, however, they may tell us more. We made such adjustments, company by company, wherever they seemed necessary, and the following discussion is based on seasonally adjusted data.

FEWER COMPANIES WITH RISING PROFITS IN LATE BUSINESS EXPANSION, MORE IN LATE CONTRACTION

Quarter by quarter changes

The seasonally adjusted data reveal a great diversity of profit experience that can be summarized in several ways. We shall begin with what is perhaps the simplest and most obvious procedure. In each quarter we can count the number of companies whose profits were higher than in the preceding quarter. (We count an enterprise that suffered a deficit in one quarter, but a larger deficit in the preceding quarter, as having increasing profits.) The number with rising profits can then be expressed as a percentage of all companies in the sample. In the second quarter of 1930, for instance, 59 of the 185 companies in our 1929-37 sample had higher profits (or smaller losses) than in the first quarter of 1930. The percentage with profits higher than in the preceding quarter was

NOTES TO TABLE 1

[a]From Arthur F. Burns and Wesley C. Mitchell, *Measuring Business Cycles* (NBER, 1946), p. 78.

[b]Compiled from Moody's *Manuals,* except as noted. At end of period covered by sample.

[c]From Bureau of Internal Revenue, *Statistics of Income,* various years. Companies filing balance sheets.

[d]Not available.

[e]Republic Steel, 1923, 1924; Bethlehem Steel, 1926, 1927, 1929; Shell Union Oil, 1933; E. I. Dupont de Nemours, 1937, 1938.

therefore 100 times 59 ÷ 185, i.e., 32. When such percentages for the various quarters are plotted, they form a curve in which, although it is highly irregular, we discern major waves (Chart 1). We mark the crest of each wave (the quarter in which rising profits were most common) and the trough of each wave (the quarter in which rising profits were least common) with an asterisk. The quarter in which the fewest companies had rising profits usually preceded the trough in business by a long interval. The quarter in which the largest percentage of companies had rising profits came well before the business peak.[3]

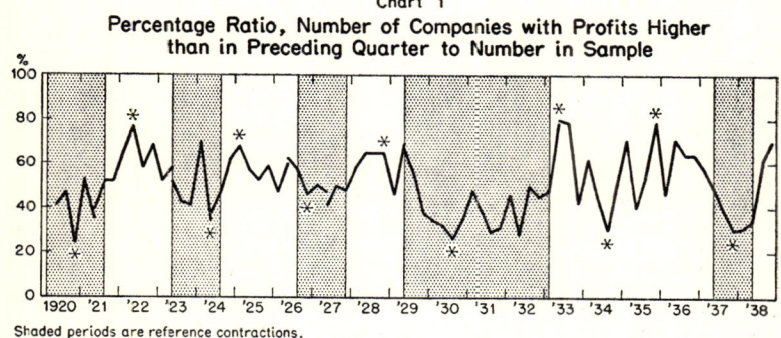

Chart 1
Percentage Ratio, Number of Companies with Profits Higher than in Preceding Quarter to Number in Sample

Shaded periods are reference contractions.

The location of these turning points in the percentage of companies suggests a typical sequence of events. When economic activity at large begins to rise, the number of companies with improving profits is rising and continues to rise during the earlier stages of the business expansion. Long before the decline in economic activity at large, however, the number of companies with improving profits begins to diminish. The fall in the number continues to the end of the expansion in business and on into the earlier stages of the following contraction. Long before economic activity revives, however, the

[3]Because of the overlap in our samples, percentages like those in Chart I can be computed, for any year except 1920 and 1938, from either of two or in some cases any of three samples. For each year we used the largest and latest sample. Thus the percentages for the fourth quarter of 1933 were computed, not from the 1927-33 sample of 155 companies or the 1929-37 sample of 185 companies, but from the 1933-38 sample of 244 companies.

number of companies with growing profits again begins to increase.

Broader movements

This method of classifying companies recognizes every fluctuation, every minor irregularity, in a company's profits. By another method, we can ignore the minor fluctuations and concentrate attention on the larger upswings and downswings. The second method requires a little explanation. Our first step is to chart the seasonally adjusted profits of each company. When we examine such a chart we usually find that the company's history can be divided into periods of rising and periods of falling profits. Months of outstandingly high earnings we call peaks, months of conspicuously low earnings, troughs. We now say that a company's profits were 'in expansion' in every quarter between a trough and the next peak. We say they were 'in contraction' in every quarter between a peak and the next trough. In marking peaks and troughs we follow a set of rules, one of which is that peaks must be at least fifteen months apart, and so must troughs.[4] In other words, each full cycle (measured from peak to peak or from trough to trough) must be at least fifteen months long. For this and other reasons, many minor fluctuations do not win recognition as expansions or contractions.

When the peaks and troughs, if any, in the profits of a company have been marked, we classify that company, in each quarter, according to whether its profits were expanding or at a peak, on the one hand, or contracting or at a trough, on the other. This is the second method of classification, and it produces somewhat different results than the first. In the profits of the Phillips Petroleum Company, for example, an expansion runs from a trough in the fourth quarter of 1923 to a peak in the third quarter of 1926 (Chart 2). But profits fell in certain quarters — in the second, third, and fourth quarters of 1924 and the third and fourth of 1925. By the first method the company would be classified as having falling profits in these five quarters; by the second method, it would be classified as having expanding profits.

[4] For the rules, see pp. 56-66 of the volume mentioned in Table 1, note a.

Chart 2
Profits of Phillips Petroleum Company

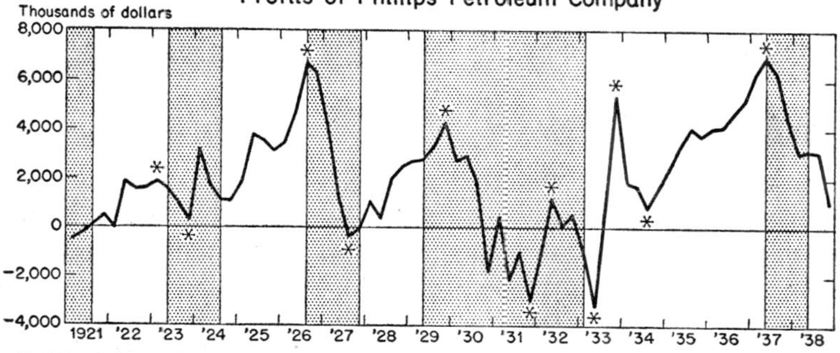

Shaded periods are reference contractions.

When all companies have been classified by the second method, the percentage with expanding or peak profits can be computed for each quarter. Plotting the resulting percentages (Chart 3), we obtain a curve smoother than the curve on Chart 1. High and low points (marked by asterisks) are easier to designate on the new curve. The story it tells however, is similar to the earlier one. At the beginning of a business expansion, the number of companies with profits in expansion or at peak is rising. It continues to rise during the earlier stages of the business expansion, but declines during the later stages. The number continues to decline during the earlier stages of the following business contraction, but rises during the later stages of that contraction.[5]

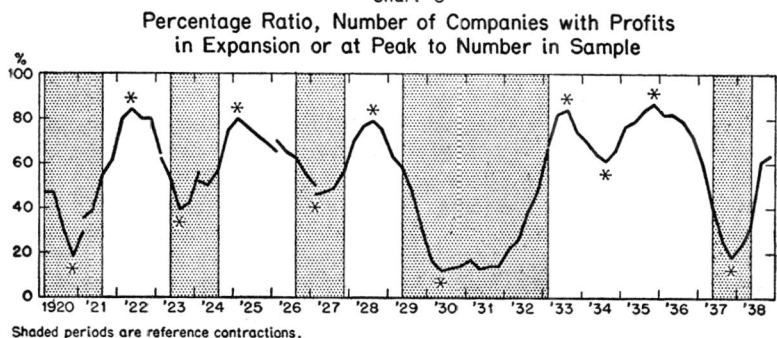

Chart 3
Percentage Ratio, Number of Companies with Profits in Expansion or at Peak to Number in Sample

Shaded periods are reference contractions.

[5] Computations for each quarter based on latest and largest sample; see note 3.

TURNING POINTS IN PROFITS OF INDIVIDUAL COMPANIES CLUSTERED ABOUT TURNS IN BUSINESS

When the number of companies with expanding or peak profits increases from one quarter to the next, the number with profits at trough in the first quarter must have exceeded the number at peak.[6] If the number with profits in expansion or at peak increases for a long period, troughs must have exceeded peaks for an almost coinciding period. Conversely, if the number with profits contracting or at trough increases for a considerable period, peaks must have exceeded troughs for a similar period. Chart 3 therefore tells us that in each of several quarters before and after a business peak, some companies arrived at the peak of their profits, and that profit peaks were more common than troughs both before and after the business peak. Profit troughs were similarly clustered about the business trough.

But sometimes a company has two or more peaks near a business peak, or two or more troughs near a business trough. In such cases it might be preferable to regard one of the turns as corresponding to the business turn and ignore the others. Colonial Beacon Oil Company, for example, had a trough in the second quarter of 1931, another in the third quarter of

---

[6] If we classify companies by their status in any one quarter, then subclassify them by their status in the next quarter we get the following exhaustive subclassification. A moment's consideration will show that the change in the number in expansion or at peak equals $(A+B+C+D) - (C+D+E+F)$ or $(A+B) - (E+F)$.

	FIRST QUARTER	SECOND QUARTER
A	At trough	In expansion
†B	At trough	At peak
C	In expansion	In expansion
D	In expansion	At peak
E	At peak	In contraction
†F	At peak	At trough
G	In contraction	In contraction
H	In contraction	At trough

†Instances in these categories are very rare, almost impossible.

1932, a third in the fourth quarter of 1934, and still another in the second quarter of 1936 (Chart 4). In such cases, we re-

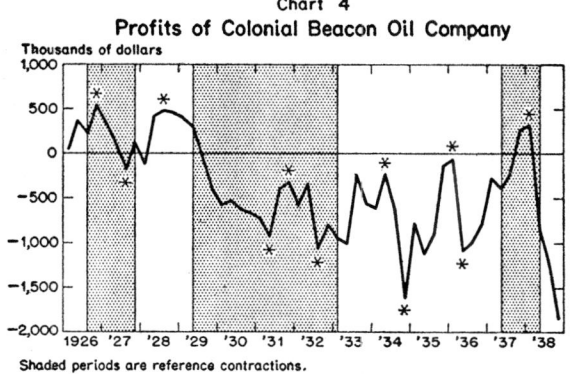

Chart 4
Profits of Colonial Beacon Oil Company
Shaded periods are reference contractions.

gard the turning point in profits nearest in time to the turning point in business as corresponding to the latter. We count Colonial as having a trough corresponding to the reference trough I33 in the third quarter of 1932. Occasionally, two turns in profits were equally near the business turn. American Safety Razor Corporation, for example, had a trough in IV26, four quarters earlier than the reference trough IV27, and another in IV28, four quarters later than the reference turn (Chart 5). In this case we regarded the deeper trough, in 1926, as 'corresponding'.

Turns in profits occurred in numerous quarters both be-

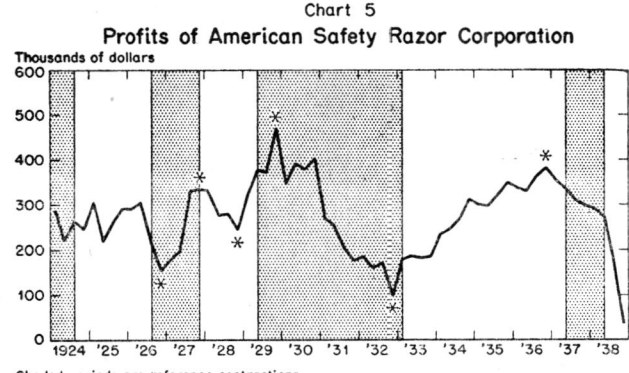

Chart 5
Profits of American Safety Razor Corporation
Shaded periods are reference contractions.

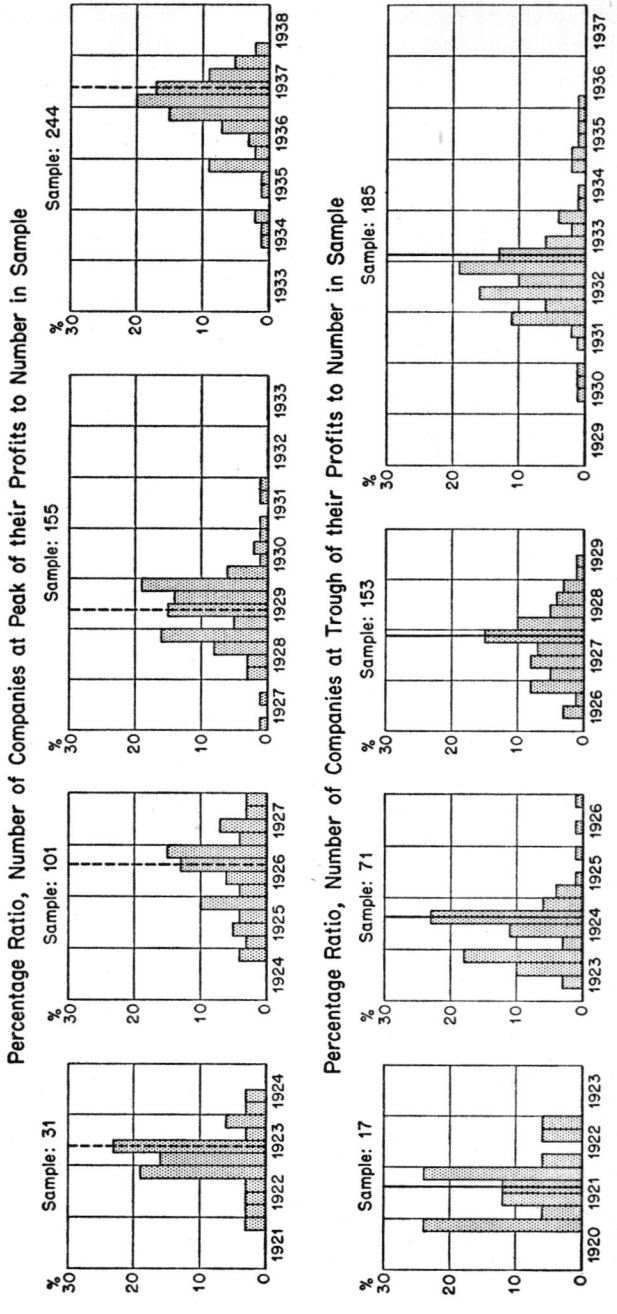

Chart 6
Scattering of Turns in Profits

fore and after the business turn to which they 'correspond' (Chart 6). Nevertheless there was a noticeable concentration around the business turns. Peaks in the profits of individual companies were much more common near a reference peak than near a reference trough; and troughs in profits were much more common near the reference low points. In a very rough way, turning points in profits became more and more frequent up to the quarter of the turn in business, then became less and less frequent as the business turn receded into the past. If we had larger samples we might find a smoother change in frequency.[7]

ALWAYS SOME EXCEPTIONAL COMPANIES

At every stage of the business cycle the fortunes of some companies, temporarily at least, ran counter to the main stream. The quarter by quarter data indicate that in the quarter with fewest rises during the great 1929-37 depression, 26 percent of the corporations had rising profits. In the quarter of the 1920's most favorable to profits, 23 percent had diminishing earnings.[8] When we disregard minor fluctuations exceptions are fewer but there are still some. In every quarter of the 1920's the profits of at least 16 percent of the companies were contracting or at a trough. In every quarter of the 1930's the profits of at least 12 percent were expanding or at a peak.

In the case of every business turn except 1933 some firms had no corresponding turn in their net income. About one-fifth did not have any turn corresponding to the 1926 business peak, and almost one-third missed the business trough in

---

[7] Quite a few of the fourth-quarter percentages on Chart 6 jut beyond their neighbors. Corporations sometimes make year-end accounting corrections that affect the fourth-quarter figures. Our seasonal adjustments apparently fail to neutralize these effects (which are highly irregular) completely. If the adjustments had been more successful the rise in frequency of profit turns before, and the decline in frequency after, a business turn might have been smoother.

[8] A company's profits seldom remained constant. The interval from the curve up to the 100 percent line, therefore, approximately measures the percentage of companies in each quarter whose profits were smaller than in the preceding quarter.

1927 (Table 5, lines 19 and 20). Sometimes the absence of a turn means that the profits of a company grew in both contraction and expansion. The earnings of Frank G. Shattuck Company, for example, increased in both 1926-27 and 1927-29 (Chart 7). In other instances the lack of a turn may mean that earnings declined in both expansion and contraction. In still others it may mean the movement was so irregular that we are unwilling to designate a 'corresponding' turn.

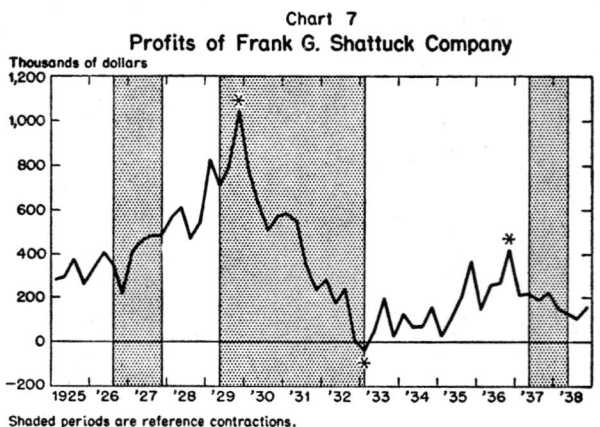

Chart 7
Profits of Frank G. Shattuck Company

Shaded periods are reference contractions.

NO CONSISTENT LEAD OR LAG IN AGGREGATE PROFITS

Although numerous companies experienced declining profits while business activity was still in its ascendant phase, the aggregate profits of all the companies studied continued to grow practically up to the end of the business expansion (Chart 8). The increases in the profits of the remaining companies exceeded the decreases in the profits of the companies whose earnings were waning. In contraction, similarly, aggregate profits diminished up to the end, even though a gradually increasing number of companies were becoming more prosperous. The turning point in aggregate profits coincided with the reference turn in five instances, preceded it by one quarter in 1921 and 1937 and two quarters in 1932-33, followed it by one quarter in 1929. There was no consistent lead, no consistent lag.

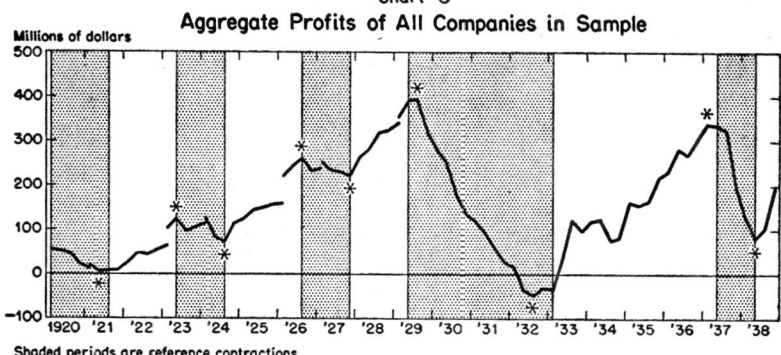

Chart 8
Aggregate Profits of All Companies in Sample

Shaded periods are reference contractions.

All our samples include two very large corporations — General Motors and United States Steel. They held at first an overwhelming and even later a large percentage of the assets belonging to all the companies included (Table 1, line 10). In our calculations regarding the number of companies in expansion or at peak, or at a 'corresponding' turn, a large company, of course, counts for no more than a small one. In considering the dates of turns in aggregate profits it may be appropriate to exclude the earnings of the two giants. In our worksheets we have a chart, similar to Chart 8, pertaining to the profits of all sample companies except these two. Its peaks and troughs differ somewhat from those on Chart 8 but they do not differ systematically from the reference turns. They lead the latter four times, coincide with them four times, and follow them once. There was one interval of three quarters, another of two, the rest were only one quarter long (Table 2, col. 4 and 5).

Although aggregate profits continued to grow after the number of companies with rising profits began to decline, the subsequent growth was less rapid, except in 1932-37 (Table 3). The fall in the aggregate was, likewise, less rapid after the number of companies with growing profits began to increase, except in 1937-38.

Table 2
Turning Points in Profits

NATURE OF TURN	DATE OF TURN IN					NO. OF QUARTERS BETWEEN DATES IN COLUMNS					
	NO. OF COMPANIES WITH		AGGREGATE PROFITS		BUSINESS (REFERENCE CHRONOLOGY)						
	Profits higher than in preceding quarter	Profits in expansion or at peak	Incl. G.M. & U.S.S.C.	Excl. G.M. & U.S.S.C.		(1) & (3)	(2) & (3)	(1) & (4)	(2) & (4)	(1) & (5)	(2) & (5)
	(1)	(2)	(3)	(4)	(5)	(6)	(7)	(8)	(9)	(10)	(11)
Trough	4Q 1920	4Q 1920	2Q 1921	4Q 1920	3Q 1921	2	2	0	0	3	3
Peak	2Q 1922	2Q 1922	2Q 1923	4Q 1922	2Q 1923	4	4	2	2	4	4
Trough	2Q 1924	3Q 1923	3Q 1924	3Q 1924	3Q 1924	1	4	1	4	1	4
Peak	1Q 1925	1Q 1925	3Q 1926	2Q 1926	3Q 1926	6	6	5	5	6	6
Trough	4Q 1926	1Q 1927	4Q 1927	4Q 1927	4Q 1927	4	3	4	3	4	3
Peak	4Q 1928	3Q 1928	3Q 1929	3Q 1929	2Q 1929	3	4	3	4	2	3
Trough	3Q 1930	2Q 1930	3Q 1932	1Q 1933	1Q 1933	8	9	10	11	10	11
Peak	4Q 1935	4Q 1935	1Q 1937	1Q 1937	2Q 1937	5	5	5	5	6	6
Trough	4Q 1937	4Q 1937	2Q 1938	2Q 1938	2Q 1938	2	2	2	2	2	2

TABLE 3

Aggregate Profits: Change per Quarter in Earlier and in Later Quarters of Each Business Phase

DATE	CYCLICAL STATUS OF		COS. IN SAMPLE		CHANGE FROM PRECEDING DATE ($000)	QUARTERS FROM PRECEDING DATE	CHANGE PER QUARTER ($000)
	Aggregate profits	No. of cos. in expansion or at peak	No.	Agg. profits ($000)			
2Q 1921	At Trough	Rising	31	4928			
2Q 1922	Rising	At Peak	31	49245	44317	4	11079
2Q 1923	At Peak	Falling	31	75714	26469	4	6617
2Q 1923	At Peak	Falling	71	124955			
3Q 1923	Falling	At Trough	71	96650	−28305	1	−28305
3Q 1924	At Trough	Rising	71	66613	−30037	4	−7509
3Q 1924	At Trough	Rising	101	71630			
1Q 1925	Rising	At Peak	101	124232	52602	2	26301
3Q 1926	At Peak	Falling	101	196010	71778	6	11963
3Q 1926	At Peak	Falling	153	261444			
1Q 1927	Falling	At Trough	153	239613	−21831	2	−10916
4Q 1927	At Trough	Rising	153	213868	−25745	3	−8582
4Q 1927	At Trough	Rising	155	222450			
3Q 1928	Rising	At Peak	155	321850	99400	3	33133
3Q 1929	At Peak	Falling	155	380675	58825	4	14706
3Q 1929	At Peak	Falling	185	394633			
2Q 1930	Falling	At Trough	185	249617	−145016	3	−48339
3Q 1932	At Trough	Rising	185	-48700	−298317	9	−33146
3Q 1932	At Trough	Rising	185	-48700			
4Q 1935	Rising	At Peak	185	197229	245929	13	18918
1Q 1937	At Peak	Falling	185	311082	113853	5	22771
1Q 1937	At Peak	Falling	244	340016			
4Q 1937	Falling	At Trough	244	194812	−145204	3	−48401
2Q 1938	At Trough	Rising	244	81054	−113758	2	−56879

POSSIBLE EXPLANATIONS OF EARLY CYCLICAL CHANGES

Encroachment of costs on prices

Wesley C. Mitchell expressed the view in 1913 that during the course of a business expansion the cost of doing business sooner or later begins to increase more or less generally throughout industry. The rise in cost, he thought, is not necessarily accompanied by a general decline in profits. Quite possibly, profits in the aggregate might be at their highest just before business activity begins to recede. But not all enterprises, he reasoned, would be able to offset rising costs by raising the prices they charge for their products. Some would be prevented by law, governmental regulation, custom, or high sensitivity of buyers to advances in prices. Their profits must begin to decline even though the aggregate profits of all are still growing. Their difficulties would make their banking and commercial creditors more reluctant than before to accommodate them. Distrust of the future, curtailment of capital expenditures and other adverse developments, spreading along the many lines of interdependence among enterprises, might lead to a general recession. Conversely, during the later stages of a business contraction, Mitchell believed, costs tend to fall. The decline in cost would not in all cases be translated into correspondingly lower prices received; the profits of some firms would begin to rise. In one way or another, the companies with improving fortunes might presently become focal points in a business revival.[9]

Our findings support those of Mitchell's surmises on which they have a direct bearing. The number of companies with diminishing profits does begin to rise before the end of expansion. Despite the increasing number of firms with falling profits, the aggregate profits of all the firms studied continue to rise until the end. In contractions, too, the sequence of events is about what Mitchell expected.

Scatter of turning points in production

The early declines we find in the profits of some companies, however, do not necessarily reflect a squeeze between costs and prices. An early rise in cost per unit of goods sold, unaccompanied by an equal or larger rise in the price received for it, will, to be sure, reduce profit per unit and may reduce the aggregate profits of a company. On the other hand, an early decline in the physical volume of goods a company sells will reduce its aggregate profit even if there is no change in unit profit and may reduce the aggregate even if profit per unit increases. We know that in every expansion the sales of some industries reach peaks at various early dates, then decline. The scattering of turning points in the sales of individual enterprises is doubtless more pronounced. The early declines

[9] Wesley C. Mitchell, *Business Cycles* (University of California Press, 1913), pp. 457-514, 562-9, or *Business Cycles and their Causes* (reprint of Part III of the same volume, 1941), pp. 8-74, 139-47.

in the profits of some corporations may reflect early declines in production sold, pressure of cost against prices, or both. (In enterprises with heavy overhead cost, the effect of declining volume would often be reenforced by an accompanying decline in unit profit.) One explanation may fit the facts (which we do not have) about prices, costs, and volume in some instances, another explanation may fit them in other instances. Conversely, the early rise we observe in the profits of some corporations during business contractions may signify a more favorable relation of prices received to unit costs, a rise in volume, or both.

PROFITS IN DURABLES DID NOT LEAD PROFITS IN OTHER INDUSTRIES

It might be illuminating to know whether the companies with early turns in their profits have other characteristics in common — whether, for example, the profits of some branches of industry usually decline before those of others. Unfortunately our data do not permit us to explore such questions in detail. The number of companies for which we have figures in a particular industry, such as the manufacture of foods or of hardware and tools, is too small to support a generalization about profits in that industry. We have, however, classified every company broadly either as a producer of durable goods primarily or as a producer of nondurable goods (producers of services are assigned to the latter group). There was no consistent difference between the two classes. In some cycles producers of durables had earlier turns than producers of nondurables; but in other cycles it was the latter who had the earlier turns (Table 4; Table 5, lines 21 and 22; Table 6).

CAN PROFITS FORECAST BUSINESS CYCLES?

The consistent leads on Charts 1 and 3 raise a hopeful question: can one forecast turning points in general business activity by following the fortunes of a group of companies and counting, quarter by quarter, the number with rising profits? In fact the predictive value of such information is rather limited.

TABLE 4

Date of Most Common Turning Point in Profits of Producers
of Durables and of Nondurables

REFERENCE TURN		QUARTER IN WHICH LARGEST NO. OF COS. HAD CORRESPONDING TURN IN PROFITS[a]		LEADER	LENGTH OF LEAD (QUARTERS)
Date	Kind	Durables	Nondurables		
3Q 1921	Trough	4Q 1921	4Q 1920	Nondurables	4
2Q 1923	Peak	2Q 1923	4Q 1922	Nondurables	2
3Q 1924	Trough	3Q 1924	4Q 1923	Nondurables	3
3Q 1926	Peak	4Q 1925, 4Q 1926[b]	4Q 1926	Durables?	4?
4Q 1927	Trough	4Q 1927	1Q 1928	Durables	1
2Q 1929	Peak	4Q 1928	4Q 1929	Durables	4
1Q 1933	Trough	4Q 1932	1Q 1933	Durables	1
2Q 1937	Peak	1Q 1937	4Q 1936, 1Q 1937[b]	Nondurables?	1?

[a] As indicated by two charts in our files, one for each class of company, similar in design to Chart 6 pertaining to all companies.
[b] Number same in both quarters.

A possible forecasting procedure

If a predictive effort were made it would probably be better to employ the method underlying Chart 1 than the method underlying Chart 3. The latter involves determining in each quarter the specific cycle status of each company. This can be done only if peaks and troughs in its profits have been designated. As we have noted, the profits of individual companies are often highly irregular. A quarter cannot confidently be recognized as a peak (or trough) until several later quarters have elapsed. But if one must wait to determine the status of individual companies, one must wait also to count the number in expansion or at peak. The event to be predicted might be upon us before the 'prediction' was made. It must be conceded, however, that the smoother curve produced by the method of Chart 3 is likely to contain fewer minor irregularities that might be mistaken for major turns.

Even if the method of Chart 1 were adopted, the problem of recognizing turns promptly would still have to be faced, though in only one series of figures: the percentage of companies with profits higher than in preceding quarter. A simple if arbitrary rule might be: in a business expansion, let the first quarter showing a rise in the percentage, followed immediately by a decline, be taken as the peak in the percentage; in a contraction, let the first quarter showing a decline, followed

TABLE 5: Frequency of Turning Points in Profits in Early, Median, and Late Quarters Producers of Durables and of Nondurables

	Kind of turn	Trough	Peak	Trough	Peak	Trough	Peak	Trough	Peak
(1)		3Q 1921	1Q 1923	2Q 1924	3Q 1926	4Q 1927	2Q 1929	4Q 1932	1Q 1937
(2)	Median quarter*								

NUMBER OF COMPANIES

	Producers of durables								
	With turn in								
(3)	Earlier quarters	3	2	9	27	30	32	53	52
(4)	Median quarter	2	3	7	7	16	16	22	29
(5)	Later quarters	4	9	16	14	15	31	16	38
(6)	Some quarter (3) + (4) + (5)	9	14	32	48	61	79	91	119
(7)	No quarter	1	3	7	9	19	3	0	2
(8)	In sample (6) + (7)	10	17	39	57	80	82	91	121
	Producers of nondurables								
	With turn in								
(9)	Earlier quarters	4	8	15	9	9	23	35	54
(10)	Median quarter	0	2	1	6	7	7	14	19
(11)	Later quarters	3	3	11	18	20	41	45	43
(12)	Some quarter (9) + (10) + (11)	7	13	27	33	46	71	94	116
(13)	No quarter	0	1	5	11	27	2	0	7
(14)	In sample (12) + (13)	7	14	32	44	73	73	94	123
	Durables & nondurables								
	With turn in								
(15)	Earlier quarters	7	10	24	36	49	55	88	106
(16)	Median quarter	2	5	8	13	23	23	36	48
(17)	Later quarters	7	12	27	32	35	72	61	81
(18)	Some quarter (15) + (16) + (17)	16	27	59	81	107	150	185	235
(19)	No quarter	1	4	12	20	46	5	0	9
(20)	In sample (18) + (19)	17	31	71	101	153	155	185	244

RATIO OF EARLY TO ALL TURNS

(21)	Durables (3) ÷ (6)	.333	.143	.281	.562	.492	.405	.582	.437
(22)	Nondurables (9) ÷ (12)	.571	.615	.556	.273	.413	.324	.372	.466
(23)	All corporations (15) ÷ (18)	.438	.370	.407	.444	.458	.367	.476	.451

*Less than half of all the companies (durables plus nondurables) with corresponding turns had them before this quarter; more than half had them before *or in* this quarter.

TABLE 6

Peaks and Troughs in (A) the Number of Companies with Profits Higher than in Preceding Quarter, (B) the Number with Expanding or Peak Profits, 1921-38: Producers of Durables and of Nondurables

LEVEL OF NUMBER	QUARTER IN WHICH NO. OF COMPANIES REACHED LEVEL[a]		LEADER	LENGTH OF LEAD (QUARTERS)
	Durables	Nondurables		
NUMBER WITH PROFITS HIGHER THAN IN PRECEDING QUARTER				
Trough	2Q 1921	4Q 1920	Nondurables	2
Peak	2Q 1922	1Q 1922, 2Q 1922[b]	Nondurables?	1?
Trough	4Q 1923	2Q 1924	Durables	2
Peak	1Q 1925	2Q 1926	Durables	5
Trough	1Q 1927	2Q 1927	Durables	1
Peak	3Q 1928	2Q 1928	Nondurables	1
Trough	3Q 1931	2Q 1932	Durables	3
Peak	4Q 1935	4Q 1935	Neither	0
Trough	4Q 1937	1Q 1938	Durables	1
NUMBER WITH EXPANDING OR PEAK PROFITS				
Trough	4Q 1920, 1Q 1921[b]	4Q 1920	Nondurables?	1?
Peak	4Q 1922	1Q 1922	Nondurables	3
Trough	4Q 1923	2Q 1923	Nondurables	2
Peak	1Q 1925	2Q 1926	Durables	5
Trough	1Q 1927	3Q 1927	Durables	2
Peak	3Q 1928	4Q 1928	Durables	1
Trough	2Q 1930	4Q 1930	Durables	2
Peak	4Q 1935	4Q 1935	Neither	0
Trough	4Q 1937	4Q 1937	Neither	0

'Extra' peaks and troughs in 1933 and 1934 are not included.

[a]As indicated by separate charts for durables and nondurables, similar in design to Charts 1 and 3.

[b]Number same in both quarters.

by a rise, be taken as the trough. Suppose that an economic analyst, compiling and plotting the data underlying Chart 1 as they became available from quarter to quarter, had adhered to this rule, beginning in 1920; how would he have fared?

Before one can answer the question, one must note that it is difficult to say how he would have proceeded in 1933-37. He would have found a peak in the percentage of companies in the second quarter of 1933, just as we do in retrospect. But we know that it was an 'extra' peak; there was no business peak reasonably soon after it. Business conditions were, however, mixed; one might say there was a quasi-contraction shortly after the second quarter of 1933. Assume the analyst recognized a quasi-contraction; where would he have placed his next peak in the percentage of companies? It would depend upon where he placed the quasi-trough. Most likely he would have found a peak in the number of companies in the first quarter of 1935. The other decisions he would have made are summarized in Table 7, column (1). With two exceptions his turning points would have been the same as those on Chart 1.

TABLE 7

Hypothetical Forecasts of Business Turns

NATURE OF TURN	HYPOTHETICAL DATE OF		NO. OF QUARTERS BY WHICH HYPOTHETICAL DATE PRECEDED BUSINESS TURN	
	Turn in number of companies (1)	Forecast (2)	Date in (1) (3)	Date in (2) (4)
Trough	4Q 1920*	2Q 1921	3	1
Peak	2Q 1922	4Q 1922	4	2
Trough	4Q 1923	2Q 1924	3	1
Peak	1Q 1925	3Q 1925	6	4
Trough	4Q 1926	2Q 1927	4	2
Peak	4Q 1928	2Q 1929	2	0
Trough	3Q 1930	1Q 1931	10	8
Peak	1Q 1935	3Q 1935	9	7
Trough	4Q 1937	2Q 1938	2	0

Dates of business turns are given in Table 2, Col. 5.

For nature of hypothesis, see text.

*Doubtful; if data were available for the first quarter of 1920 and if they showed a higher percentage of companies than in the second quarter, the latter would be the hypothetical date.

Variable leads

The interval between the date the analyst would have designated in the number of companies and the actual date of the following business turn was highly variable, as the accom-

Length of lead, in quarters	2	3	4	5	6	7	8	9	10
Number of instances	2	2	2	0	1	0	0	1	1

panying summary from Table 7, column (3), indicates. The turning point in the percentage of companies with rising profits may tell us that a turn in business is coming; but this, in an economy in which business cycles are known to prevail, is hardly news. It does not tell us with any precision when a turn in business is coming.

On the other hand, a prediction that a business turn would occur at some time during the year after the date of the forecast would have been correct in six of nine instances. Perhaps a range of twelve months and a record of two successes out of three may be useful for some purposes.

Delayed availability

For certain kinds of events there is an inevitable lag between the time they occur and the time it becomes known that they have occurred. Our analyst could not decide that a quarter was a peak until he had a figure for the next quarter; and figures for earnings in a quarter are not published until the quarter has closed. The analyst could not name his turn in the number of companies and forecast an approaching turn in business until two quarters after the turn in the number of companies. In 2 instances out of 9 he would have made his 'forecast' in the quarter in which the business turn occurred: in 2 others he would have anticipated the business turn by only one quarter (Table 7, col. 4).

In defense of the forecasting procedure it might be replied that there is a lag in the recognition of high and low points in business also. They are identified only in retrospect. Therefore, even when the evidence of a turn in the number of companies first becomes available in the quarter in which business itself turns, that evidence might make it possible to identify the business turn more promptly. This defense would be valid if the lead were fairly constant from cycle to cycle. But it is not. When it became apparent to our imaginary analyst, in the second quarter of 1938, that a trough in the percentage of companies had occurred in the last quarter of 1937, his experience did not tell him how soon to expect a trough in business. It might still be two years away.

Profits one piece of evidence

Changes in the percentage of companies with rising profits, then, do not forecast business conditions with respectable precision. But people who are obliged to make decisions in which the prospective course of business is a factor might nevertheless weigh information of this character together with other evidence. Further research, too, may yield an explanation of variations in the length of lead. If it does, the forecasting or identifying value of data on the distribution of changes in profits among companies will be enhanced.[10]

A simplified approach to the seasonal problem

The procedure we followed may be unnecessarily complex and expensive for forecasting. We adjusted the reported profits of each company for seasonal variation, then counted the number whose adjusted profits increased. Instead, we could count the number of companies whose profits, as reported, increased for seasonal or other reasons; we could express that number as a percentage of all companies for which we had data; and finally we could adjust that percentage itself for seasonal variation. We did this for the firms in our largest sample (244 corporations, 1933-38). The result-

---

[10] An analyst of current business conditions who watched the kind of evidence we have discussed would want to know as promptly and definitely as possible how any forecast he ventured was turning out. He would need to recognize the turn in 'business' soon after it occurred. In this paper we have used the 'reference' turns of Burns and Mitchell who, in fixing their turns, considered the evidence of economic events following by a considerable interval the dates on which they eventually decided, and survey a wide range of economic activities. If our analyst wished a quicker determination, he could make his forecast apply to some single, important, measurable aspect of economic activity, such as carloadings, factory employment, or an index of industrial production. Such a measure should have turning points that never come early and never late in the procession of turns in many kinds of activity. No single series of figures will meet this requirement. A group of activities would be better. Its components would often have their respective turns in different quarters. The business turn could be defined as the median turn for the group. If there were seven activities and one reached a trough in March, two in April, one in July, and the others later or not at all, July would be the business trough. Geoffrey H. Moore, in Statistical Indicators of Cyclical Revivals and Recessions (NBER, *Occasional Paper* 31, 1950), discusses more fully the reasons for preferring a group, and presents one.

ing curve (Chart 9) is similar in general contour to the part of the curve on Chart 1 that pertains to the same years. Both forecast the 1938 business trough, although the new curve leads it by only one quarter instead of two. Both show two 'extra' turns in 1933-34 (on the new curve, however, the first extra turn is somewhat uncertain, for lack of earlier data, and it apparently came one quarter later than its analogue on Chart 1).

Chart 9
Number of Companies (out of 244) with Profits Higher than in Preceding Quarter
Two Methods of Seasonal Adjustment Compared

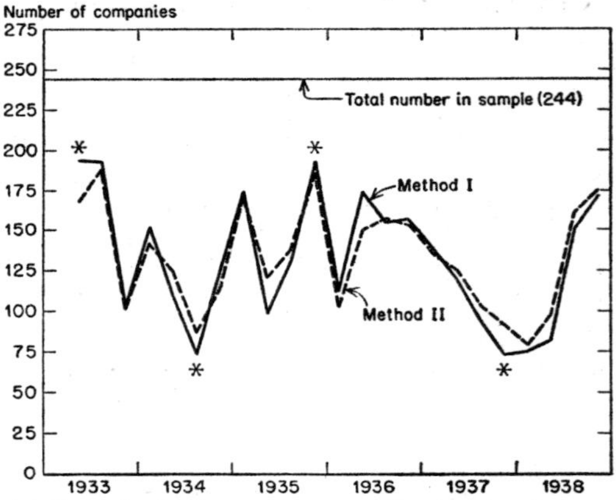

Method I: Profits of each company seasonally adjusted, number of companies with rises counted.
Method II: Number of companies with rise in reported (unadjusted) profits counted, number then seasonally adjusted.

The new procedure makes it possible to broaden the base of our calculations. We held down the size of our earlier samples by requiring that data must be available for a corporation over at least one entire business cycle. Although adopted for another purpose, this requirement was almost necessary to provide enough information to compute proper seasonal adjustment factors. For our present purpose we can drop it, since we are no longer adjusting each company's earnings. We now accept, as part of the data on change from any quarter to the next, data for any company whose profits, for those two quarters, appear in the National City Bank file. We count the number of companies with higher profits in the second quarter and the number for which there are data on both quarters. We express the first number as a percentage of the second, and seasonally adjust the series of percentages so obtained.[11] From 1923 to 1938 peaks or troughs in the seasonally adjusted percentage usually preceded those in business (Chart 10). The new method therefore indicates the same relation as the old. But it falls down in one instance: in the fourth quarter of 1927 the new trough in the percentage of companies with rising profits coincided with the trough in business.

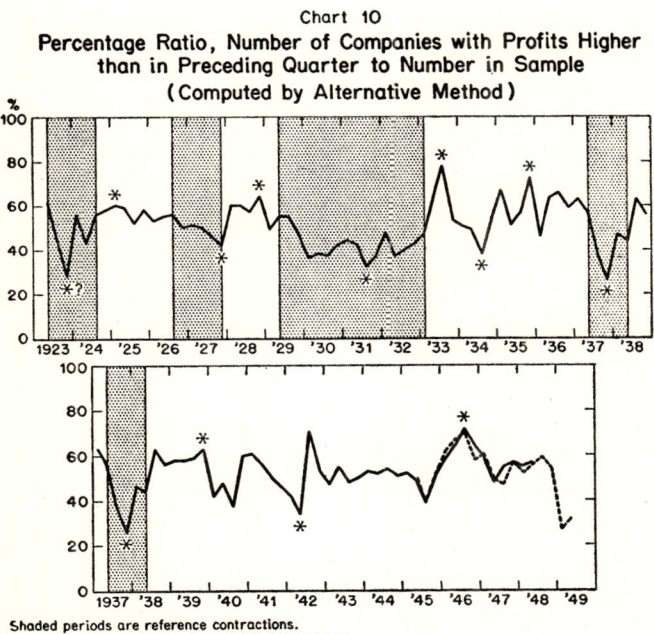

Chart 10
Percentage Ratio, Number of Companies with Profits Higher than in Preceding Quarter to Number in Sample
(Computed by Alternative Method)

Shaded periods are reference contractions.
For explanation of broken line, 1945-49, see text.

[11] The total number of companies varies from one pair of quarters to the next. Some companies inevitably drop out of the Bank file from time to time and are replaced by others. Whenever this happens, the number of companies available for a *pair* of quarters is reduced. In 1923-29 the total number available ranged from 119 to 195; thereafter it always exceeded 190. We do not think the comparability of the percentages is seriously affected. The alternative would be to reduce our sample drastically, as in our earlier procedure.

Old sequence disturbed during war

Since 1938 profits have been subject to many unusual, powerful, and abruptly changing influences. A large part of industry converted from peaceful to warlike activities, then converted back. Rapidly rising prices created inventory profits.[12] Severe strikes occurred from time to time. Heavy surtaxes were added in successive steps to corporate income taxes. An excess profits tax was imposed, stepped up several times, then removed entirely. Renegotiation of contracts and tax refunds in connection with carry-over of losses complicated the tax picture. Some corporations included reserves for various contingencies in their deductions from income as reported to stockholders; some of these reserve entries were afterwards reversed, swelling the final income figures for later periods. Changes in the percentage of companies with rising profits were highly irregular (Chart 10). We find three 'specific' turns in the curve, but in doing so we pass over the crater in 1940, the sharp temporary rise to the third quarter of 1942, the low point in the third quarter of 1945, and other pronounced irregularities.

In the middle of this era, however, there was a period of relative stability. Production and employment indexes show that industrial activity was at a high and fairly steady level in 1943, 1944, and the first half of 1945 (with perhaps a mild decline in the last year and a half). Large increases in profits after taxes were impossible because of the high tax level. The percentage of companies with rising profits fluctuated unusually little, and the number with rising was about the same as the number with falling profits.

The first two of the three designated 'specific' turns since 1938 can hardly be regarded as corresponding to turns in business. Students of cycles may eventually agree that there was a business peak near the beginning of 1944 and a trough near the beginning of 1946. (Some major industries, however, expanded their production in this period.) But what

[12] Some companies minimized such profits by 'last-in first-out' accounting, but many did not.

would it mean to link the 1939 peak in the percentage of companies with a business peak four or five years later? The 1942 trough in the percentage was followed more immediately by the business quasi-peak than by the putative business trough.

The history of aggregate profits after 1939 was more or less similar to that of industrial activity (Charts 11 and 12).[13] The sharp rise in tax rates effective January 1, 1942, however, virtually halted at a relatively early date the growth of profits after taxes for the duration of the war.[14] Through

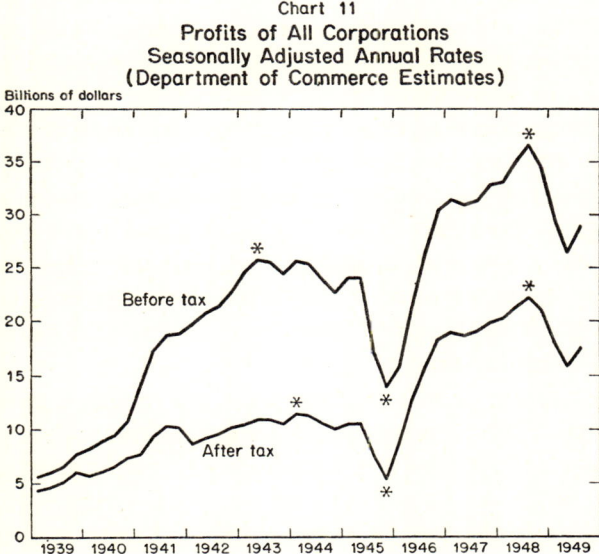

Chart 11
Profits of All Corporations
Seasonally Adjusted Annual Rates
(Department of Commerce Estimates)

[13] The data for Chart 11 are from the *Survey of Current Business,* July 1949 and later issues. The data for Chart 12 are those compiled from corporate reports by the Board of Governors of the Federal Reserve System and published in the *Federal Reserve Bulletin.* They pertain to profits after taxes. The Board has recently discontinued the larger sample, 629 corporations. Of these, 555 were classified as engaged in manufacturing or mining. All 200 in the new sample are in manufacturing. We have seasonally adjusted the Reserve Board data.

[14] The change in tax rates obviously explains the mild 1941-42 decline in profits of all corporations after taxes. It doubtless explains also a large part of the somewhat similar decline in the earnings of the 629 companies. We think the former decline too mild to be called a contraction, but recognize a contraction in the latter.

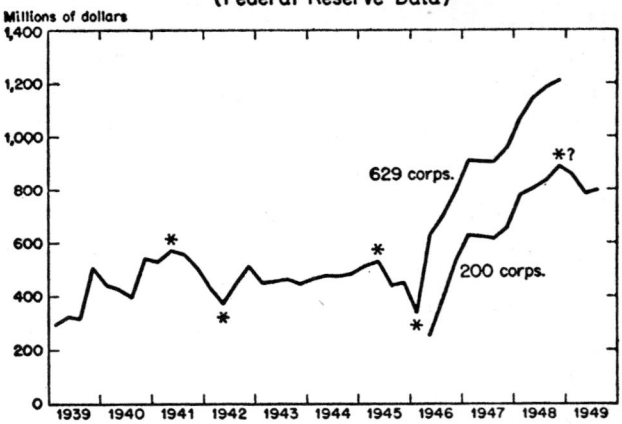

Chart 12
Earnings of Large Industrial Corporations
(Federal Reserve Data)

1945 the turning points in the percentage of companies (Chart 10) were about as poorly related to the turning points in aggregate profits as they were to the changes in business activity.

Sequence reestablished?

On the other hand, the third turn in the percentage of companies, i.e., the 1946 peak, might be regarded as heralding the peaks in business and profits which apparently occurred late in 1948. But the interval, about two years, is uncommonly long.

The National City Bank recently discontinued its 200-company sample as such and replaced it by a 400-company sample beginning in 1945. As before, to maintain a constant number of companies in the group, substitutions were necessary. Continuous information for 341 companies, however, is included. We counted, in each quarter, the number of companies whose profits (as reported, not seasonally adjusted) rose from the preceding quarter, divided by 341, and seasonally adjusted the series of percentages thus obtained. The broken line on Chart 10 indicates the result. In the period of overlap it resembles the solid line based on a smaller and changing list of companies.

It falls abruptly in the first quarter of 1949, when only 27 percent of the companies had rising profits — apparently one of the lowest percentages in the entire period 1920-49.

The percentage rose to 32 in the recent quarter of 1949. Incomplete data suggest the recovery continued. If so, a trough in the first quarter heralds the end of the business decline.

DIVERSITY AND NEW INVESTMENT

The growing diversity of profit experience in the later stages of a business expansion may have consequences that are worth mentioning, although data needed for their investigation are not presently and readily available. Declining profits on existing investment may lead corporate executives to revise downward their expectations of the additional profits to be gained from additional investment in plant and equipment. Even if long run expectations are not affected, declining profits reduce the funds available from current operations; such funds are an important means of financing new investment. Declining profits, furthermore, may impair the credit rating of a company and its ability to issue new securities on terms considered attractive by its managers. It is true that the gradual spread of declining profits from company to company does not interfere with the growth of aggregate profits. But new investment near the middle of a business expansion may be concentrated in some enterprises that have unusual long run opportunities to widen the market for their products or to improve their efficiency. It might nevertheless happen that the profits of many such enterprises began to decline early in a particular expansion. If so, the decline in their profits might help to bring about a decline in the aggregate new investment of all corporations even though aggregate profits continued for a time to increase.

NATIONAL BUREAU PUBLICATIONS ON BUSINESS CYCLES

I Books on Business Cycles

Business Cycles and Unemployment (1923)   448 pp., $4.10
Committee on Unemployment and Business Cycles of the President's Conference on Unemployment, and a Special Staff of the National Bureau

Employment, Hours and Earnings in Prosperity and Depression, United States, 1920-1922 (1923)   150 pp., 3.10
W. I. King

Business Annals (1926)   382 pp., 2.50
W. L. Thorp, with an introductory chapter, Business Cycles as Revealed by Business Annals, by Wesley C. Mitchell

Migration and Business Cycles (1926)   258 pp., 2.50
Harry Jerome

Business Cycles: The Problem and Its Setting (1927)   514 pp., 5.00
Wesley C. Mitchell

*Planning and Control of Public Works (1930)   292 pp., 2.50
Leo Wolman

*The Smoothing of Time Series (1931)
F. R. Macaulay

Strategic Factors in Business Cycles (1934)   256 pp., 1.50
J. M. Clark

German Business Cycles, 1924-1933 (1934)   308 pp., 2.50
C. T. Schmidt

Public Works in Prosperity and Depression (1935)   482 pp., 3.00
A. D. Gayer

Prices in Recession and Recovery (1936)   602 pp., 4.00
Frederick C. Mills

Some Theoretical Problems Suggested by the Movements of Interest Rates, Bond Yields and Stock Prices in the United States Since 1856 (1938)   612 pp., 5.00
F. R. Macaulay

*Consumer Instalment Credit and Economic Fluctuations (1942)   262 pp., 2.50
Gottfried Haberler

Measuring Business Cycles (1946)   592 pp., 5.00
A. F. Burns and Wesley C. Mitchell

*Price-Quantity Interactions in Business Cycles (1946)   158 pp., 1.50
Frederick C. Mills

*Changes in Income Distribution During the Great Depression (1946)   192 pp., 2.50
Horst Mendershausen

American Transportation in Prosperity and Depression (1948)   432 pp., $5.00
Thor Hultgren

Inventories and Business Cycles, with Special Reference to Manufacturers' Inventories (in press)
Moses Abramovitz

II   Books Partly Concerned with Business Cycles

**The Behavior of Prices* (1927)   598 pp., 7.00
Frederick C. Mills

**Recent Economic Changes in the United States* (1929) 2 vol.,   990 pp., 7.50
Committee on Recent Economic Changes of the President's Conference on Unemployment, and a Special Staff of the National Bureau

Seasonal Variations in Industry and Trade (1933)   480 pp., 4.00
Simon Kuznets

Production Trends in the United States Since 1870 (1934)   396 pp., 3.50
A. F. Burns

Industrial Profits in the United States (1934)   692 pp., 5.00
R. C. Epstein

Ebb and Flow in Trade Unionism (1936)   272 pp., 2.50
Leo Wolman

**The International Gold Standard Reinterpreted, 1914-1934* (1940)   2 vol., 1474 pp., 12.00
William Adams Brown, Jr.

National Income and Its Composition, 1919-1938 (1941)   1012 pp., 5.00
Simon Kuznets

**Financing Small Corporations in Five Manufacturing Industries, 1926-36* (1942)   192 pp., 1.50
C. L. Merwin

**The Financing of Large Corporations, 1920-39* (1943)   160 pp., 1.50
Albert R. Koch

Corporate Cash Balances, 1914-43: Manufacturing and Trade 1945)   148 pp., 2.00
Friedrich A. Lutz

National Income: A Summary of Findings (1946)   160 pp., 1.50
Simon Kuznets

Value of Commodity Output since 1869 (1947)   320 pp., 4.00
W. H. Shaw

Business Incorporations in the United States, 1800-1943 (1948)   196 pp., 6.00
G. Heberton Evans, Jr.

III   Papers on Business Cycles

**Testing Business Cycles* (Bulletin 31, March 1, 1929)
Wesley C. Mitchell

**The Depression as Depicted by Business Annals* (Bulletin 43, September 19, 1932)
Willard L. Thorp

Gross Capital Formation, 1919-1933 (Bulletin 52, November 15, 1934) .50
Simon Kuznets

The National Bureau's Measures of Cyclical Behavior (Bulletin 57, July 1, 1935) .50
Wesley C. Mitchell and Arthur F. Burns

Production during the American Business Cycle of 1927-1933 (Bulletin 61, November 9, 1936) .50
Wesley C. Mitchell and Arthur F. Burns

Technical Progress and Agricultural Depression (Bulletin 67, November 29, 1937) .50
Eugen Altschul and Frederick Strauss

Statistical Indicators of Cyclical Revivals (Bulletin 69, May 28, 1938) .25
Wesley C. Mitchell and Arthur F. Burns

Commodity Flow and Capital Formation in the Recent Recovery and Decline 1932-1938 (Bulletin 74, June 25, 1939) .25
Simon Kuznets

A Significance Test for Time Series and Other Ordered Observations (Technical Paper 1, September 1941) .50
W. Allen Wallis and Geoffrey H. Moore

Railway Freight Traffic in Prosperity and Depression (Occasional Paper 5, February 1942) .25
Thor Hultgren

Wartime 'Prosperity' and the Future (Occasional Paper 9, March 1943) .35
Wesley C. Mitchell

Railroad Travel and the State of Business (Occasional Paper 13, December 1943) .35
Thor Hultgren

Railway Traffic Expansion and Use of Resources in World War II (Occasional Paper 15, February 1944) .35
Thor Hultgren

Economic Research and the Keynesian Thinking of Our Times (Twenty-sixth Annual Report, June 1946)
Arthur F. Burns

The Role of Inventories in Business Cycles (Occasional Paper 26, May 1948) .50
Moses Abramovitz

The Structure of Postwar Prices (Occasional Paper 27, July 1948) .75
Frederick C. Mills

Statistical Indicators of Cyclical Revivals and Recessions (Occasional Paper 31, 1950) 1.50
Geoffrey H. Moore

Cyclical Diversities in the Fortunes of Industrial Corporations (Occasional Paper 32, 1950) .50
Thor Hultgren

New Facts on Business Cycles (Thirtieth Annual Report, April 1950)
Arthur F. Burns

Out of print.

Relation of the Directors to the Work and Publications of the National Bureau of Economic Research

1. The object of the National Bureau of Economic Research is to ascertain and to present to the public important economic facts and their interpretation in a scientific and impartial manner. The Board of Directors is charged with the responsibility of ensuring that the work of the National Bureau is carried on in strict conformity with this object.

2. To this end the Board of Directors shall appoint one or more Directors of Research.

3. The Director or Directors of Research shall submit to the members of the Board, or to its Executive Committee, for their formal adoption, all specific proposals concerning researches to be instituted.

4. No report shall be published until the Director or Directors of Research shall have submitted to the Board a summary drawing attention to the character of the data and their utilization in the report, the nature and treatment of the problems involved, the main conclusions and such other information as in their opinion would serve to determine the suitability of the report for publication in accordance with the principles of the National Bureau.

5. A copy of any manuscript proposed for publication shall also be submitted to each member of the Board. For each manuscript to be so submitted a special committee shall be appointed by the President, or at his designation by the Executive Director, consisting of three Directors selected as nearly as may be one from each general division of the Board. The names of the special manuscript committee shall be stated to each Director when the summary and report described in paragraph (4) are sent to him. It shall be the duty of each member of the committee to read the manuscript. If each member of the special committee signifies his approval within thirty days, the manuscript may be published. If each member of the special committee has not signified his approval within thirty days of the transmittal of the report and manuscript, the Director of Research shall then notify each member of the Board, requesting approval or disapproval of publication, and thirty additional days shall be granted for this purpose. The manuscript shall then not be published unless at least a majority of the entire Board and a two-thirds majority of those members of the Board who shall have voted on the proposal within the time fixed for the receipt of votes on the publication proposed shall have approved.

6. No manuscript may be published, though approved by each member of the special committee, until forty-five days have elapsed from the transmittal of the summary and report. The interval is allowed for the receipt of any memorandum of dissent or reservation, together with a brief statement of his reasons, that any member may wish to express; and such memorandum of dissent or reservation shall be published with the manuscript if he so desires. Publication does not, however, imply that each member of the Board has read the manuscript, or that either members of the Board in general, or of the special committee, have passed upon its validity in every detail.

7. A copy of this resolution shall, unless otherwise determined by the Board, be printed in each copy of every National Bureau book.

(Resolution adopted October 25, 1926 and revised February 6, 1933 and February 24, 1941)

Employment and Compensation in Education

GEORGE J. STIGLER

OCCASIONAL PAPER 33

NATIONAL BUREAU OF ECONOMIC RESEARCH, INC.

OFFICERS
1950

Boris Shishkin, *Chairman*
Harry Scherman, *President*
C. C. Balderston, *Vice-President*
George B. Roberts, *Treasurer*
W. J. Carson, *Executive Director*
Martha Anderson, *Editor*

DIRECTORS AT LARGE

Donald R. Belcher, *American Telephone and Telegraph Co.*
Oswald W. Knauth, *New York City*
Simon Kuznets, *University of Pennsylvania*
H. W. Laidler, *Executive Director, League for Industrial Democracy*
Shepard Morgan, *New York City*
C. Reinold Noyes, *New York City*
George B. Roberts, *Vice-President, National City Bank*
Beardsley Ruml, *New York City*
Harry Scherman, *President, Book-of-the-Month Club*
George Soule, *Bennington College*
N. I. Stone, *Consulting Economist*
J. Raymond Walsh, *WMCA Broadcasting Co.*
Leo Wolman, *Columbia University*
Theodore O. Yntema, *Vice President - Finance, Ford Motor Company*

DIRECTORS BY UNIVERSITY APPOINTMENT

E. Wight Bakke, *Yale*
C. C. Balderston, *Pennsylvania*
Arthur F. Burns, *Columbia*
G. A. Elliott, *Toronto*
Frank W. Fetter, *Northwestern*
H. M. Groves, *Wisconsin*
Gottfried Haberler, *Harvard*
Clarence Heer, *North Carolina*
R. L. Kozelka, *Minnesota*
Paul M. O'Leary, *Cornell*
T. W. Schultz, *Chicago*

DIRECTORS APPOINTED BY OTHER ORGANIZATIONS

Percival F. Brundage, *American Institute of Accountants*
Thomas C. Cochran, *Economic History Association*
Frederick C. Mills, *American Statistical Association*
Stanley H. Ruttenberg, *Congress of Industrial Organizations*
Murray Shields, *American Management Association*
Boris Shishkin, *American Federation of Labor*
Warren C. Waite, *American Farm Economic Association*
Donald H. Wallace, *American Economic Association*

RESEARCH STAFF

Arthur F. Burns, *Director of Research*
G. H. Moore, *Associate Director of Research*

Moses Abramovitz
Harold Barger
Morris A. Copeland
Daniel Creamer
David Durand
Solomon Fabricant
Milton Friedman
Millard Hastay
W. Braddock Hickman
F. F. Hill
Thor Hultgren
Simon Kuznets
Clarence D. Long
Ruth P. Mack
Frederick C. Mills
Raymond J. Saulnier
Lawrence H. Seltzer
George J. Stigler
Leo Wolman

Relation of the Directors to the Work and Publications of the National Bureau of Economic Research

1. The object of the National Bureau of Economic Research is to ascertain and to present to the public important economic facts and their interpretation in a scientific and impartial manner. The Board of Directors is charged with the responsibility of ensuring that the work of the National Bureau is carried on in strict conformity with this object.

2. To this end the Board of Directors shall appoint one or more Directors of Research.

3. The Director or Directors of Research shall submit to the members of the Board, or to its Executive Committee, for their formal adoption, all specific proposals concerning researches to be instituted.

4. No report shall be published until the Director or Directors of Research shall have submitted to the Board a summary drawing attention to the character of the data and their utilization in the report, the nature and treatment of the problems involved, the main conclusions and such other information as in their opinion would serve to determine the suitability of the report for publication in accordance with the principles of the National Bureau.

5. A copy of any manuscript proposed for publication shall also be submitted to each member of the Board. For each manuscript to be so submitted a special committee shall be appointed by the President, or at his designation by the Executive Director, consisting of three Directors selected as nearly as may be one from each general division of the Board. The names of the special manuscript committee shall be stated to each Director when the summary and report described in paragraph (4) are sent to him. It shall be the duty of each member of the committee to read the manuscript. If each member of the special committee signifies his approval within thirty days, the manuscript may be published. If each member of the special committee has not signified his approval within thirty days of the transmittal of the report and manuscript, the Director of Research shall then notify each member of the Board, requesting approval or disapproval of publication, and thirty additional days shall be granted for this purpose. The manuscript shall then not be published unless at least a majority of the entire Board and a two-thirds majority of those members of the Board who shall have voted on the proposal within the time fixed for the receipt of votes on the publication proposed shall have approved.

6. No manuscript may be published, though approved by each member of the special committee, until forty-five days have elapsed from the transmittal of the summary and report. The interval is allowed for the receipt of any memorandum of dissent or reservation, together with a brief statement of his reasons, that any member may wish to express; and such memorandum of dissent or reservation shall be published with the manuscript if he so desires. Publication does not, however, imply that each member of the Board has read the manuscript, or that either members of the Board in general, or of the special committee, have passed upon its validity in every detail.

7. A copy of this resolution shall, unless otherwise determined by the Board, be printed in each copy of every National Bureau book.

(Resolution adopted October 25, 1926 and revised February 6, 1933 and February 24, 1941)

Employment and Compensation in Education

GEORGE J. STIGLER
Columbia University

OCCASIONAL PAPER 33
NATIONAL BUREAU OF ECONOMIC RESEARCH, Inc.
1819 Broadway, New York 23, N. Y.

Price: $1.00

Copyright, 1950, by the National Bureau of Economic Research, Inc.
1819 Broadway, New York 23, N. Y.
All rights reserved.
Manufactured in the U.S.A. by John N. Jacobson & Son, Inc. N. Y.

Preface

In 1940 the adults in this country had on the average spent a fifth of their years in school; in another generation the fraction will exceed a fourth. This powerful yearning for formal education has given rise to a very large industry, employing a million and a half persons. Indeed, until recently teachers have been the most numerous peacetime employees of government, and education has been its most expensive peacetime function.

The measurement and explanation of the trend in the number of teachers and in their compensation are the main subjects of this study. The substance of the educational process — the quality of the product, if you will — involves wholly different problems and skills and will not be entered into.

Elementary and secondary education are considered separately from higher education. The two levels differ in many respects. Elementary and secondary education are primarily public; higher education is half private. The fraction of the population between 6 and 17 enrolled in school is so high that population movements are the chief cause of fluctuations in enrollments; only a seventh of those between 18 and 21 were in college in 1940. Elementary school teachers are usually women who have taken a formidable list of courses in pedagogical principles and practices; college professors are usually men who possess or aspire to a Ph.D.

I wish to acknowledge the helpful suggestions I have received from several Directors and members of the research staff of the National Bureau, especially Arthur F. Burns, Milton Friedman, Geoffrey H. Moore, and Donald H. Wallace. Lois Proctor and Jane Kennedy did much of the statistical work, Irving Forman drew the charts, and Martha Anderson edited the manuscript.

Contents

Preface
Part One
  Elementary and Secondary Education   1
  1 Number of Teachers   1
  2 Teachers and Enrollments   4
    Population of School Age   4
    The Fraction Enrolled in School   6
    Enrollment per Teacher   9
    Summary   10
  3 Recruitment of Teachers   11
    General Characteristics   11
    Certification   13
    Supply and Demand   14
  4 Salaries of Teachers   15
    Size of Community, Region, and Grade of School   15
    Training and Age   17
    Sex and Race   18
    Salaries since 1900   19
    Factors Affecting Comparisons with Teachers' Salaries   23
    Comparisons with Other Occupations   26

Part Two
  Higher Education   29
  1 Number of Teachers   29
  2 Institutions of Higher Education   31
  3 Recruitment and Promotion   35
    Formal Entrance Requirements   36
    Appointment and Promotion   38
  4 Salaries and Earnings   41
    Trend of Salaries   41
    Rank vs. Salary Increases   46
    Structure of Salaries   46
    Other Earnings   53
    Comparisons with Other Professions   55

APPENDIX
  A Number Employed in Elementary and Secondary Education   64
  B Effect of Legislation on Enrollments   67
  C Academic Personnel in Higher Education   71
  D College Teachers' Salaries   72

TABLE
1. Academic Personnel and Enrollments, Elementary and Secondary Schools, 1900-1946   1
2. Enrollments in Elementary and High Schools by Age of Student, 1940   5
3. Population, 5-17 Inclusive, 1900-1940   5
4. Estimated Population of School Ages, 1940-1955   6

TABLE		
5	Percentage of Population of Specified Ages Enrolled in Schools, 1900-1940	7
6	Percentage of Population 7-13 Inclusive Enrolled in Schools, 1910-1940	8
7	Enrollments per Teacher in Public Elementary and Secondary Schools, 1900-1946	9
8	Enrollment per Teacher in City School Systems, 1920 and 1938	10
9	Some Characteristics of All Teachers, 1900-1940	11
10	Distribution of States by Minimum Scholastic Requirements for Certificates for Inexperienced Teachers, 1921-1949	13
11	Supply and Demand for Public School Teachers and the Sources of Each, per 1,000 Teachers Employed, 1931	14
12	Average Salaries of Public School Teachers by Region, Size of Community, and Type of School, 1938	16
13	Average Salaries of Supervisors, Principals, and Teachers in Public Schools, 1900-1946	21
14	Educational Training of Women in Selected Occupations, 1940	26
15	Average Salaries of Urban Public School Teachers and College Teachers	27
16	Salaries of Classroom Teachers and 52-week Salaries of Women Hand Bookkeepers, 1949	28
17	Enrollments and Academic Employees in Higher Education, 1900-1946	29
18	Classification of Institutions of Higher Education by Type of Control, 1940	32
19	Enrollments, Faculty, and Expenditures of Institutions of Higher Education, 1940	32
20	Enrollments in Institutions of Higher Education, 1900-1940	33
21	Average Annual Tuition Fees in Arts Colleges	34
22	Current Income of Institutions of Higher Education, 1940	35
23	Percentage of Faculties of the Liberal Arts Colleges Holding the Ph.D. Degree, 1900-1940	36
24	Average Period between B.A. and Ph.D. for Recipients of the Ph.D. at Columbia and Harvard, 1900-1940	37
25	Inbreeding in Land-Grant Colleges Measured by Percentage of Faculty Who Received All or Part of Their Academic Training at the Institution in Which They Are Employed	39
26	Faculty by Rank, University of Illinois, 1940 and 1946	40
27	Faculty by Rank in Universities and Colleges and in Professional Schools, State of New York, Percentage Distribution, 1905-1945	40
28	Median Salaries of College Teachers in Large Public Institutions, 1908-1942	42
29	Average Salaries of College Teachers in Large Public Institutions, 1908-1922	44

TABLE		
30	Salaries of Identical Teachers, University of Illinois, 1940 and 1946	47
31	Salaries of Identical Teachers, University of Illinois, Percentage Increases, 1940-1946	47
32	Average Salaries in Degree-Granting Institutions, 1940	48
33	Average Salaries in Men's and Coeducational Colleges, 1927	49
34	Salaries of College Teachers, 1940, and Earnings of Independent Practitioners in Law, Medicine, and Dentistry, Percentage Distribution, 1941	51
35	Earnings of College Teachers who had Supplementary Earnings, 1927	54
36	Average Incomes and Salaries in Four Professions, 1929-1948	60
A	Distribution of States by Maximum Age through which Children were Required to Attend Full-time Schools	68
B	Average by States of Percentage of Children Enrolled in Schools by Age and Maximum Age through which Attendance was Compulsory, 1940	69
C	Average Percentages of Children 16-17 Enrolled in Schools in 1940, by Percentage of Nonwhite Children in 1940 and Per Capita Income Payments in 1939	70
D	Three Salary Series for College Teachers	73

FIGURE		
1	Academic Personnel and Enrollments in Elementary and Secondary Schools, 1900-1946	2
2	Average Salaries of Supervisors, Principals, and Teachers in Public Schools, 1900-1946	20
3.	Lorenz Curves of Salaries of City Public School Teachers and of Earnings of Salaried Business and Professional Workers in Minnesota, 1938-1939	25
4	Academic Personnel and Enrollments in Institutions of Higher Education, 1900-1946	30
5	Salaries of College Teachers in Large Public Institutions, 1908-1942	43
6	Lorenz Curves of Salaries of All College Teachers, 1940, and of Earnings of Independent Practitioners in Law, Medicine, and Dentistry, 1941	50
7	Lorenz Curves of Salaries of Teachers in Large and Small Private Universities and Colleges, 1940	
8	Average Salaries of Urban Public School Teachers and Teachers in Large Public Colleges and Universities, 1900-1942	57

Part One

Elementary and Secondary Education

1 *Number of Teachers*

The number of teachers, principals, and supervisors in public and private schools more than doubled between 1900 and 1940, and enrollments in public schools increased by two-thirds (Table 1 and Figure 1).[1] In addition, public schools employed about 20,000 professional administrators (superintendents, etc.) in 1940. Finally, there is a very large staff of nonacademic personnel — janitors, bus drivers, nurses, attendance officers, physicians, etc. There was about one nonacademic employee for every eight teachers in 1900, and the proportion rose to one for four by 1940.

TABLE 1
Academic Personnel and Enrollments, Elementary and Secondary Schools
(thousands)

	ACADEMIC PERSONNEL			PUBLIC SCHOOL ENROLLMENTS
	Public Schools	Private Schools	Total	
1900	443	37	480	15,503
1905	482	40	522	16,468
1910	548	46	594	17,814
1915	633	55	688	19,704
1918	681	60	741	20,854
1920	711	62	773	21,579
1922	759	70	829	23,239
1924	791	78	869	24,289
1926	853	83	936	24,741
1928	872	89	961	25,180
1930	896	89	985	25,678
1932	905	92	997	26,275
1934	884	90	974	26,434
1936	911	93	1,004	26,367
1938	923	96	1,019	25,975
1940	917	98	1,015	25,434
1942	903	98	1,001	24,562
1944	870	100	970	23,267
1946	872	102	974	23,300

[1]The methods by which these data were assembled are described in Appendix A. We consistently report a school year by its terminal year; thus 1900 refers to the school year 1899-1900.

Figure 1
Academic Personnel and Enrollments in Elementary and Secondary Schools
1900 – 1946

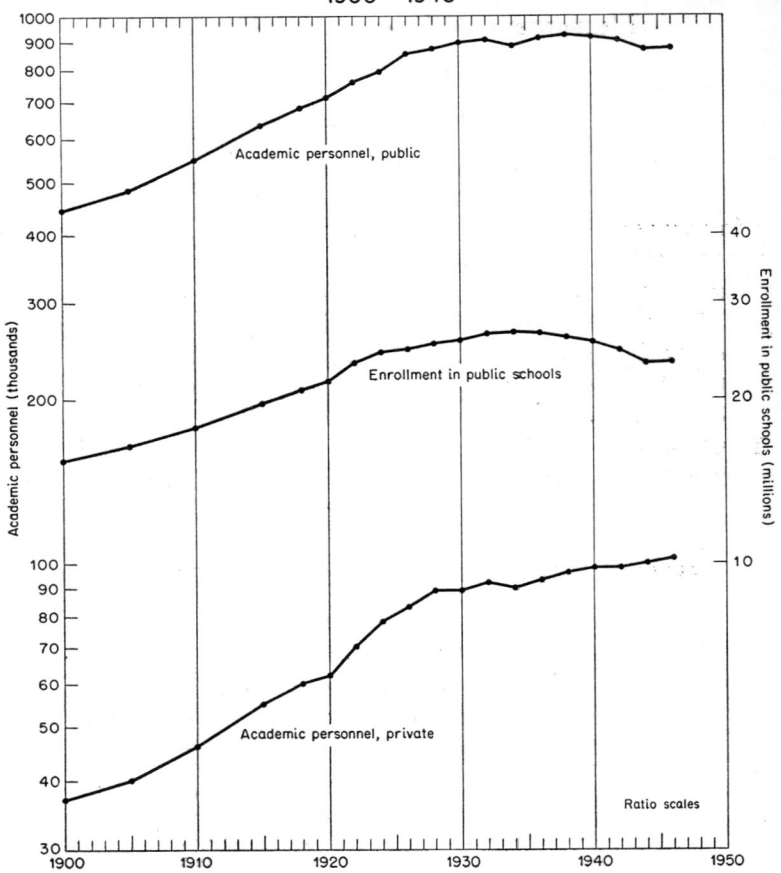

The aggregate number of people employed in elementary and secondary education at the outbreak of World War II was therefore almost one and a third million. Manhours in education increased considerably more because the average number of days in a school year in public schools rose from 144 to 175, or 21 percent.

The decline in the number of public school teachers during the war was less than proportional to the decline in enrollment. The chief direct impact of the war seems to have been a large shift from men to women teachers between 1940 and 1944: the former declined 57,000, or 31 percent, and the latter rose 26,000, or 4 percent. Since 1946 there have been large, but not yet reported, increases in enrollments and in teachers. The number of births has been rising for 15 years and rapidly for 10 years—there were 2.2 million births in 1937, 3.2 million in 1943, and a peak of 4 million in 1947, and now enrollments in elementary schools are again rising.[2]

Private and parochial schools will not be discussed because the data on number of teachers and enrollment are poor and no information is available on finances. The ratio of private to public school teachers appears to have risen substantially, especially since 1920, and enrollment in Catholic schools has risen from 8.9 percent of public school enrollment in 1920 to 9.8 percent in 1940.

Universal education is common in west European nations, but only in the United States does a majority of the population remain in school through the age of 17. The comparison of England and Wales with the United States in the adjoining table emphasizes this difference. As a result of the protracted period of

PERCENTAGE OF POPULATION IN SCHOOL

	AGE GROUP		
	14-15	16-17	18-20
England and Wales, 1931	24.9	8.1	2.9
United States, 1930	88.8	57.3	21.4

schooling in the United States, teachers are a relatively large percentage of the labor force.[3] A more important influence is the withdrawal of young people from the labor force. For example, if the proportions of those between 14 and 20 attending school in this country in 1940 had equaled the British figures for 1931, our school attendance would have been smaller by 7.7 million and our labor force would have been larger by 4 million, a reduction of 29 percent in enrollments and an addition of 8 percent to the labor force.[4]

[2] *Estimates of the Population of Continental United States: 1940 to 1948*, Bureau of the Census, Series P-25, No. 13 (Aug. 13, 1948). The number of public school teachers in cities increased 13 per cent from 1947 to 1949, according to the salary studies of the National Education Association; see Section 4.

[3] The percentages of the labor force who were teachers in the last comparable censuses were: United States, 1930, 2.02; England and Wales, 1931, 1.24; Germany, 1931, .64; France, 1931, .66.

[4] Estimated from the number working and attending school, not working and attending school, etc. (1940 Census, *Population*, IV, Part 1, Table XV) and adding all the unemployed to those not attending school.

2 Teachers and Enrollments

The number of teachers can be viewed as the product of three factors: the population of school age; the fraction enrolled in school;[5] and the number of teachers per pupil. This formal decomposition is useful because it focuses attention on three factors on which considerable information is available.

Elementary and secondary schools cannot well be treated separately before 1940 because the relationship between the age of children and their grade in school changed drastically in earlier decades. This is evident from the fact that the enrollments in public high schools rose 1,172 percent from 1900 to 1940 while the population 14 through 17 rose only 58 percent.[6] The proportion of students who completed grade school by 14 or 15 must have risen greatly.

By 1940, however, the correspondence between age and school grade was fairly well defined (Table 2): 89 percent of grade school pupils were 13 or younger and 95 percent were 14 or younger; in high schools, 80 percent were 14 to 17 inclusive and almost 90 percent 14 to 18 inclusive. A substantial number of children 15 or 16 are still in grade schools but this number will probably continue to decline,[7] so the 5-14 group supplies the overwhelming part of potential grade school enrollments. The downward drift of the age of high school students may continue, but in the absence of a fundamental change in school organization the vast majority will continue to be 14 or older; consequently the age group 14-17 inclusive can be taken as a fairly good measure of the potential supply of high school students.

POPULATION OF SCHOOL AGE

The number of children 5-17 inclusive increased an eighth or more each decade up to 1930, after which it fell 5.8 percent (Table 3). This retardation brought about a large change in the

[5] Enrollments are preferred to attendance because there is much more information on them. A study of variations among states in 1940 in the ratio of enrollments and of attendance to teachers indicates that the patterns of the two are almost identical: the coefficient of correlation is .982.

[6] The rise in the proportion of those 14-17 who were enrolled in schools was not sufficient to explain the gap between the movements of population and enrollment (Table 5).

[7] One-fourth of the 15 year olds and one-third of the 16 year olds are Negroes, although Negroes are only a tenth of the total in these age groups. Since the differences between races in the provision of schooling is diminishing, the correspondence between age and grade will become even stronger.

TABLE 2
Enrollments in Elementary and High Schools by Age of Student, 1940

AGE	ELEMENTARY SCHOOLS Number	%	HIGH SCHOOLS Number	%
5	384,160	2.1		
6	1,356,341	7.5		
7	1,902,241	10.5		
8	2,072,357	11.4		
9	2,077,573	11.5	1,391	
10	2,189,268	12.1	4,086	.1
11	2,101,271	11.6	10,125	.1
12	2,227,687	12.3	72,452	1.1
13	1,841,655	10.2	409,205	6.0
14	1,066,308	5.9	1,142,644	16.7
15	532,230	2.9	1,569,206	22.9
16	238,583	1.3	1,603,614	23.4
17	88,340	.5	1,198,009	17.5
18	35,118	.2	557,394	8.1
19	13,718	.1	172,815	2.5
20	5,815		53,341	.8
21	3,455		20,785	.3
22	2,380		10,980	.2
23	1,958		7,419	.1
24	1,784		5,933	.1
Total	18,142,242	100.1	6,839,399	99.9

Calculated on the assumption that those attending school who have completed 7 grades are in the eighth grade, etc.

age composition: those 5-14 inclusive declined 9 percent from 1930 to 1940; those 14-17 inclusive rose 4 percent. During the four decades the number of children 5-17 inclusive increased almost a half, which by itself would call for about 40 percent of the observed increase in the number of teachers.

The forecasts of population made in recent years by the Census Bureau have not been crowned with great success, but the predictions of the school age population in the near future are necessarily fairly accurate (since most of this population is already born), and deserve brief attention. The great rise in the birth rate in recent years is leading to a sharp reversal of the

TABLE 3
Population, 5-17 Inclusive, 1900-1940
(thousands)

POPULATION	1900	1910	1920	1930	1940
5-17 incl.	21,538	24,240	27,730	31,571	29,745
5-14 incl.*	16,954	18,868	22,039	24,612	22,431
14-17 incl.*	6,153	7,220	7,736	9,341	9,720

*The overlapping at age 14 should be noted.

downward trend of the school age population (Table 4): the elementary school population will regain its 1930 peak by 1950, and then increase by a fifth within five years; the secondary school population will regain its 1940 peak shortly after 1955, and then also rise rapidly.[8] It is still generally believed that the birth rate will not continue at the high level of the recent past, and if this belief (which vitiated the earlier forecasts) soon proves correct, the large increase in elementary school population by 1955 and in secondary school population by 1960 will soon thereafter be reversed. In any event, the immediate prospects are for increases of astonishing magnitude.

TABLE 4
Estimated Population of School Ages, 1940-1955
(thousands)

AGE GROUP	1940	1947	1950	1955
5-17 incl.	29,745	29,387	31,468	37,080
5-14 incl.	22,431	22,779	25,212	30,179
14-17 incl.	9,720	8,685	8,443	9,370

THE FRACTION ENROLLED IN SCHOOL

The fraction of children enrolled in school rose substantially from 1900 to 1930 (Table 5). Thereafter it was relatively stable at the elementary level (5-14 inclusive) but continued to rise at a high, though decreasing, rate at the higher ages.[9] The largest increases in the fraction enrolled were at the early school years (6-9) and the later school years (14-20); little increase in the intervening ages was possible after 1910.

At the elementary school ages the increase since 1910 in the fraction enrolled has been chiefly in the South and in rural areas generally (Table 6). The forces making for growth are apparently exhausted. If all children 7-14 inclusive attended in the same proportion as urban white children in 1940, for example,

[8]Table 4 is based upon Forecasts of Population and School Enrollment in the United States: 1948 to 1960, Series P-25, No. 18 (Feb. 14, 1949). The 1947 predictions of P. K. Whelpton (Forecasts of the Population of the United States, 1945-1975; Bureau of the Census) underestimated births between July 1, 1945 and July 1, 1948 by a fifth.

[9]The figures in Table 5 are not wholly comparable. In 1940 school enrollment was defined as enrollment in a regular school between March 1 and April 1, 1940; in 1930, the period was September 1, 1929 to April 1, 1930 and no restriction was placed on the type of school. This difference probably explains most of the decrease at certain ages. The 1910 and 1920 definitions were the same as those in 1930. Vocational schools not parts of regular schools, and also nursery schools (since children under 5 are not included) are excluded.

TABLE 5
Percentage of Population of Specified Ages Enrolled in Schools, 1900-1940

AGE	1900	1910	1920	1930	1940	% INCREASE 1910-40
5		17.0	18.8	20.0	18.0	5.9
6		52.1	63.3	66.3	69.1	32.6
7	48.1	75.0	83.3	89.4	92.4	23.2
8		82.7	88.5	94.1	94.8	14.6
9		86.2	90.4	95.6	95.6	10.9
10		90.0	93.0	97.1	95.7	6.3
11		91.2	93.9	97.5	95.9	5.2
12	79.8	89.8	93.2	97.1	95.5	6.3
13		88.8	92.5	96.5	94.8	6.8
14		81.2	86.3	92.9	92.5	13.9
15		68.3	72.9	84.7	87.6	28.2
16	41.8	50.6	50.8	66.3	76.2	50.6
17		35.3	34.6	47.9	60.9	72.5
18		22.6	21.7	30.7	36.4	61.1
19	11.7	14.4	13.8	19.8	20.9	45.1
20		8.4	8.3	13.1	12.5	48.8

enrollments in this age group would have risen only 460,000, or 2.7 percent. A similar calculation would indicate an increase of another 475,000 children 5 or 6, but the stability of the enrollments of 5 year olds is apparent in Table 5. Moreover, many school systems require that children reach their sixth birthday before entering school and this provision excludes many 6 year old children.[10] The 'market' for elementary education is saturated: enrollments will closely follow the movements of the school age population.

At the secondary school ages (14-17 inclusive), 79.3 percent

[10] Only 42 percent of the 6 year olds would attend school if the age requirement were universal and enrollment was not permitted after September 1. The changes in enrollment ratios during and after the war are given in sample Censuses. The large increase in the percentage of 6 year olds seems wholly explicable by the shift in the date of enumeration to October. Unfortunately the Census has returned to the less stringent 1930 definition of school enrollment, so some increase is to be expected on this score also. See School Enrollment of the Civilian Population: October 1947, Bureau of the Census, Series P-20, No. 19 (July 30, 1948); also April 1947, Series P-20, No. 12 (Feb. 16, 1948); October 1948, Series P-20, No. 24 (April 18, 1949).

DATE	5 YEAR OLDS	6 YEAR OLDS
April 1940	18.0	69.1
October 1945	28.3	93.2
October 1946	32.3	93.8
April 1947		67.2
October 1947	25.4	93.8
October 1948	21.6	93.4

TABLE 6

Percentage of Population 7-13 Inclusive
Enrolled in Schools, 1910-1940

	1910	1920	1930	1940
All	86.1	90.6	95.3	95.0
Urban	91.8	94.4	97.3	97.1
Rural	82.4	87.6	93.3	92.9
Northeast	93.5	94.5	97.7	97.3
South	75.1	84.1	90.8	91.0
North Central	92.7	94.6	97.8	97.3
West	89.1	93.1	96.9	97.0

were enrolled in school in 1940, or a sixth less than in the group 5-14 inclusive (95.0 percent). The percentage of urban white children 14-17 inclusive enrolled in school has been much less stable than that of younger children and therefore offers a less satisfactory estimate of the potential enrollment.[11] (Using the urban white enrollments in 1940 as an estimate of potential enrollments, total enrollments of those 14-17 inclusive would have risen 660,000, or 8.7 percent.)

Secondary school enrollments are the outcome of a multitude of factors we need not analyze; it is sufficient to mention two factors in addition to race and urbanization:[12] legislation, and income and employment. The influence of legislation is difficult to isolate, but a brief investigation (reported in Appendix B) suggests that on the whole compulsory school attendance laws have followed more than led the increase in enrollments of children over 14.

The effects of a community's income upon school enrollments are complicated. The relatively low school enrollment ratios in states with the lowest per capita incomes are easily explained by both the necessity for older children to work and the inability of

[11] The percentage of urban white children enrolled in school has risen as follows:

AGE	1920	1930	1940
7-13 incl.	94.4	97.7	97.3
14-17 incl.	62.4	77.4	86.0

[12] Urbanization and race are already allowed for by using urban white children as the measure of potential enrollments. The difference between urban and rural enrollments is not large in the younger age groups (Table 6); at higher ages it reflects income and employment in good part. In the age group 14-17 inclusive the fraction of Negroes enrolled in schools in 1940 was .84 of the fraction of white children enrolled in school, but in the South the ratio was .90 and in the remainder of the United States .95. Both sections have lower ratios than the nation because of the concentration of Negroes in the South, where the fraction of all children enrolled in school is lower.

these states to support long schooling. But when business conditions are depressed, older children tend to stay on in school because of the difficulty of finding employment. One evidence of this is that in 1940 the states with higher percentages of unemployed children 16 or 17 in the labor force were commonly also the states with higher enrollment ratios.[13] Another is that the enrollment ratio for those 16 or 17 in October 1947 was less than in April 1940,[14] and the large decline in high school enrollments during the war points in the same direction. Since the 1940 Census was taken when unemployment was large, and the preceding decennial censuses were taken in relatively prosperous times, the upward trend in the enrollment ratio after 1930 of those 14-17 inclusive is probably exaggerated. While enrollments do not press as hard on the ceiling of population as they do at the elementary level, it seems improbable that more than a 10 percent increase in enrollments in secondary schools will come from a rise in the enrollment ratio.

ENROLLMENT PER TEACHER

The enrollment per teacher in both elementary and secondary schools has been relatively stable since 1920 (Table 7). This stability in the national averages reflects the approximate canceling of a set of forces that have effected considerable changes within the various states.

TABLE 7

Enrollment per Teacher in Public Elementary and Secondary Schools, 1900-1946

	ELEMENTARY SCHOOLS	SECONDARY SCHOOLS		ELEMENTARY SCHOOLS	SECONDARY SCHOOLS
1900	37.2	25.5	1932	33.0	22.2
1910	35.1	22.0	1934	33.5	24.9
1918	34.2	19.6	1936	33.8	22.3
1920	33.6	21.6	1938	33.2	22.0
1922	34.3	22.2	1940	32.7	22.0
1924	33.9	23.5	1942	32.6	21.3
1926	32.6	22.2	1944	32.9	19.2
1928	33.1	20.7	1946	32.7	19.4
1930	33.2	20.6			

[13] The rank correlation between the percentage of unemployed persons in the labor force and the percentage enrolled in schools (in the 16-17 age group) for the 48 states was + .561. Persons 16-17 seeking work probably include a few attending school.

[14] The respective percentages were 67.6 (based upon a less stringent definition of enrollment) and 68.7; see note 9 above.

The primary factors leading to larger enrollments per teacher are associated with the growth in the size of the individual school. In part because the population is becoming more urban, in part because of improvements in transportation, and in part because of a strong movement toward consolidated schools, the number of small schools has declined sharply. The number of one-teacher schools, for example, declined about 40 percent between 1920 and 1940.[15] Enrollments per teacher run higher by a fifth in urban than in rural schools, and from two to four times as high in urban schools as in one-teacher schools.

On the other hand, within urban school systems, where the growth of school size is less important, there are conflicting trends in enrollment per teacher at various levels (Table 8). At the elementary level, enrollment per teacher is somewhat above the average for the nation but is declining; at the secondary level, it is almost 50 percent larger than for the nation and is rising. As urban and high school enrollments are still gaining relatively, these forces work in opposite directions, and only gradual and moderate changes in the over-all ratio of students to teachers are to be expected in the relevant future.[16]

TABLE 8

Enrollment per Teacher in City School Systems, 1920 and 1938

SIZE OF CITY	ELEMENTARY		SECONDARY	
	1920	*1938*	*1920*	*1938*
10,000- 30,000	37.9	33.7	24.6	28.6
30,000-100,000	36.9	33.4	24.4	29.2
100,000 & over	39.0	36.6	25.2	30.7

SUMMARY

The future trend in the number of teachers is likely to be dominated by the population of school age. The fraction of those of elementary school ages enrolled in schools cannot change substantially and the fraction of those of secondary school age enrolled in school cannot be expected to rise much — probably a tenth at the outside. Enrollment per teacher can change much

[15]No continuous series is available but series for 1 room schoolhouses and 1 teacher schools may be roughly spliced.

	1920	*1930*	*1940*	*1944*	*1946*
1 room schoolhouses	189,227	148,712			
1 teacher schools		149,282	113,600	96,302	86,563

[16]The percentage of public school teachers in high schools rose very rapidly between 1900 and 1940: from 4.8 in 1900, 8.2 in 1910, 14.9 in 1920, 25.0 in 1930, to 34.3 in 1940.

more, of course. Yet not only has the ratio been stable for almost three decades but any large decrease in the size of classrooms would encounter the obstacle of greatly increased educational costs, for teachers' salaries are considerably more than half of the cost of operating elementary and secondary schools. Thus it appears probable that the number of teachers will increase by about one-fifth in the next decade if the population forecasts (Table 4) prove to be near the mark.

3 Recruitment of Teachers

GENERAL CHARACTERISTICS

Women comprise a much larger majority of teachers in the United States than in most European countries: they were 68.1 percent of all teachers in England in 1931, and most continental countries fall well below this level. There is some evidence of a reversal of trend in this respect: women increased relatively throughout the nineteenth century and down to 1920, but a very substantial reaction set in during the 'thirties (Table 9).[17] The increase of male teachers is due in part to the growth of secondary schools, where men are relatively more numerous, and perhaps in part to the difficulty of getting employment in private industry during the 'thirties.

The median age of female teachers has risen sharply but unevenly since the beginning of the century. It has been widely

TABLE 9

Some Characteristics of All Teachers, 1900-1940

	1900[a]	1910	1920	1930	1940
Male (%)	25.5	19.9	15.5	18.2	24.7
Female (%)	74.5	80.1	84.5	81.8	75.3
White (%)	95.1	95.0	95.2	94.6	93.6
Nonwhite (%)	4.9	5.0	4.8	5.4	6.4
% of women married	4.5	6.4	9.7	17.9	24.5
Median age[b] (years)					
Male		30.1	34.1	35.2	32.6	34.3
Female		26.0	31.7	28.5	28.8	34.0

a Based upon teachers plus a relatively small number of college professors, except in the sex distribution.
b The great width of the age groups in 1900 and 1910 makes the estimate of median age very approximate; our linear interpolation probably yields overestimates.

[17] Still another reversal occurred during the war, when the number of men teachers fell sharply (see Sec. 1); and it in turn was partly reversed between 1944 and 1946.

held that the occupation is staffed chiefly by women who soon leave it for marriage: state departments of education estimated in 1930 that the average professional life of teachers was 6 years.[18] The age data do not confirm this view of the transitory nature of teaching, except to the extent that most teachers are women and on the average women leave the labor force at an earlier age than men. In 1930 the median age of teachers was only .6 years less than that of all women in the labor force (and in 1940, 1.7 years greater), a difference smaller than one would expect simply because of the rapid growth of the number of teachers. The proportion of married women has increased more than in the labor force at large, despite a growing objection in many school systems to employing married women.

On the whole the occupation seems to have been relatively fully employed; in 1930, 1.65 percent of male teachers were unemployed, 1.53 of female; in 1940, the percentages were 2.67 and 2.05.[19] Teachers' salaries in real terms increased during the decade, as we shall see, and this raises the question why more women were not attracted to the occupation so the unemployment rate would more closely approach that for all women (10.1 percent). The question cannot be definitely answered, but it is a plausible conjecture that unemployed teachers are given preference in other occupations. Teachers usually have college training, and persons with a college education had a much lower unemployment rate than the population at large.[20]

[18]More precisely, this was the average of the replies to the question, "On the average, how long do teachers remain in service in your state?" The considerable mobility of teachers between states (see below) makes the intrastate service life somewhat less than the total service life. See Teacher Supply and Demand, National Education Association, Research Bulletin, Nov. 1931, p. 338.

[19]The percentage of unemployed women teachers was 3.7 in 1940 if those on public emergency work are counted as unemployed. The data on 'usual' occupation do not reveal any marked tendency for unemployed teachers to withdraw from the labor force: of the 205,000 not in the labor force who gave teaching as their usual occupation, 149,000 were 'married with husband present', and of the remainder 16,000 were 45 to 65 and 17,000 were 65 or older.

[20]The percentage of experienced female workers who were unemployed in 1940 varied inversely with education: 9.0 percent, for those who had been only to grade school; 8.5 percent, for those who had attended high school; and 4.0 percent, for those who had attended college.

CERTIFICATION

The entrance of teachers into a particular school system is in every state controlled by the requirement that the entrant possess a certificate. Such certificates were generally required already by 1900 but with almost nominal requirements for 'low-grade' certificates and with numerous exceptions. The growing rigor of the requirements is recorded in Table 10.

TABLE 10
Distribution of States by Minimum Scholastic Requirements for Certificates for Inexperienced Teachers
(Temporary and Emergency Certificates excluded)

YEARS OF COLLEGE	NUMBER OF STATES		
	1921	1937	1949
4		5	24
3		8	7
2		11	16
1		8	1
High school graduation and less than one year of professional preparation	4	2	
4 years of high school	14	6	
No standard	30	8	
Total	48	48	48

Sources: B. W. Frazier, Development of State Programs for the Certification of Teachers, Office of Education, Bulletin 1938, No. 12, p. 73. Data for 1949 compiled from Elementary and Secondary School Teachers, BLS, Bulletin 972.

The licensing function is usually performed by state education officials, and would obviously be a convenient device for controlling the entry of new persons into the profession. Although the proposal to restrict numbers was frequently heard in the 'thirties,[21] I have seen no evidence that the licensing system has been used extensively to this end. All states (but not all cities) automatically grant one or more types of certificate on the basis of academic credits in teacher-training institutions (both within and outside the state). At present, therefore, the power to control new entrants is diffused among a thousand or more institutions of higher learning.

Of course entry of new teachers has been discouraged by the educational requirements, both as to length of training and detailed prescriptions of courses in pedagogy. These standards, however, appear to have been formulated primarily with a view

[21] See, for example, E. S. Evenden, National Survey of the Education of Teachers, Office of Education, Bulletin 1933, No. 10, VI.

to improving the quality of teachers—with what success we need not discuss.[22]

SUPPLY AND DEMAND

Numerous studies have been made of the sources from which new teachers are drawn by a school system and the reasons for vacancies.[23] The largest and most informative of these surveys, for the school year 1930-31, was based upon replies to questionnaires by half of the public school teachers in the country (Table 11).[24]

The mobility of teachers is substantial: an average of 9.1 per-

TABLE 11
Supply and Demand for Public School Teachers
and the Sources of Each, per 1,000 Teachers Employed, 1931

SOURCE	ELEMENTARY SCHOOLS Communities of				JUNIOR HIGH	SENIOR HIGH	ALL
	Open Country	Under 10,000	10,000-100,000	100,000 or more			
New teachers	372	222	100	50	148	205	205
DEMAND							
Predecessor died or retired	26	15	6	3	7	9	13
Predecessor went to college	29	13	3	1	9	11	13
Predecessor married	51	41	25	6	20	26	32
Predecessor moved to another teaching position	194	95	26	11	53	88	91
Predecessor moved to another occupation	28	14	3	1	11	19	14
New position created	17	24	20	12	31	33	23
Other	27	20	16	16	18	18	20
SUPPLY							
College or normal school	145	87	41	20	64	92	84
Moved from another teaching position	165	107	46	13	62	86	91
Moved from another occupation	42	19	6	7	13	18	20
Other	21	9	7	9	8	8	11

Source: Evenden, op. cit., p. 202; calculated from rounded data.
*The respective weights of the columns are .210, .249, .122, .147, .071, and .199. They are estimated from the number of teachers in 1930; the division of teachers between open country and urban is based on the number of children 7-13 inclusive enrolled in school in 1930 in rural farm and other areas.

[22] For a highly critical appraisal, see 'Required Courses in Education', Report of Committee Q, Bulletin of American Association of University Professors, XIX (1933), 173-200; for references to the literature calling for an expansion of such requirements, see Frazier, op. cit.

[23] To the economist perhaps the most baffling finding in certain of these studies is that the demand (appointments) has often exceeded the supply (appointees); see, for example, B. R. Buckingham, Supply and Demand in Teacher Training, Ohio State University, Bureau of Research Monograph 4 (1926).

[24] The average percentage of replies was 47.9, ranging from 5.8 for West Virginia to 79.1 for New Jersey. The South as a whole is underrepresented and the sample appears to contain other systematic biases but insufficient information is given to estimate or correct them.

cent (or about 90,000) shifted among school systems between 1929-30 and 1930-31, and another 2 percent entered teaching from other occupations. The total turnover was correspondingly high: one-fifth of all teachers entered their positions in 1930-31, and only a tenth of these newly filled positions were newly created.

There is a general drift of teachers toward larger cities, witness the higher rates of supply than of demand due to movement among teaching positions in the larger cities. This drift is confirmed by evidence on teaching experience: the median number of years of teaching experience of elementary school teachers was 5 in open country schools, 7 in communities under 10,000, 10 in cities of 10,000-100,000, and 12 to 13 in cities of 100,000 or more.[25]

4 Salaries of Teachers

The salaries of public school teachers vary systematically with the type of school, size of community, region, age and training of teacher, and numerous other factors. We shall first describe certain of the leading characteristics and determinants of this salary structure, then examine trends in salaries since 1900. Thereafter some comparisons will be made between teachers' salaries and earnings in other occupations.

SIZE OF COMMUNITY, REGION, AND GRADE OF SCHOOL

The most prominent feature of the salary structure of teachers in 1938 is the steady increase in salary with community size, for each region and type of school. In 57 of the 60 possible comparisons of salary among adjacent community sizes in Table 12, higher salaries are paid in the larger community.

The regional differences are almost equally uniform. Salaries are highest in the Northeast in each grade of school and size of community (with three exceptions), second highest in the West (with four exceptions), next highest in the North Central region (with two exceptions), and lowest in the South (with one exception). But the regional differences among the nonsouthern regions are generally smaller than the size of community differences.

The salary differences among levels of school are smaller than those among regions and community sizes,[26] but even here a

[25]Evenden, *op. cit.*, II, 30-1. The median ages in each class were 20 years higher.

[26]The differences by school grade are larger in rural schools, in part because high schools are more often consolidated school districts; see Salaries of School Employees, 1938-39, NEA, Research Bulletin, March 1939, 91 ff.

TABLE 12

Average Salaries of Public School Teachers by Region, Size of Community, and Type of School, 1938

TYPE OF SCHOOL & COMMUNITY SIZE	Northeast	South	North Central	West
Kindergarten	$2,148	$1,592	$1,688	$1,890
10,000- 30,000	1,594	639	1,273	1,454
30,000-100,000	1,803	1,233	1,454	1,695
100,000-250,000	1,892	1,601	1,552	1,745
250,000 & over	2,534	1,661	1,974	2,087
Elementary	2,212	1,268	1,707	1,981
10,000- 30,000	1,546	908	1,311	1,534
30,000-100,000	1,831	1,048	1,504	1,821
100,000-250,000	1,926	1,395	1,596	1,883
250,000 & over	2,770	1,580	2,011	2,264
Junior High	2,384	1,589	1,893	2,215
10,000- 30,000	1,817	1,141	1,498	1,658
30,000-100,000	2,026	1,290	1,714	2,247
100,000-250,000	2,059	1,468	1,869	2,176
250,000 & over	3,007	1,904	2,375	2,407
Senior & Junior-Senior High	2,282	1,686	1,980	2,381
10,000- 30,000	1,953	1,229	1,713	1,905
30,000-100,000	2,309	1,253	1,957	2,228
100,000-250,000	2,449	1,811	1,887	2,242
250,000 & over	2,822	2,160	2,518	2,670
Regular High	2,912	1,420	2,336	2,284
10,000- 30,000	1,872	1,150	1,494	1,810
30,000-100,000	2,302	1,267	1,701	2,369
100,000-250,000	2,486	1,688	2,007	2,202
250,000 & over	3,516	1,769	2,715	2,409

Source: *Biennial Survey of Education, 1937-38*. The regions are those of the 1940 Census; the community sizes those of the Office of Education, except for the class 250,000 and over, which is based on the 1940 Census.

fairly regular pattern is discernible. Salaries are lowest for kindergarten teachers, those of elementary and junior high school teachers are next in that order, and those of junior-senior and senior high schools are about equal to those of regular high school teachers.[27]

The substantial variation of salary with size of community is a general finding in income studies; presumably it is due to

[27] The difference between salaries of elementary and secondary school teachers in cities over 10,000 has been declining steadily over time. The trend continued to 1949.

	1915	1918	1928	1938
Average Salary				
Elementary School	$ 673	854	1788	1876
Secondary School	$1060	1268	2217	2249
Ratio: Secondary to Elementary School Teachers' Salary	1.58	1.48	1.24	1.20

differences in costs of living.[28] Regional differences, however, are usually fairly small when community size is held constant. Teachers are clearly an exception, perhaps because the general practice of state equalization of educational funds (whereby wealthier communities subsidize education in poorer communities) mixes regional and size of community influences. The variations of salaries with level of school are in keeping with variations in the training of teachers (see below).

TRAINING AND AGE

The differences among salaries by size of community and grade of school correspond closely with patterns of academic training. The survey of 460,000 public school teachers in 1931 revealed a steady rise in the amount of schooling of elementary school teachers with community size.[29] Teachers in junior high schools attended school an average of 15.5 years; those in senior high schools 16.2 years.

	AV. NUMBER OF YEARS TEACHERS ATTENDED SCHOOL	% OF TEACHERS WITH 4 OR MORE YEARS OF COLLEGE EDUCATION
Open country, 1 and 2 teacher schools	13.2	3.7
Open country, 3 teacher schools	14.0	11.4
Towns of less than 2,500	14.1	9.5
2,500 - 10,000	14.3	13.8
10,000 - 100,000	14.4	14.8
100,000 & over	14.6	22.0

The regional differences in salaries also parallel smaller relative differences in the amount of formal training, except that teachers in the South had on the average longer training than those in the North Central region.[30]

We would expect a stronger relationship between salary and schooling were it not for the rapid increase in the number of

---

[28]H. E. Klarman, A Statistical Study of Income Differences Among Communities, in *Studies in Income and Wealth, Volume Six;* Friedman and Kuznets, *Income from Independent Professional Practice*, Ch. 5 (NBER, 1943 and 1945, respectively).

[29]Evenden et al., II, 43.

[30] (*Ibid.*, p. 224). There appear to be serious errors in the data: the average years of school attendance are as high or higher in each region than in the country as a whole.

AVERAGE YEARS OF SCHOOL ATTENDANCE BY
REGIONS FOR TEACHERS IN CITIES OF 10,000-100,000

NORTHEAST	SOUTH	NORTH CENTRAL	WEST
15.0	14.6	14.4	14.8

school teachers before 1930.[31] Salaries rise steadily with teachers' ages, in part because of the movement from rural to city school systems, in part because of the widespread practice of granting automatic salary increases. The older teachers, however, have had less formal education, so as late as 1919, there was a consistent negative relationship between salary and academic training in cities.[32] As the number of teachers with a college degree increases, we would expect the relationship between education and salary to become more pronounced.

SEX AND RACE

The median salary of all teachers, public and private, was $1,458 for men and $972 for women in 1939.[33] The difference seems due almost exclusively to differences in type of work, grade of school, or region. Of these factors grade of school is most important: in 1940 in cities over 10,000, men were 4.4 percent of all public school teachers in elementary schools, but 41.3 percent of all teachers in the regular high schools. Men generally hold the supervisory positions in school systems, and this works in the same direction. There are also relatively few men teachers in the South, where salaries are relatively low: in 1940, of the 17 states in which fewer than a fifth of the teachers were men, 9 were in the South.[34]

[31]Many school systems have schedules that automatically increase the teacher's salary with academic training; in New York, for example, a teacher with a master's degree receives $200 more per year than a teacher with a bachelor's degree.

As will be shown below (Sec. 2, Note 40), the average increase in annual salary necessary to compensate for an additional year of training is about 5 or 6 percent; judged by this standard the $200 differential is too narrow in New York City and too wide in most of the remainder of the state.

[32]Evenden, Teachers' Salaries and Salary Schedules, NEA, Commission Series 6 (Washington, D. C., 1919), p. 79.

[33]1940 Census, *Population*, III, The Labor Force, Part 1, U. S. **Summary**, Table 73. The medians are for experienced persons in the labor force in 1939. The medians for those working 12 months in 1939 are less instructive because most teachers considered themselves, or were considered, unemployed during the summer.

[34]*Biennial Survey of Education, 1938-40* and *1940-42*, II, Ch. 7, p. 11. On the other hand, there was a somewhat higher proportion of men than women in rural schools: men were 20.4 percent of all urban teachers and 23.9 percent of all rural teachers (*ibid.*, Ch. 3, p. 39).

After allowing for these factors, the difference between salaries of men and women teachers appears to be small—probably about 5 percent larger for the former group.[35] In 11 states and a majority of city school systems, different rates of pay for men and women teachers are forbidden by law.[36]

The salaries of Negro teachers averaged only 57 percent of those of white teachers in 12 southern states in 1938.[37] However, this figure exaggerates the differences in salaries paid for teachers of different race but similar ability and working in similar schools:

1) The Negro school systems in 17 southern states had an average school term of 30.6 weeks; the white school systems in these states averaged 34.0 weeks.
2) Relatively more Negro teachers are in elementary schools. Only 8.5 percent of the Negro students were in secondary schools, whereas 21.4 percent of the white students were in secondary schools in these 17 states.[38]
3) Negro schools are more often located in rural areas or small communities than white schools (Sec. 2).
4) The formal education of Negro teachers is on the average less than that of white teachers. Of white teachers in the South in 1940, 58 percent had completed 4 or more years of college; of the Negro teachers, only 38 percent.[39]

We do not possess information to estimate the salary differences that would still be found after allowing for these factors.

SALARIES SINCE 1900

The average salary of public school teachers rose from about

[35] In the 16 states from which 50 or more replies were received from men teachers in 1 and 2 teacher open-country elementary schools in the National Survey of the Education of Teachers, men's salaries averaged 5 percent more than women's (Evenden et al., Office of Education, Bulletin 1933, No. 10, II, 251-2). The difference was considerably larger in high schools, but here it was impossible to segregate the influences of community size and administrative rank.

[36] M. L. Plunkett, Equal Pay for Women Workers, *Monthly Labor Review*, September 1946, p. 385.

[37] *Biennial Survey, 1936-38*, Bulletin 1940, No. 2, Ch. 2, p. 137.

[38] *Ibid.*, p. 138.

[39] 1940 Census, *Occupational Characteristics*.

$311 in 1900 to $1,995 in 1946 (Figure 2 and Table 13).[40] As the rise was somewhat more rapid in rural than in urban schools, the fraction rural salaries were of urban salaries rose from one-third in 1900 to almost three-fifths in 1946.

The upward march of salaries has been interrupted only once —in the 'thirties, when the average salary fell 13 percent from 1932 to 1934, then more slowly recovered. Rural teachers' salaries followed a less even course, beginning to decline earlier and failing to regain the previous peak until (1941 or) 1942.

The cost of living index compiled by the Bureau of Labor Statistics is a very shaky instrument with which to 'deflate'

Figure 2
Average Salaries of Supervisors, Principals, and Teachers in Public Schools, 1900–1946

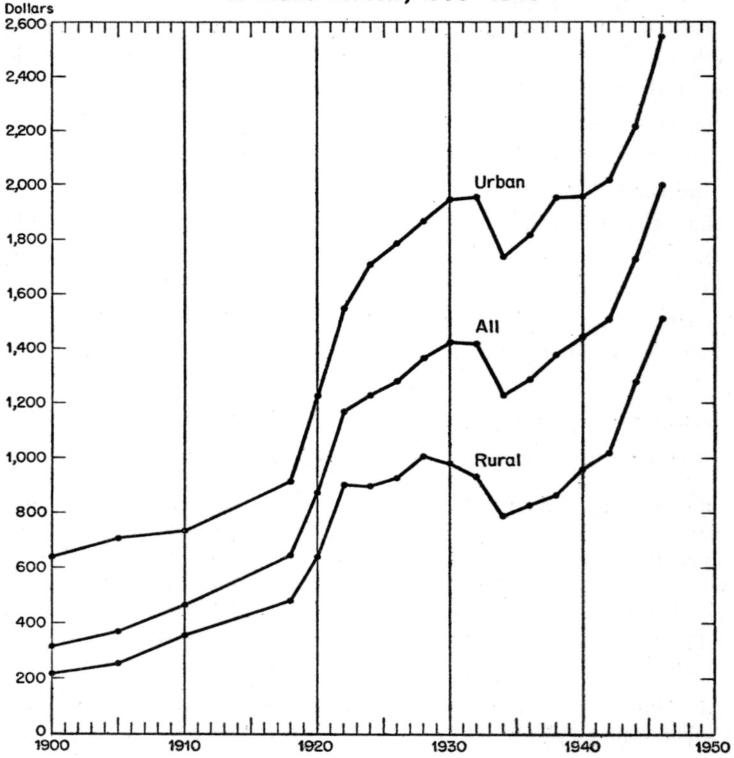

[40]These figures are really a mixture of salary and earnings: they are aggregate payrolls divided by number of teachers employed (or at times teaching positions; see App. A).

TABLE 13
Average Salaries of Supervisors, Principals and Teachers
in Public Schools, 1900-1946

	AVERAGE SALARY			COST OF LIVING INDEX (1935-39:100)	URBAN SALARIES IN 1935-39 PURCHASING POWER
	All	Rural	Urban		
1900	$ 311	$ 215	$ 638	52.6	$1,213
1905	368	252	704	59.3	1,187
1910	463	353	732	62.4	1,173
1918	641	478	911	97.8	931
1920	871	638	1,222	135.3	903
1922	1,166	899	1,545	123.6	1,250
1924	1,227	895	1,706	123.5	1,381
1926	1,277	927	1,787	128.2	1,394
1928	1,364	1,007	1,865	123.8	1,506
1930	1,420	979	1,944	122.8	1,583
1932	1,417	930	1,951	104.2	1,872
1934	1,227	787	1,735	93.9	1,848
1936	1,283	827	1,818	98.0	1,855
1938	1,374	864	1,952	103.0	1,895
1940	1,441	959	1,955	99.6	1,963
1942	1,507	1,018	2,013	110.5	1,822
1944e	1,728	1,276	2,215	124.4	1,781
1946e	1,995	1,508	2,545	129.9	1,959

Source: Salaries, *Biennial Survey of Education*. Rural includes cities under 4,000 through 1910, and cities under 2,500 thereafter to 1930. Beginning with 1930, urban includes also small cities that are part of larger school district. Cost of living index: See Table 21.

eUrban and rural salaries estimated from city and aggregate data. The National Education Association estimates average salaries to be $2,550 in 1948 and $2,750 in 1949; Teachers in the Public Schools, NEA Research Bulletin, Dec. 1949.

teachers' salaries to obtain a series on real income. Aside from its technical deficiencies, such as failure to take full account of changes in the quality of goods, it pertains to a wholly different type of consumer (a family with husband and wife, living in a large city, engaged in clerical or manual work).[41] Half of the teachers are unmarried women, and only about one-sixth of all teachers (and two-fifths of urban teachers) live in cities with more than 100,000 inhabitants. The deflation carried out in Table 13 therefore yields only a very rough estimate of the movements of real salaries of urban teachers.

Moreover, one must avoid the tendency, common in educational literature, to interpret a movement of the average salary

[41] The differences in cost of living by community size are substantial, and in particular rural teachers' salaries cannot be set against urban costs of living. In 1921 the median salary of rural teachers in Pennsylvania was only $411, but the median annual cost of room and board was only $121 (L. A. King, Status of the Rural Teacher in Pennsylvania, Office of Education, Bulletin 1921, No. 34).

as representing the movement of the salary of the average teacher. In a period when there are many departures from and new entrants into teaching, the average salary could be stable while everyone who remained in teaching received large increases by moving from small to large cities, from elementary to secondary schools, etc. These sorts of movement are believed to have occurred, but on an unknown scale, since 1940.[42]

'Real' salaries of urban teachers fell sharply during World War I but recovered very rapidly thereafter; on the average they increased two-thirds between 1918 and 1928 (and dollar salaries doubled). Thereafter the cost of living fell sooner and further than salaries, so real salaries rose another sixth by the early 'thirties. They maintained this level throughout the decade as dollar salaries kept pace with the rise in the cost of living.

Salaries have been increasing at an increasing rate since 1940; the average salaries in cities with over 2,500 inhabitants are given in the adjoining table. The large increases between 1945 and 1949 have almost fully restored these teachers' real salaries to their prewar level, as was true in the four years after World War I.

	1941	*1943*	*1945*	*1947*	*1949*
Elementary school teachers	$1,917	$1,996	$2,227	$2,552	$3,185
High school teachers	2,338	2,418	2,740	3,026	3,672

Calculated from NEA Research Bulletins, March 1941, Feb. 1943, Feb. 1945, Feb. 1947, Apr. 1949. The reports by individual cities are incomplete but cover more than half the city teachers and appear to be fairly comparable from year to year. As large cities are relatively overrepresented, the averages are higher than those for all teachers.

The present postwar rise in salaries, like that after World War I, has been accompanied by, and to a considerable degree occasioned by, widespread publicity emphasizing the loss of teachers to other occupations, the fall in real incomes, etc. The prominent role of teacher unions, however, is distinctly recent. Much the largest of these unions is the American Federation of Teachers (AFL), founded in 1916. Before 1934 this union was very small; thereafter it participated in the general expansion of union membership. In 1947 it had 42,000 paid-up members, perhaps a ninth of city school teachers.[43] The national union has been opposed to the use of the strike, but some locals (beginning

[42]For a fuller discussion of this problem, see Part 2, Section 4.

[43]For the membership each year since 1916, see *American Teacher*, Oct. 1947, p. 11.

with St. Paul in 1946) have resorted to this weapon. The most important strikes have been in St. Paul, Buffalo, Minneapolis, and Providence. The strike has been outlawed in some states, and it (and unionization of teachers) is opposed by the National Education Association (the professional society to which more than half the country's teachers belong), so its future role in salary determination is problematical.

FACTORS AFFECTING COMPARISONS WITH TEACHERS' SALARIES

Direct comparisons of teachers' salaries with those in other occupations (except college teaching) must take into account three factors peculiar to teachers' salaries: exemption from federal income taxation before 1939, the length of the working year, and the role of pensions.

The first factor, tax exemption, was of relatively small importance because before 1939 personal exemptions were large ($1,000 for individuals and $2,500 for a husband and wife during most of the period) and the initial tax rate was low (4 percent on the first $4,000 of taxable income in 1938). The savings to single teachers from tax exemption would, therefore average about 1 or 2 percent of income plus the perplexities of filing a return.

The second factor, length of the school year, is much more substantial. In 1940 public schools were in session an average of 175 days or 35 five-day weeks, but vacations within terms lengthened the period between the opening and closing of school to about 9 months. In addition, the hours of work per week in teaching (which may, however, include only work at school) were less than the average for the labor force.[44]

For purposes of comparison with other occupations it is difficult to place a monetary value on the long vacation.[45] A common practice is to compare salaries with those in other occupations on a weekly or monthly basis,[46] which is equivalent to valuing the summer vacation at the salary rate. If we adopt this convention, urban teachers' salaries on an annual basis would be about

[44] During March 24-30, 1940, 82.4 percent of female teachers worked 40 hours or less; 57.5 percent of all female workers worked 40 hours or less.

[45] The very unsatisfactory data in this field suggest that relatively few teachers take advantage of the vacation to earn supplementary income; see, for example, The Rural Teacher's Economic Status, NEA Research Bulletin, Jan. 1939.

[46] See W. Randolph Burgess, *Trends of School Costs* (Russell Sage Foundation, 1920).

12/9 = 1.33 of reported salaries and rural teachers' salaries about 12/8.4 = 1.43 of reported salaries.[47]

The varying length of the school year affects the comparison of periods and groups of teachers. The more important differences are:

1) Through time. Since the school term has been lengthening, a portion of the salary increases is for more work. Conversely, since school terms did not change appreciably after 1940 (the term was 35.1 weeks in 1944), comparisons with other occupations in which overtime was common during the war should be qualified on this score.

	1900	1910	1920	1930	1940
School term (weeks)	28.9	31.5	32.4	34.5	35.0
Annual salary ($)					
Current	311	463	871	1,420	1,441
Equivalent for 175-day school year	377	514	941	1,440	1,441

2) Between rural and urban areas. In 1940 school terms were 2.8 weeks shorter in rural than in urban areas. Annual rural salaries were 49.1 percent of urban salaries; on a weekly basis they were 53.2 percent of urban salaries.

3) Among states. There is a fairly high correlation between salary and length of the school year in rural schools,[48] but variations in both are due primarily to differences in the wealth of the states. The variation among states in salaries is only slightly greater for annual salaries than for salaries per week.

The third factor, pensions and retirement plans, is most difficult to assess. The first plan was introduced in New York City in 1894; coverage has extended gradually until about two-thirds of public school teachers were covered by 1937 and almost all by 1944.[49] Retirement allowances vary widely, but the most common pension is about half the average salary in the years immediately preceding retirement, provided the teacher has served 20 to 30 years.

The net contribution of these retirement provisions to the teacher's income cannot be estimated with any accuracy. In the

[47]Urban schools were in session in 1940 an average of 36.3 weeks; rural schools, 33.5 (in both cases 3 weeks have been added for intra-term vacations).

[48]In 1940 in 41 states for which these data were available, the rank correlation coefficient was .58.

[49]Teacher Retirement Systems and Social Security, NEA Research Bulletin, May 1937, p. 94; Statistics of State and Local Retirement Systems, 1943-44, *ibid.*, April 1945, p. 31.

first two decades virtually no such plan was on an actuarial basis,[50] and many systems still do not provide for growing liabilities. The teacher's contribution may therefore be half of current contributions to the pension fund (it actually averages somewhat less), and still pay only a quarter of the pension. As a very rough estimate, pensions add another five to ten percent to the current salaries of teachers.

In addition, there are two related characteristics of teachers' salaries that are not nearly as pronounced in private employment. The first is security of tenure: in many city systems, particularly, the tenure of the teacher has been so strongly protected by legislation that the possibility of discharge is remote. The second is the equality of their salaries. The Lorenz curve of urban teachers' salaries may be compared with those of salaried business and professional workers in Minnesota in 1938-39 (Figure 3).

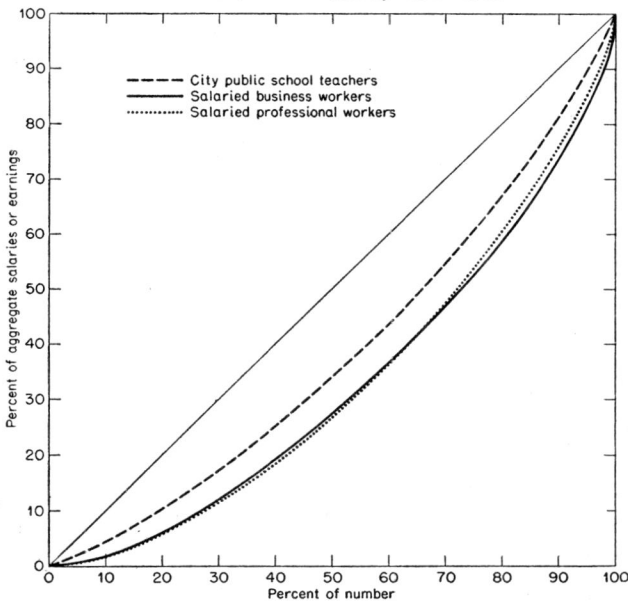

Figure 3
Lorenz Curves of Salaries of City Public School Teachers and of Earnings of Salaried Business and Professional Workers in Minnesota, 1938-1939

[50]In 1914 the New York City system had liabilities of $70 million and assets of $15 million. On the early systems, see Paul Studenski, *Teachers' Pension Systems in the United States* (Appleton, 1920), Ch. I.

It is evident that the prospects of a salary much different from the average in the occupation is small in teaching relative to business and professional employment. The effects of these characteristics, which are equally prominent in college teachers' salaries, will be discussed in Part 2.

COMPARISONS WITH OTHER OCCUPATIONS

Only a few occupations compete with teaching for college trained women on a large scale: the largest are stenographers, typists and secretaries; nurses; and other clerical workers (see Table 14). None of these occupations, moreover, is more than one-quarter staffed by college trained women. Male teachers, on the other hand, are a small proportion of college trained men: 2.5 percent of those who attended college 1 to 3 years, and 9.9 percent of those who attended college 4 or more years, were in elementary and secondary teaching in 1940.

TABLE 14
Educational Training of Women in Selected Occupations, 1940

OCCUPATION	NUMBER (000)	% OF THOSE IN OCCUPATION WHO ATTENDED COLLEGE	% OF ALL ATTENDING COLLEGE	
			1-3 years	4 or more years
All	11,279	15.0	100.0	100.0
Teachers	769	87.7	29.3	52.1
Stenographers	1,001	22.0	16.7	7.9
Clerical	697	15.4	7.7	4.3
Nurses	361	25.5	7.4	2.8
Saleswomen	729	9.1	5.2	2.2

1940 Census, *Occupational Characteristics*, pp. 75 and 81.

The economic status of teachers has risen relative to the population as a whole in the last five decades. Between 1899-1908 and 1949 teachers' salaries rose from $340 to $2,750, or 709 percent.[51] Meanwhile per capita national income rose from $242 to $1,484, or 513 percent.[52] If we roughly divide the period at 1924-33, when the respective averages were $1,341 and $581, we find that teachers' salaries rose much more rapidly than per capita income in the earlier period (294 vs. 140 percent) and more slowly in the later period (105 vs. 155 percent). Trends in the salaries of

[51] Table 13, and NEA Research Bulletin, Dec. 1949.

[52] Simon Kuznets, *National Product since 1869* (NBER, 1946), Tables II-16, 17; *Survey of Current Business*, Feb. 1950. Kuznets' figures are for national product; in 1929-38 they average $486 per capita whereas Department of Commerce data for national income average $488.

public school and college teachers are compared in more detail in Part Two.

The average salary of school teachers is relatively meaningless unless compared with salaries or earnings in fairly similar occupations, and unfortunately there are few such occupations, and fewer with adequate data. The work of college teachers is similar in many respects, and we compare their absolute salaries also in Part Two. A sample from this comparison, given in Table 15, indicates that the salaries of college teachers have averaged about $1,000 a year higher than those of public school teachers in the last two decades, and that the relative differential has been declining.

TABLE 15
Average Salaries of Urban Public School Teachers and College Teachers

	URBAN PUBLIC SCHOOL TEACHERS	COLLEGE TEACHERS		URBAN PUBLIC SCHOOL TEACHERS	COLLEGE TEACHERS
1928	$1,865	$3,045	1940	$1,955	$2,886
1930	1,944	3,065	1942	2,013	2,892
1932	1,951	3,111	1944	2,215	3,282
1934	1,735		1946	2,545	3,429
1936	1,818	2,732	1947	2,731	3,705
1938	1,952	2,861	1948		4,098
			1949	3,368	4,217

Sources: Teachers' salaries, Table 13; 1947 and 1949 from NEA Research Bulletins, Feb. 1947 and April 1949.
College teachers' salaries, Table 29 and text.

The largest number of college trained women in the labor force, outside the schools, is found in office work, but college trained women form less than one-fourth of the total (Table 14). We may offset this difference in educational training in good part by comparing teachers' salaries with salaries of the highest paid occupation reported in the large study of office workers recently made by the Bureau of Labor Statistics (Table 16).[53] In these fourteen cities, teachers' salaries consistently exceeded the salary of hand bookkeepers, without any allowances for longer vacations, pensions, or security of tenure.

The rising trend of teachers' salaries since 1900 can be explained at least in part by the increasing proportion of teachers in high schools and by the lengthening of the school year. The higher standards of academic training and the increasing propor-

[53] In an earlier study of office workers, it was reported that educational training had little influence on salaries; see Office Work in Philadelphia, 1940, U. S. Women's Bureau, Bulletin 188-5 (1942), p. 83.

TABLE 16
Salaries of Classroom Teachers and 52-week Salaries of Women Hand Bookkeepers, 1949

CITY	TEACHERS	BOOKKEEPERS	CITY	TEACHERS	BOOKKEEPERS
Atlanta	$2,632	$2,600	New Orleans	$3,204	$2,366
Boston	3,756	2,470	New York	4,618	3,120
Chicago	4,061	2,886	Philadelphia	3,642	2,574
Cleveland	3,684	2,938	Portland, Ore.	3,353	3,120
Hartford	3,996	2,652	Richmond	3,110	2,626
Los Angeles	4,294	3,250	Seattle	3,734	2,886
Minn.-St. Paul	3,847	2,340	St. Louis	3,533	2,392

Sources: Teachers' salaries, average of kindergarten, elementary, junior high school and high school teachers; NEA Special Salary Tabulations, 1-A, April 1949.
Office workers' salaries, Salaries of Office Workers in Large Cities, 1949 (BLS, Bulletins 960-1, 960-2, 960-3, 1949). Salaries are for January, February, or March 1949.
Hand bookkeeper "keeps a set of books for recording business transactions..."

tion of teachers in large cities may also have contributed to this result, although similar changes took place in the working population as a whole. As to the markedly higher salaries of teachers than of office workers we do not possess sufficient information to estimate the individual importance of factors such as differences in ability, relative social advantages of the two kinds of work, and differing determinants of salaries in private and public employment.

PART TWO

Higher Education

1 Number of Teachers

Since 1900 college professors have multiplied at a rate that is surely unprecedented in the history of established professions (Table 17 and Figure 4). By 1940 academic staffs were five times as large and enrollments six times as large as in 1900. Only one brief and mild interruption of growth (in 1933-34) has occurred in peacetime.[1] In addition to an academic staff of almost 150,000

TABLE 17
Enrollments and Academic Employees in Higher Education
(thousands)

	TEACHING STAFF	OTHER ACADEMIC EMPLOYEES	TOTAL ACADEMIC EMPLOYEES	ENROLLMENTS Total	% of population 18-21 incl.
1900	26.5	2.5	29.0	238	4.0
1905	32.9	3.9	36.8	264	4.0
1910	39.5	5.5	45.0	355	4.8
1915	43.6	6.9	50.5	404	5.5
1918	48.4	8.3	56.7	441	6.0
1920	52.5	9.5	62.0	598	8.1
1922	60.6	11.5	72.1	681	8.9
1924	68.8	13.6	82.4	823	10.3
1926	76.5	15.7	92.2	917	11.0
1928	81.7	17.5	99.2	1,054	12.1
1930	86.2	19.2	105.4	1,101	12.2
1932	90.1	20.8	110.9	1,154	12.6
1934	88.5	20.4	108.9	1,055	11.5
1936	98.1	22.9	121.0	1,208	13.0
1938	110.3	25.7	136.0	1,351	13.3
1940	118.4	28.5	146.9	1,494	15.6
1942	122.5	28.6	151.1	1,404	14.2
1944	112.0	39.0	151.0	878[a]	9.2
1946	130.1	35.2	165.3	1,677[b]	17.9

Source: Appendix C. 'Other academic employees' include those in administration, full-time research, etc.
[a]Civilian only; also 806,000 students in military programs (of which 277,000 were full year students, 529,000 short course students).
[b]Including 462,000 veterans.

[1]Annual enrollments in selected institutions confirm this statement, and also reveal a moderate decrease during World War I; see W. A. Lunden, *The Dynamics of Higher Education* (Pittsburgh Printing Company, 1939), p. 242.

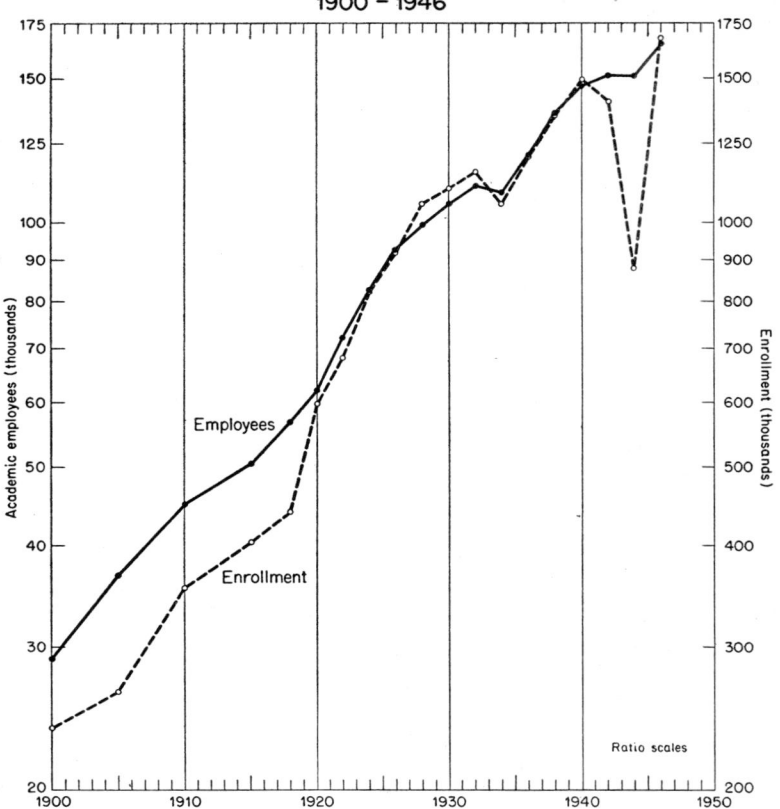

Figure 4
Academic Personnel and Enrollments in Institutions of Higher Education
1900 – 1946

in 1940, the institutions had a large but unknown number of nonacademic employees.[2]

During the war civilian enrollments fell to almost half their 1940 level, and after 1945 with the influx of veterans quickly soared to almost twice the prewar level.[3] The enrollment of

[2]The number of nonacademic employees is probably at least half the number of academic employees, if we may judge by fragmentary data (e.g., in 1940 at the University of Minnesota clerical and service employees numbered half academic employees; at Columbia University the fraction was seven-eighths).

[3]Office of Education, Statistical Circular, Nov. 20, 1946; Circular 238, Nov. 10, 1947; Higher Education, Dec. 15, 1949. Autumn enrollments run somewhat under the number reported as regular students in Table 17.

	ENROLLMENTS (THOUSANDS)		
	CIVILIAN COURSES		MILITARY
AUTUMN	Nonveterans	Veterans	COURSES
1939	1,360		
1941	1,263		
1943	738		294
1945	952	*	88
1946	998	1,080	
1947	1,215	1,123	
1948	1,386	1,022	
1949	1,600	856	

*Not reported separately; about 25,000.

nonveterans has returned to its prewar ratio to the population 18-21 inclusive.

College faculties decreased much less than civilian enrollments during the war, in part because of the expansion of nonteaching activities (research, extension work, etc.), in greater part because of the large number of students in military programs.[4] Teaching staffs have doubtless expanded greatly since the war: in the land-grant institutions (which before the war employed about a fifth of all college teachers) the number increased 69 percent from 1946 to 1949.

2 Institutions of Higher Education

Although our primary concern is with college teachers, we describe briefly by way of background the characteristics of the 1,700 institutions of higher education employing them in 1940. These institutions are a heterogeneous group: their single common characteristic is that their students have completed high school or its equivalent.

Almost half of the institutions are colleges or universities (chiefly 4-year, nonprofessional schools — the designation of college or university is self-chosen and bears no obvious relationship to observable differences in many cases), and well over half of these are still under denominational control (Table 18). Junior colleges (i.e., 2-year schools) have sprung up in large number in the last twenty-five years, and in part because of their recent development a much larger proportion (almost half) are publicly controlled.

A more informative picture of the institutions of higher education can be obtained from Table 19, where average enrollments,

[4] In addition to the 277,000 students in full year military courses in 1943-44, there were 529,000 students in short term military courses.

TABLE 18
Classification of Institutions of Higher Education
by Type of Control, 1940

TYPE OF INSTITUTION	PUBLIC CONTROL State	PUBLIC CONTROL Local	PRIVATE CONTROL Nondenominational	PRIVATE CONTROL Protestant	PRIVATE CONTROL Catholic	TOTAL
College or university	111	15	176	292	140	734
Professional school	19	1	157	67	19	263
Teachers college	156	8	12	1	4	181
Normal school	30	5	17	6	4	62
Junior college	38	173	91	118	39	459
All	354	202	453	484	206	1,699

Source: Office of Education, *Educational Directory*, Bulletin 1940, No. 1.

faculty, and expenditure are given.[5] Colleges and universities were only 43.5 percent of all institutions, but had 71.3 percent of the students, 74.2 percent of all faculty, and spent 78.2 percent of all instructional expenditure.

Public colleges and universities are on the average more than four times as large as private. But there is enormous variation within each class: the largest public college had 30,614 students,

TABLE 19
Enrollments, Faculty, and Expenditures of Institutions
of Higher Education, 1940

TYPE OF INSTITUTION	NUMBER	ENROLLMENT	FACULTY	EXP. ($000)	RATIO: EXP. TO NO. OF Students	RATIO: EXP. TO NO. OF Faculty members
Public		AVERAGES				
Colleges & universities	125	3,914	350	1,645	$420	$4,699
Professional & technological	17	838	97	469	559	4,833
Teachers colleges & normal schools	197	842	57	214	254	3,758
Junior colleges	217	494	24	75	152	3,125
Private						
Colleges & universities	597	930	87	366	394	4,209
Professional & technological	227	364	40	161	443	4,030
Teachers colleges & normal schools	40	216	26	71	327	2,713
Junior colleges	239	172	21	54	315	2,581
Public	PERCENTAGES OF AGGREGATE					
Colleges & universities	7.5	33.4	33.9	37.9		
Professional & technological	1.0	1.0	1.3	1.5		
Teachers colleges & normal schools	11.9	11.3	8.7	7.8		
Junior colleges	13.1	7.3	4.0	3.0		
Private						
Colleges & universities	36.0	37.9	40.3	40.3		
Professional & technological	13.7	5.6	7.0	6.7		
Teachers colleges & normal schools	2.4	.6	.8	.5		
Junior colleges	14.4	2.8	3.9	2.4		
Total	100.0	99.9	99.9	100.1		

[5]The numbers in Table 19 are smaller than those in Table 18 because not all institutions report to the Office of Education.

the smallest, 114; the largest private university had 36,126 students, the smallest private college, 32. Twenty-six private and 38 public colleges and universities had enrollments of 4,000 or more; together they had about 700,000 of the 1,040,000 students in all colleges and universities. In other words, the largest 9 percent of the institutions had about 70 percent of the students.

Public institutions increased in relative importance before 1920, and thereafter maintained a stable proportion of total enrollments (Table 20).[6] More detailed data indicate that enrollments in teachers colleges and normal schools have fallen off sharply relative to those in colleges, universities, and technical schools. An investigation of the cause of the shift toward public schools is not within our scope, but we may pause to notice one factor that reflects many others. The fees of public institutions are and have long been substantially less than those of private institutions (except in certain denominational schools), although fees have increased more rapidly in public schools and especially rapidly for non-resident students (Table 21).

TABLE 20

Enrollments in Institutions of Higher Education

	PUBLIC INSTITUTIONS	PRIVATE INSTITUTIONS	TOTAL
	NUMBER (THOUSANDS)		
1900	91	146	238
1920	309	289	598
1930	537	564	1,101
1940	797	698	1,494
	PERCENTAGE DISTRIBUTION		
1900	38.5	61.5	100.0
1920	51.6	48.4	100.0
1930	48.8	51.2	100.0
1940	53.3	46.7	100.0

Source: Report of the President's Commission on Higher Education, Part VI, Table 22.

The difference in fees reflects differences in the resources of the two types of institution: private institutions draw more than half their current income from student fees, public institutions less than one-fifth; public institutions receive seven-tenths of their current income from governmental appropriations, private institutions less than one-twentieth (Table 22). Endowments have been growing much more slowly than enrollments, the rate of return on endowment has fallen almost a fifth since 1926, and

[6]Public institutions began to become important after the Civil War; 42 of the land-grant colleges were founded between 1860 and 1890 (Lunden, op. cit., p. 180).

TABLE 21
Average Annual Tuition Fees in Arts Colleges

	STATE INSTITUTIONS		PRIVATE INSTITUTIONS	COST OF LIVING INDEX (1935-39:100)
	Resident students	Non-resident students		
1900	$15	$22	$130	52.6
1901	15	22	130	54.7
1902	16	26	130	55.7
1903	17	30	130	57.3
1904	17	30	131	59.9
1905	17	30	132	59.3
1906	17	30	132	59.3
1907	18	31	133	61.9
1908	18	31	133	65.0
1909	18	34	133	62.4
1910	18	35	133	62.4
1911	19	41	135	66.0
1912	19	41	135	68.1
1913	21	44	135	68.6
1914	23	51	136	70.7
1915	25	52	140	72.6
1916	25	56	146	74.0
1917	27	61	161	82.4
1918	28	62	162	97.8
1919	30	64	169	118.0
1920	33	69	203	135.3
1921	45	108	253	138.3
1922	48	120	265	123.6
1923	49	121	275	120.4
1924	49	122	289	123.5
1925	50	122	289	123.2
1926	50	123	327	128.2
1927	52	124	339	126.1
1928	52	125	341	123.8
1929	58	126	379	122.4
1930	58	126	379	122.8
1931	58	140	389	115.3
1932	59	140	391	104.2
1933	60	149	398	93.5
1934	66	180	399	93.9
1935	68	183	400	96.2
1936	68	183	407	98.0
1937	70	188	409	99.8
1938	70	194	409	103.0
1939	70	194	409	100.2
1940	73	198	412	99.6
1941	80	211	419	100.7
1942	80	212	431	110.5
1943	83	217	430	120.4
1944	85	221	431	124.4
1945	89	253	423	127.0
1946	85	249	435	129.9
1947	87	263	493	153.3
1948	104	299	526	167.0
1949	104	324	586	171.4

Notes on page 35

TABLE 22

Current Income of Institutions of Higher Education, 1940

SOURCE	AGGREGATE INCOME (MILLIONS)		% DISTRIBUTION	
	Private	Public	Private	Public
Student fees	$145.9	$55.0	52.9	18.6
Endowment earnings	64.6	6.7	23.4	2.3
Private gifts	35.3	5.1	12.8	1.7
Federal government	2.4	36.5	.9	12.4
State government	7.7	143.5	2.8	48.6
Local government	.2	24.2	.1	8.2
Sales of services	12.5	20.3	4.5	6.9
Miscellaneous	7.4	4.0	2.7	1.4
Total	275.9	295.4	100.1	100.1

Source: *Biennial Survey, 1938-40* and *1940-42*, II, Ch. IV, p. 38.

inflation has reduced real income from endowment to its lowest level in two decades.[7]

3 Recruitment and Promotion

The training of college teachers is considerably less formalized than that of elementary and secondary school teachers: there is only one conventional requirement for professorial appointment, the Ph.D., and it is not, and, as we shall see, could not have been, universally enforced. The general information available, however, suggests that college teachers form a relatively homogeneous group: chiefly male;[8] almost exclusively white (96.8

[7] Information on endowment and its earnings in 45 large private institutions is given by J. Harvey Cain, *College Investments under War Conditions* (American Council on Education, Washington, D. C., Sept. 1944).

	1926	1932	1935	1940	1943
Principal ($ mil.)	372	575	565	653	702
Income ($ mil.)	19.2	29.3	25.0	28.9	29.8
% return	5.14	5.06	4.42	4.42	4.27

[8] The 1940 Census reports females as 26.6 percent of teachers in colleges. Women are concentrated in women's and teachers' colleges; in the private institutions with enrollments over 9,000 and the public institutions with enrollments over 13,000 (each 9 in number), only 16.7 percent of the teachers were women in 1940.

Notes to Table 21
TUITION FEES
State institutions: California (Berkeley), Michigan, Minnesota, Ohio State, Texas, Wisconsin.
Private institutions: Brown, Chicago, Columbia, Harvard, Princeton, Stanford, Yale.
COST OF LIVING INDEX
To 1913: P. H. Douglas, *Real Wages in the United States* (Houghton Mifflin, 1930), p. 41.
1913 on: Bureau of Labor Statistics. Before 1915 the index is for the calendar year. Thereafter, the index opposite a given school year is for the preceding December, e.g., 100.7 was the index for December 1940.

percent in 1940); with extraordinarily equal incomes (as we shall see later); and coming chiefly from middle and working class families.9

FORMAL ENTRANCE REQUIREMENTS

Teachers in colleges and universities are usually required to be graduates of 4-year, degree-conferring institutions (and hence possessors of some kind of bachelor's degree). (The exceptions are chiefly in music, art, and foreign languages.) In addition, to be appointed to a professorial rank in a good institution, it is usually necessary to possess a Ph.D.; some indication of this is provided by an analysis of faculty members' degrees in four

TABLE 23

Percentage of Faculties of the Liberal Arts Colleges Holding the Ph.D. Degree

COLLEGE AND RANK	1900	1910	1920	1930	1940
Columbia					
Professor	75.9	76.0	83.3	85.3	87.1
Associate Professor	(50.0)	72.7	81.8	90.5	66.7
Assistant Professor	X	X	53.3	61.5	83.3
Instructor	66.7	84.6	41.7	25.5	52.9
Oberlin					
Professor	41.2	57.9	75.0	83.3	90.0
Associate Professor	(100.0)	54.5	57.1	(87.5)	(100.0)
Assistant Professor	X	X	61.5	26.3	81.0
Instructor	(14.3)	7.1	(0.0)	14.3	41.7
Smith					
Professor	47.4	56.7	64.3	71.9	73.3
Associate Professor	(100.0)	52.6	51.9	42.2	47.5
Assistant Professor	X	X	25.6	30.4	52.8
Instructor	33.3	30.8	19.2	20.0	35.9
University of Illinois					
Professor	59.1	79.2	90.7	98.4	95.0
Associate Professor	(33.3)	90.9	100.0	90.6	91.1
Assistant Professor	(28.6)	92.0	96.7	93.0	96.5
Instructor	21.4	67.3	72.2	81.0	83.8

X: Rank did not exist.
Source: College announcements. Columbia faculty is that of Columbia College, the men's undergraduate school. Percentages in parentheses based on 10 or fewer persons.

9A study in the mid-thirties of about 4,600 college teachers who were members of the American Association of University Professors gives the occupation of fathers.

Business man	26.6 percent	Lawyer or physician	9.2 percent
Farmer	24.7 percent	Professor	3.9 percent
Manual worker	12.1 percent	Chemist or engineer	3.0 percent
Clergyman	10.6 percent	Other	4.8 percent
Teacher	5.1 percent		

(B. W. Kunkel, A Survey of College Faculties, Bulletin of the Association of American Colleges, Dec. 1937, p. 510).

institutions (Table 23). Seven-eighths of the assistant professors in these schools, other than those in art, music, and foreign languages, possessed the Ph.D. degree in 1940. But this requirement is recent, and far from generally met by older professors: probably only a third of the teachers in institutions of higher learning in 1940 were Ph.D.'s, and indeed the aggregate number of Ph.D.'s conferred in the United States since 1896 (when the honorary Ph.D. was virtually abolished by general convention) is probably less than half the number of persons holding professorial rank at present.[10]

The formal requirements for the Ph.D. are typically three: two years of graduate study at the institution from which the degree is to be obtained; passage of oral or written examinations on designated subject matter and demonstration of ability to read, with the aid of a dictionary, two foreign languages; and the completion of a dissertation which, in the faculty's opinion, is an original and significant contribution to knowledge. These requirements, the young graduate student often believes, can be fulfilled in three, or at most four, years; and so they can. But because of the migration of graduate students among universities, concurrent employment (often as an instructor), and innumerable personal factors, the average period is two or three times as long (Table 24). The median period is somewhat shorter (10

TABLE 24
Average Period between B.A. and Ph.D. for Recipients of the Ph.D. at Columbia and Harvard, 1900-1940

FIELD AND INSTITUTION	1900	1910	1930	1940
Natural Sciences				
Columbia	7.6	8.0	9.4	9.2
Harvard	6.8	8.3	6.2	6.1
Social Sciences				
Columbia	4.3	9.8	10.3	12.9
Harvard	4.8	4.5	10.5	8.7
Humanities				
Columbia	4.7	9.3	13.9	14.3
Harvard	6.3	9.2	7.9	8.8
All Fields				
Columbia	6.3	9.2	10.8	11.7
Harvard	6.2	8.4	8.0	7.8

Compiled from reports of the universities.

[10]The annual number of Ph.D.'s ('Doctor's Degrees' from 1940 on) conferred has risen rapidly in recent decades. The total (estimated by linear interpolation) conferred in the four decades 1900-40 numbered about 48,000.

1900	1910	1920	1930	1940	1942	1944
342	409	532	2,024	3,290	3,497	2,305

years at Columbia, 7 years at Harvard), but still sufficient to constitute the most protracted period of preparation in any profession.[11]

The restrictive effect on entry into college teaching of the Ph.D. requirement cannot be measured by the average period required to obtain it, of course. The prospective college teacher almost invariably begins his teaching before receiving his degree; fragmentary data suggest that full-time graduate study averages only about 2 years.[12] But even if income is usually earned during the apprenticeship, the fact that it is at a lower level in rank or class of institution and in salary is of considerable importance. Nor should the retrospective statistics we have necessarily employed obscure the fair probability that the graduate student will never receive the degree, and be handicapped in his professional career.

APPOINTMENT AND PROMOTION

We have little information on the methods of recruitment of instructors in private and small institutions, but in the land-grant colleges three-fifths of all instructors were employed by

[11]The distribution of the recipients of Ph.D.'s in 1940 at Columbia and Harvard, by years between A.B. and Ph.D., is illuminating. We shall not digress to examine the reasons for the differences but one is obvious: the publication requirement at Columbia. Of those receiving the Ph.D. at Columbia in 1940, 55 percent passed their final oral examination on dissertation from 1 to 16 academic years earlier; the mean period for publication delay was .86 years, the median 1 year. The publication requirement was abolished at Columbia in 1949; Catholic University is apparently the only institution still requiring publication.

YEARS	COLUMBIA	HARVARD
2 to 4	0	13
4 to 6	25	40
6 to 8	21	31
8 to 10	19	26
10 to 12	15	14
12 to 14	12	8
14 to 16	10	11
16 to 20	23	5
20 to 30	12	1
30 to 40	2	0
Total	139	149

[12]An examination of 61 scattered entries in the Directory of American Scholars of persons receiving the Ph.D. 1930-39 indicates that the unemployed time between A.B. and Ph.D. averages 2.5 years. Since noneducational work is usually omitted, this is probably too high a figure, but on the other hand, this is a relatively successful group of teachers.

schools in which they received (or were receiving) some or all of their academic training in 1929 (Table 25).[13] At the higher ranks wider recruitment is practiced, but almost a third of even the full professors received all or part of their training at the institution at which they are employed. If the recent experience of the University of Illinois is at all typical, promotion is much the most important source of appointments to higher ranks: as of 1946, 82 percent of the new professorial appointments since 1940 were promotions; and 80 percent of the new associate professorships (Table 26). (However, in a period of rapid increase in number, external hiring is no doubt more common.)

TABLE 25

Inbreeding in Land-Grant Colleges Measured by Percentage of Faculty Who Received All or Part of Their Academic Training at the Institution in Which They are Employed

TYPE AND PORTION OF TRAINING RECEIVED AT SCHOOL WHERE EMPLOYED	RANK OF FACULTY			
	Prof.	Assoc. Prof.	Asst. Prof.	Instr.
Undergraduate				
All	15.3	20.0	23.5	28.5
Part	6.1	6.9	8.2	10.6
	21.4	26.9	31.7	39.1
Graduate				
All	9.1	14.0	20.5	30.6
Part	15.9	20.9	19.6	22.2
	25.0	34.9	40.1	52.8
Graduate & Undergraduate				
All	6.3	8.9	13.0	18.8
Part	25.8	32.6	33.6	40.3
	32.1	41.5	46.6	59.1

Source: J. H. McNeely, Faculty Inbreeding in Land-Grant Colleges and Universities, Office of Education, Pamphlet 31 (1932). The data apparently refer to 1929.

It is not difficult to list reasons why the land-grant colleges may be atypical. For example, having graduate schools, they train college teachers; on the other hand, being large institutions, they place relatively heavier weight on research accomplishments, which may work the other way. The direction of net bias is not clear, but the majority of initial appointments in all types of institutions is probably persons who were or are students.

[13] See also Report of Committee B, Methods of Appointment and Promotion, Bulletin of the American Association of University Professors, XV (1929), 175-217.

TABLE 26
Faculty by Rank, University of Illinois, 1940 and 1946

RANK IN 1940	Prof.	Assoc. Prof.	Asst. Prof.	Instr.	NOT TEACHING Emeritus	Elsewhere
Professor	118				22	11
Associate Professor	43	22			2	2
Assistant Professor	16	51	22		1	18
Instructor	2	18	81	59	2	124
Not present	13	17	55	145		

Compiled from Minutes of Trustees. Instructors include associates and assistants.

The average college teacher has taught in two or three institutions during his academic life. The extensive survey of AAUP members already referred to gives a tabulation of teachers between the ages of 50 and 60 (when additional moves are uncommon), by number of colleges in which they have taught: 24.3 percent taught in one college; 29.4 percent in two colleges; 24.9 percent in three colleges; 21.2 percent in four or more colleges.[14]

TABLE 27
Faculty by Rank in Universities and Colleges and in Professional Schools, State of New York
Percentage Distribution

	PROFESSOR	ASSOCIATE & ASST. PROFESSOR	INSTRUCTOR & TUTOR	OTHER
	UNIVERSITIES AND COLLEGES			
1905	35.0	13.2	27.3	24.6
1910	34.8	13.7	25.9	25.6
1915	32.4	20.1	26.2	21.2
1920	31.5	20.2	26.7	21.5
1925	28.8	21.7	29.8	19.7
1930	24.4	23.2	32.4	20.0
1935	21.4	25.8	30.6	19.4
1940	19.1	27.1	29.5	24.3
1945	20.9	30.0	28.2	20.8
	PROFESSIONAL SCHOOLS			
1905	36.6	7.7	28.4	27.3
1910	36.5	10.4	27.6	25.4
1915	33.5	13.7	30.2	22.7
1920	37.1	14.0	27.8	21.1
1925	34.4	18.1	34.3	13.2
1930	32.3	20.6	29.8	17.2
1935	29.7	21.0	33.2	16.1
1940	25.3	23.5	32.2	19.0
1945	22.3	29.5	31.8	16.4

Source: Annual Reports of University of the State of New York (Albany). Professional schools include architecture, dentistry, engineering, law, pharmacy, and theology; medical schools are omitted because of the large part-time faculty.

[14] Kunkel, op. cit., p. 499. A third of these teachers had taught also in one or more elementary or secondary schools.

The full professors in this sample had attained their present rank by the age of 36.7 years on the average—about 14 years after receiving their B.A. and 5 years after receiving their Ph.D. (which seven-tenths of them possessed).

The intermediate professorial ranks were relatively unused at the beginning of the century, but have grown rapidly in popularity—with colleges if not with all college teachers. The distribution of faculties by ranks in institutions in New York State shows a steady decline in the relative number of professors, and an offsetting increase in the relative number of associate and assistant professors, since 1905 (Table 27). The rise in the total number of college teachers has been so rapid, however, that one cannot infer that the professorial rank is being attained at a progressively higher age; indeed, since World War II it is probable that the proportion of full professors and their average age have both declined substantially.

4 Salaries and Earnings

A professor of moral philosophy once remarked of "that unprosperous race of men commonly called men of letters":

"Before the invention of the art of printing, a scholar and a beggar seem to have been terms very nearly synonymous. The different governors of the universities before that time appear to have often granted licenses to their scholars to beg."[15]

In this age of specialization, the mendicant functions have been restricted to the college presidents, but the belief in professional poverty continues to be widely diffused. We shall deal with this subject in as much detail as the fragmentary data permit, emphasizing the trend and structure of salaries, and comparisons with other professions.

TREND OF SALARIES

The larger public universities and colleges are the only relatively homogeneous class of institutions for which we have information over a substantial period. The information for earlier and later periods is not strictly comparable, but the broader movements of salaries appear to be reliably portrayed by Table 28 and Figure 5.

Salaries in current dollars had an upward drift before the first World War, but were roughly stable in purchasing power. From

[15]Adam Smith, *The Wealth of Nations* (Modern Library Ed.), pp. 131-2.

TABLE 28
Median Salaries of College Teachers in Large Public Institutions

	CURRENT DOLLARS				DOLLARS OF 1935-39 PURCHASING POWER			
	Prof.	Assoc. Prof.	Asst. Prof.	Instr.	Prof.	Assoc. Prof.	Asst. Prof.	Instr.
1908	2,279	1,646	1,451	891	3,506	2,532	2,232	1,371
1909	2,415	1,670	1,429	898	3,870	2,676	2,290	1,439
1910	2,417	1,737	1,438	924	3,873	2,784	2,305	1,481
1911	2,368	1,834	1,493	1,016	3,588	2,779	2,262	1,539
1912	2,382	1,791	1,503	984	3,498	2,630	2,207	1,445
1913	2,463	1,763	1,511	1,013	3,590	2,570	2,203	1,477
1914	2,530	1,862	1,567	1,008	3,579	2,634	2,216	1,426
1915	2,580	1,883	1,584	1,074	3,554	2,594	2,182	1,479
1916	2,558	1,871	1,619	1,096	3,457	2,528	2,188	1,481
1917	2,661	1,944	1,648	1,115	3,229	2,359	2,000	1,353
1918	2,677	2,012	1,714	1,114	2,737	2,057	1,753	1,139
1919	2,812	2,183	1,766	1,231	2,383	1,850	1,497	1,043
1920	3,262	2,447	2,022	1,508	2,411	1,809	1,494	1,115
1921	3,616	2,744	2,334	1,653	2,615	1,984	1,688	1,195
1922	3,835	3,007	2,484	1,794	3,103	2,433	2,010	1,451
1923	3,952	3,049	2,548	1,826	3,282	2,532	2,116	1,517
1924	4,009	3,084	2,548	1,888	3,246	2,497	2,063	1,529
1926	4,112	3,160	2,630	1,924	3,207	2,465	2,051	1,501
1927	4,230	3,197	2,675	1,908	3,354	2,535	2,121	1,513
1928	4,327	3,298	2,739	1,952	3,495	2,664	2,212	1,577
1929	4,348	3,359	2,691	2,003	3,552	2,744	2,198	1,636
1930	4,407	3,345	2,775	1,995	3,589	2,724	2,260	1,625
1931	4,480	3,418	2,815	2,069	3,886	2,964	2,441	1,794
1932	4,505	3,379	2,800	2,005	4,323	3,243	2,687	1,924
1935	3,775	2,903	2,449	1,769	3,924	3,018	2,546	1,839
1936	3,951	2,973	2,486	1,792	4,032	3,034	2,537	1,829
1937	4,166	3,144	2,556	1,842	4,174	3,150	2,561	1,846
1938	4,163	3,189	2,592	1,892	4,045	3,096	2,517	1,837
1940	4,245	3,272	2,605	1,937	4,262	3,285	2,615	1,945
1942	4,302	3,324	2,645	1,862	3,893	3,008	2,394	1,685

For salaries, see Appendix D; for implicit cost of living index, see Table 21. Data were not collected in the missing years.

the threshold of World War I (1914) to that of World War II (1940), salaries increased two-thirds to three-quarters for the various ranks of professors, and almost doubled for instructors. The upward movement was virtually unbroken except for the substantial decrease (averaging about 15 percent) from 1932 to

PERCENTAGE INCREASE, 1914-1940

RANK	CURRENT SALARY	REAL SALARY
Professor	67.8	19.1
Associate Professor	75.7	24.7
Assistant Professor	66.2	18.0
Instructor	92.2	36.4

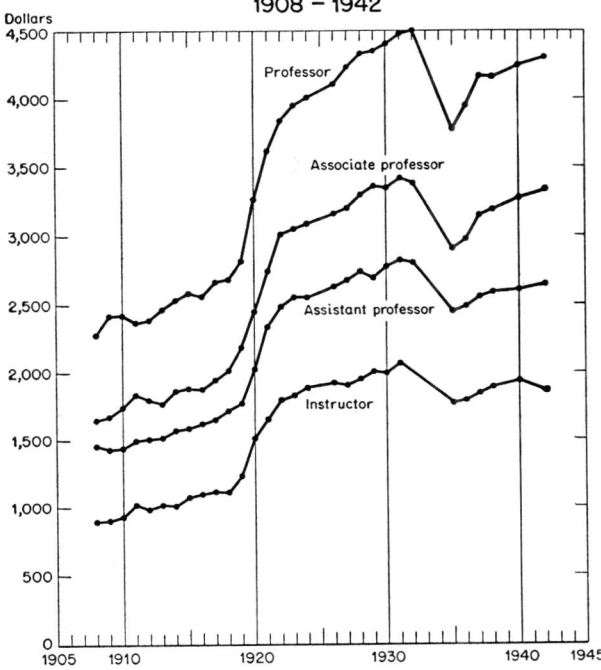

Figure 5
Salaries of College Teachers in Large Public Institutions
1908 – 1942

1935; most or all of this decrease came in 1933 and 1934.[16] Two-thirds of the aggregate increase occurred in the four years immediately after World War I (1918-22).

When the current salaries are deflated by the cost of living index, a very different pattern emerges. From 1914 to 1940 'real' salaries rose only a fourth to a third as much as salaries in current dollars. They reached their minimum in 1919 or 1920, when they were about a third below those of 1914. Thereafter the decline in the cost of living and the rapid rise in dollar salaries led to a large increase in real salaries, so the 1914 level had been

[16]From the Office of Education surveys, Economic Outlook of Higher Education, by H. G. Badger, for 1933, 1934, and 1935, one may calculate means of percentage change in modal salaries of professors in public universities and colleges. They show decreases of about 8 percent in 1933 and 12.3 percent in 1934, and a slight rise in 1935—which is consistent with our 1932-35 change. See Circulars 58 (Sept. 1932) and 121 (Sept. 1933), and Pamphlet 58 (1934).

regained by all ranks between 1928 and 1930.[17] Real salaries continued to rise for two or three years, then fell very moderately, and by 1940 new peaks had been reached.

The relative structure of salaries by rank has been surprisingly stable. The extremes in fluctuations are suggested by the adjoining table (based on Table 28). There was an upward drift in

RELATIVE SALARIES (PROFESSORS: 100)

	1914	1919	1924	1929	1932	1937	1942
Associate Professors	73.6	77.6	76.9	77.3	75.0	75.5	77.3
Assistant Professors	61.9	62.8	63.6	61.9	62.2	61.4	61.5
Instructors	39.8	43.8	47.1	46.1	44.5	44.2	43.3

the relative salaries of the lower ranks, especially of instructors, before and during World War I (if the less reliable data for this period can be trusted), but little apparent trend in the annual data thereafter.

A salary series for all ranks combined therefore differs in behavior through time from that of professors' salaries chiefly because of changes in the relative number in various ranks. The relative numbers are not known for these institutions, but we may use as approximate weights the distribution of faculty in colleges, universities, and technical schools in New York State. The combined salary series (Table 29 and Figure 8) has a less rapid

TABLE 29

Average Salaries of College Teachers in Large Public Institutions

	CURRENT DOLLARS	DOLLARS OF 1935-39 PURCHASING POWER		CURRENT DOLLARS	DOLLARS OF 1935-39 PURCHASING POWER
1908	1,656	2,548	1923	2,886	2,397
1909	1,728	2,769	1924	2,919	2,364
1910	1,746	2,798	1926	2,958	2,307
1911	1,763	2,671	1927	2,991	2,372
1912	1,748	2,567	1928	3,045	2,460
1913	1,785	2,602	1929	3,056	2,497
1914	1,821	2,576	1930	3,065	2,496
1915	1,861	2,563	1931	3,134	2,718
1916	1,860	2,514	1932	3,111	2,986
1917	1,923	2,334	1935	2,666	2,771
1918	1,943	1,987	1936	2,732	2,788
1919	2,068	1,753	1937	2,843	2,849
1920	2,410	1,781	1938	2,861	2,778
1921	2,661	1,924	1940	2,886	2,898
1922	2,834	2,293	1942	2,892	2,617

Salaries are from Table 28; distribution of faculty by rank from Table 27; cost of living index from Table 21. A simple average was taken of salaries of Associate and Assistant Professors.

[17] Of course the standard of living had actually risen by 1930; the cost of living index does not reflect improvements in quality or the introduction of new products. Nor is the index, calculated for manual and clerical workers with smaller incomes, wholly appropriate to this profession.

upward trend because of the relative decline in full professors and increase in associate and assistant professors, but does not differ greatly from that for the individual ranks.

The representativeness of the large public institutions can be roughly tested as far as the trend of salaries is concerned. From 1914 to 1920 the average salary in a large number of private institutions rose from \$1,724 to \$2,279, or 32 percent—exactly the rise in public institutions.[18] From 1920 to 1927 the percentage increase in salaries in the large public institutions and in a broad sample of 305 institutions was again tolerably close.[19] One may conclude that at least through the 'twenties the trend of salaries in colleges and universities as a whole are fairly reliably portrayed by those in large public institutions.

Comprehensive salary information is not yet available for the war and postwar periods, but a fairly accurate extrapolation of Table 29 beyond 1942 can be made from payroll data.[20] Average

SALARIES IN LAND-GRANT INSTITUTIONS

	1942	1943	1944	1945	1946	1947	1948	1949
Average salary	\$2,892	\$2,988	\$3,282	\$3,236	\$3,429	\$3,705	\$4,098	\$4,217
Av. salary in 1935-39 purchasing power	\$2,617	\$2,482	\$2,638	\$2,548	\$2,640	\$2,417	\$2,454	\$2,460

salaries rose 46 percent from 1940 to 1949 but 'deflated' salaries

[18]Trevor Arnett, Teachers' Salaries, General Education Board, Occasional Paper 8, (1928) p. 17. The agreement was of course less miraculous for specific ranks.

PERCENTAGE INCREASE IN SALARIES, 1914-1920

	PUBLIC INSTITUTIONS	ARNETT SAMPLE
Professors	40.4	30.4
Instructors	24.6	26.4

Calculated from Arnett, Teachers' Salaries, General Education Board, Occasional Paper 7, (1921).

[19]The comparison by rank is as follows:

PERCENTAGE INCREASE IN SALARIES, 1920-1927

	PUBLIC INSTITUTIONS	ARNETT SAMPLE
Professors	29.7	36.4
Associate Professors	30.6	33.9
Assistant Professors	32.3	27.3
Instructors	26.5	34.6

[20]Average salary is extrapolated by expenditures of land-grant institutions for residential instruction (which excludes plant operation, administration, extension, libraries, research, etc.) divided by the number of persons in residential instruction. This series follows the average salary closely in 1935-40. See Statistics of Land-Grant Colleges and Universities, various years. The average salary of *all* teachers in 1948 is estimated to be \$4,147 (Survey of Salaries and Occupational Attitudes of Faculty Personnel of Higher Education, 1947-48, Office of Education, Circular 254).

fell 15 percent. Data for a few large universities suggest that salaries rose most in the lowest rank and least in the highest rank, and there is some evidence of an increase in the proportion of teachers in the lower ranks.

RANK VS. SALARY INCREASES

When the workers in an occupation are classified by grade or rank, the employer may increase the salaries of individuals by within-grade increments or by promotions to a higher grade, without changing the nominal schedule of salaries by rank. The time pattern of an individual's salary is then governed by three factors: the initial levels of salary for persons of given qualifications; the rate of in-grade increments; and the rate of promotion. Many discussions of salary changes concentrate on the first factor, tacitly treating the second and third factors as stable or unimportant.

We possess little information about customary patterns of in-grade increments and of promotion in college teaching, so we cannot test the stability of these patterns.[21] A detailed analysis of the salaries paid by one large university, however, illustrates the considerable scope for salary increases through more rapid in-grade increments and promotions. The salaries of individuals receiving promotions were substantially less than those who held a given rank in both 1940 and 1946, but the latters' salaries were less than those of new personnel, in the higher ranks (Table 30). Salaries of those holding a given rank increased much more than the average salary of the rank (Table 31). It is apparent that changes in the practices of in-grade increments and promotions are important possible substitutes for changes in nominal salary levels. Common observation suggests that salary increases since the war through accelerated promotion have added substantially to the salaries of college teachers.

STRUCTURE OF SALARIES

The average salaries paid by all degree-granting institutions may be estimated from a large sample study for 1940 (Table 32). Salaries of instructors are almost equal in the various types of institution (private and public colleges and teachers colleges); the differences among type of institution become larger as one goes up the ranks, but are fairly small at all ranks if one excludes

[21]Some information for a sample of 1,351 teachers is given in Circular 254.

TABLE 30
Salaries of Identical Teachers, University of Illinois,
1940 and 1946

RANK		SALARY	
1940	1946	1940	1946
Professor	Professor	$5,418	$6,449
Associate Professor	Professor	3,815	5,247
Assistant Professor	Professor	3,305	5,257
Instructor	Professor	2,400	6,000
Not present	Professor		7,327
Professor	Not present	5,540	
Associate Professor	Associate Professor	3,681	4,330
Assistant Professor	Associate Professor	3,149	4,137
Instructor	Associate Professor	2,422	4,028
Not present	Associate Professor		4,409
Associate Professor	Not present	3,825	
Assistant Professor	Assistant Professor	3,039	3,600
Instructor	Assistant Professor	2,271	3,334
Not present	Assistant Professor		3,416
Assistant Professor	Not present	3,064	
Instructor	Instructor	1,890	2,501
Not present	Instructor		2,190
Instructor	Not present	1,896	

Source: Table 26. 'Not present' 1946 includes emeritus faculty.

the teachers colleges. If one subclassifies these categories, however, larger differences appear: in the wealthier private colleges (measured by value of plant) professors receive almost 3 times as much as in the poorer colleges.[22]

TABLE 31
Salaries of Identical Teachers, University of Illinois
Percentage Increase, 1940-1946

RANK	1940	1946	% INCREASE
Professor in 1940, present in 1946	$5,418	$6,449	19.0
Professor in 1946, present in 1940	4,810	6,049	25.8
All Professors at indicated date	5,467	6,135	12.2
Associate Professor in 1940, present in 1946	3,770	4,937	31.0
Associate Professor in 1946, present in 1940	3,134	4,162	32.8
All Associate Professors at indicated date	3,775	4,201	11.3
Assistant Professor in 1940, present in 1946	3,150	4,205	33.5
Assistant Professor in 1946, present in 1940	2,435	3,391	39.3
All Assistant Professors at indicated date	3,130	3,400	8.6
Instructor in 1940, present in 1946	2,149	3,138	46.0
Instructor in 1946, present in 1940	1,890	2,501	32.3
All Instructors at indicated date	2,037	2,280	11.9
All Faculty	3,268	3,979	21.8
All Faculty present both years	3,492	4,533	29.8

Source: Table 26.

[22] The average salary of all college teachers in 1940 was $2,855, almost the same as the average salary of teachers in land-grant colleges ($2,866; see Table 29).

TABLE 32
Average Salaries in Degree-granting Institutions, 1940

TYPE OF INSTITUTION	PROFESSOR	ASSOCIATE PROFESSOR	ASSISTANT PROFESSOR	INSTRUCTOR	ALL RANKS
Land-grant	$4,421	$3,304	$2,733	$2,000	$3,059
Universities & colleges					
Private	3,679	3,165	2,621	1,905	2,738
Public (not land-grant)	3,864	2,930	2,381	1,812	2,885
State teachers colleges	3,270	2,643	2,386	1,990	2,539
All	3,818	3,066	2,573	1,925	2,855
Detailed Classes					
Private universities & colleges					
Plant over $10 million	5,754	3,876	3,151	2,228	3,779
Plant $3 to $8 million	4,431	3,389	2,761	1,949	3,169
Plant under $1 million	1,989	1,837	1,664	1,234	1,759
Private colleges					
Men	4,361	3,271	2,707	2,101	3,081
Women	3,339	2,925	2,457	1,877	2,660

Source: College Salaries, 1939-40, Office of Education, Circular 196. The average salary of all teachers in a rank is based on the total number of teachers in each type of school, not the number in this sample of 305 schools. The aggregates are estimated from the ratio of teachers (of all ranks) in the particular schools in the sample to all teachers in the specified type of school. Thus it is assumed that the sample is representative with respect to the distribution of teachers by rank. This table covers all teachers; Table 28 covers only those on a 9-month basis of pay.

The 1940 salary structure cannot be analyzed by region, size of community, or size of school. An earlier study, however, gives some information on the regional and size of school variations in salaries (Table 33). With few exceptions, salaries are larger in the larger schools, and larger in the New England and Middle Atlantic regions than elsewhere in the country. As both variations are large, the average for professors in small schools in the South is less than half that of professors in large schools in New England. The differences by size of school are considerably smaller (relatively and absolutely) in the lower than in the higher ranks.

College teachers have relatively equal incomes. This is one element of the unusual security of the profession: one cannot be a very great financial failure or success. The contrast with the dispersion of incomes of independent practitioners in law, medicine, and dentistry is pronounced (Figure 6 and Table 34), and the contrast with salaried business workers substantial.[23] (The inequality of college teachers' earnings is probably somewhat greater than that of salaries; see below).

The extent to which incomes within a profession approaches

[23] See Figure 3 for the Lorenz curve of salaried workers in Minnesota; the Lorenz curve of college teachers is very similar to that of elementary and secondary school teachers.

TABLE 33

Average Salaries in Men's and Coeducational Colleges, 1927

RANK & COLLEGE ENROLLMENT	UNITED STATES	New England	Middle Atlantic	South	Middle West	West
Professor	$3,847					
1,000 & over	4,620	$5,632	$5,112	$3,928	$4,558	$4,184
500-1,000	3,355	4,384	3,914	3,212	2,960	3,112
Under 500	2,726	4,238	3,383	2,736	2,546	2,551
Associate Professor	3,305					
1,000 & over	3,547	4,053	4,331	2,985	3,394	3,214
500-1,000	2,741	3,377	3,127	2,430	2,488	2,648
Under 500	2,435	3,413	3,050	2,192	2,299	2,508
Assistant Professor	2,696					
1,000 & over	2,833	3,106	3,115	2,499	2,731	2,633
500-1,000	2,461	2,864	2,857	2,277	2,261	2,244
Under 500	2,169	2,783	2,322	2,056	2,107	2,421
Instructor	1,947					
1,000 & over	2,000	2,208	2,055	1,772	1,976	1,954
500-1,000	1,890	2,148	2,032	1,584	1,851	1,838
Under 500	1,623	2,200	1,724	1,553	1,664	1,239
All	3,003	3,605	3,243	2,753	2,824	2,974

Source: Arnett, General Education Board, Occasional Paper 8, Appendix. The regions are defined in *ibid.*, pp. 5-6.

equality may be viewed as determined by two factors: the directness of rivalry between members of the profession, and the importance attached to the outcome of this rivalry.[24] In law the rivalry of attorneys for litigants is direct, and the stakes are often large. In million dollar cases a lawyer who wins 60 percent of borderline cases is worth $200,000 more than one who wins 40 percent. In medicine the rivalry is less direct and personal, although still present (witness reputation, hospital connections, speed in adopting new techniques, etc.), and the stakes are very large in the buyer's eyes. Accordingly inequality is large in these fields. It is less in dentistry, where the stakes are usually much smaller in the buyer's eyes.

The two chief functions of the professor are teaching and research. Rivalry, while present in classroom performance, is mild and indirect, and indeed great success may be viewed suspiciously, perhaps as indicative of inappropriate theatricalism. The teaching abilities of a professor are usually imperfectly known, especially outside the institution where he is teaching; nor are the criteria of good teaching unambiguous. The stakes, too, are small: no matter how important it may be to give the students a good

[24] We are concerned here with what might be termed pure inequality, i.e., inequality that would be found in salaries of members of a profession who are comparable with respect to age and size of community.

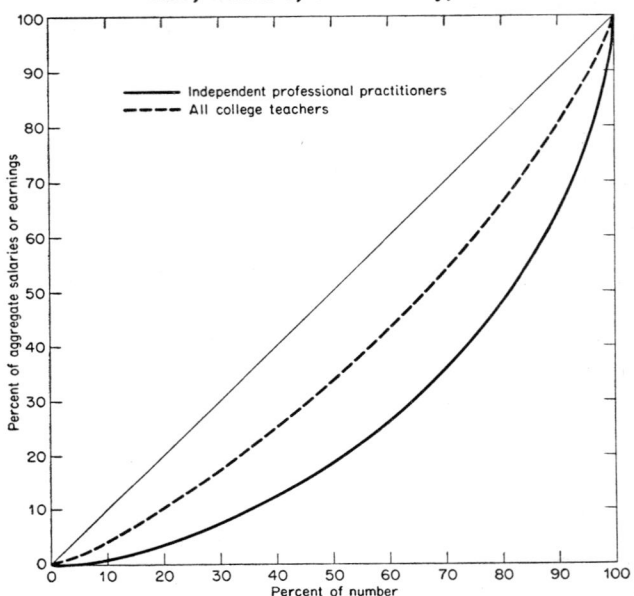

Figure 6
Lorenz Curves of Salaries of All College Teachers, 1940, and of Earnings of Independent Practitioners in Law, Medicine, and Dentistry, 1941

education, one teacher's contribution will usually be small. Research is more competitive — directly and personally in the journals, less directly in the search for new truths. The relative caliber of men is therefore more easily judged in research, but again the stakes are fairly low.[25] The prestige conferred upon a university by a distinguished faculty is very valuable, but again the contribution of one individual to this reputation is seldom large.

If this line of argument is correct, teachers' salaries should be more unequal in institutions emphasizing research than in those devoted primarily to instruction. This hypothesis can be roughly tested by comparing the Lorenz curve of 1940 salaries in seven large private colleges with that for 76 small private colleges.[26]

[25] They may become larger with the growing practice of universities of patenting and exploiting inventions of faculty members.

[26] The large institutions are Stanford, Johns Hopkins, New York University, Teachers College, Duke, Western Reserve, and the University of Pennsylvania. For the list of small schools, see *College Salaries, 1939-40*, p. 24 n.

TABLE 34

Salaries of College Teachers, 1940, and Earnings of Independent Practitioners in Law, Medicine, and Dentistry, Percentage Distribution, 1941

SALARY OR EARNINGS	COLLEGE TEACHERS All	Professorial ranks	LAW	MEDICINE	DENTISTRY
Under $1,000	2.7	1.4	11.8	11.3	6.4
1,000- 2,000	22.7	11.4	18.8	14.2	16.4
2,000- 3,000	37.1	36.5	20.3	15.6	21.8
3,000- 4,000	21.5	28.6	12.9	11.7	17.7
4,000- 5,000	9.2	12.6	8.3	9.3	12.7
5,000- 6,000	3.9	5.5	6.6	7.4	8.7
6,000- 7,000	1.5	2.1	4.8	6.6	5.7
7,000- 8,000	.7	1.0	3.4	4.9	3.6
8,000- 9,000	.4	.5	2.5	3.0	2.3
9,000-10,000	.3	.4	1.2	3.3	1.5
10,000 and over			9.5	12.7	3.2
Total	100.0	100.0	100.1	100.0	100.0

Source: See Tables 32, 36.

The larger institutions have more unequal salaries (Figure 7), although the difference is not large. Another bit of evidence pointing the same way is the slightly greater variability of salaries of full-time research men than of full-time undergraduate teachers in land-grant colleges in 1929.[27] The important conclusion is reinforced by these comparisons of inequality: college teachers' salaries approach unusually close to equality, even if no correction is made for differences in age, size of community, etc.

This equality of salary is only one of the elements of security the college teacher enjoys. In addition he is virtually certain of permanent employment once he receives 'tenure' (which usually accompanies a professorial appointment or follows automatically after a certain number of years of teaching at an institution), at least in the larger and older colleges: the discharge of a professor for incompetence or failure to perform his duties is extremely (and, from the viewpoint of the student one can argue regrettably) unusual. The absolute salary of the college teacher, unlike the earnings of the independent professional worker or most employees, does not decline after he passes his most productive

[27] See Survey of Land-Grant Colleges and Universities, Office of Education, Bulletin 1930, No. 9, Vol. 2, pp. 581-2.

	FULL-TIME Teaching	Research
Number	2,639	384
Mean salary	$2,630	$2,799
Standard deviation	$855	$1,005
Coefficient of variation	32.5	35.9

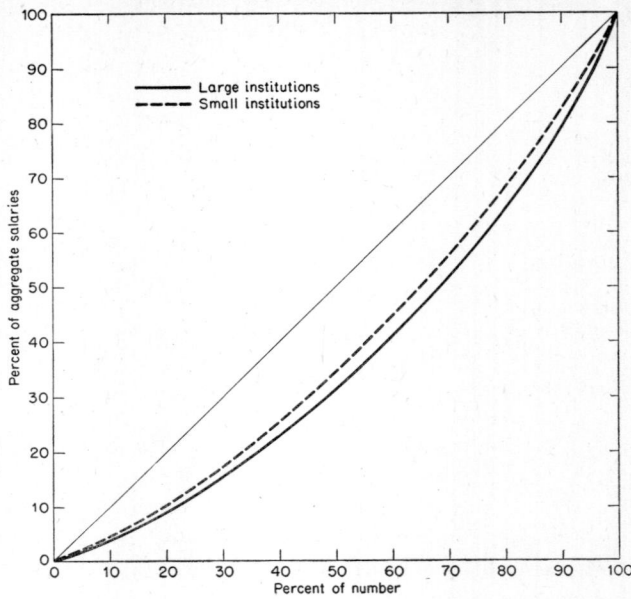

Figure 7
Lorenz Curves of Salaries of Teachers in Large and Small Private Universities and Colleges, 1940

years, although a relative decline probably occurs in a period of rising salaries.

Such extreme security, matched only in the federal judiciary and in certain civil service and seniority systems, has an uncertain effect on college teachers' earnings relative to those in riskier callings. If the possibility of great success is a real attraction to persons entering professions, as Adam Smith and innumerable followers have believed, the absence of this possibility in teaching would tend to increase college teachers' salaries enough to compensate for foregoing it. In the United States before the first World War this may well have been the effect of security; if the desire for security has since grown strong, as is often claimed, it now has the opposite effect.

We have not measured differences in teachers' salaries in various disciplines or departments. One would expect significant differences to appear from time to time, for shifts in student interests and university policies (both of which tend to be nationwide) can lead to shifts in departmental staff needs at a rate that cannot be currently met by the output of new Ph.D.'s, and of course can seldom be met by shifts of existing staff members. Absolute contraction of a department has probably been a minor problem: the vast increase in enrollments for half a century has increased the number of teachers in almost every discipline. Scraps of information for a few schools suggest that differences in salaries among departments are fairly small for professors and nearly zero at other ranks, so the impact of changing demands on inelastic supplies of new teachers must be chiefly through differences in rates of promotion.

OTHER EARNINGS

Although there is considerable information on the salaries of college teachers, little is known about their aggregate professional income. Their regular salaries are often supplemented by five types of income: salaries for teaching in the summer or in extension courses; royalties on textbooks; fees for lectures, radio talks, etc.; consultation, on a sporadic or continuing basis, with public or private bodies; and private practice in numerous fields (e.g., law, medicine, accounting, engineering). Such earnings will vary with the field of specialization: they will be smaller for historians or linguists (unless they cultivate the lecture rostrum) and larger for labor experts, lawyers, and physicians. Earnings, especially consultation fees, will vary also with professional rank and the prestige of the university, since higher ranks in the more famous institutions carry with the public greater testimony of competence.

Some measure of these outside earnings is provided by a study of teachers' incomes in 1927 (Table 35).[28] Extra income of those with outside earnings amounted to a quarter of the regular salary at each rank, and of this extra income half came from extra teaching (engaged in by two-thirds to three-quarters of the teachers). The relatively high percentage of income received by instructors from 'other' activities presumably represents chiefly earnings in nonacademic activities.

The outside earnings reported in Table 35 are averages of amounts received by teachers who reported supplementary earnings; it is impossible to determine precisely the average earnings for all teachers. The percentage of teachers receiving outside earnings was higher in the higher ranks: professors, 76.2 percent; associate professors, 70.1 percent; assistant professors, 61.7 per-

[28] Arnett, General Education Board, Occasional Paper 8.

TABLE 35

Earnings of College Teachers who had Supplementary Earnings, 1927

RANK	REGULAR SALARY	OTHER EARNINGS Total	Writing	Extra teaching	Outside lectures	Consulting work	Other
		AVERAGE EARNINGS					
Professor	$4,137	$973	$237	$429	$81	$97	$129
Assoc. Prof.	3,273	761	95	428	45	80	113
Asst. Prof.	2,749	647	72	390	26	58	103
Instructor	2,032	532	38	291	17	28	158
		PERCENTAGE RECEIVING OTHER EARNINGS					
Professor		33.0	67.9	27.3	11.1	19.6	
Assoc. Prof.		28.3	74.4	20.8	12.2	20.7	
Asst. Prof.		20.0	74.3	12.3	9.8	25.4	
Instructor		9.6	66.2	6.8	6.1	42.8	
		PERCENTAGE OF AGGREGATE EARNINGS					
Professor	81.0	19.0	4.6	8.4	1.6	1.9	2.5
Assoc. Prof.	81.1	18.9	2.4	10.6	1.1	2.0	2.8
Asst. Prof.	80.9	19.1	2.1	11.5	.8	1.7	3.0
Instructor	79.3	20.7	1.5	11.4	.7	1.1	6.2

Source: Arnett, General Education Board, Occasional Paper 8, pp. 72-3.

cent; instructors, 52.4 percent. Those who did not receive any outside earnings had somewhat lower salaries than those who did.[29] For the entire group, outside earnings averaged about 17 percent of salaries.[30]

It is highly probable that the ratio of outside earnings to regular salary has been increasing steadily. Summer school enrollments have grown much more rapidly than regular enrollments, so an increasing proportion of college teachers must have been receiving income from this, the largest source.[31]

A larger proportion of college teachers are now in large cities,

[29] Arnett, ibid., pp. 11, 72-3. Relatively more married men than single men had outside earnings. Differences in average age may explain the salary differences.

AVERAGE SALARIES, 1927

	PROF.	ASSOC. PROF.	ASST. PROF.	INSTR.
All teachers	$3,798	$3,256	$2,669	$1,941
Teachers with reported supplementary earnings	4,137	3,273	2,749	2,032

[30] A considerable number reported the receipt but not the amount of outside earnings. Outside earnings were 16.7 percent of salaries if those reporting supplementary earnings but not their amount, received only negligible amounts; 17.9 percent if this group on the average received the same amount of supplementary earnings as those who reported the amount.

[31] In 1919 there were 95,000 students in summer sessions, in 1939, 457,000 students. Therefore summer school enrollments increased twice as fast as regular enrollments in this period.

where opportunities for outside earnings are greater.[32] Moreover, the proportion of teachers in vocational fields (accounting, technology, etc.) has risen, and presumably this group has relatively larger outside earnings. One may conjecture, as a very rough guess, that the ratio of outside earnings to salary has risen from one-tenth in 1900 to perhaps one-fourth at present.

COMPARISONS WITH OTHER PROFESSIONS

Before entering on comparisons of the absolute level of college teachers' salaries with earnings in other occupations, we recapitulate briefly certain peculiarities of teachers' salaries previously discussed in connection with elementary and secondary school teachers:

Teachers in state institutions were exempt from federal personal income taxation before 1939. Because of the low federal rates and large exemptions in this period, the average value of the exemption to the recipients was small (perhaps 2 to 5 percent in the upper ranks).

College teachers have long vacations—about 3 months on the average in the summer plus several weeks during the school year. But if we recognize additional earnings, of which earnings from summer school teaching are most important, the effective vacation is reduced perhaps to 2 months.

Although a few private systems were already in operation by 1905, college teachers' pension and retirement systems really started with the establishment of the Carnegie Foundation, which began with a system of free pensions, but was eventually forced to close its list. Most retirement systems are now joint-contributory, and in most institutions teacher and institution each contribute 5 percent of the teacher's salary. About 85 percent of the teachers in universities and colleges and 95 percent of those in teachers colleges are now covered.[33] The institutions without a retirement plan have relatively low salaries. The retirement systems add about 4 percent to the average salary.

In addition to these supplements to college teachers' salaries, there are two not found in elementary and secondary education:

[32]Arnett's study shows materially higher percentages of teachers receiving outside earnings in urban than in rural areas, even with his classification (in which urban teachers are in cities of over 100,000); General Education Board, Occasional Paper 8, Table X.

[33]For a comprehensive description and discussion, see W. C. Greenough, *College Retirement and Insurance Plans* (Columbia University Press, 1948).

The college teacher often has the privilege of sabbatical leave. Commonly he receives a full year's leave at half pay or a half year's leave at full pay, not more often than every seventh year. This is not a simple increase of about one-thirteenth per teaching year, for the leave is often circumscribed: a promise is exacted to return to the institution for some period; outside earnings are prohibited; etc. About half the institutions of higher learning possess the system, but many grant sabbatical leave irregularly. In 1930 only 4.8 percent of the teachers in schools having the plan were on sabbatical leave.[34]

College teachers may receive a variety of perquisites. The most important is probably housing, which sprang into prominence as an important competitive factor in recruitment recently but extends far back into the past.[35]

There are many miscellaneous items: often lower or no tuition fees for faculty children; not infrequently access on favorable terms to university health services; occasionally preferential rates at hotels, etc.; and in at least one university (Brown) $10,000 exemption from assessments for property taxes.

Of these supplements to college teachers' salaries, the long vacation is no doubt the most important quantitatively, adding a fifth to a tenth to salaries if they are appraised at the same value as teaching time,[36] when compared with occupations with one-month vacations. Vacations have declined if, as we believe, outside earnings have increased; so on balance the ratio of these

[34]See L. B. Cooper, Sabbatical Leave for College Teachers, University of Florida Publications, Education Series, Vol. 1, No. 1 (Feb. 1932). Cooper sent inquiries to 709 institutions (excluding all junior colleges, schools for Negroes, and Catholic schools). Of the 575 institutions replying, 300 had plans of sabbatical leave, and in 193 the leave was granted regularly. In 1907 only 7 of these institutions granted sabbatical leave.

[35]Of 69 land-grant institutions 10 provided housing (on terms that were presumably generous) for some of their faculty members in 1929. (Survey of Land-Grant Colleges and Universities, Vol. 1, pp. 606-7). Before World War I the Office of Education often reported numbers of professors receiving free housing at certain universities.

[36]Summer teaching is usually paid for at the regular monthly rate; see *ibid.,* Vol. 2, pp. 417-8. This is not the only or most popular view of vacations. The late President W. R. Harper said: "In discussing the question of salaries, there is no error more ungracious and unreasonable than that which grudges the professor his vacation" (The Pay of American College Professors, *Forum,* Sept. 1893, p. 108).

monetary and nonmonetary advantages to salary has probably risen only moderately over time.

The comparison of college teachers' salaries with those of elementary and secondary school teachers is subject to least qualification for differences in working year, type of work, security of tenure, and inequality of income. One important difference, however, is that most college professors are in urban areas (79.6 percent in 1940), whereas a majority of public school teachers are in rural areas (51.5 percent in 1940). A more meaningful comparison can therefore be made between college teachers' salaries and urban public school teachers' salaries than if all public school teachers' salaries are used (Figure 8).[37] The relative difference between college and public school teachers has

Figure 8
Average Salaries of Urban Public School Teachers and Teachers in Large Public Colleges and Universities
1900 – 1942

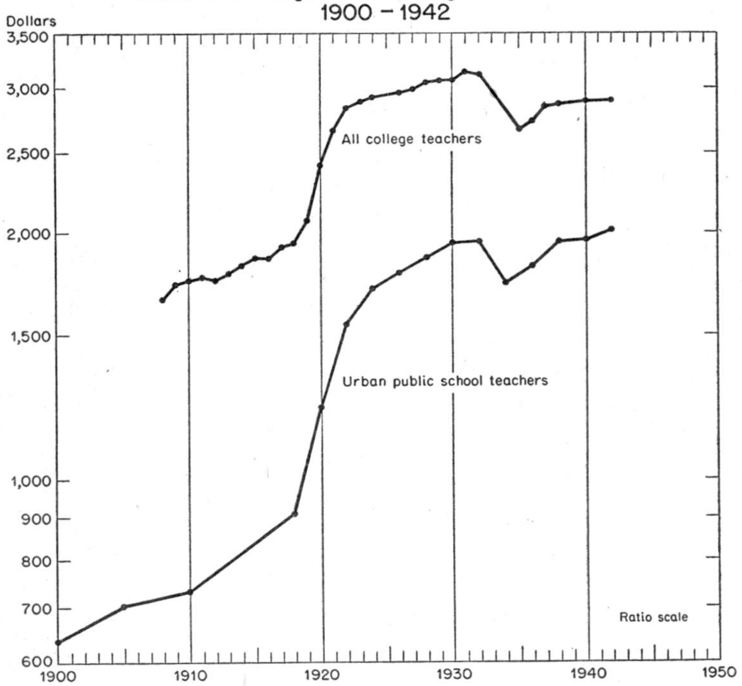

[37] Since rural school teachers' salaries rose relative to urban school teachers' salaries, the trend about to be discussed would become even more pronounced if all school teachers' salaries were used.

steadily narrowed. In 1910 college teachers' salaries were 2.4 times those of public school teachers; by 1930 the ratio had fallen to 1.6 and by 1940 to 1.5. It appears to have continued to fall since 1940.[38]

A minor part of the explanation for this decline in the ratio of college teachers' salaries to public school teachers' salaries is found in changes in formal education.[39] The academic training of the public school teacher has risen from about 1 year beyond high school in 1900 to 4 years beyond high school in 1940. The full-time academic training of college teachers has also risen, with more obtaining the Ph.D. and this degree requiring a progressively longer period of work, but on balance the differential between public school and college teachers has probably diminished. Some part of the decline in the ratio of college teachers' to public school teachers' salaries is also attributable to the convergence of teaching levels: a rising proportion of public school teachers are in high schools, and a rising proportion of college teachers in junior colleges. The rise in the average age of public school teachers relative to college teachers works in the same direction.

An important part of the explanation, however, is also that the 1910 ratio of college teachers' to public school teachers' salaries, 2.4, vastly exceeded the additional cost of training for college teaching. The additional return, as a percentage of salary, necessary to compensate a teacher for the additional training for college teaching was then on the order of 40 or 50 percent and is now on the order of 15 or 20 percent.[40] These percentages,

[38]Elementary school teachers' salaries rose 66.1 percent from 1941 to 1949, high school teachers' salaries rose 57.1 percent from 1941 to 1949, and college teachers' salaries rose 46.1 percent from 1940 to 1949.

[39]The urban school year has not changed appreciably since 1910; the trend, if any, in the college year is unknown.

[40]This percentage may be estimated roughly, using the formula given by Friedman and Kuznets (*op. cit.*, p. 142). The present value of an urban public school teacher's future salary in the late 1930's was about $50,000 (see H. Clark, *Life Earnings in Selected Occupations in the United States*, Harper, 1937). The additional formal training of college teachers is about the equivalent of 3 years if a year is allowed for the doctoral dissertation. In the formula referred to, the following estimates have been used: $V = \$50{,}000$, v (the present value of the last three years' salary in public school teaching) $= \$1{,}100$, c (the present value of the additional direct costs of college teachers' training) $= \$1{,}000$, and p (the ratio of the last three years' salary to the

moreover, are for comparable groups of college and public school teachers. They should be reduced if one compares, as we must do, the average salary of urban teachers with the average salary of all college teachers.[41]

Most public school teachers could not enter college teaching because of the traditional opposition to women on college faculties, and many could not meet the variable but apparently rising standards of the Ph.D., but many young men could choose between the two levels, and the relative attractions of college teaching were large.[42] In addition college teaching offered greater prestige, less classroom teaching, and greater opportunities for outside earnings. College teachers increased fivefold from 1900 to 1940; public school teachers doubled. The difference in salaries was probably a significant cause of this difference in rate of growth, and the difference in the rate of growth was a major factor in the declining ratio of college teachers' to teachers' salaries.

The other group with which college teachers' salaries and earnings will be compared is the independent professions — law, medicine, and dentistry. The unfortunate restriction of our information on earnings in these professions to 1929-48 (Table 36) makes comparison difficult because the temporal pattern is dominated by the relative insensitivity of professorial salaries to business fluctuations.

These cyclical effects were perhaps at a minimum in 1941, when college teachers' salaries had regained the level of the late

average salary of public school teachers) $= 1$. Then the ratio of college teachers' to teachers' salaries necessary to make the two branches equally attractive financially is 1.17.

[41]The effect of community size on salary already noted for public school teachers probably holds for college teachers. Our salary series for large public institutions probably does not include any rural college teachers. But college teachers as a class are in smaller communities than public school teachers. In 1940, 43 percent of urban public school teachers and 34 percent of urban college teachers were in cities over 100,000.

[42]The Pennsylvania studies made under the auspices of the Carnegie Foundation for the Advancement of Teaching revealed that the students in teachers colleges and the majors in education in arts colleges had lower intelligence quotients than the average college student, that their performance on the achievement tests was also low, but that the male students in education had superior records. See W. S. Learned and B. D. Wood, *The Student and his Knowledge* (Carnegie Foundation, 1938), Ch. VII.

TABLE 36
Average Incomes and Salaries in Four Professions

	LAWYERS	PHYSICIANS	DENTISTS	COLLEGE TEACHERS
1929	$5,534	$5,224	$4,267	$3,056
1932				3,111
1933	3,868	2,948	2,188	
1935	4,272	3,695	2,485	2,666
1936	4,394	4,204	2,726	2,732
1937	4,483	4,285	2,883	2,843
1938		4,093		2,861
1939	4,391	4,229	3,096	
1940		4,441		2,886
1941	4,794	5,047	3,782	
1942				2,892
1943	5,945	8,822		2,988
1944	6,504		6,649	3,282
1945	6,861		6,922	3,236
1946	6,951		6,381	3,429
1947	7,437	10,057	6,610	3,705
1948	8,121		7,039	4,098

Independent professions: E. F. Denison, Incomes in Selected Professions, *Survey of Current Business*, May 1944; William Weinfeld, Income of Lawyers, Income of Dentists, *ibid.*, Aug. 1949, Jan. 1950. The figures for physicians in 1943 and 1947 are from W. A. Richardson, Physicians' Incomes, *Medical Economics*, Sept. 1948, reduced 11.00 percent (on the basis of the 1941 relationship) for omission of physicians over 65.
College teachers: Table 29 and text.

nineteen-twenties, and the fairly sustained expansion of business had raised incomes in the independent professions well above their previous depression levels. In this year professional earnings exceeded college teachers' salaries (taking the latter to be $2,889) by the following amounts: lawyers, $1,905; physicians, $2,158; and dentists, $893.

These comparisons, however, are fatally incomplete: numerous adjustments must be made to college teachers' salaries to achieve comparability with professional earnings:

The outside earnings of college teachers are about 20 to 25 percent of their average salaries.

The vacations of college teachers exceed those in the independent professions by at least a month on the average, and amount to at least 10 percent of the average salary if valued at the rate at which teaching is usually paid.

The college contributions to college teachers' retirement funds average about 4 percent of their salaries.

The occupational expense of the college professor was on the average small (probably less than $50 per year) and his investment in equipment usually small; the earnings of independent professional workers include interest on their investment. If this investment averages $3,000, as a rough guess, at 4 percent the interest return in earnings is $120. For comparative purposes, about 2 percent should be added to college teachers' salaries.

Since college teaching is a much more rapidly growing field, its members are on the average younger. The median ages in the various professions in 1940 were college teachers, 40.8; lawyers and judges, 42.0; physicians, 44.1; dentists, 43.6. The average independent professional worker was at the age at which his earnings were at about a lifetime maximum,[43] whereas the college teacher was at a lower level relative to lifetime earnings (especially if, as is probable, salaries show no downward trend in later years of teaching comparable to that found in the independent professions). In the absence of knowledge of the life pattern of college teachers' salaries the importance of this difference cannot be estimated.

The independent professions are concentrated rather heavily in the largest communities, where income levels are relatively high; college teachers are distributed among community sizes more in proportion to the population at large. If college teachers' salaries were calculated for the same distribution among community sizes as rules in the independent professions (assuming that their salaries would show the usual size of community pattern), they would be about 15 percent higher.[44]

The full-time academic training of college teachers plus allowance of a year for the preparation of a doctoral dissertation exceeds by about a year that of dentistry and law (6 years of college), but is about 2 years less than that in medicine. In comparisons of college teachers' salaries with doctors' incomes,

[43] See Friedman and Kuznets, *op. cit.*, pp. 237 ff.
[44] Friedman and Kuznets have performed the opposite standardization, that is, calculated the incomes in the professions if their members were distributed among community sizes in the same proportion as nonrelief families (which appears to be similar to that of college teachers). The standardized income of physicians was 90 percent of their actual average income, and the corresponding percentages for dentists and lawyers are 88 and 79 respectively; *op. cit.*, p. 184.

PERCENTAGES OF MEMBERS OF THE
PROFESSIONS IN THE LARGEST COMMUNITIES, 1940

	COMMUNITY SIZE		
	Over 1,000,000	500,000–1,000,000	100,000–500,000
College teachers	9.1	4.5	13.3
Lawyers and judges	21.8	8.3	16.3
Physicians	19.4	7.4	15.7

about 10 percent should be added to the former; for comparisons with the other groups, 5 percent should be deducted.[45]

The progressive personal income tax affects net earnings after taxes (which is more pertinent than earnings before tax to the relative financial attractiveness of professions) in two ways, both favorable to college teachers. Between occupations with equal average incomes before tax, the average tax is larger the more unequal the distribution of income; and of course it increases more than in proportion to average income. Tentative calculations for 1941 indicate that the federal income tax was about 14.0 percent of the average income of lawyers, 10.8 percent of the average income of physicians, 6.0 percent of the average income of dentists, and 2.7 percent of the average salary of college teachers.[46] The second effect of the progressive income tax is to favor occupations with stable incomes relative to those with fluctuating incomes, but this effect seems to be much smaller in magnitude.[47] On these two scores, the earnings of lawyers should be reduced more than 10 percent (and those in the other independent professions by smaller percentages) in comparisons with college teaching. On the other hand, it is commonly believed that salaries are more fully reported than entrepreneurial net income.

There are two important factors on the other side. One is that our salary series does not cover persons below the rank of instructor (i.e., teaching assistants, laboratory assistants, etc.) and their inclusion might lower the average college teachers' salary appreciably.[48] The other is that outside earnings in the professions, especially law, may be substantial.

In sum, more than 50 percent must be added to the salaries of college teachers in making comparisons with earnings in inde-

[45]*Ibid.*, pp. 142 ff.

[46]These calculations assume that the earner is married and has two children, and takes into account the earned income credit. For the underlying data, see Table 34.

[47]Using the same assumptions as in the previous footnote, and employing the data on incomes of physicians from 1929 to 1937 (Friedman and Kuznets, *op. cit.*, p. 101), the physician with average income would pay a tax of 3.9 percent of his income (under 1941 rates), whereas with a stable income equal to the average for the period, he would pay a tax of 2.5 percent of his income.

[48]Although if these junior positions are usually held for several years, graduate study is also pursued, and the effects on the present value of the person's future net earnings are uncertain.

pendent professions. With this correction, in 1941 the 'net advantages' of college teaching exceeded those of dentistry, and were almost equal to those of law and medicine. It would be unsafe to generalize this finding until more ample data permit a better isolation of cyclical fluctuations in incomes, but the evidence for 1941 suggests that the net financial advantages of college teaching were not much inferior to the more prosperous independent professions.

The foregoing comparison has been made for a more or less normal year. The sensitivity of income to fluctuations in general business conditions differs greatly between the independent professions and college teaching, so comparisons in years of depression or inflation yield very different conclusions. College teachers' salaries rose from 1929 to 1932 and subsequently fell only about 15 percent, whereas earnings in the independent professions began to fall in 1930 and by 1933 had fallen 45 percent from the 1929 level.[49] Thus in 1932 college teachers' average salaries were larger than the incomes of physicians and dentists and only a fifth less than lawyers' incomes.

Conversely, during the war years college teachers' salaries fell far behind earnings in the professions (Table 36). (The different rates of increase in earnings in the various professions during the war seem directly related to the proportions of their members drawn into military service.) The gap between college teachers and the professions began to narrow after the war, but the prewar relationship had not been restored by 1948: college teachers' salaries were still a fifth lower than in 1941 relative to the average of law and dentistry, and no doubt lower still relative to medicine. These figures exaggerate the gap, for no doubt outside earnings of college teachers also respond to changing business conditions.

It is impossible to say whether college teachers have on balance lost or gained relative to the independent professions from the relative rigidity of their money salaries; if one considers the 'twenties and 'thirties, they may have gained; if one considers the 'thirties and 'forties, they probably lost. But wherever the balance lies, this stability of teachers' salaries seems ill suited to periods of large inflation and deflation such as we have experienced for several decades and may continue to enjoy for some time.

[49] See Friedman and Kuznets, *op. cit.*, p. 366.

APPENDIX A
Number Employed in Elementary and Secondary Education

PUBLIC SCHOOLS

The chief source of information on the number of teachers is necessarily the *Biennial Survey* of the United States Office of Education. The reported number of teachers, principals, and supervisors, the basic series, requires adjustment. It is the sum of teaching positions and principals and supervisors in recent years, and the sum of teachers or teaching positions and principals and supervisors in earlier years. The distinction between positions and employees seems clear, but throughout the period when both are given, the same number is reported for both classes in more than half of the states (34 in 1936). It is not known whether the number represents positions or employees in these cases. Since in at least some cases it probably refers to positions, the number in teaching is underestimated: the number of teachers runs about 10 percent higher than the number of positions in New York, for example. Only positions are reported in recent years, and this change imparts a downward bias to the series. The series used here consists of supervisors and principals plus 'employed' teachers,[1] plus also teachers in special schools.

Moreover, the series for principals and supervisors seem unreliable. Some fluctuations in state data are given in the adjoining

PRINCIPALS

	1930	1932	1934
Arizona	171		176
California	2,741	1,028	935
Iowa	281	465	290
Maryland		206	204
Texas	6,849	2,571	2,672

table. Nothing has been done to correct these figures since the obvious year-to-year changes in classification were apparently offset in good part by changes in the reported number of teachers.

The numbers reported in administrative offices also defy credi-

PROFESSIONAL ADMINISTRATIVE EMPLOYEES

	1926	1928	1930	1932
Mississippi	1,444	1,676	1,902	187
Idaho	126	4,694	177	380
Arizona	61	153	71	39
Pennsylvania	500	1,300	1,111	1,232
West Virginia	305	590	2,077	421

[1] The former two are estimated from the latter before 1920.

bility. In 1941-42, when reports were relatively complete and detailed, there were 20,518 professional employees. There does not seem to be any tolerably accurate method of estimating the number for the entire period.

PROFESSIONAL EMPLOYEES
State offices of education	1,885
Superintendents	14,949
Other professional employees	3,684
Total	20,518

The statistical work of the Office of Education has been unsatisfactory in many respects, as the foregoing examples may suggest. The Office does not fully distinguish the figures it estimates from those it collects (for example, in recent *Surveys* it does not state that school enrollment by grade in Rhode Island is estimated). The descriptions of statistics are sometimes misleading (as when a figure is given for the number of "full-time equivalent" college teachers which, in 1938, included 28 percent of such teachers not reduced to a full-time basis). The preference for medians over means (which makes combination of data so difficult) has been shown in many studies, and is indeed pervasive in educational statistics; the practice of reporting open-end classes in frequency distributions is equally popular and deplorable. The general practice of obtaining almost universal coverage on some series biennially, rather than devoting the same resources to less frequent surveys of wider scope supplemented by annual samples, has severely handicapped the student of education. The delays in publication have been great: by June 1, 1949, for example, only one chapter of the *Biennial Survey* for 1945-46 had been published. Improvements are now being made in the statistical work of the Office; it is to be hoped that they will eventually include a thorough reworking of the most important series for at least the last five decades.

PRIVATE SCHOOLS

The number of teachers in private schools is based upon the *Biennial Survey*, but obvious understatements after 1918 (e.g., in 1934) are corrected by estimating the total from the number of teachers in Catholic schools. Teachers in elementary schools in 1905 and 1915 are interpolated on the basis of the trend in their ratio to public school teachers. The early years are probably underreported. This suspicion is strengthened by the enrollment figures: in 1920 the *Biennial Survey* gives a total for all private schools that is 227,000 less than the enrollment in Catholic schools. The data in the *Survey* imply also a higher student-teacher ratio in private than in public schools in 1900, and a lower ratio in 1920. Enrollment in 1940 was 2.6 million, of which 2.3 million were in Catholic schools.

COMPARISON WITH THE POPULATION CENSUSES

The decennial Census of Occupations reports teachers (except for music, dancing art, etc.) and their numbers may be compared with those given in Table 1 of the text. The agreement is not quite as excellent as the figures suggest. The Census category

	1900	1910	1920	1930	1940
Teachers (thousands)					
Population Census	440	595	752	1,044	1,056
Biennial Survey	480	594	773	985	1,015

includes business schools, governesses, administrative officers, correspondence schools, vocational schools, and, of course, unemployed teachers. The Census figure should therefore be 5 or 10 percent higher than the Office of Education figure, but is not in the first three decennial Censuses. Nevertheless, the Census data confirm the general findings from the *Biennial Survey*.

PUBLIC NONACADEMIC EMPLOYEES

There are no continuous or complete data on nonacademic employees of public schools (and even less information for those of private schools); the *Biennial Survey,* for example, started to report numbers only in 1938, and only a third of the states reported in that year. The more important categories can be roughly estimated:

1) Janitors. The *Biennial Survey* figures for 1938 can be 'blown up' on the basis of teachers in reporting states, to yield a total of 112,000. The addition of carpenters, painters, etc. raises the total to 120,000. Alternatively, payrolls are reported in the *Biennial Survey,* and average salaries can be calculated from the salary tabulations of the National Education Association (available back to 1925), and dividing the former by the latter we get about 109,000. Both are probably underestimates, since part-time workers are incompletely reported in the *Biennial Survey* and the second procedure yields only 'full-time equivalent' employees.

2) Bus drivers. Using the 'blow-up' of *Biennial Survey* data, the number in 1938 was 91,000. Using the number of school buses (given in *Bus Facts*) multiplied by the average number of em-

ployees per bus (as given in the 1935 Census of Motor Transportation) yields 87,000 employees.

3) Other (nurses, attendance officers, clerical help, etc.). From the salary tabulations of the National Education Association a ratio to teachers can be estimated, to yield about 33,000 other employees in 1938. A 'blow-up' of the 1941-42 *Biennial Survey* data, which are more complete, yields a slightly larger figure for 1942.

It appears, therefore, that full- and part-time employees numbered about 250,000 in 1940, or a quarter of the number of teachers.

Estimating the number of janitors from payroll data, the ratio to teachers appears to be fairly constant since 1925. Using the ratio of drivers to buses to estimate bus drivers, the number drops to 15,000 in 1924, the first year in which an estimate of the number of buses is available, and the number may be presumed to have approached zero during the first World War. In the roughest of fashions these and other considerations suggest the following estimates for nonacademic personnel: in 1900, one-eighth of teachers (or 60,000); in 1910, two-fifteenths (or 80,000); in 1920, one-sixth (or 115,000); in 1930, one fifth (or 200,000); and in 1940, one-fourth (or 250,000). But the figures are so dubious that only two conclusions are safe: the number has always been large, and it has been rising more rapidly than the number of teachers.

Appendix B
Effect of Legislation on Enrollments

Two types of legislation have served directly to increase the proportion of older children attending school: compulsory school attendance laws and laws fixing the minimum age for employment in various industries. The first compulsory school attendance law was enacted in Massachusetts in 1842. Many states joined this movement in the last quarter of the century, and by 1900, 32 states and the District of Columbia had some sort of legislation requiring school attendance. The last of the remaining 16 states (15 of which were in the South) had passed compulsory attendance laws by 1919.

It is very difficult to summarize briefly the requirements imposed by these laws. Idaho may serve as an example: attendance is required of children from 8 to 18 (inclusive) for the full school term, but exceptions are made for children who (a) are 15 or older and have completed the 8th grade; (b) are 15 or older and whose help is necessary to support themselves or their parents or "where it would be for the best interest of such child to be relieved from the provisions of this article"; and (c) whose bodily or mental condition would interfere with regular school attendance. Several states waive the requirements if the child must walk more than 2, 2.5, or 3 miles to school; many states exempt children over a certain minimum age or school grade who have employment; and exceptions are sometimes made for children of widows, pages in legislatures, etc. These exceptions have been whittled down through time; consequently, the comparison of legislation in 1900, 1920, and 1940 (summarized in Table A) probably underestimates the growing scope of these laws. Moreover, the minimum term of school attendance required in 1900 was usually very short;[2] by 1920, 36 states required attendance for the entire school year; and in 1940 this requirement was universal.

TABLE A
Distribution of States by Maximum Age through which Children were Required to Attend Full-time Schools

MAXIMUM AGE	1900	1920	1940
12		2	
13	1		
14	13	9	2
15	5	7	2
16	3	29	31
17		2	8
18			6
Number of states	22	49	49
Mean age in states with laws	14.5	15.4	16.3

Along with the increase in the maximum age of compulsory attendance has gone a widening prohibition on child labor. The laws are too diverse to be summarized in a neat tabulation but it is easy to convey an impression of the great expansion of this form of control between 1900 and 1940. In the early year, 6 states had no legislation, 13 prohibited only work in mines, 5 prohibited only such employments as tight-rope walking, and no state had a minimum age for employment higher than 14. By

[2]The required terms were 12 weeks per year in 10 states, 16 weeks per year in 6 states, 20 weeks per year in 2 states, 28 weeks per year in 1 state, a full term in 1 state.

1940 every state except Wyoming had a minimum age of 14 or more for work in the broader class of factories, mines, and mercantile establishments. In 36 states the maximum age for compulsory school attendance is higher than the minimum age at which a child can work in a factory or store, and in all except one of the remaining states these ages are equal.

It is tempting to leap to the conclusion that these laws have been very effective in promoting school attendance. The percentage of children 15-18 inclusive enrolled in school was closely related in 1940 to the maximum age of compulsory school attendance (Table B). In both urban and rural-farm areas the absolute level of enrollment was higher in states with higher maximum ages for school attendance, and fell less rapidly with age. But the causal role of legislation is not so easily determined; the data in Table B are consistent with the views both that legislation compels higher enrollments and that states with high enrollments pass laws that reflect the more basic conditions leading to high enrollments.

TABLE B
Average by States of Percentage of Children Enrolled in Schools by Age and Maximum Age through which Attendance was Compulsory, 1940

MAXIMUM AGE OF COMPULSORY ATTENDANCE	AGE OF CHILDREN			
	15	16	17	18
	URBAN			
18	94.4	88.8	76.6	49.8
17	90.7	81.1	67.8	43.8
16	92.7	81.0	66.5	41.0
15	85.6	72.8	54.6	33.0
14	80.8	67.2	50.2	30.6
	FARM			
18	90.3	81.5	68.8	45.4
17	79.0	66.1	51.6	32.5
16	81.1	66.5	51.1	32.4
15	72.4	57.6	40.9	25.2
14	73.0	58.1	40.8	24.1

Of course both interpretations contain some truth. We can cite at least two kinds of evidence that the laws tend to increase enrollments. Enrollments are higher in cities with higher maximum ages of school attendance than in other cities in the same state.[3] Again, a jump in public school enrollments is often

[3] In Delaware, for example, the maximum age is 16 in Wilmington and 17 elsewhere. The effect on the percentages enrolled in school is clear.

	AGE OF CHILDREN			
	15	16	17	18
Wilmington	95.3	76.3	58.8	34.5
Other urban areas	95.8	75.2	64.6	36.8

apparent immediately after a higher compulsory age is set.[4] On the other hand, if we classify states by per capita income and the racial composition of the children (Table C) — both of which are in a sense more fundamental and persistent than school age legislation — within the cells there is no evidence of a correlation between legislation and school enrollments.[5]

TABLE C

Average Percentages of Children 16-17 Enrolled in Schools in 1940, by Percentage of Nonwhite Children in 1940 and Per Capita Income Payments in 1939

PER CAPITA INCOME	PERCENTAGE OF NONWHITE CHILDREN		
	0 to 5	5 to 15	15 & more
	PERCENTAGE ATTENDING SCHOOL		
$200-$400	71.7	57.8	55.6
400- 600	74.8	63.2	60.2
600- 825	73.3	75.2	56.7
	NUMBER OF STATES		
$200-$400	4	5	7
400- 600	16	2	3
600- 825	6	4	1

The effects of legislation cannot be separated without taking account of the many exceptions in the school attendance laws, and this intricate investigation is not necessary here. Our brief study suggests, however, that the influence of legislation is a relatively weak factor, whose presumptive significance comes largely from the correlation of maximum age in the statute with incomes and racial composition.

[4]For example, Wyoming increased the maximum age from 14 to 17 in 1923. The enrollments in secondary public schools were:

	ENROLLMENT	% INCREASE IN BIENNIUM
1918	3,376	
1920	4,476	32.6
1922	5,763	28.7
1924	8,634	49.8
1926	9,664	11.9
1928	10,644	10.1
1930	11,164	4.9

[5]The variance of the percentage of children enrolled in schools among the groups of states with various maximum ages of compulsory attendance may be compared with the variance within these groups. Although the former exceeds the latter, the variance ratio is only 1.20, with 11 and 25 degrees of freedom respectively (computed from the data underlying Table C); such a large ratio would occur by chance more than a fifth of the time. Even if income and ethnic factors are neglected, the results are the same when school enrollments in cities with populations exceeding 100,000 are analyzed. The ratio of the variance among groups of cities with different maximum ages to the variance within these groups is 1.26, with 3 and 82 degrees of freedom respectively; this ratio could arise by chance almost one-fifth of the time.

Appendix C
Academic Personnel in Higher Education

Again the chief source is the *Biennial Survey*. Since 1932 all professional employees are reported; before then only teaching staff (which excludes research, extension, and administration) was given. The ratio of teachers to all academic employees has been stable at about eight-tenths in recent years, but this ratio cannot be extrapolated backward. Extension teaching began about 1890, and full-time research was probably relatively less important early in our period.[1] The nonteaching staff was estimated roughly by extrapolating the percentage of extension to regular teachers back to zero in 1890, assuming the ratio of research staff to teachers was half as high in 1900 as in 1938, and holding the ratio of administrative staff to teachers constant. The figures in the text are reported numbers, not reduced to a full-time basis.[2] Duplications are excluded by use of the reported unduplicated totals in recent years.

A comparison may readily be made with the corresponding Census class:

	1900	1910	1920	1930	1940
Decennial Census	7,272	15,668	33,407	61,905	75,096
Biennial Survey	29,000	45,000	62,000	105,000	147,000

The discrepancy is very large, but is partly explicable in terms of differences in content. It has recently been inferred from the discrepancy that a large fraction (perhaps one-third) of faculty members have their major employment in another industry.[3] This inference seems less plausible than that graduate teaching and laboratory assistants are reported as employees to the Office of Education and as students to the Census, and that numerous teachers in religious seminaries, junior colleges, business schools, etc. are probably excluded by the Census from 'college presidents and professors'.

[1] The reported expenditures by public institutions of higher learning are first available in detail for 1928. The rise in the percentage of research to instructional expenditures from 5.9 in 1928 to 7.5 in 1935 may well be influenced by an increasing practice of budgeting research separately.

[2] The ratio of 'full-time equivalent' to all employees has been nine-tenths in recent years; no reduction was made in earlier years. The nature of the reduction to a full-time basis is ambiguous; each school makes its own decision, including the decision not to make the adjustment (see App. A).

[3] Report of the President's Commission on Higher Education (Washington, D. C., 1947), Part IV, 29.

Appendix D
College Teachers' Salaries

Salaries before 1935 are based on Viva Boothe's *Salaries and the Cost of Living in Twenty-seven State Universities and Colleges, 1913-32* (Ohio State University Press, 1932). Of the 27 institutions, 14 were land-grant schools. Median salaries in each school were reported, beginning in 1922, and their average taken. For 1914 (not 1913) through 1921, she estimated average medians from the reported maximum and minimum salaries in each institution, on the basis of the relationship among them in the 'twenties, and averaged these estimated medians. This procedure has been carried back to 1908, except that the average median was estimated directly from the average maxima and minima.[1]

Median salaries in land-grant colleges and universities are given in various reports of the Office of Education.[2] Those for individuals on a 9-month basis were chosen as a more appropriate continuation of Boothe's series than salaries of those on 11-12 month bases, since the 11-12 month basis is less common in non-land-grant schools. It is reassuring that the mean of the medians is fairly close to the mean calculated from the frequency distribution, in years when the latter is available (Table D).[3] The

MEDIAN SALARIES FOR 9-MONTH AND ALL TEACHERS

	1929		1930		1931	
	All	9-month	All	9-month	All	9-month
Professors	$4,219	$4,348	$4,342	$4,407	$4,417	$4,480
Associate Professors	3,287	3,359	3,369	3,345	3,382	3,418
Assistant Professors	2,799	2,691	2,868	2,775	2,882	2,815
Instructors	2,066	2,003	2,102	1,995	2,094	2,069

[1] The data are in annual Bulletins of the Office of Education. Miss Boothe's average maximum and minimum for 1914 differ from those calculated from the reports (so the average medians are 2.5 to 3 percent higher for 1914 in her tables); the 1908-13 salaries were raised to splice them to her series. The discrepancy may be due to her editing of the reports, in the course of which she obtained corrected data from some schools. For 1908 and 1909 only maximum salaries were available.

[2] They are summarized in the Report of the President's Commission, VI, 39.

[3] The means in this table are $125 higher than those reported in the Twenty-eighth Annual Report of the National Bureau of Economic Research, 1948, p. 33. The data are reported by $250 class intervals, and in earlier work the calculations were made on the assumption that, because of the tendency to give round-number salaries, all salaries fell at the bottom of a class interval. Although this assumption is probably more reasonable than the conventional one of a uniform distribution within the interval, the evidence seemed insufficient to depart from standard practice.

close agreement between Boothe's and the land-grant series in 1929-31 is a trifle suspicious, for the state universities as a class have salaries that average appreciably less than those of land-grant institutions.

TABLE D
Three Salary Series for College Teachers

	1929	1930	1931	1940	1942
			PROFESSOR		
Boothe	$4,348	$4,407	$4,480		
Mean salary	4,480	4,568	4,620	$4,421	$4,475
Office of Education, 9-mo. basis	4,278	4,457	4,513	4,245	4,302
			ASSOCIATE PROFESSOR		
Boothe	3,359	3,345	3,418		
Mean salary	3,369	3,434	3,451	3,304	3,359
Office of Education, 9-mo. basis	3,342	3,349	3,362	3,272	3,324
			ASSISTANT PROFESSOR		
Boothe	2,003	1,995	2,069		
Mean salary	2,092	2,155	2,135	2,000	2,018
Office of Education, 9-mo. basis	2,047	2,060	2,066	1,937	1,862
			INSTRUCTOR		
Boothe	2,691	2,775	2,815		
Mean salary	2,872	2,917	2,920	2,733	2,758
Office of Education, 9-mo. basis	2,738	2,818	2,837	2,605	2,645

THE STUDY UPON WHICH THIS PAPER IS BASED WAS MADE POSSIBLE by funds granted by The Maurice and Laura Falk Foundation of Pittsburgh. The Falk Foundation is not, however, the author, publisher, or proprietor of this publication, and is not to be understood as approving or disapproving by virtue of its grant any of the statements made or views expressed herein.

Other reports on production, employment and productivity issued with the support of grants to the National Bureau by the Maurice and Laura Falk Foundation are:

BOOKS

The Output of Manufacturing Industries, 1899-1937, by Solomon Fabricant (1940)

Employment in Manufacturing, 1899-1939: An Analysis of its Relation to the Volume of Production, by Solomon Fabricant (1942)

American Agriculture, 1899-1939: A Study of Output, Employment and Productivity, by Harold Barger and H. H. Landsberg (1942)

The Mining Industries, 1899-1939: A Study of Output, Employment and Productivity, by Harold Barger and S. H. Schurr (1944)

Output and Productivity in the Electric and Gas Utilities, 1899-1942, by J. M. Gould (1946)

OCCASIONAL PAPERS

1 *Manufacturing Output, 1929-1937,* by Solomon Fabricant (1940)

4 *The Relation between Factory Employment and Output since 1899,* by Solomon Fabricant (1941)

7 *Productivity of Labor in Peace and War,* by Solomon Fabricant (1942)

23 *Labor Savings in American Industry, 1899-1939,* by Solomon Fabricant (1945)

24 *Domestic Servants in the United States, 1900-1940,* by George J. Stigler (1946)

29 *The Rising Trend of Government Employment,* by Solomon Fabricant (1949)

The Statistical Agencies of the Federal Government: A Report to the Commission on Organization of the Executive Branch of the Government (1949) 224 pp., $2.00
F. C. Mills and C. D. Long

Taxable and Business Income (1949) 368 pp., $4.00
Dan T. Smith and J. Keith Butters

Urban Mortgage Lending by Life Insurance Companies (1950)
R. J. Saulnier 192 pp., $2.50

Business Cycles: The Problem and Its Setting (1927)
Wesley C. Mitchell 514 pp., $5.00

Production Trends in the United States Since 1870 (1934)
A. F. Burns 396 pp., $3.50

Strategic Factors in Business Cycles (1934) 256 pp., $1.50
J. M. Clark

National Income and Its Composition, 1919-1938 (1941)
Simon Kuznets 956 pp., $5.00

Cost Behavior and Price Policy (1943) 356 pp., $3.00
By the Committee on Price Determination

Business Finance and Banking (1947) 261 pp., $3.50
Neil H. Jacoby and R. J. Saulnier

Inventories and Business Cycles, with Special Reference to Manufacturers' Inventories (in press)
Moses Abramovitz

Studies In Income and Wealth
11 (1949) 464 pp., $6.00
    Six papers on the industrial distribution of manpower, real incomes in dissimilar geographic areas, national income forecasting, and the saving-income ratio.

12 (1950) 608 pp., $6.00
    Thirteen papers on national wealth.

OCCASIONAL PAPERS

30 *Costs and Returns on Farm Mortgage Lending by Life Insurance Companies, 1945-1947* (1949) $1.00
R. J. Saulnier

31 *Statistical Indicators of Cyclical Revivals and Recessions* (1950) $1.50
Geoffrey H. Moore

32 *Cyclical Diversities in the Fortunes of Industrial Corporations* (1950) $ .50
Thor Hultgren

33 *Employment and Compensation in Education* (1950)
George J. Stigler $1.00

ANNUAL REPORTS

29 *Wesley Mitchell and the National Bureau* (May 1949)
Arthur F. Burns

30 *New Facts on Business Cycles* (April 1950)
Arthur F. Burns

Behavior of Wage Rates during Business Cycles

DANIEL CREAMER

with the assistance of

MARTIN BERNSTEIN

OCCASIONAL PAPER 34

NATIONAL BUREAU OF ECONOMIC RESEARCH, INC.

OFFICERS
(1950)

Boris Shishkin, *Chairman*
Harry Scherman, *President*
C. C. Balderston, *Vice-President*
George B. Roberts, *Treasurer*
W. J. Carson, *Executive Director*
Martha Anderson, *Editor*

DIRECTORS AT LARGE

Donald R. Belcher, *American Telephone and Telegraph Co.*
Oswald W. Knauth, *New York City*
Simon Kuznets, *University of Pennsylvania*
H. W. Laidler, *Executive Director, League for Industrial Democracy*
Shepard Morgan, *New York City*
C. Reinold Noyes, *Princeton, New Jersey*
George B. Roberts, *Vice-President, National City Bank*
Beardsley Ruml, *New York City*
Harry Scherman, *Chairman, Book-of-the-Month Club*
George Soule, *Bennington College*
N. I. Stone, *Consulting Economist*
J. Raymond Walsh, *WMCA Broadcasting Co.*
Leo Wolman, *Columbia University*
Theodore O. Yntema, *Vice-President—Finance, Ford Motor Company*

DIRECTORS BY UNIVERSITY APPOINTMENT

E. Wight Bakke, *Yale*
C. C. Balderston, *Pennsylvania*
Arthur F. Burns, *Columbia*
G. A. Elliott, *Toronto*
Frank W. Fetter, *Northwestern*
H. M. Groves, *Wisconsin*
Gottfried Haberler, *Harvard*
Clarence Heer, *North Carolina*
R. L. Kozelka, *Minnesota*
Paul M. O'Leary, *Cornell*
T. W. Schultz, *Chicago*

DIRECTORS APPOINTED BY OTHER ORGANIZATIONS

Percival F. Brundage, *American Institute of Accountants*
Thomas C. Cochran, *Economic History Association*
Frederick C. Mills, *American Statistical Association*
Stanley H. Ruttenberg, *Congress of Industrial Organizations*
Murray Shields, *American Management Association*
Boris Shishkin, *American Federation of Labor*
Warren C. Waite, *American Farm Economic Association*
Donald H. Wallace, *American Economic Association*

RESEARCH STAFF

Arthur F. Burns, *Director of Research*
Geoffrey H. Moore, *Associate Director of Research*

Moses Abramovitz
Harold Barger
Morris A. Copeland
Daniel Creamer
David Durand
Solomon Fabricant
Milton Friedman
Millard Hastay
W. Braddock Hickman
F. F. Hill
Thor Hultgren
Simon Kuznets
Clarence D. Long
Ruth P. Mack
Frederick C. Mills
Raymond J. Saulnier
Lawrence H. Seltzer
George J. Stigler
Leo Wolman

Relation of the Directors to the Work and Publications of the National Bureau of Economic Research

1. The object of the National Bureau of Economic Research is to ascertain and to present to the public important economic facts and their interpretation in a scientific and impartial manner. The Board of Directors is charged with the responsibility of ensuring that the work of the National Bureau is carried on in strict conformity with this object.

2. To this end the Board of Directors shall appoint one or more Directors of Research.

3. The Director or Directors of Research shall submit to the members of the Board, or to its Executive Committee, for their formal adoption, all specific proposals concerning researches to be instituted.

4. No report shall be published until the Director or Directors of Research shall have submitted to the Board a summary drawing attention to the character of the data and their utilization in the report, the nature and treatment of the problems involved, the main conclusions and such other information as in their opinion would serve to determine the suitability of the report for publication in accordance with the principles of the National Bureau.

5. A copy of any manuscript proposed for publication shall also be submitted to each member of the Board. For each manuscript to be so submitted a special committee shall be appointed by the President, or at his designation by the Executive Director, consisting of three Directors selected as nearly as may be one from each general division of the Board. The names of the special manuscript committee shall be stated to each Director when the summary and report described in paragraph (4) are sent to him. It shall be the duty of each member of the committee to read the manuscript. If each member of the special committee signifies his approval within thirty days, the manuscript may be published. If each member of the special committee has not signified his approval within thirty days of the transmittal of the report and manuscript, the Director of Research shall then notify each member of the Board, requesting approval or disapproval of publication, and thirty additional days shall be granted for this purpose. The manuscript shall then not be published unless at least a majority of the entire Board and a two-thirds majority of those members of the Board who shall have voted on the proposal within the time fixed for the receipt of votes on the publication proposed shall have approved.

6. No manuscript may be published, though approved by each member of the special committee, until forty-five days have elapsed from the transmittal of the summary and report. The interval is allowed for the receipt of any memorandum of dissent or reservation, together with a brief statement of his reasons, that any member may wish to express; and such memorandum of dissent or reservation shall be published with the manuscript if he so desires. Publication does not, however, imply that each member of the Board has read the manuscript, or that either members of the Board in general, or of the special committee, have passed upon its validity in every detail.

7. A copy of this resolution shall, unless otherwise determined by the Board, be printed in each copy of every National Bureau book.

(Resolution adopted October 25, 1926 and revised February 6, 1933 and February 24, 1941)

Behavior of Wage Rates during Business Cycles

DANIEL CREAMER
with the assistance of
MARTIN BERNSTEIN

OCCASIONAL PAPER 34

NATIONAL BUREAU OF ECONOMIC RESEARCH, INC.

My colleagues, A. F. Burns, Geoffrey H. Moore, and Leo Wolman in particular, have contributed in important ways to the development of this paper. I am indebted also to Lorie Tarshis for permission to use his unpublished monthly indexes of wage rates in British manufacturing industries prepared for the National Bureau of Economic Research and to Martha Anderson for editorial assistance. H. Irving Forman drew the charts. I am grateful also for helpful comments from Donald R. Belcher, H. M. Douty, G. A. Elliot, Frank W. Fetter, Stanley H. Ruttenberg, and N. I. Stone.

Daniel Creamer

Price: $1.00

Copyright, 1950, by National Bureau of Economic Research, Inc. 1819 Broadway, New York 23, N. Y. All Rights Reserved Manufactured in the U.S.A. by The Academy Press

CONTENTS

1	Difference between Wage Rates and Average Hourly Earnings	2
2	Data on Wage Rates and Average Hourly Earnings in Manufacturing Industries, United States	5
3	Wage Rates turn later than Business Activity and Employment in Manufacturing Industries, United States	6
4	Similar Lags in the Railroad Industry	22
5	Lags also in British Manufacturing Industries	25
6	Average Hourly Earnings as Indicators of Turning Points in Wage Rates	32
7	Cyclical Amplitudes of Wage Rates and Average Hourly Earnings	34
8	Average Hourly Earnings in a Postwar Contraction	38

APPENDIX

A	Wage Rate Indexes, with Notes on their Construction, and Average Hourly Earnings in Manufacturing, United States	40
B	Wage Rate Indexes, with Notes on their Construction, and Average Hourly Earnings on Class I Railroads, United States	56
C	Cost of Fringe Benefits in Anthracite Coal Mining	60
	Notes on Sources of Data and Methods of Estimating	63

TABLE

1 Cyclical Turning Points in Business Activity, Employment, Wage Rates, and Average Hourly Earnings, All Manufactures, 1919-1938, and Nine Manufacturing Industries, United States, 1919-1930   7

2 Turning Points in Business, Manhours Worked and Wage Rates, Class I Railroads, United States, 1920-1938   22

3 Cyclical Turning Points in British Business Activity and Wage Rates, Seven Branches of British Manufactures, 1920-1939   28

4 Relative Amplitudes of Cyclical Fluctuations in Wage Rates and Average Hourly Earnings, Class I Railroads, United States, 1922-1937   35

5 Amplitude of Fluctuations of Corresponding Specific Cycles in Average Hourly Earnings, Wholesale Prices, and Factory Production and Employment, United States, 1919-1939   37

6 Average Hourly Earnings, Employment, and Production, All Manufacturing Industries, Relative Declines in Specific Cycle Contractions, 1920-1949   39

APPENDIX

A Wage Rate Indexes and Average Hourly Earnings, All Manufactures and Nine Manufacturing Industries, United States   43

B Index of Wage Rates, Employees on an Hourly Basis, Average Hourly Earnings, Employees on an Hourly and Daily Basis: Class I Railroads, United States, 1920-1939   58

C Expenditures of Employers on Wage Supplements, Anthracite Coal Mining, 1939 and 1948   62

CHART

1 Indexes of Wage Rates and Factory Employment and Average Hourly Earnings, All Manufactures, United States, 1919-1939   12

2 Indexes of Wage Rates and Factory Employment and Average Hourly Earnings in Selected Manufacturing Industries, United States, 1919-1931   14

3 Index of Wage Rates and Average Hourly Earnings, All Manufactures, United States, 1923-1931   16

4 Index of Wage Rates, Average Hourly Earnings, and Total Manhours Worked, Class I Railroads, United States, 1920-1939   23

5 Indexes of Wage Rates in Seven Industrial Groups and Percentage of Insured Workers Unemployed, United Kingdom, 1920-1941   26

UNEVENNESS IN THE RATE OF CHANGE IN THE PRICES OF VARIOUS GOODS and services is sometimes advanced as a partial explanation of the changing levels of business activity.[1] The failure of wage rates to respond quickly to change in the pace or direction of movement of business is cited as one of the outstanding examples. However, empirical investigation of the movement of wage rates during business cycles in the United States has been stymied because a measure of changes in wage rates has not been readily available. Previous discussions have relied largely upon average hourly earnings, but wage rates and average hourly earnings are not identical. An investigator must therefore face the question, how well does the movement of hourly earnings represent that of wage rates? The question is of some significance because data on average hourly earnings for the recent past and the near future will continue to be more abundant than materials on wage rates. Hence if we can establish firm relations between the movements of the two series, we can extend our knowledge of the behavior of wage rates by utilizing the fuller body of data on hourly earnings.

We are concerned therefore with two questions: the cyclical behavior of wage rates and the parallelism of the cyclical movement of wage rates and average hourly earnings. To advance our understanding of these matters on an empirical level, we must have a measure of wage rate movements for some years and for some industries covered also by statistics on average hourly earnings. To this end we have constructed monthly indexes of wage rates in all manufacturing industries in the United States, in each of nine branches of manufactures and in interstate railroads, and we utilize similar indexes for manufacturing industries in the United Kingdom.

From an analysis of these materials for the two decades between World War I and II the pattern of the cycical behavior of wage rates emerges. Typically, wage rates turned a substantial number of months later than business activity and employment. The average lag behind business activity for aggregate manufactures, for example, was 9 months in the United States and 11 months in

---

[1] See, e.g., Wesley C. Mitchell, 'Wider Aspects of Business Cycles', *Business Cycles and Their Causes*, Ch. 5, a reprint of Mitchell's *Business Cycles*, Part III (University of California Press, 1941), pp. 149-65. Price disparities were central to Mitchell's own account of what happens during business cycles; moreover, he reduced the core of the business cycle theories of Spiethoff, Sombart, Carver, and Irving Fisher to these terms; see especially pp. 162-5.

the United Kingdom. The lag in turns of wage rates on Class I railroads in the United States was even longer.

With respect to our technical problem of parallelism our analysis suggests that for industry aggregates and at the major turning points of business activity the turning points in average hourly earnings are a reliable indicator of those in wage rates. They are a somewhat less reliable indicator for industry subgroups. We conclude also that the cyclical amplitudes of wage rates and average hourly earnings are closely similar although this judgment rests largely on circumstantial evidence.

If the cyclical amplitudes of average hourly earnings can be taken to approximate those of wage rates, the cyclical amplitude of wage rates in manufacturing have been considerably smaller than those of factory production and employment or of wholesale prices of raw materials and, with minor exceptions, of semifinished goods. In contractions this has been true also of the declines in wage rates compared with the declines in the wholesale prices of finished commodities, but in half of the expansions the amplitudes of wage rates substantially exceeded those of the wholesale prices of finished commodities. The relation was reversed at minor expansions.

1 *Difference between Wage Rates and Average Hourly Earnings*
The time and piece rate are the two basic systems of wage payment. The time rate, the basis of compensation for a specified period of labor, usually an hour, is generally expressed as an hourly rate. The wages of workers hired by the day or week can be expressed as an hourly rate merely by dividing the standard wage payment for the day or week by the standard number of hours worked per day or week.

The basic hourly rate, 'straight time', is the remuneration for an hour's labor performed during the day shift in the course of the normal workweek. Hours worked in excess of the hours comprising the standard workweek are usually compensated at a higher rate, 'overtime', figured as a specified percentage of the straight-time hourly rate. Work on an evening or night shift also is frequently compensated at premium rates, determined by adding an absolute amount, called a 'shift differential', to the straight-time hourly rate. These arrangements make the straight-time hourly rate the pivotal time rate.

The piece rate, the price paid per unit of physical output, is the simplest form of an incentive method of payment. The more a worker produces in a given period, the higher his wage receipts. For this reason it is difficult to translate a piece rate into a time rate, or vice versa, and therefore to combine the two types of rate into a composite wage rate or index.[2]

Whether this translation has been done correctly by the reporting establishments cannot be determined. What we have done is to take the reported percentage changes from month to month in wage rates, whether time or piece, weight and chain them to obtain an index of wage rates (App. A). Wage rate indexes of this character can be constructed for individual manufacturing industries as well as for aggregate manufactures. At best, they measure only average changes in the schedules of wage rates, not changes in average wage rates caused by relative shifts in high and low wage industries, establishments, or occupations.

Management is more directly concerned with measuring the average cost of employing labor for a stated period, say an hour, or the average labor cost per unit of output. The latter measure cannot be derived satisfactorily in time series form because of deficiencies in our data; the former, labor cost per hour, however, has been adequately measured, at least between World War I and II, by average hourly earnings.[3]

Hourly earnings are computed by dividing total wage receipts in

---

[2] According to surveys by the National Industrial Conference Board in 1924 and 1935, about 56 percent of factory wage earners were paid on a time-rate basis, the rest on some form of incentive basis. In the establishments covered, employing upward of 700,000 workers, the percentage paid on a time-rate basis was virtually identical in the two surveys (*Monthly Labor Review,* Department of Labor, Vol. 41, No. 3, Sept. 1935, pp. 697-700).

A Bureau of Labor Statistics survey in 1945-46 of a much larger sample, 15,600 establishments employing 3.2 million workers, disclosed that 70 percent received a time-rate wage (ibid., Vol. 65, No. 5, Nov. 1947, pp. 535-8). It is uncertain how much of the difference can be attributed to differences in the sample and how much to a change in policy largely induced by the more extensive unionization of factory workers in the late 'thirties.

[3] In the years following World War II neither concept, wage rates or average hourly earnings, serves its former purpose in many industries because some of the 'fringe' payments to labor, to provide various types of social security, are excluded from the statistics on hourly earnings and wage rates. For the relative size of such payments in one industry see Appendix C.

a given period by the number of hours worked.[4] Changes in average hourly earnings in a given industry reflect not only changes in hourly rates and in piece rates but also the influence of various other factors. If, for example, the premiums paid for overtime or for extra shifts, or the prevalence of work compensated at premium rates change, straight-time rates will not be affected but hourly earnings will. Shifts in the relative number of high and low paid workers or of high and low wage plants also would affect average hourly earnings even though rates remained the same. Changes in the relative amount of work compensated on time- and piece-rate bases would have similar effects since hourly earnings at an identical task tend to be higher for piece workers.[5] Changes in the productivity of piece-rate workers are another factor that might cause hourly earnings and wage rates to diverge. The up- and downgrading of jobs is another example of change that influences the relative movement of hourly earnings but not nominal wage rates. In other words, a given task, without any alteration in the requirements, may be designated by an occupational title that qualifies it for a higher (upgrading) or a lower hourly rate (downgrading).

Another important difference is the fact that changes in wage rate schedules in a given industry are not continuous and are usually in response to substantial alterations in the previous relationships between the supply of and the demand for labor. Average hourly earnings, on the contrary, tend to change continuously, reflecting the adjustments induced by even moderate changes in the level of production. The extent to which the differences in the two concepts are the source of differences in cyclical behavior depends upon the cyclical pattern of the factors that are superimposed upon wage rates to yield hourly earnings.

Since average hourly earnings in a given industry are more sensitive than wage rates to changes in the level of production, it is questionable how well relative movements in hourly earnings represent relative movements in wage rates. Any difference in relative movements could, of course, be ascertained by comparing the two series in identical industries.

[4] 'Hours worked' actually means hours paid for in the case of time-rate workers and nominal hours in the case of piece-rate workers. That is, it includes 'stand-by time' when no work is performed.
[5] For evidence see Effect of Incentive Payments on Hourly Earnings, BLS *Bulletin* 742 (1943), p. 9.

2 Data on Wage Rates and Average Hourly Earnings in Manufacturing Industries, United States

From 1919 to 1935 the Bureau of Labor Statistics compiled data monthly on changes in wage rates based on reports from establishments in its employment and payroll sample. It published the number of establishments reporting specified percentage changes in rates from January 1919 to April 1923; we weighted the percentage changes in rates by the number of establishments affected. From April 1923 to August 1931 we used the number of employees affected as weights and carried the establishment-weighted indexes forward through December 1923 to observe the effect of the shift in weights. After August 1931 the BLS published the relative changes in wage rates and employees affected only for all manufacturing industries combined. In July 1935 it discontinued the series because of inherent deficiencies and in the belief that the average hourly earnings series instituted in 1932 covered much the same ground. Hence our indexes for the nine industries end with August 1931 and for all manufactures with July 1935 (App. A).

One inherent deficiency is the unavoidable assumption that establishments not reporting a change in wage rates made no change. Since the reports are monthly and since changes in wage rates are fairly infrequent one would expect the proportion of establishments not making any change in a given month to be large. Nevertheless, our assumption may understate the proportion somewhat since some firms that changed wage rates may simply have failed to report.[6] The effect would be to make our indexes more stable than they should be, but to what degree we do not know.[7]

The only monthly series on average hourly earnings in manufacturing that cover most of these years, and are therefore available for comparison with the wage rate indexes, are those compiled by the National Industrial Conference Board. From its 25 industry series we selected 9 for which the size of the samples seems most adequate and the coverage comparable in definition with the BLS

[6] For the percentage of all factory workers affected by changes in wage rates, see Appendix A.

[7] This inference involves the further assumption that a majority of the firms not reporting changes in a given month instituted changes in the same direction in which the index moved. This assumption seems plausible in the light of Section 7 where we could not explain the differences in amplitude of the cyclical movements in wage rates and average hourly earnings by the differences in concepts.

industry designations. For these 9, monthly movements in wage rates and in average hourly earnings can be compared (Table 1 and Charts 1-2). The deficiencies of samples in individual industries are probably less serious when the 25 industries are combined into a single series for all manufacturing, although the manufacture of food products, clothing, and construction materials seems under-represented. In the absence of a more satisfactory series, we compare average hourly earnings for all manufacturing compiled by the NICB with the index of wage rates for all manufacturing based on the industry samples of the BLS, which has a broader coverage.

Because our interest is centered in cyclical behavior these series must be adjusted to eliminate possible seasonal movements; i.e., seasonally adjusted average hourly earnings are compared with the unadjusted index of wage rates since the latter does not seem to require adjustment.

3 Wage Rates turn later than Business Activity and Employment in Manufacturing Industries, United States

Let us examine first the movement of wage rates. Among the first impressions we get from Charts 1 and 2 is that wage rates declined sharply from 1920 to 1922, made a substantial but partial recovery by 1923, and continued at the 1923 level with minor variations until 1930 or thereabouts when the impact of the Great Depression began to affect their level. On closer inspection, however, we find that the minor movements during this period of relative stability, 1923-30, have a cyclical character. This is illustrated by Chart 3 which shows the movement for these years for all manufactures computed to 2 decimal places and plotted on a generous scale.[8] The amplitudes of the cyclical phases are so very small that we are compelled to distinguish between the major and minor cyclical movements in wage rates. The former are the movements that correspond to the contraction of business activity from January 1920 to July 1921, the succeeding expansion from July 1921 to May 1923, and the contraction initiated in June 1929. The minor cyclical move-

---

[8] Cycles appear during this period in 5 of the 9 individual industries when the data are computed to 2 decimal places and plotted on a generous scale: automobile, iron and steel, paper and pulp, silk and rayon, and woolen and worsted manufactures (Table 1).

TABLE 1

Cyclical Turning Points in Business Activity, Employment, Wage Rates, and Average Hourly Earnings All Manufactures, 1919-1938, and Nine Manufacturing Industries, United States, 1919-1930

LEVEL OF BUS. ACT.	DATE OF TURNING POINT IN						LEAD (−), LAG (+), OR COINCIDENCE (0), MONTHS							
	Bus. act.[a]	Empl.[b]	Wage rates		Average hourly earn.		Rates & bus. act.		Earn. & bus. act.		Rates & empl.		Rates & earn.	
			SM	A	SM	A	SM	A	SM	A	SM	A		A

ALL MANUFACTURES

Trough	4/19	3/19			c	c			c	c				
Peak	1/20	1/20	10/20	10/20	10/20	10/20	+9	+9	+9	+9	+9	+9	0	c
Trough	7/21	7/21	4/22	4/22	c	c	+9	+9	c	c	+9	+9	c	c
Peak	5/23	6/23	1/24	1/24	11/24	12/23	+8	+8	+18	+7	+7	+7	+1	+1
Trough	7/24	7/24	12/25	12/25	9/25	9/25	+17	+17	+14	+14	+17	+17	+3	+3
Peak	10/26	1/26			8/27		+3		+10		+12			
Trough	11/27	1/28			2/28		+14		+3					
Peak	6/29	8/29	1/30	6/30	4/30	8/30	+7	+12	+10	+14	+5	+10	−2	−2
Trough	3/33	7/32	5/33	5/33	6/33	6/33	+2	+2	+3	+3	+10	+10	−1	−1
Peak	5/37	7/37	c	c	3/38	10/37	c	c	+8	+5	c	c	c	c
Trough	6/38	6/38	c	c	2/39	2/39	c	c	+8	+8	c	c	c	c
Average							+8.6	+9.5	+9.6[d]	+9.4[d]	+10.1	+10.3		+0.2

AUTOMOBILES

Trough	4/19	5/19			c				c	c				
Peak	1/20	1/20	9/20	9/20	7/20		+8	+8	+6	+9	+8	+8	+2	+2
Trough	7/21	1/21	4/22	4/22	c		+9	+9	c	c	+15	+15	c	c
Peak	5/23	1/24	9/23	5/23	2/24		+4	0	+9	+7	−4	−8	−9	−9
Trough	7/24	7/24	12/24		9/24		+5		+2		+5			
Peak	10/26	11/25												
Trough	11/27	10/27												
Peak	6/29	2/29	6/30	7/30	7/30		+12	+13	+13		+16	+17	0	
Average							+7.6	+7.5	+7.5	+8.0	+8.0		

TABLE I (cont.)

DATE OF TURNING POINT IN — LEAD (—), LAG (+), OR COINCIDENCE (0), MONTHS

LEVEL OF BUS. ACT.	Bus. act.[a]	Empl.[b]	Wage rates SM	Wage rates A	Average hourly earn. SM	Average hourly earn. A	Rates & bus. act. SM	Rates & bus. act. A	Earn. & bus. act. SM	Earn. & bus. act. A	Rates & empl. SM	Rates & empl. A	Rates & earn. A
					BOOTS AND SHOES								
Trough	4/19	3/19			c				c				
Peak	1/20	12/19	12/20	12/20	2/21		+11	+11	+13		+12	+12	−2
Trough	7/21	1/21			c		+13[e]	+13[e]	c				c
		9/21											
		4/22	8/22[e]	8/22[e]									
Peak	5/23	4/23	1/24	11/23	3/24		+8	+6	+10		+4	+4	−4
Trough	7/24	7/24			11/25[f]				+16[f]		+9	+7	
		3/25											
		4/26											
Peak	10/26	12/26			7/26				−3				
Trough	11/27	8/28			4/27				−7				
Peak	6/29	11/29	2/30	2/30	1/30		+8	+8	+7		+3	+3	+1
Average							+10.7	+9.5	+6.0		+8.3	+6.5	
					ELECTRICAL GOODS								
Peak	1/20	10/20	c	c	10/20		c	c	+9				c
Trough	7/21	10/21	c	c	c		c	c	c				c
Peak	5/23	8/23		6/23			+1	+1				−2	
Trough	7/24	11/24			5/25								
					1/26								
Peak	10/26	1/26											
Trough	11/27	5/27											
Peak	6/29	7/29	9/30	11/30	6/30		+15	+17	+12		+14	+16	+5
Averages													

		DATE OF TURNING POINT IN						LEAD (−), LAG (+), OR COINCIDENCE (o), MONTHS					
LEVEL OF BUS. ACT.	Bus. act.[a]	Empl.[b]	Wage rates		Average hourly earn.		Rates & bus. act.		Earn. & bus. act.		Rates & empl.		Rates & earn.
			SM	A	SM	A	SM	A	SM	A	SM	A	A
IRON AND STEEL													
Trough	4/19	5/19	8/19	8/19	c		+4	+4	c		+3	+3	c
Peak	1/20	3/20	11/20	11/20	11/20		+10	+10	+10		+8	+8	0
Trough	7/21	7/21	4/22	4/22	c		+9	+9	c		+9	+9	c
Peak	5/23	8/23	3/24	10/23	11/23		+10	+5	+6		+7	+2	−1
Trough	7/24	8/24	1/26	1/26	12/24		+18	+18	+5		+17	+17	+13
Peak	10/26	2/26	2/27		+4						+12		
Trough	11/27	12/27	6/28		+7						+6		
Peak	6/29	8/29	12/29	5/30	8/30		+6	+11	+14		+4	+9	−3
Average							+8.5	+9.5	+8.8		+8.2	+8.0	
PAPER AND PULP													
Peak	1/20	7/20	11/20	11/20	12/20		+10	+10	+11	+11	+4	+4	−1
Trough	7/21	6/21	6/22	6/22	c		+11	+11	c	c	+12	+12	c
Peak	5/23	4/23	12/23	6/23	8/23		+7	+1		+3	+8	+2	−2
Trough	7/24	7/24	11/24		c		+4				+4		
Peak	10/26	2/26											
Trough	11/27	2/28											
Peak	6/29	1/30	11/29	12/30	11/30		+5	+18	+17	+17	−2	+11	+1
Average							+7.4	+10.0	+10.3		+5.2	+7.2	
RUBBER TIRES AND TUBES													
Trough	7/21	2/21	c	c	c		c	c	c		c		c
Peak	5/23	3/23	7/23	7/23	8/23		+2	+2	+3		+4	+4	−1
Trough	7/24	7/24		9/23	10/23			−10	−9			−10	−1
Peak	10/26	12/25			12/27[h]				h				
Trough	11/27	7/26			7/28[h]				h				
Peak	6/29	4/29		6/30	3/31		+12	+12	+21			+14	−9
Average							+1.3	+1.3	+5.0			+2.7	

TABLE I (concl.)

DATE OF TURNING POINT IN

LEAD (−), LAG (+), OR COINCIDENCE (0), MONTHS

LEVEL OF BUS. ACT.	Bus. act.[a]	Empl.[b]	Wage rates		Average hourly earn.		Rates & bus. act.		Earn. & bus. act.		Rates & empl.		Rates & earn.
			SM	A	SM	A	SM	A	SM	A	SM	A	A

SILK AND RAYON

Trough	4/19	2/19											+1
Peak	1/20	5/20	10/20	10/20	9/20		+9	+9	+8		+5	+5	c
Trough	7/21	1/21, 9/21, 8/22	8/22[e]	8/22[e]	c		+13[e]	+13[e]	c	c	c	0	−6
Peak	5/23	5/23	4/24	6/23	12/23		+11	+1	+7		+11	0	
Trough	7/24	7/24	9/24		12/24		+2		+5		+2	+1	
Peak	10/26	1/26	11/26		1/27		+1		+3		+10		
Trough	11/27	2/28					+3				+20		
Peak	6/29		5/29	4/30	9/29, 3/30[f]		−1	+10			−2	+9	+1[1]
Average		7/29					+5.4	+8.2	+5.8		+6.6	+3.8	

SLAUGHTERING AND MEAT PACKING

Trough	7/21	12/21	c	c			c	c	c		c	c	c
Peak	5/23	9/23		5/23	c	6/23	c	c	c	+1	c	−4	−1
Trough	7/24	7/26											
Peak	10/26												
Trough	11/27												
Peak	6/29	11/29	3/30	3/30	3/30		+5	+9	+9	+9	+1	+5	0
Average[g]													

WOOLENS AND WORSTEDS

| Peak | 1/20 | c, 1/21, 9/21 | 10/20 | 10/20 | c | | +9 | +9 | c | c | c | c | c |
| Trough | 7/21 | 7/22 | 8/22 | 8/22 | 8/22 | | +13 | +13 | +13 | +13 | +1 | +1 | 0 |

Peak	5/23	7/23	3/24	5/23	5/23	+10	0	+8	−2	0
Trough	7/24	7/24 3/25 3/26		7/25 10/25	6/24 4/25 8/26^h		−1			+3 −10
Peak	10/26	1/27			12/27^h	+17				
Trough	11/27	9/28	4/29		12/29^i	+5	+12	+7 +1	+8	−1^i
Peak	6/29	10/29	11/29	6/30	7/30^i					
Average						+10.8	+8.5	+4.2	+2.3	

AVERAGE FOR 9 INDUSTRIES

Peak	1/20		+9.5	+9.5	+7.4	+7.4
Trough	7/21		+11.3	+11.3	+9.2	+9.2
Peak	5/23		+7.4	+1.8	+5.8	+6.1	0
Trough	7/24		+7.2		+3.0	+7.0	
Peak	10/26		+9.0			+11.0	
Trough	11/27		+6.7	+12.2	+13.3	+4.6	+10.2
Peak	6/29						
Averages at all turning points in 9 industries			+8.0	+8.0	+7.2	+6.8	+5.6	−0.9

SM: standard method; A: alternate method.

a The turning points in business activity are NBER reference cycle dates.

b BLS employment indexes were used for all manufactures, automobiles, boots and shoes, iron and steel, silk and rayon, and slaughtering and meat packing; NICB employment indexes for rubber products, electrical goods, woolens and worsteds, and paper and pulp. All employment indexes were corrected for seasonal fluctuations.

c The data are insufficient or unavailable to determine turning points.

d The lags between the turning points in earnings and the 5/37 and 6/38 turning points in business activity are not included in the average.

e The 8/22 trough in wage rates corresponds to the 7/21 trough in business activity.

f The 11/25 trough in average hourly earnings corresponds to the 4/26 trough in employment.

g Average omitted since it would be based on only two observations.

h No corresponding turn in business activity.

i Although the turning point in hourly earnings does not correspond to any turning point in business activity, it does correspond to a turning point in wage rates.

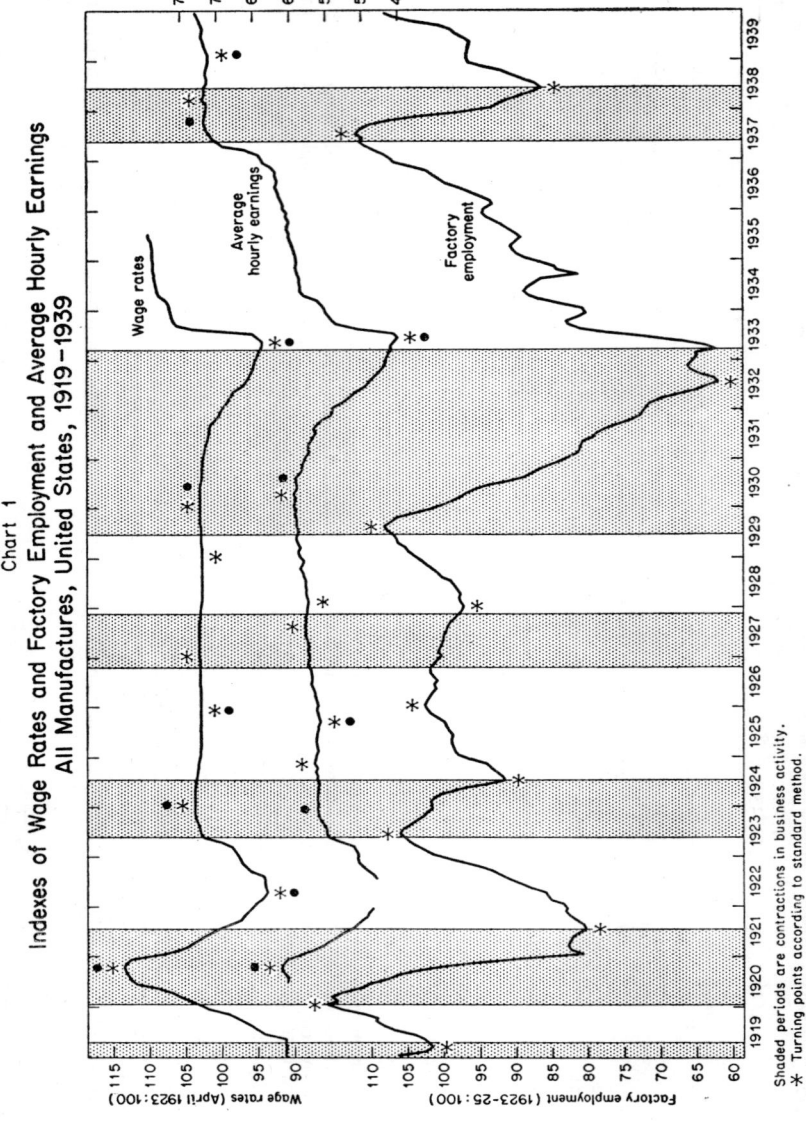

Chart 1

Indexes of Wage Rates and Factory Employment and Average Hourly Earnings
All Manufactures, United States, 1919–1939

ments are those that correspond to movements in business activity between May 1923, the end of the recovery from the postwar deflation of World War I, and June 1929, the inception of the Great Depression.

Recognition of the two orders of cycles in wage rates is the reason for introducing two dates for the beginning and end of certain cyclical movements. In the first instance the standard NBER procedure for marking off cyclical phases was applied to our indexes of wage rates (computed to 2 decimal places), average hourly earnings, and employment.[9] The dates of these turning points in all cycles, major and minor, mark the dates of reversal in the direction of the cyclical movements of each series. However, the strict application of the standard procedure to minor cycles in wage rates and average hourly earnings does not in all cases designate changes that are most significant for us since the cyclical movements prior and subsequent to the turning point may be of very slight amplitude because both wage rates and hourly earnings tend to fluctuate within a relatively narrow range and are subject to erratic movements. If the series were smoothed, the turning points might well differ from those based on the original data. The standard procedure, in effect, selects turning points in the unsmoothed series while the alternate procedure allows implicitly for smoothing by using the dates that terminate or initiate substantial changes in wage rates or hourly earnings. That is, we marked off the beginning and end of plateau-like movements that characterize some phases of minor cycles. Such points do not necessarily coincide with the turning points that mark reversals in direction (Table 1). The degree of parallelism of movement between wage rates and average hourly earnings can best be judged by using the alternate turning points.

This difference in method may be illustrated by our selection of turning points in the wage rate index for the iron and steel industry. The period that creates difficulties is 1923-30. When the index computed to 2 decimal places for these years is plotted on a generous scale, our standard method would select the following turning points: peak, March 1924; trough, January 1926; peak, February 1927; trough, June 1928; peak, December 1929. Accord-

[9] For a description of this procedure, see Burns and Mitchell, *Measuring Business Cycles* (NBER, 1946), Ch. 4, pp. 56-114.

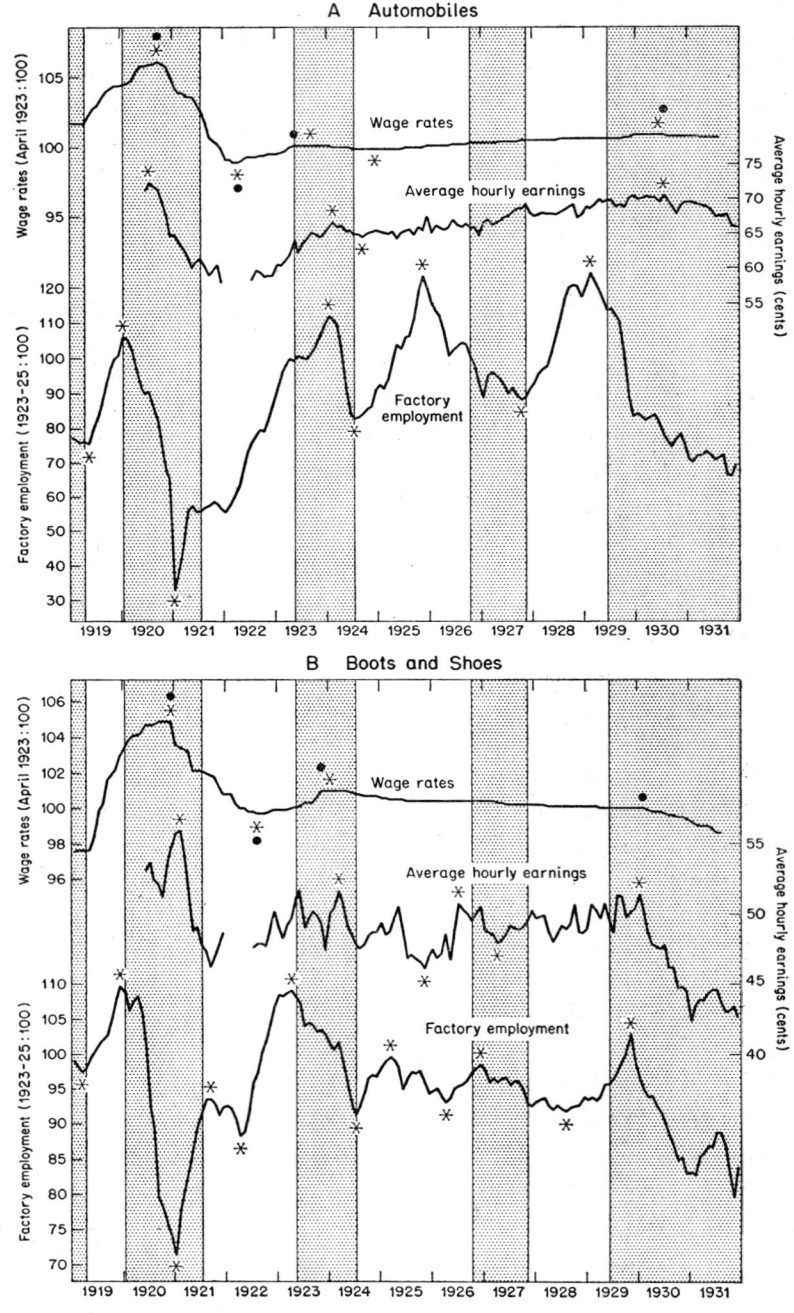

Chart 2
Indexes of Wage Rates and Factory Employment and Average Hourly Earnings in Selected Manufacturing Industries United States, 1919–1931

Chart 2 (concl.)

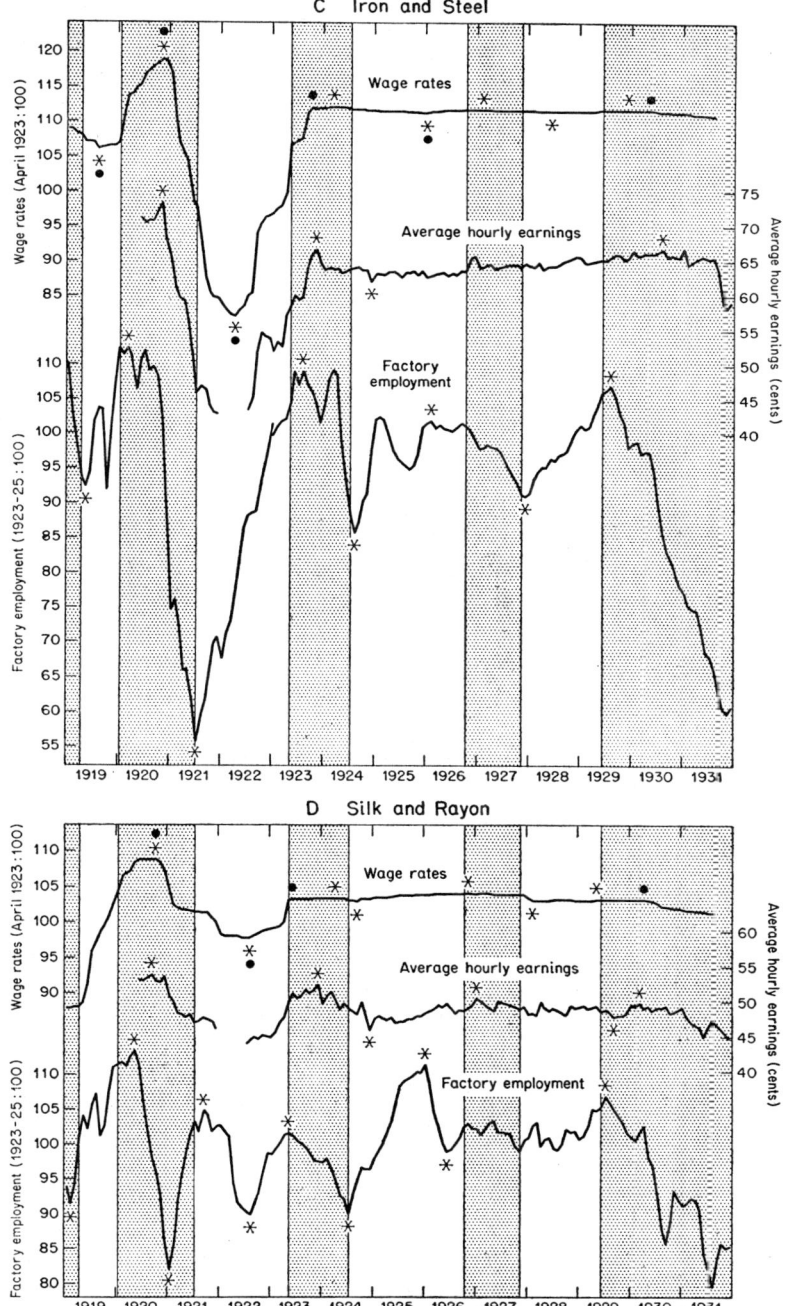

Shaded periods are contractions in business activity.
✳ Turning points according to standard method.
● Turning points according to alternate method.

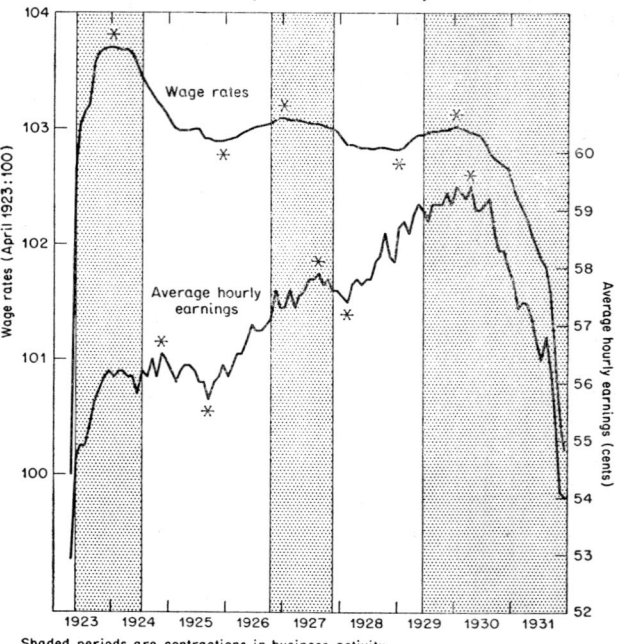

Chart 3
Index of Wage Rates and Average Hourly Earnings
All Manufactures, United States, 1923–1931

Shaded periods are contractions in business activity.
✷ Turning points according to standard method.

ing to our alternate method we reason that the series entered upon a plateau in October 1923 and this date should replace the March 1924 peak. In support we call attention to the fact that the month to month change in the index between October 1923 and March 1924 did not exceed one-tenth of a point in the index whereas before October 1923 the month to month changes were relatively much larger (see App. Table A, Iron and Steel Industry). The subsequent turning points up to the beginning of the Great Depression are disregarded because the cyclical amplitudes (the difference in standings between peak and trough or between trough and peak) are very small. Using the alternate method, we date the be-

	CONTRACTION 3/24-1/26	EXPANSION 1/26-2/27	CONTRACTION 2/27-6/28	EXPANSION 6/28-12/29
Cyclical amplitude of phase as a % of initial standing	—0.71	+0.45	—0.18	+0.09

ginning of the downturn that corresponds with the Great Depression at May 1930 rather than December 1929 because the month to month changes between the two dates were less than one-tenth of a point while after May 1930 they were at least one-tenth of a point and continued steadily downward.

As we have seen, wage rates in United States manufacturing industries turn later than business activity and employment. Moreover, at most turning points in both business activity and employment the lag has been substantial and the use of the alternate turning points does not substantially modify this general conclusion.[10] We shall confine our comments, therefore, to the results based on the standard dating of turning points, unless otherwise noted.

The wage rate index for all manufactures lagged behind business activity or factory employment at all turning points, major and minor, between 1920 and 1933. The lag behind business activity averaged 9 months, and at 6 of the 8 turns exceeded 6 months. The average lag at the major turning points was 7 months. At only one of the major turns in business activity was the lag so brief as to qualify as a rough coincidence—2 months at the trough of the 1929-33 depression. Not only did wage rates begin to rise only 2 months after the revival in business but they rose swiftly.[11] This exceptional recovery was caused by the negotiations under the terms of the National Recovery Act whereby the workweek was shortened without reducing weekly earnings. The rise in wage rates under the circumstances was automatic.

This direct intervention of the federal government in determining wage rates was an innovation that probably may be regarded as marking an institutional change in the economic environment in which wage rates change. General changes in wage rates at that point became the concern of the federal government, which has since conditioned the movement of wage rates either directly

[10] The main changes due to the alternate dating of turns are a reduction in the lag behind the peak of business activity in May 1923 in the individual industries and a lengthening of the lag at the June 1929 peak in all the series. Wage rates and employment are similarly affected.

[11] According to Chart 1 the 1929 level of wage rates was more than restored within 3 months after the low point in wage rates had been reached. This rate of recovery, however, is an exaggeration because the preceding declines are not fully reflected in the index while the rises of the recovery period are fully reported since they are due to federal legislation and public negotiation. The movements in average hourly earnings during this period probably represent the changes in wage rates more accurately.

through minimum wage legislation or indirectly through promotion of collective bargaining and social insurance (see Sec. 6).

Turning points in employment might be thought to have a more immediate effect on wage rates since they mark the point when the number of unemployed competing for jobs changes. This assumed relation is not supported by our index of wage rates for all manufactures. Wage rates turned on the average 10 months later than factory employment. At no turn was the lag less than 5 months, and the lags at the minor turns were longer than at the major turns.

The business contractions of 1920-21 and 1929-33, judged by amplitude of movement, were among the severest in our recent history. The former downturn stopped within a year and a half while the latter continued for nearly four years. Some have attributed the shorter duration of the earlier contraction to a speedier adjustment of price relationships. To appraise the validity of this thesis in general would go beyond the scope of this Paper. Our materials, however, do bear on one price series, the price of labor, and to see whether it supports or refutes the above thesis seems pertinent.

Business activity reached a peak in January 1920 but wage rates in all manufactures not until October (see Table 1). That is, industrial wage rates did not begin to decline until the recession in business activity had been under way for 9 months. The lag was of about the same length at the onset of the Great Depression. Business activity reached a peak in June 1929 and wage rates in January 1930, according to the standard procedure, or in June 1930, according to the alternate procedure, i.e., wage rates lagged 7 to 12 months. The inception of the wage rate adjustment may therefore be said to have been equally speedy or slow in both contractions.

Nonetheless, wage rates moved very differently in these two contractions. In the first, the downward adjustment, once begun, proceeded rapidly—at 1.0 percent a month. During the first half of the contraction the rate of decline per month was even higher, 1.3 percent. In the Great Depression, on the other hand, it was much less—0.2 percent from the peak in June 1930. Moreover, in the first half of this contraction the monthly rate of decrease was half of the average rate for the entire contraction.[12]

[12] As we shall see in Section 7, cyclical amplitudes and rates of change in wage rates are probably more accurately measured by average hourly earnings than by our index

This difference in the rates of decline in wage rates can be explained in large part by the differences in the movements during the months preceding the respective contractions. The peak in 1920 was the culmination of a very sharp rise initiated during World War I and continuing through the postwar inflation years. From May 1919 to October 1920, for example, wage rates increased 25 percent, and the subsequent deflation must be read against the background of this preceding upward spiral. The downturn in wage rates in 1930, in contrast, came after about 7 years of stability. The need for a realignment of wage rates, therefore, was much less obvious than in the earlier contraction. Moreover, the attitude of leading government officials and industrialists was different. At the outset of the Great Depression they exhorted employers to maintain wage rates and share employment. In the 1920-22 depression there seems to have been no such campaign.

The lagged movement of the wage rate index for all manufactures cannot be attributed to its composite character, for this delayed reaction of wage rates to changes in business activity is evident in all 9 industries. At all except 1 of the 36 corresponding turning points wage rates in each of the 9 manufacturing branches lagged behind business activity. The lags for the 9 industries averaged 8 months, almost the same as the average for the composite index: 5 or more months at all except 8 turning points; and 5 of the 8 relatively short lags were at the minor turns. The average lag ranged from 5 months in the silk and rayon industry to 11 in the manufacture of woolen and worsted goods and boots and shoes. In 3 industries— electrical goods, rubber tires and tubes, and slaughtering and meat packing—the lack of sensitivity of wage rates to changes in business activity is revealed in a failure to trace cycles instead of substantial lags. While business activity, for example, reversed its movement 5 times between 1923 and 1929, wage rates in each of these 3 industries reversed their movements only once.

Wage rates consistently lagged behind business activity on the average, at all the turning points in business activity as well as in all the industries in our sample. The lag ranged from nearly 7

---

of wage rates. However, if we substitute the former, differences in movement during the two depressions are the same although somewhat less marked. For example, in the 1920-22 contraction the rate of change per month was —1.0 percent; for the first half —1.7. In the Great Depression the comparable figures were —0.7 and —0.5.

months behind the peak of business activity in June 1929 to 11 months behind the trough in July 1921. Our observations are too few, unfortunately, to tell whether it has been lengthening, shrinking, or has remained about the same, or whether its length differs significantly at peaks and troughs of business activity.

As in all manufactures, wage rates in all 9 industries lagged behind employment and by about the same interval on the average as behind business activity (see Table 1). This is true also for each of the 9 industries except woolen and worsted goods, in which the average lag was 4 months; the average lag behind turns in business activity was 11 months. The depressed state of the woolen and worsted goods industry during the 1920's probably accounts for its somewhat greater sensitivity; in addition, it has more cycles than business activity.

The lag of wage rates at peaks of employment suggests that the downward pressure of shrinking employment opportunities on wage rates does not take effect, on the average, until about 6 months after employment itself has begun to decline.

Some of the major reasons for this sluggish reaction of wage rates to altered conditions in business activity and employment seem clear. The chief one may well be that cyclical turning points are recognized only after the event; during the transition from one phase to another, an employer cannot know whether a change in the level of his business activity will prove to be a minor fluctuation or a sustained change. The diversity of dates at which activity in each firm changes would certainly contribute to the creation of lags in wage rates. Near the peak of prosperity, for example, the firms of a given industry whose activity has declined may be loath to reduce wage rates because they want to retain the goodwill of their employees and hope that the downturn is minor and temporary. On the other hand, firms continuing to expand their business may grant increases in wage rates, thereby causing the average wage rate for the industry to rise. In unionized manufacturing industries, of which there were few between 1919 and 1935,[13] negotiations for

[13] Factory workers organized in trade unions were estimated to constitute only 11 to 16 percent of all factory workers between 1923 and 1933, and by 1935 wage agreements covered only about a quarter of all factory workers. Only in the clothing industry, excluding boots and shoes, was as much as a half of the labor force unionized; in the printing and publishing trades, long regarded as a stronghold of union-

higher wage rates under contracts that expire before the peak may be initiated before the peak but not be concluded until after the downturn. If the wage contract expired after the peak, the downward adjustment of wage rates would automatically lag.

At cyclical troughs too, certain factors make wage rates lag behind business activity or employment. The upturn is usually not recognized as such when it occurs, and employers are still keenly conscious of the necessity of reducing costs because of the lively competition due to large unused capacity. Competition for jobs is equally keen because of widespread and, in many instances, prolonged unemployment. The continued decline in retail prices after employment begins to expand and the rise in 'take-home' pay due to a fuller workweek are other reasons why wage earners do not effectively resist further reductions in hourly rates.[14] Moreover, in

---

ism, only 25 to 31 percent of the workers were members of unions. Leo Wolman, *Ebb and Flow in Trade Unionism* (NBER, 1936), pp. 128, 224, 226, and 227.

This is one of our reasons for not utilizing the BLS series on union wage rates. These data have other serious limitations for our purposes: in only two trades, building and printing, do they extend back of 1929. Thus their industrial coverage is narrow. Of more consequence is the fact that union wage rates are reported only once a year. For an analysis of cyclical timing annual data are much too crude. The nominal character of union wage rates also poses a problem. In the building trades, particularly, deviations from union rates have been notorious.

However, if one is willing to ignore all their defects, these two series confirm our findings on the lag of wage rates behind general business.

DATES OF CYCLICAL TURNING POINTS

LEVEL OF BUSINESS ACTIVITY		UNION HOURLY WAGE RATES		LEVEL OF BUSINESS ACTIVITY		UNION HOURLY WAGE RATES	
		Building trades	Printing trades			Building trades	Printing trades
Peak	1907		*	Trough	1921	1922	
Trough	1908		*	Peak	1923		
Peak	1910		*	Trough	1924		
Trough	1911		*	Peak	1926		
Peak	1913			Trough	1927		
Trough	1914			Peak	1929	1931	1931
Peak	1918			Trough	1932	1933	1933
Trough	1919			Peak	1937		
Peak	1920	1921		Trough	1938		

* Data not available.
Source: *Handbook of Labor Statistics, 1947* (Department of Labor), Table C-8, p. 100.

[14] The consumer price index usually lags behind cyclical turning points in business activity; e.g., at the 5 peaks in business activity between 1920 and 1937, the timing of its turning points was respectively +5, +9, −6, +2, and +5; and at the 5 troughs between 1921 and 1938, +14, +1, +17, +1, and +12 (a plus indicates a lag; a minus a lead; the unit of measurement is a month).

industries where wage rates are controlled by collective agreements it would be sheer coincidence if a contract expired exactly at the trough of employment or of business activity. And contracts expiring before the trough would hardly be renewed at higher rates.

4 Similar Lags in the Railroad Industry

Wage rates in the railroad industry too turn later than business activity or employment (Chart 4). Our index of wage rates for railroads was computed in much the same way as our index for manufactures. However, because railroad wage negotiations are so centralized and public the record of changes in wage rates on Class I railroads is more nearly complete (see App. B).

Wage rates in the railroad industry did not trace mild cycles in the middle 1920's or short phases such as the contraction of 1937-38. Nor did the wage rate index reflect the May 1923 peak. With these exceptions, wage rates turned at each major turn in business: January 1920, July 1921, June 1929, and March 1933 (Table 2). However, they turned 14-31 months later, the lag averaging sightly more than 19 months.[15] Indeed, the lags in 1920 and 1922 are so long that wage rates may be said to run counter to business activity. Compared with the turning points in railroad employment (manhours worked) the lags in wage rates were somewhat shorter but still substantial, ranging from 8 to 29 months.

The average lag in railroad wage rates was about twice that in manufacturing. At two peaks the downturn came 8 and 24 months

TABLE 2

Turning Points in Business, Manhours Worked and Wage Rates Class I Railroads, United States, 1920-1938

BUSINESS ACTIVITY		TURNING POINTS IN R.R.		LAG OF WAGE RATES BEHIND	
Level	Turning points	Manhours worked	Wage rates	Business activity	Manhours worked
				(months)	
Peak	1/20		6/21	17	
Trough	7/21	1/22	9/22	14	8
Peak	5/23	8/23			
Trough	7/24	6/24			
Peak	10/26	7/26			
Trough	11/27	4/28			
Peak	6/29	8/29	1/32	31	29
Trough	3/33	4/33	6/34	15	14

[15] If the beginning of the wage rate plateau in October 1937, which continued until the latter part of 1941, is taken as a peak, the lag would be 5 months behind the peak of business activity in May 1937.

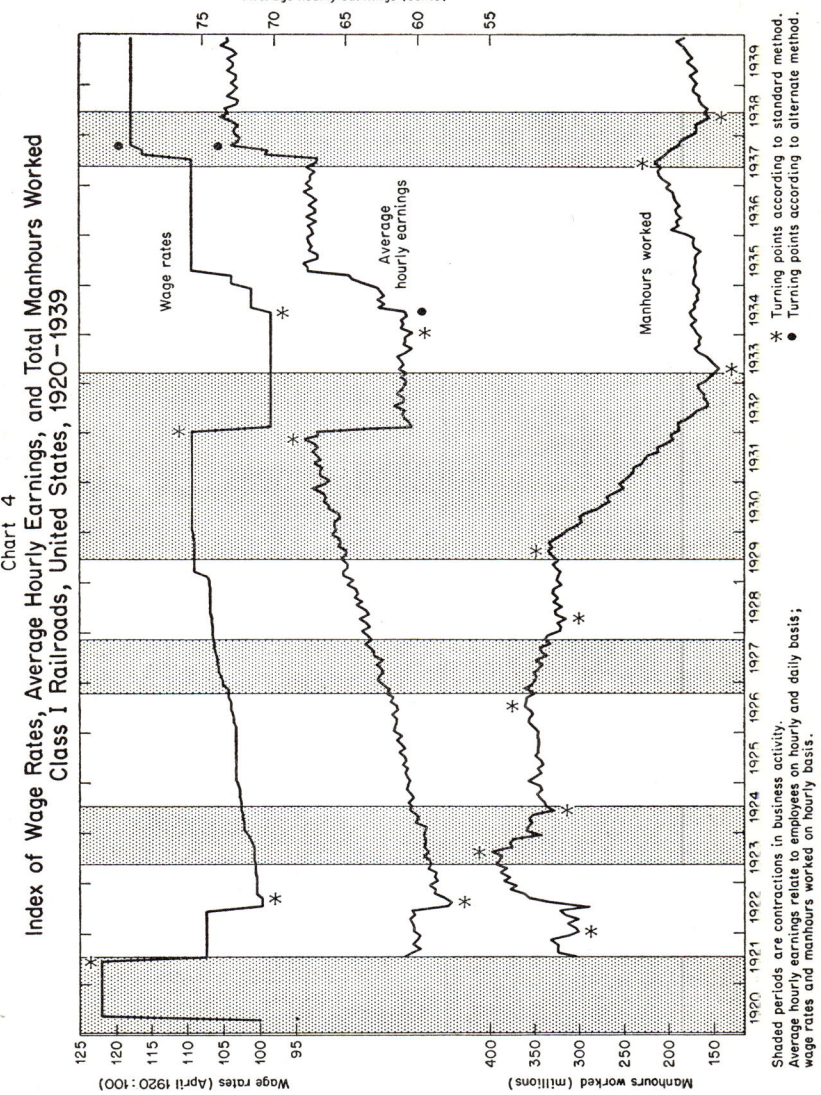

Chart 4
Index of Wage Rates, Average Hourly Earnings, and Total Manhours Worked
Class I Railroads, United States, 1920–1939

after the turn in factory wage rates; at two troughs the upturn in railroad wage rates came 5 and 13 months later.

The longer lags of railroad wage rates can be traced to institutional differences. Unlike the manufacturing industries during the greater part of these two decades, railroad wage rates have been changed only after prolonged negotiations between management and unions. For in the railroad industry about half of all workers were members of trade unions between 1923 and 1933 and about 70 percent were covered by trade union agreements by 1935.[16] Wage negotiations typically were carried on with the carriers organized in regional or national associations, and the federal government has maintained an elaborate system of mediation to forestall the collapse of collective bargaining.

A second institutional difference also serves to lengthen negotiations on wage rates: changes in prices of railroad service, freight rates and passenger fares, must be approved by the Interstate Commerce Commission.

How collective bargaining may create lags is well illustrated by the negotiations of the 1937 changes in wage rates, which are not unrepresentative of the process. Harry E. Jones, Executive Secretary, Bureau of Information of the Eastern Railways, describes the negotiations (*Wages and Labor Relations in the Railroad Industry, 1900-1941*, pp. 104-5):

"Wages for all classes of railroad employees having been restored on April 1, 1935, to the levels prevailing in 1931, and the year 1936 having witnessed some revival in business, railroad labor in the spring of 1937 presented demands for wage increases. These demands were, in the first instance, presented by the fourteen nonoperating organizations on March 4, 1937. . . . These demands were followed on March 22nd by demands from the four transportation brotherhoods and the switchmen. . . . Negotiations with respect to the two sets of demands proceeded separately.

The negotiations with the nonoperating organizations reached an impasse on June 29th, when the National Mediation Board proffered its services. As a result an agreement was reached on August 5, 1937, which was ratified by the general chairmen of the organizations on August 13th, and which established increased rates of pay effective as of August 1st. . . .

[16] Wolman, op. cit., pp. 123 and 131.

Meanwhile, negotiations had been proceeding with the engine and train service organizations. A strike vote was taken which authorized the executives of the brotherhoods to call a strike in the event that the negotiations failed to produce a satisfactory solution. Mediation was proffered by the National Mediation Board on August 25th, and an agreement was finally closed on October 3rd . . . (retroactive to October 1).

Hardly had these wage increases been placed in effect than a severe business recession set in during the fall and winter of 1937."

Indeed, by March 1937 railroad traffic began to decline, and by June railroad employment had reached its peak; the recession in general business activity is dated from May 1937. Thus increases in wage rates, demanded at the peak in traffic and 3 months before the decline in employment, became effective 2 to 4 months after the peak of employment and 5 to 7 months after the falling off of rail traffic.

This process seems to have hardened with the passage of the Railway Labor Act in 1926 which formalized the collective bargaining procedures and federal mediation, reducing sensitivity to pressures for downward adjustments. Thus, the reduction of wage rates in the first major depression was initiated 17 months after the peak in business activity while the first reductions in the Great Depression were not instituted until 31 months after the high point of the preceding boom.[17] Moreover, the severe but short-lived contraction of 1937-38 caused merely a leveling off, not a reduction, in railroad wage rates.

This experience in the railroad industry suggests that as changes in manufacturing rates become more and more subject to collective bargaining the lags may become even longer.

5 Lags also in British Manufacturing Industries

Wage rates in British manufacturing industries constitute a third sample that can be analyzed for its timing behavior. A monthly index of wage rates in 64 minor industries and 12 major industry groups was prepared some years ago by Lorie Tarshis for the National Bureau of Economic Research. We have, however, confined our investigation to the 7 major industry groups that comprise

[17] As in manufactures, railroad wage rates prior to the 1920-21 contraction had increased very rapidly whereas during the 'twenties they rose little.

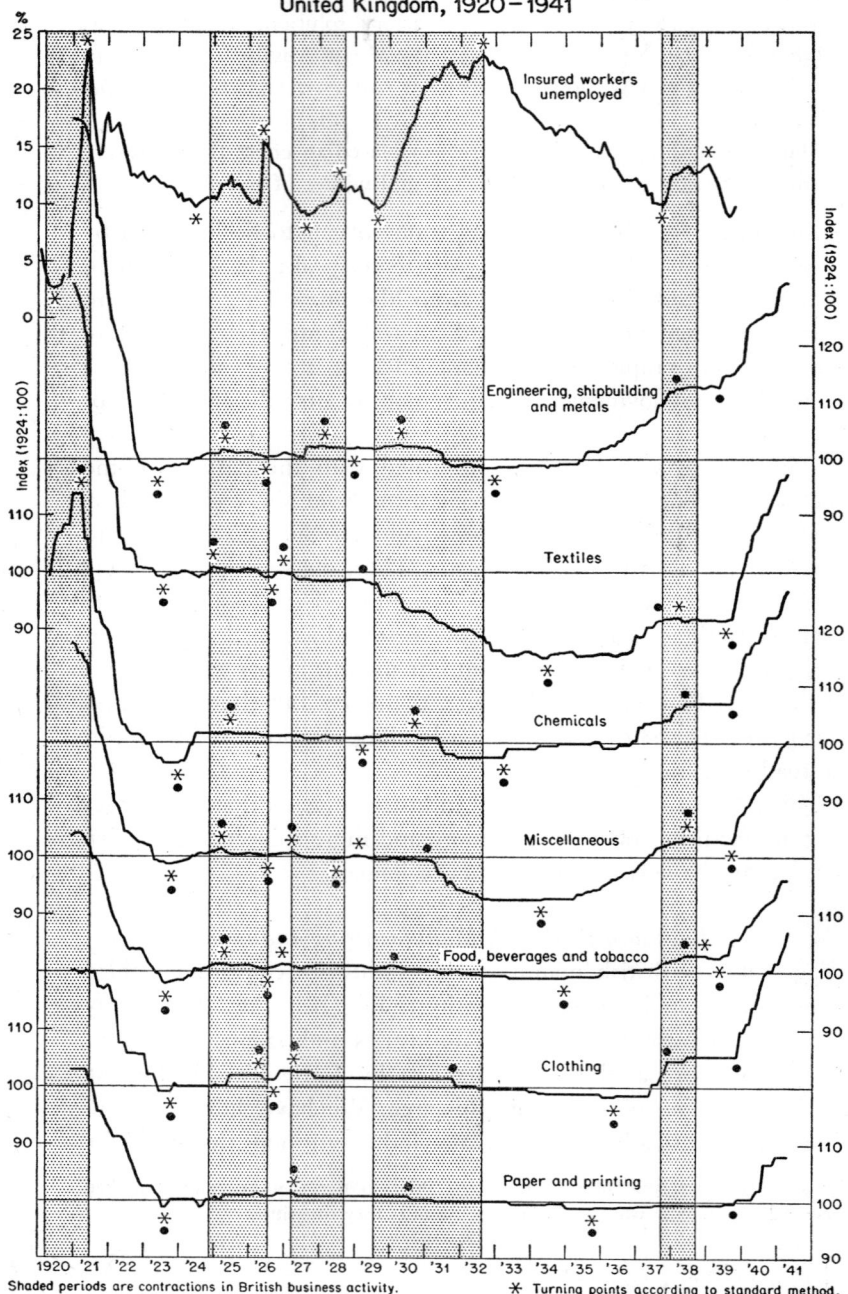

Chart 5
Indexes of Wage Rates in Seven Industrial Groups and Percentage of Insured Workers Unemployed
United Kingdom, 1920–1941

Shaded periods are contractions in British business activity.
✶ Turning points according to standard method.
● Turning points according to alternate method.

British manufactures and to the years 1920-41 (Chart 5).[18] A composite index for all British manufactures is not available for these years.

There are several similarities and several differences in the movements of wage rates in British and in United States manufactures. In both, for example, wage rates declined sharply from the latter part of 1920 to 1922 or 1923, then recovered somewhat. In the United States, however, the recovery occurred earlier and was more substantial. Following this recovery, wage rates in both countries entered upon a period of stability until 1929-30 when they were appreciably reduced. Once again the recovery from the Great Depression took place earlier and more rapidly in the United States. Thereafter the period covered by the wage rate series in the two countries no longer coincides.

Another similarity appears when the plateau-like movement of wage rates in British manufactures during the stable period 1924-29 is plotted on a generous scale. It is actually composed, as in the United States, of cycles with very narrow amplitudes. In this instance too we obtain more information if we distinguish between turning points that mark off major and minor cyclical phases. Because of these minor cycles, strict adherence to the standard procedure introduces some artificiality into the selection of some of the turning points. For example, according to the standard practice, peaks in wage rates corresponding to the mid-1929 peak in British business occurred in only 3 of the 7 industry groups. However, in all 7 groups wage rates changed significantly in response to the Great Depression. In our view it is more meaningful in these circumstances to select as the turn the point marking a substantial change in the rate of movement rather than the point marking a turn. We have entered in Table 3 therefore the dates that end the plateau-like movement in 1929-30 and those that initiate or end a similar movement during the 1937-38 contraction. It is the timing based upon these turning points that we analyze.

Lag of wage rates behind turns in business activity has been a common characteristic of British manufactures also in the two

---

[18] Tarshis' method consisted essentially of monthly interpolations of annual indexes of wage rates prepared by E. C. Ramsbottom. His monthly interpolations, based on changes in wage rates reported in the *Ministry of Labour Gazette*, have not been published but may be consulted at the National Bureau of Economic Research.

Table 3

Cyclical Turning Points in British Business Activity and Wage Rates Seven Branches of British Manufactures, 1920-1939

LEVEL OF BUS. ACT.	DATE OF TURNING POINT IN			LEAD (−), LAG (+), OR COINCIDENCE (0), MONTHS Rates & activity	
	Bus. act.*	WAGE RATES SM	A	SM	A
		CHEMICALS			
Peak	3/20	3/21	3/21	+12	+12
Trough	6/21	12/23	12/23	+30	+30
Peak	11/24	6/25	6/25	+7	+7
Trough	7/26				
Peak	3/27				
Trough	9/28	3/29	3/29	+6	+6
Peak	7/29	9/30	9/30	+14	+14
Trough	8/32	3/33	3/33	+7	+7
Peak	9/37		5/38		+8
Trough	9/38		9/39		+12
Average				+12.7	+12.0
		CLOTHING			
Trough	6/21	10/23	10/23	+28	+28
Peak	11/24	4/26	4/26	+17	+17
Trough	7/26	9/26	9/26	+2	+2
Peak	3/27	4/27	4/27	+1	+1
Trough	9/28				
Peak	7/29		10/31		+27
Trough	8/32	5/36	5/36	+45	+45
Peak	9/37		11/37		+2
Trough	9/38		11/39		+14
Average				+18.6	+17.0
	ENGINEERING, SHIPBUILDING, AND METALS				
Trough	6/21	5/23	5/23	+23	+23
Peak	11/24	4/25	4/25	+5	+5
Trough	7/26	6/26	6/26	−1	−1
Peak	3/27	2/28	2/28	+11	+11
Trough	9/28	12/28	12/28	+3	+3
Peak	7/29	4/30	4/30	+9	+9
Trough	8/32	12/32	12/32	+4	+4
Peak	9/37		2/38		+5
Trough	9/38		5/39		+8
Average				+7.7	+7.4
	FOOD, BEVERAGES, AND TOBACCO				
Trough	6/21	8/23	8/23	+26	+26
Peak	11/24	4/25	4/25	+5	+5
Trough	7/26	7/26	7/26	0	0
Peak	3/27	12/26	12/26	−3	−3
Trough	9/28				
Peak	7/29		2/30		+7
Trough	8/32	12/34	12/34	+28	+28
Peak	9/37	12/38	5/38	+15	+8
Trough	9/38	5/39	5/39	+8	+8
Average				+11.3	+9.9

28

LEVEL OF BUS. ACT.	DATE OF TURNING POINT IN			LEAD (—), LAG (+), OR COINCIDENCE (0), MONTHS Rates & activity	
	Bus. act.*	WAGE RATES SM	A	SM	A
		PAPER AND PRINTING			
Trough	6/21	8/23	8/23	+26	+26
Peak	11/24				
Trough	7/26				
Peak	3/27	4/27	4/27	+1	+1
Trough	9/28				
Peak	7/29		7/30		+12
Trough	8/32	10/35	10/35	+38	+38
Peak	9/37				
Trough	9/38		10/39		+13
Average				+21.7	+18.0
		TEXTILES			
Trough	6/21	7/23	7/23	+25	+25
Peak	11/24	12/24	12/24	+1	+1
Trough	7/26	8/26	8/26	+1	+1
Peak	3/27	12/26	12/26	—3	—3
Trough	9/28				
Peak	7/29		3/29		—4
Trough	8/32	6/34	6/34	+22	+22
Peak	9/37	3/38	8/37	+6	—1
Trough	9/38	7/39	9/39	+10	+12
Average				+8.9	+6.6
		MISCELLANEOUS			
Trough	6/21	10/23	10/23	+28	+28
Peak	11/24	3/25	3/25	+4	+4
Trough	7/26	7/26	7/26	0	0
Peak	3/27	3/27	3/27	0	0
Trough	9/28	6/28	6/28	—3	—3
Peak	7/29	2/29	1/31	—5	+18
Trough	8/32	4/34	4/34	+20	+20
Peak	9/37	6/38	6/38	+9	+9
Trough	9/38	9/39	9/39	+12	+12
Average				+7.2	+9.8
		AVERAGE FOR SEVEN INDUSTRIES			
Trough	6/21			+26.6	+26.6
Peak	11/24			+6.5	+6.5
Trough	7/26			+0.4	+0.4
Peak	3/27			+1.2	+1.2
Trough	9/28			+2.0	+2.0
Peak	7/29			+6.0	+11.9
Trough	8/32			+23.4	+23.4
Peak	9/37			+10.0	+5.2
Trough	9/38			+10.0	+11.3
All turning points in 7 industries				+11.2	+11.1

* Reference cycle dates for Great Britain from Burns and Mitchell, *Measuring Business Cycles*, pp. 512-3.

decades between the two world wars. If we count the terminal points of plateaus as turns, wage rate series for the 7 groups contained 55 turning points that corresponded with turning points in British business activity. At only 6 did turns in wage rates precede and at only 3 did the turns coincide. That is, at 84 percent of the turning points wage rates lagged behind business activity. The average lag at all corresponding turns was 11 months.

The fluctuations in wage rates, moreover, bear much the same lagged relationship to turns in factory unemployment (see Chart 5) as they did to turns in business activity, allowing, of course, for the inverted pattern of the former. Owing to the long lag, much of the deflation of wage rates after World War I coincided with a very substantial reduction in the percentage of the insured population that was unemployed; i.e., from a high of about 23 percent to a low of about 10, which level persisted until the Great Depression. Despite the continuance of substantial unemployment workers maintained their wage rates at a relatively stable level until about 1930 when wage rates began to be depressed in the face of a rising tide of unemployment which returned to the 23 percent level. And as unemployment receded to the chronic level of 9 percent wage rates recovered until 1938 when a temporary plateau was reached; meanwhile unemployment was rising moderately.

The substantial lag of wage rates behind business activity is not due merely to the averaging process. For in each of the 7 industry groups the lag was typical. In no group was the average lag as short as 6 months and in 3 groups it was as long as a year or more.

Despite the considerable average lags in each industry, the wage rate lag behind business activity has been merely nominal at certain turning points. For example, at the turns marking off minor cyclical phases—July 1926, March 1927, and September 1928—the lags on the average were very short, none exceeding 2 months. Indeed, the 3 coincident turns mentioned above occurred at these minor turns, as did 4 of the 6 leads. At all the turning points of major phases, on the other hand, the average lag in wage rates was substantial, ranging from 5 to 27 months. The longest lags, about 2 years, occurred at the troughs in June 1921 and August 1932, the terminal points of the severest depressions in these decades. This contrast in the length of lags in wage rates at minor and major turning points is puzzling. Apparently, wage rates in British manufactures have been more sensitive to relatively small changes in the fortunes of British business activity than to sweeping changes. However, we must bear in mind that our procedure interprets even minute movements as cyclical fluctuations if they are appropriately timed with respect to changes in general business. The changes in wage rates in such instances may be caused by the decisions of a very few enterprises. This illustrates how unsmoothed, raw data may yield unreasonable results.

A comparison of the lags in factory wage rates behind business activity in the United States and United Kingdom is not without interest. If for the United States we use the lags of the index of wage rates for all manufactures and for the United Kingdom the average lags for the 7 industry groups, our comparison involves lags at 4 major turning points. At the 2 peaks the rise in wage rates

LEVEL OF BUSINESS ACTIVITY	DATE OF TURNING POINT IN ACTIVITY		LAG OF WAGE RATES BEHIND ACTIVITY MONTHS	
	U.K.	U.S.	U.K.	U.S.
Trough	6/21	7/21	26.6	9.0
Peak	11/24	5/23	6.5	8.0
Peak	7/29	6/29	11.9*	12.0*
Trough	8/32	3/33	23.4	2.0

* Based on alternate turning points.

in both countries halted about the same number of months after the respective peaks in business activity. After the low points in business, however, wage rates in the United States began to rise many months earlier than wage rates in the United Kingdom.

If extent of unionization were the chief determinant of the timing of turning points in wage rates, the lag of British factory wage rates behind British business activity would be longer than the comparable lags in wage rates in United States manufactures. In the United Kingdom, for example, 42.1 percent of manufacturing employees were members of trade unions in 1924, 38.4 percent in 1930, and by 1935, when business activity was still at a relatively low level, the percentage had become 27.7 of all employed workers.[19] Between 1923 and 1933, 11 to 16 percent of workers in United States factories were organized in trade unions.

[19] The percentages for 1924 and 1930 are from Leo Wolman, 'Union Membership in Great Britain and the United States', NBER *Bulletin 68*, Dec. 27, 1937, App. Table IV. The percentage for 1935 was computed. Trade union membership figures are from the *Ministry of Labour Gazette*, XLV, Oct. 1937, p. 404; employment figures from the *Annual Abstract of Statistics*, Central Statistical Office, No. 84, 1935-46, pp. 107-9 and 114-6.

As already noted, the brief wage rate record available for analysis fails to support completely the expectation of longer lags in British wage rates, for the lags at the 2 peaks in both series are of about the same length. Only at the 2 troughs does it confirm this expectation in some degree. And here, we must repeat, the unusually short lag of United States factory wage rates at the 1933 trough is attributable to the direct intervention of the federal government through the NRA.

Despite some differences, all 3 samples of wage rate data have a common pattern in the timing of cyclical change: typically wage rates lagged behind business activity by a substantial number of months.

6 Average Hourly Earnings as Indicators of Turning Points in Wage Rates

Two aspects of cyclical fluctuations are of special interest, their timing and amplitude. We investigate the former first. Average hourly earnings in all manufactures traced as many cycles between 1920 and 1935 as our composite index of wage rates, and the cycles in the two series correspond whether we use the standard method of selecting turning points or our alternate method. To find out whether the turning points in the 2 series occurred at about the same time we use the alternate turns whenever turns compete. For it is more meaningful to compare the dates that mark appreciable changes in rates and earnings than the dates that mark reversals in direction without regard to the magnitude of the change. Turning points in a series 2 months before or after the corresponding turning points in the other are considered roughly coincident. Of the 5 major turning points only 4 can be determined precisely and at all 4 the timing is roughly coincident.[20] At the minor turning points, however, there was not even rough coincidence.

We may conclude that in aggregate manufactures the major turning points of average hourly earnings are a reliable indicator of major turns in wage rates and these will usually correspond, with a lag, to major reversals in business activity. This should be a help-

[20] Turning points cannot be determined precisely from January through June 1922 because we do not have any data on average hourly earnings. However, since in aggregate manufactures the standing at July 1922 is the lowest recorded near the turn, the turn had to occur between December 1921 and July 1922. Were the precise turn known, it would probably coincide roughly with the turn in wage rates.

ful guide in analyzing the past since in retrospect it is possible to distinguish between minor and major reversals in average hourly earnings. For current series this distinction is much more difficult to draw although it may be somewhat easier in this area of analysis since typically average hourly earnings do not turn until 9 months after business activity, an interval that may be sufficient to permit a firm judgment on whether a current reversal is major or minor.

The behavior of wage rates in all manufacturing at the peak of business in May 1937 and at the trough in June 1938 must be inferred, for our index could not be computed after July 1935. Average hourly earnings suggest that wage rates ceased to rise and entered upon a plateau in the autumn of 1937. Thus wage rates continued to rise for about 5 months after business began to recede. They continued at the October 1937 level, 22 percent above the 1929 level, with only minor changes until the first quarter of 1939, when the plateau-like movement ended. That is, they did not rise until about 8 months after business had begun to revive. The large number joining trade unions in the mass production industries after 1935 apparently had not yet caused any lengthening in the lag of wage rates in the technical sense in which we measure lags by our alternate method. However, this is the first major contraction in business activity during the 2 interwar decades when wage rates did not decline. The rise in trade union membership and the continuing drive for members were probably the chief reasons for maintaining the level of wage rates throughout the 1937-38 contraction in the face of sharp curtailments in production and employment.

For some analytical purposes it is necessary to work with subgroups of total manufactures; it would be useful therefore to know the degree to which wage rates and average hourly earnings have had roughly coincident turning points in each of the 9 groups of manufacturing industries. If we restrict ourselves to major turning points selected by our alternate method, the 9 industry groups passed through 23 turns, and at 17 turning points, 74 percent, wage rates and average hourly earnings roughly coincided. Rates and earnings had only 4 corresponding turns at minor turning points, and at only 1 did they roughly coincide. Moreover, the predominance of rough coincidence at the major turning points in business activity characterized all the subgroups except electrical goods and rubber tires and tubes. However, since we did not have more than

33

3 observations in any subgroup, the basis for this conclusion is rather tenuous.

INDUSTRY GROUP	CORRESPONDING TURNS OF RATES & EARNINGS AT MAJOR TURNING POINTS IN BUSINESS (number)	ROUGH COINCIDENCES
All manufactures	4	4
Automobiles	3	2
Boots and shoes	3	2
Electrical goods	1	0
Iron and steel	3	2
Paper and pulp	3	3
Rubber tires and tubes	2	1
Silk and rayon	3	2
Slaughtering and meat packing	2	2
Woolens and worsteds	3	3

The timing of cyclical turns in average hourly earnings at major turning points in business activity seems to be a somewhat less reliable indicator of the timing of cyclical turns in wage rates for individual branches than for aggregate manufactures. In the railroad industry, however, they seem to have been a reliable guide. For example, all turning points in wage rates and in average hourly earnings either coincided or differed by no more than 2 months (Chart 4). That is, every substantial change in average hourly earnings coincided with a similar change in wage rates.

Although the movement of hourly earnings reflects various adjustments made by management to changes in the level of production, at the major turning points our materials on manufactures and railroads indicate that the main determinant of the reversal in the movement of hourly earnings seems to be the reversal in the movement of wage rates themselves.

7 Cyclical Amplitudes of Wage Rates and Average Hourly Earnings
Our data have little to say positively about the similarity in the amplitude of cyclical fluctuations in wage rates and average hourly earnings. Charts 1 and 2 suggest that the relative changes in average hourly earnings in manufacturing are substantially larger than in wage rates during corresponding cyclical phases. Unfortunately, the assumption required in constructing our indexes of wage rates in manufacturing—that the establishments that did not report a change in wage rates in a given month made no change—causes the index to understate seriously the actual magnitude of changes in wage rates. The series on average hourly earnings are not sub-

ject to this sort of bias but, as pointed out above, other factors may produce differences in the magnitude of changes in earnings as compared with wage rates. Changes in overtime pay, in the relative number of skilled and unskilled workers or of high and low wage plants, in the relative number of time- and piece-rate workers, in the productivity of piece workers, and up- or downgrading may affect hourly earnings. Their net effect upon the amplitude of hourly earnings relative to that of the type of index we have been able to construct (see App. A) is not clear, and the empirical data are too fragmentary to settle the matter.

The data for the railroad industry are more enlightening. As previously explained, under-reporting in the wage rate index for Class I railroads must, under the circumstances, be negligible. In this index, therefore, our sampling error is deemed to be very small. In 2 of the 3 cyclical phases the amplitudes of average hourly earnings and wage rates are virtually identical (Table 4). In the third phase, the long expansion from the end of 1922 to the end of 1931, average hourly earnings had an 86 percent larger relative amplitude.

TABLE 4

Relative Amplitudes of Cyclical Fluctuations in Wage Rates and Average Hourly Earnings, Class I Railroads, United States, 1922-1937

	PHASE OF CYCLE IN		RELATIVE AMPLITUDE*	
	Rates	Earnings	Rates	Earnings
Expansion	9/22- 1/32	8/22-11/31	9.6	17.9
Contraction	1/32- 6/34	11/31- 6/34	10.0	10.3
Expansion	6/34-10/37	6/34-10/37	19.7	20.0

* Total change during the phase expressed as a percentage of the standing of the series at the beginning of the phase.

However, half of the excess in this long phase occurred after March 1929 and for a reason that is probably peculiar to the railroad industry: the postponement of maintenance work during contractions. Average hourly earnings continued upward between March 1929 and January 1932 although wage rates were virtually constant. The continued rise in hourly earnings can be explained by the relatively larger decline in the manhours worked by the lowest paid (those receiving 54 cents or less per hour in 1929) than in those worked by all other hourly workers. Thus, the manhours worked by the lowest paid accounted for 46 percent of the manhours worked by all other hourly workers in August 1929, the peak of this percentage; by January 1932, when the rise in average hourly earnings halted, this percentage was reduced to 36.[21] The decline is explained by the fact that most of the lowest paid workers are engaged in maintaining ways and structures, and this work was reduced to a minimum.

In manufacturing industries, on the contrary, maintenance workers constitute a relatively small percentage of the total labor force; consequently, cycles in maintenance work would not cause substantial cyclical changes in the composition of the labor force. On the other hand, the changing productivity of workers paid by the piece, a factor that conceivably could make for larger amplitudes in average hourly earnings than in wage rates, would be operative in many branches of manufactures but would figure scarcely at all in the railroad industry.

These considerations suggest that the cyclical amplitudes of rates and earnings are probably about the same except when the occupational composition of the labor force is altered substantially, which in most branches of manufactures seems unlikely during the short period of a business cycle.[22] This assumption is our justification for presenting the cyclical amplitudes of average hourly earnings in manufactures as though they measured the cyclical amplitudes of wage rates. To establish the relative magnitude of the adjustment of wage rates to the changing vicissitudes of business activity, we compare the amplitudes of corresponding cycles in average hourly earnings in manufactures (the price of an hour's labor) first with manufacturing activity represented by factory production and employment, secondly with the prices of materials used in manufacturing represented by the indexes of wholesale prices of

[21] These computations are based upon statistics compiled monthly by the Interstate Commerce Commission. The data have been corrected for seasonal movements.

[22] The smallness of the seasonal correction in our series on average hourly earnings supports our contention that the occupational composition of the labor force in manufacturing industries does not change substantially during short periods since the considerations affecting occupational selectivity in dismissals and hirings at seasonal peaks and troughs are much the same as at cyclical peaks and troughs. It is this selectivity that brings about whatever seasonal movement exists in average hourly earnings. How important the seasonal element has been can be judged by the seasonal amplitudes of our 10 series on average hourly earnings: all manufactures, 0.4; automobiles, 3.0; boots and shoes, 2.9; electrical goods, 1.0; iron and steel, 2.0; paper and pulp, 0; rubber products, 2.2; silk and rayon, 2.1; slaughtering and meat packing, 1.4; woolen and worsted goods, 1.2.

raw and semifinished commodities, and thirdly with the index of wholesale prices of finished goods which represents the prices received for factory production.

Manufacturing activity has fluctuated much more, relatively, than hourly earnings in both expansion and contraction (Table 5). Obviously the same would hold for the full cycle. This has been true also for the wholesale prices of raw materials and with minor exceptions for the wholesale prices of semifinished goods. In other words, of the two principal elements of direct costs, labor and materials, the price of materials has been subjected to relatively larger adjustments both upward and downward and over the entire cycle than the price of labor.

TABLE 5

Amplitude of Fluctuations of Corresponding Specific Cycles in Average Hourly Earnings, Wholesale Prices, and Factory Production and Employment, United States, 1919-1939

PHASE OF SPECIFIC CYCLE	DATE OF CORRESP. PHASE OF BUSINESS ACTIVITY	AV. HRLY. EARN.	AMPLITUDE OF CYCLE RELATIVES				
			WHOLESALE PRICES OF			FACTORY	
			Raw materials	Semi-fin. goods	Fin. goods	Prod.	Empl.
Contraction	1/20- 7/21	−24.0	−71.0	−104.8	−50.1	−39.1	−33.9
Expansion	7/21- 5/23	+15.1	+20.6	+33.0	+8.7	+47.4	+26.2
Contraction	5/23- 7/24	−0.8	−8.6	−20.7	−7.6	−19.0	−13.3
Expansion	7/24-10/26	+3.3	+13.0	+6.0	+7.2	+23.3	+10.0
Contraction	10/26-11/27	−0.4	−14.0	−15.8	−7.4	−5.1	−5.0
Expansion	11/27- 6/29	+3.0	+8.3	+1.9	+3.6	+25.8	+11.5
Contraction	6/29- 3/33	−25.0	−62.4	−47.8	−36.9	−69.8	−49.9
Expansion	3/33- 5/37	+42.1	+54.2	+42.0	+27.9	+80.5	+54.9
Contraction	5/37- 6/38	−0.8	−27.4	−18.6	−10.7	−47.6	−27.7

Based on the business cycle files of the NBER.

Our third comparison of average hourly earnings and wholesale prices of finished goods provides an interesting variation. In all 5 declines the prices received for factory production have decreased, relatively, much more than the price of labor; indeed, in 3, the decline in hourly earnings was scarcely perceptible. However, in 2 of the 4 expansions the relative rise in the price of labor was significantly larger than in the prices received for factory output. The opposite relation obtained in the 2 minor expansions. When we measure amplitudes over the full cycle—adding the amplitude of expansion to the amplitude of contraction without regard to sign— we find that, measuring from trough to trough, hourly earnings had a smaller amplitude than the wholesale prices of finished goods in 3 of the 4 full cycles. In short, there was usually less adjustment in the price of labor than in the price of factory output.

To explore the implications of these differences for business cycle analysis calls for a broader and deeper framework than is appropriate for this Paper.

8 *Average Hourly Earnings in a Postwar Contraction*
From our analysis of the two decades between World War I and II we turn to the brief period following World War II. In this period there has been at least one contraction in general business— in 1948-49.[23] Factory production reached a peak in October 1948 and declined 17 percent to a low in July 1949; factory employment declined 13.5 percent between its high point of January 1948 and its low of November 1949.[24] Average hourly earnings, on the other hand, did not have any sustained decline, remaining, with negligible deviations, upon the plateau they entered in the last quarter of 1948 until the fourth quarter of 1949.

AVERAGE HOURLY EARNINGS, PRODUCTION AND NONSUPERVISORY WORKERS, ALL MANUFACTURING INDUSTRIES

	1948	1949	1950
January	$1.302	$1.405	$1.418
February	1.308	1.401	1.420
March	1.310	1.400	1.423
April	1.314	1.401	1.434
May	1.324	1.401	1.441
June	1.340	1.405	
July	1.356	1.408	
August	1.373	1.399	
September	1.386	1.407	
October	1.390	1.392	
November	1.397	1.392	
December	1.400	1.408	

Source: *Monthly Labor Review*.

If in measuring average hourly earnings we could take account of the growing importance of 'fringe benefits,' the plateau would probably be replaced by a gently upward slope (App. C). The decline in general business, however, continued only about 9 months, a period that just about equals the average lag of average hourly earnings behind turns in general business (Table 1). Factory employ-

[23] There is some indication of a contraction in 1945-46. We pass over that period because the cyclical movements are ambiguous and their interpretation uncertain owing to continued enforcement of price and other controls.

[24] Based on seasonally adjusted indexes of factory production and employment published in the *Federal Reserve Bulletin*.

ment declined 22 months, a period that greatly exceeds the average lag of average hourly earnings behind turns in employment, although the rate of decrease during 1948 was slight. However, it must be borne in mind that wholesale prices of manufactured goods declined only moderately, 10 percent, during this recession in general business.

Did the movement of average hourly earnings during 1948-49 conform to the prewar pattern? As a partial answer we present the relative declines in average hourly earnings, factory production, and factory employment during contractions beginning with the 1920-21 depression (Table 6). The severe contraction of factory production and employment in 1920-21 was short-lived. The corresponding adjustment in average hourly earnings, though belated, was swift (see Sec. 3). The 1923-24 contraction in employment and production was moderate, yet the decline in average hourly earnings did not exceed 1.5 percent of the peak value and the same rigidity of wage rates accompanied the minor contraction of 1926-27. In the Great Depression the relative decreases in factory production and employment exceeded the comparable decreases in the 1920-21 depression by a half and a third respectively. The relative reduction in average hourly earnings, however, was roughly of the same order of magnitude as in 1920-21 although the earlier contraction lasted 21 months and the Great Depression 38 months. The reaction of average hourly earnings was sluggish in the 1937-38 contraction also. The downward adjustment did not exceed 1 percent, although the curtailment of production and employment was about as sharp and extensive, relatively, as in the 1920-21 depression.

Table 6

Average Hourly Earnings, Employment, and Production All Manufacturing Industries, Relative Declines in Specific Cycle Contractions, 1920-1949

Approxmiate date of contraction	Percentage decline from peak to trough		
	Average hourly earnings	Employment	Production
1920-21	—21.6	—31.0	—35.4
1923-24	—1.4	—13.7	—18.9
1926-27	—0.9	—5.3	—6.2
1929-33	—24.2	—42.9	—55.7
1937-38	—1.0	—23.1	—35.8
1948-49	negligible	—13.5	—16.8

As we have already noted, the downward adjustment in average hourly earnings during the postwar contraction of 1948-49 was scarcely perceptible despite fairly substantial declines in factory production and employment, declines about equal to those of the contraction of 1923-24. This postwar experience, therefore, is similar to the prewar trend toward greater rigidity of wage rates in business contractions, although to generalize on the basis of a period so brief and current is hazardous at best.

Appendix A

Wage Rate Indexes, with Notes on their Construction, and Average Hourly Earnings in Manufacturing, United States

Wage rate indexes for 9 manufacturing industries from 1919 to 1931 and, in the case of all manufactures, to 1935, are constructed from data published by the Bureau of Labor Statistics in its *Monthly Labor Review*. Between August 1931 and July 1935, when this series was discontinued, data on the percentage change in wage rates for all manufactures only were available.

From 1919 to June 1922 the BLS presented changes in wage rate schedules in narrative form. The following excerpt selected at random is typical (*Monthly Labor Review*, XIV, 3, March 1922, pp. 121-2):

"During the period December 15, 1921 to January 15, 1922 there were wage changes made by some of the establishments in 10 of the 14 industries.

Iron and steel—an increase of 1½ percent was granted to 64 percent of the men in one plant. A reduction of 19 percent was made to 4 percent of the force in one mill, while another mill reduced the wages of 45 percent of the employees 15 percent. Twelve plants reported a decrease of 10 percent affecting all employees. . . ."

The same information was published in tabular form from June 1922 to March 1923. Thereafter until August 1931 the tables included information on the percentage of workers affected by changes in wage rates. Our table, showing the BLS column headings, contains hypothetical data to illustrate our computation. The essential information for the construction of an index of wage rates is given in columns 4 and 7. Thus for industry A the weighted average per-

INDUSTRY	ESTABLISHMENTS Total no. report. (1)	No. report. changes in wage rates (2)	% CHANGE IN WAGE RATES Range (3)	Av. (4)	Total no. (5)	EMPLOYEES AFFECTED AS % OF ALL EMPLOYEES In estab. report. changes in wage rates (6)	In all estab. report. (7)
			INCREASES				
A	200	15	7-12	10	10,000	73	20
B	350	16	8-11	9	6,200	42	5
C	150	9	5-7	6	3,200	67	7
			DECREASES				
A	200	6	4-7	5	5,000	82	10
D	175	15	2-8	6	2,000	25	3
E	400	4	1-6	4	800	30	2

centage change is 1.5: the algebraic sum of the product, 150, is divided by the total weights, 100. The index of wage rates for, say, February, would therefore be 1.5 percent higher than the index for January.

Rate of Change from col. 4 (1)	% of Employees Affected (weights) from col. 7 (2)	Product (1 x 2) (3)
+10	20	200
−5	10	−50
0	70	0
Total	100	150

Wage rates in April 1923 are taken to equal 100 and the monthly link relatives are chained to this base. When a relative monthly increase or decrease is less than 0.1 percent it is cumulated until it amounts to 0.1 percent, then included in the index.

For the period before April 1923 the only index we can construct is cruder, because employee weights for combined changes in the wage rates of individual establishments are lacking. As is clear from the excerpt quoted above, the relative change in wage rates in establishments reporting changes can be reduced to the percentage change for each establishment, affected and unaffected workers alike, by multiplying the reported change by the percentage of workers affected. In terms of the quotation, the 1.5 percent increase affecting 64 percent of the workers in one plant becomes a plant-wide increase of 0.96 percent (.015 times 64 percent). The average change for establishments reporting changes in a given industry is an unweighted average of the plant-wide percentage changes. The latter percentage for establishments reporting changes is combined with the zero change for establishments not reporting any change by using the relative number of establishments in each category as weights. The monthly link relatives derived in this manner are chained to the same base, April 1923. These computations were carried out for each of the 9 branches of manufacturing and for all manufacturing.

The two indexes are not spliced. They are, however, presented for an overlapping period of 8 months in 1923, during which their relative movements in each industry are very similar but at somewhat different levels.

The data are such that we cannot directly combine time and piece rates into a composite index. Establishments report merely the average percentage change in wage rates of affected occupations. In many instances the affected occupations must include occupations paid at time rates as well as at piece rates. We do not have any way of knowing how establishments computed the average announced changes in wage rates that they reported to BLS.

There are two correct procedures. One, which seems more feasible, involves converting the affected piece rates before and after change into hourly earnings on the basis of some norm of hourly output. The hourly piece rate earnings before and after change would be combined respectively with the affected time rates before and after change weighted by the number of manhours worked at the affected occupations. The percentage difference between the composites before and after the changes in wage rates would be the average change for the occupations subject to change.

The other procedure involves converting the affected hourly rates before and after change into piece rates on the basis of some norm of output in the time-rate occupations. Changes in the two types of rate could then be averaged weighted by earnings of the affected occupations.

In our opinion, a payroll clerk entrusted with preparing an answer to the BLS inquiry would hardly apply so much statistical sophistication to a voluntary report. More probably, the reported change in wage rates for a given establishment was merely an average of the percentage change of individual rate changes weighted, perhaps, by the number employed in each occupation subject to change. If our presumption is correct, the possible difference in the bases of the individual percentages would not be taken into account. Despite this presumed deficiency an index compounded from average percentage changes of this character would probably be adequate for a study of the timing of changes in wage rates. However, for the analysis of the amplitude of fluctuations in wage rates this deficiency may be serious, although the direction and degree of bias is not known.

The sampling error, on the other hand, is presumed to be such that the indexes understate the amplitudes of fluctuation. Some evidence for this view is presented in Section 7. Our judgment is based also on the percentage of factory workers affected by changes in wage rates in the course of a year disclosed by data compiled by the BLS. The relative number subject to changes in wage rates between 1924 and 1930 seems too small. However, we do not know of any data that could be an independent check.

Percentage of All Factory Workers Affected by Changes in Wage Rates, United States, 1923-1935

1923 (last 7 mo.)	35.8	1930	4.9
1924	8.8	1931	23.0
1925	6.9	1932	39.5
1926	4.0	1933	76.8
1927	2.8	1934	25.7
1928	3.8	1935 (first 7 mo.)	9.4
1929	4.2		

Table A

Wage Rate Indexes and Average Hourly Earnings
All Manufactures and Nine Manufacturing Industries,
United States

Base of index of wage rates is April 1923:100. Average hourly earnings (in cents) are corrected for seasonal variations in all industries except all manufactures during 1920-21 and 1931-39 and the entire paper and pulp series, in both of which seasonal movement is virtually nonexistent.

Source: See text, Sec. 2, and App. A.
a Constructed on firm basis.
b Constructed on employee basis.
See Appendix A for full description.
n.a.: not available.

Table A

ALL MANUFACTURES

	Jan.	Feb.	March	April	May	June	July	Aug.	Sep.	Oct.	Nov.	Dec.
1919												
Rate, 13 ind.[a]	91.2	91.2	91.1	91.2	91.1	94.0	95.0	95.9	97.1	98.2	99.4	102.0
1920												
Rate, 13 ind.[a]	103.2	104.7	106.0	107.0	109.2	111.9	112.7	113.0	113.3	113.5	113.3	112.6
Earnings					60.3	60.2	60.6	61.1	61.1	60.8	60.1
1921												
Rate, 13 ind.[a]	108.0	105.8	104.6	103.7	102.8	101.6	100.3	99.0	97.6	97.0	96.5	96.1
Earnings	58.1	56.6	55.3	54.5	53.3	52.6	51.2	50.7	49.9	49.2	49.0	48.6
1922												
Rate, 13 ind.[a]	95.4	94.6	94.1	93.8	93.9	94.1	94.1	94.2	96.1	96.8	97.3	97.5
Rate, all mfg.[a]							93.9	94.1	95.4	96.2	96.7	97.0
Earnings	n.a.	n.a.	n.a.	n.a.	n.a.	n.a.	47.9	48.3	49.3	49.8	50.4	50.6
1923												
Rate, 13 ind.[a]	97.9	98.3	98.7	100.0								
Rate, all mfg.[a]	97.5	98.0	98.6	100.0								
Rate, all mfg.[b]					102.6	103.0	103.1	103.2	103.6	103.7	103.8	103.8
Earnings	50.5	50.9	51.2	52.9	54.7	54.9	54.9	55.2	55.7	55.9	56.1	56.2
1924												
Rate, all mfg.[b]	103.8	103.8	103.8	103.8	103.8	103.7	103.6	103.5	103.4	103.3	103.3	103.2
Earnings	56.1	56.2	56.2	56.1	56.1	55.8	56.2	56.1	56.4	56.1	56.5	56.4
1925												
Rate, all mfg.[b]	103.1	103.1	103.0	103.0	103.0	103.0	103.0	102.9	102.9	102.9	102.9	102.9
Earnings	56.2	56.0	56.2	56.3	56.3	56.2	56.0	56.0	55.7	56.0	56.1	56.3
1926												
Rate, all mfg.[b]	102.9	102.9	102.9	102.9	102.9	103.0	103.0	103.0	103.0	103.0	103.0	103.0
Earnings	56.1	56.3	56.5	56.5	56.7	57.0	56.9	56.9	57.0	57.1	57.6	57.3
1927												
Rate, all mfg.[b]	103.1	103.1	103.1	103.1	103.1	103.1	103.1	103.1	103.1	103.0	103.0	103.0
Earnings	57.3	57.6	57.3	57.5	57.6	57.8	57.8	57.9	57.7	57.8	57.6	57.6

BOOTS AND SHOES

1919 Rate[a]	97.5	97.6	97.6	97.6	98.5	99.9	100.2	101.6	101.9	102.2	103.0	
1920 Rate[a]	103.4	103.9	104.1	104.1	104.2	104.7	104.7	104.7	104.9	104.9	104.9	104.9
Earnings							53.1	52.4	52.1	51.2	53.6	54.8
1921 Rate[a]	103.6	103.4	103.3	103.2	102.1	102.1	102.1	102.0	101.9	101.8	101.3	100.8
Earnings	55.8	55.9	54.5	51.6	48.8	49.1	47.7	47.4	46.2	47.1	47.9	48.7
1922 Rate[a]	100.8	100.8	100.2	100.0	100.0	99.8	99.8	99.7	99.7	99.7	99.8	99.9
Earnings	n.a.	n.a.	n.a.	n.a.	n.a.	n.a.	47.6	47.9	47.9	47.7	49.2	50.2
1923 Rate[a]	99.9	99.9	99.9	100.0	100.0	100.1	100.2	100.2	100.2	100.4	100.8	100.8
Rate[b]												
Earnings	49.0	48.3	49.3	49.7	51.1	51.7	49.0	49.7	50.2	49.9	49.3	47.4
1924 Rate[b]	101.0	101.0	101.0	101.0	101.0	100.9	100.8	100.8	100.7	100.7	100.7	100.7
Earnings	50.1	50.5	51.7	50.8	49.1	48.5	47.8	47.5	47.8	48.5	48.7	48.7
1925 Rate[b]	100.6	100.6	100.5	100.5	100.5	100.5	100.4	100.4	100.4	100.4	100.4	100.4
Earnings	49.4	48.5	48.8	49.8	50.6	48.8	46.8	47.1	46.8	46.6	46.1	47.0
1926 Rate[b]	100.4	100.4	100.4	100.4	100.4	100.4	100.4	100.4	100.4	100.4	100.4	100.4
Earnings	47.5	46.9	47.2	48.6	46.7	48.8	50.7	50.3	50.0	49.5	50.1	50.6
1927 Rate[b]	100.4	100.4	100.4	100.3	100.3	100.2	100.2	100.2	100.2	100.2	100.2	100.2
Earnings	48.8	48.7	48.5	47.9	48.1	48.6	49.2	49.0	48.9	49.1	49.5	50.3
1928 Rate[b]	100.2	100.2	100.2	100.1	100.1	100.1	100.1	100.1	100.1	100.1	100.1	100.1
Earnings	49.7	49.8	49.9	48.7	48.0	48.7	49.2	48.9	49.3	50.7	48.8	48.7
1929 Rate[b]	100.1	100.1	100.1	100.0	100.0	100.0	100.0	100.0	100.0	100.0	100.0	100.0
Earnings	49.0	50.7	50.3	49.7	50.8	49.6	48.6	51.4	51.3	49.7	50.2	50.4
1930 Rate[b]	100.0	100.0	99.9	99.8	99.8	99.8	99.7	99.6	99.6	99.5	99.5	99.4
Earnings	51.4	50.4	48.6	47.8	47.6	47.5	47.8	46.2	46.2	44.7	44.8	44.5
1931 Rate[b]	99.3	99.1	99.0	99.0	99.0	98.9	98.6	98.6				
Earnings	42.3	43.5	43.9	43.8	44.4	44.6	44.6	43.7	43.0	43.1	43.4	42.7

TABLE A (cont.)
ELECTRICAL GOODS

	Jan.	Feb.	March	April	May	June	July	Aug.	Sep.	Oct.	Nov.	Dec.
1920 Earnings	60.7	58.8	55.0	55.5	55.2	61.0	60.9	62.3	63.1	63.1	62.5	61.9
1921 Earnings	n.a.	n.a.	n.a.	n.a.	n.a.	55.1	54.9	52.4	52.5	50.6	50.3	49.7
1922 Rate[a]	98.7	98.9	99.3	100.0	101.5	97.9	98.0	98.0	98.4	98.6	98.6	98.7
Earnings	51.3	51.8	52.8	100.0	102.6	n.a.	49.1	49.4	50.1	50.6	41.2	41.3
1923 Rate[a]	103.0	103.0	103.1	103.1	103.1	101.9	102.0	102.0	102.0	102.0	102.1	102.1
Rate[b] Earnings	60.3	60.4	60.3	60.2	57.3	102.9 57.4	102.9 57.4	103.0 58.4	103.0 59.6	103.0 60.3	103.0 60.2	103.0 60.2
1924 Rate[b] Earnings	103.1 60.2	103.1 60.5	103.1 60.9	103.1 61.1	103.1 59.7	103.1 60.4	103.1 59.9	103.1 59.9	103.1 59.3	103.1 60.0	103.1 60.0	103.1 60.1
1925 Rate[b] Earnings	103.1 58.1	103.1 58.2	103.1 58.6	103.1 58.8	103.0 61.5	103.0 60.5	103.0 60.4	103.0 60.3	103.0 58.4	103.0 60.0	103.0 59.8	103.0 59.6
1926 Rate[b] Earnings	103.4 60.7	103.4 60.9	103.4 60.4	103.1 58.8	103.2 58.6	103.3 59.5	103.3 59.2	103.3 59.3	103.3 59.7	103.4 59.4	103.4 59.9	103.4 59.8
1927 Rate[b] Earnings	103.5 60.9	103.5 61.2	103.5 61.6	103.5 60.7	103.5 61.1	103.5 60.9	103.5 60.9	103.5 61.0	103.5 61.1	103.5 61.2	103.5 61.7	103.5 61.4
1928 Rate[b] Earnings	103.7 62.1	103.8 62.4	103.8 61.5	103.5 61.4	103.5 61.5	103.5 61.6	103.5 61.2	103.5 60.7	103.5 61.5	103.5 61.6	103.5 62.1	103.6 62.4
1929 Rate[b] Earnings	104.3 63.8	103.8 62.4	103.8 61.5	103.8 61.8	103.8 62.1	103.9 61.8	103.9 62.5	104.1 63.2	104.1 63.9	104.1 63.4	104.1 63.4	104.1 63.8
1930 Rate[b] Earnings	104.3 63.8	104.3 63.9	104.3 65.0	104.3 65.1	104.3 64.8	104.3 65.1	104.3 64.6	104.3 64.3	104.3 65.0	104.3 64.3	104.3 64.3	104.2 64.1
1931 Rate[b] Earnings	104.1 64.5	104.1 64.2	104.0 64.4	104.0 63.7	103.9 63.6	103.8 62.4	103.8 62.5	103.7 62.3	62.7	63.1	63.0	62.3

RUBBER TIRES AND TUBES (RATES), ALL RUBBER PRODUCTS (EARNINGS)

	Jan	Feb	Mar	Apr	May	Jun	Jul	Aug	Sep	Oct	Nov	Dec
1920 Earnings						71.4	69.9	68.1	68.6	67.9	65.4	63.2
1921 Earnings	61.1	58.2	59.2	60.0	60.4	61.1	58.8	60.1	54.7	52.5	52.4	52.3
1922 Rate[a]	n.a.	n.a.	n.a.	n.a.	n.a.	98.1	98.2	98.8	98.8	98.9	98.9	98.9
1922 Earnings				n.a.	n.a.	n.a.	58.5	58.9	57.9	57.5	58.6	58.9
1923 Rate[a]				100.0	100.3	100.3	100.4	100.3	99.8	99.8	99.7	99.7
1923 Rate[b]	98.9	99.2	99.8	100.0	100.2	100.2	100.3	100.3	98.3	98.3	98.2	98.2
1923 Earnings	58.4	57.2	63.2	63.4	65.2	66.2	62.7	66.4	61.9	61.4	61.8	63.1
1924 Rate[b]	98.2	98.2	98.2	98.2	98.2	98.2	98.0	98.0	98.0	98.0	98.0	97.8
1924 Earnings	63.8	63.2	61.7	62.2	63.2	63.9	65.4	62.1	63.7	65.1	65.1	65.3
1925 Rate[b]	97.8	97.8	97.8	97.7	97.7	97.7	97.7	97.6	97.6	97.6	97.6	97.6
1925 Earnings	63.9	64.0	63.7	64.4	65.1	65.9	66.3	65.3	66.0	66.5	65.7	65.7
1926 Rate[b]	97.6	97.6	97.6	97.6	97.6	97.6	97.6	97.6	97.6	97.6	97.6	97.5
1926 Earnings	64.0	65.9	67.4	66.7	66.6	65.9	63.4	65.4	66.6	66.5	67.4	65.9
1927 Rate[b]	97.5	97.4	97.4	97.4	97.4	97.4	97.4	97.4	97.4	97.4	97.4	97.3
1927 Earnings	65.5	65.7	65.1	65.5	66.2	66.2	65.9	67.2	65.5	66.1	65.7	67.7
1928 Rate[b]	97.3	97.2	97.2	97.2	97.2	97.2	97.2	97.2	97.2	97.2	97.2	97.2
1928 Earnings	66.5	64.8	65.7	65.8	63.3	63.9	63.2	63.9	65.4	66.0	66.1	65.8
1929 Rate[b]	97.2	97.2	97.2	97.2	97.2	97.2	97.2	97.2	97.2	97.2	97.2	97.2
1929 Earnings	66.5	67.0	66.3	65.0	65.7	65.6	66.1	66.0	66.5	65.7	66.8	65.5
1930 Rate[b]	97.2	97.2	97.2	97.2	97.2	97.2	96.8	96.8	96.8	96.8	96.8	96.8
1930 Earnings	65.7	65.6	65.5	66.9	66.5	66.1	66.6	67.4	65.4	65.3	63.9	64.3
1931 Rate[b]	96.8	96.7	96.7	96.7	96.7	96.7	96.7	96.7				
1931 Earnings	67.4	66.6	68.0	67.4	64.8	64.3	63.5	64.1	64.6	63.3	63.9	63.6

TABLE A (cont.)

SILK AND RAYON

	June	July	Aug.	Sep.	Oct.	Nov.	Dec.	Jan.	Feb.	March	April	May
1919 Rate[a]	87.8		87.8	87.8	87.9	87.9	88.6	97.2	98.8	99.6	100.9	102.7
1920 Rate[a]	104.3		106.5	106.9	107.1	108.4	108.8	108.8	108.8	108.8	106.7	
Earnings								53.3	53.8	52.9	52.8	53.7
1921 Rate[a]	105.1		102.3	101.9	101.7	101.7	101.6	101.4	101.3	101.3	100.6	100.0
Earnings	50.7		50.2	48.3	48.2	47.8	48.1	47.1	47.7	47.4	47.2	46.0
1922 Rate[a]	98.1		98.0	98.0	98.0	98.0	97.8	97.8	98.1	98.5	98.8	98.9
Earnings	n.a.		n.a.	n.a.	n.a.	n.a.	n.a.	44.5	45.0	44.7	45.2	45.0
1923 Rate[a]	99.1		99.2	99.4	100.0	102.0	102.1	102.2	102.2	102.2	102.3	102.3
Rate[b]					100.0	103.1	103.2	103.2	103.2	103.2	103.3	103.3
Earnings	44.9		45.6	47.1	47.7	50.0	51.2	50.8	51.8	51.2	51.5	52.4
1924 Rate[b]	103.3		103.3	103.3	103.3	103.3	103.3	103.0	102.9	103.3	103.3	103.3
Earnings	49.6		50.8	51.4	50.0	48.8	49.8	48.5	48.1	49.9	48.1	45.8
1925 Rate[b]	103.4		103.4	103.4	103.4	103.5	103.6	103.7	103.7	103.7	103.8	103.8
Earnings	47.7		47.9	47.5	47.4	47.7	47.0	47.1	47.5	47.5	47.9	47.9
1926 Rate[b]	103.8		103.8	103.9	103.9	103.9	103.9	103.9	103.9	103.9	104.0	103.9
Earnings	48.5		48.7	48.9	49.5	49.2	49.6	48.2	48.9	48.8	49.1	49.5
1927 Rate[b]	103.9		104.0	104.0	104.0	103.9	103.9	103.9	103.9	103.9	103.9	103.9
Earnings	50.5		50.1	49.6	49.0	48.6	50.2	49.7	49.3	49.2	48.8	49.3

		Jan	Feb	Mar	Apr	May	Jun	Jul	Aug	Sep	Oct	Nov	Dec
1928	Rate[b]	103.2	103.0	103.0	103.0	103.0	103.1	103.1	103.1	103.1	103.1	103.1	103.0
	Earnings	48.2	48.3	48.0	49.9	48.6	48.7	48.4	49.0	48.4	48.1	49.4	49.0
1929	Rate[b]	103.0	103.0	103.0	103.0	103.1	103.1	103.1	103.1	103.1	103.1	103.1	103.1
	Earnings	49.2	49.4	49.0	49.1	48.6	48.4	47.8	48.8	48.4	48.0	48.0	48.3
1930	Rate[b]	103.1	103.1	103.1	103.1	103.0	102.9	102.2	102.2	102.0	101.9	101.9	101.9
	Earnings	49.6	49.3	49.8	49.0	49.3	48.7	49.3	49.2	48.2	48.5	48.5	48.7
1931	Rate[b]	101.7	101.6	101.6	101.5	101.5	101.4	101.3	101.3				
	Earnings	49.2	47.7	46.9	46.6	46.3	44.8	46.4	47.4	46.5	46.1	45.4	44.7

SLAUGHTERING AND MEAT PACKING

		Jan	Feb	Mar	Apr	May	Jun	Jul	Aug	Sep	Oct	Nov	Dec
1920	Earnings	57.1	57.2				58.3	58.1	58.5	57.9	57.8	57.9	57.4
1921	Earnings	n.a.	n.a.	51.9	50.2	50.0	49.0	48.1	48.4	48.6	48.4	48.2	44.7
1922	Rate[a]	99.0	99.1	99.1	100.0	n.a.	98.7	98.7	98.7	98.8	98.9	98.9	98.9
	Earnings	44.6	44.4	44.5	47.4	n.a.	43.9	44.2	44.1	44.1	44.1	44.0	43.8
1923	Rate[a]	104.8	104.9	104.9	103.7	103.7	103.7	103.8	103.8	103.8	103.8	103.8	103.8
	Earnings	48.9	49.5	49.2	47.8	48.3	48.5	48.0	48.7	48.6	48.5	48.1	48.6
1924	Rate[b]	104.8	104.9	104.9	104.9	104.9	105.0	105.0	105.0	105.0	105.0	105.0	105.0
	Earnings	48.9	49.5	49.2	49.4	48.1	49.4	50.0	49.4	50.0	49.9	50.6	51.4
1925	Rate[b]	105.1	105.1	105.1	105.1	105.1	105.1	105.1	105.1	105.1	105.1	105.1	105.2
	Earnings	51.1	50.8	51.1	50.7	50.9	50.1	50.5	51.3	50.7	51.3	51.4	50.7
1926	Rate[b]	105.2	105.2	105.2	105.2	105.2	105.3	105.3	105.3	105.4	105.4	105.4	105.5
	Earnings	50.7	50.4	50.8	50.5	51.2	51.2	50.8	51.0	50.6	51.0	51.7	51.3

TABLE A (concl.)

	Jan.	Feb.	March	April	May	June	July	Aug.	Sep.	Oct.	Nov.	Dec.
1927 Rate[b]	105.5	105.5	105.5	105.5	105.5	105.5	105.5	105.5	105.5	105.5	105.5	105.5
Earnings	51.3	51.5	51.2	50.5	50.5	50.4	51.1	50.8	51.2	51.1	50.6	50.9
1928 Rate[b]	105.5	105.5	105.5	105.5	105.5	105.5	105.5	105.5	105.5	105.5	105.5	105.5
Earnings	51.0	51.2	51.0	50.8	51.1	50.9	51.1	51.7	51.4	51.5	51.4	50.9
1929 Rate[b]	105.5	105.5	105.5	105.5	105.5	105.5	105.5	105.5	105.5	105.6	105.6	105.6
Earnings	51.2	51.1	52.0	51.1	51.1	51.7	51.1	51.5	51.3	51.4	52.7	53.1
1930 Rate[b]	105.6	105.6	105.6	105.5	105.5	105.4	105.4	105.3	105.3	105.2	105.2	105.2
Earnings	52.9	53.4	53.8	53.2	53.5	53.0	53.0	52.4	53.1	53.1	51.8	51.8
1931 Rate[b]	105.2	105.2	105.2	105.1	105.1	105.0	105.0	104.9				
Earnings	52.5	52.4	52.3	52.0	51.4	51.3	51.5	51.3	51.5	50.9	46.6	45.9

WOOLENS AND WORSTEDS

	Jan.	Feb.	March	April	May	June	July	Aug.	Sep.	Oct.	Nov.	Dec.
1919 Rate[a]	83.9	83.9	83.9	83.9	83.9	96.8	96.8	97.0	97.2	97.2	97.2	110.9
1920 Rate[a]	110.9	110.9	110.9	111.1	111.1	126.0	126.0	126.0	126.0	126.0	125.6	125.6
Earnings						58.0	57.9	57.6	57.6	58.0	56.9	57.0
1921 Rate[a]	100.6	98.5	98.1	98.1	98.1	98.1	98.1	98.1	98.1	98.1	98.1	98.1
Earnings	50.9	47.9	46.9	46.9	47.7	47.5	46.0	45.9	46.1	46.5	46.2	46.3
1922 Rate[a]	98.1	98.1	97.7	97.7	97.7	97.7	97.6	97.6	98.2	98.2	98.3	98.5
Earnings	n.a.	n.a.	n.a.	n.a.	n.a.	n.a.	45.5	45.2	45.7	46.6	46.2	47.2
1923 Rate[a]	98.6	98.7	98.9	100.0	107.2	107.3	107.3	107.3	107.3	107.4	107.4	107.4
Rate[b]				100.0	109.4	109.4	109.5	109.5	109.5	109.5	109.5	109.5
Earnings	46.4	46.3	47.1	48.3	52.6	52.1	52.4	52.1	52.5	52.4	52.3	52.1

1924											
Rate[b]	109.5	109.5	109.5	109.5	109.5	109.5	109.4	109.4	109.4	109.4	109.4
Earnings	51.4	51.5	51.3	49.5	48.9	48.8	49.5	51.1	50.8	50.7	50.5	51.0
1925											
Rate[b]	109.4	109.4	109.4	109.4	109.3	109.3	106.7	106.6	105.5	105.5	105.5
Earnings	51.1	50.8	50.7	51.1	50.7	50.8	50.4	49.4	49.1	48.5	48.6	47.3
1926											
Rate[b]	105.5	105.5	105.5	105.6	105.6	105.6	105.5	105.5	105.5	105.5	105.5
Earnings	47.2	47.7	48.5	48.4	48.4	47.9	47.9	46.9	47.7	48.3	48.5	49.0
1927											
Rate[b]	105.5	105.4	105.4	105.4	105.4	105.2	105.2	105.2	105.2	105.2	105.2
Earnings	48.6	48.7	48.5	48.8	49.4	49.3	49.9	49.3	49.6	49.5	49.6	50.4
1928											
Rate[b]	104.9	104.8	104.8	104.8	104.8	104.8	104.8	104.8	104.8	104.8	104.8
Earnings	49.6	49.1	48.6	49.0	48.9	48.6	48.3	48.8	48.3	49.0	49.4	49.6
1929											
Rate[b]	104.8	104.8	104.8	104.8	104.9	104.9	104.9	104.9	104.9	104.9	104.9
Earnings	48.7	48.7	48.5	49.4	48.6	49.1	47.7	47.8	47.8	48.3	47.6	47.1
1930											
Rate[b]	104.9	104.9	104.9	104.9	104.9	104.9	104.8	104.8	104.8	104.7	104.7
Earnings	48.5	48.7	48.7	49.5	49.1	48.7	50.1	49.9	49.3	49.0	49.4	48.9
1931											
Rate[b]	104.2	103.5	103.4	103.4	103.3	103.2	103.1	103.1			
Earnings	48.6	48.1	48.3	47.1	47.2	47.0	47.0	47.6	47.2	47.7	45.1	44.3

APPENDIX B

Wage Rate Indexes, with Notes on their Construction, and Average Hourly Earnings on Class I Railroads, United States

In constructing an index of wage rates for all employees on Class I railroads paid by the hour, our starting point is the decision of the Railway Labor Board, effective May 1, 1920, granting a 22 percent increase to all railroad employees. Making April 1920 the base, we compute the index for May 1920 (centered at the middle of the month) to be 122.0. All subsequent changes are converted to link relatives and chained to this base. The effective dates of changes in wage rates are used rather than the dates of the decisions or bargaining agreements that brought them about.

Information on changes in wage rates is from *Wages and Labor Relations in the Railroad Industry, 1900-1941* by H. E. Jones (Bureau of Information of the Eastern Railroads), and *Historical Development of the Railroad Wage Structure* by B. M. Jewell and G. M. Cucich (American Federation of Labor, Railway Employees' Department, Chicago, 1941). When absolute changes in cents per hour or day are given, the wage rate before the change is estimated from *Wage Statistics of Class I Steam Railways in the United States* (ICC monthly release), in addition to these two sources. The percentage change in wage rates can then be estimated.

The percentage of all Class I railroad workers affected by changes in wage rates is necessary for weighting purposes. Whenever a change involves a given occupation on all railroads the weights can be computed directly from the ICC monthly release. When a change affects only workers in a given occupation in one of the three regions (East, West, or Southeast) or on a specific railroad the weights are estimated by assuming that the relative composition of occupations on each railroad and in each region is identical with that for all Class I railroads. The ratio of industry-wide employment in a given occupation to total railroad employment (Class I) is then multiplied by the ratio of employment on a given railroad or in a given region, as the case may be, to total railroad employment. This procedure is illustrated by an example showing how the weighted percentage change in the index of wage rates from January to February 1927 was computed. The sum of the products, .307, divided by the total weights, 100, is +0.3 percent. Since the index for January 1927 is 105.1, February 1927 becomes 105.4.

	FIREMEN IN EAST	CONDUCTORS & TRAINMEN IN SOUTHEAST	OTHER R.R. EMPLOYEES	TOTAL
1) % change in wage rates	+7.5	+7.5	0	
2) Ratio: emp. in region affected to total emp. on Class I roads (%)	43.0	19.8		
3) Ratio: no. of emp. in given occupation to total emp. on Class I roads (%)	4.1	11.7		
4) % of emp. affected, weights (2 x 3)	1.8	2.3	95.9	100.0
5) Product (1 x 4)	.135	.172	0	.307

In the case of clerical and station employees, signalmen, and telegraphers receiving increases from individual railroads during 1923-30, a tally is made for each occupation, listing chronologically (by effective dates) the specific railroads affected and the amount or percentage of increase in wage rates. As in constructing the manufacturing wage rate indexes, when the increase is less than 0.1 percent from one month to another, it is cumulated until 0.1 percent is reached. When, during 1923-24 and again in 1926, no precise effective date is mentioned for the increase granted by individual roads, ultimately affecting all workers in the mechanical trades, the weighted percentage change is distributed equally over each period. In 1926, for example, the weighted percentage change in wage rates received by this group, 1.2, is distributed so that March, June, September and December reflect 0.3 percent increases.

Data on the number of employees on individual roads and in the three regions of the United States are from *Statistics of Railways in the United States* (ICC annual reports). For the tallies, tables in the Jewell-Cucich study are used.

Table B

Index of Wage Rates, Employees on an Hourly Basis, Average Hourly Earnings, Employees on an Hourly and Daily Basis:* Class I Railroads, United States, 1920-1939

Base of index of wage rates is April 1920:100; average hourly earnings in cents are corrected for seasonal variation

	Jan.	Feb.	March	April	May	June	July	Aug.	Sep.	Oct.	Nov.	Dec.
1920 Rate	122.0	122.0	122.0	100.0	122.0	122.0	122.0	122.0	122.0	122.0	122.0	122.0
Earnings	n.a.	n.a.	n.a.	n.a.	n.a.	n.a.	n.a.	n.a.	n.a.	n.a.	n.a.	n.a.
1921 Rate	107.4	107.4	107.4	122.0	122.0	122.0	107.4	107.4	107.4	107.4	107.4	107.4
Earnings	60.3	60.3	60.4	n.a.	n.a.	n.a.	60.9	60.4	59.8	60.4	60.0	59.9
1922 Rate	100.5	100.5	100.6	100.6	107.4	107.4	99.8	99.8	99.8	100.5	100.5	100.5
Earnings	58.6	58.8	58.7	59.3	60.2	60.4	57.8	57.6	58.2	58.9	58.8	59.2
1923 Rate	102.2	102.2	100.6	100.6	100.6	100.8	100.8	100.8	100.8	101.1	101.4	101.6
Earnings	59.5	59.4	58.7	59.3	59.1	59.2	59.6	59.3	59.6	59.5	59.5	59.6
1924 Rate	102.2	102.2	102.2	102.4	102.4	102.6	102.6	102.6	102.8	102.8	102.8	103.0
Earnings	59.5	59.4	60.2	60.0	60.1	60.6	60.4	60.7	60.3	60.5	60.8	60.7
1925 Rate	103.3	103.3	103.3	103.3	103.3	103.3	103.3	103.3	103.3	103.3	103.3	103.3
Earnings	60.6	60.8	60.9	60.7	61.1	60.8	60.9	61.3	60.9	61.2	61.5	61.1
1926 Rate	103.3	103.3	103.6	103.6	103.7	104.0	104.0	104.0	104.3	104.3	104.3	105.1
Earnings	61.7	61.6	61.5	61.5	61.8	61.4	61.5	61.9	61.7	62.2	61.9	62.4
1927 Rate	105.1	105.4	105.7	105.7	105.8	105.8	105.9	106.2	106.3	106.3	106.4	106.5
Earnings	62.8	62.7	62.4	62.5	62.9	62.4	63.1	63.1	63.3	63.7	63.2	63.5
1928 Rate	106.5	106.5	106.6	106.6	106.9	106.9	106.9	106.9	106.9	106.9	106.9	107.0
Earnings	63.9	63.3	63.6	64.1	63.4	63.6	64.3	63.8	64.4	64.2	64.3	64.9

	1	2	3	4	5	6	7	8	9	10	11	12
1929												
Rate	107.0	107.2	109.1	109.1	109.1	109.1	109.1	109.1	109.1	109.1	109.2	109.2
Earnings	64.5	65.2	65.2	64.8	64.9	65.3	65.0	65.0	65.5	65.4	65.5	66.0
1930												
Rate	109.4	109.4	109.4	109.4	109.4	109.4	109.4	109.4	109.4	109.4	109.4	109.4
Earnings	65.7	65.8	65.8	65.4	65.5	66.2	66.6	66.6	66.4	66.6	67.4	66.4
1931												
Rate	109.4	109.4	109.4	109.4	109.4	109.4	109.4	109.4	109.4	109.4	109.4	109.4
Earnings	66.1	66.8	66.8	66.7	67.2	66.7	67.1	67.4	66.9	67.2	67.9	66.9
1932												
Rate	109.4	98.5	98.5	98.5	98.5	98.5	98.5	98.5	98.5	98.5	98.5	98.5
Earnings	67.0	60.4	60.6	61.0	61.1	60.9	61.7	61.0	61.0	61.5	61.1	60.9
1933												
Rate	98.5	98.5	98.5	98.5	98.5	98.5	98.5	98.5	98.5	98.5	98.5	98.5
Earnings	60.8	61.2	60.8	61.4	61.0	61.2	61.5	60.8	60.4	61.0	60.9	60.9
1934												
Rate	98.5	98.5	98.5	98.5	98.5	98.5	101.3	101.3	101.3	101.3	101.3	101.3
Earnings	60.4	61.2	61.0	61.2	60.8	60.9	62.8	62.3	62.8	62.3	62.6	62.8
1935												
Rate	104.0	104.0	104.0	109.5	109.5	109.5	109.5	109.5	109.5	109.5	109.5	109.5
Earnings	63.9	64.7	64.8	67.7	68.0	67.0	67.0	67.6	67.4	67.4	67.6	67.7
1936												
Rate	109.5	109.5	109.5	109.5	109.5	109.5	109.5	109.5	109.5	109.5	109.5	109.5
Earnings	67.3	67.4	67.7	67.1	67.8	67.2	67.2	67.6	67.0	67.4	68.0	67.4
1937												
Rate	109.5	109.5	109.5	109.5	109.5	109.5	109.5	109.5	116.3	116.3	117.9	117.9
Earnings	67.9	67.5	67.5	67.2	67.8	67.1	67.0	67.0	70.7	70.6	73.1	72.4
1938												
Rate	117.9	117.9	117.9	117.9	117.9	117.9	117.9	117.9	117.9	117.9	117.9	117.9
Earnings	72.8	72.8	72.5	73.0	73.8	73.2	73.5	72.6	72.5	73.3	72.8	72.6
1939												
Rate	117.9	117.9	117.9	117.9	117.9	117.9	117.9	117.9	117.9	117.9	117.9	117.9
Earnings	73.1	72.7	72.7	73.3	72.9	72.9	73.3	72.6	72.9	73.7	73.2	73.3

Source: For rates, see Appendix B; earnings derived from ICC data by U.S. Department of Commerce, *Survey of Current Business*.

*Executives, officials, and staff assistants are excluded.

n.a.: not available.

Appendix C

Cost of Fringe Benefits in Anthracite Coal Mining

Fringe payments is a phrase that has gained currency to describe payments to wage earners by employers as a supplement to wages paid on the basis of hours worked or production completed. The stipulations concerning wage rates are regarded as the heart of the wage contract while the stipulations concerning the supplements are deemed to be on the periphery or fringe. During 1949 wage supplements have occupied the center of the stage in collective bargaining negotiations. However, supplements in some form, as we define them for purposes of measurement, have existed for at least several decades. Demands for fringe benefits, originating in the deep-seated desire of workers for security and leisure, could be pressed in recent years because of the great strength of trade unions and full employment. Moreover, the policy of wage stabilization during the war years served to focus attention on the possibilities of altering the fringes of the contract without touching its heart.

Until wage supplements began to loom large in the total picture employers could regard average hourly earnings as a close approximation to the average cost of employing labor for an hour. As wage supplements become more important, average hourly earnings become less adequate as an approximation to the cost of an hour's labor. For to the employer supplements are additional costs of employing labor and are not reflected in average hourly earnings.

We define wage supplements as the benefits in cash or kind received by wage earners as a result either of state or federal legislation or of collective bargaining negotiations. The expenditures on benefits are paid in whole or in part by employers. The following is a reasonably comprehensive list of wage supplements:

I   Wage supplements provided by legislation
    A   Workmen's compensation
    B   Old-age and survivors insurance
    C   Unemployment compensation
    D   Sickness insurance

II Wage supplements provided by collective agreements
   A Pension and retirement payments
   B Disability payments
   C Group life insurance
   D Hospitalization
   E Medical care
   F Travel time
   G Paid vacations
   H Paid holidays

The first three wage supplements, or rights thereto, provided by legislation are received by a very high percentage of wage earners except those employed in agriculture, domestic service, or nonprofit institutions. Sickness insurance, the most recent of these social security schemes, is operative in only a few states. The share and amount of these expenditures borne by employers is published in government reports. The extent of wage supplements under collective agreements varies from industry to industry, and from firm to firm within a given industry. Information on which wage supplements are in force in a given industry can be obtained from the collective agreement and the expenditures of the employer estimated. The estimate, however, will be more or less accurate only if the industry is completely unionized, or virtually so, and the collective agreement is industry-wide.

The anthracite coal industry fulfills these requirements; accordingly, we chose it to illustrate the difference between average hourly earnings and average labor cost per hour worked and the changes in these magnitudes in recent years.

Employers spent 39 cents on wage supplements in anthracite coal mining in 1948 and only 8 cents in 1939 for each hour worked by each wage earner (Table C). Therefore the average cost of an hour's labor in 1948 was not $1.81, as indicated by the BLS figures on average hourly earnings, but $2.20 (average hourly earnings, $1.81, plus expenditure on supplements per manhour worked, 39 cents). Similarly, in 1939 the average hourly cost was $1.00, not 92 cents, the amount reported as average hourly earnings.

Thus, in the course of a decade, expenditures on wage supplements quintupled while average hourly earnings about doubled. Relatively, expenditures on wage supplements were two and a third

TABLE C
Expenditures of Employers on Wage Supplements, Anthracite Coal Mining, 1939 and 1948

	TYPE OF WAGE SUPPLEMENT	EXP. OF EMPLOYERS 1939	1948
1	Workmen's compensation	$5,470,000	$13,742,000
2	Old-age and survivors insurance	1,100,000	2,230,000
3	Unemployment compensation	3,530,000	2,294,000
4	Health and welfare fund	....	8,397,000
5	Paid vacations	....	6,254,000
6	Travel time	....	18,220,000
7	Total wage supplements	$10,100,000	$51,137,000
8	Total manhours worked	123,969,000	132,239,000
9	Exp. on wage supplements per manhour worked (7 ÷ 8)	$.08	$0.39
10	Average hourly earnings	0.92	1.81
11	Exp. on wage supplements per manhour worked as % of av. hourly earnings (9 ÷ 10)	8.7%	21.5%

times as large in 1948 as in 1939. In the latter year, for example, expenditures on supplements per manhour added 8.7 percent to hourly earnings; 10 years later, 21.5 percent.

An investigator relying solely on average hourly earnings statistics as currently compiled would find that the cost of labor per hour had increased 97 percent between 1939 and 1948. If expenditures on wage supplements are included, the cost of a manhour of labor has risen 120 percent. The evidence suggests that expenditures on wage supplements continued to increase in 1949. Thus, if royalty payments into the Health and Welfare Fund in 1948 had been at the 1949 rate, 20 cents per ton, instead of the 1948 rate, 10 cents, on all tonnage mined from January 1 to July 15 and 20 cents thereafter, expenditures on all wage supplements per manhour worked would have been 41 cents—nearly 23 percent of average hourly earnings in 1948 and 22 percent of average hourly earnings in 1949.

In 1948 about three-fifths of expenditures on wage supplements were incurred for workmen's compensation and travel time. In less hazardous industries and when payment for travel time is less common, such as most branches of manufacturing, supplementary labor costs would constitute a smaller proportion of average hourly earnings.

Notes on Sources of Data and Methods of Estimating

The numbered paragraphs that follow correspond to the lines in Table C.

The first three wage supplements represent legislative social security programs operative in Pennsylvania, the seat of most anthracite coal mines. The last three wage supplements are stipulated in the collective agreement between the owners of anthracite coal mines and the anthracite coal miners represented by the United Mine Workers. The terms of the collective agreements operative in 1939 and 1948 were summarized for us by the Division of Industrial Relations, Bureau of Labor Statistics, Department of Labor.

1) Workmen's compensation: derived by applying the average premiums for workmen's compensation and occupational disease insurance to the annual payrolls of production workers.

Payrolls in 1948 were estimated by multiplying total manhours worked each month by average hourly earnings for the given month and adding the 12 monthly totals. For our estimates of total manhours worked each month see 8. Average hourly earnings in anthracite mining were compiled by the BLS. The average premium for workmen's compensation in 1948 was $3.58 per $100 of payroll; the average premium for occupational disease insurance was $1.62 (letter from the Coal Mine Section, Pennsylvania Compensation Rating and Inspection Bureau, Harrisburg).

Payrolls in 1939, from the 1939 Census of Mineral Industries, represent payments to wage earners only. The premiums in 1939, reported by the Rating Bureau in correspondence, were $9.51 for the first half of the year and $7.22 for the second half for workmen's compensation and $0.90 during the entire year for occupational disease insurance. The Bureau cautions, however:

"Several things must be taken into consideration in order to make an intelligent comparison between rates in effect in 1939 and in 1948. In 1939 there was a much smaller amount of insured anthracite business than there is at the present time. At that time, most of the mines were rather small and the loss experience in that type of mine has always been unfavorable. At the present time, the larger part of the underground mining that is insured is covered by fifteen or twenty medium-sized or large mines. This in itself accounts for a tremendous improvement in the loss experience."

In the light of this information it seemed that errors would be minimized by applying the average workmen's compensation premium of 1948 to the payroll total for July-December 1939 and this premium, increased 31.72 percent ($9.51÷$7.22), to the January-June 1939 payroll. The annual payroll was divided into semi-annual payrolls on the basis of the BLS monthly payroll indexes for 1939. The occupational disease insurance premium, $0.90, reported for that year was applied to the annual 1939 payroll. The estimate for 1939 is probably somewhat low.

2) Old-age and survivors insurance: payroll taxes paid by employers were obtained by correspondence with the Division of Research and Statistics, Social Security Administration, Federal Security Agency. They include also the taxes paid on the payrolls of nonproduction employees. To confine the costs to production workers we multiplied the reported total for 1939 by 93.87 percent, the ratio of wage earners to all employees reported for anthracite mining in the 1939 Census of Mineral Industries. The comparable percentage for 1948, according to the BLS, was 94.75. The use of this adjustment percentage assumes that the relation between taxable wages of production workers and total taxable wages is the same as the above relation based on the number employed. This adjustment probably does not remove all the taxes paid on the taxable earnings of nonproduction workers, especially in 1939.

3) Unemployment compensation: payroll taxes paid by employers; source and adjustments as in 2.

4) Health and welfare fund: financed by employers by royalty payments on tonnage mined. The royalty was 10 cents per ton from January 1 to July 15, 1948 and 20 cents per ton thereafter. The weekly and monthly production figures are compiled by the Bureau of Mines and published in the *Mineral Industry Surveys*. There was no such fund in 1939.

5) Paid vacations: the collective bargaining agreement, as summarized by the Bureau of Labor Statistics, provides that:

"Vacation compensation shall be at the rate of one hundred ($100) dollars per year for each employee and payment of the full amount of $100 per year shall be predicated on an employee having worked in each of the twenty-four semi-monthly pay periods in the year ending June 15.

Where an employee has not worked in all of the semi-monthly periods for any cause, compensation payable to him shall be a pro rata share of the $100 on the number of pay periods actually worked for his employer in said year provided . . . that no vacation compensation shall be payable to any employee who has worked for his employer in less than six semi-monthly pay periods in each vacation year."

We do not know of any data that classify anthracite mine workers employed as of a specific date by the number of pay periods worked in the preceding 12 months. However, from the statistics compiled by the Bureau of Old-Age and Survivors Insurance it is possible to classify these workers by the number of calendar quarters in which they had some work during the calendar year. The latest available distribution is for 1947. In using this distribution we are obliged to assume that some work in a calendar quarter means work in all pay periods in a calendar quarter. This is probably a reasonably good assumption in years of full employment such as 1947 and 1948. Whatever overstatement results from this assumption is offset in part at least by the further assumption that no one working for only one quarter worked for as many as 6 semi-monthly pay periods. The percentage distribution of workers by employment in 4, 3, 2, and 1 quarters applied to the average number of wage earners in 1948 (estimated by the BLS) yields an estimate of the number of workers entitled to vacation pay of $100, $75, $50, and $0, respectively. The sum of the products of the number of workers and the respective amounts of vacation pay yields an estimate of total vacation pay. There was no provision for paid vacations in 1939.

6) Travel time: the collective bargaining agreement stipulates that: "The present travel time shall be $1.339 per shift with the understanding that contract workers, in keeping with the custom and practice, shall be paid this amount per start. This is on the basis of an accepted and agreed travel time for all inside employees of forty-five (45) minutes per day, at a rate of $1.191 per hour at rate and one-half, taking into account the extreme difficulty of measuring accurately the actual travel time of individual underground workers."

The cost of travel time then is the product of the number of man-shifts for underground workers and $1.339. The Bureau of Mines compiles each year statistics on the average number of days worked and of underground workers. The ratio of underground workers to all production workers in 1948 was applied to the estimate of all production workers in 1948 (BLS) to obtain an estimate of the average number of underground workers in 1948. The latter figure multiplied by the average number of days worked equals the number of manshifts. This, in turn, multiplied by $1.339 yields the estimated cost of travel time. There was no provision for travel time in 1939.

8) Total manhours worked: total manhours paid for was first estimated. This was accomplished for 1948 in the following manner: For each month the average length of the workweek was multiplied by the number employed and by the number of weeks in the month. The sum of these 12 products equals the estimated manhours paid for. Manhours paid for minus the manhours involved in paid vacations and in travel time yields manhours worked. The manhour equivalent of paid vacations was derived by dividing the cost of paid vacations (line 5) by average hourly earnings in June and July 1948 (BLS). The amount of travel time equals the number of manshifts multiplied by 45 minutes.

In 1939 manhours worked and paid for are identical. The total is reported in the 1939 Census of Mineral Industries.

10) Average hourly earnings: the figures for 1939 and 1948 are from BLS compilations.

Shares of Upper Income Groups in Income and Savings

SIMON KUZNETS

OCCASIONAL PAPER 35

NATIONAL BUREAU OF ECONOMIC RESEARCH, INC.

OFFICERS
(1950)

Boris Shishkin, *Chairman*
Harry Scherman, *President*
C. C. Balderston, *Vice-President*
George B. Roberts, *Treasurer*
W. J. Carson, *Executive Director*
Martha Anderson, *Editor*

DIRECTORS AT LARGE

Donald R. Belcher, *American Telephone and Telegraph Co.*
Oswald W. Knauth, *New York City*
Simon Kuznets, *University of Pennsylvania*
H. W. Laidler, *Executive Director, League for Industrial Democracy*
Shepard Morgan, *New York City*
C. Reinold Noyes, *Princeton, New Jersey*
George B. Roberts, *Vice-President, National City Bank*
Beardsley Ruml, *New York City*
Harry Scherman, *Chairman, Book-of-the-Month Club*
George Soule, *Bennington College*
N. I. Stone, *Consulting Economist*
J. Raymond Walsh, *WMCA Broadcasting Co.*
Leo Wolman, *Columbia University*
Theodore O. Yntema, *Vice-President—Finance, Ford Motor Company*

DIRECTORS BY UNIVERSITY APPOINTMENT

E. Wight Bakke, *Yale*
C. C. Balderston, *Pennsylvania*
Arthur F. Burns, *Columbia*
G. A. Elliott, *Toronto*
Frank W. Fetter, *Northwestern*
H. M. Groves, *Wisconsin*
Gottfried Haberler, *Harvard*
Clarence Heer, *North Carolina*
R. L. Kozelka, *Minnesota*
Paul M. O'Leary, *Cornell*
T. W. Schultz, *Chicago*

DIRECTORS APPOINTED BY OTHER ORGANIZATIONS

Percival F. Brundage, *American Institute of Accountants*
Thomas C. Cochran, *Economic History Association*
Frederick C. Mills, *American Statistical Association*
Stanley H. Ruttenberg, *Congress of Industrial Organizations*
Murray Shields, *American Management Association*
Boris Shishkin, *American Federation of Labor*
Warren C. Waite, *American Farm Economic Association*
Donald H. Wallace, *American Economic Association*

RESEARCH STAFF

Arthur F. Burns, *Director of Research*
Geoffrey H. Moore, *Associate Director of Research*

Moses Abramovitz
Harold Barger
Morris A. Copeland
Daniel Creamer
David Durand
Solomon Fabricant
Milton Friedman
Millard Hastay
W. Braddock Hickman
F. F. Hill
Thor Hultgren
Simon Kuznets
Clarence D. Long
Ruth P. Mack
Frederick C. Mills
Raymond J. Saulnier
Lawrence H. Seltzer
George J. Stigler
Leo Wolman

Relation of the Directors to the Work and Publications of the National Bureau of Economic Research

1. The object of the National Bureau of Economic Research is to ascertain and to present to the public important economic facts and their interpretation in a scientific and impartial manner. The Board of Directors is charged with the responsibility of ensuring that the work of the National Bureau is carried on in strict conformity with this object.

2. To this end the Board of Directors shall appoint one or more Directors of Research.

3. The Director or Directors of Research shall submit to the members of the Board, or to its Executive Committee, for their formal adoption, all specific proposals concerning researches to be instituted.

4. No report shall be published until the Director or Directors of Research shall have submitted to the Board a summary drawing attention to the character of the data and their utilization in the report, the nature and treatment of the problems involved, the main conclusions and such other information as in their opinion would serve to determine the suitability of the report for publication in accordance with the principles of the National Bureau.

5. A copy of any manuscript proposed for publication shall also be submitted to each member of the Board. For each manuscript to be so submitted a special committee shall be appointed by the President, or at his designation by the Executive Director, consisting of three Directors selected as nearly as may be one from each general division of the Board. The names of the special manuscript committee shall be stated to each Director when the summary and report described in paragraph (4) are sent to him. It shall be the duty of each member of the committee to read the manuscript. If each member of the special committee signifies his approval within thirty days, the manuscript may be published. If each member of the special committee has not signified his approval within thirty days of the transmittal of the report and manuscript, the Director of Research shall then notify each member of the Board, requesting approval or disapproval of publication, and thirty additional days shall be granted for this purpose. The manuscript shall then not be published unless at least a majority of the entire Board and a two-thirds majority of those members of the Board who shall have voted on the proposal within the time fixed for the receipt of votes on the publication proposed shall have approved.

6. No manuscript may be published, though approved by each member of the special committee, until forty-five days have elapsed from the transmittal of the summary and report. The interval is allowed for the receipt of any memorandum of dissent or reservation, together with a brief statement of his reasons, that any member may wish to express; and such memorandum of dissent or reservation shall be published with the manuscript if he so desires. Publication does not, however, imply that each member of the Board has read the manuscript, or that either members of the Board in general, or of the special committee, have passed upon its validity in every detail.

7. A copy of this resolution shall, unless otherwise determined by the Board, be printed in each copy of every National Bureau book.

(Resolution adopted October 25, 1926 and revised February 6, 1933 and February 24, 1941)

Shares of Upper Income Groups in Income and Savings

SIMON KUZNETS
University of Pennsylvania

OCCASIONAL PAPER 35

NATIONAL BUREAU OF ECONOMIC RESEARCH, INC.

1950

Throughout the study whose results are summarized in this paper I had the patient and expert assistance of Elizabeth Jenks and Lillian Epstein. Miss Jenks bore the brunt of the work and of the numerous revisions of estimates and analysis. Without her and Miss Epstein's help the study would never have been completed; and this paper might never have seen the light of day.

An earlier version of this paper was presented for discussion at the meeting of the Conference on Research in Income and Wealth in spring 1949. I profited greatly from various critical suggestions made at that meeting.

The detailed report and the summary paper were reviewed by a committee of the National Bureau staff. Helpful comments were received from Ruth Mack and Thor Hultgren, and particularly from Geoffrey Moore. Martha Anderson as usual labored hard to eliminate infelicities of style and ambiguities of expression.

I wish to express my sincere thanks for all the assistance.

S. K.

Price: $1.00

Copyright, 1950, by National Bureau of Economic Research, Inc. 1819 Broadway, New York 23, N. Y. All Rights Reserved Manufactured in the U.S.A. by The Academy Press

THE DISTRIBUTION OF INCOME AMONG THE INDIVIDUALS AND HOUSEHOLDS that go to make up the nation is one of our important statistics. Unless economic activity is looked upon as a pastime or a vocation whose pursuit is its own reward, compensation for personal participation or for the use of property is in a sense its *ultima ratio*. Income tends to be a criterion of an economy's performance and influences an individual's pattern of consumption and savings, and to an important degree his efficiency as a producer. The distribution of income by size is one of the points at which we can observe the flow of the product of the economy to consumers and producers, and at which we can, therefore, discern a key link in the economic mechanism, helpful in understanding some of its workings and in appraising some of its advantages and disadvantages.

The importance of a size distribution of income is matched by the difficulty of getting reliable and continuous measures, especially in a society that traditionally has tended to minimize state interference. Its members are the sole adequate source of information about the income receipts of individuals and households; and in an individualistic free society they are neither eager nor always able to tell all about their income, in strict accordance with the economist's concept. Indeed, most of our accurate economic information comes not from individuals but from enterprises, which keep accounts because they are essential to survival and growth as well as to daily living. And enterprises being, in a sense, creatures of society and of its sovereign organs, can be easily called to account. They cannot provide us, however, with a distribution of income among individuals and households, which may receive income from various sources, or with data on the social characteristics of recipients whose home life is their own.[1]

[1] A free economic society in which individuals have a fair amount of liberty as consumers and producers and in which it is, therefore, indispensable to analyze the distribution of income by size as a basis for ascertaining the patterns of consumer and producer behavior is exactly the type of society in which getting such information is difficult because of the natural resistance of its members. In an authoritarian society individuals as consumers and producers have much less freedom and it may be less important to analyze the size distribution of income as a system of production incentives or as a basis for relating consumption and investment patterns, but it is easier to get the data. This paradox may have some intriguing aspects in that the existence of free agents in a society may enhance both the value of studying their behavior and the difficulty of getting the data; and the subjection of free agents to authoritarian control acts both to facilitate the supply of data and to reduce the need for them.

All this is by way of explaining why the investigation whose results are summarized below[2] is confined largely to the upper income groups. For them alone do we have, in this country, continuous information on their number and income for a fairly long period. With this information, derived from federal income tax returns by individuals, we can estimate their shares in total income on a basis that, despite several qualifications inherent in the data, is fairly comparable from year to year. Information on the large proportion of the income population below the top has become available for only a few recent years, and even for these it is too scanty for detailed analysis.

The percentage shares of upper income groups in total income can be estimated annually for 1919-47; and, in less detail, back to 1913. Subject to some limitations, they can be estimated also in the countrywide aggregates of employee compensation, entrepreneurial income, dividends, interest, and rent. We can, therefore, observe the average structure of the size distribution, as revealed by shares of upper income groups, in total income and in various types. The average level and structure of the shares of the upper and lower groups is the first topic discussed in Part A, and the two major findings may be put briefly:

1) The average income shares (income ex capital gains and before taxes) of upper income groups between the two world wars were: the top 1 percent of the population, 15 percent of income, top 5 percent, 30 percent of income.

2) The shares of upper income groups were largest in the countrywide aggregate of dividends: the top 1 percent of the population received on the average 65 percent of total dividends paid to individuals, the top 5 percent, 77 percent. Their shares were lowest in the countrywide total of employee compensation, averaging about 6½ percent for the top 1 percent and 17 percent for the top 5 percent group.

These findings can be interpreted properly if it is recognized that in distinguishing the top 1 and 5 percent groups, we reach well down the income scale. As shown in Appendix Table 1, the *lowest* units in the top 1 percent group received incomes which, on a *per capita* basis, ranged (for 1919-38) from somewhat over $2,000

[2] A two volume report under the same title is now being prepared for publication at the National Bureau of Economic Research.

to somewhat over $4,000, i.e., from over $8,000 to over $16,000 for a family of four. For the lowest units in the top 5 percent group, per capita incomes ranged from about $1,250 to about $2,000, i.e., from $5,000 to $8,000 for a family of four. Furthermore, the percentage shares of the top 1 and 5 percent groups cited above are averages for 1919-38: as indicated below, the shares declined markedly during World War II and postwar years.

The size of income shares and even of their changes in any distribution depend upon the recipient unit used (the individual, family, consuming unit, etc.); the scope of income (including or excluding income in kind, capital gains, other transfer items, etc.); the extent to which several types of income from various sources combine to swell the total income of a given recipient unit; and the period over which income is cumulated (a year, two years, etc.). In addition to such statistical characteristics of the size distribution, we consider others that reveal the demographic and social composition of income classes—sex, age, education, size of family, location (rural, urban, cities of different size), occupation, industrial attachment, and the like. The effects of the statistical characteristics of the distribution on the shares of upper income groups and of their social characteristics must both be taken into account in interpreting income inequality—all of which form the second group of topics discussed in Part A. The conclusions do not lend themselves to a brief summary. But in general they show the large degree to which income inequality, as measured here, is due to our use of income for a single year and the composition of upper income groups: more persons at productive ages, with higher formal education and experience, and consuming units whose place of residence entails high costs of living.

In Part B we deal with changes in the shares of upper income groups, in both total income and countrywide aggregates of various types of income. While the period covered is at most some three decades, the diversity of the patterns of change and of the income types gives a rather complex picture—treated here only in broad outline and suggesting two major findings:

3) The shares of upper income groups declined substantially from 1939 to 1944 or 1945, and by 1948 had recovered little. From 1939 to 1945 the share of the top 1 percent group dropped from over 13 to 9.5 percent and the share of the top 5 percent group,

from over 28 to 19.5 percent. If capital gains and taxes are allowed for, the decline was even sharper—from over 12 to over 7 percent for the top 1 and from over 27 to about 17 percent for the top 5 percent group.

4) During business cycles in the interwar period income shares of upper income groups changed, on the whole, little. That of the top 1 percent group was irregularly related to business cycles; shares of the upper income groups below the top 1 percent tended to move counter to business cycles, as did that of the top 5 percent group as a whole.

To know how the country's income is distributed among individuals and families and how its distribution changes is useful only if we can better explain the behavior of income recipients as producers and as consumers. Of the possible implications of our findings concerning income shares of upper income groups, we have explored only one, that for the level and short term movements of individuals' savings. This necessarily entailed scrutinizing data on the patterns of individuals' savings—with special attention to savings of upper income groups as contrasted with savings of all groups. The bearing of these data, and of the level and movements of shares of upper income groups, on the role of their savings during business cycles, is set forth in Part C, with the following tentative conclusions:

5) During business cycles the savings-income ratios for the upper income groups fluctuated much less relatively than those for the lower income groups. This, together with the stability of the income shares of upper income groups, suggests that their savings constituted a fairly stable proportion of the total income of individuals. Consequently, the extreme variability during business cycles of the savings-income ratio for the total population must have been due largely to violent changes in the savings-inome ratios for lower income groups.

6) In view of the distinct probability that savings of upper and of lower income groups seek different investment channels, the changing distribution during business cycles of total individual savings between savings by upper and lower income groups should be recognized as affecting the savings-investment flow.

In Part D the major avenues of further work in the field, whether along the lines pursued here or along others, are briefly discussed. While Part D may seem out of place in a summary, we venture to include it for two reasons: it qualifies our results and, in revealing the ignorance that appears to prevail in so vital a field of economic intelligence, may serve to stimulate more work.

A AVERAGE INCOME SHARES OF UPPER INCOME GROUPS

1 *Average Levels*

The averages are for the two interwar decades, 1919-38. We exclude information for years before 1919 and since 1938 in order to eliminate the marked effect of the wars on the distribution of income by size.

Shares of upper income groups are based upon comparisons between federal tax data and countrywide aggregates of income receipts by individuals. The definition of individuals' incomes corresponds to that of national income: receipts for the participation of individuals or of their property in the productive process. This means, unless otherwise noted, including employee compensation, entrepreneurial income, dividends, interest, and rent; excluding capital gains and other transfers, and not allowing any deductions except of business expenses.

Tax data are available for return units, classified by net income, as defined for tax purposes. We reduce classes of returns to classes of persons represented on the returns (income recipients and dependents); record the total income (as defined above) for each class; calculate per capita income for each class; array the classes downward by size of per capita income, then interpolate for the top 1, 3, 5, etc. percent of the total population. At each partition line we estimate the total income reported above that line; the proportion this income constitutes of the countrywide aggregate is the share of the income group above the partition line. This procedure yields the shares we call the 'basic' variant because it is the variant for which we can exploit most fully the detailed data in the annual tabulations of federal income tax returns (Table 1, col. 1, lines 1-5).

During 1919-38 these tax returns covered almost exclusively nonfarm residents, and countrywide aggregates of individuals' income receipts for the nonfarm population are available. Therefore, we can compare the income and population represented on federal tax returns not only with total income and population but also with

5

Table 1

Average Annual Income Shares, Upper Income Groups
Total and Nonfarm Population, 1919-1938

		% of Countrywide Income Received		
	Percentage Bands of Total and Nonfarm Population	Basic variant (1)	Economic income variant (2)	Disposable income variant (3)
		TOTAL POPULATION		
1	Top 1 percent	13.1	15.0	14.3
2	2nd & 3rd percentage band	6.6	8.3	8.4
3	4th & 5th percentage band	4.9	6.5	6.4
4	Top 5 percent	24.7	29.8	29.1
5	Lower 95 percent	75.3	70.2	70.9
		NONFARM POPULATION		
6	Top 1 percent	13.3	15.1	14.3
7	2nd & 3rd percentage band	6.6	8.1	8.2
8	4th & 5th percentage band	4.5	6.0	6.0
9	Top 5 percent	24.4	29.2	28.5
10	Lower 95 percent	75.6	70.8	71.5

Because of rounding, details in this and the following tables do not necessarily add to the totals.

the income and number of the nonfarm population. For the basic variant we draw new partition lines, at percentages of nonfarm instead of total population, and divide the new totals by total nonfarm income (col. 1, lines 6-10).

The basic variant is merely a first approximation to the comparison desired. We made several adjustments in the totals taken from the tax data: to include some omitted income items (compensation of nonfederal government employees and imputed rent on owner-occupied houses); to allow for a finer division of return classes by distinguishing within each net income class between head of family and nonhead returns; and to make some allowance for the effect of using as a basis of classification net income as defined for tax purposes instead of economic income. These several adjustments give a better approximation to the shares of upper groups in a distribution of economic income by size of income per capita; but they make it impossible to use the full detail in the tabulations of tax returns on the composition of income by type. Adding these adjustments to the shares as estimated in the basic variant yields the 'economic income' variant (col. 2).

Both basic and economic income variants measure income shares as they flow from the productive process, not shares as they are finally received by individuals after various transfers and deductions (payment of taxes, gains and losses from sales of assets, gifts, etc.). From income tax data we can calculate only two of these transfer items: payments of federal income taxes by individuals and realized gains and losses on sales of assets. Modifying the shares in the economic income variant to allow for these two items yields the 'disposable income' variant (col. 3) which of course does not cover all the gaps between economic and disposable income.

If income were distributed equally, each percentage group in the population would receive a corresponding percentage of total income. That is, the top 1 percent, representing 1 percent of the population, would receive just 1 percent of income, not the 13-15 percent shown in Table 1; the 2nd and 3rd percentage band would receive 2 percent of total income, not 6½-8½ percent; and so on. The amount by which the shares in Table 1 exceed levels equal to the percentages the recipients constitute of the population thus measures the inequality in the distribution of income, as far as it is reflected in the shares of upper income groups.

More realism can be lent to the evidence in Table 1 by considering the underlying absolute figures. Per capita income averaged about $550 (current prices) in 1919-38. Taking the economic income variant for total population as the most relevant, we find that the top 5 percent group received 29.8 percent of total income. Its average per capita income was, therefore, $3,300, i.e., ($550 × 29.8 ÷ 5), or over $13,000 for a family of four. For the top 1 percent the average ratio of the actual income share to the 'equality' share was 15:1; hence its average per capita income was somewhat over $8,000, i.e., ($550 × 15), or $33,000 for a family of four. Average income levels for any year and any percentage band covered in Table 1 can be similarly calculated (see App. Table 1).

The income of the various groups can be described also in terms of partition values. The average income (economic income variant, total population) at the lower end of the top 1 percent band was about $3,200; i.e., the top 1 percent included returns which, on the average, had per capita incomes of $3,200 or more; or, for a family of four, $12,800 or more. The lower partition value for the 2nd and 3rd percentage band averaged $2,000 per capita; i.e., this band included returns whose per capita incomes averaged $2,000-$3,200. The lower partition value for the 4th and 5th percentage band, and hence for the top 5 percent group, averaged $1,670 per capita; i.e., this band included returns whose per capita incomes averaged

$1,670-$2,000; the top 5 percent group as a whole included returns whose per capita incomes averaged $1,670 or more.

The contrast between the income shares of the upper and lower income groups shifts with the percentage partition line: the contrast between the incomes of the top 1 and the lower 99 percent is greater than that between the incomes of the top 5 and the lower 95 percent; that between incomes of the top 5 and the lower 95 percent is greater than that between the incomes of the top 10 and the lower 90 percent. Any reference to inequality of incomes between the 'rich' and 'poor' should specify at which percentage of population in the array the partition line is drawn.

Table 1 reveals three other relations. First, shares of upper income groups are invariably higher in the economic income than in the basic variant. The distribution represented by the former reflects more clearly differences in economic income per capita; hence the inequality in the distribution is sharper, undiluted by defects in the unit and basis of classification employed in the basic variant.[3] As between the economic and disposable income variants there is a slight drop in the share of the top 1 percent, and a partly compensating rise in the share of the 2nd and 3rd percentage band—effects largely of the impact of federal income taxes during the period under observation.[4] For the top 5 percent group the difference in level of shares between these two variants is relatively slight.

Second, the shares diminish rapidly as we descend to lower percentage bands in all three variants. For example, in the economic income variant the drop is from 15 percent for the top 1 percent to slightly over 4 per percentile for the 2nd and 3rd percentage band, to slightly over 3 per percentile for the 4th and 5th percentage band. Presumably the decline in per percentile shares in the lower bands, not shown in Table 1, would be progressively milder unless it accelerates sharply in the lower tail of the distribution, which covers persons with net losses.

[3] Only a very minor part of the difference is due to the inclusion in the numerator for the economic income variant of nonfederal employee compensation—omitted from the numerator for the basic variant.

[4] That the deduction of federal income taxes reduces the share of the top 1 percent group so little, and those of the 2nd and 3rd, and 4th and 5th percentage bands not at all, is due partly to the low tax rates during most of the interwar period; but largely to the inclusion in the top 5, and even in the top 1 percent group, of units well down the scale of total income (and still lower down the scale of net taxable income).

Third, for the top 5 percent, although not for the top 1 percent, the shares in the variants for the nonfarm population are slightly lower than those for the total population. In general, the smaller the population group for which the income distribution is studied, the less the inequality, i.e., the narrower the dispersion. This is plausible because the larger the population group, the more heterogeneous its components are likely to be, and the more room for wider dispersion between low and high income groups. This association between the size of a population and the relative amplitude of income dispersion in it does not always hold: differences in economic structure unassociated with the size of the population may introduce disturbing effects. But it should be kept in mind in comparing income inequality among population groups differing materially in size.

For the upper income groups in Table 1 we can observe shares in countrywide aggregates of various types of income for both the total and the nonfarm population, but only for the basic variant (Table 2). The results for the nonfarm population differ relatively little from those for the total, and it would unduly complicate this summary to present and discuss those for both. Consequently, we postpone their presentation and discussion to the report itself.

The shares of upper income groups in countrywide aggregates of various types of income differ widely. While the top 1 percent

Table 2

Average Annual Percentage Shares of Upper Income Groups in Countrywide Aggregates of Various Types of Income
Basic Variant, Total Population, 1919-1938

	Type of income	Top 1 Percent (1)	2nd & 3rd Percentage Band (2)	4th & 5th Percentage Band (3)	Top 5 Percent (4)	Lower 95 Percent (5)
1	Total income	13.1	6.6	4.9	24.7	75.3
2	Employee compensation	6.5	5.6	4.8	16.9	83.1
3	Entrep. income	13.7	8.1	5.2	26.9	73.1
4	Rent	17.9	11.4	8.9	38.3	61.7
5	Interest	27.5	8.5	5.5	41.5	58.5
6	Dividends	64.7	8.2	3.6	76.6	23.4
7	Entrep. income & rent	14.2	8.5	5.6	28.3	71.7
8	Dividends & interest	46.1	8.4	4.5	58.9	41.1
9	Service incomes	8.1	6.2	4.9	19.1	80.9
10	Property incomes	40.1	8.8	5.3	54.2	45.8

received on the average about 13 percent of total income it received only 6.5 percent of employee compensation but about 65 percent of total dividends paid to individuals. The spread in the shares of various types of income received by the 2nd and 3rd, and 4th and 5th percentage bands is much narrower. The top 5 percent group received about 25 percent of total income, 17 percent of employee compensation, and about 77 percent of all dividends paid to individuals.

Despite these wide differences, the shares of upper income groups in the various types of income are significantly higher than the equality share. For example, though the 6.5 percent the top 1 percent group received of employee compensation is much smaller than its share of any other income type, it is still 6.5 times the equality share. Indeed, the smallest excess over the equality share is in the share of the 4th and 5th percentage band in dividends, and even here the share is 1.8 times the equality level. In other words, the upper income groups in Table 2 receive on the average much more than 'equal' shares of *any* type of income distinguished. Naturally, this conclusion holds for the groups as wholes, not for units within them: there must be numerous units at the top that receive only one type of income.

The shares of each income type in Table 2 suggest the *minimum* inequality in their distribution by size. Since the top 1 percent, selected on the basis of an array of *total* income per capita, receives on the average 6.5 percent of employee compensation, it would be getting *at least* 6.5 percent of total employee compensation, and probably appreciably more, if the distribution were confined to this type. As we pass to the lower percentage bands, shares of each income type decline consistently, suggesting that the minimum inequality shown in Table 2 is perhaps not far from the actual inequality that would be established in the distribution of each income type separately. In the light of this observation it is of interest that the inequality in the distribution of income, as revealed by the shares of the top 1 and 5 percent groups, becomes progressively greater as we pass from employee compensation to entrepreneurial income, to rent, to interest, and finally to dividends.

The upper income groups receive very large shares of property incomes. If we assume that the capital, i.e., dividend-, interest-, and rent-yielding capital separately, held by the upper and lower income groups have similar yields, the top 5 percent group must own very large shares of the income-yielding capital held by individuals: over three-quarters of dividend-yielding capital, over four-tenths of interest-yielding capital, and almost four-tenths of rent-yielding capital. And if we combine all income-yielding capital, implying that the yields of the three categories are not too different, the top 5 percent holds over half of all income-yielding capital held by individuals. Hence the inequality in the ownership of income-yielding capital is much greater than the inequality in the distribution of total current income. The major qualification to be borne in mind is that the shares are of capital held by individuals, excluding holdings by corporations and other associations from which individuals may benefit, e.g., via insurance policies, though the amounts may not show up in any accountable flow of income receipts.

Since shares of upper income groups in countrywide aggregates of income of various types and in total income differ widely, the income structure of the upper income groups, the total population, and the lower income groups must differ significantly (Table 3). For all population groups (col. 1) employee compensation is the largest source of incomes, about two-thirds; entrepreneurial income less than a fifth; and all property incomes combined (rent, dividends, and interest) slightly less than a sixth. The income structure of the top 1 percent is significantly different: only about

Table 3
Average Annual Percentage Proportions of Various Types of Income in Total Income, Upper Income Groups and Total Population
Basic Variant, Total Population, 1919-1938

	Type of income	Total Population (1)	Top 1 Percent (2)	2nd & 3rd Percentage Band (3)	4th & 5th Percentage Band (4)	Top 5 Percent (5)	Lower 95 Percent (6)
1	Employee compensation	66.0	33.0	56.3	63.8	45.4	72.8
2	Entrep. income	18.2	19.0	22.5	19.1	19.9	17.6
3	Rent	3.0	3.9	5.2	5.3	4.5	2.5
4	Interest	6.5	13.2	8.2	7.1	10.6	5.1
5	Dividends	6.3	30.9	7.8	4.6	19.5	2.0
6	Entrep. income & rent	21.2	22.9	27.7	24.4	24.5	20.1
7	Dividends & interest	12.8	44.1	16.0	11.8	30.1	7.1
8	Service incomes	84.2	51.9	78.8	83.0	65.3	90.4
9	Property incomes	15.8	48.1	21.2	17.0	34.7	9.6

a third of its income comes from employee compensation, and almost a half from property. As we descend the income scale the proportion of employee compensation increases and that of property incomes diminishes. Presumably, if we could study the percentage bands below the top 5 percent we would find the proportion of employee compensation continuously increasing, that of entrepreneurial income declining after a while, and that of property incomes continuously decreasing, except in the incomes of semi-retired and retired persons at the lower end of the income scale who might be deriving a large part of their total income from savings.

The income structure of the top 1 percent group is unique in two ways. First, as already mentioned, this group receives an unusually large share of property incomes, particularly dividends, and a relatively small share of employee compensation. Second, for this group alone is the allocation of total income among the five types of income unusually equal: each of four types accounts for more than a tenth of total income, whereas for all the lower income groups only two income types contribute more than a tenth. This characteristic, obviously true of the top 1 percent group as a whole but not necessarily true even of the majority of units within it, means that if there are any compensating movements in the size of various types of income, the total income of the top 1 percent is likely to reflect them. The total income of lower income groups or of the entire population, in contrast, is likely to be dominated by the movement of just one income type, employee compensation; the effects of the next large type, entrepreneurial income, run a weak second. In the 2nd and 3rd percentage band the income structure begins to resemble that for the total population; and in the 4th and 5th percentage band the similarity becomes quite close.

From Tables 2 and 3 we can calculate the arithmetic effects of either omitting or redistributing property incomes, that is, see what happens to the shares of upper income groups if, *with everything else held the same,* property holdings by individuals are eliminated or the proceeds distributed equally among the population (Table 4).

If property incomes, defined as dividends, interest, and rent, are removed completely from the income distribution, the shares of the upper income groups, assuming that the ones originally at

Table 4

Average Annual Percentage Shares of Income Assuming Removal or Equal Distribution of Property Incomes
Basic Variant, Total Population, 1919-1938

Income Shares	Top 1 Percent (1)	2nd & 3rd Percentage Band (2)	4th & 5th Percentage Band (3)	Top 5 Percent (4)	Lower 95 Percent (5)
1 In total income as given	13.1	6.6	4.9	24.7	75.3
PROPERTY INCOMES DEFINED AS DIVIDENDS, INTEREST, & RENT					
2 Assuming removal	8.1	6.2	4.9	19.2	80.8
3 Assuming equal distribution	7.0	5.5	4.4	16.9	83.1
PROPERTY INCOMES DEFINED AS ABOVE PLUS PART OF ENTREPRENEURIAL INCOME					
4 Assuming removal	6.7	5.7	4.9	17.3	82.7
5 Assuming equal distribution	5.7	5.1	4.4	15.1	84.9

the top remain there, are reduced (line 2). The major reduction, for obvious reasons, is in the share of the top 1 percent—from 13.1 to 8.1 percent; the reduction in the shares of the other upper percentage bands is quite minor. If we keep property incomes but redistribute them equally among all population groups, the reduction in the shares of the upper income groups becomes larger (line 3). Even here, however, the reduction in the shares of the percentage bands below the top is minor, and the share of the top 5 percent group is reduced from about 25 to 17 percent, or less than a third.

If we widen property incomes to include some part of entrepreneurial income,[5] then either eliminate this larger property income total or redistribute it equally among the entire population, the reduction in the shares of the upper income groups becomes more appreciable (lines 4 and 5). On this most extreme assumption, the share of the top 5 percent group is reduced from 25 to 15 percent, or about four-tenths.

The reductions in Table 4 are overestimated throughout, for various reasons. First, including all net rent with property incomes may be unwarranted because this item covers some compensation for entrepreneurial activity. Second, the allowance we made for including and distributing the property part of entrepreneurial income is much too large, overestimating both the part and the

[5] We assumed, for the purpose, that the share of entrepreneurial income received by the upper income groups *in excess of* the share they received of employee compensation represented the property part of entrepreneurial income. For the amounts, see Table 2, lines 2 and 3.

inequality in its distribution. Third, if we omit or redistribute a given income item, we should re-array the income classes, since an income unit or group that was high in the array before the omission or redistribution may have moved down. In other words, in keeping our upper groups the same 'before' and 'after', we underestimated the true shares after property incomes had been omitted or redistributed. The underestimate may be as large as 2 or 3 percentage points in the income share for the top 5 percent group.

Nevertheless, the reduction in the shares of the upper income groups is relatively moderate and a large proportion of the inequality between the top 5 and lower 95 percent groups remains even after we omit or redistribute property incomes. The relative addition to the share of the lower 95 percent is quite moderate, from a fourteenth to an eighth of its income before the omission or redistribution. Only if property incomes are transferred to a small proportion of the lower income groups can they constitute a sizeable addition.

These conclusions obviously follow from two characteristics of the income structure: the small weight property incomes have in the total and the unequal distribution of service incomes (employee compensation and entrepreneurial income). Had property incomes constituted a much larger proportion of total income, while remaining as unequally distributed as they are in Table 2, the effects of omission or redistribution on the shares of upper income groups would have been much greater. Were service incomes distributed more equally, the distribution of income *after* property incomes were omitted or redistributed would have been less unequal. Needless to say, Table 4 shows the purely arithmetical effects of omission and redistribution, telling nothing about the far-reaching repercussions on the productivity of either men or capital, or on any possible associated shifts in the distribution of service incomes proper.

2 *Effects of Statistical Characteristics*

The estimates discussed so far are derived by arraying return units (which are close to, but not identical with, family units) by economic income per capita for a given year. They manifestly depend upon the unit, the definition of income, the inclusion of various income sources in the total, and the use of a given year's rather than a given biennium's or triennium's income. This section explores, in an illustrative rather than definitive way, the effects of these four choices.

a) *Recipient unit*

Income may be distributed among the individuals who receive it or among families, however defined, each family taken as a unit and its income pooled for that unit; or among consuming units, however defined, with income pooled for each unit; or among any other units larger than a single individual. In dealing with units larger than a single individual we can convert their income to a per capita, per equivalent consumer, or some other basis, then group the families and similar units as so many bundles of persons or equivalent consumers, etc., by the size of income per capita or per consumer.

Table 5 presents two illustrative comparisons. In the first, the identical population and pool of income are distributed in two ways: among all recipients by size of income per recipient and

Table 5

Effect of Income Unit on Percentage Share of Top Income Group

		Share of Top 5 Percent in Distribution of			
		All units (1)	Family units (2)	Av. Number per Unit (3)	Av. Number per Family (4)
	I From Recipient to Spending Unit				
	Census Sample, Average for 1947 and 1948				
1	Recipients, by money income per recipient	19.2	18.8	1.50	1.64
2	Consuming units, by money income per unit	16.3	15.1		
	II From Spending Unit to Person				
	A *Minnesota, 1938-39*				
3	Economic units, by total income per unit	17.8	17.3	3.12	3.66
4	Persons, by per capita income per economic unit	19.4	19.5		
	B *Consumer Purchases Study, 1935-36*				
5	Consuming units, by total income per unit	26.7	26.7	3.19	3.94
6	Persons, by per capita income per consuming unit	30.1	28.6		
	C *Census Sample, Average for 1944, 1945, 1947, and 1948*				
7	Consuming units, by money income per unit	16.8	15.5	3.14	3.59
8	Persons, by per capita income per consuming unit	18.0	17.3		

among all consuming units by size of income per unit.[6] The share of the top 5 percent group is distinctly larger in the former (lines 1 and 2). This comparison covers only two years and is based upon a relatively small sample. But it stands to reason that a distribution of income among recipients is likely to be less equal than that among larger consuming units: many recipients, e.g., retired persons, have small property incomes and many others are subsidiary earners, and both groups may include dependent members of larger family or consuming groups. This category of extremely low income units would be proportionately smaller among consuming units than among recipients. For this reason alone, the shares of upper groups of recipients (compared with the average per recipient) would tend to be larger than the shares of upper groups among families and similar consuming units.

The second comparison is between a distribution of income among families or consuming units by total income per family or consuming unit and among persons by size of per capita income per family or consuming unit. The three illlustrations of this comparison in Table 5 all point to the same conclusion: the share of the top 5 percent group in a distribution of persons by per capita income per unit is larger than in a distribution of units by total income per unit. This implies that as we convert the distribution of consuming units or families to a per capita income basis, many of the units that had a large total income and consisted of several persons are shifted downward; and the extremes of the distribution are exaggerated in that a correspondingly large number of units, presumably with a few persons each, shift into the top brackets, at a level significantly above the average than was the case with the large income families.[7]

The size of the differences in Table 5 is not firmly established. But the relatively small spread, between a fourteenth and an eighth (col. 1), may well be typical, and two inferences can be drawn.

[6] In this case, consuming units include families defined as groups of 2 or more persons related by blood, marriage, or adoption, and residing together; and individuals not belonging to families.

[7] For one recent sample, the Survey of Consumer Finances, the share of the top 5 percent in a distribution of persons by per capita income per consuming unit is somewhat smaller than in a distribution of consuming units by total income per unit. However, for the top *10 percent* group, the share in the distribution of persons is larger than in the distribution of consuming units.

First, if the unit of the distribution is changed, the shares assigned to the upper groups are altered significantly; and, most probably, also the shares of the groups at the extreme lower end of the distribution. Any comparisons must, therefore, be carefully scrutinized for the unit of the income size distribution. Second, changing units may mean substantial shifts in the members of the groups at the upper and lower levels. In a distribution of units by total income per unit the upper groups will contain a fair proportion of large units with small per capita incomes; and in a distribution of persons by size of per capita income per unit these large units will tend to move out of the upper groups and be replaced by others. This difference in the composition of the upper and lower income groups is relevant in any study of their social characteristics since they will differ with the unit of the distribution—recipient, family, etc.

Perhaps the most important point brought out by Table 5 is the difficulty of selecting the proper unit in a size distribution of income. A recipient unit leaves much to be desired, for recipients combine in different numbers and proportions into larger groups that pool their incomes and that make decisions concerning the allocation of income among various types of expenditure or between expenditures and savings. Yet it is hard to identify these pooled units, since income may be pooled for one type of expenditure and not for others. Furthermore, these pooling units differ with respect to the number of producers and consumers in each. Dividing by the number of persons to get per capita income is a crude adjustment: differences among families or consuming units in the number of *persons* may well be greater than differences in the number of equivalent *consumers* or *producers*. Hence, our calculations, based upon a distribution of income per capita, may exaggerate the inequality as compared, say, with that in a distribution of income per consumer-equivalent. Though the exaggeration cannot be substantial, we must still search for the proper unit to use in such size distributions as will be helpful in explaining the behavior of individuals as producers and as consumers.

b) *Effects of scope of income*

The effects of excluding and including various income items have been indicated both in the distinction between the economic and disposable income variants and in the illustrative calculations of the

Table 6

Effect of Scope of Income on Percentage Shares of Upper Income Groups

Income Shares	Top 1 Percent (1)	2nd-5th Percentage Band (2)	Top 5 Percent (3)	Ratio: Total to Other Income (4)
I Total and Money Income, Economic Units Classified by Size of Total Income, Minnesota, 1938-39				
Urban Units				
1 In total income			17.8 ⎫	1.06
2 In money income			18.4 ⎭	
Rural Nonfarm Units				
3 In total income			16.0 ⎫	1.11
4 In money income			17.3 ⎭	
II Total and Economic Income, Economic Units Classified by Size of Total Income, Minnesota, 1938-39				
5 In total income	7.0	10.8	17.8 ⎫	1.06
6 In economic income	6.6	11.4	18.0 ⎭	
III Total and Net Income, Tax Definition, State Income Tax Returns, Delaware, Average for 1936-38				
7 In total income, returns by total income	31.4	12.6	44.0 ⎫	1.16
8 In net income, returns by net income	25.8	13.3	39.1 ⎭	

consequences of omitting or redistributing property incomes. Table 6 therefore merely reenforces what is perhaps an obvious and already established point.

The first set of comparisons is between the distribution of total income and of money income, excluding all receipts in kind. In general, the shares of upper income groups in a distribution of money income are larger than those in a distribution of total income, the size of the difference being associated with the relative contribution of money and nonmoney income to the total. Income in kind is received more commonly at the lower total income levels and tends to be proportionately larger at low than at high income levels. Hence its inclusion tends to raise the income position of the lower brackets relative to that of the upper brackets and reduces correspondingly the shares of upper income groups. This observation is important in recent years when most sample distributions of income by size are confined to money income. The difference in Table 6 between the shares in total and in money income is an underestimate because the distribution of both is by size of total income, thus reducing the shares of upper income groups in money income below what they would be in a distribution by size of money income alone.

The second comparison is for total and economic income, the former including various transfer items (inheritances, relief payments, and the like). Unfortunately, the size and variety of noneconomic receipts for Minnesota are quite small. Yet the effect of excluding them (again underestimated because both total and economic income are classified by size of total income) on the share of the top 1 percent and of the 2nd through 5th percentage band is different. The former is reduced and the latter increased because noneconomic receipts are of two distinct types: large items which lift the recipient into a high income category in one year (inheritances, large capital gains, and the like) and the items that tend to be small, chiefly gifts, relief payments, etc. The first, because they are large, are associated with the current year's top group of total income recipients; the second go to the groups at lower income levels. These characteristics of various noneconomic receipts may well be typical for other years and for wider areas than those covered in Table 6.

The third comparison is between a distribution of total income and of net income, as defined for tax purposes, both being distributions of one and the same population total. (It is this requirement that limits possible comparisons, the only one readily available being that for Delaware for 1936-38.) The top 1 percent receives a significantly smaller share of net income, tax definition, than of total income. Obviously, the differential benefit of permissible deductions from total income is much greater for the topmost income group than for the groups below. The share of the 2nd through 5th percentage band, in contrast, is appreciably larger in the distribution of net income, tax definition. Delaware has a peculiar size distribution of income in that the upper groups have very large shares (the shares in Table 6 are in total income reported on tax returns but in view of the wide coverage of the income tax, they are not far from those in total income for the state). It is, therefore, difficult to say whether the same relation would hold for similar comparisons over wider areas.

The differences in Table 6 are merely illustrative. But in combination with the other evidence already considered, they suggest two conclusions. First, the effects on shares of upper income groups of including or excluding given income items depend upon: (a) the size of the item relative to the income total before inclusion or exclusion: all other conditions being equal, the larger the item the greater the effect; (b) the inequality or dispersion in the distribution of the item that is included or excluded: all other conditions being equal, the greater the dispersion, the greater the positive effect of inclusion (negative effect of exclusion); and (c) the association between the inequality in the distribution of the item and of the income total before inclusion or exclusion: positive association raises the positive effect of inclusion (negative effect of exclusion), and negative association raises the negative effect of inclusion (positive effect of exclusion). Knowledge of or plausible hypotheses about these several factors would permit a reasonable judgment concerning the probable effects of including or excluding any given item.

The second conclusion applies more specifically to our estimates. While numerous transfers, exchanges, etc. intervene between economic and disposable income, the major ones are realized gains and losses from sales of assets and tax payments. After these two are accounted for, the percentage shares of upper income groups in the distribution of either economic or disposable income are not likely to be much affected by the minor items that should be considered. Provided we realize that the flow of current income is merely one factor influencing the behavior of producers and consumers, the estimates of shares of upper income groups of the type presented here are not likely to be modified much by questions concerning income scope, at least of the kind that can be and have been raised in studies in this field.

c) *Effect of combining income types*

As we have observed, the total income of upper groups, particularly the top 1 percent, is less dominated by one or two types than the income of the total population. However, as also noted, this does not necessarily imply that the units at the top levels typically receive their incomes from several sources. Though each unit receive income of one type only, the income structure of the top 1 or 5 percent might still be exactly as it is in Table 3.

Units in the upper income groups, at least in the top 1 percent, do receive income from several sources (Table 7, lines 1-4). The upper levels of the tax population are set to correspond roughly with the top 1 or 2 percent of the total population of the given area. The proportion of multi-type returns is much larger at the top levels of the

Table 7
Extent of Combining Types of Income and Its Effect
on Percentage Share of Top Income Group

		Federal Tax Data 1936 (1)	Wisconsin State Tax Data Av. for 1929, 1935, & 1936 (2)	Delaware State Tax Data Av. for 1936-38 (3)
	I Extent of Combination			
1	% of returns, top group	6.5	4.8	2.4
2a)	% of single type returns, top group	15.0	18.5	8.9
b)	% of single type returns, all returns	57.0	60.8	74.3
3a)	% of two type returns, top group	28.5	24.5	30.7
b)	% of two type returns, all returns	24.2	23.5	16.2
4a)	% of three or more type returns, top group	56.5	57.0	60.4
b)	% of three or more type returns, all returns	18.8	15.8	9.5
	II Effect of Combination			
5	Share of top group in total income on all tax returns (%)			
	a) Actual		23.5	39.0
	b) Assuming no combination of types at top		20.8	35.7
	c) Assuming full combination of types at top		36.7	47.7

tax population than for the tax population as a whole; and this contrast would be even greater between the top 1 or 5 percent band and the total population of the country.

Does this prevalence of multi-type returns—the combination of income of various types and presumably from different sources—contribute greatly to the high incomes at the upper levels? When one and the same unit at the upper levels receives different types of income, is its total income share much larger than when from a single source?

According to experimental calculations based on Wisconsin and Delaware state tax data, income shares at upper levels are not appreciably larger because income is derived from several sources. Allowing the combination of types to raise total income as much as possible, i.e., combining the largest payments of income of various types with the largest number of types, we raise the share of the top income group in Wisconsin from about 21 (assuming no combination at all) to 37 percent, and that in Delaware from about 36 to about 48 percent. The actual shares are 23.5 and 39.0 percent, respectively. Thus, of the maximum possible contribution of combination to raising income at the top levels, only about a sixth was realized in Wisconsin and somewhat over a fourth in Delaware.

While Table 7 contains groups corresponding to the top 1 percent group alone, the findings would obviously apply even more forcefully to the top 5 percent group.

This suggests that even at upper income levels, where receipts from several sources are common, one source usually dominates, accounting for the preponderant proportion of the given unit's total income, and receipts from any other source are secondary at best. Consequently, the large income recipients in, say, the top 1 percent band, must comprise several groups: those dependent chiefly upon employee compensation, entrepreneurial income, and rent, interest, or dividends. It also follows that the *proportion of units* dependent upon each of the several types of property income is appreciably higher in the top group. Furthermore, the degree of concentration or inequality in the holdings of income-yielding property is even higher than is suggested by Table 2. For if a large proportion of all dividends received by the top 1 percent is received by a small component of that group—the component for whom dividends are the dominant source of total income—a large share of the countrywide total of dividends must be received by a group that forms only a small fraction of 1 percent of the country's total population. This conclusion is naturally qualified by the prevalence of multi-source receipts at the upper income levels which has some effect on the high incomes at these levels. But it seems valid enough as an hypothesis meriting exploration.

To the degree that the total income of a large majority of all units is heavily dominated by just one type the distribution suggests the existence of distinct groups characterized by the kind of income they depend upon for their livelihood: property income groups, on the one hand, and service income groups, on the other; groups that rely largely on venture, equity capital of the kind that yields dividends, and those that rely largely on fixed return, bond type of capital that yields most of the interest received by individuals. However, it must be remembered that our data are for income for a current year rather than for a longer period and are not a safe ground for assuming economic classes characterized by long term dependence upon a given income type.

d) *Effect of period of income cumulation*

Since the upper income groups are selected each year by the size of their current income, they will always include units that would not be there except for transient circumstances. If we lengthened the period during which income used for classification by size is cumulated, the lifting of shares of upper income groups by the inclusion of temporarily favored units would be reduced. Hence we would expect that shares of upper income groups in a size distribution for, say, a quinquennium or decade would be significantly smaller than the shares in a distribution of the kind used here.

This conclusion is patent from the customary drop of income levels whenever we trace to a later or earlier year the average income of a top income group of a given year (Table 8, lines 1-4). For purposes of summary we selected the fourth year following the year that is the basis of the size of income classification (initial year). Diverse as the samples are, the three sizeable samples (lines 2-4) show roughly the same decline in the level of the mean—from 20 to 40 percent in four years. Whenever the sample covers a longer period, the regression ends in about the fourth or fifth year, reflecting the effects of shorter term changes associated with business cycles.

Table 8
Effect of Length of Period of Income Cumulation on Share of Top Income Group

	Sample	% of Units in Top Group (1)	Initial year of classification (2)	4th year following (3)	Average of (2) & (3) (4)	Ratio: (4) to (2) (5)
			Ratio: Per Unit Income of Top Group to Av. Per Unit Income			
1	Federal sample, 1,240 returns, 1914-19, initial year base	4.6	8.3	4.4	6.35	0.76
2	Federal sample, 4,063 returns, 1916-24, initial year base	3.0	8.6	5.9	7.25	0.84
3	Financial Survey of Urban Housing, av. for 33 cities, 1929-33, initial year base	5.0	4.07	3.28	3.68	0.90
4	Wisconsin sample, 13,184 returns, 1929-35, initial year base	4.9	4.62	2.81	3.72	0.80
5	Wisconsin sample, 13,183 families, 1929-31, ratio: per unit income of top 5 percent to av. per unit income					
	a) 1 year distribution, 1929		4.66*			
	b) 2 year distribution, 1929-30		4.20*			
	c) 3 year distribution, 1929-31		4.00*			

* Relates to period for which income is cumulated.

The decline in the income means does not, however, tell us what the shares of upper income groups would be if we based the distribution on the average income for four years instead of on the income for a single year. We know that these shares would be appreciably smaller, but not how much.

The amount is suggested by the average level of the share of a given top percentage band, based on a given year's income, for the full period over which regression occurs. This would mean, to use lines 2-4 of Table 8, that the income level of the initial year would be reduced in the fourth year to about 70 percent, or an *average* share for the four years of about 85 percent. In other words, the share of the top 5 percent group would shrink about a seventh as we pass from a single to a four year income base. Line 5 is confirmatory evidence. The decline in the share of the top 5 percent in the shift from a one to a three year income base is about 14 percent of the level on the one year base (from 4.66 to 4.00).

Here again the comparisons are merely illustrative. But two conclusions are warranted. First, as we shift from an income base of a single year to one of a longer period, from what might be called income incidence to income status, the shares of upper income groups decline significantly; and so does inequality in the distribution by size, as far as it is reflected in the shares of upper income groups (and no doubt the shares of the groups at the lower tail of the distribution would increase, for the same reason). Second, if we think of income periods long enough to cancel out short term changes associated with business cycles but short enough to avoid averaging out genuine secular movements in the income levels of the various units, i.e., of about four to five years, the change in the share of the 5 percent group is about that shown in Table 8, a reduction of a sixth to a seventh of the share based on a single year's income.

3 Social Characteristics of Upper Income Groups
a) *Sex, age, and education*

In interpreting income inequality as reflected by shares of upper income groups, we should note that these groups are selective—contain a much larger proportion than the total population of persons in their prime productive ages (from about 35 through about 64) and equipped with the qualities more intensive formal education can provide (Table 9).

Table 9
Sex, Age, and Educational Level Composition
Top Income Group and Total Income Population (percentages)

	Sex, Age, and Education Classes	Minnesota, 1938-39 EARNERS Top 5.2 percent	Total	Census Sample, Av. for 1947 & 1948 (lines 1-9), & 1946 Nonfarm (lines 10-14) INCOME RECIPIENTS Top 5-6 percent	Total
	I Sex				
1	Male	97.3	79.3	95.4	68.0
2	Female	2.7	20.7	4.6	32.0
	II Age				
3	Under 20 years	0.0	3.1	0.0	6.8
4	20-24	0.6	10.1	1.2	11.8
5	25-34	10.6	21.8	16.9	22.0
6	35-44	31.2	23.6	31.5	20.1
7	45-54	32.0	20.8	27.6	16.6
8	55-64	18.1	13.2	16.3	12.3
9	65 & older	7.5	7.3	6.4	10.4
	III Education Classes, All Earners 25 & Older				
10	Under 7 years elementary school			3.2	15.8
11	7 & 8 years elementary school			15.1	28.7
12	1 to 3 years high school			12.3	18.6
13	4 years high school			25.2	22.0
14	1 year or more college			44.2	15.0

Whatever may be said about the relative potential productive power of women and men, in our society the training and obligations of the former prevent them from acquiring experience and skills comparable with those attainable by the latter. Hence, the larger proportion of men in the top 5 percent of income earners or recipients than in the total population (lines 1 and 2) means that the upper income groups contain a relatively larger share of the working and earning population of the more skilled and experienced type.

The same may be said of the age structure of the top income group compared with that of all income recipients (lines 3-9). The former has a much larger proportion of persons at the prime of life. Perhaps the sole qualification is that the 25-34 age class accounts for a smaller proportion of the top income group than of the total income receiving or earning population. Yet age should be viewed as an index of the accumulation of skill and experience as well as a matter of sheer physical strength. One may, therefore, argue that the 25-34 year class still includes a large proportion of persons who, however formally trained, may be in the early, learning years of their lifetime jobs. And the three decades from 35 to 64 do represent the periods within which the peaks of skill and experience are attained and within which, particularly in the later years of that span, the decline in productive power due to purely physical handicaps is still moderate and savings begin to accumulate.

Persons with longer formal training form a much larger proportion among the top income group (lines 10-14). For example, college trained persons are almost a half of the top income group and only about a seventh of the total income receiving population.

Table 9, in terms of income recipients or earners rather than consuming units or returns on a per capita basis, reflects different income distributions from the ones discussed above. Nor are the various characteristics—sex, age, and education—properly cross-classified to reveal the effect of each separately. Finally, these illustrative examples are from small samples for just one to three years. But all these qualifications, however they may affect the specific magnitudes, do not impair the main conclusion: the upper income groups are highly selective in that they are dominated by the sex, age (representing accumulated experience and skill), and education classes that are among the most productive in the total income earning and receiving population. In other words, a significant part of the high incomes at the upper levels is to be attributed to the fact that individuals at the height of their productive power constitute such a large proportion of the group.

This obvious conclusion is often overlooked in interpreting inequalities in distributions of income by size. One implication is plain. Were we to consider an income distribution not for all recipients but confined to those who might justifiably be described as full-time, able-bodied, maturely experienced income earners; eliminate from it the young who are still learning and the old and semi-retired who are designedly or otherwise limiting their efforts; exclude such female and male, chiefly the former, income earners who are only temporarily and secondarily in the labor market; and finally, adjust for the differential cost of education and delay in initiating earning activities, the distribution would display much less inequality than the distributions with which we deal here; and the shares of upper income groups would be materially smaller than the shares shown here. How much we cannot tell, though Table 9 makes it evident that the reduction would be substantial.

b) *Occupational characteristics*

The occupational distribution of the top income group, as compared with that of the total population, reveals the dominance of two broad groups: business and professional persons (Table 10). All three comparisons demonstrate similar tendencies except that for 1947 and 1948 the much better economic position of farmers puts a higher proportion of them among the top income group than among the total population—the opposite of the situation in 1935-36.

Table 10

Occupational Distribution of Top Income Group and of Total Population (percentages)

	Occupational Group	Consumer Purchases Study, 1935-36 FAMILIES		Census Sample			
				Av. for 1947 & 1948* INCOME RECIPIENTS		1948* HEADS OF FAMILIES	
		Top 2.7 percent (1)	Total (2)	Top 5-6 percent (3)	Total (4)	Top 2.9 percent (5)	Total (6)
1	Wage earning	2.4	32.2	4.8	29.2	9.4	27.2
2	Farming	10.9	21.0	13.3	8.8	13.3	12.0
3	Clerical	8.3	12.3	3.9	10.1	3.1	5.8
4	Business, salaried	22.9	3.8	15.2	3.4	16.0	4.8
5	Business, independent	23.3	8.1	20.8	5.4	24.1	7.5
6	Professional, salaried	10.6	3.4	11.1	4.8	7.8	4.5
7	Professional, independent	16.0	1.1	6.4	0.8	9.7	1.1
8	All other nonrelief	5.5	2.9	19.2	16.0	10.3	20.0
9	Relief	0.0	15.3	......	......	......	......
10	In armed forces or not employed	......	......	5.2	21.4	6.4	17.2

* Recorded as of April of the following year.

Notes on the Classification of the Detailed Census Occupations for Comparison with 1935-36

Wage earning: operatives and kindred workers, domestic service workers, service workers except domestic, and laborers except farm and mine.
Farming: farmers and farm managers, and farm laborers and foremen.
Clerical: clerical and kindred workers.
Business salaried and independent, and professional independent: as specified in the Census data.
Professional salaried: salaried and semiprofessional workers.
All other nonrelief: salesmen and saleswomen, craftsmen, foremen and kindred workers.

This distinctive occupational distribution of upper income groups not only confirms what was observed in connection with educational characteristics but also brings to light some new factors that must be considered in interpreting the inequality of a size distribution of income. The large proportion of persons in professional occupations in the top income group is to be associated chiefly with the high cost of preparation and training and in this sense substantiates the comparisons of educational status in Table 9.[8] The larger proportion of persons in business occupations, whether independent or salaried, in the top income group may reflect the greater age and experience required for relatively high positions in the salaried business hierarchy or for the attainment of an independent position at the head of a firm; and partly the compensation for risks inherent in entrepreneurial activity. Current year income, in the case of entrepreneurial groups, must compensate for any losses that may be incurred at other times. The size distribution of a single year's income in business occupations may characteristically be one in which large losses at the small lower tail are compensated by risk allowances for the majority of the units that enjoy a positive income. In contrast to a distribution in which no such risk is involved, it would tend to put a higher proportion of units among the upper groups.

c) *Size of family and location*

These characteristics are relevant when we view income recipients as consumers, not as producers. For the size of family or consuming unit in which an individual participates has a definite effect upon per capita expenditures; and so does location, as is evident in costs and living patterns in the country vs. the city, or in a small city vs. a metropolis. Illustrations, confined to only three years and rather narrow samples, are provided in Table 11.

In the first comparison (lines 1-5) it must be recognized that the distribution is of the number of *persons* in categories classified by the size of the family or consuming unit. Thus, column 1 shows that in 1935-36 of all persons classified as constituting the top 5 percent of the income distribution, as many as 45 percent were single individuals, i.e., over five times as many proportionately as there were in the total population. While this overstates the proportion of single individuals owing to defects in the 1935-36 estimates, their marked concentration among the top 5 percent is confirmed by the data for 1947 and 1948.

In general, the smaller the family or consuming unit the greater

---

[8] For a detailed analysis of the extent to which incomes of professional practitioners represent compensation for extra costs entailed in longer training, see Milton Friedman and Simon Kuznets, *Income from Independent Professional Practice* (NBER, 1945), Ch. 4, pp. 95-173; and more recently, G. J. Stigler, Employment and Compensation in Education, *Occasional Paper 33* (NBER, 1950).

Table 11: Size of Family and of Community Residence Composition Top Income Group and Total Population

		Consumer Purchases Study, 1935-36		Census Sample, Av. for 1947 & 1948	
		(1)	(2)	(3)	(4)
	I % Distribution of Persons by Size of Unit				
		(Top 5 percent)	Total	(Top 5 percent)	Total
1	Single individuals	45.2	8.0	19.4	5.6
2	2 person families	18.0	12.2	44.2	16.4
3	3-4 person families	24.5	33.8	36.4	41.8
4	5-6 person families	8.5	26.6	0.0	23.6
5	7 & over person families	3.8	19.4	0.0	12.6
	II % Distribution of Families by Size of Community				
				(Top 11.6 to	
		(Top 7.2 percent)	Total	12.7 percent)	Total
6	Metropolises	23.1	11.2	19.8	12.0
7	Large cities	27.8	19.0	12.9	11.0
8	Middle size cities	9.8	10.9	14.6	12.8
9	Small cities	12.5	16.6	25.3	24.5
10	Rural nonfarm communities	15.3	19.3	15.6	22.2
11	Farms	11.5	23.0	11.7	17.5

Line 6 includes cities of 1.5 million and over (1935-36) and 1 million and over (1947-48); line 7, cities of 100,000-1,500,000 (1935-36) and 250,000-1,000,000 (1947-48); line 8, cities of 25,000-100,000 (1935-36) and 50,000-250,000 (1947-48); line 9, all other cities down to 2,500.

the excess of the proportion of persons belonging to it among the upper income groups over that in the total; and the larger the family or consuming unit the greater the deficiency in the proportion of persons belonging to it among the upper income groups over that in the total. In other words, the association between the number of persons in a family or consuming unit and income per capita is negative. But this does not imply a direct causal connection: the connection may be through related factors of the type already discussed (education, occupation, etc.) or through location.

Two aspects of the location factor in its association with income differentials can be studied: differences due to living on farms, in the country, and in cities of different size; and regional differences. In general, regional proportions in the distribution among all units and among the top income group do not differ much, *provided* we adjust for inter-regional differences in the relative weight of large and small communities. Differentials associated with the size of community factor, in contrast, are substantial and significant, even within regions.

In Table 11 distributions of families alone, excluding single individuals, are compared: that is, the proportions in the top income group and in the total population in communities of different size are studied net of the difference between families and individuals, but not of differences in size among families themselves. We find as we expected that a much larger proportion of top income families than of all families live in metropolises. There is a similar but less pronounced concentration of large city residents in the top income group. By contrast and in compensation, the proportion of rural dwellers is much lower than in the total population.

d) *Expenditure differentials*

The structure of upper income groups in their distribution among family units of different size, among residents of various types of community, and among occupational strata affects our interpretation of the inequality of income as revealed by their large income shares. The conditions under which these groups receive their large incomes impose upon them expenditures that are necessarily much larger than those of the lower income groups, either for exactly the same bundle of goods or for about the same level of satisfaction and different bundles of goods. For example, because a much larger proportion of upper income groups are single individuals or members of two person families, they may pay higher prices for the same supply of goods *per capita* than larger family units; and there may be an adverse price differential for identical goods because a much larger proportion of upper income groups live in big cities. Likewise, even when the various income groups purchase different goods, some part of the bigger bundle purchased by upper income groups may be due to their residing in big cities or in small family units and are in the nature of expenses of a mode of life—a business expense rather than a final consumer good. For example, expenditures on carfare, high rent, and many other appurtenances of metropolitan life are for goods that are completely dispensable to a rural dweller and merely compensate for some disadvantages of urban life.

To measure expenditure differentials due to each of these three possible elements of higher expenditure levels for upper income groups—higher prices of identical goods, additional costs of goods that are in the nature of 'business expenses', and differences in supply of additional *final* goods—is impossible with the present data or at least within the scope of this report. The expenditure differentials summarized in Table 12 are for a single year, 1935-36, and take account of only one, though a significant, adjustment. The expenditures are calculated at identical levels of per capita income for each binary comparison. To illustrate: at an income level of $300 per capita, families spent $305 per capita, including gifts and taxes; individuals, $349 per capita, 14 percent more (col. 1); expenditures per person in families were $314 in urban communities as against $284 on farms, or 11 percent more (col. 2), and $332 in metropolises as against $307 in small cities, or 8 percent more (col. 3). Hence, within each comparison, differences in per capita expenditures cannot be associated with differences in per capita income; they must be due to one of the three factors mentioned—different prices, 'costs', or propensities to consume (differences in the real volume of final goods purchased at a given income level).

At the same level of per capita income, individuals spent 14-36

Table 12
Percentage Differential in Expenditures per Capita at Same Levels of per Capita Income, Different Size of Family, Size of Community, and Occupational Groups, 1935-1936

Per Capita Income Level	Percentage Excess in per Capita Expenditures			
	Individuals over families (1)	Families in urban communities over farm (2)	Families in metropolises over small cities (3)	Families in higher income type occupations over lower (Chicago) (4)
$100		28	87	
200		13	23	
300	14	11	8	
400		18	4	
450				0
500			6	
550				4
600	14	32	7	
650				5
700			6	
750				6
850				11
900	21	50	10	
950				7
1,000			11	
1,200	27		9	
1,300		69	10	
1,600	31			
1,800			20	
2,500	36			
4,500	25			
10,000	27			

31

percent more per capita than families; families in urban communities 11-69 percent more than families in farm communities; and families in large cities 4-87 percent more than families in small cities. Finally, in Chicago, per capita expenditures at identical income levels by families in business and professional occupations were 4-11 percent more than those in 'lower income' type occupations. All these figures are of illustrative rather than descriptive value. Yet, the general differences they suggest are real and lasting: at identical levels of per capita income, individuals tend to spend more per capita than families; small more than large families (according to our report, though Table 12 does not show it); urban more than rural families; large city more than small city families; higher income occupation more than lower income occupation families. Some part of these differentials may be due to differences in prices of identical goods and to the higher 'cost' of identical levels of living. These parts of the expenditure differentials reduce the purchasing power of upper as compared with lower income groups; and our measures of inequality in the distribution of income should be adjusted accordingly, if they are to reflect differences in spending units' command over consumer goods. Unfortunately, we cannot tell how large this interclass difference in purchasing power of money is, and how large is the consequent reduction in income inequality viewed as inequality in command over consumer goods.

B CHANGES IN INCOME SHARES OF UPPER INCOME GROUPS

The chart portrays annual movements in income shares of upper income groups for all three variants. The most conspicuous movement is the decline after 1939. During the two decades between the wars the shares of the various top percentage bands shifted somewhat from the first to the second decade. There were also shorter term changes which can be studied most effectively within a reference frame of cycles in general economic activity. The changes in income shares of upper income groups are, therefore, described for recent years, the two interwar decades, and business cycles.

1 *Movement after 1939*

Measures of the movement since 1939 in shares of upper income groups, summarized in Table 13, end with 1945 because detailed data from federal income tax returns needed for calculating all three

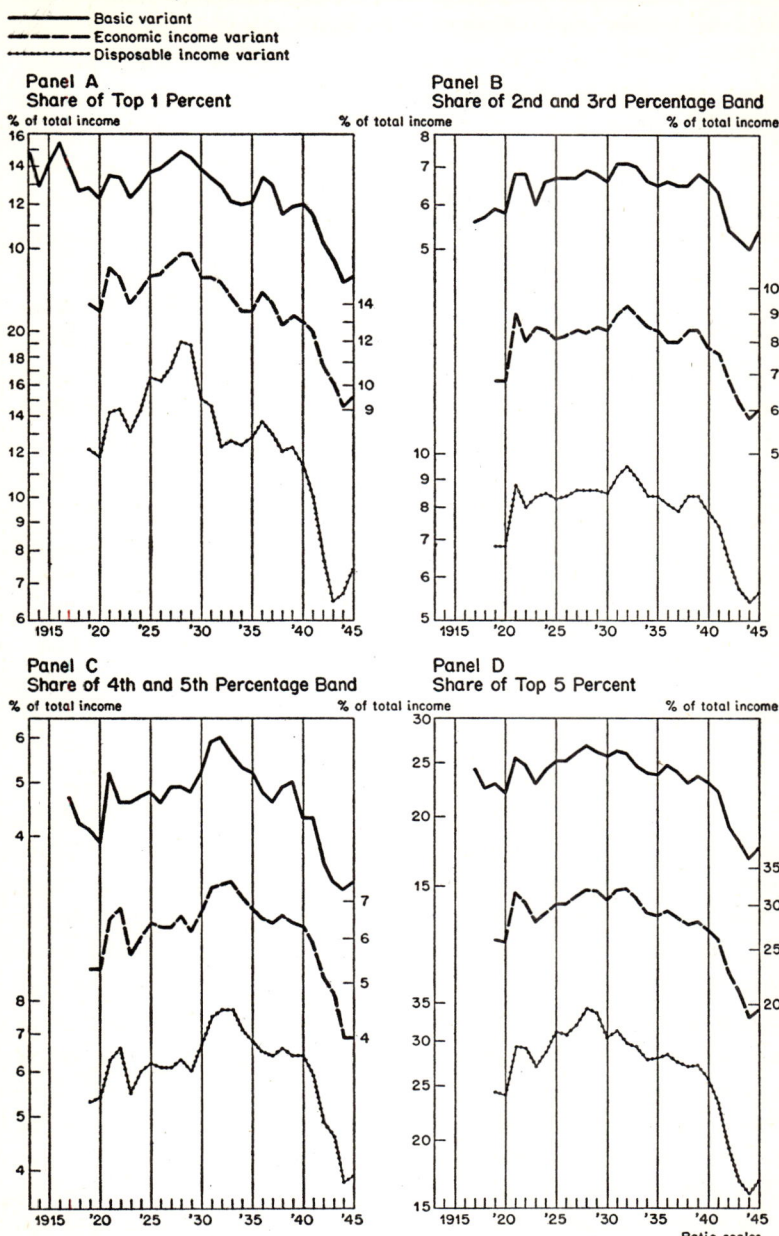

Income Shares of Upper Income Groups, Total Population
Three Variants, 1913–1945
— Basic variant
— — — Economic income variant
·········· Disposable income variant

Table 13
Changes since 1939 in Percentage Shares of Upper Income Groups in Total Income and in Countrywide Aggregates of Various Types of Income

	Top 1 Percent (1)	2nd & 3rd Percentage Band (2)	4th & 5th Percentage Band (3)	Top 5 Percent (4)	Lower 95 Percent (5)
I Change from 1939 to 1945					
Basic Variant					
1 Level, 1939	11.9	6.8	5.0	23.7	76.3
2 Change, 1939-45	−3.0	−1.4	−1.7	−6.1	+6.1
Economic Income Variant					
3 Level, 1939	13.3	8.4	6.4	28.1	71.9
4 Change, 1939-45	−3.8	−2.4	−2.4	−8.6	+8.6
Disposable Income Variant					
5 Level, 1939	12.3	8.4	6.4	27.1	72.9
6 Change, 1939-45	−4.9	−2.8	−2.5	−10.3	+10.3
II Change from 1939 to 1947					
7 Change in share, basic variant	−3.3	−1.2	−1.5	−6.0	+6.0
Change in Shares in Countrywide Aggregates of Various Types of Income					
8 Employee compensation	−2.5	−2.6	−2.1	−7.2	+7.2
9 Entrep. income & rent	+0.8	+2.3	+0.3	+3.4	−3.4
10 Dividends & interest	−6.8	+1.7	−0.8	−5.9	+5.9
Change in Percentage Proportions of Various Types of Income in Total Income					
11 Employee compensation	−5.4	−18.7	−11.0	−10.3	+1.0
12 Entrep. income & rent	+17.7	+20.4	+14.0	+17.9	+1.3
13 Dividends & interest	−12.3	−1.8	−3.0	−7.5	−2.5

variants are not available for later years. However, for the basic variant we can extend the measures another two years on the basis of preliminary releases.

The shares declined markedly from 1939 to 1945 in all three variants (lines 1-6). The relative decline was large for the top 1 percent: about a fourth of the 1939 level in the basic variant; almost three-tenths in the economic income variant; and almost four-tenths in the disposable income variant, where the heavier impact of federal income taxes is reflected. And the decline in the shares of the 2nd and 3rd, and 4th and 5th percentage bands, relatively to their 1939 levels, was equally large, ranging from about a fifth to four-tenths in the different variants. For the top 5 percent group, the decline was about a fourth for the basic variant; slightly over three-tenths for the economic income variant; and almost four-tenths for the disposable income variant.

With the lapse of another two years the decline of the shares in the basic variant remained about as large as in 1939-45 (line 7). That in the share of the top 1 percent became somewhat larger, and that in the shares of the 2nd and 3rd, and 4th and 5th percentage bands somewhat smaller; that in the share of the top 5 percent group was about the same as in 1939-45. Recent sample studies suggest a decline, rather than a rise, in the shares of upper income groups from 1947 to 1948.[9]

Was this decline offset by the increase in undistributed profits of corporations, most of which should be charged to these upper income groups in view of their preponderant holdings of dividend-bearing stock of business enterprises? The question can be answered crudely and approximately by imputing corporate savings to the upper income groups in the proportion their receipts constitute of the countrywide total of dividends paid to individuals. This procedure exaggerates their share in such undistributed incomes, since some net corporate savings must be charged to stock held by insurance companies, banks, nonprofit corporations, etc.

In 1939-45, when shares in the disposable income variant declined absolutely 4.9, 2.8, and 2.5 percentage points for the top 1, 2nd and 3rd, and 4th and 5th percentage bands respectively (Table 13, line 6), inclusion of corporate savings reduced the decline in the shares of the top 1 percent and the 2nd and 3rd percentage band only slightly (to 4.5, and 2.7 percentage points respectively), and did not affect the decline in the share of the 4th and 5th percentage band. When the series are extended through 1946, on the basis of the change in the basic variant adjusted to include corporate savings, the sharp rise in corporate savings reduces the decline in the shares to 3.5, 2.1, and 2.2 percentage points respectively. Data are not yet available to extend these calculations but the appreciably bigger rise in corporate savings in 1947 suggests still further reductions in this decline. However, even allowing for these reductions, which exaggerate the significance of corporate savings to upper income groups, the decline from 1939 remains substantial, both absolutely and relatively.

This decline was obviously not due to an absolute drop in

[9] See the 1949 Survey of Consumer Finances, *Federal Reserve Bulletin*, July 1949, p. 786. For the upper tenth, the share in money incomes declined from 33 percent in 1947 to 32 percent in 1948. However, figures from the Surveys are not fully consistent with our estimates. Like ours, they show a rise in the share of the upper tenth from 1945 to 1946; but unlike ours, they show a rise also from 1946 to 1947.

income. The incomes of both lower and upper groups have increased since 1939; but the relative rise in the former must have been appreciably larger than in the latter. In the disposable income variant the rise in income taxes fell more heavily on the upper income groups, accentuating the decline beyond that shown in variants based on income before taxes.

There is evidence that the changes during the years associated with World War I were similar. The share of the top 1 percent in the basic variant, the only one for which we have estimates, declined from a peak of 15.4 percent in 1916 to a low of 12.3 in 1920. In 1928 it recovered, temporarily, to 14.9—close to its peak level; and in 1924, eight years after the peak, it was 12.9, about a sixth below the peak. During the recent period the share of the top 1 percent reached a trough in 1944, 8.7 percent, or 26.9 percent below its 1939 level, 11.9; and after a temporary recovery to 9.1 in 1946, dropped to 8.6 in 1947, or 27.7 percent below its 1939 level. Thus the recent decline was longer and larger than in the period associated with World War I. The income shares of the 2nd and 3rd, and 4th and 5th percentage bands (basic variant), which reached lows of 5.0 and 3.2 percent respectively in 1944, recovered to levels of 5.5 percent and 3.5 percent in 1947, but were still from a fifth to three-tenths below their 1939 levels.

In which income types did the shares of upper income groups decline during 1939-47? The question is answered in lines 8-10. For all three upper income groups the share in the countrywide total of employee compensation dropped (line 8): the relative decline is evident if it is remembered that the average share (1919-38) of the top 1 percent in employee compensation was 6.5 percent and that of the top 5 percent group, 17 percent. The decline was thus almost four-tenths for the top 1 percent and somewhat over four-tenths for the top 5 percent. The shares of upper income groups, except the 2nd and 3rd percentage band, in the countrywide total of dividends and interest also declined substantially but much less relatively (line 10). The shares in the combined total of entrepreneurial income and rent, in contrast, rose consistently (line 9) although the changes are not large either absolutely or relatively, except for the 2nd and 3rd percentage band.

Since the upper percentage bands are classified by size of current income, their personal composition is not completely continuous from year to year. Hence, the rise in the shares of some income types and the decline in the shares of others are not necessarily changes in the relative shares of a given group of individuals: the changes may represent a movement into the upper income groups of individuals whose incomes are largely from a given income type, say entrepreneurial income, and the movement out of the upper levels of units whose incomes are largely from another source, say employee compensation or dividends. The actual situation is probably a mixture of the movement of units into and out of the upper income groups and of changes in the proportion of countrywide aggregates of income of various types received by units who remain in the upper income levels in both years of the comparison.

The changes in lines 8-10 spell shifts in the income structure of the various income groups (lines 11-13). The share of employee compensation in the total income of upper income groups declined appreciably from 1939 to 1947, whereas its share in the total income of the lower 95 percent of the population rose. The share of the combined total of dividends and interest in the total income of both the upper and lower groups declined. The share of the combined total of entrepreneurial income and rent, dominated by the former, in the total income of upper groups increased substantially; in that of the lower 95 percent, only slightly.

2 Changes from 1919-28 to 1929-38

Twenty years are too short a period to establish secular trends. Nevertheless, it may be of interest to see whether there were any drifts during 1919-38 in the income shares of upper income groups. We compared two decennial averages in the expectation that any major trends could be observed in even such a simple calculation (Table 14).

The share of the top 1 percent declined from the average level of the first decade to that of the second in each variant. The decline was small both absolutely and relatively, except for the disposable income variant where the shift from capital gains in the 1920's to capital losses in the 1930's naturally produced a much bigger decline. If the period since 1939 is treated as a continuation of the two decades 1919-38 the share of the top 1 percent in total income has declined substantially over the period as a whole, i.e., since 1919-28 and through 1947-48.

Table 14

Changes from 1919-28 to 1929-38 in Percentage Shares of Upper Income Groups in Total Income and in Countrywide Aggregates of Various Types of Income

		Top 1 Percent (1)	2nd & 3rd Percentage Band (2)	4th & 5th Percentage Band (3)	Top 5 Percent (4)	Lower 95 Percent (5)
		Basic Variant				
1	Av. level, 1919-28	13.4	6.5	4.6	24.6	75.4
2	Av. level, 1929-38	12.9	6.7	5.2	24.8	75.2
3	Change	−0.6	+0.2	+0.6	+0.3	−0.3
		Economic Income Variant				
4	Av. level, 1919-28	15.3	8.0	6.1	29.5	70.5
5	Av. level, 1929-38	14.7	8.5	6.9	30.1	69.9
6	Change	−0.7	+0.5	+0.8	+0.6	−0.6
		Disposable Income Variant				
7	Av. level, 1919-28	14.9	8.1	6.0	29.0	71.0
8	Av. level, 1929-38	13.7	8.6	6.9	29.2	70.8
9	Change	−1.2	+0.5	+0.9	+0.2	−0.2
		Change in Shares in Countrywide Aggregates of Various Types of Income				
10	Employee compensation	+0.6	+1.4	+1.2	+3.2	−3.2
11	Entrep. income	−2.3	−1.8	−0.6	−4.6	+4.6
12	Rent	+4.3	+1.6	+2.7	+8.6	−8.6
13	Dividends	−11.0	−1.5	−0.0*	−12.5	+12.5
14	Interest	−7.1	−2.6	−1.3	−11.0	+11.0
		Change in Percentage Proportions of Various Types of Income in Total Income				
15	Employee compensation	+6.4	+14.3	+11.4	+10.3	+0.9
16	Entrep. income	−6.0	−10.2	−8.2	−7.5	−2.5
17	Rent	−1.5	−2.8	−2.5	−2.0	−1.9
18	Dividends	+1.0	−0.2	+0.2	−0.2	+1.3
19	Interest	+0.1	−1.0	−0.9	−0.6	+2.1

* Less than −0.05

The shares of the 2nd and 3rd, and 4th and 5th percentage bands, in contrast, rose from the first to the second decade. While absolutely small, these rises are a substantial proportion of the average level of the shares, particularly in the economic and disposable income variants. As far as change since 1939 may be viewed as part of that for the entire, almost thirty year, period, the decline in the shares of these bands during recent years is a reversal of the movement during 1919-38.

Because of the opposite movements in the shares of the top 1 percent and of the other upper percentage bands, the drift in the share of the 5 percent group was rather small, so small that it is perhaps safest to conclude that there was no significant trend either upward or downward during the two interwar decades.

Changes in the shares *within* each income type were fairly consistent for all upper percentage bands (lines 10-14). Their shares in the countrywide totals of employee compensation and rent were larger in the second than in the first decade—and these increases are fairly substantial when viewed as proportions of the average shares for the period. The shares in entrepreneurial income, dividends, and interest were smaller in the second than in the first decade. Movements in the shares of upper income groups in the countrywide aggregates of income of various types since 1939 represent partly a continuation of the trends in Table 14, partly a reversal. The recent decline in the shares of upper percentage groups in the countrywide aggregate of employee compensation is a reversal of the drift during 1919-38; likewise, the recent increase in the shares of upper income groups in the countrywide aggregate of entrepreneurial income and rent is a reversal of the downward drift that would be shown in the combined total from 1919-28 to 1929-38. But the recent decline in the shares of upper income groups, except the 2nd and 3rd percentage band, in the countrywide aggregate of dividends and interest may be viewed as a continuation of the downward drift in Table 14.

Changes in the shares in the countrywide aggregates of income of various types (lines 10-14) mean shifts in the income structure of total income (lines 15-19). On the whole, the upper income groups derived in the second decade a larger proportion of their income from employee compensation and a smaller proportion from entrepreneurial income, rent, dividends, and interest, the most consistent shifts being the rise in the former and the decline in the shares of entrepreneurial income and rent. The lower 95 percent too derived a larger proportion of its income from employee compensation and a smaller proportion from entrepreneurial income and rent but the relative magnitude of these changes was markedly different from that in the income structure of the top 5 percent. Changes in the proportions of dividends and interest were in the opposite direction to and appreciably bigger than those for the top 5 percent.

3 Changes during Business Cycles

With annual rather than monthly data and for a period as short as that covered here, cyclical variations in the shares of upper income groups cannot be analyzed adequately. But we can observe how these shares changed during cycles in general business conditions, and learn enough to form at least reasonable hypotheses subject to further check.

From 1919 through 1938 the reference chronology of the National Bureau traces five cycles in general business activity. For each we can study the change per year in the income shares during expansion, contraction, and the 'differential movement' per year, i.e., the amount by which the per year change during the contraction falls short of or exceeds the per year change during the preceding expansion. We measured these movements in percentage shares of income received by upper income groups as absolute changes, without reducing them to the base of the average for each cycle, as is customary in NBER procedure. The measures summarized in Table 15 tell us how much, on the average, the upper income shares changed during reference phases or cycles. These absolute changes in shares can be compared with the average levels by referring to lines 1, 8, and 15.

With qualifications to be noted below, the income shares of the upper groups moved, on the whole, counter to business cycles, i.e., declined during expansions and rose during contractions. The statement applies to *percentage* shares of total income received by upper income groups, not to their absolute incomes, which rose during expansions and declined, or were retarded in their rise, as is the case in mild recessions, during contractions. What happens, obviously, is that when incomes rise during cyclical expansions, the relative rise in incomes of upper groups is not as large as in incomes of lower groups; and when incomes decline during cyclical contractions, or are retarded in their rise, the relative decline in upper level incomes is not as large, or the retardation in their rise is not as large, as in incomes of lower groups.[10]

While the income shares of upper groups in all three variants run, on the whole, counter to business cycles, the shares for the several upper percentage bands differ significantly in their patterns and in the amplitude of their average change. The share of the top 1 percent almost never moved consistently either with or counter to business cycles; the number of cycles having the sign of the average change never exceeds 3 out of 5 (col. 1). Other evidence of incon-

---

[10] Using entirely different data, Horst Mendershausen also found that from 1929 to 1933 the share of total income received by the 'upper' group increased. See his *Changes in Income Distribution during the Great Depression* (NBER, 1946).

Table 15

Average Change per Year during Business Cycles in Percentage Shares of Upper Income Groups, 1919-1938

		Top 1 Percent (1)	2nd and 3rd Percentage Band (2)	4th and 5th Percentage Band (3)	Top 5 Percent (4)	Lower 95 Percent (5)
		BASIC	VARIANT			
1	Average share, 1919-38	13.1	6.6	4.9	24.7	75.3
	Av. Change, Expansions					
2	Value	−0.10	−0.11	−0.18	−0.40	+0.40
3	No. of cycles with same sign as line 2	2	3	5	3	3
	Av. Change, Contractions					
4	Value	+0.05	+0.34	+0.48	+0.87	−0.87
5	No. of cycles with same sign as line 4	3	4	5	3	3
	Differential Movement					
6	Value	+0.16	+0.46	+0.66	+1.27	−1.27
7	No. of cycles with same sign as line 6	2	4	5	3	3
		ECONOMIC	INCOME	VARIANT		
8	Average share, 1919-38	15.0	8.3	6.5	29.8	70.2
	Av. Change, Expansions					
9	Value	−0.16	−0.12	−0.11	−0.39	+0.39
10	No. of cycles with same sign as line 9	3	3	3	3	3
	Av. Change, Contractions					
11	Value	+0.39	+0.62	+0.44	+1.46	−1.46
12	No. of cycles with same sign as line 11	3	4	5	4	4
	Differential Movement					
13	Value	+0.55	+0.74	+0.56	+1.84	−1.84
14	No. of cycles with same sign as line 13	3	5	4	4	4
		DISPOSABLE	INCOME	VARIANT		
15	Average share, 1919-38	14.3	8.4	6.4	29.1	70.9
	Av. Change, Expansions					
16	Value	+0.20	−0.10	−0.11	−0.01	+0.01
17	No. of cycles with same sign as line 16	3	3	3	3	3
	Av. Change, Contractions					
18	Value	+0.30	+0.59	+0.42	+1.31	−1.31
19	No. of cycles with same sign as line 18	3	5	4.5	3	3
	Differential Movement					
20	Value	+0.10	+0.69	+0.54	+1.32	−1.32
21	No. of cycles with same sign as line 20	2	5	4	4	4

Differential movement is calculated by subtracting the change per year during the expansion from the change per year during the following contraction. A *minus* sign, therefore, signifies positive conformity, in that the rate of change declines from expansion to contraction; a *plus* sign signifies inverted conformity, in that the rate of change increases from expansion to contraction.

sistency is the much smaller amplitude of the average change in the top 1 percent than in the 2nd and 3rd or 4th and 5th percentage band (relative to the average level of the shares): the cyclical movements of the share of the top 1 percent are so diverse that some cancel and the average change is small. The inconsistency is apparent in the chart: the share of the top 1 percent tended to run counter to business cycles during 1919-24, with them during 1929-38 (also during 1913-14 for the basic variant). One is forced to conclude that there seems little consistent relation between changes in the income share of the top 1 percent and business cycles. The shares of the 2nd and 3rd, and 4th and 5th percentage bands, on the contrary, moved fairly consistently counter to business cycles, and it is this behavior that lends consistency to the movement of the share of the top 5 percent group as a whole, at least in the economic and disposable income variants which are of most interest for our analysis.[11]

How do shares of the upper income groups in countrywide aggregates of income of various types move during business cycles? If we adopt as our criterion of consistent behavior that for at least 4 out of the 5 cycles in the period change be in the same direction, we find that the shares of all upper percentage bands in the countrywide total of employee compensation rose *consistently* during contractions; and showed a rise from the rate of change (usually a decline) during expansions to the rate of change (uniformly a rise) during contractions (Table 16, lines 1-7). The shares of upper income groups in the countrywide total of rent also ran counter to business cycles: here too there was a rise fairly uniformly during contractions and in the differential movement from expansion to contraction (lines 15-21).

[11] The inverted pattern is more prominent in the share of the 4th and 5th percentage band than in that of the 2nd and 3rd; and one could reasonably surmise that it might characterize the 6th and 7th and lower percentage bands as long as we stay in the income distribution above the cyclically sensitive wages, salaries, and entrepreneurial income which are reached at somewhat lower income levels. Were it possible to extend the upper income groups to cover the top 10 rather than the top 5 percent, the inverted pattern might well be more prominent and more consistent than it is for the top 5 percent group.

Estimates for the basic variant, available through the 10 percent line from 1919 through 1924, confirm the surmise in some degree. During the two cycles covered in this period the shares of both the top 5 and 10 percent groups ran counter to business cycles without exception. But for the 5 percent group the average differential movement per year was $+3.47$, relative to an average level of the share of 23.7 percent; that for the 10 percent group was $+5.18$, for an average level of the share of 33.2 percent. The relative amplitude of the counter-cyclical movement for the 10 percent group was thus slightly wider.

Table 16

Average Change per Year during Business Cycles in Percentage Shares of Upper Income Groups in Countrywide Aggregates of Various Types of Income, Basic Variant, 1919-1938

		Top 1 Percent (1)	2nd and 3rd Percentage Band (2)	4th and 5th Percentage Band (3)	Top 5 Percent (4)	Lower 95 Percent (5)
		EMPLOYEE COMPENSATION				
1	Average share, 1919-38	6.5	5.6	4.8	16.9	83.1
	Av. Change, Expansions					
2	Value	−0.21	−0.13	−0.19	−0.52	+0.52
3	No. of cycles with same sign as line 2	4	3	3	3	3
	Av. Change, Contractions					
4	Value	+0.39	+0.46	+0.49	+1.34	−1.34
5	No. of cycles with same sign as line 4	5	5	5	5	5
	Differential Movement					
6	Value	+0.60	+0.59	+0.68	+1.86	−1.86
7	No. of cycles with same sign as line 6	5	5	5	5	5
		ENTREPRENEURIAL INCOME				
8	Average share, 1919-38	13.7	8.1	5.2	26.9	73.1
	Av. Change, Expansions					
9	Value	+0.12	+0.23	−0.18	+0.17	−0.17
10	No. of cycles with same sign as line 9	4	4	4	2	2
	Av. Change, Contractions					
11	Value	+0.34	−0.20	+0.47	+0.61	−0.61
12	No. of cycles with same sign as line 11	3	3	4	3	3
	Differential Movement					
13	Value	+0.23	−0.44	+0.66	+0.45	−0.45
14	No. of cycles with same sign as line 13	3	4	4	3	3
		RENT				
15	Average share, 1919-38	17.9	11.4	8.9	38.3	61.7
	Av. Change, Expansions					
16	Value	+0.32	−0.31	−0.16	−0.16	+0.16
17	No. of cycles with same sign as line 16	4	4	2	3	3
	Av. Change, Contractions					
18	Value	+0.75	+1.11	+0.76	+2.62	−2.62
19	No. of cycles with same sign as line 18	4	4	4	4	4
	Differential Movement					
20	Value	+0.43	+1.42	+0.92	+2.77	−2.77
21	No. of cycles with same sign as line 20	4	4	4	4	4
		DIVIDENDS				
22	Average share, 1919-38	64.7	8.2	3.6	76.6	23.4
	Av. Change, Expansions					
23	Value	−0.40	−0.18	−0.23	−0.80	+0.80
24	No. of cycles with same sign as line 23	3	2	5	3	3
	Av. Change, Contractions					
25	Value	−2.75	+0.38	+0.55	−1.82	+1.82

Table 16 (concl.)

		DIVIDENDS (CONCL.)				
		(1)	(2)	(3)	(4)	(5)
26	No. of cycles with same sign as line 25	4	2	4	4	4
	Differential Movement					
27	Value	−2.36	+0.55	+0.78	−1.02	+1.02
28	No. of cycles with same sign as line 27	3	2	4	3	3
		INTEREST				
29	Average share, 1919-38	27.5	8.5	5.5	41.5	58.5
	Av. Change, Expansions					
30	Value	−0.70	−0.25	−0.04	−0.98	+0.98
31	No. of cycles with same sign as line 30	3	5	4	2	2
	Av. Change, Contractions					
32	Value	−1.72	+0.28	+0.24	−1.20	+1.20
33	No. of cycles with same sign as line 32	4	2	4	4	4
	Differential Movement					
34	Value	−1.03	+0.53	+0.28	−0.22	+0.22
35	No. of cycles with same sign as line 34	4	3	3	4	4

Employee compensation and rent are the only two income types in which the shares of all upper percentage bands moved consistently during business cycles. The shares in total entrepreneurial income changed, on the whole, counter to business cycles, but the movement was consistent for only the 4th and 5th percentage band. Those in total dividends and interest moved, on the whole, with business cycles, but the movement was consistent for only the top 1 percent (and the 5 percent group as a whole, whose holdings of dividends and interest are dominated by those of the top 1 percent); the shares of the 2nd and 3rd, and 4th and 5th percentage bands moved counter to business cycles.

These differences in pattern explain in part the lack of consistency in the business cycle behavior of the share of the top 1 percent in total income, in contrast to the consistency of the inverted pattern in the shares of the 2nd and 3rd, and 4th and 5th percentage bands. Looking down the columns in Table 16, one observes that for the top 1 percent the shares in some income types (employee compensation and rent consistently, and entrepreneurial income inconsistently) ran counter to business cycles, whereas those in dividends and in interest moved with business cycles. In contrast, the share of the 4th and 5th percentage band in all types of income changed counter to business cycles.

C Shares of Upper Income Groups in Savings

Short term movements in the apportionment of income between expenditures and savings have long been recognized as influencing business cycles. We may now consider what the changes in upper income shares which we have just discussed imply for short term cyclical changes in savings.

1 Setting of the Problem

Does movement of income shares of upper groups counter to business cycles mean that their shares in total savings also move counter to business cycles?

The answer would presumably be affirmative as long as changes in the savings-income ratios (proportions of income that are saved) for the upper income groups, which presumably move with business cycles, do not have an amplitude wider than that of the savings-income ratios for the lower groups. For the share of any given income group in total savings is a fraction, of which the numerator is the product of its share in total income and the proportion of its income that is saved, and the denominator is the over-all savings-income ratio for the total population. For example, if the income share of the top 5 percent group is 30 percent and it saves a third of its income, its savings, as a share of the total income of all individuals, will be 10 percent (30 percent x 0.33). If the population as a whole saves 15 percent of its income, the top 5 percent group's share in total savings will be (30 x 0.33)/15, or two-thirds.

The particular question to be explored here is how the savings-income ratios at upper income levels vary over time. These ratios can be studied for either (a) given percentile groups, i.e., the top 1, 5, etc., percent of the population in each year; or (b) groups at a given relative income level, i.e., groups that in each year derive incomes x times the average income per capita (referred to below as income multiple position). Measures under (a) would be more directly relevant for the analysis here. But the several deficiencies in the sample data on expenditures and savings permit much greater comparability if we use measures under (b). For this reason, in trying to formulate the question to be explored here, we couch Table 17 largely in terms of savings-income ratios at income multiple positions.

We record in columns 1, 4, and 7, the percentage shares of total

Table 17: Savings of Upper Income Groups as Percentages of Total Income of Individuals Assuming Constancy of Savings-Income Ratios at Upper Income Levels, 1919-1945

	Top 1 Percent			2nd & 3rd Percentage Band			4th & 5th Percentage Band			Top 5 Percent Savings as % of Total Income Assuming Constancy of Savings-Income Ratio for Given		Rank of Share (Increasing Order) of Top 5 Percent Group in Total Savings Assuming Constancy of Savings-Income Ratio for Given	
	% share of total income, economic income variant (1)	Savings-income ratio (%) (2)	Savings as % of total income (1) x (2) (3)	% share of total income, economic income variant (4)	Savings-income ratio (%) (5)	Savings as % of total income (4) x (5) (6)	% share of total income, economic income variant (7)	Savings-income ratio (%) (8)	Savings as % of total income (7) x (8) (9)	Income multiple (10)	Percentage band (11)	Income multiple (12)	Percentage band (13)
1919	14.0	42.10	5.9	6.8	25.80	1.7	5.3	21.60	1.1	8.8	9.0	6	6
1920	13.6	41.86	5.7	6.8	25.80	1.8	5.3	21.60	1.1	8.6	8.9	10	10
1921	16.2	43.06	7.0	9.0	29.46	2.7	6.5	25.40	1.7	11.3	10.8	26	26
1922	15.6	42.84	6.7	8.0	28.00	2.2	6.8	25.80	1.7	10.7	10.4	20	20
1923	14.0	42.10	5.9	8.5	28.60	2.4	5.6	22.80	1.3	9.6	9.6	12	12
1924	14.7	42.48	6.2	8.4	28.60	2.4	6.0	24.00	1.4	10.1	9.9	19	19
1925	15.7	42.88	6.7	8.1	28.00	2.3	6.4	25.00	1.6	10.6	10.4	14	14
1926	15.8	42.92	6.8	8.2	28.30	2.3	6.3	24.60	1.5	10.6	10.4	18	18
1927	16.5	43.15	7.1	8.4	28.60	2.4	6.3	25.00	1.6	11.1	10.7	17	17
1928	17.2	43.34	7.4	8.3	28.30	2.3	6.6	25.40	1.7	11.5	11.1	21	21
1929	17.2	43.34	7.4	8.5	28.60	2.4	6.2	24.60	1.5	11.4	11.0	15	15
1930	15.6	42.84	6.7	8.4	28.60	2.4	6.7	25.40	1.7	10.8	10.5	23	23
1931	15.6	42.84	6.7	9.0	29.46	2.7	7.4	27.00	2.0	11.3	10.8	22	22
1932	15.3	42.72	6.5	9.3	30.01	2.8	7.5	27.35	2.1	11.4	10.8	24	24
1933	14.4	42.33	6.1	8.9	29.18	2.6	7.6	27.35	2.1	10.7	10.3	27	27
1934	13.6	41.86	5.7	8.5	28.89	2.5	7.1	26.20	1.9	10.0	9.7	25	25
1935	13.6	41.86	5.7	8.4	28.60	2.4	6.8	25.80	1.8	9.8	9.6	13	13
1936	14.7	42.48	6.2	8.0	28.00	2.2	6.5	25.40	1.7	10.2	10.0	8	8
1937	14.1	42.16	6.0	8.0	28.00	2.2	6.4	25.00	1.6	9.8	9.7	11	11
1938	12.8	41.38	5.3	8.4	28.60	2.4	6.6	25.40	1.7	9.4	9.3	16	16
1939	13.3	41.68	5.5	8.4	28.60	2.4	6.4	25.00	1.6	9.5	9.4	9	9
1940	13.0	41.50	5.4	7.8	27.70	2.2	6.3	24.60	1.5	9.1	9.1	7	7
1941	12.5	41.19	5.1	7.6	27.35	2.1	5.9	23.40	1.4	8.6	8.7	5	5
1942	10.8	39.84	4.3	6.8	25.80	1.8	5.1	21.00	1.1	7.1	7.6	3	3
1943	10.1	39.12	3.9	6.2	24.60	1.5	4.8	20.30	1.0	6.4	7.1	2	2
1944	9.1	37.92	3.4	5.8	23.40	1.4	4.0	17.00	0.7	5.5	6.4	1	1
1945	9.5	38.40	3.6	6.0	24.00	1.4	4.0	17.00	0.7	5.8	6.6	4	4

Notes to Table 17

COLUMN	
2, 5, 8	Multiples of average income were derived by dividing the percentage of economic income received (col. 1, 4, and 7) by the percentage of population receiving it. To each multiple a savings-income ratio was assigned, set, on the basis of sample evidence in the report (partly summarized in Table 18), at 17 percent for the multiple of 2, 24 percent for the multiple of 3, 28 percent for the multiple of 4, 30.8 percent for the multiple of 5, 33.2 percent for the multiple of 6, 35 percent for the multiple of 7, 37.8 percent for the multiple of 9, 39 percent for the multiple of 10, and 45 percent for the multiple of 25, and interpolated with an allowance for decreasing increments in the savings-income ratio as the multiple increases.
10	Sum of columns 3, 6, and 9.
11	Sum of products for each year of columns 1, 4, and 7 and a *constant* savings-income ratio. The constant ratio for column 1, 41.859 percent, is the arithmetic mean of column 2 for 1919-45; that for column 4, 27.735 percent, the arithmetic mean of column 5; and that for column 7, 24.037 percent, the arithmetic mean of column 8.
12 & 13	a) To the NBER estimates of individuals' savings for 1919-38 (*National Income and Its Composition, 1919-1938*, Table 39, p. 276) and the Department of Commerce estimates of personal savings for 1929-45 (*Survey of Current Business*, July 1949, Table 3, p. 10) was added the Department of Commerce series on depreciation of owner-occupied dwellings as shown for 1929-41 in National Income Supplement to *Survey of Current Business*, July 1947, Table 39, p. 47, for 1942-45 in *Survey of Current Business*, July 1949, Table 39, p. 25, and extrapolated back to 1919 by an index based on depreciation on all residences (Solomon Fabricant, *Capital Consumption and Adjustment*, NBER, 1938, Table 29, p. 160) and the ratio of imputed rent to all rent paid on urban dwellings as computed from data underlying the NBER series on total imputed rent. b) The series for 1919-38 and 1929-45 calculated in (a) were divided by aggregate payments to individuals including depreciation on owner-occupied dwellings from sources cited in (a). c) The percentages for 1919-38 and 1929-45 calculated in (b) were converted to indexes with 1919-38 as base. d) The index for 1919-38 calculated in (c) was extrapolated through 1945 by the index for 1929-45. e) Columns 10 and 11, each converted to an index with 1919-38 as base, were divided by the index for 1919-45 calculated in (d), and the ratios ranked in increasing order, to yield columns 12 and 13, respectively.

income, economic income variant, received by the several upper income groups. These shares, when related to the percentage of the population covered, determine for each year the income multiple position (e.g., in 1919, the income multiple position of the top 1 percent was 14.0; of the 2nd and 3rd percentage band, 3.4). From the scattered sample evidence on expenditures and savings, summarized in Table 18, we can estimate the savings-income ratios corresponding to the given income multiple positions—on the assumption that the levels of these ratios, derived primarily from evidence for the 1930's and early 1940's, are held constant for the period covered in Table 17. This evidence, together with the assumption just stated, is the source of columns 2, 5, and 8. Multiplying the annual entries in columns 1, 4, and 7 by those in columns 2, 5, and 8, we obtain the hypothetical savings of the several upper income groups expressed in percentages of total income of individuals (col. 3, 6, and 9). Adding these estimates, thus expressed, for the three upper income groups, gives the savings of the top 5 percent group (col. 10).

To repeat, column 10 shows the hypothetical savings of the top 5 percent of the population on the assumption that the average proportion of income it saves is determined by its *income multiple position;* and that the savings-income ratio for a given income multiple position is *constant,* at a level suggested by sample studies available since 1929. It is of interest to see what the hypothetical estimate would be on a somewhat different assumption: that the savings-income ratio is constant for a given *percentile* group. This assumption can be easily applied, by using in columns 2, 5, and 8 a *constant* savings-income ratio. Setting the latter at a level equal to the arithmetic mean for the period, multiplying columns 1, 4, and 7 by the constant savings-income ratio for each, and adding the three products, we get the entries in column 11. The latter shows the hypothetical savings of the top 5 percent group, expressed in percentages of total income of individuals, on the assumption that the savings-income ratios for the upper percentage groups are constant over time at levels suggested by the sample studies since 1929.

It will be seen from Table 17 that the hypothetical savings of upper income groups, on the assumption of constancy of the savings-income ratios either at a given income multiple position (col. 10) or for a given percentile group (col. 11), when expressed in percentages of the total income of individuals, vary but little except for the years since 1939. What variation there is is counter-cyclical (observe the rises in 1921 and 1924, the declines in 1920 and 1923, and the almost complete absence of decline during the great depression of 1929-33). The results in columns 10 and 11 would be little affected by any reasonable assumptions concerning the *average levels* of the savings-income ratios of the upper income groups. Unfortunately, there is no reliable series on total savings of individuals with which columns 10 and 11 can be directly compared, at least no series with an average level of the savings-income ratio consistent with the evidence yielded by the samples summarized in Table 18 (and used in

Table 17). But for purposes of rough comparison, we took the crude estimates of total savings of individuals, derived as the difference between aggregate income receipts and consumer expenditures plus taxes; added depreciation on owner-occupied houses; expressed the totals as percentages of all income payments to individuals; converted these percentages to an index with 1919-38 as base; took the ratio of entries in columns 10 and 11 (also converted to indexes with 1919-38 as base) to this index of all individuals' savings as a percentage of their incomes; and ranked the ratios in increasing order.[12]

The entries in columns 12 and 13 indicate a decline after 1939 in the share of total savings accounted for by the top 5 percent group; and, what is more important here, a movement counter to business cycles. The years of depression (1921, 1924, 1932-33, 1938) are marked by high ranks, indicating a high proportion of upper group savings to total savings. In contrast, the years of prosperity (1919-20, 1923, 1929, 1936-37) are marked by low ranks.[13]

The question we propose to explore can now be posed. Is the assumption made in Table 17 at all realistic: that the savings-income ratios for the upper income positions or groups move relatively little during the short periods associated with business cycles? If they are relatively stable in the short run, the share of upper group savings in total savings must vary widely and run counter to business cycles. Only if the savings-income ratios of upper income positions or groups vary with business cycles and much more widely than the savings-income ratios of the lower income positions or groups will this greater variability tend to offset the counter-cyclical movements of their income shares and give them a constant share in total savings of individuals.

The question then reduces itself to one concerning the relative short term variability of savings-income ratios for the upper and lower income groups respectively.

It is the relative variability, not the absolute changes in savings-income ratios that should be compared, as can be seen from the fol-

[12] The use of ranks instead of the actual ratios was due to lack of confidence in the absolute magnitude of the ratios derived—stemming from lack of confidence in the absolute magnitude of the levels of countrywide savings of individuals.

[13] There is some hint that the decline in the proportion of upper income group savings to total savings reaches a trough somewhat before the peak in general business conditions (1919 rather than 1920, 1936 rather than 1937). But the data are too crude to reveal leads or lags.

lowing simple example. If total savings are 15 percent of aggregate income payments, and the top 5 percent group saves a third of its total income of 30 percent, thereby contributing 10 of the over-all 15 percent, the lower 95 percent group must save 5 percent of the aggregate income of individuals out of its total income of 70 percent; i.e., its savings-income ratio is roughly 7 percent. Assume that the savings-income ratios for both the top 5 and the lower 95 percent groups are reduced or increased, absolutely, 3 percent. The savings-income ratios then become either 30 and 4, or 36 and 10 percent, respectively. If they decline and the distribution of income between the two groups remains the same, the over-all savings-income ratio becomes 11.8 percent, instead of 15, of which 9 percent is contributed by the top 5 percent group and 2.8 percent by the lower 95 percent group—a shift in the proportion in total savings in favor of the top group because the *relative* reduction in its savings-income ratio is much less than that of the lower 95 percent group (3 out of 33 percent, or an eleventh, as compared with 3 out of 7 percent, or over four-tenths). If the savings-income ratios rise, the over-all savings-income ratio becomes 17.8 percent, instead of 15, of which 10.8 percent is contributed by the top 5 percent group and 7 percent by the lower 95 percent group—a sharp cut in the relative contribution of the former because the *relative* rise in its savings-income ratio is so much smaller. This example shows, and it can be demonstrated algebraically, that if the short term movements of the savings-income ratios for both upper and lower income groups are in the same direction, equal *absolute* changes will mean that changes in the savings shares of the upper income groups run counter to the absolute changes in the savings-income ratios. Only equal relative changes of savings-income ratios will leave the proportions of upper and lower income group savings in the total of all savings unaffected.

2 *Savings-Income Ratios for Upper and Lower Income Groups*
Table 18 brings together the savings-income ratios revealed in several samples covering intermittently the period from 1929 to 1948. While these samples claim countrywide coverage, they differ significantly in the income concept, number of returns, and adequacy of coverage. For example, the Brookings Institution distribution was based originally upon income including gains and losses from sales of assets, and we had to adjust it to reduce it to the basis of eco-

nomic income. The samples for 1945-48 cover the distribution of money income alone, and no adjustment for their exclusion of income in kind was made.

Table 18

Savings as Percentages of Income, Relative Levels of Income per Consuming or Spending Unit, Various Samples, 1929-1948

	Multiples of Arithmetic Mean Income per Consuming or Spending Unit	Brookings Study 1929 (1)	Consumer Purchases Study 1935-36 (2)	Survey of Spending and Saving in Wartime 1941 (3)	1942, 1st Qu. (4)	Survey of Consumer Finances			
						1945 (5)	1946 (6)	1947 (7)	1948 (8)
1	0.25	—30.4	—32.1	—15.6	—25.1	4.9	—9.3	—14.8	—22.2
2	0.50	—1.3	—7.4	0.2	—0.1	7.9	1.9	1.4	—1.3
3	0.75	8.1	—1.5	5.3	8.3	10.7	7.0	4.6	3.2
4	1.00	11.6	3.5	5.0	10.9	12.9	10.8	7.0	6.4
5	1.50	16.3	9.4	10.7	15.9	15.7	15.9	10.2	10.8
6	2.00	19.5	14.1	13.9	18.2	19.6	19.7	14.0	14.0
7	3.00	23.6	21.9	19.3	22.7	28.6	24.9	21.5	18.5
8	4.00	29.0	27.2	24.8	27.2				
9	7.00	37.0	37.5						
10	10.00	38.5	39.8						
11	25.00	43.1	49.2						
		Arithmetic Means of Above for Wider Groups							
	LINES								
12	2-4 (av. multiple 0.75)	6.1	—1.8	3.5	6.4	10.5	6.6	4.3	2.8
13	6-7 (av. multiple 2.50)	21.6	18.0	16.6	20.4	24.1	22.3	17.8	16.2
14	6-8 (av. multiple 3.00)	24.0	21.1	19.3	22.7				
15	8-10 (av. multiple 7.00)	34.8	34.8						

One general adjustment was introduced to improve the comparability of the samples. First, the arithmetic mean income of each total sample population was adjusted to equal the per consuming unit income of a continuous series of individuals' aggregate incomes, in this case the Department of Commerce series. Then each sample income subgroup was described by its ratio to the arithmetic mean income per consuming unit for the total population. Consequently, the savings-income ratios for the several income classes in each sample distribution were associated with their average incomes expressed as ratios of the countrywide per consuming unit income derived from Department of Commerce estimates. The savings-income ratios were then established for standard multiples by simple interpolation.

Four conclusions are obvious. First, the savings-income ratios are significantly higher at the upper income multiples than at the lower. This carries with it a no less obvious but often overlooked implication that savings are less equally distributed than income. If the savings-income ratios were the same at different levels of per unit income, the relative spread in the distribution of savings and of income would be identical. But if they are higher at higher levels of per unit income, the shares of upper income groups in total savings must be considerably larger than their shares in total income. The order of magnitude is readily calculated. As the top 5 percent group received, on the average, about 30 percent of total income (economic income variant), its income multiple position was 6. At this income multiple position, the savings-income ratio is about a third. Hence, savings by the top 5 percent group would be about 10 percent of total individuals' income. If savings by all individuals are about 15 percent of total income, the maximum average level that we can reasonably assume from evidence of the samples, the proportion accounted for by the top 5 percent group would be two-thirds. In other words, the share of the top 5 percent group in total savings would be over twice as large as its share in aggregate income, three-tenths.

Second, the rise in the savings-income ratios with the rise in income is larger in the lower than in the higher ranges of the income multiples. From the income multiple of 0.5 to that of 1.0 (doubling), the savings-income ratio rises from close to or well below zero (barring 1945, an exceptional year still marked by war restrictions) to well above zero and in most years to over 5 percent. From the income multiple of 2.0 to that of 4.0 the savings-income ratio fails to double, and above the income multiple of 4.0, its rise is quite gentle. The slope of the line connecting savings-income ratios with relative income position declines as we ascend the income scale.

Third, the spread in the savings-income ratios is somewhat wider when we classify income groups by their standing relative to average *per capita* income than by their standing relative to per consuming or spending unit income.[14] This is in line with the usual greater

[14] This statement is based on the results of more detailed calculations. Since the results are close to those in Table 18, it did not seem necessary to summarize them here. They reenforce the conclusions with respect to differences in the levels of savings-income ratios for upper and lower income groups respectively, the damping

52

sensitivity of a distribution based on per capita income in reflecting income as a determinant of expenditures and savings than of a distribution based on total income per consuming or spending unit where large families with large total but low per capita income may be classified at upper income levels.

The fourth and most relevant conclusion is the greater stability over time of the savings-income ratios at the upper income levels than at the lower. At the multiple of 0.50 (omitting the 0.25 multiple as too low for yielding reliable savings-income ratios), the range is from 1.9 to —7.4 percent (again disregarding 1945 as an exceptional year); at the multiple of 1.0, from 3.5 to 11.6 percent, already narrower; at the multiple of 1.5, from 9.4 to 16.3 percent, still narrower; at the multiple of 2.0, from 13.9 to 19.7 percent, still narrower; at the multiple of 3.0, from 18.5 to 24.9 percent, slightly wider absolutely but narrower relatively; and so on, with increasing narrowing of even the absolute, let alone the relative ranges, as we pass to the higher income multiples. This narrowing of absolute changes in savings-income ratios as we ascend the income scale is even more evident for the wider groups in lines 12-15. And while Table 18 does not include years of marked cyclical trough, it does cover years with quite a range in the over-all savings-income ratio— from about 7 percent in 1948 to about 17 percent in 1929. Furthermore, according to additional information from a special Brookings Institution sample of questionnaire returns for 1928-32, the absolute and certainly the relative range of changes over time in the savings-income ratio are much narrower at the upper than at the lower income levels. What lends the conclusion more significance is that this diminution in the range seems systematic and gradual as we rise from the lowest to the highest income multiples; and that changes revealed by different samples and sample years in the over-all savings-income ratios reflect business cycles and are not random.

This conclusion is necessarily tentative in view of the small body of data upon which it is based and is subject to one exception. If gains or losses on sales of assets are very large at the upper income levels, and are treated by recipients as bona fide income to be spent currently, the savings-income ratios of upper income groups would be reduced during cyclical expansions and raised during contrac-

---

of the slope of the rise in the ratios at upper income levels, and the narrower range of changes in these ratios for the upper income groups.

tions, thereby introducing a variability not recorded in the savings-income ratios in terms of *economic* income in Table 18. But even this exception, which would make for a counter-cyclical movement of savings-income ratios for upper income groups, would merely strengthen the final conclusion, that the shares of upper income groups in total savings decline during expansions and rise during contractions.

The factors that make for stability, or narrow short term changes, in the savings-income ratios at upper income levels can be summarized only briefly here. First, it can be demonstrated by simple algebra that with a given change in income and constant expenditures, the resulting change in savings-income ratios would be absolutely, and of course relatively, smaller for an income group whose savings-income ratio is high than for one whose ratio is low. Second, the savings-income ratio for lower income units may vary more during short term cycles because they cannot curtail consumption proportionately to income during bad times, and having contracted debts or reduced their assets materially, are impelled to build them up again during good times. The resulting relative stability of consumption (keeping it in bad times above the relative cut in income and in good times below the relative rise in income) makes for a wide cyclical swing in the savings-income ratio. The upper income units need not hold so rigidly to their consumption patterns, since they can ordinarily dispense with a large proportion of goods. Third, even if not directly affected by realized gains and losses on sales of assets, the upper income units, as large property holders, are affected by fluctuations in asset values; and may increase or reduce their consumption with short term fluctuations of the business cycle, thus contributing to a relatively constant savings-income ratio. Fourth, since we deal here with units classified by current year income, shifts into and out of income groups should be considered. These shifts, which in general increase the short term variability of the savings-income ratio, affect most heavily the groups at the two extremes of the income distribution. But the effect at the upper extreme is mitigated by the fact that beyond a certain income multiple range, the savings-income ratio does not rise or rises very slowly; and migration within this range would not have much effect on the savings-income ratio. The effect of migration on the variability of the savings-income ratio at the lower end of the income distribution may be larger because of the steep slope of the line connecting the savings-income ratio with relative income size, i.e., with the income multiple.

3 Implications

The evidence in Table 18 and the arguments just adduced corroborate the assumption that savings-income ratios at upper income *multiples* vary less during business cycles than those at lower income positions. In so far as upper income *groups* can be characterized by their average income levels, they are at high income multiples; hence *if* their relative income position were constant during business cycles, their savings-income ratios would vary with a much narrower relative amplitude than would the savings-income ratios of the lower income groups. Furthermore, the income multiple position of upper income groups is not constant but on the whole (with qualification for the irregular behavior of the share of the top 1 percent) changes counter to business cycles. The movements in the savings-income ratios of the upper income groups are then a product of two sets of opposite changes: (a) the counter-cyclical changes of their income shares (multiple positions); (b) the changes in the savings-income ratios at given upper income multiples, which move with business cycles. We cannot tell with any assurance what the net balance of these opposite movements is in setting the cyclical pattern of changes in savings-income ratios of upper income groups: in most violent cyclical shifts, the positive conformity of savings-income ratios for a given multiple position probably outweighs the counter-cyclical pattern of shifts in income shares, i.e., in income multiple positions, thereby making savings-income ratios for upper income groups move with business cycles.

But even so, our analysis clearly suggests that the savings of the upper income groups will vary less during business cycles than those of lower income groups (both expressed as percentages of the aggregate income of individuals). The reasons are two: (a) the inverted movement of the shares of upper groups in total income tends to offset the positive movement of the savings-income ratio for given income multiples, whereas for the lower income groups both the share of aggregate income received and the savings-income ratio move with business cycles; (b) the savings-income ratio varies less for upper income multiples than for lower, and the difference in the *relative* variation must be quite large.

As far as the savings of upper income groups, expressed as percentages of the total income of individuals, are stable or vary little whereas those of lower income groups vary markedly with business cycles, two further conclusions follow. First, the marked fluctuation in the over-all savings-income ratio for individuals in positive conformity to business cycles must be due largely to variations in the savings-income ratios for the lower income groups; it can be due only in small part to variations in either the income shares or the savings-income ratios of upper income groups. Second, the proportions of total savings by individuals accounted for by upper and lower income groups respectively must change significantly during business cycles: as total savings and their ratio to the aggregate income of all individuals rise during expansions, the share of savings contributed by upper income groups must decline; as total savings of individuals and their ratio to total income decline during contractions, the share contributed by upper income groups must rise.

These conclusions are subject to several qualifications. Our sample data were scanty, particularly in their coverage of the top income group and of cyclical contractions; they had to be adjusted, necessarily crudely, in different ways to fit the income concepts used here. Furthermore, the period covered by our analysis is quite short, yielding surmises rather than firm generalizations. Yet one aspect of the conclusions must be emphasized. If the average level of the savings-income ratio for upper income groups (say top 5 or 10 percent) is 25 or 30 percent, and that for lower income groups is 5 percent or less, the *relative* variability of the savings-income ratio for the former can hardly be as wide as for the latter. Consequently, the greater relative variability of savings-income ratios for the lower income groups is so highly probable as to be almost in the nature of an algebraic necessity; and the inference concerning the counter-cyclical movement of upper group shares in total savings necessarily follows.

By way of final illustration we present Table 19, which in a sense restates data used in Table 18; but it brings out more distinctly the connection between changes in the over-all savings-income ratio and in the proportion of total savings accounted for by the upper income groups. For the two samples that cover more than one year and for which changes can therefore be studied without any adjustment for comparability, we assembled measures of the over-all savings-income ratio and of shares of the upper tenth and lower nine-tenths in savings and income. These were taken from the sample distributions, and the groups are classified by income per consuming or spending unit.

Table 19

Shares of Savings Accounted for by Top Income Group in Periods of Change in the Over-all Savings-Income Ratio
Two Samples (percentages)

Sample	Over-all Savings-Income Ratio (Sample Population) (1)	Top Tenth			Lower Nine-Tenths		
		Share of savings (2)	Share of income (3)	Savings-income ratio (4)	Share of savings (5)	Share of income (6)	Savings-income ratio (7)
	SURVEY OF SPENDING AND SAVING IN WARTIME						
	Farm						
1 1941	13.8	56.0	23.4	33.1	44.0	76.6	8.0
2 1942, 1st Qu.	—10.2	*	33.7	47.3	*	66.3	—39.3
	Rural Nonfarm						
3 1941	5.8	68.6	23.2	17.1	31.4	76.8	2.4
4 1942, 1st Qu.	11.2	47.9	24.0	22.4	52.1	76.0	7.7
	Urban						
5 1941	9.0	78.4	31.6	22.4	21.6	68.4	2.9
6 1942, 1st Qu.	13.9	68.3	31.5	30.1	31.7	68.5	6.4
	SURVEY OF CONSUMER FINANCES						
7 1945	15	46	29	23.8	54	71	11.4
8 1946	12	63	32	23.6	37	68	6.5
9 1947	9	77	33	21.0	23	67	3.1
10 1948	7	80	32	17.5	20	68	2.1

* Not shown because of difference in signs: for column 2 there are positive savings 156.9 percent as large as the negative total; for column 5 there are negative savings 256.9 percent as large as the negative total.

Whenever the over-all savings-income ratio rises from one year to the next, the proportion of total savings of individuals accounted for by savings of the upper income groups declines; and whenever it declines, the proportion rises. The consistent negative association is due to: (a) a negative association between changes in the income share of the upper income groups and changes in the over-all savings-income ratio; (b) a consistently narrower relative, and often absolute, change in the savings-income ratio of the upper income groups than in that of the lower groups.

The significance of Table 19 is limited by the small size of the samples and particularly by the presence of war years in the period covered. Nevertheless, it strengthens the basic conclusion of the analysis of income and savings of upper income groups: short term variations in the proportions they contribute to total savings of individuals are large and run counter to variations in the over-all savings-income ratio, hence counter to business cycles.

Further implications of this conclusion are beyond the scope of this discussion. However, they seem, at least at first glance, to be far-reaching. The savings of upper and of lower income groups tend to flow into different kinds of investment: upper income groups are the chief recipients of dividends which in turn constitute a large share of their property incomes. Of the property incomes of lower income groups, on the contrary, dividends constitute a small share. Similar evidence concerning differences in the composition of assets held by upper and lower income groups is provided in the 1949 Survey of Consumer Finances (see *Federal Reserve Bulletin*, Aug. and Sept. 1949). Cyclical shifts in the proportion of total savings accounted for by upper income groups may mean shifts in the proportion of individuals' savings available for different types of investment, and an analysis of the relation between the new supply of savings and of investment opportunities during business cycles must consider cyclical shifts in savings coming from the upper and from the lower income groups.

There are similar consequences in the distribution of consumer expenditures between those by upper and by lower income groups. The counter-cyclical movement of income shares and the more stable savings-income ratios for upper than for lower income groups mean that in expansions a decreasing share of income is offset by only a moderate rise in the savings-income ratio, whereas for the lower income groups an increasing share of income may be offset by a sharp rise in the savings-income ratio. The shares of upper income groups in consumption expenditures may rise during expansions, or at least through a substantial part of them, and decline during contractions. However, their average share in expenditures is much smaller than their average share in savings; hence the shifts in the distribution of the former are likely to be much less marked than those in the distribution of total savings by individuals.

D Directions of Further Inquiry

An empirical investigation in economics often leaves more questions unanswered than it answers, opening a wider vista than the canvas originally covered and requiring further explorations. The main reason for this embarrassing situation is the changing complexity of economic reality and the paucity of data and resources available for empirical study, which together make it difficult to elaborate an acceptable theory, a tested framework that delimits an area of knowledge and fully defines its components. Had we such a framework, any empirical investigation would be seen to cover some of the field and to reduce the area of ignorance, rather than unveil new areas and new aspects of hitherto unrecognized ignorance. In the absence of such a framework, the more one learns the more one realizes one does not know.

This remark does not imply that economic research is not worth while: after all, what is learned can and should be used, no matter how much else we may be ignorant of. The remark is made here rather to show the impossibility, at the end of this investigation as at the end of many another, of listing all potential lines of further inquiry: there are too many for any list to be of much use. We try rather to mention the most obvious directions of further work, obvious because they are forced upon our attention by difficulties encountered in trying to establish our findings; are brought out by the data or techniques for areas we ourselves did not explore; or seem so logical an extension of findings to other sectors of the economy as to call for further study, even if different data and techniques are required.

1 Testing the Findings

Little is or can be said specifically in this summary about the reliability of our estimates or the technical steps taken to attain them. But it must be evident from our presentation that we encountered considerable difficulty in constructing estimates with a high degree of reliability and in unearthing data for checking the several hypotheses. Hence, the first and most obvious line of further inquiry is to test the findings in the light of new data for the future that will increasingly become our past or new data for the longer past.

The broad areas for testing are three. One is the comparability of data reported on federal income tax returns with those underlying the estimates of countrywide income receipts of individuals. This investigation and several others examined these two bodies of data and tried to improve their comparability, but the task is far from finished. Current steps providing for a more systematic audit of federal income tax returns will make possible for the first time a careful estimate of shortages in tax reporting by individuals. It is hoped that the use of these data, together with further scrutiny of the countrywide estimates, will resolve the discrepancies and assign them to the proper size classes and types of income. The results of such further work are not likely to upset the broad conclusions drawn in this investigation; nor would adjustments indicated by audits for current years necessarily apply to data for the past. But comparisons of totals on federal tax returns with countrywide estimates of aggregate payments to individuals are an obvious step toward a combined analysis of the two bodies of data, and perhaps the only valid basis for continuous estimates of the income shares of upper income groups. Hence, such further testing of the comparability of these data is needed not only as a further check upon the findings for the past, but even more as a base for continuous estimates and analysis for the future.

The effects of statistical and social characteristics of upper income groups upon their income shares constitute the second area for testing. Our analysis is patchy, partly because data are few and partly because only so many years and resources can be devoted to any empirical study. But limited as it is, it reveals how large the effect of taking income for a period longer than just the current year; of excluding from the income distribution groups who are either in the 'learning' stage or are already semi-retired or retired; of considering differences in purchasing power of money between the upper and lower income classes. The incomes men and women receive from their participation in economic activity, either by working or by lending their property, determine the effectiveness of their contribution to economic production in the future and are a major factor in shaping their actions as buyers and consumers. But any interpretation of the size distribution of income as influencing the behavior of people as producers and consumers requires not only measuring the shares but also associating them with the demographic, economic, and social characteristics of the several income size classes. Further work in this direction, even if confined to the upper income groups, is needed to lend more realism and permit more intensive analysis than was feasible in this investigation.

The third area for testing consists of the patterns of savings- (and the implied patterns of consumer expenditure-) income ratios for the upper and lower income groups. More information is needed on the temporal stability of savings-income ratios of upper income groups as compared with their variability among the lower income groups, as well as analysis to show more explicitly why these should be the behavior patterns. Data must be gathered for more checking, and related sectors in the distribution of income between savings and expenditures and within expenditures among outlays on different types of goods analyzed, so that we can understand why upper income groups allocate their income between savings and expenditures as they do.

2 *Extending the Analysis along Present Lines*

Measuring income shares of upper income groups by comparing data on tax returns with estimates of the income of the total population is a technique that can, without substantial modification, be extended in two directions. It can be applied, first, to each of the forty-eight states in this country or to combinations of them in regions; second, to other countries for which both individual income tax returns and estimates of total individuals' incomes are available.

State totals of income receipts by individuals have been estimated for 1919-21, and annually since 1929. The tabulations of federal income tax returns classify returns by the filer's state of residence throughout the years covered by the federal income tax, and in as full detail as for the country as a whole at least since 1926. To compare for each state the several variants in the detail employed here for the country would be unwarranted not only because of the labor involved and lack of detail for some years but even more because the margins of error are wider for the state units than for the nation in both the income tax data and the estimates for all individuals. Moreover, the state estimates for property incomes and the federal income tax data are partly interdependent, whereas federal tax data and the countrywide estimates of individual incomes are independent. But if the comparisons for the states were confined to the basic variant, dealt with shares in total income alone (disregarding shares in state totals of various types of income), and deliberately neglected some of the finer points in the procedures used here for the countrywide comparisons, the results, procurable with moderate labor, would still be of substantial value. They would permit us to associate differences in the shares of upper income groups, defined in standard percentage bands, for the several states at a given time with the economic and social characteristics of the states. Comparisons for several years would enable us to study differences in the movement of the shares of upper income groups in states and regions, and the factors that determine them.

The extension of the analysis to other countries is contingent upon the availability of reliable and independent sets of data for both terms of the comparison. Lack of knowledge about data for other countries makes me hesitate to speak about this matter with assurance. However, in most industrially advanced countries where fairly effective individual income tax systems have long existed, total individuals' incomes are likely to be estimated. The big question is whether the two sets of data are independent, particularly whether the countrywide totals are not themselves based in large part upon income tax data; and the other bases of estimates are perhaps of doubtful validity. Whatever the case, comparisons similar to those in the report may well be feasible for other countries; and application to them of this or similar techniques should yield results of high value. The results might lengthen the period over which changes in the income shares of upper income groups could be observed, and reveal these changes for economies that differ significantly from ours—in the phase of their development, in social and economic structure, and in the degree to which the state, through taxation or other measures, has tried to shape the distribution of income and wealth.

3 *Extension to Other Sectors of the Income Distribution*

Through most of the period studied here, federal income tax data cover a relatively small proportion of the population, and we can measure the income shares of the top groups alone. Even for the few recent years for which the coverage reaches much further down the size distribution of income there are grounds for believing that the relative error in reporting increases as we descend the income scale.

Consequently, it is still safer to measure the shares of a relatively small top percentage group alone.

Obviously the main direction of further inquiry is to analyze income shares and the determining factors for sectors below the small top group; and it is equally obvious that for this purpose new data and techniques are requisite. It is neither possible nor appropriate to discuss them at length here. Were they easily available, we would have used them, and this summary would cover a much larger segment of the income size distribution.

But some general comments can be made. Public interest in the size distribution of income has tended to emphasize the upper and the lower extreme tails, the top groups that derive large incomes and the groups at the bottom that suffer from inadequate incomes. Such emphasis arises from natural apprehension about a possibly dangerous concentration of economic power at the top, and from concern about the human misery that may result from the shortcomings of our economic and social system at the bottom. But the emphasis may be justified even if one is merely interested in the causes and consequences of income size, regardless of welfare, justice, or power. For it is at the extremes that the causes and effects of income size are most conspicuous.

The most natural supplementation of this investigation would be to study the income shares of low income groups, if there is need to limit the study instead of trying to cover the full range of the income size distribution. Whether or not there is any advantage in studying the low income groups before other sectors, much of what has been said in this summary concerning the upper income groups is, by analogy, relevant to an analysis of groups at the bottom of the income scale. Their income shares may vary over time much more than do those at the top; and over the short term of business cycles, they would move counter to upper income shares. But statistical and social characteristics seem just as relevant in interpreting the low average level of incomes at the bottom of the scale as in interpreting the high level incomes at the top: the low income groups may have a disproportionately large component of transitorily depressed incomes, of learner and retired groups, and of people residing in areas with an appreciably lower price level or cost of living. Likewise, the observations concerning the temporal stability of savings-income ratios at the upper income levels bear with them the complementary consequence of high variability at the very low income levels.

In all these respects a study of shares in income and savings of income groups at the bottom of the income size distribution would in a sense be a continuation of this investigation, serving both to complement and test our findings. It would necessarily have to employ different data, for the groups involved are not covered by income tax statistics, no matter how wide the coverage of the law. On the other hand, sample field studies are likely to cover these groups more fully. And the attention of society, directed at such of these lower groups as need assistance, has yielded and will continue to yield data not forthcoming for either the middle or the upper ranges of the income size distribution.

For reasons explained at the beginning of this section, we could easily list many more topics for further study in the field. But the many of importance not even mentioned, e.g., the internal shifting within the distribution of income, will be recognized if one basic concept emphasized throughout this investigation is kept in mind. We conclude this summary by trying to express this concept in a few words.

A distribution of income by size is an integral part of a rather complex set of interrelations in a country's economy, a set that functions amidst continuous change, whether long or short term. An economy is a system of interrelated parts whose relative weights and influences change in different ways, even if some pattern can be observed. Differences in size of income are one aspect under which differences in the components of the economy—among occupations, industries, age and sex groups, education, etc.—emerge, and these differences, whose combined effects are reflected in the size distribution of income, shift both in the long term growth and in the short term changes associated with business cycles. Hence, to conceive differences in income as significant in and of themselves, as having a meaning outside the structural differences in a country's economy that find expression in them is to overlook their most telling aspect. To justify a given inequality in the distribution of income by general references to inequality in ability, or to condemn it by general references to egalitarian principles, is equally superficial. In a dynamic society the various structural components (industries, occupations, etc.) grow at different rates and undergo different changes in the short run; hence income will always be unequally distributed, and inequality will change in smaller or greater degree over time. But this does not mean that all present income differentials are indispensable to satisfactory growth in the long run or to adaptation in the short run. The essence of the matter is not in the inequality but in what it stands for—differences in production and consumption power and incentive among the various groups and the bearing upon the functioning of the economy as judged by its basic purposes.

It is this concept of the income size distribution as a summary expression of various components of a changing economy that is the chief concept of the investigation summarized here. The unfolding of all its implications would perhaps yield the best general guide for further research in the field.

Appendix Table 1

Per Capita Income of Total Population and at Lower Partition Line of Top 1 and 5 Percent Groups, 1919-1945 (dollar value)

	Per Capita Income, Total Population			Per Capita Income at Lower Limit of Given Percentage Band			
				TOP 1 PERCENT		TOP 5 PERCENT	
	Basic variant	Economic income variant	Disposable income variant	Basic variant	Economic income variant	Basic variant	Economic income variant
	(1)	(2)	(3)	(4)	(5)	(6)	(7)
1919	606	620	611	2,591	2,978	1,185	1,549
1920	627	645	635	2,628	3,110	1,197	1,650
1921	490	510	497	2,288	3,055	1,206	1,574
1922	520	540	536	2,488	3,043	1,151	1,751
1923	593	614	609	2,552	3,443	1,254	1,576
1924	586	609	612	2,740	3,460	1,264	1,657
1925	610	633	648	3,090	3,779	1,411	1,969
1926	627	647	660	3,329	4,048	1,411	1,976
1927	622	642	657	3,232	4,017	1,459	1,951
1928	630	648	677	3,300	4,002	1,477	2,032
1929	659	678	692	3,348	4,199	1,509	2,027
1930	583	601	587	2,905	3,617	1,332	1,773
1931	480	494	470	2,390	3,043	1,287	1,659
1932	368	378	355	1,747	2,280	1,008	1,300
1933	357	366	352	1,668	2,127	885	1,246
1934	409	418	408	1,898	2,368	1,023	1,385
1935	443	452	446	2,038	2,547	1,107	1,469
1936	498	507	503	2,416	2,871	1,144	1,582
1937	538	549	539	2,544	3,011	1,181	1,701
1938	491	502	494	2,258	2,809	1,156	1,577
1939	519	531	524	2,472	3,004	1,254	1,637
1940	557	569	555	2,618	3,050	1,181	1,752
1941	679	692	659	3,172	3,714	1,321	1,847
1942	862	878	812	3,466	4,148	1,434	2,062
1943	1,036	1,055	941	4,062	4,686	1,580	2,363
1944	1,118	1,141	1,036	4,174	4,729	1,664	2,124
1945	1,139	1,162	1,071	4,654	5,155	1,719	2,139

Appendix Table 2
Income Shares of Top 1 and 5 Percent Groups
Total Population, Three Variants, 1919-1945

	PERCENTAGE OF COUNTRYWIDE INCOME RECEIVED BY					
	Top 1 Percent			Top 5 Percent		
	Basic variant (1)	Economic income variant (2)	Disposable income variant (3)	Basic variant (4)	Economic income variant (5)	Disposable income variant (6)
1919	12.8	14.0	12.2	22.9	26.1	24.3
1920	12.3	13.6	11.8	22.1	25.8	24.0
1921	13.5	16.2	14.2	25.5	31.7	29.3
1922	13.4	15.6	14.4	24.8	30.4	29.0
1923	12.3	14.0	13.1	22.9	28.1	27.0
1924	12.9	14.7	14.3	24.3	29.1	28.7
1925	13.7	15.7	16.5	25.2	30.2	31.1
1926	13.9	15.8	16.3	25.2	30.2	30.8
1927	14.4	16.5	17.2	26.0	31.2	31.9
1928	14.9	17.2	19.1	26.8	32.1	34.1
1929	14.5	17.2	18.9	26.1	31.9	33.5
1930	13.8	15.6	15.1	25.7	30.7	30.3
1931	13.3	15.6	14.6	26.2	32.0	31.2
1932	12.9	15.3	12.3	26.0	32.1	29.6
1933	12.1	14.4	12.6	24.6	30.8	29.3
1934	12.0	13.6	12.4	24.0	29.1	27.8
1935	12.1	13.6	12.8	23.8	28.8	27.9
1936	13.4	14.7	13.7	24.8	29.3	28.3
1937	13.0	14.1	13.0	24.1	28.5	27.4
1938	11.5	12.8	12.1	23.0	27.8	27.0
1939	11.9	13.3	12.3	23.7	28.1	27.1
1940	12.0	13.0	11.5	23.0	27.1	25.7
1941	11.5	12.5	10.0	22.2	26.0	23.2
1942	10.2	10.8	7.9	19.2	22.7	19.2
1943	9.5	10.1	6.5	18.0	21.1	16.8
1944	8.7	9.1	6.7	16.8	18.9	15.9
1945	8.9	9.5	7.4	17.6	19.5	16.8

Contents

A	Average Income Shares of Upper Income Groups	5
	1 Average Levels	5
	2 Effects of Statistical Characteristics	14
	a Recipient unit	15
	b Effects of scope of income	17
	c Effect of combining income types	20
	d Effect of period of income cumulation	22
	3 Social Characteristics of Upper Income Groups	24
	a Sex, age, and education	24
	b Occupational characteristics	27
	c Size of family and location	28
	d Expenditure differentials	30
B	Changes in Income Shares of Upper Income Groups	32
	1 Movement after 1939	32
	2 Changes from 1919-28 to 1929-38	37
	3 Changes during Business Cycles	39
C	Shares of Upper Income Groups in Savings	45
	1 Setting of the Problem	45
	2 Savings-Income Ratios for Upper and Lower Income Groups	50
	3 Implications	55
D	Directions of Further Inquiry	59
	1 Testing the Findings	59
	2 Extending the Analysis along Present Lines	61
	3 Extension to Other Sectors of the Income Distribution	62

APPENDIX TABLES   66

The Labor Force
in
War and Transition
Four Countries

CLARENCE D. LONG
Professor of Economics
The Johns Hopkins University

OCCASIONAL PAPER 36

NATIONAL BUREAU OF ECONOMIC RESEARCH, INC.

OFFICERS
1952

Harry Scherman, *Chairman*
C. C. Balderston, *President*
Percival F. Brundage, *Vice-President*
George B. Roberts, *Treasurer*
W. J. Carson, *Executive Director*

DIRECTORS AT LARGE

Donald R. Belcher, *American Telephone and Telegraph Company*
Oswald W. Knauth, *Beaufort, South Carolina*
Simon Kuznets, *University of Pennsylvania*
H. W. Laidler, *Executive Director, League for Industrial Democracy*
Shepard Morgan, *New York City*
C. Reinold Noyes, *Princeton, New Jersey*
George B. Roberts, *Vice-President, National City Bank*
Beardsley Ruml, *New York City*
Harry Scherman, *Chairman, Book-of-the-Month Club*
George Soule, *Bennington College*
N. I. Stone, *Consulting Economist*
J. Raymond Walsh, *New York City*
Leo Wolman, *Columbia University*
Theodore O. Yntema, *Vice President-Finance, Ford Motor Company*

DIRECTORS BY UNIVERSITY APPOINTMENT

E. Wight Bakke, *Yale*
C. C. Balderston, *Pennsylvania*
Arthur F. Burns, *Columbia*
G. A. Elliott, *Toronto*
Frank W. Fetter, *Northwestern*
H. M. Groves, *Wisconsin*
Gottfried Haberler, *Harvard*
Clarence Heer, *North Carolina*
R. L. Kozelka, *Minnesota*
Paul M. O'Leary, *Cornell*
T. W. Schultz, *Chicago*

DIRECTORS APPOINTED BY OTHER ORGANIZATIONS

Percival F. Brundage, *American Institute of Accountants*
Frederick C. Mills, *American Statistical Association*
S. H. Ruttenberg, *Congress of Industrial Organizations*
Murray Shields, *American Management Association*
Boris Shishkin, *American Federation of Labor*
Donald H. Wallace, *American Economic Association*
Frederick V. Waugh, *American Farm Economic Association*
Harold F. Williamson, *Economic History Association*

RESEARCH STAFF

Arthur F. Burns, *Director of Research*
Geoffrey H. Moore, *Associate Director of Research*

Moses Abramovitz
Harold Barger
Morris A. Copeland
Daniel Creamer
David Durand
Solomon Fabricant
Milton Friedman
Millard Hastay
W. Braddock Hickman
F. F. Hill
Thor Hultgren
Simon Kuznets
Clarence D. Long
Ruth P. Mack
Frederick C. Mills
Raymond J. Saulnier
Lawrence H. Seltzer
George J. Stigler
Leo Wolman

Relation of the Directors to the Work and Publications of the National Bureau of Economic Research

1. The object of the National Bureau of Economic Research is to ascertain and to present to the public important economic facts and their interpretation in a scientific and impartial manner. The Board of Directors is charged with the responsibility of ensuring that the work of the National Bureau is carried on in strict conformity with this object.

2. To this end the Board of Directors shall appoint one or more Directors of Research.

3. The Director or Directors of Research shall submit to the members of the Board, or to its Executive Committee, for their formal adoption, all specific proposals concerning researches to be instituted.

4. No report shall be published until the Director or Directors of Research shall have submitted to the Board a summary drawing attention to the character of the data and their utilization in the report, the nature and treatment of the problems involved, the main conclusions and such other information as in their opinion would serve to determine the suitability of the report for publication in accordance with the principles of the National Bureau.

5. A copy of any manuscript proposed for publication shall also be submitted to each member of the Board. For each manuscript to be so submitted a special committee shall be appointed by the President, or at his designation by the Executive Director, consisting of three Directors selected as nearly as may be one from each general division of the Board. The names of the special manuscript committee shall be stated to each Director when the summary and report described in paragraph (4) are sent to him. It shall be the duty of each member of the committee to read the manuscript. If each member of the special committee signifies his approval within thirty days, the manuscript may be published. If each member of the special committee has not signified his approval within thirty days of the transmittal of the report and manuscript, the Director of Research shall then notify each member of the Board, requesting approval or disapproval of publication, and thirty additional days shall be granted for this purpose. The manuscript shall then not be published unless at least a majority of the entire Board and a two-thirds majority of those members of the Board who shall have voted on the proposal within the time fixed for the receipt of votes on the publication proposed shall have approved.

6. No manuscript may be published, though approved by each member of the special committee, until forty-five days have elapsed from the transmittal of the summary and report. The interval is allowed for the receipt of any memorandum of dissent or reservation, together with a brief statement of his reasons, that any member may wish to express; and such memorandum of dissent or reservation shall be published with the manuscript if he so desires. Publication does not, however, imply that each member of the Board has read the manuscript, or that either members of the Board in general, or of the special committee, have passed upon its validity in every detail.

7. A copy of this resolution shall, unless otherwise determined by the Board, be printed in each copy of every National Bureau book.

(Resolution adopted October 25, 1926 and revised February 6, 1933 and February 24, 1941)

The Labor Force
in War and Transition
Four Countries

What! a young knave, and begging!
Is there not wars? Is there not employment?
Doth not the King lack subjects?
                    FALSTAFF

CLARENCE D. LONG
Professor of Economics
The Johns Hopkins University

OCCASIONAL PAPER 36

NATIONAL BUREAU OF ECONOMIC RESEARCH, INC.
1952

This paper owes much to the careful work of my assistants, Esther McPherson Donahue and Susan Dischka. H. Irving Forman drew the charts. Martha Anderson edited the manuscript. Arthur F. Burns, Solomon Fabricant, Thor Hultgren, Frederick C. Mills, Geoffrey H. Moore, Theodore W. Schultz, Boris Shishkin, George Stigler, and Leo Wolman read the manuscript at one stage or another and made comments in keeping with the best traditions of the National Bureau.

CLARENCE D. LONG

Price: $1.00

Copyright, 1952, by National Bureau of Economic Research, Inc.
1819 Broadway, New York 23, N. Y. All Rights Reserved
Typography by Oscar Leventhal, Inc.
Printing by Basso Printing Corporation
Library of Congress Catalog Card Number: 52-6745

CONTENTS

1	Summary	1
2	The Labor Force before World War II	5
	Labor Force Concept and Coverage	6
3	The Labor Force in Mobilization: United States, Great Britain, Germany	8
	Mid-1939 to the Invasion of Russia	9
	To the Triumph in North Africa	18
	To the Victory in Europe	22
	Labor Force, Armed Forces, and Unemployment	25
4	The War Peak: United States, Great Britain, Canada, Germany	32
	Wartime Additions by Age and Sex Earning Groups	36
5	Weakness of German Manpower Policy Explained	37
6	Increase in Hours during World War II: United States	45
7	Demobilization	46
8	The Korean War and Possibilities for Further Expansion	48

TABLE

1	Labor Force by Employment and Military Status: Four Countries, Both Sexes 14 and Older	16
2	Additions to Employment and Labor Force by Sources: Both Sexes 14 and Older	18
3	Need for Females in Housework Based on Population to be Cared for: United States, April 1940-1951	28
4	Need for Houseworkers as Factor Determining Size of Female Labor Force: United States, April 1940-1951	30
5	Peak Excess of World War II Labor Force (including armed forces) over Prewar or Early War	34
6	Peak Excess of World War II Labor Force (including armed forces) per 1,000 Population of Similar Age and Sex	37
7	Additions of Females to Labor Force in World War II and Two Factors Accounting for Them	40

8	Allotments and Allowances to Dependents of Armed Force Members: United States, Great Britain, Canada, Germany	42
9	Wartime Gain in Equivalent Fulltime Employment due to Increase in Hours (parttime and overtime combined): United States, April 1940-1946	46
10	Change in Equivalent Fulltime Employment due to Change in Extent of Parttime: United States, April 1940-1945	47
11	Wartime Gain in Equivalent Fulltime Employment due to Overtime: United States, April 1940-1945	47
12	Labor Force in Early Wartime by Employment and Military Status: Both Sexes 14 and Older, United States, April	49
A1	Labor Force by Employment and Military Status: United States, 1940-1951; Quarterly Averages, All Data except Armed Forces Adjusted for Seasonal Variation	52

CHART

1	Labor Force, Armed Forces, and Unemployed	9
2	Civilian Employment by Industrial Divisions, World War II	14
3	Armed Forces and Labor Force, Annual Increases, World War II: United States	26
4	Females Needed in Housework Based on Population to be Cared for: United States, April 1940-1951	29
5	Female Labor Force and Number Available: United States, April 1940-1951	31
6	Ratio of Labor Force to Armed Force Increases and Annual Decreases in Unemployment: United States, April 1940-1945	32
7	Labor Force per 1,000 Population 14 and Older, World War II	33

1 SUMMARY

In five years of World War II up to April 1945 the equivalent of 25 million fulltime workers moved into civilian and military employments in the United States, raising the number of equivalent jobholders from 45 to 70 million, that is, to more than three for every two workers occupied in the spring of 1940.

These additions enabled civilian employments to augment their strength 13 million (nearly 30 percent) while the armed forces were calling up 12 million men. Over 5 million equivalent workers came from increases in hours, mostly overtime, nearly 8 million from reemployment of idle persons already in the labor force in 1940, 11.5 million from expansion in the labor force itself. The labor force includes wage and salary earners (on both public and private payrolls), employers, and self-employed persons whether full or parttime or seeking work.

Employed persons, including civilian and military, increased 42 percent in the United States, slightly more than in Canada, three times as much as in Britain, and four times as much as in Germany (counting in Germany active armed forces and 7 million foreigners; counting only citizens, the number of Germans mobilized for employment barely rose at all). The civilian employed increased a sixth in the United States and possibly a fifth in Canada. Britain and Germany were less fortunate. The former, with slower population growth and less prewar unemployment than the two North American nations, had suffered an actual diminution of about 4 percent by 1943 and 8 percent by 1945, made up in the earlier year by the average worker putting in 9 percent more hours. German civilian employed fell, by mid-1943, over a fifth below 1939; if foreigners are counted, a fifteenth. Compensating extensions in hours were minor. The workweek gained no more than 4 percent in the first 2 years and lost most of that by 1944.

The 11.5 million expansion in the wartime labor force of the United States was half again the combined increases of Great Britain, Canada, and Germany (even counting the foreigners pressed into work in that country). Part of the huge American rise was due to rapid population growth.

Excluding the part due to population growth, the labor force rose 8.5 million in the United States, 1.8 million in Britain, and 0.6 million in Canada. In relation to working age population, the American labor force rose from 54.1 percent before the war to 62.3 percent at the war peak, or 8.2 percent compared with 6.8 in Canada and 4.7 percent in Great Britain. In some degree, however, the comparison with prewar is favorable to the United States and Canada and unfavorable to Great Britain, for the formers' labor force proportions were depressed in 1940 or 1939 whereas the latter's was expanded somewhat in view of the war mobilization already partly in effect. Based on the postwar (1947) labor force proportions, the wartime excess is 6.4 percent in the United States, 5.4 percent in Britain, and 5.1 percent in Canada.

On any basis of comparison Germany made the poorest record for getting wartime additions. Its labor force lost natives, even debiting it with no war deaths; counting foreigners, its expansion was still much less than that in the United States. This failure to get additional Germans to work or seek work cannot be attributed to emigration, Allied bombing, 'high' birthrates, small reserves of women in the peacetime labor force, or somewhat more complete mobilization at the start of the war.

The inflows to the labor force were dominated by the military draft. Until the armed forces were enlarged, the labor force expanded negligibly. With the demobilization of nine-tenths of the peak armed strength the United States labor force shrank eight-tenths of its excess over prewar (disregarding the population growth). United States additions to the labor force averaged for the war about 70 for every 100 men taken into the armed forces. The relation between the labor force and the draft was not uniform, however. Indeed its variations reveal the influence of unemployment. The number who moved into the labor force for each 100 conscripted by the armed forces was relatively large — between 70 and 119 — in the early part of the war when unemployment was shrinking rapidly, and relatively small — about 50 — in the last two years when unemployment was close to a minimum and therefore no longer declining. The average for the five years was 72, almost the same as for Canada during 1939-45. The ratios of labor force to armed force increases in the other two countries were very different: in Great Britain, 47 during 1939-43 and a substantial negative amount during the last two years; in Germany, zero or negative during 1939-44.

Females in this country were a bit over half the addition to the labor force (including the part due to the population growth), eight-tenths in Britain. Excluding the part due to population rise, for every hundred females at work before the war the United States added 35, Britain 21, and Canada 19 (compared with 1941); Germany relinquished 1. For every hundred males the United States added 9, Canada 6, Britain 2, and Germany 0.3.

Besides increases in employment and hours, there were large transfers into more essential jobs. The major shifts to war production in all four countries probably occurred within industries. Nevertheless, there was no lack of inter-industry mobility. In the United States all industry groups except agriculture took on personnel during the first years. By 1943 industrial employment (manufacturing, mining, and construction) had exceeded 1939 levels by about half. By 1945 transportation had expanded almost three-fourths; services (government, professional, and domestic) over a fourth; trade, distribution, and finance held their own.

In Great Britain industrial employment went down after 1942; in 1945 it was below 1939, though the fluctuations were never wide. Agriculture, services, and transportation remained about the same during the six years, and commerce, trade, and finance lost heavily up to 1943. Britain built up its war industries and agriculture by severely curtailing domestic services, construction, trade, distribution, finance, and the manufacture of clothes, food, and beverages.

The Germans were less ingenious, or determined, than the British in restricting nonessentials. Throughout the war, domestic service, employing chiefly native Germans, was almost undisturbed. Agriculture and industry parted with workers at first, but by the war's end had just about gotten them back. Employment fell in most service industries, also in commerce, trade, and finance. Transportation made negligible gains.

Compulsion was not important in recruiting wartime labor. The United States never required civilians to work. Germany had universal conscription on paper but did not thoroughly enforce it until after the Allied landing, when it was too late to use the extra labor effectively. Half of Britain's additions were made before the National Service Act. Even after that, its policy was still persuasion. Coercion was not relied upon extensively until the last two years, during which, paradoxically, the labor force as a whole and essential employment were both declining.

Four factors may have influenced movements to the labor force: reserves of extra workers among students, housewives, and the elderly; numbers of young children, husbands, and brothers requiring care at home and preventing girls and women from taking gainful work; liberality of government to dependents of fighting men; and strength of enemy blows. These explain the large proportion added to the labor force in the United States which had more females outside its peacetime labor force than the British or Germans, so that more could go into industry in wartime despite a higher proportion of child cares. It was less openhanded than Germany or Canada in caring for dependents, though by no means niggardly. And it avoided the German and Canadian practice of reducing dependents' allowances if they worked for pay.

Most additions came when the enemy was hitting hardest. In Britain six in ten of the labor force additions were made before the USSR was forced into the war; in this country two in three during the two years up to the Italian surrender in mid-1943; in Germany the few native workers after the Stalingrad disaster. Canada, an auxiliary belligerent, distributed its expansion fairly evenly throughout the first five years of the war.

The homewardbound forces of the three English-speaking victors trailed the exodus of civilians. The latter quit war industries first, shifting into less essential sectors as pipelines filled, then left the labor force itself as sisters, wives, and fiancees went home to await the returning warriors. The entire shrinkage of the labor force occurred in the United States between March 1945 and May 1946. It took longer in Canada and Britain but was about complete by early 1947.

Aside from the part due to population growth, the great bulk of the labor force excess over prewar turned out to be temporary in all three countries. (No satisfactory postwar comparisons can be made for dismembered Germany.) In America the labor force did not go all the way back to its 1940 proportion of the population, misleading many into believing it was still expanded from the war. This belief arose from failure to perceive that the labor force at the turn of the 1940's was somewhat depressed, probably by the widespread unemployment.

So far in the Korean conflict the labor force has shown indications of retracing its early World War II patterns by rising as the armed forces expand. However, its ratio to armed force recruitments was less than half that in 1941-42, possibly because in April 1940 the labor force proportion was depressed whereas in April 1950 it was already mildly inflated. During the four years ahead, if a major war comes, this country probably could, by drawing on its reserves inside and outside the labor force, conscript 9 million more men without diminishing the civilian employment of 60 million in April 1951. It could get another 5 million equivalent workers by increasing hours. This 8 percent potential rise in civilian employment is less than the almost 30 percent increase in the five years after April 1940. Still, if it is assumed that the mobilization is now, relatively speaking, about where it was in the spring after Pearl Harbor, the effective employment yet possible is on a par with that realized after April 1942.

2   THE LABOR FORCE BEFORE WORLD WAR II

In spring 1939 the United States had a little over 44 million employed and nearly 10 million unemployed.[1] Its labor force, the sum of these two figures, was somewhat below what it would have been had the same proportion of working age population been at work or seeking work as in such years of peace and low unemployment as 1930 or 1947.[2] A third of a million were in uniform. Germany by early summer had reduced unemployment to almost nil, restored its slightly depressed labor force to the same proportion of the population as in 1925,[3] and mustered a military force which, though still far under its subsequent strength, was

---

[1] My tables for the United States (1, A, and 2, A), which are based on Work Projects Administration and Bureau of the Census monthly sample surveys of about 25,000 households, do not begin until 1940 and, in order to keep clear of the summer influx, which is particularly large in this country, compare Aprils instead of midyears. The labor force, armed forces, unemployment, and civilian employment in April 1939 are computed to be 54.1, 0.3, 9.7, and 44.1 million respectively. It was assumed that between April 1939 and 1940 the labor force rose 0.7 million from the growth in population. Armed forces and unemployed were taken from the *Economic Almanac for 1950* (National Industrial Conference Board), p. 164; civilian employment was the residual.

[2] The proportion of population 14 and older in the labor force in April 1940, as revised by the Census to be comparable to the 1945 enumeration technique, was 54.1 percent, 1.8 percent below the 55.9 percent measured by the same technique in 1947 and 2.0 percent below the 56.1 percent in 1930. I revised the labor force in 1930 to make it comparable to the 1945 technique. With a working age population in 1940 of 101 million, this deficiency in the labor force proportion involves 1.8 million workers. Since the 1939 labor force is estimated by extrapolating backward from 1940 on the basis of mere population change, the estimated deficiency would be approximately the same. See Section 2 for an explanation of the 1945 measurement technique.

[3] Leo Wolman has disclosed that early increases in employment claimed by the Nazis were really a statistical reclassification in which formerly idle persons doing makework comparable to the United States WPA were regarded as employed: 'The Meaning of Employment and Unemployment', *The State in Society* (Oxford University Press, 1940). By 1939 approaching war had probably made German employment reasonably genuine.

the most effective at that time. Britain, with one in sixteen workers idle,[4] the labor force somewhat above the proportion of the population to which it was to return after the war, and armed ranks expanding, had its manpower only partly ready when in the first hours of September the Nazi divisions crossed into Poland and set off World War II.

This paper reviews the labor force changes in these three countries during six years of arming and fighting. It also compares the additions in the United States, Great Britain, Germany, and Canada at the peak; and inquires how the first two built up their labor forces by large relative amounts, Canada by smaller numbers, and Germany by none at all. First, however, it may be useful to explain what is meant by the 'labor force'.

LABOR FORCE CONCEPT AND COVERAGE

The concept varies in some degree among the four countries, though without invalidating analysis of wartime changes. In the United States the labor force includes, as of a certain week, both 'employed' and 'unemployed'. The latter covers those reported seeking jobs and able and willing to work for going wages. The former embraces wage and salary earners, military and civilian personnel of government, employers and self-employed such as farmers and practicing physicians, and children and wives on farms or in family stores working without pay to produce a marketable product. The labor force takes in persons, mostly employed, who are on vacation, temporarily ill, on strike, or weather-bound. It leaves out children under 14, housewives and students as such, retired or disabled persons, and inmates of institutions. It excludes men and women in illegal occupations such as gambling or prostitution (as far as they report their activities to household interviewers). It does not deduct for fractional employment of parttime workers.

In spring 1940 the Work Projects Administration began to collect monthly data from a sample of about 25,000 of the nation's households, using an interview method instituted at the decennial enumeration. The Census Bureau subsequently took over the survey and in mid-1945 modified the interview technique so as to rely less on the commonsense or caprice of enumerators. In the first month of the modified technique

[4] The British unemployment figures for 1939 did not include persons in industries or occupations not covered by unemployment insurance. If these were included, the unemployment rate would have been somewhat higher than 6 percent.

a test survey, asking families both old and new questions, indicated that the new schedule swelled the estimate by 2 million, mostly wives and students who also did some parttime work. Accordingly, the Bureau revised the earlier data upward. It is this revised series that we use.

The United States data are thus from official census sources.⁵ In Britain no census of the labor force had been taken between 1931 and 1951. Estimates for 1939-48 were therefore constructed from the 'working population', compiled from records of unemployment insurance administration, private employers, and government agencies including armed forces.⁶

The Canadian labor force and armed force for June 1941 are from the Decennial Census, and for June 1942-45 from 'Estimates of the Canadian Labour Force and its Composition 1941-7', a mimeographed table prepared by the Research and Statistics Branch, Department of Labour, Ottawa. The latter are merely rough projections from the Census of 1941, are not strictly comparable in definition with the quarterly surveys instituted in November 1945, and exclude both students and women gainfully occupied on farms or in farm homes. The August 1939 employment and armed forces are from 'Estimated Manpower Distribution' also of the latter agency. Unemployment for that date could

---

⁵ United States: *Sixteenth Census, 1940, III, Part I,* p. 99; *Monthly Report on the Labor Force,* Population, Series 59, also Series P-57; *Labor Force Bulletin 6,* July 1945, pp. 12-15; *Current Population Reports,* Series P-50; unpublished Census estimates of the age distribution of the armed forces and of the population.

⁶ Great Britain: *Annual Abstract of Statistics, 1935-46,* No. 84; *Monthly Digest of Statistics; National Register, 1939, Report; Registrar General's Statistical Review of England and Wales, 1943, 1945* (London); *Ministry of Labour Gazette;* H. Frankel, 'The Industrial Distribution of the Population of Great Britain in July, 1939', *Journal of the Royal Statistical Society,* 1945, p. 392.

Until 1948 unemployment insurance did not cover women working parttime, men 65 and older, women 60 and older, private indoor domestic servants, employers or self-employed, non-manual employees earning over £420 a year, established civil servants, permanent employees of local authorities, railways, and public utilities, excepted by certificate, teachers, armed forces, female professional nurses, policemen, and farmers' sons and daughters. Most of these omitted classes were approximated from the overlap in 1948 between the more and the less comprehensive coverages; but private domestic servants, men 65 and older, and women 60 and older were calculated separately. The mid-1945 labor force contained a few Irish, Norwegians, French, Dutch, and Belgians, but left out civilians and armed forces killed, as well as prisoners of war working in Britain. To adjust for the practice of counting a woman working parttime as half a member, after 1939 she was treated as a regular worker for comparison with United States data.

be calculated only roughly, by assuming that it bore the same ratio to 1941 as trade unions' idleness. Because of the weakness of the 1939 estimate of labor force, the crudeness of the annual interpolations and the lack of age and sex detail during 1942-44, most of the wartime analyses are confined to comparisons of June 1945 with June 1941.[7]

The labor force data of Germany are from the official census of 1939 and from the Kriegswirtschaftliche Kräftebilanz (War Economy Manpower Balance Sheet) of the Statistisches Reichsamt for 1940-44. The latter "were not always reliable and had frequently changing conceptual and territorial coverage", were based on questionnaires to be returned by employees, self-employed professional workers, and the like, on the membership lists of industrial, trade, and cultural organizations, and were subject to some gaps and duplications among organizations. The data were used in the study as adjusted for the above discrepancies by the *Strategic Bombing Survey*. They cover all gainfully occupied persons counting, beginning 1944, a small number of home workers, i.e., persons engaged in industrial work at home.[8]

3 THE LABOR FORCE IN MOBILIZATION: UNITED STATES, GREAT BRITAIN, GERMANY

It is convenient to divide the half dozen years of war into three 2-year periods: the first ending with Germany's attack on Russia, the second with its surrender in North Africa, the third with its defeat in Europe. The last few months of World War II get incidental attention, for Japan's surrender was an anticlimax to the German collapse. This section describes in some detail the assembling of labor resources by the three major countries and carries a statistical account for Canada in Charts 1, 7, and Tables 1, 2, 5-8.

---

[7] Canada: *Canada Yearbook, 1945* and *1947; Census of Canada, 1941,* VII, Occupations, 12; *Canadian Statistical Review; Labour Force Bulletin;* Department of Labour, Ottawa: *Labour Force Gazette, Estimates of the Canadian Labour Force and its Composition, 1941-47* (mimeographed).

[8] Germany: *Statistisches Jahrbuch fuer das Deutsche Reich, 1938; Wirtschaft und Statistik,* Feb. 1941, p. 50, Dec. 1940, p. 519; *Effects of Strategic Bombing on the German War Economy, U. S. Strategic Bombing Survey* (Overall Economic Effects Division, Oct. 31, 1945), Appendix Tables 1, 6, pp. 199, 202, 207; *Statistical Yearbook of the League of Nations, 1941-42* (Geneva, 1943), Table 3, p. 26; Frank Notestein, *Future Population of Europe and the Soviet Union* (Geneva, 1944), pp. 264-5.

Chart 1
Labor Force, Armed Forces, and Unemployed
A United States, 1940-1951, Quarterly Averages*

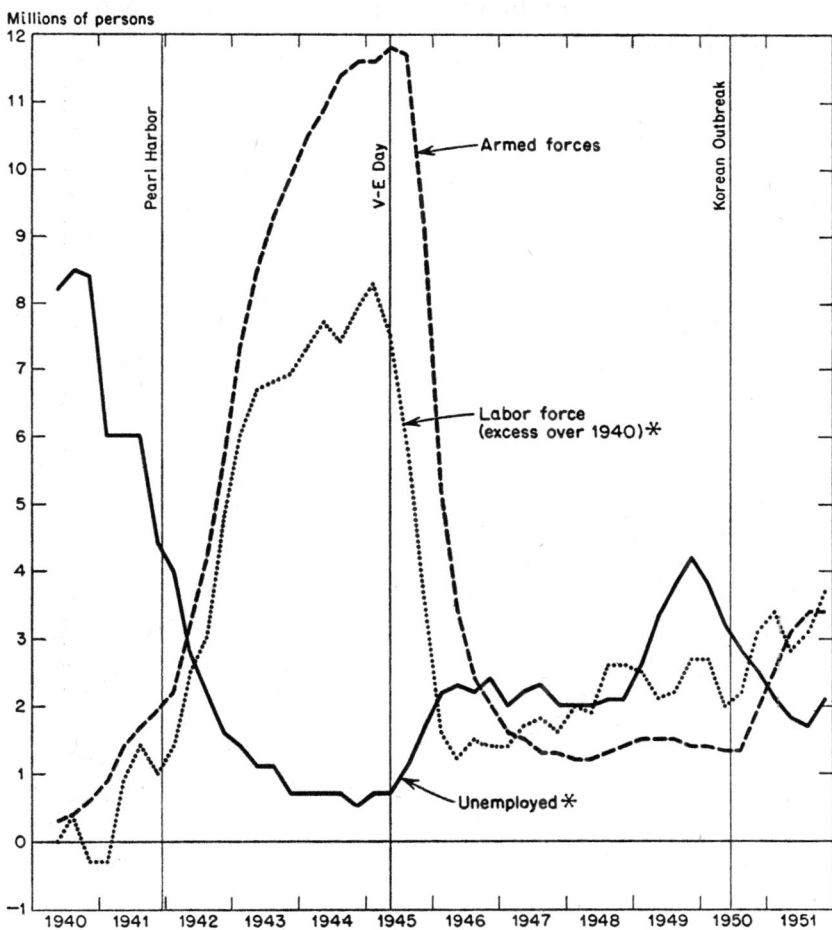

For sources of data and some discussion of their nature, see Section 2; notes 1-8, 42.
* Population changes eliminated from labor force; both labor force and unemployed adjusted for seasonal variation.

MID-1939 TO THE INVASION OF RUSSIA

During April 1939-41 the United States drafted a million men and took 4.5 million into civilian employment besides. About six in ten of the increase came from reduction in unemployment and the rest from a rise

Chart 1 (cont.)
Labor Force, Armed Forces, and Unemployed
B Great Britain, 1939–1948*
Armed Forces and Unemployed Quarterly Beginning Mid-1945

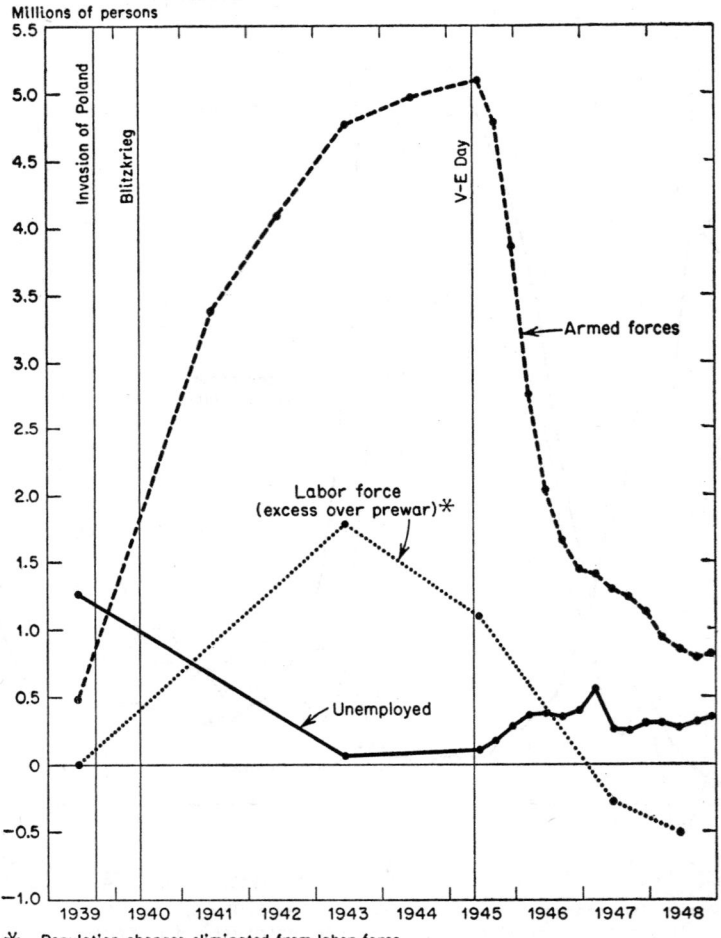

* Population changes eliminated from labor force.

in the labor force. The only industry that did not gain workers was agriculture, which gave up almost half a million (Chart 2). Acquisitions were least, under a tenth, in trade, distribution, and finance, public utilities, mining, and services; most in transportation (a ninth), manufacturing (a fourth), and contract construction (nearly two-thirds).

Chart 1 (cont.)
Labor Force, Armed Forces, and Unemployed
C Canada, 1939-1950, Quarterly Beginning 1945*

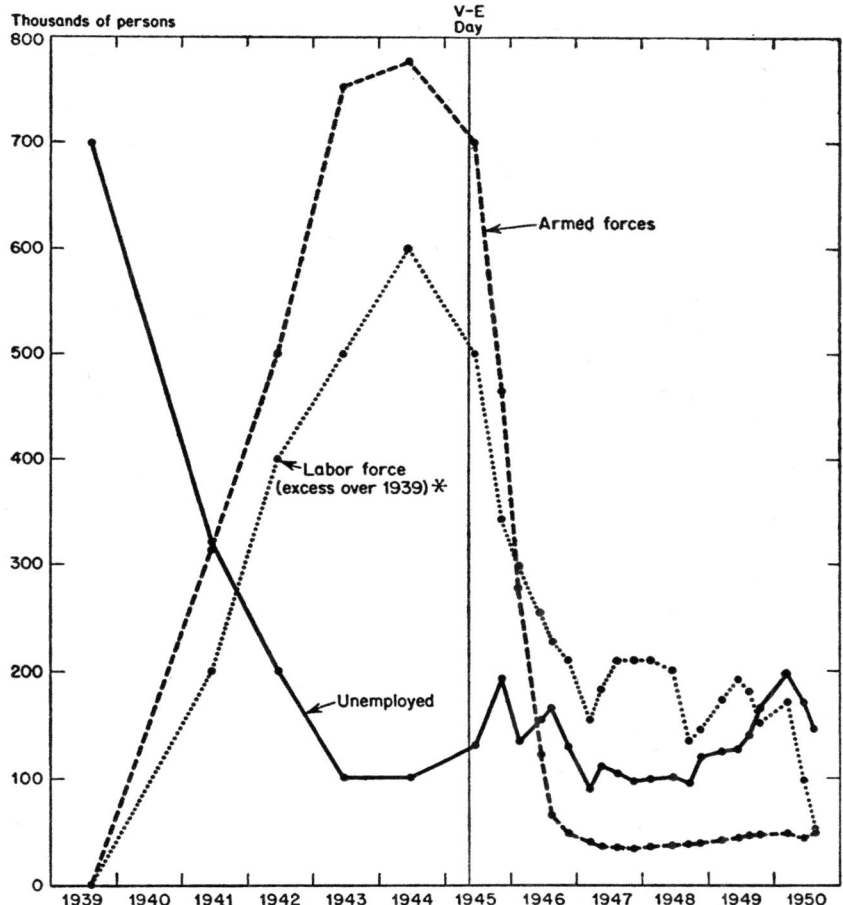

* Population changes eliminated from labor force; beginning 1945 both labor force and unemployed adjusted for seasonal variation.

Combined trade, distribution, and finance reached a peak during 1941.

A pinch of skilled craftsmen, felt particularly in the metal trades, was relieved by upgrading workers and breaking down complex jobs and training persons to do semiskilled suboperations. Location of defense demands in areas of short supply stimulated tremendous migration. In general, however, the critical items were not labor but raw materials,

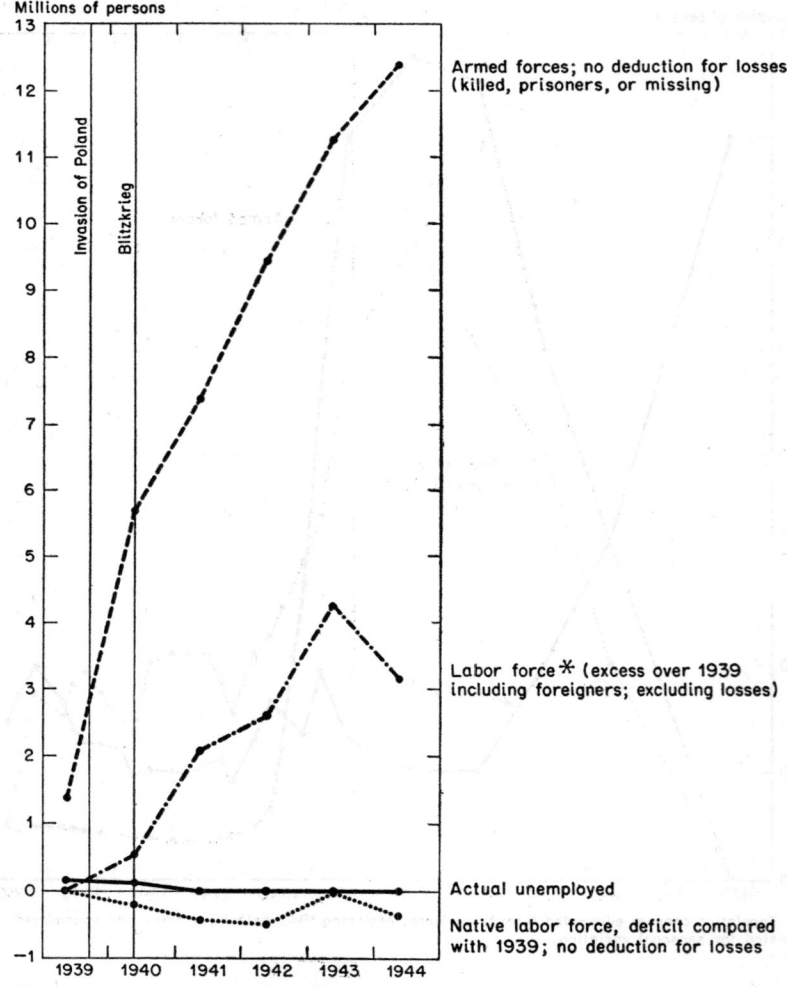

Chart 1 (concl.)
Labor Force, Armed Forces, and Unemployed
D   Germany, May 1939-1944*

* Population changes eliminated from the labor force.

machine tools, components, ships, freight cars, and (in defense areas) housing and public facilities.[9]

[9] Historical Reports on War Administration, No. 1: *The United States at War (Development and Administration of the War. Program by the Federal Government)*, prepared under the auspices of the Committee of Records of War Administration by the Bureau of the Budget, War Records Section (G. P. O., 1946), pp. 173-5.

Britain's economy in this time of its defiance was under intense strain but did not suffer from general labor scarcity until July 1941.[10] Limiting factors throughout 1940 were skilled workmen, especially in aero engine and ordnance factories, and in industrial facilities: steel, alloy steel, machine tools, fabricated items. These bottlenecks kept a famine of unskilled and semiskilled labor from manifesting itself until nearly two years after the start of the war.

Over 3 million men and women went into its armed forces. Only a few were at the expense of civilian employment, for possibly two-thirds came from reemployment and shifts out of non-industrial areas, the other million from a 4 percent net increase in the proportion of population in the labor force, about half of labor force accretions for the war. Employment declined in most industries, particularly those in which payroll accessions in the United States were moderate — commerce, distribution, and banking — and public utilities, miscellaneous services, and mining (not charted separately). Some industries that gained a lot in this country lost a lot in Britain, notably construction (not charted separately). On the other hand, agriculture, which gave up workers here, took on a few in Britain during this period and continued to do so for the duration. Increases were concentrated in fewer industries: engineering, vehicles, and shipbuilding and government (not charted separately) each expanded employment about a third.

The heavy emphasis on defense production called for mass shifts of workers to new industries. In these transfers compulsion played a role not to be entirely ignored. During those first years, however, it "was proceeding but slowly. Its influence in the big migration into war industry between mid-1940 and mid-1941 must not therefore be overestimated . . . industrial conscription was operating as yet only on the difficult margins of the war economy."[11] In the sense that workers had rather

[10] History of the Second World War, United Kingdom Series: *British War Economy*, ed. by W. K. Hancock and M. M. Gowing (His Majesty's Stationery Office, London, 1949), pp. 291-2.

[11] *Ibid.*, p. 309. "The award of government contracts, fortified by grants of priority for materials and labour, was perhaps the most important of all the forces that were building up munitions employment. For many workers, perhaps for the majority, transfer from civilian industry to war industry did not mean either a change of neighborhood or of factory or of occupation; it was the factory itself that was switched over. . . . The change was frequently a matter of the product, rather than of the processes upon which labour was engaged. Workers did also, of course, change their jobs, their factories and their neighborhoods. A variety of 'pulls' and 'pushes' moved them. Patriotism drew many into war work, the desire to shelter from the Forces drew a few. Higher wages . . . were often a powerful incentive. Meanwhile, the decline of the unessential industries exerted a steady 'push'."

Chart 2
Civilian Employment by Industrial Divisions, World War II

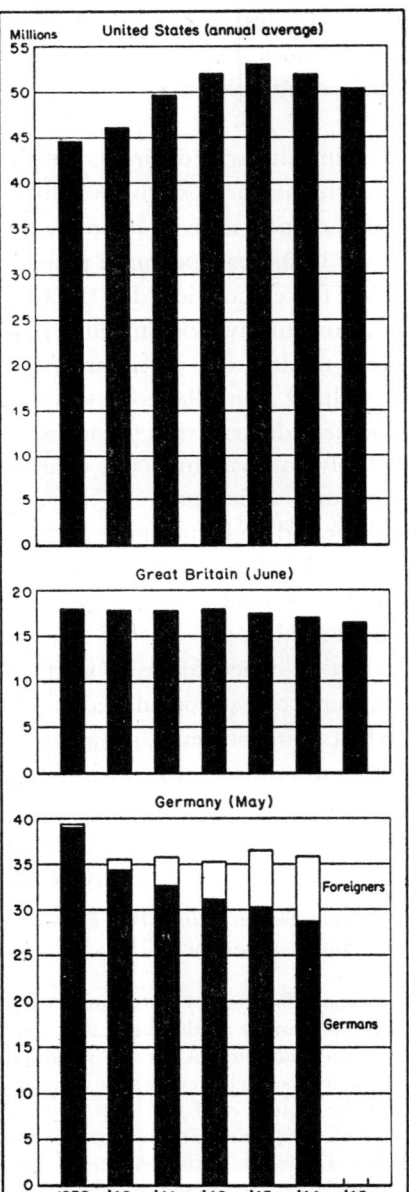
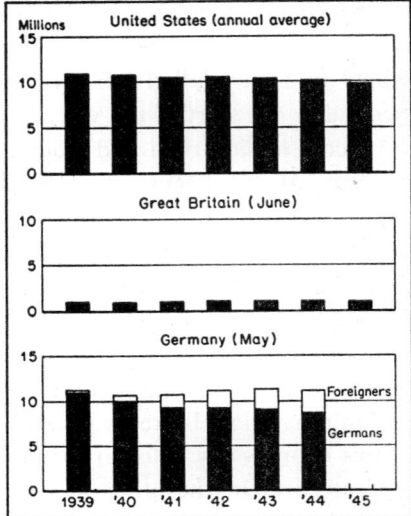
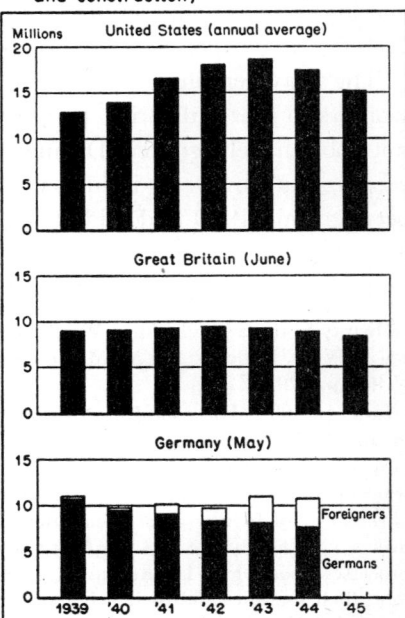

Chart 2 (concl.)
Civilian Employment by Industrial Divisions, World War II

D Services (government and administrative services, domestic and miscellaneous services; in Germany also handwork)

E Transportation

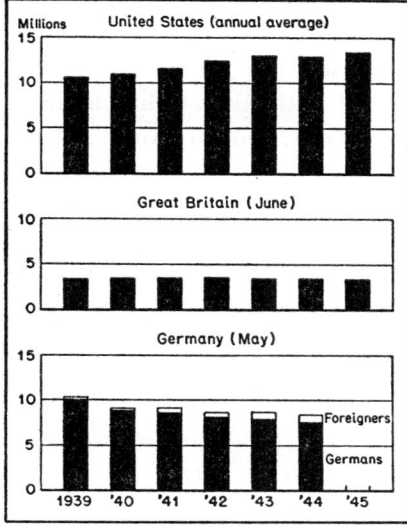

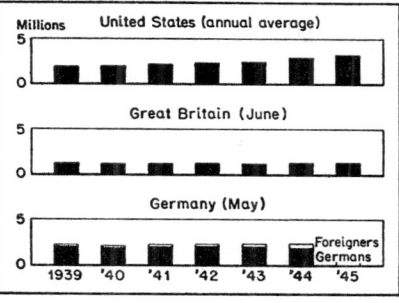

F Commerce, Trade, Distribution, Banking, and Finance

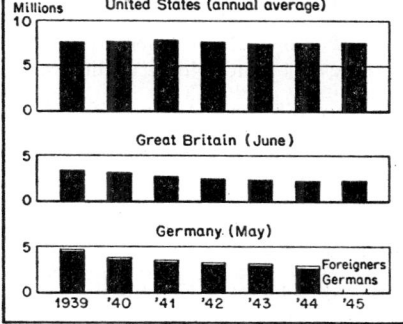

Sources: United States, *Economic Almanac for 1950,* p. 162,
Great Britain, *Annual Abstract of Statistics,* No. 86, 1938-1948, p. 97,
Germany, *Strategic Bombing Survey,* pp. 204-5.

wide choice of time and place, their movement must for the most part be regarded as voluntary.

Germany, as a result of its victories, did not experience real manpower stringency during this biennium. The use of steel output to sustain current consumption rather than to expand facilities, the enormous capacity in conquered and intimidated countries, and the herds of foreign replacements imparted a sense of strength that could not have made it easy to call on civilians for sacrifices. Focusing of production in the most efficient plants to save fuel, labor, and transportation was opposed by management and minor party leaders (as in the United States and, for a time, in Britain). In 1940 it was urged that women be conscripted and the workweek lengthened in order to replace drafted labor. But virtually nothing of this sort was done; instead, more emphasis was laid upon recruiting non-Germans. The easy going administration of the war, especially in the first years, was reflected in the mere 4 percent rise of output up to 1941.

Indeed, Germans were not drawn into the work force even as fast as they increased among the working age population, and the civilian labor force was not replenished for any citizens called to its armed forces. 'Industry' (manufacturing, mining, and construction), despite reinforcement by nearly 1 million aliens, parted with almost that number. Employment decreases were particularly severe, about a fourth, in hand work and in combined trade, banking, and insurance. A net half a million left agriculture despite reinforcement by three times as many foreigners. Clearly women did not go into work in sufficient number to make up for men drawn into the army, navy, and air force. Females

Table 1

Labor Force by Employment and Military Status: Four Countries
Both Sexes 14 and Older (millions of persons)

A UNITED STATES, APRIL 1940-1945

	1940	1941	1942	1943	1944	1945
Total labor force (civilian & military)	54.8	56.3	58.8	63.2	65.2	66.3
Armed forces	0.3	1.3	2.9	8.3	10.9	12.1
Labor force (civilian)	54.5	55.0	55.9	54.9	54.3	54.2
Unemployed	8.4	6.4	3.1	1.0	0.7	0.5
Employed	46.1	48.6	52.8	53.9	53.6	53.7
Labor force increase over 1940	......	1.5	4.0	8.4	10.4	11.5
Due to population growth	......	0.7	1.3	1.9	2.5	3.0
Excess over part due to population growth	......	0.8	2.7	6.5	7.9	8.5
Unemployment compared with 1940	......	−2.0	−5.3	−7.4	−7.7	−7.9
Employment increase over 1940						
Civilian	......	2.5	6.7	7.8	7.5	7.6
Total (civilian & military)	......	3.5	9.3	15.8	18.1	19.4

B GREAT BRITAIN, JUNE 1939-1945

	1939	1943	1945
Total labor force (civilian & military)	22.9	25.2	24.6
Armed forces	0.5	4.8	5.1
Labor force (civilian)	22.4	20.4	19.5
Unemployed	1.2	0.0	0.1
Employed	21.2	20.4	19.4
Labor force increase over 1939	......	2.3	1.7
Due to population growth	......	0.5	0.6
Excess over part due to population growth	......	1.8	1.1
Unemployment compared with 1939	......	−1.2	−1.1
Employment increase over 1939			
Civilian	......	−0.8	−1.8
Total (civilian & military)	......	3.5	2.8

C CANADA, AUG. 1939, JUNE 1941-45

	1939	1941	1942	1943	1944	1945
Total labor force (civilian & military)	4.4	4.7	5.0	5.1	5.3	5.3
Armed forces	0.0	0.3	0.5	0.7	0.8	0.7
Labor force (civilian)	4.4	4.4	4.5	4.4	4.5	4.6
Unemployed	0.7	0.3	0.2	0.1	0.1	0.1
Employed	3.7	4.1	4.3	4.3	4.4	4.5
Labor force increase over 1939	......	0.3	0.6	0.7	0.9	0.9
Due to population growth	......	0.1	0.2	0.2	0.3	0.4
Excess over part due to population growth	......	0.2	0.4	0.5	0.6	0.5
Unemployment compared with 1939	......	−0.4	−0.5	−0.6	−0.6	−0.6
Employment increase over 1939						
Civilian	......	0.4	0.6	0.6	0.7	0.8
Total (civilian & military)	......	0.7	1.1	1.3	1.5	1.5

D GERMANY, MAY 1939-1944

	1939	1940	1941	1942	1943	1944
	NATIVES MOBILIZED (MILITARY LOSSES NOT DEDUCTED)[a]					
Total labor force (civilian & military)	40.5	40.5	40.5	40.7	41.5	41.4
Armed forces mobilized	1.4	5.7	7.4	9.4	11.2	12.4
Labor force (civilian)	39.1	34.8	33.1	31.3	30.3	29.0
Unemployed[b]	0.2	0.1	......	......	......	......
Employed	38.9	34.7	33.1	31.3	30.3	29.0
Labor force increase over 1939	......	0.0	0.0	0.2	1.0	0.9
Increase called for by population growth	......	0.3	0.6	0.8	1.1	1.3
Deficit below increase called for by population growth	......	−0.3	−0.6	−0.6	−0.1	−0.4
Unemployment compared with 1939	......	−0.1	−0.2	......	......	......
Employment increase over 1939						
Civilian	......	−4.2	−5.8	−7.6	−8.6	−9.9
Total (civilian & military)	......	0.1	0.2	0.4	1.2	1.1
	NATIVES AND FOREIGNERS (MILITARY LOSSES DEDUCTED)					
Total labor force (civilian & military)	40.8	41.6	43.4	44.2	46.1	45.2
Armed forces active	1.4	5.6	7.2	8.7	9.6	9.1
Labor force (civilian)	39.4	36.0	36.2	35.5	36.5	36.1
Labor force increase over 1939	......	0.8	2.6	3.4	5.3	4.4
Due to population growth	......	0.3	0.6	0.8	1.1	1.3
Excess over part due to population growth	......	0.5	2.0	2.6	4.2	3.1

For sources of data and some discussion of their nature and adjustment, see text Section 2; notes 1-8, 42.

[a] The purpose in not deducting military losses is to show the labor force contributed by the German population. The number actually available for work or military service was, of course, smaller by the number of war dead or missing, which were (in thousands) 1939, 0; 1940, 85; 1941, 185; 1942, 800; 1943, 1,680; 1944, 3,285.

[b] Unemployment was assumed to be negligible after 1940.

employed on family farms as parttime 'helping members' had always been supposed to constitute a hidden reserve that could shift to industry without taking much away from agriculture, but no more than a few hundred thousand were, in fact, released. Little help came from increases in hours. The average workweek was lengthened only 4 percent from March 1939 to its high for the war, 49.5 hours in September 1941. As an interesting commentary on the Nazi myth of total warfare, domestic service, almost entirely native German, relinquished relatively few in this or subsequent periods.[12]

TO THE TRIUMPH IN NORTH AFRICA

A general labor deficit did not appear in the United States between April 1941 and 1943.[13] More moved into its labor force than in any other period — nearly 7 million. This almost matched the rise in armed forces, so that civilian employment could profit by the entire 5 million decline in unemployment (Tables 1 and 2). Gains of a tenth were registered in services and transportation, and of a fourth in manufacturing. But mining, public utility, and agricultural employments barely

[12] *Strategic Bombing Survey,* pp. 21-33, 35, 215.

[13] *The United States at War,* p. 173. "Officials concerned with manpower [in, say, 1942] were shadow-boxing with a problem which had not yet developed. There was a great output of plans and much controversy over what should be done and who should do it, but few actions of any importance were taken. Yet this lack of action did not appreciably retard war production. Workers continued to show up at the factories, employers continued to hire and train them, and Government for the most part observed the process from the sidelines."

Table 2

Additions to Employment and Labor Force by Sources
Both Sexes 14 and Older (all data except percentages in millions of persons)

A UNITED STATES, APRIL 1940-1945

		1940-41	1941-42	1942-43	1943-44	1944-45	1940-45
1	Employment (civilian & military) rise	3.5	5.8	6.5	2.3	1.3	19.4
2	Unemployment fall	2.0	3.3	2.1	0.3	0.2	7.9
3	Labor force rise	1.5	2.5	4.4	2.0	1.1	11.5
4	Due to population growth	0.7	0.6	0.6	0.6	0.5	3.0
5	Excess over part due to population growth	0.8	1.9	3.8	1.4	0.6	8.5
6	Taken into armed forces	1.0	1.6	5.4	2.6	1.2	11.8
7	Civilian employment rise	2.5	4.2	1.1	−0.3	0.1	7.6
8	Labor force rise as % of additions to armed forces (line 5 ÷ 6)	80	119	70	54	50	72

B GREAT BRITAIN, JUNE 1939-1945

		1939-43	1943-45	1939-45
1	Employment (civilian & military) rise	3.5	−0.7	2.8
2	Unemployment fall	1.2	−0.1	1.1
3	Labor force rise	2.3	−0.6	1.7
4	Due to population growth	0.5	0.1	0.6
5	Excess over part due to population growth	1.8	−0.7	1.1
6	Taken into armed forces	4.3	0.3	4.6
7	Civilian employment rise	−0.8	−1.0	−1.8
8	Labor force rise as % of additions to armed forces (line 5 ÷ 6)	47	−200	30

C CANADA, AUG. 1939, JUNE 1941-45

		1939-41	1941-42	1942-43	1943-44	1944-45	1939-45
1	Employment (civilian & military) rise	0.7	0.4	0.2	0.2	0.0	1.5
2	Unemployment fall	0.4	0.1	0.1	0.0	0.0	0.6
3	Labor force rise	0.3	0.3	0.1	0.2	0.0	0.9
4	Due to population growth	0.1	0.1	0.0	0.1	0.1	0.4
5	Excess over part due to population growth	0.2	0.2	0.1	0.1	−0.1	0.5
6	Taken into armed forces	0.3	0.2	0.2	0.1	−0.1	0.7
7	Civilian employment rise	0.4	0.2	0.0	0.1	0.1	0.8
8	Labor force rise as % of additions to armed forces (line 5 ÷ 6)	67	100	50	100	100	71

D GERMANY, MAY 1939-1944

		1939-40	1940-41	1941-42	1942-43	1943-44	1939-44
		NATIVES MOBILIZED (MILITARY LOSSES NOT DEDUCTED)					
1	Employment (civilian & military) rise	0.1	0.1	0.2	0.8	−0.1	1.1
2	Unemployment fall[a]	0.1	0.1	……	……	……	0.2
3	Labor force rise	0.0	0.0	0.2	0.8	−0.1	0.9
4	Due to population growth	0.3	0.3	0.2	0.3	0.2	1.3
5	Excess over part due to population growth	−0.3	−0.3	0.0	0.5	−0.3	−0.4
6	Taken into armed forces	4.3	1.7	2.0	1.8	1.2	11.0
7	Civilian employment rise	−4.2	−1.6	−1.8	−1.0	−1.3	−9.9
8	Labor force rise as % of additions to armed forces (line 5 ÷ 6)	−7	−18	−0	28	−25	−4
		NATIVES AND FOREIGNERS (MILITARY LOSSES DEDUCTED)					
1	Labor force rise	0.8	1.8	0.8	1.9	−0.9	4.4
2	Due to population growth	0.3	0.3	0.2	0.3	0.2	1.3
3	Excess over part due to population growth	0.5	1.5	0.6	1.6	−1.1	3.1
4	Added to armed forces	4.2	1.6	1.5	0.9	−0.5	7.7
5	Labor force rise as % of additions to armed forces (line 3 ÷ 4)	12	94	40	178	220	40

For sources of data and some discussion of their nature and adjustment see Section 2; notes 1-8, 42.

[a] Unemployment was assumed to be negligible after 1940.

held their own (agriculture despite wholesale deferment). Trade, distribution, and finance parted with a small percentage. Construction dwindled almost to 1939 levels. Some industries had their top employments in the middle of this biennium.

As the conflict passed through different stages, British workers shifted out of nonessential into higher priority areas. Main expansions up to mid-1943 took place in the armed forces, agriculture, government, and the manufacture of metals, vehicles, ships, and chemicals. Losses continued to be suffered in food, clothing, and shoe manufacturing, utilities, construction, commerce, distribution, and other services. Transportation and mining employment held their own. Altogether, Britain made the remainder of its labor force increments, about a million, and apparently attained its peak mobilization at the close of this period.

Nevertheless a gap opened between labor needs and supply two years before there was even a moderate divergence in the United States (see below). Failure to fill requirements began in Birmingham and Sheffield areas and led quickly to the manpower survey of mid-1941, the first step in allocating supply where it was most needed. This survey forecast large new demands for 1942. Partly as a result, Britain passed its National Service Act just before Japan's attack on Hawaii, extending obligation of defense work to all persons 18 and 60, raising the age for military service from 41 to 50, and applying conscription to women 20-30, with option to enter Auxiliary Service, civil defense, or essential industry. By Pearl Harbor day, shortages had intensified, become acute in coal mining, shipbuilding, aircraft production, and armed services. Plans to relieve them with labor from construction, which had been due to shrink, were shelved by the need to build camps and airfields for American forces, scheduled to begin disembarking in 1942. A second manpower budget, drawn up in mid-1942 for the next 18 months, indicated additional demand for 2.7 million workers and extra supply of only 1.6 million. To cut demand and allocate output to industries with the most urgent requirements, Supply Ministries were told to economize on labor or curtail contracts. "Manpower had become an almost continuous preoccupation of the War Cabinet."[14]

Britain even turned to women with household responsibilities. The manpower authority interviewed them during late 1941 and early 1942 and, when they had free time, asked them to take parttime work, em-

---

[14] *British War Economy*, pp. 313, 438-49.

phasizing inducement rather than compulsion. Britain exempted workers doing 30 hours or less per week from Unemployment Insurance Acts and Essential Work Orders in order to relieve them from insurance deductions and from fear that they could not withdraw if the burden of working both in and out of the home became too heavy. Parttime employment grew three quarters of a million.[15] "The extent of the mobilization was considerably greater than was achieved during the first world war. . . . Women were brought directly into the war effort to a far greater extent . . ." (*ibid.*, pp. 3-4).

NUMBER OF PARTTIME WORKERS IN BRITISH EMPLOYMENT
UNADJUSTED FOR LENGTH OF TIME WORKED

1941	1942	1943		1944		1945
June	June	June	December	June	December	June
Negligible	380,000	750,000	840,000	900,000	870,000	900,000

In autumn 1941 Hitler ordered a production cutback in the belief that victory was in sight, but rescinded it after the Moscow defeat in early 1942. Instead of taking effective measures to recruit nationals, however, Germany stepped up immigration. Its attempt to draw in women through the registration of January 1943 had negligible results. The labor force reached its maximum with a million workers and fighters more than in 1939. As this increase was under that which could have come through population growth, its native labor force remained below the proportion of working age population that had prevailed in 1939. It was a small amount below that level even before battle deaths are deducted, and when these are taken out, nearly 2 million. Another 3 million aliens were drawn into work, but civilian employment climbed only a few hundred thousand — to the highest it was to achieve. Minor gains were realized in agriculture, transportation, and industry, major ones in armed forces administration. In May 1943 employment in agriculture and industry counting foreigners, was at about 1939 levels. But extensive use of Poles, French, Belgians, Dutch, and other nationals could not prevent employment from falling a tenth in trade, banking, and insurance, or in administration and services, and a sixth in handwork. Hours worked by the average wage earner went back to prewar levels, as the workweek of females steadily shortened through the war.[16] Even domestic help fell off a bit!

[15] *Ministry of Labour and National Service Report, 1939-46*, p. 65. Counting two parttime workers as one fulltime, following the British, yields 190,000 for June 1942, 375,000 for June 1943, and so on.
[16] *Strategic Bombing Survey*, pp. 35, 215.

TO THE VICTORY IN EUROPE

During the last two years of war the labor forces of the three countries did not change much. The United States gained 3.1 million new workers and its total labor force grew almost up to V-E Day but since nearly 4 million men were taken by the armed forces civilian employment arrived at its maximum in 1943. Munitions employment also got to its summit in the last months of that year.[17] Transportation continued to add to payrolls; and services, trade, distribution, and finance recovered slightly. All other industries, particularly manufacturing, mining, construction, and agriculture, yielded up workers. Employment declined even in government.

Labor, not theretofore critically short, became in autumn 1943 an 'ultimate' limit on production; on the Pacific Coast female workers were scarce in all industries. As the drafts to the services outpaced inflows to the labor force and reductions in unemployment, civilian employment fell behind for the first time, dropping over a million in 1944 (Table 2). "The labor reserves with which the United States had entered the war had been fully mobilized . . . everybody who would willingly take a job already had a job, and door-to-door recruiting campaigns conducted by the Civil Service Commission and the War Manpower Commission yielded negligible results." Marked outflows from war production centers began with the Italian surrender and Russian successes,[18] and during 1943-45 half the personnel of manufacturing firms were quitting each year, four times the rates in 1940 and double those after the cessation of hostilities.[19]

By spring 1944 the acute phase of labor scarcity had passed. Spot shortages were made up to some extent by spot measures: special deferments from the draft; emergency campaigns by the Employment Service for particular plants and industries; Army furloughs for skilled workers; and special wage boosts allowed by the War Labor Board. The real relief of the stringency, however, probably came from the debouching of pro-

---

[17] *The United States at War,* p. 433 (Chart 51). Munitions production, which had been increasing faster than munitions employment, declined from 1944 to mid-1945 at about the same rate as employment.

[18] *Ibid.,* pp. 421-33.

[19] Bureau of Labor Statistics, *Fact Book on Manpower, 1951,* p. D-4. The Boeing Plant in Seattle hired 250,000 in the 3 years after June 1940 but had only 39,000 workers in mid-1943 (*The United States at War,* p. 432).

duction pipelines which had been filling during the preceding several years, not from any canny disposition of manpower. A few contracts were diverted to surplus labor areas, but on the whole such attempts were defeated by opposition of Congressmen, business men, and even industry divisions of the War Production Board (p. 434). In regions such as the West Coast, programs of the War Manpower Commission to allocate tight supply through urgency lists and employment ceilings had limited success, for the WMC, powerless to enforce priorities or require employers to hire exclusively through Employment Offices, was regarded by both industry and the WPB as a mere recruiting agency.

Congress, doubtless reflecting the temper of its constituents, refused repeatedly to conscript labor. It furthermore exempted farmers from the draft and backed up Selective Service Boards in deferring for dependency rather than occupation: "The great majority of men over 30 continued for the remainder of the war in the deferred classes — nominally on the basis of occupational essentiality, rather liberally interpreted, but actually on the basis of age and family status."

As the end of the European phase came in sight, workers hesitated more and more to take temporary situations. As it neared, production schedules were cut and unemployment cropped up here and there.[20] The munitions industries, from which 1.5 million had departed between late 1943 and early 1945, gave up a million in the last three months before V-E Day.

In Britain the armed forces took on a few hundred thousand. Employment held its own in agriculture, transport, and shipping, but gave ground in the other industries, in defense manufacturing most of all. "It became apparent that Great Britain had reached the limits of mobilization; during the rest of the year recruitment from the nonindustrial population would not be sufficient to offset the normal wastage from industry. Before long the labour force would decline." The workweek, up 9 percent since 1938, was also at its limit by mid-1943, especially in view of the spare hours spent at homeguard exercises and fire watching.[21]

The dim prospects led to stricter budgeting of labor as well as in-

[20] *Ibid.*, pp. 433, 442-3, 445-9.
[21] *British War Economy*, pp. 447, 454. According to my estimates, population 14-64, which had grown only 300,000 during the preceding 4 years, actually shrank from mid-1943 to mid-1945. The population of young males and females 14-24 declined throughout the war under the erosion of birth deficits during the two preceding decades.

creased pressure, even "regretful ruthlessness", on females to take essential work or to migrate from surplus labor areas, such as Wales, into the Midland, Northwestern, and London areas where labor needs were even more concentrated than population. Most women who could go elsewhere were already employed. It was necessary to shift them to the tight areas, putting into their jobs those who were tied by child and household cares to their own neighborhoods. Despite the National Service Act and in face of moral pressure to get girls and women into war duties, both essential employment and the labor force fell off; the latter had dropped perhaps half a million by V-E Day. "Lack of replacements for ordinary industrial wastage was probably as important as actual labour withdrawals in decreasing labour force of the less essential industries."[22]

Up to May 1944 Germany's combined labor and fighting forces dwindled slightly, the civilian labor force of its own nationals somewhat more. A few hundred thousand females left industry, transport, and domestic service, some others took on home work or returned to agriculture, but the over-all proportion of its females in work did not change. Albert Speer, Minister for Armament and War Production, reported to Hitler in July 1944 that 588,000 able-bodied men 18-34 could be combed out to the armed forces and replaced by women. His proposal that 300,000-400,000 domestic servants and 30,000 college girls be diverted to war production was in vain. Not until the last year of war did Germany take drastic measures. When Allied successes followed the landings in France, foreign replacements became a trickle. A real shake-up was instituted and large sections of industry closed — newspapers, printing, amusements, railroad travel, teaching, and research. By this time bombing was disrupting factory routine, paralyzing key industries, and interfering with mobility, the consequence being that much of the labor turned loose by austerity measures became unemployed. Between March 1943 and 1944 average hours worked per week went down half way to prewar levels in both production and consumption. They declined for all workers, male and female, skilled and unskilled. From January 1945 on, the war economy was disintegrating.[23]

The Allies experienced their best victories, the Germans their worst defeats, in this period, but all three major countries lost manpower from manufacturing, and fought to some extent with guns and materials put

[22] *Ibid.*, p. 460. [23] *Strategic Bombing Survey*, pp. 38-9, 215.

into pipelines in the preceding four years. Only the United States expanded its total labor force.

LABOR FORCE, ARMED FORCES, AND UNEMPLOYMENT

In none of the three countries whose nationals moved into gainful occupations in extra numbers during the war have any such inflows been recorded in time of peace. In each of the three, as will subsequently become manifest, the labor force gave up virtually all its wartime gains as soon as, even before, the armed forces disbanded. Only in the United States are data adequate to test the association in detail (Charts 1 and 3).

Until the armed forces enlarged, the labor force of this country about held its own, aside from population increase. Most of the influx occurred in the years when recruiting camps were jammed with inductees (Chart 3). It does not seem too much, therefore, to suppose that it was brought about by the military draft. The immense levies drew young men from schools into the armed forces and therefore into the labor force; reduced the number at home for whom women had to keep house; took away the main breadwinner of many families, putting new burdens of earning upon wives, sisters, and mothers; and, by removing husbands, fiances, and boyfriends, created a vacuum in the social life of women which millions filled by taking defense jobs.

It has been this writer's observation that the burden of housekeeping is determined primarily by the number for whom beds must be made, meals cooked, shirts ironed, and food and clothes purchased, and only secondarily by the size of the house or its equipment — vacuum cleaners, electric ironers, and automatic dishwashers. If millions of boys and men were conscripted, fewer houseworkers would be needed and more women would presumably be available for the labor force. How can this hypothesis be tested statistically?

In 1940 the ratio of the number of females engaged in housework to the number of persons living in private households of two or more was 0.228, slightly under one houseworker for four persons. Multiplying the household population by 0.228 yields an estimate of females needed in housework. Tested against an actual number in Table 3 (lines 3 and 4), the figure is strikingly close, in most years within 2 percent (Chart 4). Not even in the first demobilization years, when women were leaving jobs to get homes ready for their menfolk, was the excess as much as 5 percent.

Chart 3
Armed Forces and Labor Force, Annual Increases
World War II, United States

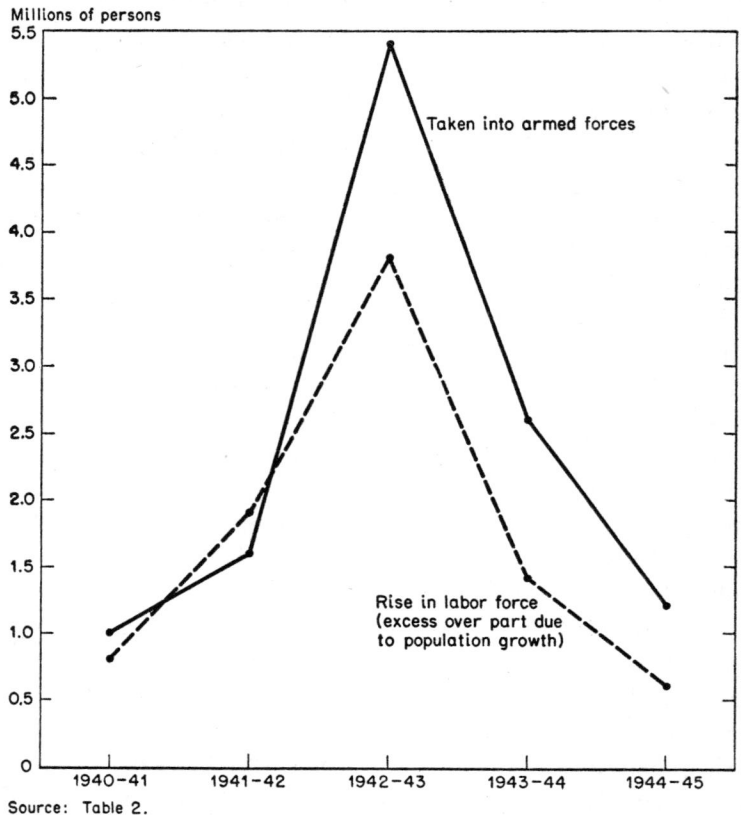

Source: Table 2.

The difference between total active females 14 and older (excluding the disabled and institutional inmates) and the number of houseworkers needed, plus the number attending school, is assumed to be available for the labor force. The actual labor force may of course be smaller, for there will always be some women who do not wish or feel competent to earn a living. Nevertheless, during World War II the number in the labor force fluctuated with the number available (Table 4, lines 4 and 5, and Chart 5). Aside from population growth and the decline of girls attending school, it seems possible to attribute nearly all the increase in the labor force during April 1940-45 to the shrinkage in the requirement for female houseworkers as a result of millions of men being drained out of private homes to the armed forces. The relation after the war is less impressive. During 1946-47 women quit jobs more rapidly than men left the armed forces and in larger number than were required to keep house for the returning servicemen. Undoubtedly this excessive outflow from the labor force was a reaction to the years of work and separation. During 1948-51, on the other hand, females increased more rapidly in the labor force than in the number available, until in April 1950 and 1951 the gap was nearly closed and barely more than half a million females were unaccounted for.

But the association with the armed forces was apparently not independent of changes in unemployment. The United States had only partly recovered from the great depression of the 1930's when Hitler's divisions broke through into the Low Countries. Over 7 percent of its work force were still seeking jobs 19 months later when the Japanese dropped their bombs on Hawaii. Although my studies elsewhere have shown that the peacetime labor force has borne a stable ratio to the working age population from one high employment period to another, they have shown also that it shrinks a bit when jobs become hard to find, then expands again when employment recovers and people with new hope rejoin the labor market.[24] The labor force of this country has been close to 56 percent of the population 14 and older in years of peace and high employment such as 1947 or 1930 (1930 data adjusted to the 1945 measurement technique). In April 1940, however, it was only 54.1 percent, hence 1.8 percent too low. The deficiency may have been due to the fact that since one in six persons already in the job market could not get work 1.8 million persons may have been discouraged from even seeking it, remaining out of the labor force altogether.

Certainly, the ratio to armed force increases was high in years such as 1940-43 when unemployment was falling most rapidly, highest of all (1.19) in 1941-42 when 3⅓ million idle persons were being absorbed into jobs, and relatively low, close to 0.50, in the last two years when few unemployed were left to be absorbed (Chart 6).

[24] C. D. Long, The Labor Force in Wartime America, NBER *Occasional Paper 14,* March 1944; 'The Labor Force and Economic Change', Chapter 13, *Insights into Labor Issues,* ed. by R. A. Lester and Joseph Shister (Macmillan, 1948); 'Labor Force, Income, and Employment' (mimeographed manuscript, NBER, 1950, now being revised).

Table 3

Need for Females in Housework Based on Population to be Cared for United States, April 1940-1951 (millions of persons)

	1940	1941	1942	1943	1944	1945	1946	1947	1948	1949	1950	1951
1 Population in private households of 2 or more	124.6	124.7	124.4	120.7	119.5	118.7	127.7	135.4	138.2	140.8	143.4	144.7
2 Ratio of houseworkers to population in households (1940)	0.228											
3 Est. need for houseworkers (line 1 × 0.228)	.....	28.4	28.4	27.5	27.2	27.1	29.1	30.9	31.5	32.1	32.7	33.0
4 Actual number in housework	28.4	28.8	28.6	27.5	27.8	26.7	30.5	32.4	32.7	33.3	33.0	33.1
5 Excess of actual over need	.....	0.4	0.2	0	0.6	−0.4	1.4	1.5	1.2	1.2	0.3	0.1
6 % excess is of need	.....	1.4	0.7	0	2.2	−1.5	4.6	4.6	3.7	3.6	0.9	0.3

Source of data on which calculations were based: Bureau of the Census.

Chart 4
Females Needed in Housework Based on Population to be Cared for United States, April 1940-1951

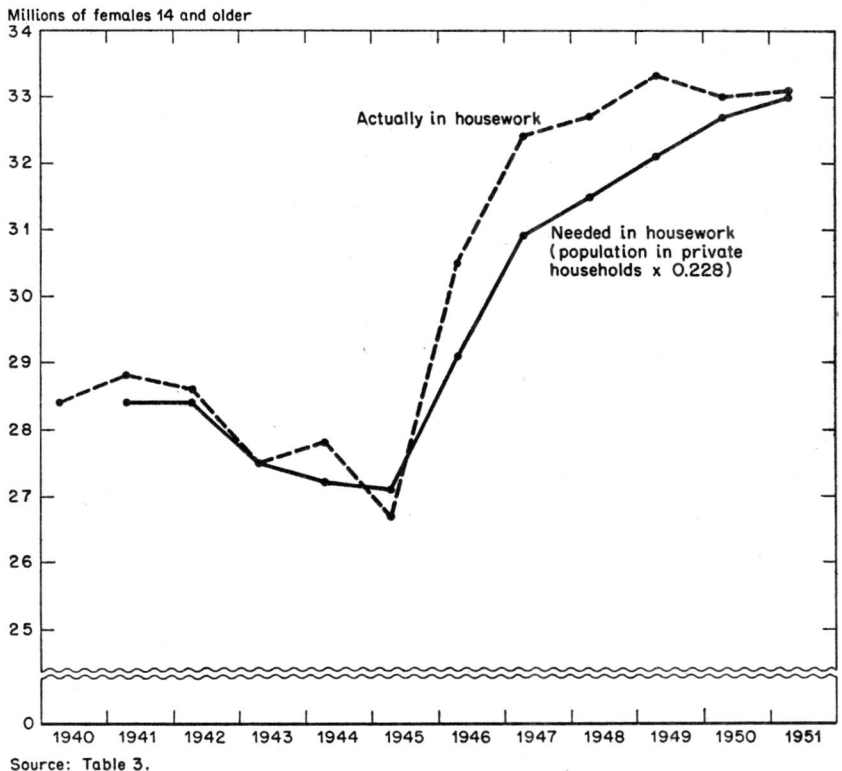

Source: Table 3.

To be sure, the rise in the armed forces was doubtless partly responsible for reducing unemployment in the early years of World War II. Many idle persons were absorbed directly into the military, many others into tank arsenals and electronic assembly lines, to supply the armies that were in the making. Thus unemployment may not have been an independent factor. But independent or not, it was a factor and it would not be safe to ignore the effect that reemployment of 8 million had on the size and rapidity of the labor force increase. Suppose that at the outbreak of World War II the United States had had only 4, instead of 15, percent unemployed and that its labor force had been at the same proportion of the population as ordinarily prevails in years of peace and

Table 4

Need for Houseworkers as Factor Determining Size of Female Labor Force
United States, April 1940-1951 (millions of females)

	1940	1941	1942	1943	1944	1945	1946	1947	1948	1949	1950	1951
1 Females 14 & older (excl. disabled & inst. inmates)	49.5	......	50.8	51.4	51.9	52.5	53.0	53.7	54.2	54.8	55.5	56.1
Minus:												
2 School attendance	4.6	n.a.	4.5	3.7	3.5	3.4	4.1	4.0	3.7	3.7	3.9	3.9
3 Needed in housework (Table 3, line 3)	28.4*	......	28.4	27.5	27.2	27.1	29.1	30.9	31.5	32.1	32.7	33.0
4 Residual 'available' for labor force	16.5	......	17.9	20.2	21.2	22.0	19.8	18.8	19.0	19.0	18.9	19.2
5 Actual labor force	13.8	......	15.5	18.2	18.6	19.8	16.7	16.3	17.2	17.2	18.1	18.6
6 'Available' but not in labor force	2.7	......	2.4	2.0	2.6	2.2	3.1	2.5	1.8	1.8	0.8	0.6

Source of data on which calculations were based: Bureau of Census.
n.a.: not available.
*Actual number in housework.

Chart 5
Female Labor Force and Number Available
United States, April 1940-1951

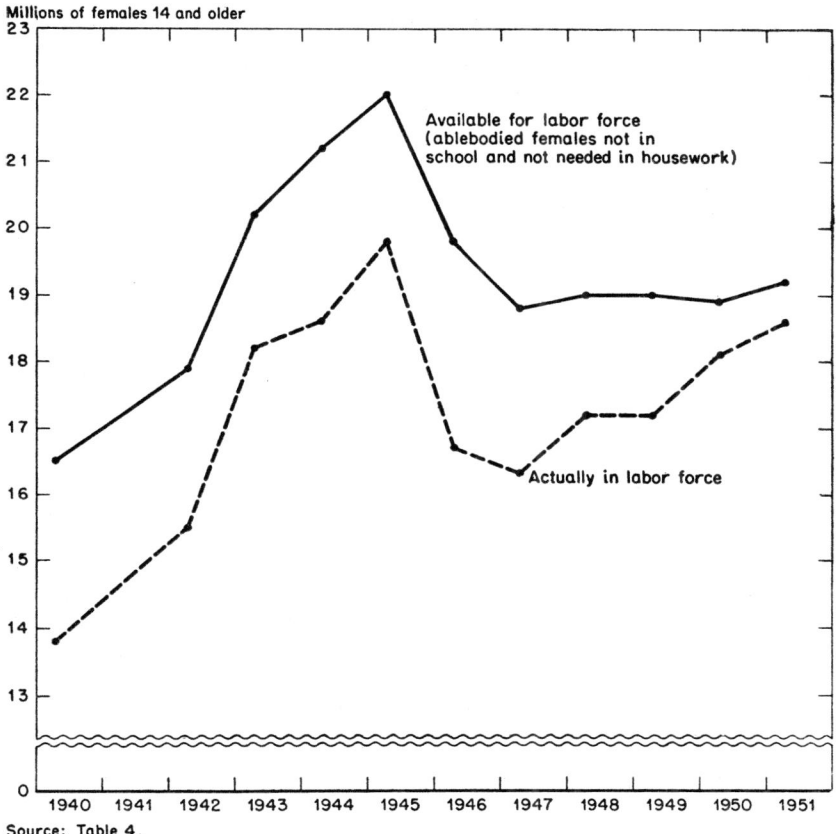

Source: Table 4.

high employment. Could the labor force have been expected to rise as fast as it did in those early war years? We shall have an opportunity to test this in the Korean War, for when the Communist equipped battalions swept across the 38th parallel, unemployment in the United States was no more than a third of its pre-World War II level and its labor force was 3 million larger than if 1940 proportions had prevailed. It will be interesting to see whether the labor force increases bear as high a relation to armed force inductions as in the early years of World War II.

Chart 6
Ratio of Labor Force to Armed Force Increases and Annual Decreases in Unemployment United States, April 1940-1945

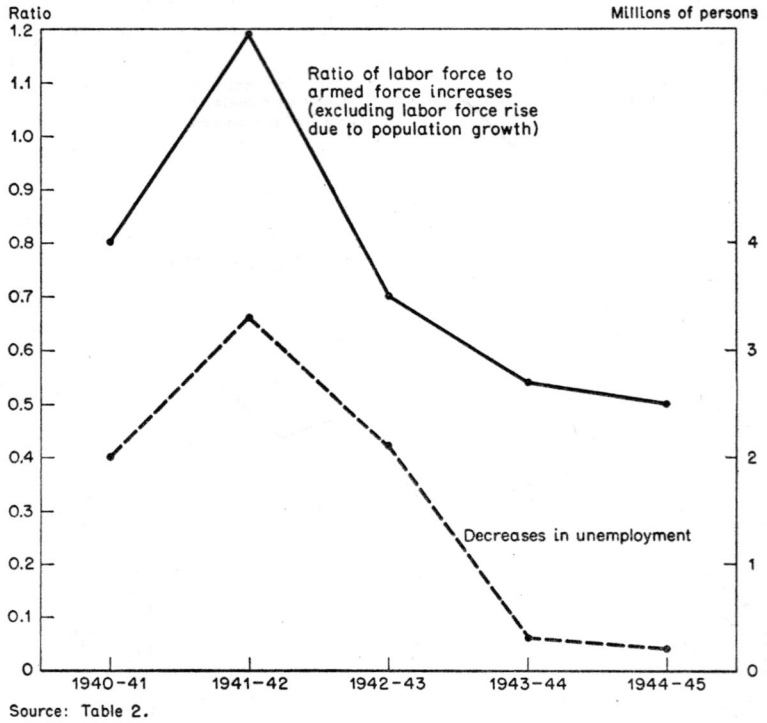

Source: Table 2.

4 THE WAR PEAK: UNITED STATES, GREAT BRITAIN, CANADA, GERMANY

In World War I the United States, Great Britain, and Germany did not add appreciably to their labor forces, the illusion of an over-all increase having arisen from transfers out of domestic service and other paid employment to factories and shipyards.[25] In all three countries the civilian labor force was depleted by the full number drafted, and labor needed in war work had to be pulled from the small pool of prewar unemployed or from industries turning out goods of less urgency.

During World War II, on the contrary, the labor forces unquestionably increased (Chart 7), though the number varied widely among the countries. Nonexistent in Germany unless one counts foreigners, and

[25] *Occasional Paper 14,* pp. 39 ff.

Chart 7
Labor Force per 1,000 Population 14 and Older, World War II

■ Armed forces

A United States, April 1940-1951

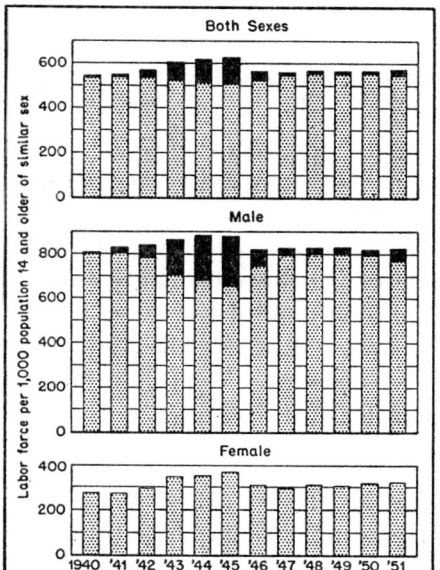

B Great Britain, June 1939-1948

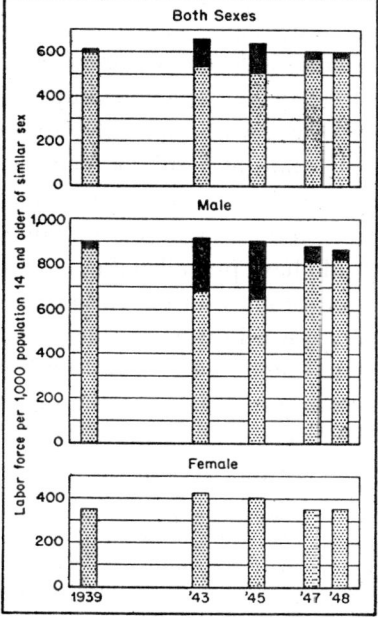

C Canada, August 1939, June 1941-1950

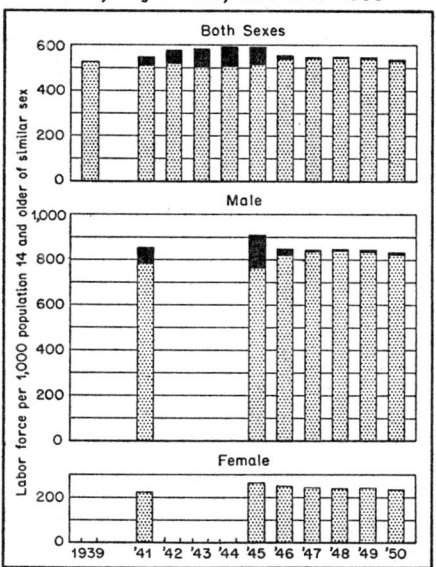

D Germany, May 1939-1944
(labor force including armed forces but excluding foreigners)

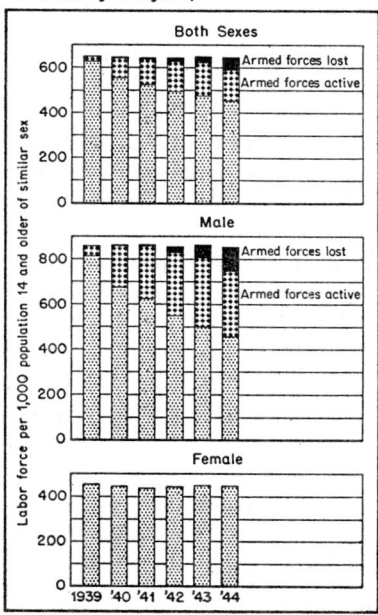

Source: See text notes 5 and 6.

substantial in Canada, in Britain it was impressive though smaller than usually imagined, and in the United States largest of all.

In April 1940 the American armed forces were hardly worth numbering. Five Aprils later, as the *Wehrmacht* was breaking up, they had taken on a dozen million which, added to the gains of the civilian sector, had brought employment up altogether by 19.4 million (Table 2 A, line 1). Much was due to the absorption of many millions unemployed in 1940, but 11.5 million represented extra workers who had come in during the five intervening years. Leaving out further the part due to population growth, 8.5 million was the excess over the labor force that would have prevailed if the population 14 and older had contributed the same proportion of workers as in April 1940 — 54.1 percent.[26] This nation was in the enviable position of staffing one of the largest military establishments in history and at the same time placing a sixth more persons in civilian jobs than in 1940. Over half of the labor force additions were females, one for every three who would have been in gainful work on the basis of prewar participation rates (Table 5).

[26] These statistics were revised by the Census to be comparable to 1945. They manifest an upturn in the proportion of the population in the labor force during 1940 and 1941. In the data underlying *Occasional Paper 14* the increase was less (p. 50 and App. B), the discrepancy arising chiefly from the new technique which made the July 1945 labor force nearly 2 million bigger. For comparability, the earlier data were raised by the Census back to 1940, and the above difference distributed in such a way that the labor force was enlarged about a million more in April 1943 than in March 1940 ('Labor Force, Employment and Unemployment in the United States, 1940 to 1946', *Current Population Reports*, Series P-50, No. 2, Sept. 11, 1947, p. 9)

Table 5

Peak Excess of World War II Labor Force (including armed forces) over Prewar or Early War (millions of workers)

	U. S. April 1, 1945[a]	G. B. June 1, 1943[b]	Canada June 1, 1945[c]	Germany May 1, 1943[d]		
				A	B	C
A Both Sexes 14 and Older						
Actual number						
Both sexes	66.3	25.2	5.3	41.5	39.9	46.1
Males	46.4	16.7	4.2	26.7	25.1	29.8
Females	19.9	8.5	1.1	14.8	14.8	16.3
Excess, incl. rise due to population growth						
Both sexes	11.5	2.3	0.7	1.0	−0.6	5.3
Males	5.5	0.7	0.4	0.8	−0.8	3.7
Females	6.0	1.6	0.3	0.2	0.2	1.6
Excess, excl. rise due to population growth						
Both sexes	8.5	1.8	0.4	−0.1	−1.7	4.2
Males	3.8	0.3	0.3	0.1	−1.6	3.0
Females	4.7	1.5	0.1	−0.2	−0.1	1.2

B MAJOR AGE-SEX EARNING GROUPS
Actual number
Males 25-64	33.5	11.9	2.8
Others	32.8	13.3	2.5
Young persons 14-24	16.7	7.0	1.6
Elderly persons 65+	2.9	1.2	0.3
Women 25-64	13.2	5.1	0.6

Excess, incl. rise due to population growth
Males 25-64	2.4	0.3	0.2
Others	9.1	2.0	0.5
Young persons 14-24	4.4	0.2	0.2
Elderly persons 65+	0.7	0.4	0.1
Women 25-64	4.0	1.4	0.2

Excess, excl. rise due to population growth
Males 25-64	0.5	0.0	0.0
Others	7.8	1.8	0.4
Young persons 14-24	4.6	0.3	0.2
Elderly persons 65+	0.5	0.2	0.1
Women 25-64	2.7	1.3	0.1

ª Excess over April 1940. The United States mobilized a slightly larger labor force inasmuch as 300,000 men were killed. Their inclusion would not alter the picture materially.

ᵇ Excess over June 1939. For information on British parttime workers, military and civilian war losses, and foreign workers and war prisoners, see *Labor Force, Income, and Employment,* Appendix H.

ᶜ Excess over June 1941. The Canadian labor force concept excludes student workers and farm women employed on family farms. Canada mobilized a slightly larger labor force than is reflected in these figures on active strength inasmuch as 40,000 were killed. Their inclusion would not alter the picture materially.

ᵈ Excess over May 1939. These data do not reflect some concealed possible shifts in the German female labor force to the extent that 'agricultural helping wives' transferred to industry. The same shifts occurred in the United States but undoubtedly some farm wives, who would be excluded from the United States or Canadian peacetime labor force, were in the German labor force before the war and might, if their peacetime work was trivial, constitute a real addition to the labor force without being recognized in these statistics. However, no more than a few hundred thousand did, in fact, shift from agriculture; and indication that females may not have worked harder on their family farms is had in the fact that the exodus of German men from farms was just about made up by foreign labor.

The actual labor force data are based upon a threefold classification:

A Labor force mobilized from native population, military losses not deducted; civilian losses by May 1943 negligible.

B Labor force maintained in active strength from native population, military losses deducted; civilian losses by May 1943 negligible.

C Labor force deducting military losses and counting foreigners and prisoners of war; civilian losses by May 1943 negligible.

The labor force influx exceeded by far that of the other three countries together even if foreigners are counted in the German work force (Tables 1, 5). In percentages of working age population, however, additions in Britain compare favorably to those in this country (Table 6). Britain also drew more females 25-64 into its labor force per 1,000

35

of those ages in the population, despite smaller reserves. In a larger sense Britain aroused its people most completely to action, for its peak wartime labor force was a larger proportion of native population than that of any of the other three countries.[27] Germany lost from its native labor force even if killed and missing are not deducted, and heavily if they are.[28] Only by including foreigners in the labor force can its additions be compared to those of the United States (Tables 5 and 6, A, col. C).

WARTIME ADDITIONS BY AGE AND SEX EARNING GROUPS

No information was available on the age of the German labor force during World War II. Detail on the other three countries (Tables 5, 6) elicits first that, aside from population growth, few additions were drawn from males 25-64. Men 65 and older represented also, except in Canada, a minor source, furnishing in the United States no more than did males 25-64. Most of the extra labor came from young persons 14-24 and women 25-64. The former was the source of over half of all United States accretions, the latter, of nearly 40 percent; hardly more than a tenth came from men of prime ages and the elderly together. Most fresh manpower was thus, in fact, woman- and childpower. In Canada one in every two entering the labor force during 1941-45 was a youth. Women supplied the same number as elderly men. In Great Britain young persons were among the least important additions, no doubt because most children 14 or older were already gainfully occupied in peacetime. Seven in every ten entrants were women 25-64.

[27] Moreover, 47 percent of its workers in civilian nonagricultural industries, classified by uses of products, were in war employments, compared with 38 percent in Canada and 34 percent in this country. 'The Impact of the War on Civilian Consumption in the United Kingdom, the United States, and Canada', *A Report to the Combined Production and Resources Board,* Morris A. Copeland, Chairman, September 1945, pp. 152-6.

[28] To show that Germany's failure to enlarge its labor force was due to other factors than military losses one set of figures is presented in which the war dead are not deducted. Incidentally, the failure to recruit native females puts figures quoted during the war in an unfavorable light. According to uncited German sources in *The Economist* (March 6, 1943, p. 300), 2.2 million women, including conscripts for compulsory labor service and 'helpers' in the *Wehrmacht,* were brought into employment from the labor reserve that existed in August 1939. "Thus, it is obvious that only married women are available [in Germany] in large numbers. Married women without children or with one child, have already been drawn into some kind of war work. . . ."

Table 6

Peak Excess of World War II Labor Force (including armed forces) per 1,000 Population of Similar Age and Sex

	United States April 1, 1945[a]	Great Britain June 1, 1943[b]	Canada June 1, 1945[c]	Germany May 1, 1943[d]		
				A	B	C
A BOTH SEXES 14 AND OLDER						
Actual proportion						
Both sexes	623	658	594	649	639	672
Males	879	916	909	861	853	874
Females	370	423	265	449	449	473
Excess over prewar proportion						
Both sexes	82	47	46	0	−10	21
Males	70	19	55	2	−6	14
Females	96	73	42	−4	−4	19
B MAJOR AGE-SEX EARNING GROUPS						
Actual proportion						
Men 25-64	958	974	970			
Others	459	509	411			
Young persons 14-24	639	872	646			
Elderly persons 65+	289	260	378			
Women 25-64	374	377	218			
Excess over prewar proportion						
Men 25-64	18	3	10			
Others	111	66	66			
Young persons 14-24	176	43	91			
Elderly persons 65+	43	50	111			
Women 25-64	91	102	42			

See Table 5, notes.

5 WEAKNESS OF GERMAN MANPOWER POLICY EXPLAINED

The failure of Germany to augment its labor force with citizens calls for careful scrutiny, especially in view of the Nazis' supposed dictatorial advantage and reputation for total warfare. We must be sure, first, that it was not because civilians were stricken by bombing or sent out to conquered territories.

Emigration can be disposed of fairly quickly. "According to a slogan coined by Chancellor Hitler and frequently repeated by National Socialist leaders, 'the conquests of the German sword must be consolidated by the plough'. The German victories throughout Europe did not, however, lead to any appreciable volume of German settlement apart from the resettlement of Germans abroad. . . . There are, of course, millions of Germans from the Reich in the territories conquered, annexed, or occupied by Germany, but the overwhelming majority of them are directly connected with the military operations" (p. 27). "The number of Germans working abroad in commercial undertakings should not be overestimated, since it must be remembered that retail trade, which commonly absorbs the great majority of people engaged in commerce, is left in the hands of local merchants" (p. 33).[29] Thus, apart from those in the armed forces, most Germans in occupied lands were police and other government officials; employees on military railways; civilian auxiliaries to the army; or overseers, foremen, and skilled workers building fortifications and armament factories. For such construction the chief administrative arm was the Todt Organization. In May 1943 one of its officials could say that "it is today undoubtedly the biggest employer in the world". Nevertheless, it had few citizens in foreign countries; more than four-fifths of its employees in late 1942 were aliens. Even its small supervisory minority came in good part not from the fatherland but from places like Poland where they were classed as racial Germans for purposes of National Socialist statistics.[30] On November 30, 1944 the Todt Organization Regional Construction Corps employed no more than 47,423 nationals outside the Reich.[31] "With few exceptions, they have been sent under orders and are performing work to which they have been assigned. . . ."[32] Though abroad, they were almost certainly counted in the German labor force.

Civilian casualties also are not responsible. Injuries from air raids were about 1 million, but less than half occurred before summer 1944, and of these no more than half affected the labor force. Since two-thirds of those wounded survived, a large number of the 250,000 pre-1944 labor force casualties doubtless returned subsequently to work.[33]

As reasons for the poor showing of Germany the *Strategic Bombing Survey* stressed several factors. The National Socialists had been preaching that woman's place was at home and were loath to reverse themselves. Party members at all levels got female relatives exempted — a bad example. Allied bombing impeded the release of wives and daughters from household responsibilities by making housekeeping conditions difficult.

[29] Eugene M. Kulischer, *The Displacement of Population in Europe* (International Labour Office, Studies and Reports Series O, No. 8, Montreal, 1943). About 600,000 persons of German stock repatriated from conquered countries may be ignored, since nearly all were resettled in outside areas, chiefly Poland.
[30] *The Exploitation of Foreign Labour by Germany* (International Labour Office, Studies and Reports, Series C, No. 25, Montreal, 1945), pp. 72, 74.
[31] *Strategic Bombing Survey,* Appendix Table 50.
[32] Kulischer, *op. cit.,* p. 31.
[33] *Ibid.,* p. 39

These explanations are more ingenious than convincing. The Nazis were doubtless embarrassed to urge women to take jobs, but Hitler was not given to sticking to logic at all costs, and without question would have jettisoned his *Kinder, Kueche, und Kirche* slogan had he been really apprehensive at an early date. Difficulties of keeping house under bombing also rank low. The British persuaded females to take jobs despite damaging air attacks. Although the Germans ultimately sustained heavier raids, the proportion of girls and women in their labor force shrank in the years when bombing was negligible and sporadic, and actually rose as it grew in frequency and fury.

Various statistical explanations, such as the peacetime reserve of those not in the labor force, merit more consideration.

Boris Shishkin offers the suggestion that Germany's additions may have been meager because it had already been in "full mobilization" before the outbreak. Actually, except for having achieved full employment, it was far from attaining a complete muster of its manpower. Its armed forces had expanded to barely an eighth the number they were ultimately to call into service, and its May 1939 labor force proportion was not in excess of that found by the Census in 1925, a year of peacetime high employment. Indeed, the failure during the war to keep up with the small growth in working age population resulted in a labor force proportion in 1943 of only 0.5 to 1.0 percent above that in the deep depression a decade before.

It might be argued next that the peacetime German labor force is traditionally so high, in boom or depression, that when war comes its population has no reserves to draw upon. This line of argument is not, however, strong enough to hold. As the *Strategic Bombing Survey* remarked (p. 31), women workers were a large proportion of the prewar German female population only in agriculture. The nonfarm population turned out to have the same percentage of workers 14 and older as in Britain for females and not much higher for males. Britain, moreover, has one of the very highest peacetime labor force proportions, yet it added more during wartime than Canada, which has a very small normal labor force in relation to population.

At first glance the more definite cause suggested by the *Strategic Bombing Survey* (p. 35) — "the relatively high birth rate under the Nazi regime" — derives support from the experience of Britain, which with low birthrates got its labor force proportion up to higher levels than any other country here considered. In point of fact, however, the "vast broods" are an easily exploded myth. Far from having a "number of children under 14 . . . probably higher than anywhere else in the 'western world' ", the Germans had fewer, relatively to females of working age, than the Americans or Canadians and not many more than the British. Birthrates under the Nazis were barely at reproduction rates.[34] Moreover, with a lighter child burden on their women — 437 children 0-9 per 1,000 females 14-64 in May 1945 compared with 503 in the United States in April and 573 in Canada in June — they lost female workers while this country and Canada gained them.

On the other hand, related to women *outside the labor force,* child care responsibilities were greater in Germany than in the United States or Britain (Table 7, line 2). Furthermore, among the four nations there was a very good (inverse) rank association between additions to the labor force from each 1,000 females not gainfully occupied (employed or unemployed) under peacetime conditions of high employment, and the number of children they must presumably nurse and cook for (Table 7, lines 1 and 2). These differences in responsibilities were, however, too small to explain the very large contrasts in labor force additions. For example, German women had the same relative child care responsibilities as Canadian, yet left the labor force while the latter contributed a third as many persons to the labor force per 1,000 as women in the United States.

[34] *Population Index* (Office of Population Records, School of Public Affairs, Princeton University, 1947), XIII, Table 3, p. 168.

Table 7

Additions of Females to Labor Force in World War II and Two Factors Accounting for Them

		U. S. April 1945	G. B. June 1943	Canada June 1945	Germany New Boundaries May 1943
1	Female labor force additions per 1,000 females outside the labor force under peacetime conditions of high employment	103	112	32	—8
2	Children 0-13 to be cared for per 1,000 females outside the labor force under peacetime conditions of high employment	872	704	935	935
3	Allowance-income index (Table 8)	100	104	193	198

As a matter of fact, though freedom from child cares might enable a woman to take a job, it would not ensure that she would actually work unless she was under pressure to earn her keep. Could it be that in some countries relatively liberal allowances to dependents of fighting men make it possible for wives, sisters, daughters, and parents to live without working and that in other countries less ample stipends drive them into the labor market? Here caution is in order. Difficulty lurks in hundreds of pay and subsidy combinations, as well as in wide variations between living standards; what would appear stingy to an American might strike a German as bountiful. It is more meaningful, therefore, to relate allowances to peacetime incomes. The ratios in Table 8 were computed by dividing prewar disposable income per equivalent adult male into minimum allowances plus allotments granted a wife and two children of lower rank service men during the first years of the war, when most accretions were made. These allowances, together with the child cares of females outside the labor force, help explain why, compared with the United States, Britain drew in a large percentage of unoccupied females, Canada a low percentage, and Germany none at all (Table 8).

If the American ratio is taken as 100, Britain was somewhat more generous. Supplementary grants, adjusted to current needs and prior commitments such as for rent, illness, taxes, and insurance, raised its subsidies, relative to income, still further above the moderate liberality of the United States. Canada, whose labor force additions were small compared with those of the United States, paid almost double its allowances (in relation to workers' incomes). Germany, which enjoyed no significant labor force addition, paid the most ample of all and made them available besides to wide categories not covered in other countries — to wives of railway guards, of Red Cross and post office workers, and of men in the labor and air protection services; to stepchildren, adopted and illegitimate children; and to other dependent relatives. Founded on the principle that soldiers' families must maintain their prewar living standards and widows their customary social levels, its subventions were even more munificent than the index suggests.[35]

The influence of service allowances may seem to contradict the finding in 'Labor Force, Income, and Employment' that the labor force has been insensitive to changes in income. However, incomes are, for the most part, rewards for working. Allowances, on the other hand, were

[35] *Monthly Labor Review,* Dec. 1943, p. 1130.

Table 8

Allotments and Allowances to Dependents of Armed Force Members
United States, Great Britain, Canada, Germany

	U. S. 1942	G. B. 1943	Canada 1941	Germany 1939
Allotment & allowance (monthly) to wife & 2 children of lower rank enlisted personnel	72[a]	186[b]	78.50[c]	147[d]
Disposable monthly income per equivalent adult male	196[a]	488[b]	111[c]	202[d]
Ratio: allowance to disposable income	0.367	0.381	0.707	0.728
Index (U. S.: 100)	100	104	193	198

Source of data on allotments and allowances, Helen Tarasov, 'Family Allowances: An Anglo-American Contrast', *Annals of the American Academy of Political and Social Science, May 1943*, pp. 9-21; D. C. Cline, 'Allowances to Dependents of Servicemen in the United States', *ibid.*, pp. 1-8; *Monthly Labor Review*, Dec. 1943, pp. 1129-30; *Social Security Bulletin*, April 1941, pp. 11-78; Dec. 1942, p. 22. *Labour Gazette,* Sept. 1944, p. 1171. Hedwig Wachenheim, 'Allowances for Dependents of Mobilized Men in Germany', *International Labour Review,* 49 (March 1944), No. 3, pp. 323-38.

[a] In U. S. dollars. Ranks below the top three grades of enlisted personnel. Amounts of deduction and allowance did not vary with enlisted men's pay grades. Deductions were not rigidly compulsory, but servicemen with Class A dependents were "expected to participate". Allowances were tax exempt, as, for all practical purposes, were salaries of enlisted personnel and lower ranks of officers.

[b] In shillings. Ranks below sergeant; wife's allowance increased somewhat with rank of serviceman; children's allowances varied only with number of children up to three. Allotments were optional; if serviceman did not make an allotment, the government did not grant an allowance. War Service Grants were available to family or dependents up to 260 s. per month on proof of hardship; and, if justified by living standard before service, so were funeral and sickness allowances. Allowances to dependents other than wife, very much circumscribed and based on need, were tax exempt.

[c] In Canadian dollars. Ranks below warrant officer, Class I. Allotments, amounting to 15 days' pay, were compulsory. Allowances increased with rank. They were exempt from income taxes, as, for all practical purposes, were salaries of the lower ranks of military personnel.

[d] In Reich marks. Ranks below sergeant; men of higher rank were expected to support their families from their pay. Allowances were tax exempt. See text.

for status and in some cases withdrawn in part if dependents took gainful jobs.

The United States did not penalize dependents, regardless how much they earned.[36] Britain docked them for extra income[37] but, like this country, set their allowances so low that they were obliged to work in order

[36] Public Law No. 625, 77th Cong., 2nd Sess., June 23, 1942.

[37] The limit on the monthly income of dependents beyond which allowances would be reduced was set (depending on rank), first at 65s, 80s 2d, 101s 8d; then at 69s 4d, 86s 8d, and 108s 4d (Cmd. 6260, the British War Office, *Monthly Labor Review,* Sept. 1941, p. 720).

to live. Each therefore had systems well designed for recruiting wartime labor. In Canada and Germany, however, a wife could get much of her ration without working and since there was also a scarcity of things to buy, often lacked incentive to earn. Both gave less to dependents who worked for pay. The former gave all servicemen the same amounts for children but varied allowances for wives and other relatives according to rank, and applied a means test: up to the end of 1942 total income could not be more than double the basic rate.[38] The latter, in an autumn 1939 amendment, let the applicant choose between a grant based on family responsibilities in relation to local living costs and one based upon the wages last earned by the person called up. Both methods weighed income from all sources; two-thirds of a wife's monthly wage could be deducted, one-third of a child's (*ibid.*, Dec. 1939, p. 1364; March 1940, p. 602).

Why did the Nazi government establish such a short sighted scheme? Why did it not institute incentives and compulsions to expand the native labor force?

Theoretically, it enjoyed absolute power. It had introduced compulsory labor service as early as 1935, extending it in 1939 to all ages and to females. Nevertheless, not until late did it use these powers or even press women into work in less direct ways. It did, of course, take measures to get its nationals into the labor force. These, on paper, make a formidable list. At the outbreak of war, 15,000 day nurseries had accommodations for 500,000 children; by 1943, 22,000 nurseries for 1,000,000; by 1944, 32,000 nurseries for 1,200,000 children. Many women were said to work parttime in offices — on an average over 30 hours a week. Beginning with 1941 young girls were required to work at least six months. The obligation was later extended to a year and to girls as young as 17. Vacation work was compulsory for school children. Boys became tram conductors and auxiliary policemen. Fairly early in the conflict all retired men under 70 had to register for employment. Old men's corners were organized in workshops to enable those past retirement to work at a slower pace and, of course, at lower pay. The Manpower Director was repeatedly replaced. About 1941 the post was filled with a Nazi Party leader in order to bypass the bureaucracy.

Opinion, or propaganda, fluctuated. In the early days of the war

---

[38] From the beginning of 1943 allowances were cut only if the dependent earned more than $40 a month; *ibid.*, June 1943, pp. 1114-6.

the press derided the British for their chaotic labor market, flaunting Germany's own alleged increase of women in civilian employment. Later it acknowledged, for example, that on only 18 of 105 Pomeranian farms did all residents help with the root crop and on the other 87 only 40 percent. Up to the end of 1943 it was beseeching women to register and complaining that the wealthy were moving to avoid registration. In May 1944 it admitted that war work in the home, promoted for two years, was carried on by fewer than 300,000 persons.[39] Such sidelights render less puzzling the huge deficits in the civilian labor force, compared in Table 1 with those of the three Allies.

Clearly not until after its defeat at Stalingrad — too late — did it even begin to enforce compulsory conscription of women. In mid-war their deployment by Britain was said to be "more militaristic than anything considered as useful or dignified in Germany" (*Economic Journal,* 1942, p. 23). Nor were wives and mothers induced to volunteer for parttime, the sole way really feasible in view of the many alibis they could plead. Some regulations were strict without being effective, it being conceded that women were staying out of employment for fear of becoming "slaves of their labor book". In contrast, Britain was then, as we noted, relieving married women of unemployment compensation payments and freeing them from essential work orders (so they could enter the labor force with confidence that it was not a trap door); moreover, it exempted them from taxes on annual earnings up to £80.[40]

The real reason for Germany's manpower shortcomings may well be its conviction during the crucial years that it need not mobilize completely in order to win.

Until the first defeat there was a general belief, almost a promise to the people, that hostilities would be short and confined to Europe. The belief led to preparation in 'width' rather than 'depth': from the beginning industry was converted not to extending steel and other industrial capacity, but to making finished articles, thereby yielding quick and plentiful output of powder and shot without detracting from Nazi popularity with business men or labor. This is the comfortable preparation which many have always imagined a dictatorship could avoid, in

---

[39] H. W. Singer, 'The German War Economy in the Light of Economic Periodicals', *Economic Journal, 1941,* pp. 24, 408; *1942,* pp. 21, 186-7, 192, 194; *1944,* p. 209.
[40] *The War and Women's Employment,* N. S. I. (International Labour Office, Montreal, 1946), pp. 24-5.

view of its supposedly arbitrary powers. When it finally dawned on the Germans that the industrial base was too narrow, there was no longer time to broaden it; to do so would have taken manpower and steel from immediate output and worsened the shortages. The Nazis did not, therefore, draw upon all their reserves, at least not until late 1944: at first because it seemed unnecessary in view of their successes in the field and apparent abundance of foreign labor; subsequently because it was obviously too late. It is tempting to conclude that countries do not exert more effort in war than they have to, that the Germans were in the end partly undone by their early conquests and the resulting trainloads of prisoners and booty.[41]

6 Increase in Hours during World War II: United States

Gains from a longer workweek are estimated by deducting employment measured in persons from employment measured in equivalent fulltime workers (Table 9). These accretions reached a maximum in 1943 of 7.6 million equivalent workers (line 14), then declined to 5.5 million in 1945. Why were some of the gains that had been made during 1940-43 lost during 1944-45?

The answer may be found by separating parttime from overtime work. Little was gained or lost during 1940-43 as a result of changes in the extent of parttime employment but during 1944-45 the time lost rose (Table 10), apparently in some degree because young people and women had become a larger element in the civilian labor force and men a smaller element. Many young people could work only after school and on Saturdays. Some women, burdened by children and home duties, could spare no more than a few days a week; and women always take more time off for ill health than men. Finally, keen demand for labor is usually accompanied by higher absenteeism and turnover. The gains

[41] Germany used foreign labor not only directly but also indirectly: it confiscated commodities or bought them at low prices; an eighth of its pig iron and about 5 percent of its machine tools came from occupied Poland, France, Belgium, and the Netherlands; early it captured stocks of oil, copper, and other strategic materials. During 1939-44 foreign contributions to national product ranged from 16 to 25 percent (*Strategic Bombing Survey*, pp. 21, 22, 260). These imports, even though all were not costless, unquestionably took the place of some native labor. Nevertheless, its plunder was not enough to meet its war needs and, though it faced desperate labor scarcities from 1942 on, it was unable or unwilling to call on its substantial reserves among its own nationals.

Table 9

Wartime Gain in Equivalent Fulltime Employment due to Increase in Hours (parttime and overtime combined): United States, April 1940-1946

	1940	1941	1942	1943	1944	1945	1946
AGRICULTURE							
1 Av. weekly hours	54.0	55.0	56.7	60.0	56.1	53.5	52.6
2 Employed persons (millions)	8.7	8.9	9.1	8.8	8.4	8.7	8.2
3 Manhours (millions)	470	490	516	528	471	465	431
4 Equivalent fulltime employed (millions)	8.9	9.2	9.7	10.0	8.9	8.8	8.1
5 Equivalent fulltime compared with actual employed (millions)	+0.2	+0.3	+0.6	+1.2	+0.5	+0.1	−0.1
NONAGRICULTURE							
6 Av. weekly hours	40.0	41.5	43.5	46.5	46.1	45.6	42.9
7 Employed persons (millions)	37.3	39.6	43.7	45.0	45.3	44.9	45.9
8 Manhours (millions)	1492	1643	1901	2093	2088	2047	1969
9 Equivalent fulltime employed (millions)	35.5	39.1	45.3	49.8	49.7	48.7	46.9
10 Equivalent fulltime compared with actual employed (millions)	−1.8	−0.5	+1.6	+4.8	+4.4	+3.8	+1.0
TOTAL CIVILIAN							
11 Employed persons (millions)	46.0	48.5	52.8	53.8	53.7	53.6	54.1
12 Equivalent fulltime employed (millions)	44.4	48.3	55.0	59.8	58.6	57.5	55.0
13 Equivalent fulltime compared with actual employed (millions)	−1.6	−0.2	+2.2	+6.0	+4.9	+3.9	+0.9
GAIN IN EMPLOYMENT DUE TO HOURS INCREASES							
14 Compared with 1940 (millions)	......	+1.4	+3.8	+7.6	+6.5	+5.5	+2.5
15 Compared with 1941 (millions)	......	......	+2.4	+6.2	+5.1	+4.1	+1.1

Source of data on which the calculations were based: Bureau of Census, Current Population Surveys. Fulltime hours were assumed to be 53 a week in agriculture, 42 a week in nonagriculture.

due to overtime (Table 11, line 4) rose rapidly during 1940-43, slightly in 1944, and fell off somewhat by 1945, though they were offset in some degree during 1944 and 1945 by the time lost through continued dilutions of the labor force with women and young people.

7 DEMOBILIZATION

Between mid-1944 and 1945, Canada's armed forces discharged a fifth of their personnel. Its labor force failed to keep pace with population

Table 10

Change in Equivalent Fulltime Employment due to Change in Extent of Parttime: United States, April 1940-1945 (millions)

	Employed less than Fulltime by Average Hours		1940	1941	1942	1943	1944	1945
	Worked	Lost						
1	0*	42*	1.0	0.5	0.8	0.8	1.4	1.3
2	7	35	1.0	1.2	1.3	1.2	1.5	1.7
3	25	17	4.9	5.0	5.2	4.1	5.6	6.0
	Equivalent Fulltime Workers							
4	Lost through parttime		3.8	3.5	4.0	3.5	4.9	5.1
	Gained through Reduction of Parttime							
5	Compared with 1940		......	+0.3	−0.2	+0.3	−1.1	−1.3
6	Compared with 1941		......	......	−0.5	0	−1.4	−1.6

Source of data on which calculations are based: Bureau of Census, Current Population Surveys.
*Have a job but not at work.

growth, and during the rest of 1945 shrank rapidly. By autumn 1946 it had returned to the 1941 proportion of population. The armed forces still held a few thousand men (Chart 1).

Britain's combined industrial and military labor force touched its summit in late 1943. When the armed forces began to let personnel go home after V-J Day, it was a quarter demobilized. Many workers leaving manufacturing and mining did not abandon the labor force but shifted to transport, nonessential construction, services, and distribution. By early 1947 the labor force had lost its war gains, though the armed ranks were still somewhat larger than before the conflict.

The United States yielded up a bit of its excess labor force in the two months before V-E Day; by V-J Day a third had disappeared. The armed forces did not stop inducting until almost the end and still held several

Table 11

Wartime Gain in Equivalent Fulltime Employment due to Overtime
United States, April 1940-1945 (millions)

		1941	1942	1943	1944	1945
1	Gain due to increased hours (Table 9, line 14)	1.4	3.8	7.6	6.5	5.5
2	Less gain due to decreased parttime (Table 10, line 5)	0.3	−0.2	0.3	−1.1	−1.3
GAIN DUE TO OVERTIME						
3	Compared with 1940	1.1	4.0	7.3	7.6	6.8
4	Compared with 1941	......	2.9	6.2	6.5	5.7

Source of data on which calculations are based: Bureau of Census, Current Population Surveys.

million men in late spring 1946 when the labor force had returned to peacetime proportions. As in Canada, the civilian sector was overdisbanded. After 1946 the total labor force stayed above the prewar proportion of population, unemployment was less than 4 percent of the labor force, and the armed forces still retained over a million men. During the 12 or 18 months after victory the labor force tended to anticipate the precipitous flight from military service.

Very little can be discovered about the labor force demobilization of Germany during the months following the defeat. Official enumerations made in 1946 covering all four zones of occupied Germany, plus Berlin, disclosed that the combined labor force proportion of population 14 and older, standardized for age and sex, was 4 percent below the labor force participation in the same areas in May 1939. (Wirtschaftswissenschaftliches Institut der Gewerkschaften, *Deutschland in Zahlen,* 1950 [Köln, 1951] pp. 12-13, 31.) The fact, however, that this deficiency was much larger than in the United States, Britain, or Canada could have been due (a) to the postwar industrial disorganization of Germany, (b) to the possession by Germans of far more money than they could spend, in view of the restricted quantity of goods offered at controlled prices, or (c) to the taking of the census in late October, by which time the labor force may have lost many agricultural helpers normally at work in May, the month in which the prewar count was made.

8 THE KOREAN WAR AND POSSIBILITIES FOR FURTHER EXPANSION

At the threshold of the Korean conflict, in April 1950, the labor force contained 63.5 million workers[42] of which 1.3 million were in the armed

---

[42] The monthly figures for April 1940 through April 1951 are from Census Current Population Surveys and rest on interviews with about 25,000 households. The accuracy of sample surveys is always suspect and the 1950 enumeration of the nation's households does nothing to settle them, for a preliminary release, also resting on a sample though a much larger one, reports 3.5 million fewer in the April 1950 labor force on the basis of the same concept and measurement technique (Series PC-7, No. 2, April 11, 1951, pp. 1-2). The Census ascribed the cause of this paradoxical discrepancy to the poor quality and inexperience of the 130,000 temporary interviewers as well as their responsibility for questions on housing, income, and agriculture. The Survey enumerators, in contrast, were a "small, well-trained group with, on the average, more than 12 months of specialized experience in the enumeration of the labor force. . . . As was the case a decade earlier, when the monthly survey results were compared with the 1940 Decennial Census data, it appeared that the more skilled interviewers had had greater success in handling the labor force questions for population groups whose activity is difficult to measure and, in consequence,

forces (Table 12). By the end of the next 12 months, the armed forces were nearly 3 million strong, and 1.2 million new workers and work seekers had moved into the labor market. The rise in the labor force from the population growth was a bit larger than in early World War II but the additions in excess of the population growth were much smaller: a half million, representing an increase in people's willingness to be in the labor force. The ratio of the labor force to the armed force enlargement was well under that in 1940-41 or 1941-42. Though there was as yet no general labor shortage, stringencies were afflicting key occupations. As defense orders take hold, there will be a great need for extra manpower. What are the prospects for further expansion?

A paragraph of caution is directed at those who would use the World War II experience to project employment and labor force increases

Table 12

Labor Force in Early Wartime by Employment and Military Status
Both Sexes, 14 and Older, United States, April

	World War II			Korean War		
	1941	1942	Change	1950	1951	Change
A MILLIONS OF PERSONS						
Labor force (civilian & military)	56.3	58.8	2.5	63.5	64.7	1.2
Armed forces	1.3	2.9	1.6	1.3	2.9	1.6
Labor force (civilian)	55.0	55.9	0.9	62.2	61.8	−0.4
Unemployed	6.4	3.1	−3.3	3.5	1.8	−1.7
Employed	48.6	52.8	4.2	58.7	60.0	1.3
B PERCENTAGE OF POPULATION 14 AND OLDER						
Labor force (civilian & military)	55.0	56.8	1.8	56.6	57.1	0.5
Armed forces	1.3	2.8	1.5	1.2	2.6	1.4
Labor force (civilian)	53.7	54.0	0.3	55.4	54.5	−0.9
Unemployed	6.3	3.0	−3.3	3.1	1.6	−1.5
Employed	47.4	51.0	3.6	52.3	52.9	0.6

had obtained a more nearly complete count of persons who were employed or who were looking for work. . . . Both groups of enumerators obtained practically the same results for employed males 25 years of age and over. . . ."

Skillful sample surveys *can,* of course, be more accurate than hasty enumerations, but it does not ease the mind to discover that the excess increased from 1.0 percent in 1940 to nearly 6 percent in 1950, yielding a differential in April 1950 of nearly 5 percent or roughly 3 million. Either the Survey interviewers further improved their quality or the measurement technique, when carried out faithfully, tends to drag in increasing numbers of borderline workers. Though the same technique was applied in the 1950 Census, it may not lend itself to the 'quickie' interviews of decennial enumerators.

during future wars. In April 1951, following the Korean outbreak, there were only a fourth as many unemployed as in April 1940, and the labor force proportion was 3.0 percent of the population 14 and older above that eleven years before. Of the reserves that might have existed if pre-World War II conditions had been reproduced, 6.2 million formerly unemployed and 3.4 million outside the labor force were presumably at work in April 1951. Nearly 10 million of the World War II additions to civilian and military employment had thus already been absorbed.

Nevertheless, prospects are now good for filling another 9 million jobs in the event of a major war. About 3 million may be expected to come into the labor force during the next four years from the new population. Another 5 million might well enter if the armed forces were raised to a maximum by calling up 9 million more men (on the basis of the 0.5 to 0.6 ratio of labor force to armed force increases that prevailed in the later years of World War II). Still another million and a quarter civilian employed would come from a fall of unemployment to the trough in World War II.

With these potential reinforcements, the armed forces could add another 9 million to its present 3 million without depressing civilian employment below the 60 million in April 1951. Lengthening the workweek 5 hours, fully practicable only under considerable strain, could supply another 5 million equivalent workers. (The average person in nonagricultural industries is now working the same number of hours as in the spring before Pearl Harbor.) Essential employments could also get more personnel by converting automobile plants to tank production and diverting domestic servants, bartenders, unproductive farm workers, and the like, to munitions industries. However, too sharp a curtailment of laundry, cleaning, catering, plumbing, painting, and other services would add burdens to housework, so that fewer women and young persons could work outside the home. An overlong workweek would depress the hourly productivity of those employed[43] and keep out of jobs many women who must have time after work to shop and cook. Depletion of high schools, colleges, and technical institutes for many years would cut off future skilled workers and trained leaders. Consequently,

[43] Hours of Work and Output, BLS *Bulletin 917*. Clarence D. Long, *Manpower Needs and the Labor Supply* (American Enterprise Association, 4 East 41st St., New York, Dec. 1951), pp. 28-30.

in increasing the labor supply attention has to be given to keeping all its parts in balance. The manpower potential is far more fully utilized than in 1940 and certain skills are already short. Still, in all-out war, 14 million equivalent fulltime workers, a quarter of present employment, might be added to military and civilian occupations.[44] Reserves of this relative size give an economy great flexibility. They surely exist in no other land and, with them in prospect, the United States is entitled to face a total mobilization with considerable confidence.

[44] *Ibid.,* pp. 15-24.

Table A1

Labor Force by Employment and Military Status: United States, 1940-1951
Quarterly Averages, All Data except Armed Forces Adjusted for Seasonal Variation

A MILLIONS OF PERSONS 14 AND OLDER

| | Labor Force (civilian & military) | | | Armed Forces | Civilian Labor Force | Unem- ployed | Civilian Employed |
	Both sexes	Male	Female	Male	Both sexes	Both sexes	Both sexes
1940							
II	55.9	41.7	14.2	0.3	55.6	8.2	47.4
III	56.4	42.2	14.2	0.4	56.0	8.5	47.5
IV	55.9	42.2	13.7	0.6	55.3	8.4	46.9
1941							
Av.	57.4	42.8	14.6	1.5	55.9	5.6	50.3
I	56.1	42.2	13.9	0.9	55.2	6.0	49.2
II	57.4	42.9	14.5	1.4	56.0	6.0	50.0
III	58.1	43.2	14.9	1.7	56.4	6.0	50.4
IV	57.8	42.7	15.1	1.9	55.9	4.4	51.5
1942							
Av.	60.1	44.1	16.0	3.8	56.3	2.6	53.7
I	58.4	43.4	15.0	2.2	56.2	4.0	52.2
II	59.6	43.8	15.8	3.2	56.4	2.8	53.6
III	60.3	44.2	16.1	4.2	56.1	2.2	53.9
IV	62.2	45.0	17.2	5.6	56.6	1.6	55.0
1943							
Av.	64.4	45.7	18.7	8.8	55.6	1.0	54.6
I	63.6	45.3	18.3	7.3	56.3	1.4	54.9
II	64.4	45.5	18.9	8.5	55.9	1.1	54.8
III	64.7	45.7	19.0	9.3	55.4	1.1	54.3
IV	64.9	46.1	18.8	9.9	55.0	0.7	54.3
1944							
Av.	65.9	46.4	19.5	11.0	54.9	0.7	54.2
I	65.5	46.4	19.1	10.3	55.2	0.7	54.5
II	66.0	46.6	19.4	10.9	55.1	0.7	54.4
III	65.8	46.2	19.6	11.4	54.4	0.7	53.7
IV	66.4	46.6	19.8	11.6	54.8	0.5	54.3
1945							
Av.	65.2	45.9	19.3	11.1	54.1	1.0	53.1
I	67.0	46.9	20.1	11.6	55.4	0.7	54.7
II	66.3	46.4	19.9	11.8	54.5	0.7	53.8
III	64.7	45.7	19.0	11.7	53.0	1.1	51.9
IV	62.6	44.5	18.1	9.0	53.6	1.7	51.9
1946							
Av.	60.8	44.0	16.8	3.2	57.6	2.3	55.3
I	60.8	43.8	17.0	5.2	55.6	2.2	53.4
II	60.5	44.0	16.5	3.4	57.1	2.3	54.8
III	60.9	44.1	16.8	2.4	58.5	2.2	56.3
IV	61.0	44.2	16.8	2.0	59.0	2.4	56.6
1947							
Av.	61.6	44.7	16.9	1.4	60.2	2.1	58.1
I	61.2	44.4	16.8	1.6	59.6	2.0	57.6
II	61.6	44.8	16.8	1.5	60.1	2.2	57.9
III	61.8	44.8	17.0	1.3	60.5	2.3	58.2
IV	61.8	44.7	17.1	1.3	60.5	2.0	58.5

	Labor Force (civilian & military)			Armed Forces Male	Civilian Labor Force Both sexes	Unemployed Both sexes	Civilian Employed Both sexes
	Both sexes	Male	Female				
1948							
Av.	62.8	45.2	17.6	1.3	61.5	2.1	59.4
I	62.3	44.9	17.4	1.2	61.1	2.0	59.1
II	62.3	44.9	17.4	1.2	61.1	2.0	59.1
III	63.2	45.5	17.7	1.3	61.9	2.1	59.8
IV	63.3	45.5	17.8	1.4	61.9	2.1	59.8
1949							
Av.	63.6	45.5	18.1	1.5	62.1	3.5	58.6
I	63.4	45.5	17.9	1.5	61.9	2.6	59.3
II	63.2	45.5	17.7	1.5	61.7	3.3	58.4
III	63.5	45.5	18.0	1.5	62.0	3.8	58.2
IV	64.2	45.6	18.6	1.4	62.8	4.2	58.6
1950							
Av.	64.5	45.9	18.6	1.5	63.0	3.0	60.0
I	64.4	45.7	18.7	1.4	63.0	3.8	59.2
II	64.0	45.7	18.3	1.3	62.7	3.2	59.5
III	64.3	46.0	18.3	1.3	63.0	2.8	60.2
IV	65.4	46.1	19.3	1.9	63.5	2.5	61.0
1951							
Av.	66.0	46.7	19.3	3.1	62.9	1.9	61.0
I	65.9	46.3	19.6	2.5	63.4	2.1	61.3
II	65.4	46.6	18.8	3.1	62.3	1.8	60.5
III	66.0	47.0	19.0	3.4	62.6	1.7	60.9
IV	66.7	47.0	19.7	3.4	63.3	2.1	61.2

Seasonal indexes were computed by averaging ratios of original figures to 4 term moving averages; see Arthur F. Burns and Wesley C. Mitchell, *Measuring Business Cycles* (NBER, 1946), pp. 46-50.

B PERCENTAGE OF POPULATION 14 AND OLDER OF SIMILAR SEX

	Labor Force (civilian & military)			Armed Forces Male	Civilian Labor Force Both sexes	Unemployed Both sexes (% of labor force)
	Both sexes	Male	Female			
1940						
II	55.2	82.4	28.1	0.6	54.9	14.7
III	55.6	83.2	28.0	0.8	55.2	15.1
IV	54.9	83.0	26.9	1.2	54.3	15.0
1941						
Av.	55.9	83.5	28.5	2.9	54.5	9.8
I	55.0	82.8	27.2	1.8	54.1	10.7
II	56.1	83.9	28.3	2.7	54.7	10.5
III	56.6	84.3	29.0	3.3	54.9	10.3
IV	56.1	83.1	29.3	3.7	54.3	7.6
1942						
Av.	58.0	85.3	30.8	7.3	54.4	4.4
I	56.6	84.3	29.0	4.3	54.5	6.8
II	57.6	84.8	30.4	6.2	54.5	4.7
III	58.1	85.4	30.9	8.1	54.1	3.6
IV	59.8	86.8	33.0	10.8	54.4	2.6

| | Labor Force (civilian & military) | | | Armed Forces | Civilian Labor Force | Unemployed Both sexes |
	Both sexes	Male	Female	Male	Both sexes	(% of labor force)
1943						
Av.	61.5	87.5	35.7	16.8	53.2	1.7
I	61.0	87.1	35.0	14.0	54.0	2.2
II	61.6	87.3	36.0	16.3	53.5	1.7
III	61.7	87.5	36.1	17.8	52.8	1.7
IV	61.7	88.0	35.6	18.9	52.3	1.1
1944						
Av.	62.4	88.3	36.7	21.0	51.9	1.0
I	62.2	88.4	36.1	19.6	52.4	1.1
II	62.5	88.6	36.6	20.7	52.2	1.1
III	62.2	87.8	36.9	21.7	51.4	1.1
IV	62.6	88.4	37.1	22.0	51.7	0.7
1945						
Av.	61.1	86.7	35.9	20.8	50.8	1.7
I	63.1	88.9	37.6	22.0	52.2	1.1
II	62.3	87.8	37.1	22.3	51.2	1.1
III	60.6	86.3	35.4	22.1	49.6	1.7
IV	58.5	83.9	33.6	17.0	50.1	2.7
1946						
Av.	56.5	82.6	30.9	6.1	53.5	3.7
I	56.7	82.4	31.5	9.8	51.9	3.6
II	56.3	82.6	30.5	6.4	53.1	3.8
III	56.5	82.7	30.9	4.5	54.3	3.6
IV	56.5	82.7	30.8	3.7	54.6	3.9
1947						
Av.	56.7	83.2	30.8	2.7	55.4	3.5
I	56.5	82.9	30.7	3.0	55.0	3.3
II	56.8	83.5	30.6	2.8	55.4	3.6
III	56.8	83.4	30.9	2.4	55.6	3.7
IV	56.7	83.0	31.0	2.4	55.5	3.2
1948						
Av.	57.3	83.6	31.7	2.4	56.1	3.3
I	57.1	83.3	31.5	2.2	56.0	3.2
II	56.9	83.1	31.4	2.2	55.8	3.2
III	57.6	84.0	31.8	2.4	56.4	3.3
IV	57.5	83.8	31.9	2.6	56.2	3.3
1949						
Av.	57.4	83.2	32.1	2.7	56.0	5.5
I	57.5	83.6	32.0	2.8	56.1	4.1
II	57.1	83.3	31.6	2.7	55.7	5.2
III	57.2	83.0	32.0	2.7	55.8	6.0
IV	57.6	83.0	32.9	2.6	56.3	6.5
1950						
Av.	57.4	82.8	32.7	2.6	56.1	4.8
I	57.6	82.9	33.0	2.5	56.3	5.9
II	57.0	82.6	32.1	2.3	55.9	5.0
III	57.1	82.9	32.1	2.3	56.0	4.4
IV	58.0	82.9	33.7	3.4	56.3	3.8
1951						
Av.	58.1	83.5	33.4	5.6	55.4	2.9
I	58.2	83.1	34.1	4.5	56.0	3.2
II	57.6	83.4	32.6	5.5	54.9	2.8
III	58.0	83.9	32.9	6.1	55.0	2.6
IV	58.5	83.7	34.0	6.1	55.5	3.1

Index

Absenteeism, 45
Active armed forces, Germany, 1
Aero engines, 13
Agriculture, 10, 13, 14, 18, 20, 48
Aircraft production, 20
Airfields, building of, 20
Air raids, injuries from, 38
Aliens, 21; in Germany, 16
Allotment, 41
Allowances, 4, 40, 41, 42n, 43
Amusements, 24
Armament factories, 38
Armed forces, 6, 9, 10, 11, 12, 16, 18, 20, 21, 31, 42n
Automobile plants, 50
Auxiliary service, 20

Belgians, 7n; in Germany, 21
Belgium, 45n
Berlin, 48
Birmingham, England, 20
Birthrates, Germany, 2, 39, 40; Great Britain, 39
Blitzkrieg, 10, 11, 12
Boeing Plant, Seattle, 22n
Bombing, 2, 24, 38, 39
Booty, 45
Bottlenecks, 13
Boys at work, Germany, 43
Budget, Bureau of, 12n
Business men, 22, 44

Camps, building of, 20
Canada
    allotments, 42
    allowances, 40, 41, 42
    armed forces, 7, 11, 17, 19, 33, 34, 37, 46, 47
    civilian employment, 17, 19
    earning group, by age-sex, 35, 36, 37
    employed, 7, 17, 19
    females in labor force, 40

Canada, *cont.*
    labor force, 7, 8, 11, 17, 19, 33, 34, 35n, 36, 37, 40, 46
    additions, 41
    peacetime, 39
    peak excess, 34, 35, 37
    population growth, 17, 19, 34, 35, 36
    unemployed, 7, 11, 17, 19
Casualties, from air raids, 38
Catering, 50
Census
    Canada, 7
    Germany, 8, 39, 48
    Great Britain, 7
    United States, 5n, 6, 7, 7n, 49n
Chemicals, manufacture of, 20
Child and home care duties, 4, 40, 41, 45
Children, 3, 6, 40, 43; illegitimate, 41
Civil defense, women in, 20
Civilian auxiliaries, Germany, 38
Civilian employment, 14, 18, 21, 34
Civilian labor force, Germany, 16
Civilian losses, 35n
Civilian nonagricultural industries, 36n
Civilians, exodus from labor force, 4
Civilians, stricken by bombing, 37
Civil servants, Great Britain, 7n
Civil Service Commission, United States, 22
Cleaning, 50
Cline, D. C., 42
Clothes, 20
Coal mining, shortages of labor in, 20
College girls, Germany, 24
Communist, 31
Complex jobs, breaking down, 11
Compulsion, 3, 21, 36n, 43
Congress, 22, 23
Conquered countries, industrial capacity of, 15
Conscription, 13, 20

55

Construction, 10
Contracts, 23
Copeland, Morris A., 36n
Copper, 45n

Day nurseries, Germany, 43
Deaths, battle, 21
Deductions from pay, 42n
Defense demands, location of, 11
Defense orders, 49
Defense production, 13
Deferment, 20, 22, 23
Demand for labor, 11
Demobilization, 47, 48
Dependents, 4, 42, 42n, 43
Depression, 27, 39
Dictatorship, 44
Disabled persons, 6, 26
Disposable income, 41, 42
Domestic help, 7n, 21, 24, 50
Draft, military, 22
Dutch, 7n, 21

Economist, London, 36n
Elderly persons, 3
Emigration, Germany, 2, 37
Employees, 7n, 8, 38
Employers, 1, 18n
Employment, 6, 13, 16, 21, 22, 23, 24, 49
Engineering, 13
Enlisted personnel, 42, 42n
Enumerators, 6
Equivalent adult male, 41
Essential industry, women in, 20
Essential Work Orders, Great Britain, 21
Europe, 8, 44

Fabricated items, 13
Factories, 13n, 32
Farmers, 6, 7n, 50; exempt from draft, 23
Females, 2, 18, 22, 24, 34, 40, 41
Finished articles, 44
Fire watching, Great Britain, 23
Food, Great Britain, 20
Foreigners, in Germany, 1, 2, 12, 15, 16, 24, 45; in Great Britain, 35n
Foremen, Germany, 38
France, 7n, 21, 24, 45n
Frankel, H., 7n

Fuel, Germany, 15
Full mobilization, Germany, before 1939, 39
Furloughs, military, 22

Gainfully occupied; *see* Labor force
Gambling, 6
Gap between need and supply, Great Britain, 20
Germany
 administration, 21
 agriculture, 3, 14, 16, 18, 21, 24, 35n, 39
 allotments, 42
 allowances, 40, 41, 42
 armed forces, 12, 17, 19, 24, 33, 34, 37, 38, 39
 banking, 15, 16, 21
 civilian employment, 1, 15, 17, 19
  labor force, 24, 32, 44
  war losses, 35n, 38
 commerce, 3, 15, 38
 construction, 14, 16
 consumption, 15
 distribution, 15
 domestic service, 3, 15, 18, 24, 32
 employed, 8, 17, 32
 factories, 32
 finance, 3, 15
 fishing, 14
 foreigners in labor force, 32, 33, 35n, 36, 45n
 forestry, 14
 full employment, 39
 gainfully occupied, 8
 government services, 15
 handwork, 15, 16, 21
 home work, 24
 hours, 24, 43
 industry, 3, 18, 24, 32, 44
 insurance, 16, 21
 labor force, 2, 8, 12, 17, 19, 24, 32-4, 35n, 36-41, 48
  active, 35n
  additions, 41
  native, 35n, 36, 43
  peak excess, 34, 35, 37
  wives, 44
  women, 36n, 39, 40

56

Germany, *cont.*
  manpower, 39, 44, 45
  manufacturing, 14, 16
  military
    employment, 17, 19
    losses, 35n, 36
  mining, 14, 16
  mobilization, need for, 44
  parttime work, 43, 44
  population growth, 17, 19, 39
  prisoners-of-war, 35n
  production, 15
  services, 3, 21
  skilled workers, 38
  steel, 44, 45
  trade, 3, 15, 16, 21
  transportation, 3, 15, 24
  unemployed, 5, 12, 17, 19, 24, 32
  work week, 1
Girls in school, 26
Government, 7, 13n, 18, 38
Gowing, M. M., 13n
Grants, 41, 43
Great Britain
  agriculture, 3, 13, 14, 20, 23
  allotments, 42
  allowances, 40-2
  armed forces, 7, 7n, 10, 13, 16, 19, 20, 23, 33, 34, 37, 47
  banking, 13, 15
  beverages, 3
  civilians
    employed, 13, 14, 16, 19
    killed, 7n
    labor force, 32
  clothes, 3
  commerce, 3, 13, 15, 20
  construction, 3, 13, 14, 20, 47
  defense manufacturing, 23
  distribution, 3, 13, 15, 20, 47
  domestic service, 3, 15, 32
  earning groups, age-sex, 35-7
  employed, 16, 32, 36n
  employers, 7n
  females, 35
  finance, 3, 15
  fishing, 14
  food, 3
  forestry, 14

Great Britain, *cont.*
  government services, 13, 15, 20
  industries, 3, 13, 23, 32
  labor force, 6, 10, 16, 19, 32-3, 36, 39, 40, 47
    peacetime, 39
    peak excess, 34-7, 47
  manpower, 6
  manufacturing, 14, 47
  mining, 13, 14, 20, 47
  population, 16, 23n, 34, 35-7
  public utilities, 13, 20
  services, 3, 13, 15, 20, 47
  shipping, 23
  trade, 3, 15
  transportation, 3, 15, 20, 23, 47
  unemployed, 6n, 10, 16, 19, 32
  unemployment insurance, 7, 7n
  war economy, 23n
  women, 36

Hancock, W. K., 13n
Hawaii, 27
High employment, peacetime, 40
Hitler, 21, 24, 27, 37, 39
Homeguard exercises, 23
Home workers, German, 8
Hostilities, expected to be short, 44
Hours, 1, 18, 21
Household, 6, 48n
Housekeeping, 25, 38
Housewives, 3
Housework, 25, 50

Illegal occupations, 6
Illness, 41
Immigration, Germany, 21
Incentives to work, 21, 43
Income, 41, 43
Industrial base, Germany, 45
  disorganization, 48
  division, 14
  employment, 3, 13, 47
Industry, 16, 21, 24
Inmates of institutions, 6, 26
Insurance, 21, 41
Interindustry mobility, 3
International Labour Office, 38n, 44n
Interview technique, 6

Irish, 7n
Italian surrender, 4, 22

Japan, 8, 27

Key industries paralyzed, Germany, 24
   occupations, 49
Kinder, Kueche, Kirche, 39
Korean War, 4, 9, 31, 48, 49, 50
Kriegswirtschaftliche Kräftebilanz, 8
Kulischer, Eugene, M., 38n

Labor
   budgeting, 23
   conscription, 23
   deficit, 18
   drafted, 15
   Germany, 15, 44
   market, 27, 41, 44
   mobility, 24
   reserves, 8, 22
   scarcity, 13, 22, 45n
   supply, 51
   ultimate limit of production, 22
   withdrawal, 24
Labor force, 18
   additions, 4, 40
   concept, 6
   coverage, 6
   depressed, Germany, 5
   enumeration technique, 5n, 27, 48n, 49n
   excess, 9
   increment, 13, 20, 25
   peacetime, 4, 35n, 39
   projected, 7, 49
   proportions, 2
   reserves, 50
   sources, 7
   summer influx, 5n
Laundry, 50
Lester, R. A., 27n
Living standards, 41, 42n
London, 24
Long, C. D., 27n, 32n, 34n, 50n
Losses, German, armed forces, 12, 15, 17n, 35n
Low countries, 27

Machine tools, 13, 45n
Management, Germany, 15
Manhour, 46
Manpower, 7, 18n, 20, 23
Manpower Director, Germany, 43
Manufacturing, 10, 18, 22, 24
Marketable product, 6
Married women, 36n, 44
Means test, for allowances, 43
Men, 65 and older, 7n
Metals, 11, 20
Midland, Great Britain, 24
Migration, 11, 13
Military service, age of, 20
Mining, 10, 18
Mobilization, 5, 20, 21
Monthly Report on the Labor Force, 7n
Moscow defeat, 21
Munitions employments, 13n, 22n, 23, 50

National product, German, foreign contribution to, 45n
Nationals, German, recruiting of, 2, 12, 21
National Service Act, 3, 20, 24
National Socialists, 37, 38
Nazis, 5n, 37, 39, 43, 44
Netherlands, 45n
Newspaper industry, German, 24
Nonagriculture, 39, 46, 50
Nonessential areas, Great Britain, 20
Nonindustrial areas, 13, 23
North Africa, 8
Northwestern areas of Great Britain, 24
Norwegians, 7n
Notestein, Frank, 8n
Nurses, Great Britain, 7n

Occupied Germany, 4 zones, 48
Oil, Germany, 45n
Ordnance factories, 13
Output, rise of, Germany, 16
Overseers, Germany, 38
Overtime, 1, 45-7

Pacific Coast, 22
Painting, 50
Parttime employment, 21, 35n, 45-7
Party Nazi, 15, 38

Patriotism, 13n
Pay grades, 42n
Pearl Harbor, 5, 9, 20, 50
Physicians, 6
Pig iron, 45n
Plumbing, 50
Poland, 6, 10, 12, 38, 38n, 45n
Poles in Germany, 21
Police, 7n, 38
Pomeranian farms, 44
Population changes, 1, 9, 10, 11, 12, 13, 21
Population Index, Princeton, 40n
Population, working age, 1, 16, 21
Preparation for war, Germany, 44
Prices, controlled, Germany, 48
Printing, 24
Priority areas, Great Britain, 20
Prisoners, 7n, 12, 45
Private employers, 7
Production cutback, 21, 23
Productivity, 50
Professional workers, 8
Propaganda, Germany, 43
Public utilities, 10, 18

Railroad travel, Germany, 24
Ration, 42n
Raw materials, 11
Reclassification of idle persons, Germany, 5n
Recruiting, 4, 22, 25
Red Cross, 41
Reemployment, 1, 13, 29
Registrar General, 7n
Registration of women, 44
Reich, 37, 38
Rent, 41
Replacements, lack of, 24
Reserves, 3, 45
Retail trade, 38
Retired persons, 6, 43
Russia, 8, 9, 22

Sample survey, 5n, 48n, 49n
School attendance, 26, 30, 43
Seasonal variation, adjustment for, 9, 11, 52
Selective Service Boards, 23

Self-employed, 1, 7n, 8
Semi-skilled, 11
Service men, 41
Services, 10, 18
Sheffield, 20
Shipbuilding, 13, 20, 32
Shishkin, Boris, 39
Shister, Joseph, 27n
Shoe manufacturing, 20
Shortages, 20
Singer, H. W., 44n
Skilled workers, 11, 24, 50
Soldiers' families, 41
Speer, Albert, 24
Spot shortages, 22
Stalingrad, 4, 44
Statistisches Jahrbuch, 8n
Statistisches Reichsamt, 8
Steel industry, 13, 15
Strategic Bombing Survey, 8, 15, 21n, 45n
Students, 3, 7, 35n
Supply, areas of short, 11, 20
Supply ministries, 20
Surplus labor areas, 24
Survey enumerators, 48n, 49n

Tarasov, Helen, 42
Taxes, 41
Taxes, exemption, Great Britain, 44
Teachers, Great Britain, 7n; Germany, 24
Temporary interviewers, 48n, 49n
Temporary situations, 23
Thirty-eighth parallel, 31
Todt Organization, 38
Total warfare, 18, 37
Trade, distribution, finance, 10, 11
Training, 11
Transfers of labor, compulsory, 13
Transportation, 10, 18, 21
Turnover, 45

Unemployed, 1, 6, 8-12, 18, 27
Unemployment compensation, 6n, 21, 44
United States
   agriculture, 3, 10, 14, 22, 46
   allotments, 42
   allowances, 40-2

United States, *cont.*
  armed forces, 1, 2, 4, 5n, 8, 16, 18, 21, 25-7, 29, 32-4, 37, 47-50, 52-4
  banking, 15
  Bureau of the Census, 28, 30, 34, 46-8
  civilian employment, 1, 5, 5n, 9, 16, 18, 21, 22, 46, 50, 52-4
    labor force, 32, 45, 48, 49, 52-4
  commerce, 15
  construction, 3, 10, 14, 20, 22
  demobilization, 2, 25, 46
  distribution, 3, 10, 11, 15, 20, 22
  domestic services, 3, 15, 22
  earners, wage and salary, 6
  earning groups, age-sex, 35-7
  employed, 3, 6, 16, 18, 22, 27, 32, 33, 45-7, 49, 50-2
  employers, 6
  equivalent workers, 5, 45-7, 50-1
  essential jobs, 2
  extra workers, 34
  females, active, 26
    available for labor force, 30-1
    in housework, 25, 28-31
    in labor force, 27, 30, 31, 34, 36
  finance, 3, 10, 11, 15, 20, 22
  fishing, 14
  forestry, 14
  government, 3, 15, 22
  high employment, 27, 31
  hours, 3, 5, 45-7
  housewives, 6
  houseworkers, 26, 28, 30
  industries, 20, 22, 32
  labor force, 1, 2, 4-9, 16, 18, 22, 25-7, 29, 31-5, 40, 48, 49, 50, 52-4
    additions, 2, 34, 40, 41
    depressed, 4
    excess, 4, 34, 35, 37, 47
    increase, 29, 31, 32
    measurement technique, 1945, 34n
    outflow from, 27
    peacetime, 27, 29, 35n, 48
    postwar comparison, 4
    proportion of, 4, 5n, 27, 31, 34n, 37, 48, 50
    reserves, 4
    shortage, 49
    shrinkage, 4, 27

United States, *cont.*
  labor market, 49
  males, by age, 36
  manpower, 36, 49, 51
  manufacturing, 3, 10, 14, 22
  military draft, 2, 25
    employment, 1, 50
  mining, 3-10, 14, 22
  mobilization, 8, 51
  munitions employment, 22
  new workers, 22, 49
  parttime workers, 6
  population growth, 2, 4, 5n, 16, 25, 26, 32, 34-6, 49, 50
    working age, 4, 5n, 27, 35
  private households, persons living in, 25, 28
  professional services, 3
  public utilities, 10
  seeking jobs, 6, 27, 49
  self-employed, 6
  services, 3, 10, 15, 22, 50
  students, 6, 7
  trade, 3, 10, 11, 15, 20, 22
  transportation, 3, 10, 15, 22
  unemployed, 2, 4-6, 8, 9, 16, 18, 22, 23, 27, 29, 31, 32, 34, 48-50, 52-4
  wages 6
  wives, 6, 7, 25
  women, in defense jobs, 25
    not at work, 26, 27
Universal conscription, 3
Unskilled labor, 13
Upgrading, 11
Urgency lists, 23
U.S.S.R., 4

Vacation, 6, 43
V-E Day, 9, 10, 11, 22, 24, 47
Vehicles, 13, 20
V-J Day, 47

Wachenheim, Hedwig, 42
Wage and salary earners, 1, 21
Wage boosts, 22
Wales, 24
War Cabinet, 20
War industry, 4, 13

War Labor Board, 22
War Manpower Commission, 22, 23
War mobilization, 2
War peak in four countries, 32
War Production Board, 23
War production center, 22
War service grants, 42n
Wehrmacht, 34, 36n
West Coast, 23
Widows, Germany, 41
Wives, 35n

Wolman, Leo, 5n
Women, 2, 7, 15, 16, 20, 21, 24, 35, 38, 41, 43-6, 50
Workers, 13-14, 18n, 20
'Working population,' Great Britain, 7
Work Projects Administration, 5n, 6
Workshops for old men, 43
Workweek, 15, 18, 21, 23, 45, 50
World War I, 1
World War II, 4, 6, 8, 26, 29, 31-4, 36, 37, 40, 45, 49

Recent and Prospective National Bureau Publications

Wesley Clair Mitchell: The Economic Scientist (1952) Arthur F. Burns (ed.)	398 pp.,	$4.00
Conference on Research in Business Finance (1952) Universities-National Bureau Committee for Economic Research	512 pp.,	$6.00
Federal Grants and the Business Cycle (1952) James A. Maxwell	128 pp.,	$2.00
A Study of Moneyflows in the United States (1952) Morris A. Copeland	736 pp.,	$7.50
Commercial Bank Activities in Urban Mortgage Financing (1952) Carl F. Behrens	152 pp.,	$2.50
What Happens during Business Cycles: A Progress Report (1951) Wesley C. Mitchell	422 pp.,	$5.00
Conference on Business Cycles (1951) Universities-National Bureau Committee for Economic Research	448 pp.,	$6.00
The Nature and Tax Treatment of Capital Gains and Losses (1951) Lawrence H. Seltzer	576 pp.,	$7.50
The Transportation Industries, 1889-1946: A Study of Output, Employment, and Productivity (1951) Harold Barger	304 pp.,	$4.00
Deterioration in the Quality of Foreign Bonds Issued in the United States, 1920-1930 (1951) Ilse Mintz	112 pp.,	$2.00
Urban Real Estate Markets: Characteristics and Financing (1951) Ernest M. Fisher	208 pp.,	$3.00
History and Policies of the Home Owners' Loan Corporation (1951) C. Lowell Harriss	224 pp.,	$3.00
Corporate Income Retention, 1915-43 (1951) Sergei P. Dobrovolsky	142 pp.,	$2.50
Shares of Upper Income Groups in Income and Savings (in press) Simon Kuznets		

Studies In Income and Wealth

12	Thirteen papers on national wealth (1950)	608 pp.,	$6.00
13	Ten papers dealing with income distribution by size (1951)	608 pp.,	$6.00
14	Seven papers on wealth (1951)	286 pp.,	$3.50

Technical Paper

7 *Factors Affecting the Demand for Consumer Instalment Sales Credit* (1952) Avram Kisselgoff	$1.50

National Bureau of Economic Research, Inc.
1819 Broadway, New York 23, N. Y.

Trends and Cycles
in
Corporate
Bond Financing

W. BRADDOCK HICKMAN

OCCASIONAL PAPER 37

Financial Research Program

NATIONAL BUREAU OF ECONOMIC RESEARCH, INC.

OFFICERS, 1952

Harry Scherman, *Chairman*
C. C. Balderston, *President*
Percival F. Brundage, *Vice-President*
George B. Roberts, *Treasurer*
W. J. Carson, *Executive Director*

DIRECTORS AT LARGE

Donald R. Belcher, *American Telephone and Telegraph Company*
Oswald W. Knauth, *Beaufort, South Carolina*
Simon Kuznets, *University of Pennsylvania*
H. W. Laidler, *Executive Director, League for Industrial Democracy*
Shepard Morgan, *New York City*
C. Reinold Noyes, *Princeton, New Jersey*
George B. Roberts, *Vice-President, National City Bank*
Beardsley Ruml, *New York City*
Harry Scherman, *Chairman, Book-of-the-Month Club*
George Soule, *Bennington College*
N. I. Stone, *Consulting Economist*
J. Raymond Walsh, *New York City*
Leo Wolman, *Columbia University*
Theodore O. Yntema, *Vice President-Finance, Ford Motor Company*

DIRECTORS BY UNIVERSITY APPOINTMENT

E. Wight Bakke, *Yale*	Gottfried Haberler, *Harvard*
C. C. Balderston, *Pennsylvania*	Clarence Heer, *North Carolina*
Arthur F. Burns, *Columbia*	R. L. Kozelka, *Minnesota*
G. A. Elliott, *Toronto*	Paul M. O'Leary, *Cornell*
Frank W. Fetter, *Northwestern*	T. W. Schultz, *Chicago*
H. M. Groves, *Wisconsin*	Jacob Viner, *Princeton*

DIRECTORS APPOINTED BY OTHER ORGANIZATIONS

Percival F. Brundage, *American Institute of Accountants*
Frederick C. Mills, *American Statistical Association*
S. H. Ruttenberg, *Congress of Industrial Organizations*
Murray Shields, *American Management Association*
Boris Shishkin, *American Federation of Labor*
Donald H. Wallace, *American Economic Association*
Frederick V. Waugh, *American Farm Economic Association*
Harold F. Williamson, *Economic History Association*

RESEARCH STAFF

Arthur F. Burns, *Director of Research*
Geoffrey H. Moore, *Associate Director of Research*

Moses Abramovitz	F. F. Hill
Harold Barger	Thor Hultgren
Morris A. Copeland	Simon Kuznets
Daniel Creamer	Clarence D. Long
David Durand	Ruth P. Mack
Solomon Fabricant	Frederick C. Mills
Milton Friedman	Raymond J. Saulnier
Millard Hastay	Lawrence H. Seltzer
W. Braddock Hickman	George J. Stigler

Leo Wolman

Relation of the Directors to the Work and Publications of the National Bureau of Economic Research

1. The object of the National Bureau of Economic Research is to ascertain and to present to the public important economic facts and their interpretation in a scientific and impartial manner. The Board of Directors is charged with the responsibility of ensuring that the work of the National Bureau is carried on in strict conformity with this object.

2. To this end the Board of Directors shall appoint one or more Directors of Research.

3. The Director or Directors of Research shall submit to the members of the Board, or to its Executive Committee, for their formal adoption, all specific proposals concerning researches to be instituted.

4. No report shall be published until the Director or Directors of Research shall have submitted to the Board a summary drawing attention to the character of the data and their utilization in the report, the nature and treatment of the problems involved, the main conclusions and such other information as in their opinion would serve to determine the suitability of the report for publication in accordance with the principles of the National Bureau.

5. A copy of any manuscript proposed for publication shall also be submitted to each member of the Board. For each manuscript to be so submitted a special committee shall be appointed by the President, or at his designation by the Executive Director, consisting of three Directors selected as nearly as may be one from each general division of the Board. The names of the special manuscript committee shall be stated to each Director when the summary and report described in paragraph (4) are sent to him. It shall be the duty of each member of the committee to read the manuscript. If each member of the special committee signifies his approval within thirty days, the manuscript may be published. If each member of the special committee has not signified his approval within thirty days of the transmittal of the report and manuscript, the Director of Research shall then notify each member of the Board, requesting approval or disapproval of publication, and thirty additional days shall be granted for this purpose. The manuscript shall then not be published unless at least a majority of the entire Board and a two-thirds majority of those members of the Board who shall have voted on the proposal within the time fixed for the receipt of votes on the publication proposed shall have approved.

6. No manuscript may be published, though approved by each member of the special committee, until forty-five days have elapsed from the transmittal of the summary and report. The interval is allowed for the receipt of any memorandum of dissent or reservation, together with a brief statement of his reasons, that any member may wish to express; and such memorandum of dissent or reservation shall be published with the manuscript if he so desires. Publication does not, however, imply that each member of the Board has read the manuscript, or that either members of the Board in general, or of the special committee, have passed upon its validity in every detail.

7. A copy of this resolution shall, unless otherwise determined by the Board, be printed in each copy of every National Bureau book.

(Resolution adopted October 25, 1926 and revised February 6, 1933 and February 24, 1941)

Committee on Research in Finance

In the planning and conduct of its studies in finance the National Bureau benefits from the advice and guidance of its Committee on Research in Finance. The members of the Committee are:

RALPH A. YOUNG, Chairman — *Director, Division of Research and Statistics, Board of Governors of the Federal Reserve System*

RAYMOND J. SAULNIER, Secretary — *Barnard College, Columbia University; Director, Financial Research Program, National Bureau of Economic Research*

BENJAMIN HAGGOTT BECKHART — *Columbia University; Economic Consultant, The Chase National Bank*

ARTHUR F. BURNS — *Columbia University; Director of Research, National Bureau of Economic Research*

WILLIAM J. CARSON — *University of Pennsylvania; Executive Director, National Bureau of Economic Research*

GEORGE W. COLEMAN — *Economist, Mercantile Trust Company*

EDISON H. CRAMER — *Chief, Division of Research and Statistics, Federal Deposit Insurance Corporation*

ERNEST M. FISHER — *Columbia University*

E. A. GOLDENWEISER

F. CYRIL JAMES — *Principal and Vice-Chancellor, McGill University*

WALTER LICHTENSTEIN

WALTER MITCHELL, JR. — *Managing Director, Controllers Institute of America*

SHEPARD MORGAN

WILLIAM I. MYERS — *Dean, College of Agriculture, Cornell University*

JAMES J. O'LEARY — *Director of Investment Research, Life Insurance Association of America*

GEORGE BASSETT ROBERTS — *Vice-President, The National City Bank; Treasurer, National Bureau of Economic Research*

HAROLD V. ROELSE — *Vice-President, Federal Reserve Bank of New York*

CASIMIR A. SIENKIEWICZ — *President, Central-Penn National Bank of Philadelphia*

WOODLIEF THOMAS — *Economic Adviser, Board of Governors of the Federal Reserve System*

DONALD S. THOMPSON — *Vice-President, Federal Reserve Bank of Cleveland*

JOHN H. WILLIAMS — *Graduate School of Public Administration, Harvard University; Economic Adviser, Federal Reserve Bank of New York*

JOHN H. WILLS — *Second Vice-President, Northern Trust Company*

LEO WOLMAN — *Columbia University; Research Staff, National Bureau of Economic Research*

DONALD B. WOODWARD — *Second Vice-President, Mutual Life Insurance Company of New York*

Trends and Cycles in Corporate Bond Financing

W. BRADDOCK HICKMAN

OCCASIONAL PAPER 37

Financial Research Program

NATIONAL BUREAU OF ECONOMIC RESEARCH, INC.

1952

Price: $.75

Copyright, 1952, by National Bureau of Economic Research, Inc.
1819 Broadway, New York 23, N. Y. All rights reserved.
Typography by Oscar Leventhal, Inc.
Printing by John N. Jacobson & Son, Inc.
Library of Congress catalog card number: 52-9767

ACKNOWLEDGMENTS

The study on which this paper is based was conducted under generous grants from the Life Insurance Association of America; the American Life Convention; the Association of Reserve City Bankers; J. Reed Morss, President, Boston Five Cents Savings Bank; the Savings Banks Trust Company of New York; and the Trust Investment Study Committee of the New York State Bankers Association. It was supported, as well, by general funds of the National Bureau of Economic Research. The underlying tabulations, which will be presented in a complete report, were prepared on equipment provided by the International Business Machines Corporation. The New York State Banking Department, the American Bankers Association, and the Life Insurance Investment Research Committee cooperated actively in the work of the project.

The data of the study were largely compiled by the Corporate Bond Project, a Work Projects Administration study sponsored by the Federal Deposit Insurance Corporation, supervised by the National Bureau of Economic Research, and carried on with the cooperation of several public agencies and private investment services.

In the preparation of this paper and throughout the investigation, I have benefited greatly from the advice and encouragement of my fellow economists, both inside and outside the National Bureau. In particular, I wish to thank Donald R. Belcher, Arthur F. Burns, William J. Carson, Lewis N. Dembitz, Solomon Fabricant, Raymond W. Goldsmith, Geoffrey H. Moore, George B. Roberts, Raymond J. Saulnier, Elizabeth T. Simpson, Melville J. Ulmer, Leo Wolman, and members of the National Bureau's Technical Committee on Corporate Bond Research. Acknowledgment is also due to Martha S. Jones and Georgette M. Welscher for aid in the statistical computations, to Ruth W. Harris for the preparation of the charts, and to Mary Phelps for editorial assistance.

W. BRADDOCK HICKMAN

Contents

Trends in Corporate Bond Outstandings	2
Industrial Development	4
Growth in Corporate Size	6
Price Level Changes	8
Corporate Liquidity, Earnings, and Taxes; Capital Market Conditions	8
The Position of Corporate Funded Debt Relative to Total Debt: Elements of Stability and Elements of Change	11
Relations between Bond Offerings and Extinguishments	13
Interest Rates and Bond Financing	16
Cyclical Fluctuations in Corporate Bond Financing	20
Aggregate Default and Settlement Experience on Corporate Bond Investments	25
Appendix: Basic Data for Charts 1, 5, and 7	32

List of Charts

1. Corporate Bond Outstandings by Major Industry Group, and Index of Wholesale Prices, 1880-1951	3
2. Percentage Share of Major Industry Groups in Corporate Bond Outstandings, 1900-1951	5
3. Average Size of Corporate Bond Issues Outstanding, by Major Industry Group, 1900-1944	9
4. Total Debt of the American Economy, and Its Major Components, 1917-51	12
5. Corporate Bonds: Net Changes in Outstandings, New-Money Offerings, and Yields, 1900-1950	17
6. Average Cyclical Patterns for Bonds and Stocks during Cycles in General Business Activity	23
7. Corporate Bond Defaults: Outstandings, New Defaults, and Settlements, 1900-1944	27

WHAT have been the broad trends in the aggregate volume of corporate bonded indebtedness in the United States since 1900? How do present levels compare with those of the past? What shifts have occurred in the major industry and size components of this aggregate and in the position of corporate bonds relative to other types of indebtedness? What are the principal factors influencing the volume of new bonds offered to investors and the volume of old bonds extinguished? In particular, how have these debt series behaved during business cycles and over longer periods? And what implications does their behavior have for our understanding of the relation between interest rates and corporate financing? Finally, what has been the aggregate experience of investors in corporate bonds as reflected in cash interest receipts, in the volume of bonds going to default, and in the time required to settle default situations? This paper is a summary of a larger study that seeks to provide answers to these questions. In its brief compass the discussion is necessarily limited to the bare essentials; detailed analyses and tables will appear in the complete report.[1]

The coverage of our investigation is broadly limited to bonds issued by domestic profit-seeking corporations in the railroad, public utility, and industrial fields, and to the parts of such issues that are held by domestic investors (individuals and financial intermediaries). We exclude bonds issued by the financial and real

[1] The full report, entitled *The Volume of Corporate Bond Financing since 1900*, and now being prepared for publication by the National Bureau, is the first of a series of three related volumes on the corporate bond market. It will present and analyze previously unavailable materials on bond offerings, extinguishments, and outstandings, classified by such major groupings as industry, type of issue, size of issue, and method and purpose of offering. Subsequent monographs will provide detailed breakdowns of the characteristics of the securities included in these aggregates and an analysis of their behavior over selected periods.

estate groups, by government, and by eleemosynary and other non-profit-seeking organizations. Bonds held by government and by the issuing corporation are excluded also, as are domestic bonds payable in a foreign currency.

A corporate bond is a long-term, negotiable debt instrument running between the issuing corporation and the bondholder. The most popular type is a "straight" bond, which has a fixed coupon rate and single maturity date; such issues account for 90 to 95 percent of the total par amount for all types. Bond issues may also mature serially (serial bonds); interest payments may vary in some predetermined way with earnings (income bonds); or the issues may be offered explicitly for the purchase of such equipment as the rolling stock of railroads, street railways, etc. (equipment obligations); but these minor types of issues account in the aggregate for only 5 to 10 percent of the principal amount of bonded debt outstanding.

TRENDS IN CORPORATE BOND OUTSTANDINGS

Our special compilations of data on outstandings cover the period January 1900 – January 1944, and reasonably reliable extrapolations can be made backward to 1880 and forward to the beginning of 1951.[2] By piecing together these data, we find (Chart 1) that outstandings traced out a very simple trend over this seventy-year period. Since rail debt, which is the only part that can be shown before 1900, was such a large proportion of the total in the early years, we infer that the funded debt of all industries moved upward continuously from 1880 to 1895 with the rail debt, and, after a possible dip in the following year, again moved upward to 1900. The chart then shows a continuous increase from $6 billion to a peak of $32 billion at the beginning of 1932. Outstandings then turned downward, and except for a brief reversal in 1938 continued their fall to a trough of $24 billion at the close of World War II. After that they shot upward, reaching an all-time high of about $36 billion at the beginning of 1951.

Over the period 1900-1944, for which our data are complete,

[2] Except as otherwise noted, data on outstandings refer to the situation at the beginning of the year.

CHART 1 — Corporate Bond Outstandings by Major Industry Group, and Index of Wholesale Prices, 1880-1951

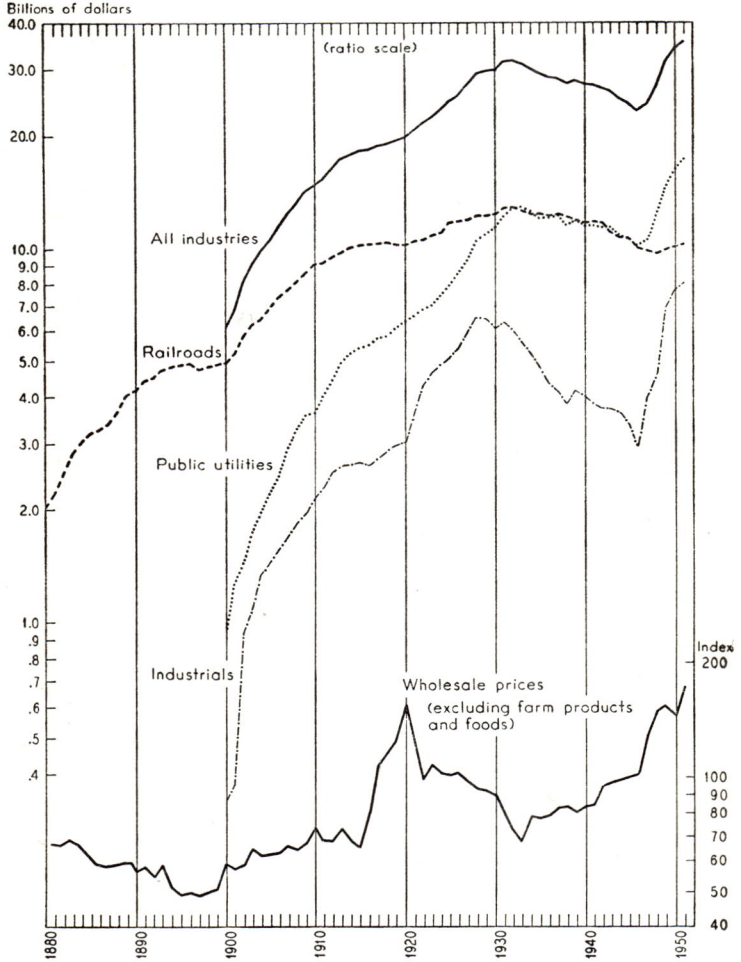

On the vertical scale, equal distances represent equal ratios of change.

Outstandings are January figures, par amount, and include issues of all types (see Table 1, Appendix). The price index, 1913-51, covers wholesale prices of commodities other than farm products and foods (Bureau of Labor Statistics, January prices, 1926 = 100). For earlier years, this index was estimated from movements in the BLS "all commodities" index.

the curve of total outstandings, and of each of the major industry components, described somewhat less than one full swing upward and downward, following patterns of long-term growth roughly similar to those observed in many other economic time series. An initial period of rapid growth was followed successively in each case by gradually retarded growth up to a peak and by mild contraction.

Over shorter periods within the years 1900-1944, bond outstandings behaved somewhat less regularly than this summary statement would indicate. But such movements against the trend as were observed were not sufficiently pronounced to disturb the underlying pattern. It is suggestive that the high growth rates that followed World War II were similar to those observed around the turn of the century. Moreover, these rates already show some signs of tapering off; but this does not necessarily mean, of course, that the past pattern of growth and retardation will be repeated.

Although no systematic attempt was made during the investigation to trace the effects of the many factors governing the broad movements in corporate bond outstandings, it is tempting to speculate about them in this summary statement. Among the factors that have clearly played an important role are: general economic and technological developments in industry; the increasing size of business concerns; fluctuations in the price level; corporate liquidity, earnings, and taxes; and the condition of the capital markets. It may be of interest to comment on each of these at least generally.

Industrial Development

General industrial developments have had a pronounced effect on the capital requirements of business and hence on the volume and composition of outstanding obligations. Generally speaking, industries with relatively heavy fixed-capital requirements (those having high ratios of plant and equipment accounts to total assets) have been the most dependent on long-term financing. For example, during the present century the railroads have had ratios of fixed assets to total assets ranging closely around 90 percent, and ratios of book value of stocks and bonds to total assets ranging closely

CHART 2 — Percentage Share of Major Industry Groups in Corporate Bond Outstandings, 1900-1951

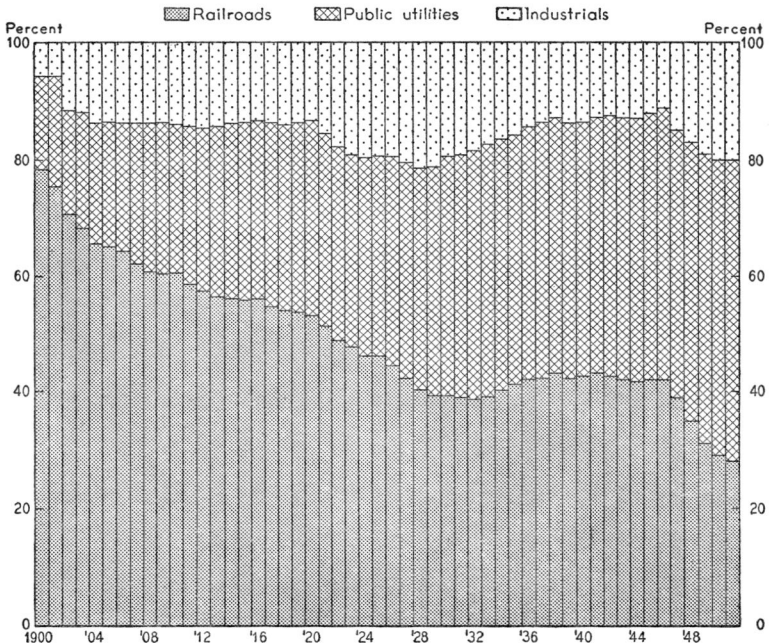

Outstandings include straight issues only, January figures, par amount; from special tabulations to be presented in the book on which this paper is based.

around 70 percent.[3] Comparable ratios for the electric light and power industry are respectively 80 percent and 80 percent; for large manufacturing corporations, 60 percent and 60 percent; and for large trade, 45 percent and 55 percent.[4] Again speaking generally, industries with relatively heavy fixed-capital requirements have been the largest issuers of corporate bonds. Thus, until very

[3] As used here, "book value" includes the par value of bonds and of stocks having par value, and the stated value of no-par stocks. Proprietary reserves and surplus accounts are excluded.

[4] Data for railroads are from *Statistics of Railways;* for the private electric light and power industry from *U.S. Census of Electrical Industries;* for manufacturing and trade from sample data covering 84 large manufacturing corporations and 27 large trade corporations, collected by the National Bureau of Economic Research.

recently the ratio of the long-term debt of the railroads to their total assets has ranged narrowly around 40 percent. Approximately the same figure applies to the electric utilities, but the ratio stands at only about 10 percent for large manufacturing corporations and at about 2 percent for large trade.

It is clear, then, that those developments that have encouraged the expansion of industries with heavy fixed-capital requirements have also encouraged corporate bond financing. The railroads expanded rapidly between 1880 and 1900, and their funded debt expanded apace; at the beginning of the century, as Chart 2 shows, rail bonds accounted for nearly 80 percent of the total of all straight corporate bonds outstanding. By then the railroads were largely "in being," so that rail debt subsequently grew much less rapidly than that of the other industry groups, and now (in 1951) it accounts for only about one-quarter of total outstandings.

At the beginning of the century, public utilities (mostly street railways at that time) accounted for 16 percent of outstanding bonds, industrials making up but 5 percent. Like the rails, the public utilities are heavy users of fixed capital. Along with rapid technological developments in the electric light and power industry, and the expansion of street railway and telephone and telegraph systems, went an increasing use of the corporate bond as a device for capital financing. These developments were so rapid that public utility outstandings expanded over tenfold between 1900 and 1932, while for rails the increase was only twofold. And though public utility debt contracted slightly more rapidly than rail debt from then until the close of World War II, the postwar expansion was much greater. From 16 percent of total outstandings at the beginning of the century, the share of public utility bonds in corporate bonded debt has increased to more than 50 percent, the remainder being almost equally divided between rails and industrials.

Growth in Corporate Size

The influence of growth in the size of corporations on outstandings is somewhat more difficult to trace statistically, principally because comprehensive data on size of firms and their indebtedness are not available for most of the period studied. Sample data for large and small manufacturing concerns, however, collected by the National Bureau, suggest the effect of increasing size. During 1926-35 the large concerns (those with total assets exceeding $10 million) had a ratio of aggregate funded debt to aggregate total assets of about 10 percent, while for the small concerns (with assets of less than $250,000) the ratio was about 5 percent, so that an increase in average size seems to encourage the wider use of bond financing. Doubtless this is due in good part to the fact that large corporations generally have relatively heavier fixed-capital requirements than small concerns, and freer access to the organized securities markets.

Besides exerting a stimulating effect on outstandings, the growth in the size of corporations issuing bonds has brought about a rise in the average size of issue (Chart 3). Between 1900 and 1944 the average size of straight issues for the combined industries increased from $2.3 million to $8.5 million. Rail issues increased at an almost uniform rate over this period from an average size of $3.0 million at the beginning to $11.7 million at the end. The average utility issue ranged narrowly between $1.0 million and $1.5 million during the first two decades of the century but increased rapidly thereafter until it stood at $8.1 million by 1944. Industrial issues had a somewhat more checkered history, with no systematic tendency for their size to increase until about 1940.

So far as we can determine, the principal factor underlying the rise in average size of issue was not simply a rise in the size of the productive unit per se but an increase in average size of enterprise through corporate consolidation. The effects of consolidation are most easily traced in the railroad field, where the funded debt of the merged roads was systematically refunded into large "blanket mortgage" issues, and in the public utility field in cases where large issues of holding companies replaced small issues of operating companies. The average size of industrial issues rose abruptly between 1900 and 1904 because of the formation of the giant trusts, many of which were financed largely by bond issues. When the trusts were dissolved, on the other hand, the large issues were exchanged for stocks and bonds of the operating companies, with the result that the average size of industrial issues shrank by 50 percent between 1904 and 1912.

7

Price Level Changes

In addition to their many other effects, prices have two direct effects on bond financing. Generally speaking, the higher the price level at the time of financing, the greater will be the volume of financing required by a given firm. Second, the higher the level of current prices, the lower the burden of past financing. No systematic attempt was made to eliminate these price influences from the series utilized in our investigation; certain technical problems, such as the selection of the correct price index and the complexity of an appropriate weighting system, make this unfeasible. However, an examination of the index of wholesale prices as given in Chart 1 shows that unadjusted dollar figures may be grossly misleading. For example, the dollar volume of corporate funded debt increased threefold between 1900 and 1920, but debt in real terms was about the same at the end of the period as it had been at the beginning. There were, of course, important changes within the period: debt in terms both of current and of constant dollars more than doubled by 1914; by 1920, though the current figures showed a further increase, debt in constant dollars had fallen back to its 1900 level. From 1920 until 1932 debt in current dollars increased by only 60 percent, but the increase in terms of constant dollars was much greater—250 percent—because of declines in the price level at the beginning and end of the period. Because of the rise in the price level after 1932, the contraction in constant dollar debt through the end of World War II was even sharper than in the current dollar figures. It is particularly suggestive that, notwithstanding the abrupt run-up in the dollar volume of outstandings after World War II, the deflated total in 1951 was about equal to that for such years as 1946, 1923, and 1910, and was less than half of the deflated dollar volume at the peak year, 1932.

Corporate Liquidity, Earnings, and Taxes
Capital Market Conditions

Along with other factors corporate earnings, corporate cash balances, tax considerations, and the condition of the equity market have had an important influence on corporate bond outstandings.

CHART 3 — Average Size of Corporate Bond Issues
Outstanding, by Major Industry Group, 1900-1944

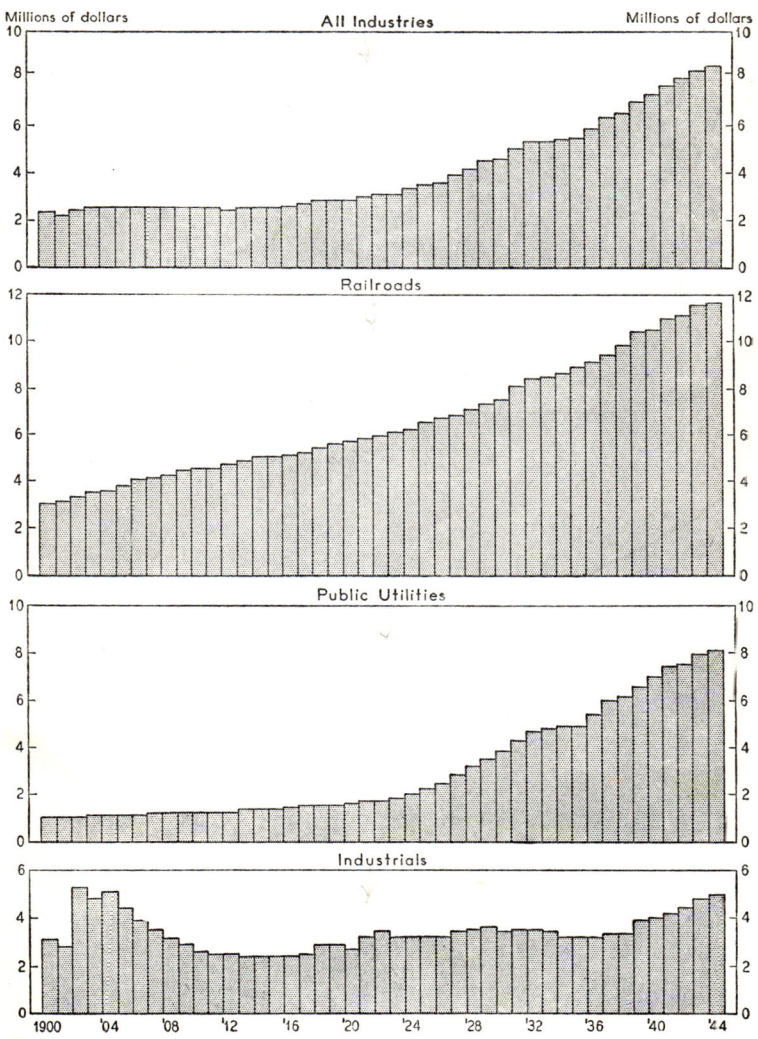

Data are January figures, par amount, and include straight issues only; from special tabulations to be presented in the book on which this paper is based.

Throughout most of the period of secular expansion 1900-1932, cash balances appear to have been drained off by expanding inventories and trade credit, so that corporations necessarily resorted to the banking system for short-term funds and to the stock and bond markets for fixed-capital requirements. During the thirties the situation was reversed. In the industrial field, and to some extent among utilities as well, inventories and trade credit contracted, while capital programs were deferred; thus cash balances partly were used to repay debt obligations, and outstandings of all maturities declined.[5] At the same time, corporations hampered by comparatively heavy fixed charges and low cash throw-off from operations, for example many railroads and street railways, were unable to meet payments on their outstanding bonds. Many of these obligations were later settled by part payment in stock or by write-downs, which furthered the decline in bond outstandings.

Throughout World War II the net cash receipts of railroads expanded markedly, and again many railroads were able to retire debt. In other fields, expanding cash requirements induced by the war effort were met partly out of swollen cash balances inherited from the thirties, and partly through federal advances and prepayments to war contractors, deferral of tax liabilities, and increased retained earnings. When the enormous capital expansion programs got under way at the close of the war, the wartime sources proved inadequate, and corporations turned again to the capital markets. Small and medium-sized corporations had recourse to the banking system; large corporations financed themselves principally by direct placements of bond issues with financial intermediaries, thus causing bond outstandings to rise abruptly. The rise in corporate tax rates and the deductibility of interest charges in arriving at taxable income, the growing institutionalization of savings, the upward surge of commodity prices, and the relatively low level of stock prices as compared with bonds, all served to encourage bond and discourage stock financing during the postwar period.

---

[5] For a discussion of the banking side of this story, see Neil H. Jacoby and Raymond J. Saulnier, *Business Finance and Banking* (National Bureau of Economic Research, Financial Research Program, 1947) pp. 10-13.

THE POSITION OF CORPORATE FUNDED DEBT RELATIVE TO TOTAL DEBT: ELEMENTS OF STABILITY AND ELEMENTS OF CHANGE

Two things stand out clearly when one examines the position of corporate bonds relative to other types of debt (Chart 4). The first is the stability in the composition of private debt; the second is the enormous rise in the ratio of public to private debt.

These observations are based on a comparison of our data with net debt estimates of the Department of Commerce. On the chart, total corporate debt is broken down into bonds and "other corporate debt," the latter covering short-term debt and such unfunded long-term items as direct mortgage loans, receivers' certificates, term loans, and other long-term notes to banks.[6] As the chart indicates, bonds and other corporate debt have moved similarly since 1917, the latter being slightly more volatile principally because of variations in short-term debt. With minor exceptions, the funded debt of railroad, public utility, and industrial corporations has usually accounted for about two-thirds of corporate long-term debt (not shown separately on the chart), and the latter has constituted a similar proportion of total corporate debt.

Rough stability is also exhibited in the relationship between corporate and private noncorporate debt. (In the private noncorporate category are included the debt of unincorporated business units, real estate mortgage debt of individuals, and consumer debt.) Before 1931 these two components of private debt were approximately equal, but from then until the close of World War II noncorporate debt was lower. In the postwar period this relationship was reversed, mainly because of the sharp rise in residential mortgages. Between the beginning of 1946 and the beginning of 1951, private noncorporate debt increased by 98 percent, corporate short-term debt by 73 percent, total corporate debt by 59 percent, and corporate bonds by only 52 percent.

In contrast with the relative stability of the various components

---

[6] The Department of Commerce estimates include, and our bond estimates exclude, the debt of financial and real estate corporations. Hence the difference — other corporate debt — covers, besides the items listed, an undetermined amount of bonds of the financial and real estate groups.

11

CHART 4 — Total Debt of the American Economy, and Its Major Components, 1917-51

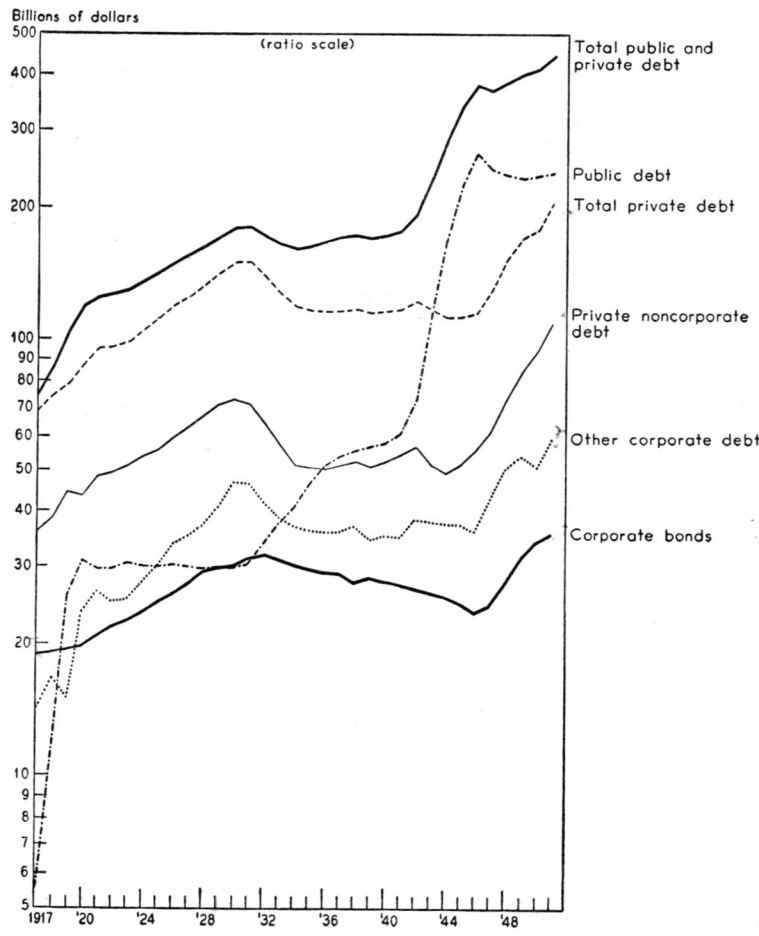

On the vertical scale, equal distances represent equal ratios of change.

All series other than corporate bonds are U. S. Department of Commerce estimates of net public and private debt after adjustment to exclude corporate reserves for taxes, dividends, etc. (*Survey of Current Business*, September 1945, p. 12, October 1950, pp. 9-15, and September 1951, pp. 20-24).

Corporate bonds are par amount of outstandings, January figures, including issues of all types (see Table 1, Appendix).

For note on "other corporate debt" see text footnote 6.

of private debt in most years, a marked shrinkage of private as against public debt characterizes the period covered by Chart 4. In 1917, corporate debt accounted for about 44 percent of total debt (public and private), and private noncorporate debt for about 48 percent, so that the private components together accounted for about 92 percent, and public debt for only 8 percent. Thereafter, except for a minor reversal in the twenties, the share of the public sector in total debt moved gradually upward until it stood at 34 percent just before World War II. In the years of heavy war financing by the federal government the share of the public sector increased much further, reaching its high point, 70 percent of total debt, at the close of the war. Since then a pronounced expansion in the dollar volume of private debt and a moderate contraction in public debt have lowered the share of public debt to 54 percent of the total (at the beginning of 1951).

The position of corporate bonds has also changed drastically. We estimate that they accounted for about 25 percent of total debt in the years immediately preceding World War I and for only 6 percent at the close of World War II. Since then, their share, like the shares of the other components of private debt, has expanded slightly. At the beginning of 1951 they accounted for about 8 percent of total debt.

RELATIONS BETWEEN BOND OFFERINGS AND EXTINGUISHMENTS

The volume of funded debt outstanding at any moment measures on the one hand the total indebtedness of business corporations arising from their past offerings of corporate bonds (less repayments), and on the other hand the volume of past savings held in this form by the investing public. To interpret the behavior of these "stock" figures, we must study the "flows" by which they are generated.

For this purpose the net and gross flows into and out of the "stock" of bond outstandings have been measured at various levels. Our basic gross estimates are monthly and annual series of total offerings (including bonds offered both for new-money purposes and for refunding old bonds), and of total extinguishments (including both bonds actually extinguished in an economic sense and those refunded into new bonds).[7] The difference is the net change in outstandings, which, when added to the volume of bonds outstanding at the beginning of a period, generates the series on outstandings described in the preceding section. Separate estimates of the volume of refundings (old bonds refunded into new bonds) enable us to transform the two gross flow series into series on new-money offerings (total offerings less refundings) and on net repayments (total extinguishments less refundings). All of these series are measured in terms of par amounts (the principal amount promised by the obligor at maturity); in addition, three cash series are utilized. We have measured the gross cash proceeds obtained by business corporations from the sales of their bonds, their gross cash payments at extinguishment, and the difference between these, or net cash receipts of corporations from sales of bonds.

During the period 1900-1944, for which we have full information, the total par amount of straight bonds offered to (and purchased by) the investing public aggregated $72 billion, while total extinguishments of straight bonds aggregated $55 billion. Thus the net change in outstandings was only $17 billion. Refundings accounted for $32 billion of total offerings or extinguishments; it follows that only $40 billion or 55 percent of total offerings was for new-money purposes, and that only $23 billion or 41 percent of the total volume of bonds extinguished was actually repaid without refunding.

During the years 1900-1944 the gross amount of cash received by business corporations from the sale of bonds was $60 billion, or 84 percent of the par amount of total offerings. The remaining 16 percent was accounted for principally by bonds offered in direct exchange for old bonds. On the other side of the ledger, the gross amount of cash paid out by business corporations at extinguishment was $40 billion, or 73 percent of the par amount of total

[7] "Total extinguishments" include bonds retired through maturity, call, conversion, exchange, payment of bondholders after liquidation, or a change in the contract not provided for in the original indenture, such as an extension of the maturity of the issue or a change in the coupon rate. Extinguished bonds are said to be "refunded" to the extent that they are replaced by new bonds; all other extinguished bonds are said to be "repaid."

extinguishments. The remaining 27 percent was accounted for largely by direct exchange of old bonds for new bonds. It follows that the net cash realized by business corporations from sale of bonds was about $20 billion, as compared with a net change in outstandings of $17 billion; bonds were in effect "sold" at approximately a 20 percent premium over the amounts repaid to investors. We find, however, that in most years the net cash flow corresponds closely to the net change in outstandings. We may therefore focus attention largely on the behavior of the net change in outstandings, for which our estimates are most complete, with reasonable assurance that the corresponding cash flows are moving in the same direction.

Our analysis of the interrelationships among the various bond series yields some pertinent information on a practical matter, that of the selection of an appropriate series to be used as an indicator of the net volume of bond financing. In many credit markets, namely those where old loans run off rather smoothly and the volume of refunding activities is not large, a series on new credit granted (analogous to our total offerings) is a reliable index of net credit change. The volume of refunding activity in the bond market, however, is large, and bond offerings statistics must be interpreted with caution. In 1936, for example, total offerings reached unusually high levels, but the proceeds of nearly all of these offerings were used simply to refund outstanding issues. Since repayments exceeded new-money offerings, outstandings actually declined. In 1918 the reverse situation obtained: total offerings were held to a low level by the Capital Issues Committee, but new-money offerings exceeded repayments, so that the volume of outstandings actually rose.

Clearly the best measure of the impact of bond financing on the economy is either the net change in outstandings or the closely related series on net cash flow. Unfortunately, our data for these series terminate at the end of 1943, and estimates for later years are not yet available.[8] Our analysis of new-money offerings, which measures the gross volume of bonds offered for new-money pur-

[8] Estimates of net cash flow are being prepared by the Securities and Exchange Commission but have not yet been released for general use.

poses, shows that this series is rather highly correlated with the net change in outstandings. During the period studied, about five-eighths of the year-to-year variation in the net change in outstandings can be imputed to changes in new-money offerings and only about three-eighths to repayments. To put it differently, new-money offerings moved in the same direction as the net change in 33 of the 43 years for which our data can register the movements. It follows that a series on new-money offerings, such as that currently prepared by the *Commercial and Financial Chronicle,* may be of use as a rough indicator of the direction of change in outstandings until more precise statistics become available.

INTEREST RATES AND BOND FINANCING

The interrelated statistics developed in this study should prove useful in the analysis of the relationships between interest rates and bond financing. A preliminary examination of these matters, which is all that can be undertaken here, will suffice to show that the relationships are complicated, and to indicate some promising leads for further investigation.

Some of the basic data are presented in Chart 5, where high-grade bond yields are compared with the net changes in outstandings and with the closely related series on gross new-money offerings. In interpretation of this chart it is desirable to distinguish the long-run drifts in the series from the shorter ups and downs. At this point we shall concern ourselves mainly with the former; in the next section we take a look at the short-run movements.

To the extent that bond yields (the cost of long-term money) are effective regulators of the demand for bond financing, the higher the yield, the lower will be the net change in outstandings; and conversely, the lower the yield, the higher will be the net change in outstandings. The chart shows that between 1900 and 1920 the trend in bond yields was upward while that of both new-money offerings and the net changes in outstandings was on the whole downward. During 1920-32 bond yields moved sharply downward and then leveled off (rising sharply in 1931-32), while new-money offerings and net changes in outstandings first rose rapidly and then fell. From 1932 to 1945 bond yields declined

CHART 5 — Corporate Bonds: Net Changes in Outstandings, New-Money Offerings, and Yields, 1900-1950

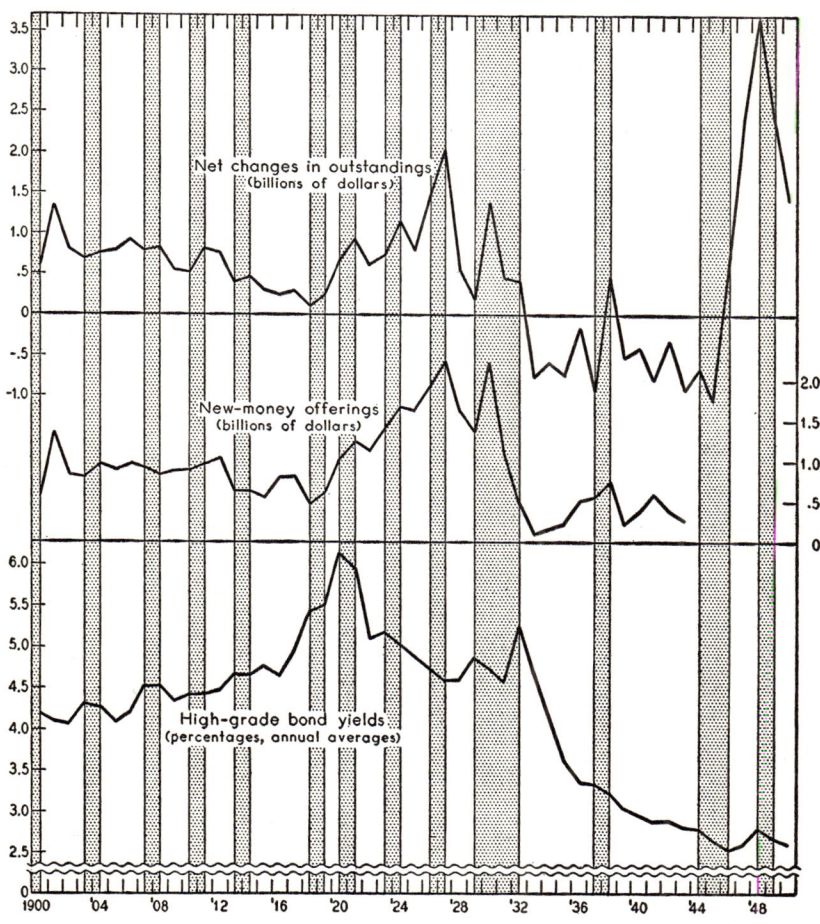

Figures are for all industries combined (see Table 2, Appendix). The series of net changes in outstandings and for new-money offerings include straight bonds only, par amount. Yield series is a weighted average of Standard and Poor's Corporation high-grade railroad, public utility, and industrial bond yields, with National Bureau estimates of outstandings as weights.

Shaded areas, representing contractions in general business activity, and white areas, representing expansions, are from Arthur F. Burns and Wesley C. Mitchell, *Measuring Business Cycles* (National Bureau of Economic Research, 1946), p. 78.

almost continuously, while new-money offerings and net changes rose during 1933-38 and then declined irregularly. After World War II, yields moved moderately upward through 1948 and downward through 1950, while over the same years the net changes rose and fell enormously.

Although some of these movements suggest that interest rates operated to restrict the demand for long-term money, it is also true that corporations borrowed most in the twenties when interest rates were above average levels, and less in earlier and later periods when interest rates were lower. For the period 1900-1950 as a whole, it is evident that the relation between interest rates and bond financing was affected significantly by other strategic forces influencing the demand for long-term money. For example, in the period 1900-1920 stock prices were generally higher than they had been at most times in the late nineteenth century, so that the situation was conducive to stock rather than bond financing. Again, during World War I the bond market was controlled and this reinforced the effect of the rise in interest rates during the war. When control was lifted, bond yields rose rapidly, yet the decline in stock financing after 1919 induced a substantial advance in bond financing. During the twenties the upward trend in business activity, no doubt reinforced by the decline in bond yields, stimulated bond financing until 1927; but in 1927-29, while business activity continued upward, bond financing fell off abruptly as interest rates stiffened and stock financing boomed. In the depressed thirties, despite the low level of interest rates and of stock financing, bond financing was at an extremely low ebb. Finally, in the postwar years the upward trend of business activity, a corporate tax structure favoring bonds rather than stocks, and a relatively unfavorable market for new stock financing all contributed to the boom in bond financing.

A full-dress analysis of all factors affecting bond financing would carry us well beyond the scope of this paper. For the present we conclude simply that the observed long-run movements in bond yields were not in themselves sufficient to explain satisfactorily the observed movements in bond financing. This, of course, does not mean that bond yields play no role in determining the demand for long-term money, nor does it establish that associated changes in money rates in other markets, or credit conditions in general, may not have far-reaching effects. Moreover, even if bond financing should, upon detailed investigation, prove to have been relatively insensitive to the rather moderate changes in bond yields that have occurred in the past, the possibility that large and rapid movements might have more pronounced effects should not be overlooked.

Data to be presented in the volume on which this paper is based indicate that a secular decline in interest rates may, in the long run, have a pronounced effect on bond financing. As interest rates decline, bonds rising above call price are successively refunded into lower yielding obligations. It follows that a secular decline in interest rates, such as occurred in the thirties, will ultimately lower the interest burden on debtor corporations, thus tending to increase profit margins and to encourage general corporate expansion. However, the process of refunding an appreciable portion of outstanding debt is a time-consuming one. We find, for example, that the impact of the downward revision of interest rates in the thirties was not fully felt until the postwar period of credit inflation.

Another implication of a secular decline in interest rates is that the associated reduction in debt burden may occur most promptly and be greatest for firms having the most favorable earnings records and prospects. In the late thirties, for instance, firms in the industrial and utility groups reduced their interest costs considerably while the railroads, partly because of their low credit standing and partly because many of their bonds were noncallable, effected only a slight reduction.

Finally, the results of a secular decline in interest rates must also be judged from the point of view of the investor. The downward adjustment of interest rates in the thirties and early forties reduced the burden of corporate funded debt, as measured by the ratio between interest actually paid and outstandings, from 4.6 percent in 1932 to 3.7 percent in 1943. This decline of nearly 20 percent in interest costs, while desirable from the point of view of the debtor corporation, represented an equal decline in the income received by corporate bond investors.

These findings contribute something to our understanding of the influence of the long-term rate of interest on the net flow of funds to industry through the bond market, and suggest some of the difficulties with monetary theories that posit a uniform and simple causal relationship between bond yields and bond financing. The relationship so far as it is observable in our data appears neither very simple nor very stable. Further evidence to this effect will be developed in the next section.

CYCLICAL FLUCTUATIONS IN CORPORATE BOND FINANCING

The series on corporate bond outstandings, although influenced by the business cycle, is dominated by trend movements. The business cycle affects more strongly the net change in outstandings and the related series on offerings and extinguishments.

Total offerings of corporate bonds and each of the two component series — bonds offered to refund other bonds, and bonds offered to raise new money — exhibit negative conformity to the business cycle. This means that as the pace of general business activity quickens, the volume of bonds offered in the market typically falls; contrariwise, as the pace of general business activity slackens, the volume of bonds offered typically rises. The same behavior characterizes the gross cash proceeds obtained by corporations from sale of bonds. On the other hand, total bond extinguishments, bond repayments (total extinguishments less refundings), and gross cash payments by corporations at extinguishment all show the reverse pattern of behavior. Typically they are positively conforming series, rising during business expansions and falling during business contractions.

The cyclical behavior of the net change in outstandings (which, as we have seen, may be interpreted either as the difference between total offerings and extinguishments or as the difference between new-money offerings and repayments) is governed by the behavior of its components. During business cycle expansions, offerings usually fall while extinguishments rise, so that the net changes in outstandings fall. Conversely, during business cycle contractions, offerings rise while extinguishments fall, so that the net changes in outstandings rise. The average cyclical pattern of the net change in outstandings is exhibited in Chart 6.[9] Roughly the same pattern characterizes the net cash flow to the corporate sector of the economy from sale of corporate bonds. Thus, both net cash receipts and net par amount of bond financing are inverted with respect to the pace of general business activity.

These findings throw new light upon the familiar theory that "credit," in a generic sense, plays a dominant role in the business cycle. Clearly a distinction needs to be drawn between the various types of credit. Many types of financing — for example short-term and stock financing — appear to behave in the way theory would indicate; but bond financing runs a contrary course to other types and thus acts, so to speak, as a stabilizing force.

Some idea of the stabilizing role of the bond market during business cycles may be gained by comparing turning points in the bond and stock series with turning points in general business cycles. If we take a stand at the point in the general business cycle at which stock offerings turn upward, the financial process typically appears to unfold as follows. Soon after the upturn in stock offerings and while general business activity is still falling, the net changes in bond outstandings turn downward. The immediate cause is a rise in extinguishments, possibly induced by the repayment of some funded debt from the proceeds of stock offerings. Since certain corporations are still financing their capital programs via the bond market at this time, bond offerings continue to rise through early business expansion. As stock prices become increasingly attractive, corporations turn from bond to stock financing; bond offerings turn downward; and the net changes in bond outstandings continue to fall. These movements persist until a late stage in business expansion, when stock offerings and stock prices fall. In the next stage, proceeds from the stock market are no longer obtainable for the retirement of bonds; bond extinguishments turn downward; and the net volume of bond financing begins to rise. Bond offerings

[9] For a description of the derivation of such patterns, see Arthur F. Burns and Wesley C. Mitchell, *Measuring Business Cycles* (National Bureau of Economic Research, 1946). Essentially the method consists in removing the seasonal from the series, calculating the relative standing of the series at nine stages within each business cycle, and striking an average of the relative standings at each stage over all cycles covered by the series.

continue to fall, however, since the bond market moves sympathetically with the stock market at this point. Soon after the business peak, the bond market stabilizes, and bond offerings turn upward, thus reinforcing the rise of the net changes in outstandings. These movements continue until late in business contraction, when the stock market recovers. The entire process is then re-enacted during the next business cycle.

It will be observed from the preceding discussion that the stock market complements the bond market over business cycles. In our opinion, the strategic variable governing the relative volume of financing in these two markets is either the ratio of stock to bond prices or the level of stock prices alone. A comparison of the relevant lines on Chart 6 will show these relationships: When the ratio of stock to bond prices moves upward from one cycle stage to the next, the ratio of bond financing to stock offerings usually moves downward. And conversely, when the ratio of stock to bond prices moves downward, the ratio of bond financing to stock offerings moves upward. This finding, which is amply borne out by the evidence, may be explained on the basis of the differential costs of financing in the two markets. The significant point is that bond prices alone (or bond yields alone) appear to play a relatively minor role in this story. Indeed, during the cycle, corporations frequently borrow more heavily when bond yields are high than when bond yields are low. As the chart shows, bond prices and the net changes in outstandings move in the same direction during parts of the cycle, and in the opposite direction during others. Detailed study of monthly data reveals that the timing relationships can be viewed in either of two ways: (1) The net changes consistently lead the corresponding turns in bond prices by fairly long intervals; or (2) the net changes lag behind the opposite turns in bond prices, also by fairly long intervals. These complex timing relationships cannot be adequately explained, we believe, by any simple theory of the response of bond financing to bond yields, or without reference to the dominating influence of the stock market. In our view it is necessary to substitute a theory of differential money costs for a bond yield theory in order to account for the cyclical behavior of the bond market.

CHART 6 — Average Cyclical Patterns for Bonds and Stocks during Cycles in General Business Activity

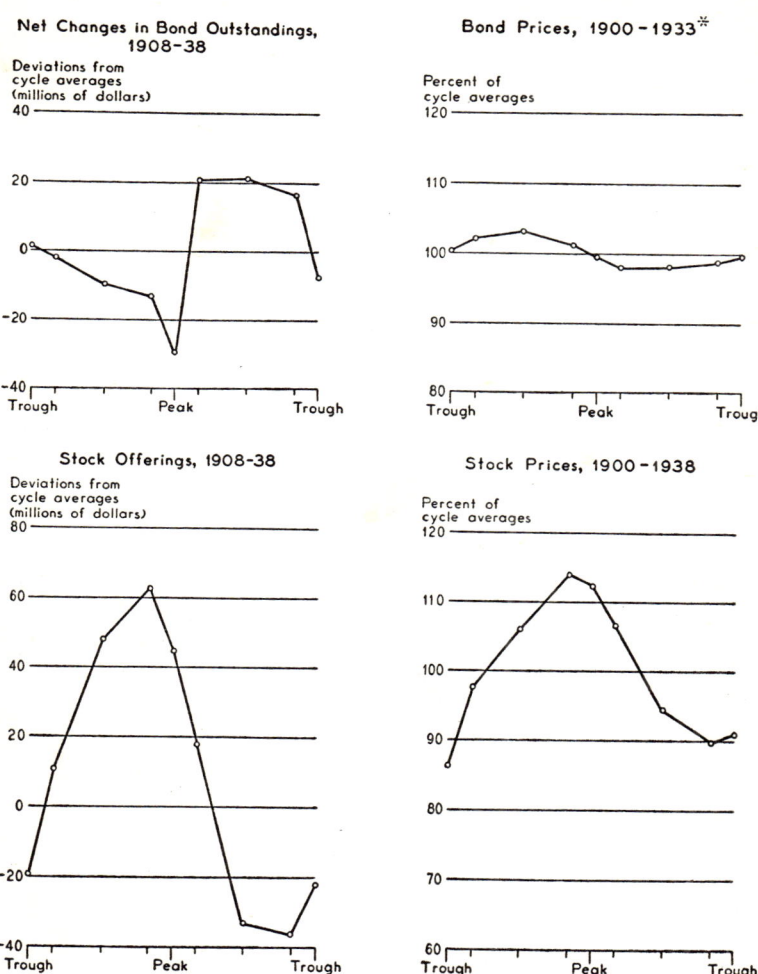

*For bond prices, the last two points in the pattern cover 1900-1927 adjusted to the level of the preceding point.

Index of common stock prices from Alfred Cowles 3rd and Associates, *Common-Stock Indexes* (Bloomington, Indiana, 1939); bond prices from inverted index of yields of high-grade corporate and municipal bonds, Standard and Poor's Corporation; stock offerings (including those for refunding purposes) United States, Canadian, and foreign from *Journal of Commerce*; net changes in bond outstandings from monthly data to be presented in the book on which this paper is based.

Much empirical research remains to be done before we can obtain a well-rounded picture of the behavior of money and credit during business cycles.[10] What, for example, happens to bank credit and short-term interest rates in each cycle stage, and what is the relationship of these factors to funded debt and equity funds? How are these various credit series influenced by the changing cash requirements of business corporations over the cycle? One may conjecture that as business expands, cash is absorbed increasingly into inventories and trade credit; that corporations replenish their depleted cash accounts through the banking system and the stock market; and that surplus funds obtained from these sources are used to retire funded debt. During business contractions, on the other hand, the stock market ceases to be an attractive source of funds; banks allow marginal loans to run off; and the gap is partially filled through the liquidation of inventories and trade credit and the flotation of bonds.

The foregoing analysis describes the typical behavior of bond financing during the cycles of the period 1900-1938. An important exception, however, occurred after the stock market collapse of 1929. At first the net volume of bond financing increased in the usual way, but in late 1931 the bond market broke badly as the result of a tightening of the money markets and a general deterioration of credit. The bond market therefore could not perform its typical contracyclic function at the business trough of 1932. During the next cycle, 1932-38, and on through the wartime cycle, 1938-46, bond financing again followed its typical pattern, moving downward during business expansions and upward during business contractions. During the following transitional cycle, 1946-49, however, the series again behaved atypically. Indeed, in that cycle the net volume of bond financing reached an all-time high in 1948 at the crest of the business expansion. The postwar experience raises important questions as to the applicability of the earlier relation-

---

[10] A contribution in this direction has recently been made by Ilse Mintz in *Deterioration in the Quality of Foreign Bonds Issued in the United States, 1920-1930* (National Bureau of Economic Research, 1951). Mrs. Mintz observed a complementary relation between flotations of foreign bonds and of domestic stocks in the cycles of the twenties.

ships to the economy of the future. Rising commodity prices and taxes, and the relatively low level of stock prices, we have seen, have all encouraged bond and discouraged stock financing since the war. Similar changes have affected the relationship between stock and bond financing in the past and may well affect it in the future.

AGGREGATE DEFAULT AND SETTLEMENT EXPERIENCE ON CORPORATE BOND INVESTMENTS

A corporate bond default is defined as the failure to pay principal or interest promptly when due. Comprehensive data on corporate bond defaults in major industry and size groups will be presented in the volume on which this paper is based. The series are of the interrelated "stock-flow" type used generally throughout the investigation. They provide annual estimates of the volume of bonds outstanding in default, of new defaults, of default settlements (bonds previously in default that were restored to good standing, extinguished through reorganization, etc.), and of the net change in outstanding defaults (new defaults less default settlements). Ancillary estimates are also provided for special categories of new defaults and settlements. More detailed breakdowns by minor industry groups and other classifications will be presented in a later monograph. Chart 7 gives the picture for all industries combined, and the discussion will bring in some of the differences between major industry groups.

Between 1900 and the onset of the Great Depression the aggregate volume of corporate bonds outstanding in default was quite small, both in absolute and in relative terms. During this period the average par amount of bonds outstanding in default was only $0.4 billion or 2.7 percent of total outstandings. With the financial difficulties of the early thirties, outstanding defaults climbed rapidly to a peak level in 1936 of about $4 billion or 15 percent of outstandings. Although there was a mild improvement in 1936-37, the situation again deteriorated and the amount outstanding in default in 1940 was about as large as in 1936. After that, default settlements generally exceeded new defaults, so that the volume of outstanding defaults declined.

Since rail bonds dominated the market for corporate bonds over most of the first three decades of this century, one would expect them to occupy a predominant position in corporate bond defaults. Actually, they accounted for less than half of the total volume of bonds outstanding in default in the majority of the years from 1900 to 1933. The proportion of rail bonds in default during this period was usually well below that of the other major industry groups, rarely exceeding 4 or 5 percent. Between 1931 and 1940 the status of rail bonds deteriorated rapidly, the percentage in default climbing from 0.5 to 27.9. Moreover, very few of the rail defaults had been settled by the end of the period covered by our records: at the beginning of 1944, 26 percent of rail bonds were still in default. The volume of utility bonds outstanding in default was fairly heavy in the early twenties and again in the mid-thirties (about 8 percent and 7 percent respectively), largely because of the poor performance of street railways in these years. With industrial bonds the greatest difficulties came in the early thirties, the volume of defaults climbing from $0.1 billion in 1931 to $1.1 billion in 1934, or from 2 to 24 percent of industrial outstandings. By 1944, however, all but $0.1 billion of the defaults had been settled. At that time only 4.8 percent of industrial bonds were in default; for utilities, the proportion was only 3.5 percent. This is in marked contrast to the rails.

As in the case of the net change in outstandings and its two components — offerings and extinguishments — the effects of the business cycle are clearly apparent in the series on new defaults, default settlements, and net changes in outstanding defaults. The net change in outstanding defaults in any year is highly correlated with the volume of new defaults, and both series show high negative conformity to the business cycle, reaching peaks at or near business troughs, and troughs at or near business peaks. The volume of default settlements lags behind new defaults, but the lag is irregular owing to extreme variations in the length of time required to settle distress situations through corporate reorganization, etc. The latter series, therefore, shows positive but low conformity with business cycles.

From the investors' point of view, a better measure of default

CHART 7 — Corporate Bond Defaults: Outstandings, New Defaults, and Settlements, 1900-1944

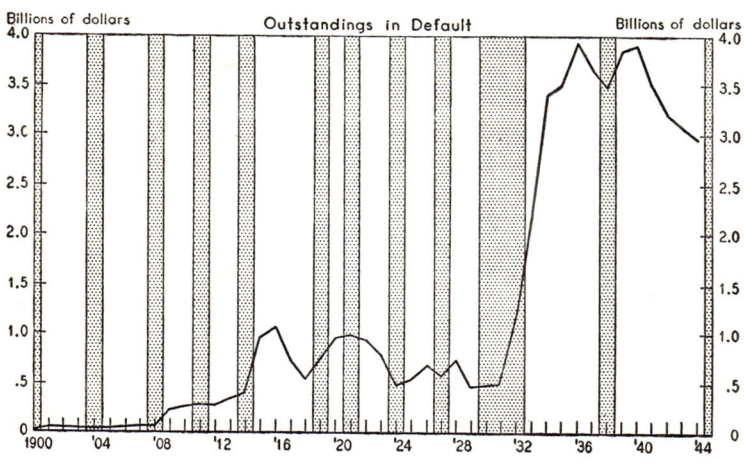

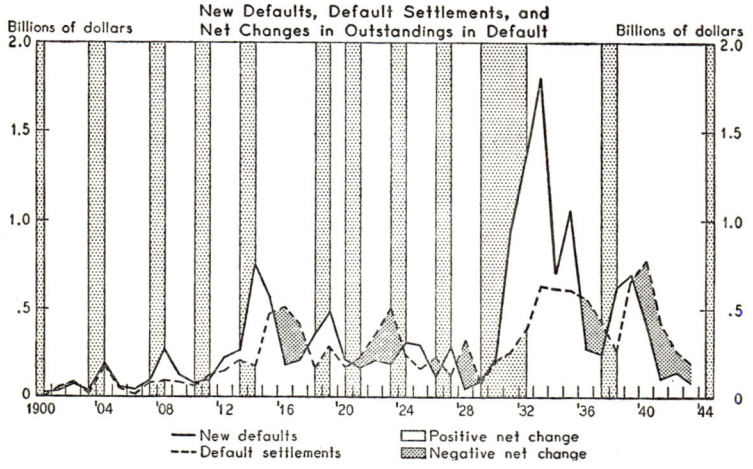

— New defaults
--- Default settlements
☐ Positive net change
▨ Negative net change

Data are for all industries combined and include straight issues only, par amount (see Table 3, Appendix). Outstandings in default are January figures; other series are totals for the year.

Shaded areas in the time scale, representing contractions in general business activity, and white areas, representing expansions, are from Arthur F. Burns and Wesley C. Mitchell, *Measuring Business Cycles* (National Bureau of Economic Research, 1946), p. 78.

experience than the absolute volume of defaults is given by the rate at which bonds go to default and the rate at which these defaults are settled. As measured by the average annual default rate calculated over the entire period 1900-1943, default experience was best on utility bonds and poorest on bonds in the industrial group. During the first three decades of the century, rail bonds had clearly the best record. Their average annual default rate for this period was only 0.9 percent as against 1.5 percent for utilities and 2.1 percent for industrials. This relative performance was reflected in conservative investment opinion in the period before the Great Depression, when rail bonds were favored while industrials were frowned upon by conservative investors, by the compilers of the legal lists of bonds eligible for savings bank and trust fund investment, and by the investment rating agencies.

On the basis of the depression experience, there was a pronounced shift in investor preferences from rail bonds to utilities and industrials. According to their average annual default rate calculated over the years 1930-43, utility bonds had much the best experience (a default rate of 1.6 percent per annum), and they came to occupy a preferred position as outlets for funds seeking low-risk investment. Trends in outstandings since World War II, and present market-yield differentials, indicate that industrial bonds are now also a preferred class of investment, while rail bonds have taken a decidedly secondary position. It will therefore surprise some investors to learn that the default experience with rail bonds during the depressed thirties was actually superior to that with industrials. Both rail and industrial bonds did poorly in these years, but the 3.2 percent average annual default rate for rails compared favorably with the 3.5 percent rate for industrials.

In seeking an explanation for the superior market performance of industrial bonds as compared with rails in recent years, one must take into account the fact that the rate at which bonds go to default measures only one aspect of over-all investor experience. Our analysis of default rates was therefore supplemented by a parallel analysis of annual settlement rates. (The annual settlement rate is the proportion of defaulted bonds outstanding at the beginning of the year that were settled during the year.) Averages of these annual settlement rates for the major industry groups follow:

PERIOD	All industries	Railroads	Public utilities	Industrials
1900-1929	33.2%	28.0%	30.9%	35.8%
1930-1943	14.1	8.4	20.9	27.0

As the table indicates, rail bonds had the lowest settlement rate of the three major industry groups in both periods shown, whereas industrial bonds had the highest. In short, rail bonds went to default slightly less frequently than industrials but remained in default over much longer periods.

In general, the statistical records on settlement rates emphasize the importance of the average level of earnings in the settlement of defaults. Industrial corporations' earnings were unstable in the thirties, but recovered rapidly, and many of their bonds were quickly restored to good standing. From these findings we infer that defaults were settled more quickly by obligors having a relatively simple capital structure, and by obligors not subject to close public regulation, than by others.

Another measure of investor experience with corporate bonds is provided by the record of interest payments on funded debt. In the present investigation, certain monthly and annual series on interest payments have been developed, primarily for use in national income studies where previously available data of this type have been unusually weak. These statistics, which cover the aggregate volume of interest payments promised by obligors (contractual payments) and the volume of interest actually paid (actual payments), also throw light on the ability of business enterprise to service funded debt. The difference between contractual and actual payment is, of course, the amount of interest in default.

These series amplify and confirm our findings as to industrial differences in corporate bond defaults. They also show that, despite the unusual financial disturbances of the Great Depression, the record of American business enterprise in servicing its funded debt has been remarkably good. Between January 1900 and January 1944 contractual interest payments aggregated $40.8 billion, and actual interest payments $38.4 billion. Thus over 94 percent of all contractual interest was paid during this period, leaving only 6 percent in arrears. Moreover, in none of the years in question did the portion of contractual interest actually paid fall below 84 percent, while in 32 of the 44 years it exceeded 95 percent. This record does not take account, of course, of reductions in contract rates through corporate reorganizations. It appears remarkable, however, when compared with that of the foreign dollar bonds offered in this country during the twenties. As late as 1950 only 58 percent of the debt service on these obligations was being met.

In the preceding paragraphs we have considered such measures of investor experience as default rates, settlement rates, interest receipts, and the period from default to settlement. While each of these statistics measures an important aspect of investor experience, account should also be taken of the price paid for the investment at offering and the value of receipts at extinguishment. Realized yield statistics, which fully reflect all of these payments, and their timing, will be examined in a later report.

APPENDIX

TABLE 1—PAR AMOUNT OF OUTSTANDINGS OF CORPORATE BONDS OF ALL TYPES, CLASSIFIED BY MAJOR INDUSTRY GROUP, JANUARY FIGURES, 1880-1951*

(in millions)

YEAR	All industries	Railroads	Public utilities	Industrials
1880		$2,026.7		
1881		2,211.4		
1882		2,515.0		
1883		2,827.0		
1884		3,058.9		
1885		3,205.9		
1886		3,290.3		
1887		3,392.7		
1888		3,658.3		
1889		4,040.2		
1890		4,218.8		
1891		4,461.3		
1892		4,524.9		
1893		4,722.6		
1894		4,814.5		
1895		4,898.0		
1896		4,935.5		
1897		4,772.3		
1898		4,835.7		
1899		4,923.9		
1900	$6,244.2	4,932.2	$969.7	$342.3
1901	6,852.1	5,209.9	1,262.4	379.8
1902	8,205.7	5,837.0	1,431.5	937.2
1903	9,106.2	6,275.8	1,741.8	1,088.6
1904	9,841.7	6,527.7	1,973.9	1,340.1
1905	10,621.9	6,976.9	2,211.3	1,433.7
1906	11,469.0	7,439.6	2,467.9	1,561.5
1907	12,480.1	7,825.0	2,951.1	1,704.0
1908	13,370.2	8,221.7	3,305.2	1,843.3
1909	14,241.4	8,676.1	3,597.7	1,967.6
1910	14,880.4	9,055.2	3,682.5	2,142.7
1911	15,529.0	9,189.4	4,043.8	2,295.8
1912	16,499.6	9,507.4	4,470.8	2,521.4
1913	17,395.7	9,802.3	4,987.2	2,606.2
1914	17,914.2	10,054.1	5,237.9	2,622.2
1915	18,364.9	10,258.4	5,424.3	2,682.2

TABLE 1 (concluded)

YEAR	All industries	Railroads	Public utilities	Industrials
1916	$18,596.9	$10,384.7	$5,564.0	$2,648.2
1917	18,923.1	10,381.1	5,779.0	2,763.0
1918	19,193.7	10,388.7	5,917.8	2,887.2
1919	19,434.5	10,349.3	6,086.8	2,998.4
1920	19,743.3	10,333.5	6,382.3	3,027.5
1921	20,753.4	10,474.4	6,578.5	3,700.5
1922	21,796.9	10,572.8	6,911.2	4,312.9
1923	22,541.7	10,841.7	7,043.6	4,656.4
1924	23,545.5	11,114.3	7,523.8	4,907.4
1925	24,881.3	11,785.3	8,003.3	5,092.7
1926	25,807.8	11,812.9	8,632.2	5,362.7
1927	27,318.8	11,950.1	9,429.4	5,939.3
1928	29,353.6	12,216.3	10,546.6	6,590.7
1929	29,848.1	12,224.5	11,027.4	6,596.2
1930	29,964.7	12,348.8	11,464.9	6,151.0
1931	31,423.6	12,767.8	12,349.5	6,306.3
1932	31,741.9	12,812.0	12,780.3	6,149.6
1933	31,158.0	12,600.0	12,872.1	5,685.9
1934	30,189.2	12,430.2	12,508.6	5,250.4
1935	29,459.8	12,408.3	12,170.1	4,881.4
1936	28,718.9	12,211.7	12,111.4	4,395.8
1937	28,606.4	12,261.2	12,170.1	4,175.1
1938	27,705.5	12,168.5	11,666.9	3,870.1
1939	28,123.2	11,978.0	11,963.6	4,181.6
1940	27,567.3	11,867.7	11,651.6	4,048.0
1941	27,373.1	11,878.0	11,594.4	3,900.7
1942	26,837.2	11,709.7	11,368.7	3,758.8
1943	26,432.8	11,313.0	11,371.6	3,748.2
1944	25,387.4	10,764.7	10,958.8	3,663.9
1945	*24,700.0*	*10,650.0*	*10,650.0*	*3,400.0*
1946	*23,500.0*	*10,200.0*	*10,300.0*	*3,000.0*
1947	*24,400.0*	*9,850.0*	*10,550.0*	*4,000.0*
1948	*27,200.0*	*9,700.0*	*12,200.0*	*5,200.0*
1949	*31,400.0*	*9,950.0*	*14,450.0*	*6,900.0*
1950	*34,200.0*	*10,100.0*	*16,200.0*	*7,800.0*
1951	*35,800.0*	*10,250.0*	*17,350.0*	*8,100.0*

* Data for 1900-1944 are from special tabulations of the National Bureau of Economic Research. Italics distinguish the data for other years. Those for 1945-51 are extrapolations based on unpublished materials of the Securities and Exchange Commission; railroad data for 1880-99 are rough estimates based on balance sheet figures in Poor's *Manual of Railroads,* 1900.

TABLE 2—Par Amount of Net Changes in Outstandings and of New-Money Offerings of Straight Corporate Bonds, and Yields of High-Grade Corporate Bonds, All Industries Combined, Annually, 1900-1950*

(dollar figures in millions)

YEAR	Net change in outstandings	New-money offerings	High-grade bond yields (annual average)
1900	$578.5	$588.8	4.19%
1901	1,312.1	1,336.7	4.09
1902	807.4	825.5	4.06
1903	692.2	803.4	4.28
1904	761.9	948.7	4.26
1905	786.5	888.7	4.09
1906	920.6	974.5	4.20
1907	799.4	907.4	4.53
1908	822.6	834.3	4.53
1909	550.8	862.9	4.33
1910	512.2	862.3	4.42
1911	823.6	959.7	4.42
1912	769.9	1,020.8	4.46
1913	396.4	632.7	4.65
1914	472.0	628.2	4.64
1915	285.0	540.7	4.76
1916	247.7	788.7	4.64
1917	280.0	799.2	4.93
1918	105.6	465.0	5.42
1919	225.2	614.6	5.49
1920	687.3	1,018.4	6.13
1921	923.4	1,245.9	5.96
1922	623.7	1,138.3	5.12
1923	715.8	1,395.8	5.18
1924	1,158.7	1,668.8	5.02
1925	797.7	1,615.4	4.88
1926	1,456.9	1,949.9	4.73
1927	2,027.9	2,247.9	4.59

TABLE 2 (concluded)

YEAR	Net change in outstandings	New-money offerings	High-grade bond yields (annual average)
1928	$549.1	$1,615.4	4.59%
1929	168.7	1,359.5	4.86
1930	1,360.5	2,207.8	4.71
1931	459.2	1,063.5	4.55
1932	−406.7	479.6	5.26
1933	−765.9	89.5	4.68
1934	−595.2	137.5	4.13
1935	−728.4	207.1	3.61
1936	−166.6	517.9	3.34
1937	−944.2	551.4	3.33
1938	476.1	767.6	3.23
1939	−522.6	214.0	3.04
1940	−494.8	376.8	2.94
1941	−818.9	577.4	2.87
1942	−324.2	367.3	2.88
1943	−924.8	260.0	2.81
1944	*−650.0*	......	2.79
1945	*−1,040.0*	......	2.64
1946	*700.0*	......	2.53
1947	*2,430.0*	......	2.60
1948	*3,660.0*	......	2.82
1949	*2,400.0*	......	2.67
1950	*1,420.0*	......	2.61

* Par amount series for 1900-1943 are from special tabulations of the National Bureau of Economic Research; italics distinguish the 1944-50 figures, which are extrapolations based on unpublished materials of the Securities and Exchange Commission. Yield series is a weighted average of Standard and Poor's Corporation high-grade railroad, public utility, and industrial bond yields, with National Bureau estimates of outstandings as weights.

TABLE 3—Par Amount of Straight Corporate Bonds Outstanding in Default, New Defaults, Default Settlements, and Net Changes in Outstandings in Default, All Industries Combined, Annually, 1900-1944*

(in millions)

YEAR	Outstanding in default, beginning of year	New defaults during year	Settlements during year	Net change in outstanding defaults over year
1900	$21.6	$25.3	$.9	$24.4
1901	46.0	36.7	41.7	—5.0
1902	41.0	78.0	85.7	—7.7
1903	33.3	15.7	20.6	—4.9
1904	28.4	194.4	194.3	.1
1905	28.5	58.5	49.0	9.5
1906	38.0	24.5	11.5	13.0
1907	51.0	90.9	86.1	4.8
1908	55.8	271.8	98.3	173.5
1909	229.3	116.1	90.1	26.0
1910	255.3	83.3	65.1	18.2
1911	273.5	102.3	110.3	—8.0
1912	265.5	225.2	153.2	72.0
1913	337.5	265.4	206.3	59.1
1914	396.6	746.4	183.3	563.1
1915	959.7	571.9	474.2	97.7
1916	1,057.4	193.1	512.8	—319.7
1917	737.7	206.2	405.1	—198.9
1918	538.8	359.3	164.6	194.7
1919	733.5	491.4	282.0	209.4
1920	942.9	205.3	174.1	31.2
1921	974.1	179.5	222.0	—42.5
1922	931.6	213.5	350.5	—137.0
1923	794.6	197.1	507.5	—310.4

TABLE 3 (concluded)

YEAR	Outstanding in default, beginning of year	New defaults during year	Settlements during year	Net change in outstanding defaults over year
1924	$484.2	$303.4	$238.0	$ 65.4
1925	549.6	292.3	163.3	129.0
1926	678.6	125.4	225.8	−100.4
1927	578.2	284.0	130.1	153.9
1928	732.1	57.1	319.7	−262.6
1929	469.5	96.8	84.0	12.8
1930	482.3	228.1	221.1	7.0
1931	489.3	940.2	255.0	685.2
1932	1,174.5	1,352.7	387.9	964.8
1933	2,139.3	1,901.4	629.6	1,271.8
1934	3,411.1	710.4	617.0	93.4
1935	3,504.5	1,055.9	615.5	440.4
1936	3,944.9	288.5	565.0	−276.5
1937	3,668.4	253.4	431.5	−178.1
1938	3,490.3	620.2	268.1	352.1
1939	3,842.4	698.9	653.9	45.0
1940	3,887.4	420.6	790.4	−369.8
1941	3,517.6	106.8	419.7	−312.9
1942	3,204.7	145.3	265.7	−120.4
1943	3,084.3	82.1	200.2	−118.1
1944	2,966.2			

* From special tabulations of the National Bureau of Economic Research.

Productivity and Economic Progress

FREDERICK C. MILLS

OCCASIONAL PAPER 38

NATIONAL BUREAU OF ECONOMIC RESEARCH, INC.

OFFICERS, 1952

Harry Scherman, *Chairman*
C. C. Balderston, *President*
Percival F. Brundage, *Vice-President*
George B. Roberts, *Treasurer*
W. J. Carson, *Executive Director*

DIRECTORS AT LARGE

Donald R. Belcher, *American Telephone and Telegraph Company*
Oswald W. Knauth, *Beaufort, South Carolina*
Simon Kuznets, *University of Pennsylvania*
H. W. Laidler, *Executive Director, League for Industrial Democracy*
Shepard Morgan, *New York City*
C. Reinold Noyes, *Princeton, New Jersey*
George B. Roberts, *Vice-President, National City Bank*
Beardsley Ruml, *New York City*
Harry Scherman, *Chairman, Book-of-the-Month Club*
George Soule, *Bennington College*
N. I. Stone, *Consulting Economist*
J. Raymond Walsh, *New York City*
Leo Wolman, *Columbia University*
Theodore O. Yntema, *Vice President-Finance, Ford Motor Company*

DIRECTORS BY UNIVERSITY APPOINTMENT

E. Wight Bakke, *Yale*
C. C. Balderston, *Pennsylvania*
Arthur F. Burns, *Columbia*
G. A. Elliott, *Toronto*
Frank W. Fetter, *Northwestern*
H. M. Groves, *Wisconsin*

Gottfried Haberler, *Harvard*
Clarence Heer, *North Carolina*
R. L. Kozelka, *Minnesota*
Paul M. O'Leary, *Cornell*
T. W. Schultz, *Chicago*
Jacob Viner, *Princeton*

DIRECTORS APPOINTED BY OTHER ORGANIZATIONS

Percival F. Brundage, *American Institute of Accountants*
Frederick C. Mills, *American Statistical Association*
S. H. Ruttenberg, *Congress of Industrial Organizations*
Murray Shields, *American Management Association*
Boris Shishkin, *American Federation of Labor*
Donald H. Wallace, *American Economic Association*
Frederick V. Waugh, *American Farm Economic Association*
Harold F. Williamson, *Economic History Association*

RESEARCH STAFF

Arthur F. Burns, *Director of Research*
Geoffrey H. Moore, *Associate Director of Research*

Moses Abramovitz
Harold Barger
Morris A. Copeland
Daniel Creamer
David Durand
Solomon Fabricant
Milton Friedman
Millard Hastay
W. Braddock Hickman

F. F. Hill
Thor Hultgren
Simon Kuznets
Clarence D. Long
Ruth P. Mack
Frederick C. Mills
Raymond J. Saulnier
Lawrence H. Seltzer
George J. Stigler

Leo Wolman

Relation of the Directors to the Work and Publications of the National Bureau of Economic Research

1. The object of the National Bureau of Economic Research is to ascertain and to present to the public important economic facts and their interpretation in a scientific and impartial manner. The Board of Directors is charged with the responsibility of ensuring that the work of the National Bureau is carried on in strict conformity with this object.

2. To this end the Board of Directors shall appoint one or more Directors of Research.

3. The Director or Directors of Research shall submit to the members of the Board, or to its Executive Committee, for their formal adoption, all specific proposals concerning researches to be instituted.

4. No report shall be published until the Director or Directors of Research shall have submitted to the Board a summary drawing attention to the character of the data and their utilization in the report, the nature and treatment of the problems involved, the main conclusions and such other information as in their opinion would serve to determine the suitability of the report for publication in accordance with the principles of the National Bureau.

5. A copy of any manuscript proposed for publication shall also be submitted to each member of the Board. For each manuscript to be so submitted a special committee shall be appointed by the President, or at his designation by the Executive Director, consisting of three Directors selected as nearly as may be one from each general division of the Board. The names of the special manuscript committee shall be stated to each Director when the summary and report described in paragraph (4) are sent to him. It shall be the duty of each member of the committee to read the manuscript. If each member of the special committee signifies his approval within thirty days, the manuscript may be published. If each member of the special committee has not signified his approval within thirty days of the transmittal of the report and manuscript, the Director of Research shall then notify each member of the Board, requesting approval or disapproval of publication, and thirty additional days shall be granted for this purpose. The manuscript shall then not be published unless at least a majority of the entire Board and a two-thirds majority of those members of the Board who shall have voted on the proposal within the time fixed for the receipt of votes on the publication proposed shall have approved.

6. No manuscript may be published, though approved by each member of the special committee, until forty-five days have elapsed from the transmittal of the summary and report. The interval is allowed for the receipt of any memorandum of dissent or reservation, together with a brief statement of his reasons, that any member may wish to express; and such memorandum of dissent or reservation shall be published with the manuscript if he so desires. Publication does not, however, imply that each member of the Board has read the manuscript, or that either members of the Board in general, or of the special committee, have passed upon its validity in every detail.

7. A copy of this resolution shall, unless otherwise determined by the Board, be printed in each copy of every National Bureau book.

(Resolution adopted October 25, 1926 and revised February 6, 1933 and February 24, 1941)

Productivity and Economic Progress

FREDERICK C. MILLS

OCCASIONAL PAPER 38

NATIONAL BUREAU OF ECONOMIC RESEARCH, INC.
1952

Price: $.75

Copyright, 1952, by National Bureau of Economic Research, Inc.
1819 Broadway, New York 23, N. Y. All rights reserved.
Typography by Oscar Leventhal, Inc.
Printing by John N. Jacobson & Son, Inc.
Library of Congress catalog card number: 52-14251

Contents

		PAGE
I	Factors in the Growth of Production	2
	Output, effort input, and productivity	2
II	Increments to National Product, and their Components	5
III	Uses of Productive Resources	9
	Maintenance, defense, and progress	9
	The margin above maintenance needs	12
	On the role of the productivity increment in progress	19
IV	Conclusion	21

Note 1	On the present estimates of gross national product	23
Note 2	Estimates of productivity	24
Note 3	Estimation of the labor input increment and the productivity increment	31

PRODUCTIVITY AND ECONOMIC PROGRESS*

Over the last half century the real national product of the United States increased five-fold, while population doubled. Output per capita of the population increased two and one-half times. Here was the basis of a substantial advance in economic power and in levels of consumption. Over this same period the total volume of human effort going into production (measured by manhours of labor input) increased by 80 per cent. The great gain in total output was won with an increase in labor input well below the increase in population. Here is evidence of a gain in welfare in another dimension — a saving of effort and a lightening of the toil by which the material needs of life are satisfied.

The major instrument used in the winning of these dual gains was enhanced productivity. During this period there was an unbroken advance in average physical output per manhour of work done. Decade by decade the effectiveness of productive effort increased. In the final decade output per manhour of labor input was 2.81 times what it was fifty years before.

The movements thus briefly summarized reflect four basic trends in the growth of the economy of the United States (see table

---

* This paper is one of a series of National Bureau studies dealing with production and productivity. This series has been supported in large part by funds granted by The Maurice and Laura Falk Foundation of Pittsburgh. The Falk Foundation is not, however, to be understood as approving, by virtue of its grant, any of the statements made or views expressed herein.

In a paper presented at a meeting of the American Economic Association at Boston, in December 1951, I drew upon some of the materials utilized in this report, and presented preliminary estimates of some of the quantities here given. Concepts, procedures, and estimates have been modified somewhat in the present essay. A fuller discussion of the topics here dealt with may be expected in a subsequent National Bureau publication.

I am indebted to Maude R. Pech for assistance in this study.

REAL GROSS NATIONAL PRODUCT, POPULATION, LABOR INPUT, AND
PRODUCTIVITY, UNITED STATES, BY DECADES, 1891-1950

Decade	Gross national product (billions of 1929 dollars)	(relative)	Population (relative)	Total man-hours of labor input (relative)	Output per manhour (relative)
1891-1900	294	100.0	100.0	100.0	100.0
1901-1910	455	154.8	120.6	126.1	122.8
1911-1920	603	205.1	143.4	140.5	146.0
1921-1930	838	285.0	165.4	145.1	196.4
1931-1940	843	286.7	181.9	122.8	233.5
1941-1950	1,493	507.8	201.4	180.5	281.3

above). These trends are examined in the pages that follow. We there attempt to determine the magnitudes of some of the elements of growth, to outline the uses to which we have put our expanding productive power and, in so doing, to define some aspects of the pattern of progress over this half century of economic expansion.

I

FACTORS IN THE GROWTH OF PRODUCTION

Economic resources may be used for maintenance, for defense, or for material progress. Maintenance includes the support of the population (which may be a growing population) at an established consumption level and the full upkeep of an existing stock of capital equipment. It could, indeed, include defense, because military protection is necessary to the preservation of an existing way of life, but there are advantages in treating defense in a separate category of uses. Economic progress is possible when there is a margin of output over and above the needs of maintenance and defense.

Output, effort input, and productivity

Progress in this sense is not, of course, defined by the rate of change in total output. Yet, with a growing population, an increasing supply of physical goods and services is a basic requirement of material growth. I first note, therefore, certain conditions bearing on the growth of production.

The aggregate physical output of an economy may be expanded by an increase in the input of human effort or by an increase in output per unit of labor input. We may expend more effort or we may resort to the diverse factors that render human effort more productive. Manpower input[1] may be increased by fuller use of an existing labor force (i.e., by drawing upon the unemployed), by expansion of the labor force, or by a lengthening of working hours. Except during limited periods, expansion of output in the United States over the last half century has been achieved primarily by means of rising productivity; the instrument of augmented manpower has played a secondary role. The forces enhancing output per unit of work time have been many. In their aggregative influence as elements of productivity they have been the major factor in our recent material growth.

The distinction between effort and the unit effectiveness of effort as factors in the productive process cuts across the conventional classification of factors into land, labor, capital, and enterprise, and corresponds in no wise to that division. From the present view we have but two interacting agents: on the one hand, the mental and physical effort exerted by all grades and levels of producers; on the other, the combination of elements that determine the effectiveness of this effort in production. The latter, the productivity factor, comprehends the quality and magnitude of available natural resources, the amount and quality of capital equipment used, the skill, intelligence and training of all personnel, and the quality of organization and management. Effort and the productivity factor are, of course, not additive; they are related in a multiplicative way. They are integral components of every unit of the ultimate product.

[1] In this study I use manpower input, as defined by manhours of work time on the part of the total employed labor force, as a measure of human effort expended in production. This quantity is meant to include all labor entering into the productive process. It includes the efforts of managers as well as wage earners, of proprietors as well as employees. No attempt is made to distinguish qualities of work input.

In their usual form, indexes of output, of effort input, and of productivity define relative changes in these elements over time.[2] Such measures were cited in the opening paragraphs of this paper. In addition, it is useful to deal with absolute increments to output, and to divide them into two components, one associated with increases in the quantity of effort input, the other with increases in output per manhour of work done. These two components of a production increment are termed, for convenience, the *labor input increment* and the *productivity increment*. The former is the absolute increase in output between two stated periods that would have resulted from the recorded increase in labor input, had the employed labor force been working at a productivity level equal to the average of the two periods compared. The latter is the absolute increase in output that would have resulted from the recorded gain in output per manhour, had this gain been utilized by a working labor force equal to the average of the two periods compared. (Either of the two components may, of course, decrease, in which case we should have a decrement instead of an increment.) The productivity increment is the "technological margin", the concrete resultant of the diverse influences that determine the effectiveness of productive operations. It is, at once, the substance for which producing and consuming groups compete and the mainspring of material progress.[3]

I should emphasize that the productivity increment (or decrement) is restricted to the yield of *employed* resources. Its sign will depend upon the direction of change in manhour output; its size will depend upon the absolute amounts of work input in the two periods compared. There may be such an increment (as in fact there was in the thirties) during a period of extensive and growing unem-

[2] See Note 2 at the end of this paper for a discussion of measures of productivity.

[3] It should be clear that neither the labor input increment nor the productivity increment is to be regarded as the marginal product of any of the conventional factors of production. The labor input increment could be negative when the marginal product of labor (which in this situation must relate to the result of changes over time) is positive; it could be positive with a negative marginal product. Both increments are, of course, joint products of all productive factors; neither increment is in any sense the specific product of any one factor. See Note 3 at the end of this paper for a discussion of the method here employed in estimating these quantities.

ployment. Neither a productivity index nor a productivity increment is a measure of the effectiveness with which total available resources have been used; nor does either indicate the output that might have been won had all resources been employed.

In tracing changes in a given economy we are concerned not only with the sources of the increments to national product; we are equally interested in uses. Progressively, in a growing economy, additional productive resources are opened up and new productive power is won. These resources and this power may be put to diverse uses. To some extent, too, resources carried over from earlier periods may be shifted to new uses. The pattern of resource use, as it is modified from decade to decade and from generation to generation, is one of the most revealing aspects of economic growth. We shall turn to the subject of uses after tracing the expansion of national product over the last half century and defining the parts played by labor input and productivity as contributors to changes in total product.

II

INCREMENTS TO NATIONAL PRODUCT, AND THEIR COMPONENTS

The growth of the gross national product of the United States, in real terms, has been conspicuously uneven during the twentieth century, with the major fluctuations coming in the last three decades. Decade increments and the two components of each such increment are given in the following table and are charted in Figure 1. All values relate to decade aggregates.[4]

[4] The basic national product estimates here used are those of Simon Kuznets. To Kuznets' figures, on his peacetime concept, M. Slade Kendrick's estimates of the war and defense expenditures of the federal government have been added, with a correction to prevent duplication (see Note 1 at the end of this paper). This modification gives us measures corresponding to Kuznets' wartime concept of gross national product, except that the present totals include all defense expenditures in years of peace, as well as in wartime. I am indebted to Dr. Kuznets also for the classification of elements of the national product used in later sections.

In deriving estimates of labor input I have used continuing series of the Bureau of the Census and the Bureau of Labor Statistics, and employment and hours of work estimates of Clarence Long, Leo Wolman, and others.

Decade	Gross national product increment	Labor input increment	Productivity increment
	(billions	of 1929	dollars)
1901-10 (change from 1891-1900)	+161	+85	+76
1911-20 (change from 1901-10)	+148	+57	+91
1921-30 (change from 1911-20)	+235	+23	+212
1931-40 (change from 1921-30)	+5	—141	+146
1941-50 (change from 1931-40)	+650	+437	+213

The accelerations in economic expansion, as measured by increments to real gross product, came in the first, third, and fifth decades of the century. The second decade brought modest retardation; the fourth brought a major check, with actual retrogression during the first five years. The advance of the twenties was notable, that of the forties phenomenal.

There is a sharp and revealing contrast in behavior between the two components of national product increases. One, reflecting additions or subtractions of sheer manpower, shows progressively declining increments through four decades, culminating in a decrement of major proportions in the thirties. The absolute contribution of added labor in the twenties was only about one-fourth that recorded for the decade 1901-10. Hours of work were being steadily shortened in these earlier decades, and those in the lower age groups were being withdrawn from the work force. After the first decade it was only in the forties, under the stimulus of war and defense, that we resorted primarily to the instrument of added manpower to augment production. (One reason for the very large labor input increment in the forties was, of course, the subnormal level of employment in the thirties, which provide the base of comparison for the following decade.)

The chief lifting force between the first and the fifth decades was steadily growing productivity. This increment grew from 76 billions (of 1929 dollars) in 1901-10 to 212 billions in 1921-30. Relatively, this last was the greatest productivity gain of the half century. There was a drop in the depressed thirties, but even in that decade the productivity increment was more than large enough to offset the loss of 141 billions resulting from a great decline in the

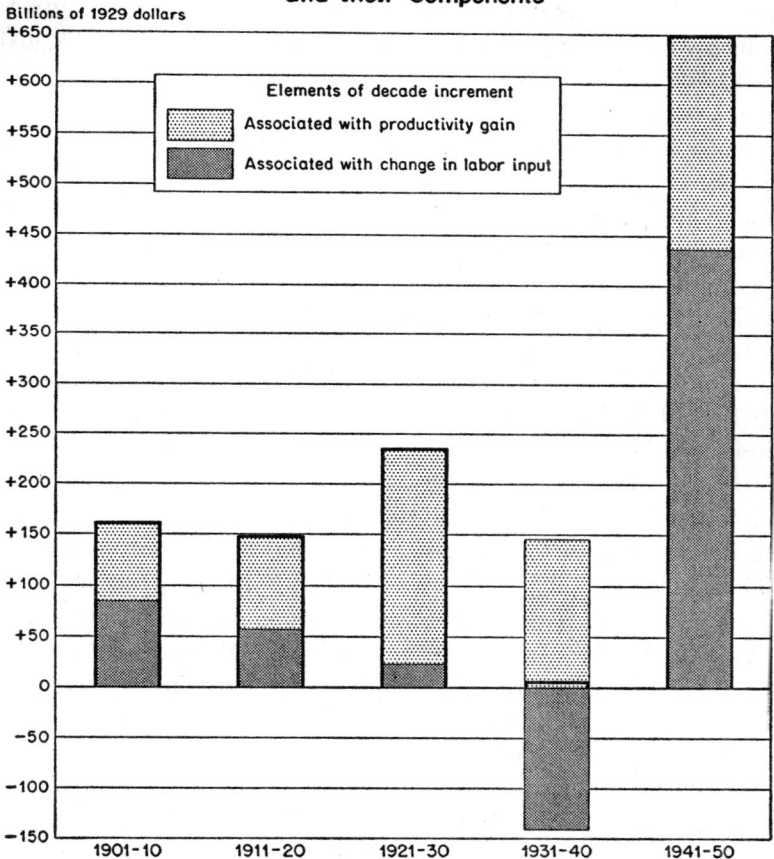

Figure 1
Decade Gains in Real Gross National Product and their Components

Each bar measures the amount by which the national product of a given decade exceeded the national product of the preceding decade.

volume of labor input. The most recent decade brought a productivity increment of 213 billion dollars, a figure approximately equal to the gain of the twenties. The employed labor force in the latest decade was the largest in our history and this, of course, served to enhance the gain resulting from the actual advance in manhour productivity. Great as it was, the productivity increment in this decade was materially exceeded by the labor input increment. Additions to manpower, supplemented by increases in output per manhour, gave us the tremendous increment to product upon which we drew for guns and butter in the forties.

I have said that the relative gains in productivity were greatest in the twenties. To the student of economic growth, indeed, special interest attaches to the period of six or eight years following the end of the first world war. In these years rates of acceleration in manhour productivity in the economy at large and in the important manufacturing sector reached their maxima, for the fifty-year period here reviewed. For the whole economy the rate of productivity gain attained almost 4 per cent a year between 1918 and 1924. In manufacturing industries output per manhour increased at a rate of 10 per cent a year for each of the three years between 1919 and 1922, an advance probably without precedent in our industrial history.

Back of these advances lay a highly favorable conjuncture of circumstances. The movement toward scientific management came to first fruition in the industrial expansion of the early twenties. The moving assembly line, dramatized by Ford a few years earlier, became a standard feature of mass production. The power available to industrial workers was greatly increased in amount and in flexibility of application. Working hours declined from 53 a week in 1914 and 1917 to an average of 47 in 1922. Occupational shifts contributed to the gain in manhour output in the general economy. In the recovery that followed the readjustment after World War I the number of persons in the relatively highly paid tertiary occupations grew, while employment in agriculture and in manufacturing lagged, or declined. The stock of real capital per worker, in the form of producers' durable equipment and industrial and commercial structures, stood at a relatively high level in the early twenties, having increased by some 40 per cent in two decades.[5] No comparable rise occurred until the notable increase that fol-

---

[5] I have here made use of Dr. Raymond Goldsmith's data on elements of estimated national wealth, in 1929 prices. See "A Perpetual Inventory of National Wealth", *Studies in Income and Wealth, Volume Fourteen* (National Bureau of Economic Research, 1951), pp. 5-73.

lowed the end of World War II. Perhaps of greater importance than the increase in the stock of capital goods was the advance in the *quality* of capital instruments. Technological improvements as well as the innovations of scientific management were widely adopted in the early twenties; such improvements were chiefly manifest in the tools of production. These diverse factors combined with others in the complex of working conditions that determine productive effectiveness to yield a remarkable productivity gain.

III

Uses of Productive Resources

The characteristics of an economic system are defined not alone by the magnitude and sources of its productive power. The purposes for which productive resources are used are the most significant indicators of its pattern of life. These purposes reflect the collective desires and needs of the individuals who make up the system. Basic wants for food, clothing and shelter, desires for satisfactions above subsistence levels, the role of instrumental goods in the productive process, and compulsions imposed by necessities of war or defense are all manifest in the patterns of use that prevail at given times. Such uses, in the aggregate, are shown by the familiar national income and national product classifications that have been developed within recent decades for this and other countries.

Maintenance, defense, and progress

A somewhat different classification of uses has been employed in this study. Here we think of economic resources as being used for three broad purposes — maintenance, defense, and progress. The population must be supported at an established consumption level; the existing stock of capital equipment must be maintained if there is not to be retrogression through depreciation and obsolescence; means must be provided for defense against attack from abroad. Only after these needs have been met is economic progress possible.

Such progress may take the form of an advance in consumption levels (i.e., an increase in average per capita expenditures for consumption goods and services) or a net increase in the stock of capital.[6]

If the "progress" made in any period is to be determined, the requirements for maintenance must first be established. For capital stock, maintenance needs can be equated to "capital consumption" — the wearing out of plant, equipment, and residential housing — during a stated period. The criterion is definite here, although one must be content with estimates of the magnitudes involved. Less precise criteria are available when we consider population maintenance. There can be no absolute and fixed definition of consumption standards. Each generation, indeed each decade and each year, brings changes in the content of living and in the subjective scales by which people judge the adequacy or inadequacy of the real incomes provided by their monetary receipts. I here assume that the consumption level attained in a given decade (as measured, in constant dollars, by average per capita expenditures for consumption goods and services) establishes a criterion of consumption needs that carries over into the decade following. This is not to say that basic requirements for the maintenance of consumption levels are always met. Claims growing out of such needs may be relinquished in periods of national emergency; in deep depression

[6] Economic growth has elsewhere been defined as an advance in the net product of goods and services per capita of the population. (Cf. J. J. Spengler, "Theories of Socio-Economic Growth", in *Problems in the Study of Economic Growth*, Universities-National Bureau Committee on Economic Research, 1949). The present definition of economic progress is similar to this in respect of consumption gains; it differs, however, in two important ways: 1) Expenditures for defense are not considered to contribute to progress. (They are, of course, an essential form of maintenance.) 2) Any formation of net capital is considered to be a component of progress, whether there is a gain per capita of the population or not. Technological improvements contributing to major advances in *quality* of capital goods could quite conceivably make possible rising per capita consumption with no accompanying increase in total capital stock. This is not likely to be the case with a growing population — certainly we stand far short of such a condition now — but in an industrial economy marked by rapid technical advance it is not essential to progress that quantitative additions to the stock of capital grow at a faster rate than population.

Under the present definition there may, of course, be progress in a net sense if there is an advance in only one of the two forms of progress, provided that this advance exceeds the decline in the other form.

output may be inadequate to meet even fundamental needs. But the historical record provides ample justification for the view that consumption levels are persistent, that they change slowly, and that gains in such levels, once realized, are defended with tenacity.[7]

[7] I have used the term "consumption level" in the sense of J. S. Davis' illuminating discussion, in his presidential address (*American Economic Review,* March 1945). In some respects the "standard of consumption", which means the scale desired and striven for, whether realized or not, would be an appropriate criterion, but available measures are restricted to levels of consumption actually realized. There is, moreover, justification for using the *attained* level, and for viewing this as including the more vigorously defended elements of a consumption standard.

A case could be made for using as criterion not the consumption level of the year or decade immediately preceding, but the highest consumption level previously attained. Duesenberry and Modigliani have suggested that consumption propensities are influenced by previous peak incomes as well as by current income levels. Tom E. Davis of Johns Hopkins has shown that the Duesenberry-Modigliani models can be further improved by substituting previous peak consumption for previous peak income ("The Consumption Function as a Tool for Prediction", *Review of Economics and Statistics,* Vol. XXXIV, No. 3, August 1952). This procedure would be particularly appropriate in dealing with the postwar forties.

The criterion here employed, it is to be noted, gives a consumption standard which changes over time. This would be true in a secular sense, of course, in an economy marked by rising living standards. It would be true, also, with reference to periodic movements. Thus a consumption level carried over from a prolonged depression would not be the same as a consumption level carried over from a period of prosperity. These differences would have a bearing upon the choices entering into the use of disposable resources at different times. Thus in a period following prolonged depression some resources would be used to restore the consumption levels of a still earlier period.

Our procedure, in which each decade average provides a consumption standard for the following decade, implies that consumption levels advance or decline in jumps. This probably approximates the truth, for advances in such standards appear to come in uneven spurts. However, the reader should recognize that the discontinuities imposed by the use of fixed ten-year intervals are arbitrary in their timing and, to some extent, in their relative magnitudes.

With reference to consumption standards I would emphasize that this study relates to a particular historical period. The consumption levels that are taken to have been marked by strong tendencies to persist are those of the five decades 1891-1900 to 1931-40. It is possible that as durable goods and luxury elements become more important in consumer standards, persistence of consumption levels will be less marked. Thus the high postwar standards may be less tenaciously defended than were the lower standards of a decade or two ago. However, it is far from certain that even high standards, entrenched by ten years of habituation, would be lightly sacrificed if per capita output should continue to increase. (Standards of *use* will, of course, be more stable than levels of *purchase.* But the distinction between use and purchase has less significance for decade intervals than it would have for shorter periods.)

Maintenance needs are relatively stable in their changes from period to period. Expenditures for defense and for progress are far more variable. In tracing changes over the last half century it will be useful to treat maintenance expenditures as a first deduction from gross national product. The margin above maintenance requirements[8] is a quantity to which special interest attaches in a study of economic development.

The margin above maintenance needs

The deductions from gross national product to care for maintenance in a given decade must provide for the support of the population of that decade at per capita consumption levels equal to those prevailing during the decade preceding and for the production of capital goods sufficient to offset in full depreciation of the preceding decade's stock of capital. The procedure, using decade aggregates, is shown in the following table. A graphic representation of the division of decade totals is given in Figure 2.

| | | Maintenance charges | | | Margin above maintenance |
Decade	Gross national product	Support of population	Capital stock	Total Col. 3 + 4	Col. 2 — 5
	(billions	of	1929	dollars)	
(1)	(2)	(3)	(4)	(5)	(6)
1901-10	455	268	43	311	144
1911-20	603	420	65	485	118
1921-30	838	527	88	615	223
1931-40	843	734	95	829	14
1941-50	1,493	803	132	935	558

[8] I have elsewhere called a variant of this concept the "disposable margin". There is justification for this term, I think, in that there is a larger element of conscious choice, individual or collective, in the allocation of resources above those required for maintenance than there is in the disposition of resources that serve established needs for consumption or capital replacement. But the term is not altogether apt, since the margin must perforce be measured retrospectively. The resources entering into it, whether used for defense or for progress, have already been committed by the time measurement is possible. It seems advisable, therefore, to use the neutral term "margin above maintenance needs" or, in short, "output margin", in preference to "disposable margin".

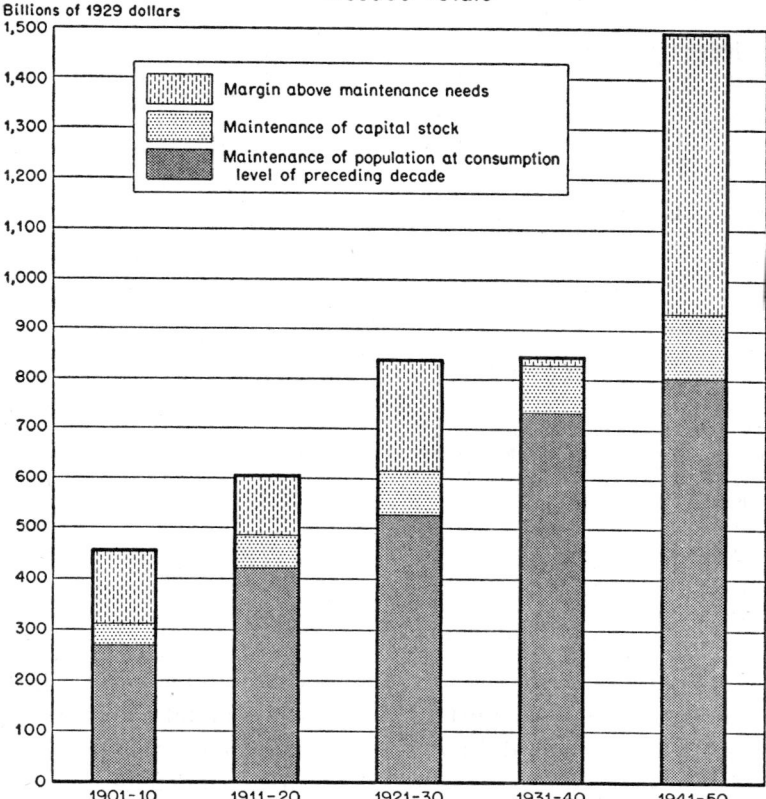

Figure 2
Uses of Real Gross National Product
Decade Totals

The entries in column 6, which define amounts by which the gross national product exceeds maintenance needs, represent margins available for new uses. Without the product represented by each of these quantities we could, in any decade, maintain the existing stock of capital equipment and support the full population at the consumption levels of the preceding decade.[9] The margins above

[9] In the thirties we did not, in fact, achieve full maintenance, for actual consumption standards in that decade were slightly below those of the twenties. We devoted to population maintenance 725 billions of 1929 dollars, not the 734 billions required for full maintenance. We did, however, increase capital stock by a small amount.

maintenance requirements have ranged from a very small fraction of gross product, in the thirties, to almost 40 per cent of gross product, in the forties. Over the five decades they have averaged 25 per cent of gross product. In every decade except the depressed thirties the margin has been substantial.

Resources providing a margin above maintenance requirements may be used for defense, or to support an increase in consumption expenditures or an expansion of capital plant. Division of the total margin, by decades, among these three uses is shown in the following table and in Figure 3. The measures given are decade aggregates. For the five decades as a whole approximately 51 per cent

			Uses of margin above maintenance		
				Progress	
	Margin above	War and	Consumption	Net capital	Total for
Decade	maintenance	defense	increase	increase	progress
	(billions	of	1929	dollars)	
1901-10	144	4	85	55	140
1911-20	118	28	37	53	90
1921-30	223	8	140	75	215
1931-40	14	11	—9	12	3
1941-50	558	228	285	45	330

of our output margin was used to raise consumption levels, 23 per cent was used to create net additions to our capital plant, and 26 per cent was used for defense.[10] About three-quarters of the margin was devoted to progress, one-quarter to national defense.

Behind these over-all proportions there have been wide decade-to-decade shifts in the uses to which the output margin has been put. Amounts spent for war and defense have varied from 4 to 228

[10] Each consumption increase in the above table is measured with reference to the preceding decade as standard, whereas the defense and capital formation figures are the total absolute amounts used for these purposes. If we use the consumption level of 1891-1900 as a fixed consumption standard for the fifty years from 1901-50, we may compare consumption changes for the whole half century with the absolute amounts used for other non-maintenance purposes. Using 1891-1900 as a base, we find that 74 per cent of the margin above maintenance needs was used to raise consumption levels, 12 per cent for net capital formation, 14 per cent for defense.

billions of 1929 dollars. Net capital formation has varied from 12 to 75 billions. Amounts devoted to consumption gains have ranged from −9 to 285 billions. Progress, as measured by the sum of the

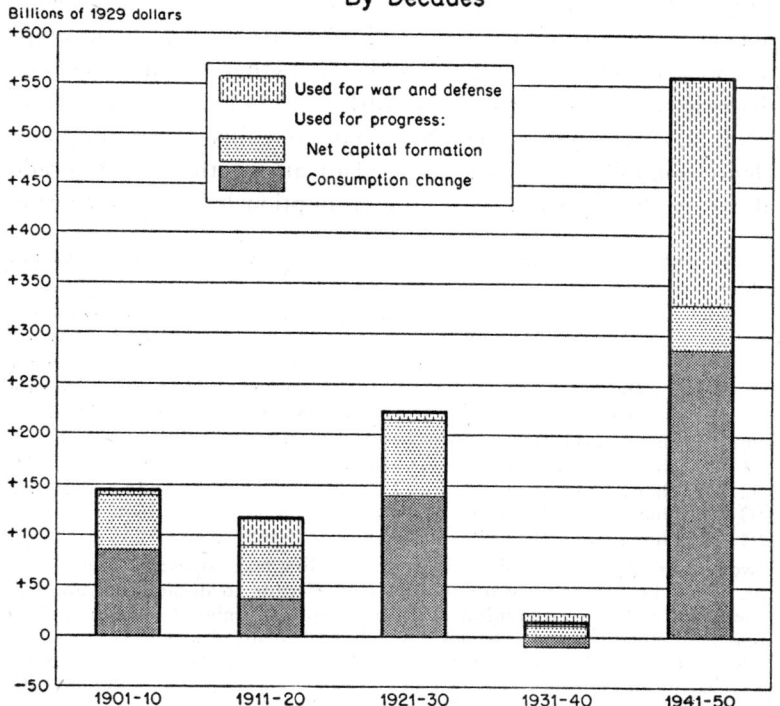

Figure 3
Uses of National Product Margin above Maintenance Needs By Decades

amounts going to raise consumption levels and to expand capital plant, was most rapid in the first, third, and fifth decades. We have moved forward in three great surges, each taking the economy to a new peak.[11]

The entries measuring decade-to-decade changes in the resources

---

[11] What I have called margins above maintenance needs are, of course, not the same as increments to gross national product. Yet the two are not far apart in magnitude. Decade increments to national product, and the three major

devoted to raising per capita consumption levels are perhaps of greatest interest. These are the immediate indexes of changes in the material well-being of members of the population at large. In maintaining capital stock we are resisting the processes of erosion. In spending for war and defense we are diverting resources to necessary protection, but these uses do not represent social or individual advances. In adding to capital we are building instruments, not end products.[12] But in augmenting resources used for consumption we are adding to the goods and services that enrich living. The three decades — first, third, and fifth — for which the "progress" totals were greatest brought the sharpest gains in consumption. Depression followed by war retarded advance in the second decade of this century. In the twenties consumption levels were sharply

---

uses to which each of these increments was put, are given in the following table.

Decade	Gross national product increment	Uses of product increment		
		Consumption	Gross capital formation	War and defense
	(billions of 1929 dollars)			
1901-10 (change from 1891-1900)	+161	+131	+28	+2
1911-20 (change from 1901-10)	+148	+104	+20	+24
1921-30 (change from 1911-20)	+235	+210	+45	—20
1931-40 (change from 1921-30)	+5	+58	—56	+3
1941-50 (change from 1931-40)	+650	+363	+70	+217

Two features distinguish this table from preceding text tables: 1) For all uses the figures here cited measure *changes* from decade to decade, not absolute amounts. 2) The consumption and gross capital formation entries include some requirements for maintenance as well as elements of progress.

Successive decade increments to national product have been mainly devoted to consumption. For the five decades as a whole no less than 72 per cent of the total of the increments to national product was devoted to consumer needs. Nine per cent was devoted to additions to gross capital, and 19 per cent to war and defense. There were, of course, variations from decade to decade, corresponding in general to decade shifts in margins above maintenance needs. The first, third, and fifth decades brought the greatest advances in both consumption expenditures and gross capital formation.

[12] The residential housing component of capital formation is an exception. Housing is an end product the use of which is spread over a number of years. For some purposes it would be useful to include residential housing among consumption goods. However, estimates of consumption including residential housing would not differ greatly from those given. Expenditures on residential construction during the last five decades have amounted to less than 5 per cent of all consumer expenditures.

advanced in a productivity spurt of exceptional intensity. Protracted depression brought retrogression in the thirties. The forties witnessed an extraordinary outburst of productive power. Drawing upon great additional resources of manpower and using improved equipment and new productive techniques, we provided war materials in massive proportions; in the same decade we lifted consumption levels to heights never before attained.[13]

We obtain a clearer view of the historical course of consumption levels by reducing the consumption increments to per capita terms, and showing each decade gain against the pre-existing level of per capita consumption. This is done in the following table; the expenditure figures are decade totals, per capita.

Decade	Per capita consumer expenditures (1929 dollars)	Change from preceding decade Absolute (1929 dollars)	Relative (per cent)
1891-1900	3,157		
1901-10	4,166	1,009	+32
1911-20	4,537	371	+9
1921-30	5,741	1,204	+27
1931-40	5,670	—71	—1
1941-50	7,692	2,022	+36

From an average per capita expenditure of $3,157 in the decade 1891-1900, there was an advance of over one thousand dollars to $4,166 in the decade 1901-10. (These are, of course, decade totals, in dollars of 1929 purchasing power. A figure for per capita expenditure per decade may be divided by ten to give the more familiar

---

[13] The major advance in consumption levels came, of course, in the second half of the latest decade, but even during the years of fighting there was a substantial net gain in the output of consumption goods. We may, roughly, break the total consumption increase of 285 billions of 1929 dollars recorded for the decade as a whole into a 93 billion dollar gain from 1941 to 1945 and a gain of 192 billions from 1946 to 1950. The base of comparison for each of the five-year periods is the decade 1931-40.

One factor contributing to the notable consumption gain in the forties was the relatively low level of consumption in the thirties, which fell slightly below the preceding decade. The thirties provide the base of comparison for the forties.

average annual per capita expenditure on consumption goods and services.) This was a gain of 32 per cent over the ten-year period. The next great advance came in 1921-30, with a jump of 27 per cent over the preceding decade. The final decade brought a gain of 36 per cent in per capita consumption expenditures, to a level of $7,692. This amounts to $769 per capita of the population per year, a notable advance over the average of $316 prevailing fifty years before. (The yardstick is, of course, a dollar of constant purchasing power.) The thesis that industrial development is necessarily marked by increasing misery would be hard to defend in the light of this record.

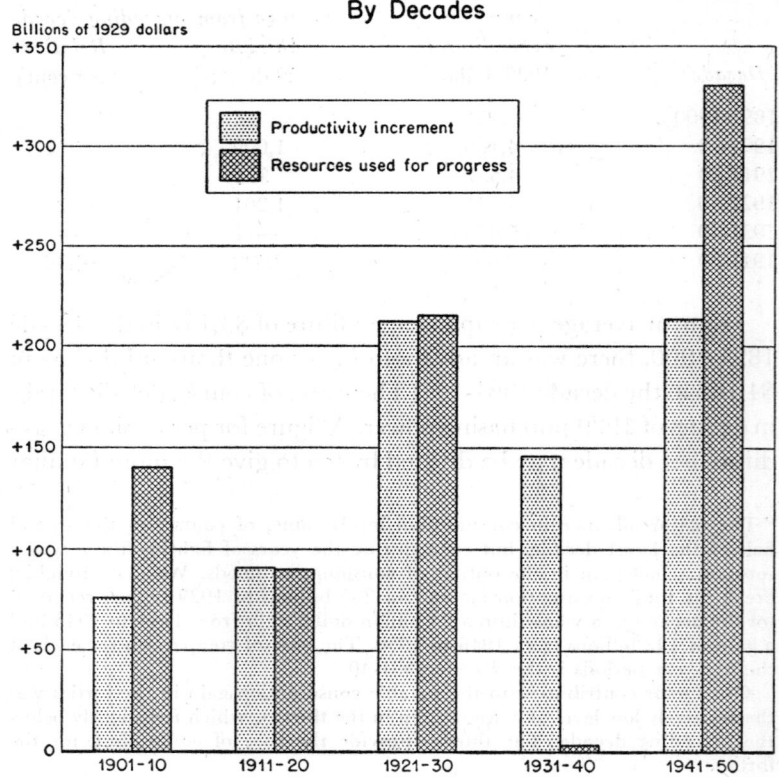

Figure 4

Productivity Increments and Resources Used for Progress By Decades

On the role of the productivity increment in progress

Decade after decade the major portion of the resources making up the margin above maintenance needs has been used for progress — to elevate consumption levels and to expand our capital plant. The resources so used are not sharply defined. We do not earmark for particular uses certain additions to labor input, certain new plants, or specified productivity gains. Nevertheless, we may ask what part has been played in the economic advances of the last fifty years by the increments to product attributable to gains in productivity. We cannot trace particular gains to particular results, but it is suggestive to compare the magnitudes of productivity gains, margins above maintenance needs, and resources used for progress. The several series, in the form of decade aggregates, are repeated in the following table. The measures relating to productivity and progress are shown graphically in Figure 4.

Decade	Productivity increment	Margin above maintenance	Resources used for progress	Productivity increment as percentage of margin above maintenance (per cent)	Productivity increment as percentage of resources used for progress (per cent)
	(billions of 1929 dollars)				
1901-10	76	144	140	53	54
1911-20	91	118	90	77	101
1921-30	212	223	215	95	99
1931-40	146	14	3		
1941-50	213	558	330	38	65

In the thirties substantially all the productivity increment was used for maintenance purposes. Omitting this decade, the sum of the productivity increments was equal to 57 per cent of the sum of the margins above maintenance needs, to 76 per cent of the sum of the resources used for progress over the half century. These percentages varied from decade to decade, but only in the forties did the productivity increment amount to less than one-half of the margin above maintenance needs. (A great increase in the volume of labor input was the chief factor in the expansion of this margin in that period.) The productivity increment equaled the full amount of the resources utilized for progress in the second and third decades; in the first decade it was more than one-half, in the fifth decade almost two-thirds, of the total amounts available for progress.

In considering productivity gains as a factor in economic and social progress, we must not regard productivity as an independent first cause, nor overlook the reverse influence of progress on productivity. We may not say that there would have been no progress in the second and third decades had there been no productivity gains, or that the increment to product available for progress would have been reduced by fifty to sixty per cent in the first and fifth decades if manhour output had not increased. For if productivity had not increased, complex related processes would have been modified. Hours of work would not have been reduced as they were in the twenties and thirties if manhour output had not gone up; the size and degree of use of the labor force would have been altered somewhat; the capital plant would not have grown as it did, and capital maintenance requirements would have been less. In the interactions of the factors in economic change, productivity gains were at once cause and effect of these associated movements in capital supply, in the labor force, and in working conditions. Yet there can be no doubt, from the relative magnitudes involved, that the productivity factor, as a closely correlated variable, has played a major part in the advances in consumption levels and the expansion of capital plant that constitute economic progress.[14] The form of progress most richly and consistently aided by

[14] Additions to output attributable to the input of new labor played a major role in meeting defense needs in the forties, and contributed materially to progress in that decade. In the thirties the labor input increment was negative. It was small in the twenties — equal to less than one-ninth of the output of resources used for progress. In the decade spanning the first world war the labor input increment, while not inconsiderable, was much smaller than the productivity increment. Only in the first and fifth decades was the input of new labor large enough to play an active role in progress.

There can be no doubt that some part of the labor input increment (a part including the labor of immigrants and of new members of the labor force with young families) is utilized for population maintenance, rather than for the lifting of consumption levels or for net capital formation — the two forms of economic progress. In periods of war a major portion of the labor input increment is allocated to defense. These considerations support the evidence provided by the statistical record that the productivity increment has been a far more potent factor than the labor input increment in economic progress in the United States over the last half century.

productivity gains has been progress in living standards. Such gains have also given steady support to the expansion of capital plant. They have helped to maintain established consumption standards when other instruments failed. The steadily re-created productivity increment has been, at once, the spearhead of progress and a reserve against emergency.

IV

In the preceding pages we have discussed the pattern of economic growth of the United States over the last half century. The materials presented bear on questions central to the appraisal of an economic system. Has it produced? Has it grown in effectiveness as a producing mechanism? It was Ernest Bevin's view that the central test of an economy is "Has it delivered the goods?". But this cannot be the sole criterion of judgment. We must ask "How has productive power been used?" This question raises issues beyond the economic. Arnold Toynbee has said that the new power found through the simplification of process that generates the growth of civilizations always presents a moral challenge. Disposable resources may be used to promote welfare or illfare. In a progressive economy, marked by steadily recurring productivity increments and expanding margins above maintenance needs, each generation faces this challenge anew.

Our economy, in its performance over the first half of the twentieth century, has clearly met Bevin's test. We have used our natural resources to produce a great and growing volume of goods and services. Apart from the protracted check that came in the thirties, the advance has been virtually unbroken. By far the greatest factor in this gain has been rising productivity. Machines, plants, administrative methods, and men have improved in productive quality; equipment has grown in quantity; flexible power has been carried to assembly line and bench. These improvements, embodied in innumerable major and minor working methods, have brought an increase in output per unit of productive effort that is probably without precedent in our history.

Appraisal of the uses to which these tremendous productive

powers have been put is not so simple. Non-economic standards of judgment must enter if the moral issues suggested by Toynbee are to be faced. We have used some of these powers for destruction, a fact that may be charged to the ill-fortune of our generation rather than to design and deliberate choice. Thanks to modern technology we have had to employ only a relatively small part of our resources to maintain and enlarge our productive plant. We have used most of our vast new powers to ease the lot of citizens at large through gains in leisure, and to improve it through diversified consumption patterns. Not all the standards expressed in this diversification might win a moralist's highest sanction. There are doubtless faults to amend. But the record leaves no doubt that much of our new productive power has gone, over this half century, to advance human welfare. In major degree, the benefits of industrial progress in the United States in this half century have served to lighten toil for producers and elevate living standards for consumers.

Note 1

ON THE PRESENT ESTIMATES OF GROSS NATIONAL PRODUCT

The estimates of gross national product used in this paper are a modification of Kuznets' basic concepts. Kuznets' peacetime concept of national product omits all war output of a nondurable character and "all nonwar expenditures of governments except those representing final products . . . or gross additions to government construction." (*National Product since 1869*, p. 23). For comparison with total labor input we wish to include the full defense output in national product; we therefore add to Kuznets' figures estimates of total war and defense expenditures. (These are unpublished estimates of M. Slade Kendrick for the period 1891-1938, estimates of the Department of Commerce for the years 1939-1950.) This addition would lead to a duplicate count of war durables, which do enter into Kuznets' estimates (peacetime concept) as elements of gross capital formation. To correct for this we deduct the equivalent of the war durables in Kuznets' series for the years 1917-21 and 1939-50, when such duplication would be considerable. We thus derive a series which differs somewhat from those of both Kuznets and Commerce — from Kuznets in that nondurable defense goods are included in our national product estimates in years of war and of peace, from Commerce in that the contribution of government to our estimates is more restricted. Kuznets' concept, which we employ except in respect to nondurable war goods, is narrower than that of Commerce in treating the contribution of government. Kuznets' present estimates extend only to 1949. We have projected his series to 1950 on the basis of a splice with the Department of Commerce series.

We have built up estimates of gross national product in constant dollars as the sum of its three deflated components. The deflators

23

used for consumer expenditures and for nonwar capital formation were Kuznets' imputed price indexes for the period 1891-1949, extended to 1950 by splicing with Commerce's deflators. The series on military expenditures was deflated by Kuznets' imputed price index for gross national product for the period 1891-1939; for 1940 an average of Kuznets' price index for war output and Commerce's price index for federal expenditures was used; for 1941-43 Kuznets' price index for war output was used; for 1943-50 we employed Commerce's price index for federal expenditures, spliced to Kuznets' price index for war output at 1943.

I should point out that the margin of error in the deflation process is inevitably wide for the war period. The accurate measurement of the prices of civilian goods is more difficult under wartime conditions than it is in peacetime, and these difficulties are compounded in dealing with the prices of munitions. The deflated measures doubtless provide a better approximation to real product than do the undeflated measures, but fairly large errors of estimate are clearly present.

Note 2

Estimates of productivity

Index numbers of productivity and estimates of productivity increments can be highly useful measures of economic change, but they are far from unambiguous. All the difficulties involved in the measurement of production changes attach to them, plus others that arise when the ratio of output to effort input is computed. Here I note some of these difficulties and certain limitations of the specific measures used in this paper.

General considerations. Index numbers derived from ratios of physical output to effort input $\frac{Q}{E}$ are accurate measures of changes in the average unit effectiveness of work done when physical output is constant in quality and composition, when the scope of the measures of effort input is constant over time, and when available measures of effort input are identical in coverage with the measures of physical output with which they are compared, or when the two are constant and fully representative proportions of the totals to which they respectively relate.[1] When these conditions are met, changes in the ratio $\frac{Q}{E}$ measure shifts in the average physical return to a unit of work time (I am assuming that effort input is measured in terms of manhours, manweeks, manmonths, or manyears of work done). The ratio may be altered by a diversity of factors. These may include changes in

- the quantity or quality of capital equipment used
- the quality of effort input (This may be a change in intensity or a change in average degree of skill. Such a change in average skill may result from a change in the competence of individuals or groups, or from a shift in the composition of the work force.)
- the ratio of effort input to productive instruments used or to natural resources used (A change in average productivity resulting from the play of diminishing returns would be included in this category.)
- the quality of natural resources or materials used
- the quantity of materials or intermediate products used to produce a standard unit of final product
- the amount of nonhuman power used or the manner of its use
- the organization of productive units
- working conditions
- the effectiveness of administration

A given change in productivity may reflect any combination of these factors. In particular, the interpretation of a given movement will be affected by the scope of the measures of effort input. In a special instance these measures could include only direct labor;

---

[1] For present purposes I am setting output solely against input of human effort. For other purposes productivity might be measured by comparing total output with the input of some other productive factor, or with the input of a combination of human effort and other factors.

variations in the role of indirect labor would then be one factor influencing the movements of the productivity index. In another case the labor equivalent of capital used up in the productive process might be included in the effort input (this would be logical when gross national product is used as a measure of output); the aim in this case would be to incorporate in E a measure of changes in the quantity of capital utilized or in the intensity of capital use, and thus to eliminate this factor as an influence on productivity. In measuring productivity in manufacturing, the effort equivalent of purchased power might be included in E, in order to eliminate the effect on productivity of possible shifts from internally generated to purchased power, or the reverse.

In the construction of closely controlled measures of productivity (of the type now being developed by the U.S. Bureau of Labor Statistics for particular industries) an attempt is made to hold constant some of the variables that bear upon productivity changes. More exact interpretation of the derived measures is then possible. In general, however, we must be content with measures of productivity that embody the results of the many indefinable changes that influence the effectiveness of work input, and that do not permit us to determine precisely which factors account for changes in productivity.

When the conditions set forth above are realized we can have accurate measures of changes in productivity, although we may not be able to specify the causal factors. When these conditions are not realized, when output is not constant in quality and in composition, when measures of output and of effort input differ in coverage, or change unequally in degree of coverage, productivity indexes become less reliable. It is fair to say that conditions for complete accuracy are seldom if ever met. Changes in quality of product are constant and elusive; any composite product of the kind represented by conventional indexes of production is subject to unceasing shifts in its make-up.[2] We may do something by judi-

---

[2] From an economy-wide or industry-wide viewpoint productivity may increase as a result of changes that shift labor from sectors of relatively low value of output per manhour to sectors of higher value of output per manhour, although there may be no change in the internal productivity of individual plants or

cious choice of weights to improve the comparability of indexes of output and of effort input, but full comparability is virtually never attained for comprehensive measures of production and of labor input. The best of our measures of productivity are imperfect and in some degree ambiguous in meaning.

Economy-wide estimates. In the present paper we have made use of measures of output, of effort input, and of productivity that purport to cover the whole economy. The estimates of output relate to a heterogeneous composite of goods and services, an aggregate that is not open to direct physical measurement. To portions of this aggregate the concept of productivity applies only equivocally. Apart from conceptual difficulties, estimating procedures are subject to considerable margins of error. Yet the question faced is important, and one to which answers will be sought: What changes have occurred over time in the economy of the United States in the average real return per unit of productive effort expended?

The adequacy of our answers to this question will depend upon the accuracy with which we can measure changes in the real output of the economy and in the amount of work done in obtaining this output. Two steps are involved in the measurement of changes in real national product — the estimation of total output (gross or net) in terms of current dollars, and the "deflation" of the elements of this total to correct for the effect of price changes. Neither of these operations can be carried through with complete accuracy. Current estimates of national product are built up from masses of detailed figures. For some processes the basic data are good, for others they are fragmentary. Errors of estimate are large for the earlier years covered, smaller for later years. No precise measure of the magnitude of these errors is available. The accuracy of estimates of national product as indexes of *change* from year to

---

subdivisions of an industry. When detailed information is available on the constituent elements of the economy or the industry, the effects of such shifts may be estimated and separated from the effects of changes in productivity ratios for plants or industrial subdivisions. See Solomon Fabricant, *Employment in Manufacturing Industries* (National Bureau of Economic Research, 1942), pp. 335-7. The increasing accuracy and expanding coverage of the Census of Manufactures are providing information more adequate for this purpose in that important field.

year or decade to decade is greater than their accuracy in absolute terms — and it is as indexes of change that we use them here.

When we use these estimates as indexes of change over time we face the second problem noted above — that of correcting for fluctuations in prices. This is done by the use of a complex set of price indexes relating to different sectors of the economy. Here, again, we can be reasonably accurate in treating data for some economic processes, while for others deflation gives at best only a rough approximation to the truth. The accuracy of the deflation procedure varies over time; accurate correction for price changes in wartime is far more difficult than it is in peacetime. The economic upheavals of World War II, in particular, were so great as to render impossible accurate correction for price changes and accurate measurement of real output. All estimates of real product for the war period are subject to wide margins of error.

The measurement of total effort input as an aggregate of undifferentiated work time expended in production is in principle simple. If we know the total number of employed members of the labor force (including all degrees of skill and all kinds of persons engaged in productive operations) and the average length of the workweek or workyear we can determine the total number of manhours or manyears of effort entering into the national product for a given period. Here, again, we must depend upon estimates that are subject to error. For recent years estimates of the total volume of employment are based upon the results of monthly sample surveys, which are blown up to cover the whole economy. For earlier years we depend upon periodic census counts of the gainfully occupied, with various corrections and interpolations. National estimates of average working hours per week or per year are built up from data and estimates for different industrial sectors. Figures on employment and hours for later years are more accurate than those for earlier years, but both current and early estimates are approximations only.[3] Indications of major changes in nationwide totals and averages may be accepted with reasonable confidence; indications of minor changes and short-period movements are less trustworthy.

[3] Details of the estimates employed in the present paper will be given in a forthcoming monograph of the National Bureau of Economic Research.

Note 3

ESTIMATION OF THE LABOR INPUT INCREMENT AND THE PRODUCTIVITY INCREMENT

The problem is that of separating an increment to output into a portion associated with an increase in labor input, and a portion associated with a productivity gain. (There are three other cases, representing other combinations of plus and minus changes in the labor input and productivity factors, but the principle involved is the same.) Since there is interaction between the two factors, which are related in a multiplicative way, there can be no definitive solution, but useful approximations to the two components of the increment may be obtained.

In brief, the procedure is as follows:

a) Estimate the increase that would have occurred in total output as a result of the given increase in labor input, but with no change in productivity. This gives what we may call Component A of the increment to gross national product.

b) Estimate the increase that would have occurred in total output as a result of the given increase in productivity, but with no change in labor input. This gives what we may call Component B.

c) Estimate the interaction component, the portion of the gain in gross national product that represents the combined result of an increment to labor input and an increment to manhour output. This gives what we may call Component C.

It is justifiable to assign Component A to the labor input factor, Component B to the productivity factor. A will vary directly with labor input, B with productivity. C, however, will vary with both factors. C is therefore arbitrarily divided, half being assigned to the labor input increment, half to the productivity increment.

This method may be illustrated with reference to decade aggregates for 1901-10 and 1911-20.

Decade	Gross national product (billions of 1929 dollars)	Labor input in total manhours (relative)	Output per manhour (relative)
1901-10	455	100.0	100.0
1911-20	603	111.4	118.9

The increment to gross national product (148 billions of dollars) is the sum of:

   Component A (455 × .114):   52 billions
   Component B (455 × .189):   86 billions
   Component C (148 — 52 — 86):   10 billions

The final estimate of the labor input increment for 1911-20 is 57 billions ($A + \frac{C}{2}$, or 52 + 5); the final estimate of the productivity increment is 91 billions ($B + \frac{C}{2}$, or 86 + 5).

As I have suggested at an earlier point, neither of these increments is to be regarded as the specific product or the marginal product of any of the conventional factors of production. Changes in the productivity ratio $\frac{Q}{MH}$, from which estimates of the productivity increment are derived, are the net result of a complex of movements, all involving relations between output and factor input that are defined conceptually by the traditional laws of return (operating over time). Thus if a change in labor input alters the ratio of effort input to natural resources or to instruments used and, through the play of diminishing returns, reduces average output per manhour of work done, these related changes will be reflected in both the labor input increment and the productivity increment (how their results will be divided between the two increments will depend on the relative magnitudes of the changes in labor input and in average return per manhour of labor input).

The method described is the mathematical equivalent of the following:
The labor input component of the increment to product between two periods is the increase in output that would have resulted from the given

increase in labor input, had the employed labor force been working at a productivity level equal to the average of manhour output in the two periods compared.

The productivity component of the increment to product is the increase in output that would have resulted from the given gain in output per manhour, had labor input been equal to its average during the two periods compared.

It may be demonstrated that the sum of the two components, as thus established, is equal to the total increment to product.

Let X = Manhours of work input, period 1
$X + \Delta X$ = Manhours of work input, period 2
Y = Output per manhour, period 1
$Y + \Delta Y$ = Output per manhour, period 2
$O = XY$ = Total output, period 1
$O + \Delta O = (X + \Delta X)(Y + \Delta Y)$
   = Total output, period 2

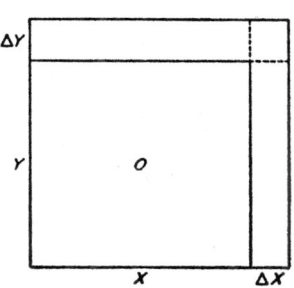

If we assume that X and Y change linearly between periods 1 and 2, then:

$$\bar{X} = X + \frac{\Delta X}{2}$$

$$\bar{Y} = Y + \frac{\Delta Y}{2}$$

The increment associated with the change in X is given by $\Delta X \left(Y + \frac{\Delta Y}{2}\right)$.

The increment associated with a change in Y is given by $\Delta Y \left(X + \frac{\Delta X}{2}\right)$.

As the sum of these two increments we have:

$$\Delta X \left(Y + \frac{\Delta Y}{2}\right) + \Delta Y \left(X + \frac{\Delta X}{2}\right) = Y\Delta X + X\Delta Y + \Delta X \Delta Y = \Delta O$$

(I am indebted to my colleague Henry Scheffé for this mode of viewing the decomposition of the increment to product.)

Beyond the formal equality thus established, the procedure has logical justification. In the limiting case in which there is no change in productivity, the entire increment to product is assigned to the change in labor input; at the other limit in which there is no change in labor input, the entire increment to product is assigned to the change in productivity. In cases falling between these limits, as we have seen, half of the small rectangle corresponding to the product of ΔX and ΔY (this corresponds to C of the procedure first noted) is assigned to each of the two factors.

The actual values, by decades, of the several components of the increments to product are given below. Component A, it will be noted, is equivalent to $Y\Delta X$, Component B to $X\Delta Y$, and Component C to $\Delta X\Delta Y$.

Decade	Increment to gross national product	Component A	Component B	Joint component C
	(billions of 1929 dollars)			
1901-10 (change from 1891-1900)	+161	+77	+67	+17
1911-20 (change from 1901-10)	+148	+52	+86	+10
1921-30 (change from 1911-20)	+235	+20	+209	+6
1931-40 (change from 1921-30)	+5	−129	+158	−24
1941-50 (change from 1931-40)	+650	+396	+173	+81

In deriving final estimates C was divided equally, for each decade, between the labor input component and the productivity component. In presenting these estimates it is recognized, of course, that labor input and productivity have changed together, and have interacted as they changed. Neither would have had the value actually recorded for a given decade had the other not been present as an active factor.

If the changes of the five decades are aggregated, we obtain from the above table the following summary of shifts between the decades 1891-1900 and 1941-1950:

Total increment to gross national product 1891-1900 to 1941-1950	Component A	Component B	Joint component C
1,199	416	693	90

Splitting the joint component C in half, and assigning half to each of the two factors, we have for the half century of growth a labor input increment of 461 billions (of 1929 dollars), a productivity increment of 738 billions. These are, respectively, 38.4 per cent and 61.6 per cent of the total increment of 1,199 billions.

Since the estimated magnitudes of the several components of an increment to national product are affected by the time unit employed, it is of interest to compare the preceding division of the half-century increment to national product with the division we should obtain by treating the half-century increment as a single lump. Relevant measures are given below:

Decade	Gross national product (billions of 1929 dollars)	Labor input in manhours (relative)	Output per manhour (relative)
1891-1900	294	100.0	100.0
1941-1950	1,493	180.5	281.3

Applying to this half-century increment the method just described, we have:

Increment to gross national product	Component A	Component B	Joint component C
1,199	237	533	429

If we split the joint component, assigning half to each of the two factors, we have for the half century a labor input increment of 451.5 billions, a productivity increment of 747.5 billions. These are, respectively, 37.7 per cent and 62.3 per cent of the total increment of 1,199 billions.

Chief interest attaches to the difference between the two values of the joint component, 90 when we move by decade steps, 429 when we move by a single half-century jump. In the latter case a much larger quantity is allocated on the somewhat arbitrary half-and-half division. Yet this division gives final values for the two components that are very close to those obtained from the presumably more accurate decade intervals.

The close agreement is in part fortuitous. Results obtained in the one case are not a check upon the other. The method of division here employed, applied to a single time period and then to subdivisions of that time period, would give identical results only where:

a) the relations between the two variables (labor input and output per manhour) are linear;

b) the separate subperiod movements mark out equal areas

35

above and below the straight line defining the net movements of the two variables between terminal dates of the whole time interval.

(The line defining the relation between labor input and output per manhour for each subperiod — here a decade — connects the appropriate corners of a rectangle similar to that represented by $\Delta X \Delta Y$ in the diagram on page 33. The limiting case, for these conditions, is that in which the movements between subperiods and between terminal dates of the whole time interval are defined by the same straight line.) In the present instance the related movements of labor input and manhour output during the last two decades of the half century departed sharply from the direction of changes during the first three decades. For the half century as a whole there was virtual equality of the deviations above and below the line marking the net fifty-year movements of the two variables; close agreement of the derived measures results. Where there is failure to agree, estimates based upon the shorter intervals would be preferred.

National Bureau Publications on Production, Employment, and Productivity

Books on Production, Employment, and Productivity

The Output of Manufacturing Industries, 1899-1937 (1940)   710 pp., $4.50
Solomon Fabricant

Employment in Manufacturing, 1899-1939: An Analysis of Its Relation to the Volume of Production (1942)   382 pp., 3.00
Solomon Fabricant

American Agriculture, 1899-1939: A Study of Output, Employment and Productivity (1942)   462 pp., 3.00
Harold Barger and Hans H. Landsberg

The Mining Industries, 1899-1939: A Study of Output, Employment and Productivity (1944)   474 pp., 3.00
Harold Barger and Sam H. Schurr

Output and Productivity in the Electric and Gas Utilities, 1899-1942 (1946)   208 pp., 3.00
J. M. Gould

Trends in Output and Employment (1947)   78 pp., 1.00
George J. Stigler

The Transportation Industries, 1889-1946: A Study of Output, Employment and Productivity (1951)   304 pp., 4.00
Harold Barger

Papers on Production, Employment, and Productivity

Manufacturing Output, 1929-1937
Occasional Paper 1, 1940   .25
Solomon Fabricant

The Relation between Factory Employment and Output since 1899
Occasional Paper 4, 1941   .25
Solomon Fabricant

Productivity of Labor in Peace and War
Occasional Paper 7, 1942   .25
Solomon Fabricant

Labor Savings in American Industry, 1899-1939
Occasional Paper 23, 1945   .50
Solomon Fabricant

Domestic Servants in the United States, 1900-1940
Occasional Paper 24, 1946   .50
George J. Stigler

The Rising Trend of Government Employment
Occasional Paper 29, 1949   .50
Solomon Fabricant

Employment and Compensation in Education
Occasional Paper 33, 1950   1.00
George J. Stigler

*Out of print.

The Role of Federal Credit Aids in Residential Construction

LEO GREBLER

STUDIES IN CAPITAL FORMATION AND FINANCING
OCCASIONAL PAPER 39

NATIONAL BUREAU OF ECONOMIC RESEARCH, INC.

OFFICERS
1953

Harry Scherman, *Chairman*
C. C. Balderston, *President*
Percival F. Brundage, *Vice-President*
George B. Roberts, *Treasurer*
W. J. Carson, *Executive Director*

DIRECTORS AT LARGE

Donald R. Belcher, *Westfield, New Jersey*
Wallace J. Campbell, *Director, The Cooperative League of the USA*
Albert J. Hettinger, Jr., *Lazard Freres and Company*
Oswald W. Knauth, *Beaufort, South Carolina*
H. W. Laidler, *Executive Director, League for Industrial Democracy*
Shepard Morgan, *New York City*
C. Reinold Noyes, *Princeton, New Jersey*
George B. Roberts, *Vice-President, National City Bank*
Beardsley Ruml, *New York City*
Harry Scherman, *Chairman, Book-of-the-Month Club*
George Soule, *Bennington College*
N. I. Stone, *Consulting Economist*
J. Raymond Walsh, *New York City*
Leo Wolman, *Columbia University*
Theodore O. Yntema, *Vice President-Finance, Ford Motor Company*

DIRECTORS BY UNIVERSITY APPOINTMENT

E. Wight Bakke, *Yale*
C. C. Balderston, *Pennsylvania*
Arthur F. Burns, *Columbia*
G. A. Elliott, *Toronto*
Frank W. Fetter, *Northwestern*
H. M. Groves, *Wisconsin*

Gottfried Haberler, *Harvard*
Clarence Heer, *North Carolina*
R. L. Kozelka, *Minnesota*
Paul M. O'Leary, *Cornell*
T. W. Schultz, *Chicago*
Jacob Viner, *Princeton*

DIRECTORS APPOINTED BY OTHER ORGANIZATIONS

Percival F. Brundage, *American Institute of Accountants*
Frederick C. Mills, *American Statistical Association*
S. H. Ruttenberg, *Congress of Industrial Organizations*
Murray Shields, *American Management Association*
Boris Shishkin, *American Federation of Labor*
Donald H. Wallace, *American Economic Association*
Frederick V. Waugh, *American Farm Economic Association*
Harold F. Williamson, *Economic History Association*

RESEARCH STAFF

Solomon Fabricant, *Acting Director of Research*
Geoffrey H. Moore, *Associate Director of Research*

Moses Abramovitz
Harold Barger
Morris A. Copeland
Daniel Creamer
David Durand
Milton Friedman
Millard Hastay
W. Braddock Hickman
F. F. Hill
Daniel M. Holland

Thor Hultgren
Simon Kuznets
Clarence D. Long
Ruth P. Mack
Frederick C. Mills
Raymond J. Saulnier
Lawrence H. Seltzer
George J. Stigler
Leo Wolman
Herbert B. Woolley

Relation of the Directors
to the Work and Publications
of the National Bureau of Economic Research

1. The object of the National Bureau of Economic Research is to ascertain and to present to the public important economic facts and their interpretation in a scientific and impartial manner. The Board of Directors is charged with the responsibility of ensuring that the work of the National Bureau is carried on in strict conformity with this object.

2. To this end the Board of Directors shall appoint one or more Directors of Research.

3. The Director or Directors of Research shall submit to the members of the Board, or to its Executive Committee, for their formal adoption, all specific proposals concerning researches to be instituted.

4. No report shall be published until the Director or Directors of Research shall have submitted to the Board a summary drawing attention to the character of the data and their utilization in the report, the nature and treatment of the problems involved, the main conclusions and such other information as in their opinion would serve to determine the suitability of the report for publication in accordance with the principles of the National Bureau.

5. A copy of any manuscript proposed for publication shall also be submitted to each member of the Board. For each manuscript to be so submitted a special committee shall be appointed by the President, or at his designation by the Executive Director, consisting of three Directors selected as nearly as may be one from each general division of the Board. The names of the special manuscript committee shall be stated to each Director when the summary and report described in paragraph (4) are sent to him. It shall be the duty of each member of the committee to read the manuscript. If each member of the special committee signifies his approval within thirty days, the manuscript may be published. If each member of the special committee has not signified his approval within thirty days of the transmittal of the report and manuscript, the Director of Research shall then notify each member of the Board, requesting approval or disapproval of publication, and thirty additional days shall be granted for this purpose. The manuscript shall then not be published unless at least a majority of the entire Board and a two-thirds majority of those members of the Board who shall have voted on the proposal within the time fixed for the receipt of votes on the publication proposed shall have approved.

6. No manuscript may be published, though approved by each member of the special committee, until forty-five days have elapsed from the transmittal of the summary and report. The interval is allowed for the receipt of any memorandum of dissent or reservation, together with a brief statement of his reasons, that any member may wish to express; and such memorandum of dissent or reservation shall be published with the manuscript if he so desires. Publication does not, however, imply that each member of the Board has read the manuscript, or that either members of the Board in general, or of the special committee, have passed upon its validity in every detail.

7. A copy of this resolution shall, unless otherwise determined by the Board, be printed in each copy of every National Bureau book.

(Resolution adopted October 25, 1926 and revised February 6, 1933 and February 24, 1941)

This is a preliminary report on a joint study of capital formation and financing in residential real estate by the Institute for Urban Land Use and Housing Studies, Columbia University and the National Bureau of Economic Research, Inc. The study is part of a large investigation of trends and prospects in capital formation and financing made possible by a grant from the Life Insurance Association of America.

Price: $1.00

Copyright, 1953, by National Bureau of Economic Research, Inc.
1819 Broadway, New York 23, N. Y. All rights reserved.
Typography by Oscar Leventhal, Inc.
Printing by Basso Printing Corporation

THE ROLE OF FEDERAL CREDIT AIDS IN RESIDENTIAL CONSTRUCTION

LEO GREBLER
Institute for Urban Land Use and Housing Studies
Columbia University

Studies in Capital Formation and Financing
Occasional Paper 39
National Bureau of Economic Research, Inc.   1953

Contents

		Page
1	**Scope of the Paper**	13
2	**New Housebuilding under FHA and VA Programs**	16
	Effects on the Volume of Construction	20
	Widening the Market	21
	Sales Housing Versus Rental Housing	26
3	**Importance of Federal Programs in Mortgage Finance**	29
	Mortgage Funds for New Housebuilding	30
	Influence in Home Mortgage Lending Activity	34
	Government-Insured Loans in the Mortgage Debt	34
	Influence on Sources of Funds	36
	The Government's Role in the Secondary Market	42
	Influence on Cost and Terms of Financing	49
4	**A Note on the Future of Federal Credit Aids**	54
	A Trend?	55
	Limits to Present Types of Aids	59
	Consequences for Capital Formation and Financing	62

IN THE PREPARATION OF THIS PAPER I have benefited greatly from advice and criticism of a number of colleagues and experts. I wish particularly to thank Solomon Fabricant, Simon Kuznets, Geoffrey H. Moore, and Raymond J. Saulnier of the National Bureau staff for careful review of drafts and many helpful comments. Valuable suggestions were made by David M. Blank and Louis Winnick, my associates in the preparation of a monograph on *Capital Formation and Financing in Residential Real Estate,* from which this paper is derived. I am indebted to James J. O'Leary, Director of Investment Research of the Life Insurance Association of America, and to Raymond W. Goldsmith for their keen interest in this paper and incisive comments. The charts were drawn by H. Irving Forman.

Finally, I acknowledge gratefully the assistance rendered by Allan F. Thornton, Director of the Division of Research and Statistics, Federal Housing Administration, and by members of research staffs of other federal agencies who were consulted on points of fact and analysis. No one but the author, however, bears responsibility for the interpretation of data and the judgments expressed in this paper or for any of its shortcomings.

L. G.

Introduction

1

This paper is a product of a wider inquiry initiated by the National Bureau of Economic Research in mid-1950, at the request of the Life Insurance Association of America and with its generous assistance. The inquiry deals with long term trends in capital formation and financing in the United States — in the hope that establishing these trends and analyzing the relevant factors may contribute to a better understanding of current problems and to a more intelligent view of the future. Even if we find, as we well may, that the patterns of change revealed by the past are too complex and the factors at play too uncertain in their bearing to permit specific projections, whatever we learn should serve to enrich and revise current notions and theories, and thus provide a sounder basis upon which both research and policy may be planned.

The inquiry is organized primarily about the major capital-using and demanding sectors of the economy — agriculture, mining, manufacturing, public utilities, residential real estate, government, and the foreign sector. Each is the subject of a study designed to analyze the factors that have determined trends in capital formation and financing in the sector and to indicate, so far as possible, the significance of these factors for the future. In tracing trends in real capital formation we try to reach back to 1870; in dealing with trends in financing, we must, in most cases, stop at 1900 and have great difficulties extending the record even that far back.

In addition to the sector studies, the inquiry comprises two others, of somewhat wider scope. One deals with intermediate financial institutions, and attempts to establish trends in external financing channeled through these various institutions and to link them, so far as possible, with various groups of capital users. The other general study combines the results of all others and places them within the broader framework provided by countrywide estimates of national product and their relevant components, and of country-wide estimates of assets and debts. The whole inquiry gains much from a study of savings covering the period since 1897, recently completed by Dr. Raymond W. Goldsmith under the auspices of the Life Insurance Association of America.

The monographs which will present our results in detail will, it is hoped, be completed within a year or two. For earlier circulation, we shall present some of the findings as occasional papers, of which the present is the first.

2

Professor Grebler's paper deals with what, on the scale of the inquiry, is a brief period and a narrow facet — federal credit aids in their impact on the volume and financing of new nonfarm residential construction during the past seventeen years. But within this area, the conclusions are striking, and are of general interest not only because the magnitudes of the affected processes are so massive, but also because they reflect part of a wider trend with far-reaching ramifications.

Let me state the main factual conclusions of Professor Grebler's richly documented paper, quoting his text directly whenever convenient.

1. Of the 9.5 million new dwelling units constructed in this country during the seventeen years, 1935-51, some 3.8 million, or about 40 per cent, were financed with mortgage loans insured by the Federal Housing Administration or guaranteed by the Veterans' Administration. For the six postwar years, 1946-51, when 5.8 million dwelling units were built, 2.6 millions of these, or over 45 per cent, were so financed.

2. The federal credit aid program was most important in financing new, medium priced, one-family houses in the range from

$6,000 to $12,000. The proportion of new dwelling units financed by federally insured mortgages was higher for rental than for owner-occupied housing, after World War II, but rental units were relatively few in number.

3. From 1935 through 1951, the total of insured or guaranteed mortgage loans on new construction amounted to $22 billion; $17 billion of it originated during the six postwar years, 1946 through 1951. Over the entire period, government insured or guaranteed loans averaged about 45 per cent of the total estimated flow of mortgage funds into new construction, and about 50 per cent during the six postwar years. At the end of 1950, the estimated balance outstanding of FHA and VA loans on existing and new construction, over $22 billion, was roughly 40 per cent of the aggregate residential mortgage debt.

4. "The exclusion of individual lenders in the FHA program and their small share in the VA program have accentuated the tendency toward institutionalization of the residential mortgage debt. The government insurance programs, particularly FHA, have stimulated the participation of commercial banks in residential mortgage financing." (p. 36)

5. Largely through the Federal National Mortgage Association, a government owned facility, the government assisted in developing a secondary market for FHA and VA loans, which tended to widen the geographic scope of the market for mortgage loans. Even more important, the FNMA became a primary supplier of mortgage funds in some of its operations, e.g., through heavy purchases of VA loans in 1950 and 1951. This function is quite distinct from that of attracting private funds through insurance or guarantee.

6. "The federal credit aids since the middle thirties have probably accelerated the decline in residential mortgage interest rates and the liberalization of other contract terms. Lower interest rates and particularly longer contract terms on FHA and VA loans, compared to conventional mortgages, represent advantages to borrowers under these programs so far as periodic outlays are concerned. Because of the indirect influence of easy credit on prices paid for new as well as existing construction during the war and

postwar periods, however, these advantages were at least partially canceled by price effects." (p. 53)

The capsule summary above does bare justice to the findings of Professor Grebler's paper. It would hardly be possible to summarize here his illuminating comments on the effects of government credit aids on the volume of new residential construction; on its distribution between rental and owner-occupied housing, or among various price classes; on the channeling of mortgage funds through various types of financial intermediaries; or on the real costs of financing to the consumers. Nor can one condense his discussion of the changing philosophy behind this particular group of government policies — the shift from thinking largely in terms of "pump priming" under conditions of underemployment of resources to emphasis on facilitating supply, under conditions of full employment, to groups that, without special aid, would have difficulty in securing new housing. Finally, it would scarcely serve a useful purpose to try to summarize Professor Grebler's provocative discussion of the significance of this record of government credit aid for the future — particularly the possible extension of government activity beyond mere aid to private financing of new housing to measures that would stimulate new construction, not necessarily with private financing as this term is ordinarily understood. The reader, whose interest the preceding remarks are designed to stir, is urged to turn to Professor Grebler's discussion.

The principal purpose of this introduction is to indicate the relation of the findings in the paper to the main concern of the broader inquiry into capital formation and financing. In one sense this relation is obvious, for the quantities speak for themselves. From 1946 through 1950, in one quinquennium, nonfarm residential building amounted to $40 billion, out of a total of private domestic capital formation (gross) of over $180 billion, or somewhat less than a quarter. It may safely be asserted that the ratio of external financing to gross capital formation is much higher for nonfarm residential construction than for other types of business capital formation. It follows that the governmental activities with which Professor Grebler deals directly affected a quarter of all private domestic capital accumulation, and a much higher proportion of the total external capital funds used for this purpose.

Rather than stress the obvious, it may be of more interest to touch briefly upon a more difficult problem raised by Professor Grebler's paper. What does this historical incident, this rapid change during a period just a bit more than a decade and a half, mean with respect to our capacity to extract from the past results both tangible and stable enough to provide a firm basis for analyzing current problems and future prospects? This question, which haunts all research into complex and variable phenomena, is perhaps most appropriate here — when we deal with a case of rapid change, the acting agent being that apparently most unpredictable institution, the government.

3

As Professor Grebler observes, each step taken by the government in providing aids in financing new residential construction might be explained by the specific circumstances of the time. If one asks why each phase of this unprecedented program of insurance and guarantees was undertaken when it was, one can find many apparent reasons in the immediate antecedents. The drastic decline in values and the resulting threat to the whole ownership and debt structure of the country that occurred after 1929 produced conditions under which an adequate flow of funds to new construction, without aid by government, was thought by many to be far from likely. One should also note that, at least as far as the historical record back to the Civil War reveals, the decade of the 1930's was the first since the 1870's in which the drastic contraction of the long cycle in residential construction and values coincided with a severe and prolonged depression in general business conditions. Finally, it occurred when the structure of real estate debt was more fully encased than ever before in a complex network of intermediate financial institutions acting as custodians of the savings of a vast majority of the population. Under such conditions, many thought that the drastic process of deflation could only be checked by government aid, and that a satisfactory revival would not otherwise take place. Likewise, the coming of World War II and the accompanying restriction on construction; the accumulated shortage of housing facilities; the expected pressures upon limited productive resources in the postwar reconstruction; the restrictive effects of rent control; and many other facets of the economic and political scene provided a setting without which the governmental aid programs might not have been undertaken.

It is patent that other specific explanations could be added to or substituted for those mentioned. Less apparent is the implication of this wealth of specific explanations. That each step in governmental activity in this, as in many other fields, can be traced to a variety of antecedents — some immediate and others with roots in the longer past — makes all the more difficult reduction to a few determining factors. We are faced here with the familiar problem of generalizing from specific interpretations of concrete historical events. One is always struck by the multiplicity of "causes" that can be adduced for any specific historical event, or a specific chain of them. Were these "causes" reducible to one or few dominant factors, of the kind that can be observed and empirically studied — not merely glib references to "trends" and "waves of the future" — the task of deriving a tenable theory for analysis of current problems or predicting future prospects would be much simpler. Yet, however difficult the task, the first prerequisite is a clear realization of the difficulty — a full recognition of the historical setting within which the events occurred, the kind of recognition that is provided by Professor Grebler's account.

This account of the development of a new pattern of governmental aid also suggests the great capacity of society, particularly when organized with adequate room for individual and group initiative, for social invention. The record of the human mind in the fields of scientific discovery and technical invention has become so familiar that reference to it is a commonplace. Anyone who has ever observed how society deals with the succession of problems into which it seems to blunder cannot fail to be impressed by the ingenuity and inventiveness that goes into evolving new measures, new institutions, new practices. Professor Grebler's account is a story of one of these social inventions. But if our economic and social past has been materially affected by the series of social (as well as technical) inventions, an orderly pattern is bound to be all the more elusive. Discoveries and inventions, by definition, include an element of the unusual and accidental; would not this element be sufficiently strong to render the past a succession of events, each specifically explicable, but not falling easily into recognizable and simple patterns?

Clearly, a broad inquiry such as the present study of capital formation and financing must assume some discoverable order in the past, some basic and persistent forces, some recognizable pattern in the motley succession of specific events. To quote Professor Grebler: "Here, as in the interpretation of other events, it is necessary to distinguish sharply between the incidents that give rise to political actions and the more deep-seated forces that underlie the actions" (p. 56). It does not require much digging or imagination to identify the more deep-seated and persistent forces that give continuity to social life and impose some order on its course. The members of society transmit their continuing heritage from one generation to another and, expecting to do so, plan their actions accordingly. New social inventions, geared to the needs of the moment, are added to a series of other past events and thus absorbed into a common stock of experience. The past so determines the present that the choice is constrained, and the new and unusual elements, the inventive aspect of history, are to some extent kept within limits. In the particular story told by Professor Grebler, is it not clear that the whole cast of our society made some other alternatives that might have been imagined highly unlikely, e.g., complete substitution of public for private financing or a drastic reorganization of the residential construction industry under government control? If large-scale government aid to financing of new housing was novel in our history, it also had elements of the old — in that it was aid to *private* financing and attempted to preserve the organizational fabric of the industry and of the network of private finance built around it. And again, after the program was initiated under the impact of the specific conditions of the mid-1930's, did not this series of steps prove to be cumulative, so that in turn it became part of the heritage and will affect what is likely to happen in the future? It is this combination: the limitations on any new steps by the continuing past and the cumulation of new changes into a persisting contribution of the past that lends historical continuity to the whole course of economic and social change. To find this continuous pattern is the goal of empirical research.

Three brief comments in conclusion may be in order. First, one of the ways to find intellectual order, that is, to distinguish persistent from transient factors, is to lengthen the historical perspective. Such extension of the perspective permits one to study a greater variety of events and should inhibit mechanical extrapolations from short series of events. For this reason, the present inquiry into capital formation and financing attempts to cover a relatively long stretch of our economic past — although for several problems our stretch is not long enough.

Second, one may ask as to the proper definition of the term "government." As it is used, the term leads one to think of a narrowly defined institution, an industry — in which meaning it is often employed in industrial distributions of the labor force or of national income. But the same term is also applied to the *state,* the society as a whole acting under a different name from that which is used when it acts as a collection of living and consuming units, or as a group of producers organized in business firms. The extreme multiplicity and variety of governmental functions, and the claims made upon the government in a free society (rather than claims made *by* it, which are prominent in an authoritarian society) clearly suggest such interpretation. In many contexts governmental activity and policy must be viewed not as a set of decisions by a group of bureaucrats, but rather by society — whether or not under pressure of special groups. In these cases, government activity must be studied for its functional implications — examined, as Professor Grebler does, for the underlying forces, the social and economic values which drive society, through its government, to take certain actions under certain circumstances.

Third, it may seem that broad reflections of this kind have no practical bearing. Now, it is true that they are of little use in dealing with detailed and specific questions — such quandaries as whether to use index A or index B for adjustment for price changes, how to frame or whether to introduce regulation X or W, whether to count upon lower interest rates during the next year or two and arrange investments accordingly. But these fundamental notions have bearing upon the direction and standards of economic and related research, and upon the effectiveness of such research in influencing the course of economic education — in the first place of scholars in the field and eventually of society itself. Basic social decisions are made within a framework and against the background of some implicit theory or theories as to how economy and society operate; of some knowledge, no matter how crude, of the basic magnitudes; of some hypotheses about how individuals and groups will respond to changes to be imposed by the decisions. Such theory, knowledge, hypotheses are the results, in part, of thinking and research by scholars in the field, in part, of direct experience by individual members of society. The basic notions that govern the directions of research and channel the thinking are, therefore, important because they affect the framework within which far-reaching social decisions are made. Hence one may urge that in the long run, the run that affects ourselves and future members of society, a set of basic notions that forces one to consider not only the full diversity of economic experience, but also the testable distinctions between the more lasting and the more ephemeral factors in operation is of great practical importance.

The whole cast of the inquiry of which the present paper is the first instalment is colored by such notions. They cannot be stated here in precise detail, nor is their precise formulation indispensable for determining the specific course of our study. But their general import is decisive to it: decisive for an understanding of the aim of the inquiry and of what each piece contributes to that aim.

SIMON KUZNETS

Director's Comment: I do not share Dr. Kuznets' apparent faith in "our capacity to extract from the past results both tangible and stable enough to provide a firm basis for analyzing current problems and future prospects." Although the present is, of course, limited by the past, the limits would appear to be broad enough to permit an infinite variety of future courses of action. If the term "cumulative" as used by Dr. Kuznets refers to the future rather than to the past, it surely cannot be maintained that all social innovations are cumulative. History affords examples of discontinuities as well as continuities.

The above observations are not intended to detract from the value of the excellent study made by Dr. Grebler, nor from the value of the companion studies in the present series. Although we may never be able to predict the course of future social development, we do know from experience that social change generally takes place slowly. There is, accordingly, a fair degree of probability that the relationships which have obtained in the not-too-distant past will persist with slight modification into the not-too-distant future. The assumption of a certain measure of inertia in social institutions and in the social values which support them is a far cry, however, from Dr. Kuznets' assumption that there is "some discoverable order in the past, some basic and persistent forces, some recognizable pattern in the motley succession of specific events."

CLARENCE HEER

1

Scope of the Paper

Federal credit aids occupy a strategic position in residential construction. Introduced only 17 years ago, they are today deeply imbedded in the processes of capital formation and financing in residential real estate. Although the objectives, methods, and intensity of aids have changed markedly since their advent in the depression years, the aids themselves have become widely accepted as essential parts of the institutional framework in which new housing is produced and financed. The programs set up for administering them have profoundly affected not only the structure of the housebuilding industry and the sources, amount, and cost of residential mortgage funds, but even the character of the housing product.

This paper undertakes to measure the size of this new force and to trace some of its effects on housebuilding. While these can probably be said to range from the greatly increased proportion of home owners in the United States to the emergence of the large-scale "merchant" builder, this examination is focused on the effects most revealing of broad, long-term changes in capital formation and financing.

This paper also attempts to suggest what the future role of the federal government may be in the field of private residential construction. Federal credit aids express a public policy: it is in the general interest to maintain capital formation in residential real estate at a high volume. Although conceived in the depression, this policy has grown to its present dominant role over a period of rising incomes and full use of national resources. It has yet to be tested against the increasing vacancy rates, declining rents, and mounting foreclosures that in the past have signaled a shut-down of housebuilding activity. How firm a prop would credit aids prove to be in a market weakened by a large supply of housing offered at distress rentals and sale prices? Some of the facts disclosed by this study suggest that a major contraction in residential building might precipitate public demand for new financial tools, less respectful of the existing institutional pattern of mortgage finance than the present system of credit aids.

If the government's present influential role in housebuilding finance is increased, investment in residential construction may in the future become less sensitive to the competition of other potential investment uses of savings. This direct fiscal door to high-level housebuilding has already been opened wide enough to suggest that government support for new residential construction needs to be more carefully balanced against policies to maintain over-all economic stability. Some of the reasons why these two objectives may be in conflict are also discussed in this paper.

The federal programs reviewed here are the insurance of residential mortgage loans by the Federal Housing Administration, the guaranty of veterans' home loans by the Veterans Administration,[1] and the operations of the Federal National Mortgage Association in the so-called secondary mortgage market. These programs have provided assistance in financing both existing and new construction, but the analysis here is focused on their importance to the volume and financing of *new* housing. The paper is also limited to federal programs pertaining to private, nonfarm residential construction as distinguished from farm housing and public housing.[2]

Continuing government aids relevant to the future course of

[1] While there are legal and financial differences between the "insurance" of loans by FHA and the "guaranty" of loans by VA, the generic term "insurance" will sometimes be applied for convenience when the combined importance of the two programs is discussed.

[2] Discussion of the public housing and urban redevelopment programs would involve many issues and forms of government assistance greatly dissimilar to those treated here, such as direct government loans and subsidies to public agencies. With the intensification of government aids to housing, it is becoming more difficult to draw the boundary lines between private and public construction. In accordance with common usage, the distinction between private and public construction is here drawn on the basis of ownership. When title to new residential facilities is vested in private individuals or corporations or

capital formation and financing in residential construction are investigated, as distinguished from liquidated operations such as the Home Owners' Loan Corporation and RFC Mortgage Company. There is no need here for a review of all of the many activities of the federal government in this field, and of their origin and evolution.[3] Finally, the geographic distribution of government aids is outside the purview of the paper, and short-run fluctuations of residential building and mortgage lending activity that may be associated with changes in federal legislation and administrative policies are treated lightly and only to the extent that they are believed to illuminate basic and continuing issues.[4]

This paper is part of a broader study of capital formation and financing in residential real estate, which will be published as a monograph. The complete study will measure and analyze the formation and financing of capital in new private residential construction from 1890 to 1950 as part of long-term economic growth. It will also attempt to identify factors that have influenced the volume and financing of residential building activity and to assess the effect these forces will have on the future course of capital formation and financing.

---

institutions, construction is designated as private, although mortgage loans insured by a federal agency or real estate tax benefits may have been used. When title is held by a public agency, construction is designated as public, although the funds may have been raised by selling bonds to private investors. This definition is almost identical with one that uses the direct source of funds as criterion, except for the small direct home mortgage lending program of the Veterans Administration and similar small programs in various states. In these cases the owners of the real estate are private but the funds are public.

[3] Cf. for such a review Miles L. Colean, *The Impact of Government on Real Estate Finance in the United States* (National Bureau of Economic Research, 1950), particularly Chapters 5 through 8. R. J. Saulnier, "The Growth of Federal Lending, Loan Insurance and Guarantees" (National Bureau of Economic Research, Manuscript, 1952), presents comprehensive basic data on housing and other programs as well as a resume of the programs. This manuscript shows also the important position of housing in aggregate federal lending and loan insurance activities. See also C. Lowell Harriss, *History and Policies of the Home Owners' Loan Corporation* (National Bureau of Economic Research, 1950).

[4] For example, no analysis is made of year-to-year changes in the proportion of new residential construction financed by FHA-insured loans to total residential construction as they related to changes in legislation and regulation, although such an analysis would have been interesting.

2

New Housebuilding under FHA and VA Programs

From 1935 through 1951, almost 4 million new dwelling units were financed with mortgage loans insured by the Federal Housing Administration or guaranteed by the Veterans Administration. This number represents about 40 per cent of all new dwelling units built during this period, and equals more than half the entire volume constructed during the twenties. Of the 4 million dwelling units, over 2½ million were financed with FHA and VA loans made during the six postwar years 1946 to 1951. How the size of these programs changed over time is shown in Chart A and Table 1.

The number of new dwelling units financed[1] with mortgage

---

[1] The terms "financed with" and "built with" FHA insured or VA guaranteed mortgage loans require qualification. The data for new dwelling units built under FHA auspices are based on "first compliance" inspections and denote starts of dwelling units. A varying proportion of dwelling units built with FHA inspection have been sold upon completion with conventional mortgage financing or, since 1945, with mortgage loans guaranteed by the Veterans Administration. After June 1950, the data for new dwelling units built under VA auspices are also based on compliance inspections. For preceding periods, they represent rough estimates by the Housing and Home Finance Agency of the starts of new dwelling units sold with VA-guaranteed first mortgage loans. In terms of final financing of the acquisition of new residential construction, the data overstate somewhat the importance of FHA-insured loans and understate somewhat the importance of VA-guaranteed loans. Thus the combined FHA and VA totals are more accurate than the separate data for FHA and VA. Any overstatement of the combined ratio of new units financed with FHA and VA loans to total units should be small. Cases in which construction was started with either an FHA or VA loan but finally financed with a conventional mortgage are at least partially offset by cases in which houses were started with conventional loans but sold upon completion with FHA-insured mortgage financing or VA-guaranteed loans. The above qualifications apply to Chart A, Tables 1 and 8, and all text references to ratios of new dwelling units financed or built with FHA and VA loans to the total number of dwelling units. Moreover, the timing of starts as estimated by the Bureau of Labor Statistics and of starts based on FHA and VA compliance inspections is not quite synchronous. These differences are minor and do not affect the orders of magnitude.

loans insured by FHA increased rapidly from 1935 to 1941 and represented about one-third of all new dwelling units started during the three years preceding Pearl Harbor, as against 6 and 16 per cent, respectively, in 1935 and 1936. The relative importance of FHA-insured loans in the financing of new construction rose sharply during World War II in conjunction with the war housing program. During these years, more generous mortgage insurance benefits were employed under Title VI of the National Housing

TABLE 1

New Nonfarm Dwelling Units Financed under FHA and VA Programs as a Per Cent of all Privately Financed New Nonfarm Dwelling Units 1935-1951

	PER CENT OF ALL UNITS			PER CENT OF UNITS FOR OWNER-OCCUPANCY			PER CENT OF RENTAL UNITS
	FHA	VA	Combined	FHA	VA	Combined	FHA
	(1)	(2)	(3)	(4)	(5)	(6)	(7)
1935	6	....	6	7	....	7	3
1936	16	....	16	19	....	19	1
1937	18	....	18	20	....	20	6
1938	30	....	30	32	....	32	18
1939	35	....	35	37	....	37	20
1940	34	....	34	37	....	37	6
1941	36	....	36	39	....	39	6
1942	55	....	55	59	....	59	18
1943	79	....	79	82	....	82	67
1944	67	....	67	67	....	67	69
1945	20	3	23	20	3	23	15
1946	10	13	23	11	13	24	4
1947	27	25	52	23	27	50	71
1948	32	11	43	26	13	39	75
1949	36	11	47	30	13	43	69
1950	36	15	51	27	17	44	99
1951	26	15	41	20	16	36	89

SOURCE: See Table 8 for absolute numbers, sources, and notes.

Act to overcome the anticipated risks involved in the location of war housing, the reduced construction standards imposed by materials restrictions, and the credit standing of the mortgage borrowers. In 1943 almost 80 per cent of all privately financed new dwelling units were started under the FHA program.

In 1945 the home loan guarantee provisions of the Veterans Administration, under the Servicemen's Readjustment Act of 1944, began to operate. Nevertheless, the relative importance of the FHA and VA programs combined was low in 1945 and 1946, accounting for only 23 per cent of the total number of dwelling units started. From 1947 through 1951, however, approximately one-half of all privately financed new dwelling units were acquired with loans insured by FHA or guaranteed by VA, as against the maximum of one-third reached before World War II under the FHA program alone. The increased proportion of construction under these government aids was accompanied or preceded by the introduction of more liberal credit or guaranty terms for both FHA and VA mortgages, until the Korean conflict caused the introduction of credit curbs in the summer and fall of 1950. The credit restrictions and the withdrawal of rigid Federal Reserve support of government securities, which tended to raise bond yields and made investment in FHA and VA loans at fixed maximum interest rates less attractive, account for the decline in the proportion of new dwelling units financed with government-insured mortgages from 1950 to 1951.

In addition to FHA and VA loans on new construction,[2] other government aids, such as the Home Owners' Loan Corporation, the credit facilities of the Federal Home Loan Banks, and the investment of federal funds in savings and loan associations, have had an influence on the volume of residential building at various times since 1933. Their effects, however, have been less direct than those of the FHA and VA programs. Several states and cities have developed financial aids for privately sponsored new construction, particularly for the benefit of veterans, but their aggregate importance has been small. The influence of the operations of the Federal National Mortgage Association is discussed in Section III.

[2] For simplicity, the terms FHA loans and VA loans are used to denote mortgage loans insured by the Federal Housing Administration or guaranteed by the Veterans Administration.

CHART A

Number of New Nonfarm Dwelling Units Financed with Conventional and with FHA-Insured and VA-Guaranteed Loans
1935-1951

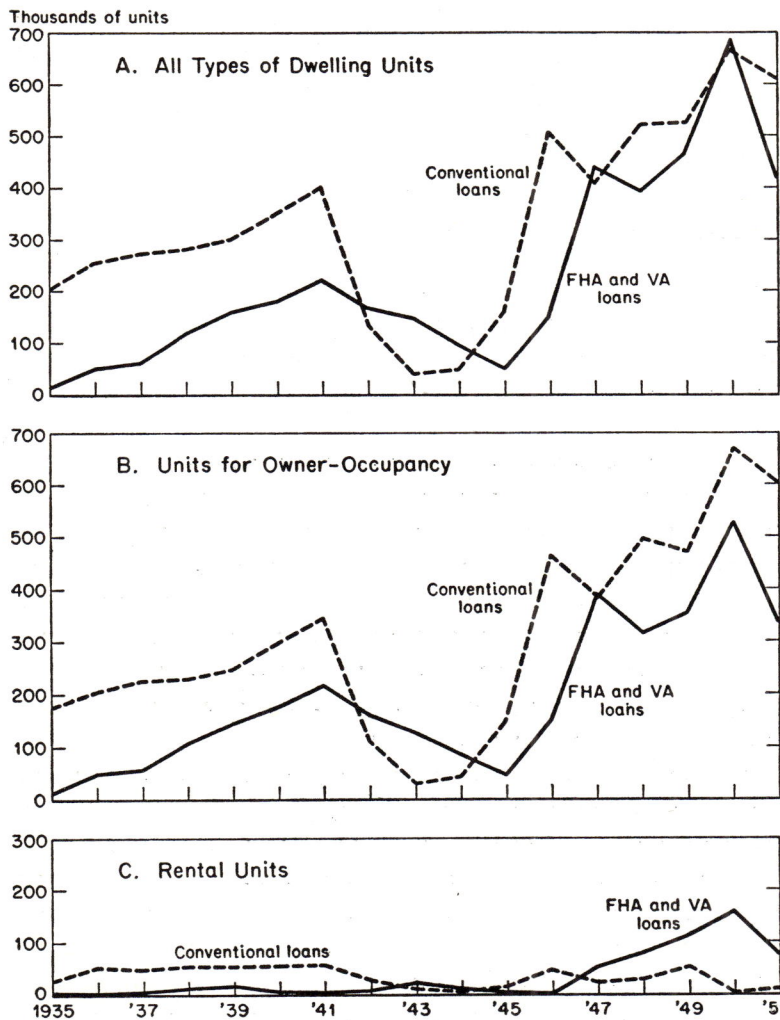

Source: Table 8
   A: Sum of columns 1 and 4 for FHA and VA, and column 5 minus sum of columns 1 and 4 for conventional.
   B: Sum of columns 2 and 4 for FHA and VA, and column 6 minus sum of columns 2 and 4 for conventional.
   C: Column 3 for FHA, and column 7 minus column 3 for conventional.

For a review of the effects of FHA and VA aids on new privately financed residential construction, at least three related questions suggest themselves. Have these programs increased the total volume of residential building over and above the level that would have been attained without them? Have they widened the market for new dwellings, by reducing carrying costs to a point where occupancy of new housing became possible for buyers and renters who otherwise would have been unable to afford new housing? Have they changed the distribution of new construction as between dwellings for sale and rent?

Effects on the Volume of Construction

The question as to the precise impact of FHA and VA aids on total residential building activity will forever remain unanswerable. There is no basis for estimating what the level and movement of residential construction would have been without the federal programs.

It would be rash to assume that all of the new construction financed with FHA and VA loans represents additional volume that would not have been produced without these aids. Much of the building sponsored under the FHA and VA programs would probably have occurred without them, for the two facilities have operated largely in a period of rising or high incomes conducive to an expanding demand for new residential construction. It would be equally rash to deduce that these programs had no influence on the volume of residential construction.

There is some reason for believing that the FHA program in the mid- and late thirties helped to accelerate the expansion of residential building — which was indeed its principal purpose. Recovery in housing construction is usually dependent upon substantial improvement in occupancy and prices and rents of existing facilities, and on the abatement of foreclosures and distress sales. By 1935 when the FHA mortgage insurance system began to operate, residential real estate markets in most areas had only moderately recovered from the Great Depression. The refinancing program of the Home Owners' Loan Corporation was still in progress. Foreclosures were still at a high level though declining. The rent index of the Bureau of Labor Statistics reached bottom in 1935 and remained low in the next few years. Residential vacancies were still high.[3] In the face of these obstacles there would probably have been even less recovery in residential construction during the second half of the thirties had it not been for the FHA program.

Moreover, if government credit aids succeeded in continuously widening the market for new housing, they tended to raise the level of new construction. Many changes in federal housing policies since the middle thirties may, in fact, be interpreted as efforts to widen the market for new residential facilities by differential credit terms favoring lower-priced dwelling units and lower income groups. It is important, therefore, to trace briefly the development of this objective and to indicate the extent to which it has been met.

Widening the Market

The change in the orientation of the FHA-insurance program furnishes an instructive record on this point. Hearings and Congressional debates leading to its enactment in 1934 reveal an almost exclusive concern with stimulation of residential construction and home purchase and modernization, as part of an economic recovery program, and with improvement of the mortgage system. There is hardly any reference to the possibility of using FHA-insurance as a device for making new or better housing available to consumers who would otherwise be unable to afford it. The emphasis was on encouragement of mortgage lenders to lend rather than on encouragement of consumers to borrow. Subsequent legislation, however, has given the FHA an increasing consumer orientation. The terms of FHA-insured loans have been more and more differ-

[3] Nonfarm real estate foreclosures totaled 229,000 in 1935 as against a depression peak of 252,000 in 1933. The number declined to 185,000 in 1936, 151,000 in 1937, and 59,000 in 1941 (Foreclosure Reports of the Home Loan Bank Board). The BLS rent index stood at 94.2 in 1935 and increased to 96.4 in 1936 and 100.9 in 1937, as against a level of roughly 140 to 150 in the twenties (1935-1939 = 100). The Real Property Inventories for 64 cities revealed an average vacancy ratio of 7.8 per cent on January 1, 1934, with a ratio of 12.9 per cent for 5-or-more family structures (David L. Wickens, *Residential Real Estate*, National Bureau of Economic Research, 1941, p. 22).

entiated between various price and rental groups on the basis of social needs rather than of mortgage loan risks (although these two criteria need not always be in conflict).[4] This differentiation has been carried so far that, under the FHA terms operative in the winter of 1952, the minimum downpayment on a house appraised at $11,000 was about five times as large as the minimum downpayment on a house appraised at less than $7,000.

The first step in this direction was a 1938 amendment to the National Housing Act, which permitted easier credit terms for newly constructed small homes.[5] The second step was the removal of the "economic soundness" requirement for loans insured under the wartime amendments to the Act. War housing financed with FHA-insured loans was to be "channeled" to war workers, many of whom would be unable to buy houses without more liberal financing and borrower credit ratings. The use of mortgage insurance for "channeling" new housing into lower income groups was transferred to the Veterans Emergency Housing Program of 1946, which stated this use as one of its specific objectives.[6] Congressional hearings on comprehensive housing legislation during the late war and the postwar periods reveal a consistent emphasis on the development of special financing tools for construction suited for "middle-income families," the groups between those served by private enterprise with existing government aids and those to be

---

[4] Lower-priced houses have a larger resale market and may therefore be sounder security for mortgages with high loan-to-value ratios.

[5] Miles L. Colean, *op. cit.*, p. 98.

[6] The program, as announced by the Housing Expediter on February 7, 1946, included the following recommendation: "Channeling the largest part of material into homes and rental housing, both farm and urban, selling for not more than $6,000 or renting for not more than $50 per month" and specified: "To provide moderately priced homes with a maximum of rental units, it is necessary for the government to offer greater incentives for the building of such housing. This can be achieved by insuring mortgages on low-cost homes for builders to the extent of 90 per cent of value. Furthermore, such mortgages must be based on necessary current costs of construction rather than on long-term economic value and they should be amortized over a long period." (Mimeographed statement of the Housing Expediter). These changes were incorporated in amendments to Title VI of the National Housing Act, enacted May 22, 1946.

served by publicly financed housing.[7] Such tools were provided in the Housing Acts of 1948[8] and of 1950.[9]

The extent to which the objective of widening the market has in fact been met is difficult to determine, even in the relatively simple case of new single-family houses for owner-occupancy. Some of the new programs are too recent to permit a judgment of their effectiveness in this respect. The credit restrictions, issued in 1950 upon the outbreak of hostilities in Korea and suspended in September 1952, and the temporary materials restrictions caused by the military preparedness programs tended to limit the use of the financing tools enacted in 1948 and 1950. Moreover, the historical data required for assessing the influence of government aids on the demand structure for new single-family houses are not available. The Federal Housing Administration reports the income distribution of purchasers of new single-family houses financed under its mortgage insurance program. Similar information exists for all purchasers in selected metropolitan districts for recent years. But there are no comprehensive time series on the distribution of incomes of buyers of new houses, of purchase prices, downpayments, and debt charges classified by government-insured and conventional mortgage financing. However, a few observations are possible by comparing the characteristics of new house

---

[7] For example, *Hearings before the Subcommittee on Housing and Urban Redevelopment of the Special Committee on Postwar Economic Policy and Planning, pursuant to Senate resolution 102*, particularly pp. 1301-5 (79 Cong., 3 Sess.). Also, *Report of the Senate Committee on Banking and Currency on S. 1592*, (General Housing Act of 1946), No. 1131 (79 Cong., 2 Sess.).

[8] Miles L. Colean, *op. cit.*, pp. 124-5, particularly Nos. 5, 6, 7 and 9.

[9] Public Law 475, 81st Congress, approved April 20, 1950. The principal features of this Act designed to widen the market are special financing provisions for cooperative housing (Section 213), and more liberal financing terms for small homes (Sections 8 and 611), as well as for rental housing projects (Section 207). These measures were taken "with the object of encouraging greater production of homes for middle-income families" (*Fourth Annual Report, Housing and Home Finance Agency*, 1950, p. 213). In addition, the law authorized a maximum of $150,000,000 in direct loans by the Veterans Administration under specified conditions, increased the guaranty for VA home loans generally from 50 per cent of appraised value not to exceed $4,000 to 60 per cent not to exceed $7,500, and extended the maximum maturity from 25 to 30 years.

TABLE 2

Distribution of Purchase Prices of
New Owner-Occupied Single-Family Houses
Financed with Mortgage Loans, by Type of Mortgage Financing
1949 and 1950

PURCHASE PRICE CLASS	FHA AND VA FIRST MORTGAGES		CONVENTIONAL FIRST MORTGAGES		FHA AND VA AS PER CENT OF TOTAL IN EACH PRICE CLASS[b]
	Number	*Per Cent*	*Number*	*Per Cent*	
(1)	(2)	(3)	(4)	(5)	(6)
Less than $ 4,000	4,000	1	54,000	17	7
$ 4,000 to $ 5,999	13,000	3	43,000	14	23
$ 6,000 to $ 7,999	126,000	31	46,000	15	73
$ 8,000 to $ 9,999	139,000	34	42,000	13	77
$10,000 to $11,999	73,000	18	39,000	13	65
$12,000 to $13,999	27,000	7	25,000	8	52
$14,000 or more	27,000	7	64,000	21	30
Total reporting	407,000	100[a]	312,000	100	57

[a] Components do not add up to 100 because of rounding.
[b] Column 2 as a per cent of the sum of columns 2 and 4.

SOURCE: Based on Bureau of the Census, *1950 Census of Housing,* Preliminary Reports, Mortgaged, Residential, Nonfarm Properties Acquired During 1949 and First Half of 1950 (Series HC-9, No. 1), Table 5. The data are from a sample survey and are subject to sampling errors detailed in the Census publication.

purchases financed with FHA and VA loans and of those financed with conventional mortgages during 1949 and 1950.

Purchases financed with government-insured loans are concentrated in the $6,000 to $12,000 price class (see Table 2). More than four-fifths of all FHA- and VA-financed purchases, and only two-fifths of purchases financed with conventional loans, fell into this category. Within this price range, the government programs operated largely in the $6,000 to $10,000 class. Almost two-thirds of FHA- and VA-financed purchases, and only 28 per cent of purchases with conventional loans, were for houses priced at $6,000 to $10,000. On the other hand, only 4 per cent of all houses purchased with government-insured loans were priced at less than

$6,000, whereas almost one-third of the houses purchased with conventional mortgages were in this price group. Only 14 per cent of all FHA- and VA-financed purchases, as against 29 per cent of all purchases financed with conventional loans, were in the price class of $12,000 or more.

About three-fourths of all new mortgaged houses bought for $6,000 to less than $12,000 were financed with government-insured loans (column 6 of Table 2). Here again, the corresponding ratios for the lower-priced and higher-priced houses are much smaller.

Thus the federal programs were operative largely in the medium price field, with emphasis on the lower range of this field. Their small share in the price class under $6,000 may be due to failure of many of these houses to meet minimum construction standards of FHA and VA. Also, large numbers of lower-priced houses are in small towns where FHA and VA facilities are less accessible or are built in locations unacceptable for mortgage insurance or guaranty. In any event, the number of all houses in this price class accounted for less than 16 per cent of the total.

Downpayments made on these purchases varied significantly with type of financing. The median downpayment was 8 per cent of the purchase price for houses bought with VA first mortgages, 22 per cent for those bought with FHA first mortgages, and 35 per cent for those purchased with conventional first mortgages.[10] These differences in conjunction with the purchase price data would suggest that reduction of downpayments through federal insurance and guarantee programs was a factor in stimulating demand for medium- and low-priced houses which otherwise would have been out of reach of many families.

Nevertheless, the evidence is by no means conclusive. The reduction of downpayments may have had the effect of causing a number of house purchasers to devote a smaller proportion of their liquid assets to this purpose than they would have done otherwise, or to

---

[10] Based on Bureau of the Census, *1950 Census of Housing,* Preliminary Reports, Mortgages, Residential, Nonfarm Properties Acquired during 1949 and First Half of 1950 (Series HC-9, No. 1), Table 12. The data are from a sample survey and are subject to sampling errors detailed in the Census publication.

buy more expensive houses.[11] Also, from a historical point of view, downpayments have been reduced much less than a comparison of maximum loan-to-value ratios for government-insured and for conventional loans would indicate. Before the institution of the federal programs, junior mortgages often filled much of the gap between purchase price and first mortgage. The substitution of high-percentage first mortgages for combinations of first and junior loans would reduce carrying charges, other things being equal. But other things have not been equal since the early thirties. The almost universal inclusion of payments on principal in debt service on single-family houses, though a sounder financing practice, has tended to absorb much of the advantage to borrowers resulting from the consolidation of multiple loans into high-percentage first mortgages at lower interest rates and for longer contract terms.[12]

Thus the extent to which the federal programs have succeeded in widening the market for new construction is not determinable from available data, but some progress in this direction has probably been made. At the same time, widening the market for new residential building has clearly emerged as a continuous and major objective of federal housing policies and one that has direct bearing on the volume of housing construction in the long run.

Sales Housing Versus Rental Housing

Have the federal programs influenced the proportions of new construction for rental and sale? The FHA has often been accused of

[11] Thus a survey of purchases from October 1950 to March 1951 revealed that about one-fourth of house purchasers had left over liquid assets valued at $1,000 or more, and about one-tenth had liquid assets valued at $2,000 or more, after purchase on terms prevalent before Regulation X (*Federal Reserve Bulletin*, July 1951, p. 779). See also Daniel B. Rathbun, "Liquid Assets: A Neglected Factor in the Formulation of Housing Finance Policies," *Journal of Finance*, December 1952, Vol. VII, No. 4. For the relationship between financing terms and purchase price, see Ernest M. Fisher, *Urban Real Estate Markets: Characteristics and Financing* (National Bureau of Economic Research, 1950), pp. 69-90.

[12] This point is examined in greater detail in a chapter "Long-Term Changes in Cost and Terms of Mortgage Financing" in the forthcoming monograph. See also "Influence on Cost and Terms of Financing," p. 49.

unduly promoting housing for owner-occupancy;[13] and the veterans home loan program is, of course, exclusively designed for purchase (although some houses bought by veterans may include additional dwelling units for rent in a small number of cases of loans on structures with more than one dwelling unit).

The facts on this point are complex. On the statistical record, the proportion of rental units in new multifamily structures to the total number of new dwelling units was lower in the period of FHA and VA operations than during any similar period since the turn of the century — about 11.5 per cent for 1935 through 1951.[14] Also, the volume of rental housing construction during the recent postwar period was relatively low compared to a similar period after World War I. From 1946 through 1951, less than 11 per cent of all new dwelling units were in multifamily structures (Table 8). From 1920 through 1925, almost double this percentage was of the rental housing type.

It does not follow, however, that government aids for rental housing were quantitatively less important in this field than in housing for sale. It is true that before World War II the proportion of FHA-financed rental construction to total rental construction was much lower than the proportion of FHA-financed building for owner-occupancy to total building for owner-occupancy (as is evident from a comparison of columns 6 and 7 of Table 1). But there was a reversal after the war. From 1947 to 1951, the proportion of FHA-financed rental construction to total rental construction was much higher than the proportion of owner-occupied housing built with both FHA and VA loans to total building for owner-occupancy. During these five years, about 80 per cent of the annual production of rental housing was financed by FHA loans.

The two phenomena of the small relative importance of rental

---

[13] See, for example, Charles Abrams, *The Future of Housing* (Harper & Brothers, 1946), pp. 224-5.

[14] See Table 8 for data 1935-1951, forthcoming monograph for data 1900-1934. Multifamily structures are defined as structures with three or more dwelling units. Structures with two dwelling units usually provide at least one unit for rent. The inclusion of these would increase the proportion of units for rent to total units, but would not change the statement that the 1935-1951 ratio was lower than that during any similar period since 1900.

housing since World War II and of the large share of FHA financing in rental housing can be reconciled. Many factors other than governmental financial aids have influenced the volume of rental housing construction. Among these are a possible long-term shift in consumers preference for single-family houses, fortified by the rise in real income and liquid assets since 1940 and the tax advantages of home ownership; the financial hazards of rental housing construction during a period of rapidly changing costs; and uncertainties over the long-run earning capacity of new projects when rent controls are removed.[15]

To meet the obstacles to rental housing construction during the postwar period, and in response to public pressure for a greater volume of rental housing, easy FHA financing arrangements under the wartime Section 608 of the National Housing Act were renewed until 1950 and even liberalized.[16] In spite of these efforts, the quantity of building for rent was relatively small, but the overwhelming proportion of this small quantity was financed by liberal FHA loans. The rewards for rental project builders using FHA financing were unusually attractive. In many cases, builders could fully or nearly "mortgage out" on loans representing 90 per cent of "necessary current costs" and were able to reap large profits on very thin equities. That these attractions did not produce any larger volume of rental housing is perhaps a measure of the postwar hazards of residential construction for rent. It is safe to conclude that the quantity of rental housing would have been even smaller if the liberal FHA aids had not existed.

[15] Cf. Leo Grebler, "Implications of Rent Control — Experience in the United States," *International Labour Review* LXV, No. 4, April 1952.

[16] Among other things, the appraisal basis was changed from "reasonable replacement cost" to "necessary current cost" and later to costs prevailing December 31, 1947, and higher maximum mortgage amounts per room were authorized.

3

Importance of Federal Programs in Mortgage Finance

Stimulation of the flow of mortgage funds into residential construction has been a principal aim of federal housing policies since the early and middle thirties. With the exception of public housing and the recent program for urban redevelopment, these policies in fact have operated almost exclusively through the use of various devices influencing the flow of private institutional mortgage funds: primarily mortgage insurance or guaranty and improved marketability of loans through the Federal National Mortgage Association.[1] As a result, government aids have had a large and increasing effect upon mortgage lending activity, sources of funds, and the amount and composition of the mortgage debt.

Another major objective of federal housing policies has been to reduce the periodic payments of mortgage borrowers, by lowering interest rates and lengthening contract terms. In fact, an increase in the ease of borrowing has been one of the means through which the federal programs have sought to raise the level of demand for new residential construction.

The precise effects of the FHA and VA programs on the volume of residential mortgage lending are as indeterminable as their impact on residential building activity. By encouraging mortgage lending during the second half of the thirties and under the special circumstances of the war housing program and by stimulating mortgage borrowing through differential terms for various price classes, the FHA has unquestionably contributed to the spectacular increase of the residential mortgage debt which totaled $56.3

---

[1] The Housing Act of 1948 added a new Title VII to the National Housing Act authorizing "yield insurance" for debt-free investments in rental housing. In this instance, federal aid was designed to stimulate the flow of equity funds. However, no such insurance had been issued by late 1952.

billion in 1950 as against less than $24 billion in 1935; and the VA home loan program with its special terms for veterans has operated in the same direction since 1945. Moreover, public funds used by the Federal National Mortgage Association during the postwar years for purchases of FHA and VA loans have directly supplemented the large private funds that were invested in residential mortgages during this period.

Mortgage Funds for New Housebuilding

From 1935 to 1951 an estimated $22 billion of mortgage loans on new residential construction were insured by the Federal Housing Administration or guaranteed by the Veterans Administration. Of this amount, over $17 billion originated during the six postwar years from 1946 to 1951. Little more than $4 billion of the grand total served to finance the construction of rental and cooperative housing projects, and all but $300 million in this category originated during the postwar period. The annual data reveal a rapid growth in the use of FHA-insured mortgages on new construction from 1935 to 1940, as would be expected in the development of a new program, and during the early years of World War II. The growth was checked by the building limitation of the late war years and the difficulties of postwar reconversion of construction activity. In the postwar period when the VA as well as the FHA program was in operation, the annual amounts of insured or guaranteed mortgages built up rapidly to a peak of $4.7 billion in 1950. A slight decline in 1951 was apparently caused by the credit restrictions on government-insured as well as conventional loans, which were introduced in the fall of 1950, and by the effect in the money market of the "unpegging" of government securities. (Chart B and Table 3).

Over the entire period from 1935 to 1950, government-insured loans on new residential construction averaged about 45 per cent of the total estimated flow of mortgage funds into new construction.[2] FHA-insured loans on new dwellings rose from 5 per cent of the total in 1935 to about 30 per cent in the immediate prewar period and supplied most of the new construction financing during

---

[2] See footnote to column 6 of Table 3 for qualifications of the data.

TABLE 3

FHA-Insured and VA-Guaranteed Loans
on New Residential Construction
1935-1951

	MILLIONS OF DOLLARS					COMBINED TOTAL AS A PER CENT OF	
	Loans on New Houses for Owner Occupancy			FHA Loans on New Rental and Co-op. Housing	Combined Total	Estimated Loans for New Construction	FHA and VA Loans on New and Existing Construction
	FHA (1)	VA (2)	Total (3)	(4)	(5)	(6)	(7)
1935	22	....	22	2	24	5.2	25.0
1936	95	....	95	2	97	11.5	31.2
1937	169	....	169	10	179	17.5	41.2
1938	227	....	227	48	275	24.2	52.8
1939	461	....	461	52	513	32.1	71.2
1940	562	....	562	12	574	30.6	76.6
1941	707	....	707	12	719	31.5	79.5
1942	751	....	751	20	771	65.3	78.8
1943	552	....	552	84	636	96.2	75.1
1944	484	....	484	46	530	97.8	69.5
1945	257	31	288	16	304	47.0	44.3
1946	120	371	491	11	502	19.2	18.3
1947	477	1,357	1,834	359	2,193	50.9	48.3
1948	1,425	944	2,369	606	2,975	48.9	64.7
1949	1,306	842	2,148	1,016	3,164	51.9	68.2
1950	1,633	1,930	3,563	1,152	4,715	48.7	70.2
1951	1,194	2,566	3,760	570	4,330	....	70.7
Total 1935-1951	10,442	8,041	18,483	4,018	22,501	44.3	61.9

SOURCES, BY COLUMN.

(1) *Fifth Annual Report,* Housing and Home Finance Agency, 1951, Table 4, p. 244. Excludes a relatively small amount of loans insured under Title I, Class 3 of the National Housing Act.

(2) Estimates derived from the total amount of VA loans closed (Table 9) and the per cent distribution of the number of loans by purpose of loan (undated mimeographed reports of VA, "Characteristics of Home Loans

SOURCES, TABLE 3, CONTINUED

Reported Closed under the VA Loan Guaranty Program"). To apply the distribution of the *number* of loans for new and existing construction to the total *amount* of loans implies that the average loan per new dwelling was the same as the average loan per existing dwelling. Consequently, the amount of loans on new construction is probably understated. The VA report lists the per cent distribution for the period November 1944 to December 1946 as a whole, and this distribution was applied to the amounts reported for 1945 and 1946. Any resulting error should be small. The amounts of the principal of guaranteed loans are shown rather than the amounts of the guaranty themselves, which are about one-half the principal amounts.

(3) Sum of columns 1 and 2.

(4) *Fifth Annual Report,* Housing and Home Finance Agency, 1951, Table 29, p. 289.

(5) Sum of columns 3 and 4.

(6) These percentages are based on tentative estimates of the flow of mortgage funds into new construction, which are to be included in the forthcoming monograph. The percentage for the total period in column 6 is based on 1935-1950. The percentages are not more than rough approximations, both because of the tenuous basis for the estimates of total mortgage loans on new construction and the differences between the timing pattern of these estimates and that of FHA and VA loan closings. On the whole the percentages conform fairly well with the percentages in Table 1, which is based on the number of dwelling units. The percentages for 1943, 1944, and 1945 in the above table, however, appear high, which is probably due to an understatement of construction expenditures during these years and a resulting understatement of total mortgage loans for new construction.

(7) For FHA: Sources quoted in footnotes for columns 1 and 4. For VA loans, Table 9.

the war. From 1947 through 1950 almost one-half of the flow of mortgage funds into new construction was in the form of FHA and VA loans (column 6 of Table 3).

Still another measure of the relative importance of government-insured loans on new construction is the volume of FHA and VA mortgages on new construction compared to the total volume of FHA and VA loans on both existing and new construction (column 7 of Table 3). For the period as a whole about three-fifths of all FHA and VA residential mortgage loans were on new construction[3] — a higher ratio than that for conventional loans. This proportion also shows a rapid rise during the prewar years, a very

[3] Under the terms of the National Housing Act, FHA-insured loans on rental housing are in effect limited to new construction, except for the refinancing of projects originally financed with FHA loans.

CHART **B**

Amounts of Conventional and FHA-Insured and VA-Guaranteed Loans on New Residential Construction 1935-1951

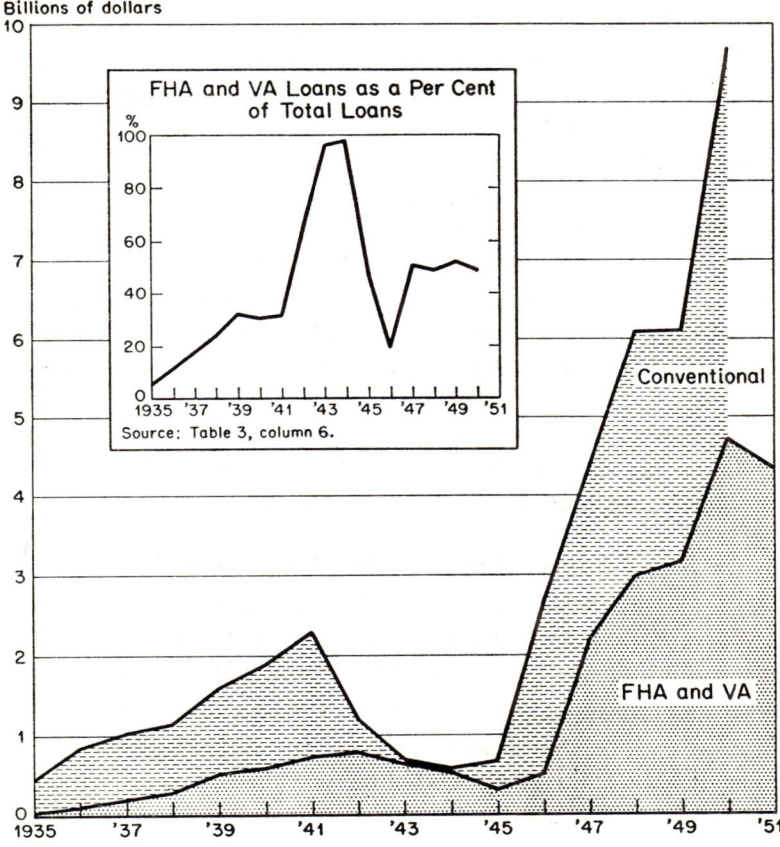

Source: For FHA and VA loans, Table 3, Column 5. For conventional loans, estimates in forthcoming monograph.

high level during the war period, and a sharp increase since 1946. From 1948 through 1951 more than two-thirds of the total amount of all FHA and VA loans went into new construction.

The government reached its dominant position in the debt financing of new residential real estate by assuming much of the risk involved in mortgage lending. Whether there are any limits to the use of this potent device, and some of the problems its use creates, will be discussed in the last section.

Influence in Home Mortgage Lending Activity

Because of the emphasis in government programs on the flow of funds into new construction, FHA and VA loans have been somewhat less important in relation to total residential mortgage lending on both existing and new residential real estate. Nevertheless, their share in total lending activity and debt has become substantial, particularly in the home-financing segment.[4]

FHA-insured loans on one- to four-family houses increased from 4 per cent of the estimated amount of all such loans made in 1935 to more than one-fifth in the immediate prewar years (see Chart C). After a decline during the war and immediate postwar period, FHA and VA loans combined rose to more than one-third of aggregate home mortgage lending activity.

Because there are no data on the annual volume of conventional loans on multifamily (rental) housing, no such comparison is possible for this segment of the residential mortgage market.

Government-Insured Loans in the Mortgage Debt

At the end of 1950 the estimated balance outstanding of FHA and VA loans totaled $22 billion and approximated 40 per cent of the aggregate residential mortgage debt.[5] The relative importance of government-insured loans in the total debt increased but slowly before the war. By 1940 less than 10 per cent of the debt was in the form of FHA loans. At the end of the war their share had risen to about 18 per cent. During the five years from 1946 to 1950, how-

[4] The terms "home financing" and "home loans" relate to mortgage loans on 1- to 4-family houses unless noted otherwise.

[5] The estimates of balances outstanding of FHA and VA loans are based on the assumption that loans not paid in full or foreclosed are amortized on schedule. In view of prepayments, the balances, and therefore the ratio of these balances to the total residential mortgage debt outstanding, are probably slightly overstated. Also, some double-counting is involved inasmuch as FHA and VA loans held by the Federal National Mortgage Association are included in the mortgage debt totals. A correction to allow for double-counting would be wholly insignificant before 1949 and would change the ratios by not more than two points in 1949 and 1950.

CHART C

Amounts of Conventional and FHA-Insured and VA-Guaranteed Loans Made on One- to Four-Family Houses 1935-1950

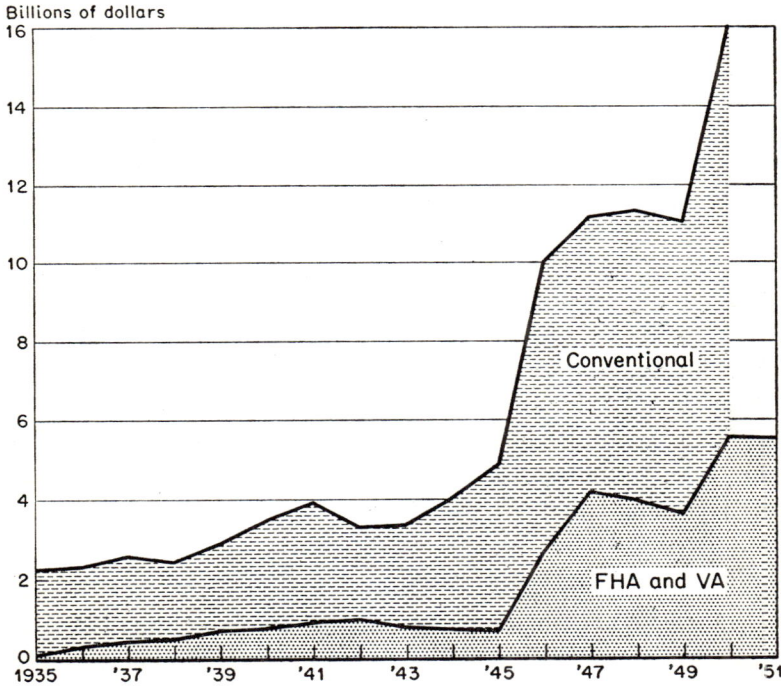

Source: For FHA and VA loans: Table 9, sum of columns 1 and 3. For conventional loans, totals as estimated by Home Loan Bank Board minus FHA and VA loans.

ever, in which the VA home loan as well as the FHA program was in operation, the balance outstanding of government-insured loans increased by more than $17 billion, or 360 per cent. Of this amount, roughly $10 billion has been in veterans' home loans (Table 4).

A more significant comparison is that between FHA and VA loan balances and total holdings of private financial institutions which represent the great bulk of portfolio lenders under the FHA and VA programs (Chart D). This comparison omits from the debt the HOLC loans, which were direct government loans, and the loans held by individuals and miscellaneous mortgage lenders who are negligible as portfolio holders though important as loan originators. On this basis, the share of government-insured loans increased from 16 per cent in 1940 to almost 30 per cent in 1945 and 50 per cent in 1950. In other words, roughly one-half of the total amount of residential mortgage loans held by financial institutions were insured or guaranteed by the federal government (column 11 of Table 4).

Over the period as a whole, the share of government-insured mortgages in the *home* mortgage debt has been larger than the share of such mortgages in the debt on multifamily dwellings. The importance of insured loans in the latter was small before and during the war but has shown a phenomenal increase since 1947. By 1950 FHA-insured loans on rental projects represented more than one-quarter of the total mortgage debt on rental housing and 40 per cent of the debt held by institutional lenders. Practically all of the more than $3 billion of FHA loans on rental housing that were outstanding at the end of 1950 was originated during the preceding four years.

Influence on Sources of Funds

Participation of various types of mortgage lenders in the FHA and, to a lesser extent, in the VA program has been at some variance with the historical shares of lenders in mortgage financing activity. The exclusion of individual lenders in the FHA program and their small share in the VA program[6] have accentuated the tendency toward institutionalization of the residential mortgage debt. The government insurance programs, particularly FHA, have stimulated the participation of commercial banks in residential mortgage financing.

The restrictions on loan-to-value ratios and maturity of mortgage loans imposed by the National Banking Act do not apply to loans insured by the Federal Housing Administration or guaranteed by the Veterans Administration. This is also true for the limita-

---

[6] From 1948 to 1950 "individuals and others" accounted for less than 1 per cent of the amount of VA home loans closed.

TABLE 4

Estimated Outstanding FHA and VA Loans by Type of Property in Million Dollars and as a Per Cent of Residential Mortgage Debt Year-Ends, 1935-1950

	HOME MORTGAGES			RENTAL MORTGAGES FHA	TOTAL FHA AND VA MORTGAGES	FHA AND VA AS A PER CENT OF			FHA AS A PER CENT OF			TOTAL FHA AND VA AS A PER CENT OF	
	FHA (1)	VA (2)	Combined (3)	(4)	(5)	Total Home Mortgages (6)	Institutional Home Mortgages (7)		Total Rental Mortgages (8)	Institutional Rental Mortgages (9)		Total Mortgages (10)	Institutional Mortgages (11)
1935	12	...	12	1	13	*	*		*	*		*	*
1936	203	...	203	2	205	1.2	2.3		*	*		0.9	1.7
1937	594	...	594	6	600	3.5	6.6		*	*		2.6	4.9
1938	967	...	967	36	1,003	5.6	10.3		*	*		4.2	8.0
1939	1,419	...	1,419	98	1,517	8.0	14.4		1.5	3.0		6.3	11.8
1940	2,295	...	2,295	107	2,402	12.1	20.5		1.7	3.1		9.5	16.4
1941	2,962	...	2,962	107	3,069	15.0	24.4		1.6	3.0		11.7	19.6
1942	3,666	...	3,666	126	3,792	18.7	29.7		2.0	3.6		14.6	23.9
1943	3,998	...	3,998	201	4,199	20.9	32.8		3.2	5.8		16.5	26.8
1944	4,146	...	4,146	241	4,387	21.6	33.9		4.0	7.2		17.4	28.1
1945	4,043	500	4,543	237	4,780	23.1	35.9		3.9	7.1		18.6	29.3
1946	3,688	2,600	6,288	214	6,502	25.7	37.8		3.3	6.0		21.1	32.1
1947	3,766	5,800	9,566	549	10,115	32.0	45.0		8.0	13.8		27.5	40.0
1948	5,251	7,200	12,451	1,144	13,595	35.4	47.7		15.1	24.6		31.7	44.2
1949	6,878	8,100	14,978	2,135	17,113	38.3	49.6		25.4	38.7		36.0	47.9
1950	8,533	10,300	18,833	3,220	22,053	40.1	50.1		34.2	46.2		39.1	49.4

*Less than 1 per cent.

Sources, Table 4, by columns:
(1), (4) Estimates in Annual Reports of the Federal Housing Administration. Home loans exclusive of small amount of Title 1, Class 3 loans. Data for 1935 to 1939 are as of June 30, for other years as of December 31. For 1935 to 1939, FHA loans are shown as percentages of the interpolated debt as of June 30 (debt at preceding and at current year-end divided by two).
(2) Letter of January 15, 1952, from Robert C. Colwell, Chief, Administrative Control Division, Loan Guaranty Service, Veterans Administration. These are rough estimates based upon "certain assumptions that loans not paid in full or extinguished by foreclosure are being amortized on schedule." Because of the general tendency toward accelerated repayment during the postwar years, the balances outstanding are probably somewhat overstated.
(3) Sum of columns 1 and 2.
(5) Sum of columns 3 and 4.
(6), (7) Total home loans outstanding as estimated by the Home Loan Bank Board, "Estimated Home Mortgage Debt and Lending Activity, 1950." Institutional loans as estimated in the forthcoming monograph, exclusive of HOLC loans.
(8), (9) Total and institutional loans on multifamily structures outstanding as estimated in the forthcoming monograph.
(10), (11) Total and institutional loans outstanding on all types of residential dwellings as estimated in the forthcoming monograph. Institutional loans exclusive of HOLC.

tions in many of the state banking laws. While similar exceptions apply to the other mortgage lending institutions, they are more potent in the case of commercial banks because their conventional mortgage lending activity is more severely limited by existing laws. The use of idle bank funds for mortgage loans was one of the prime motives in the development of the FHA insurance plan.[7] The greater assurance of a secondary market for FHA and VA loans (p. 42) made these loans more attractive to banks, by providing a means by which they could be converted into liquid assets if necessary.

During the period 1935 through 1950 commercial banks originated about one-third of the total amount of FHA-insured home mortgage loans and approximately one-half of the total amount of FHA-insured loans on rental and cooperative housing projects.[8]

[7] For example, see testimony by Marriner S. Eccles before the Senate Banking and Currency Committee (*Hearings on S. 3603,* pp. 153-5, 73 Cong., 2 Sess.).
[8] Consolidated data from Annual Reports of the Federal Housing Administration.

CHART D
Estimated Outstanding FHA-Insured and VA-Guaranteed Loans as a Per Cent of Total Residential Mortgage Debt and of Debt Held by Financial Institutions
1936-1950

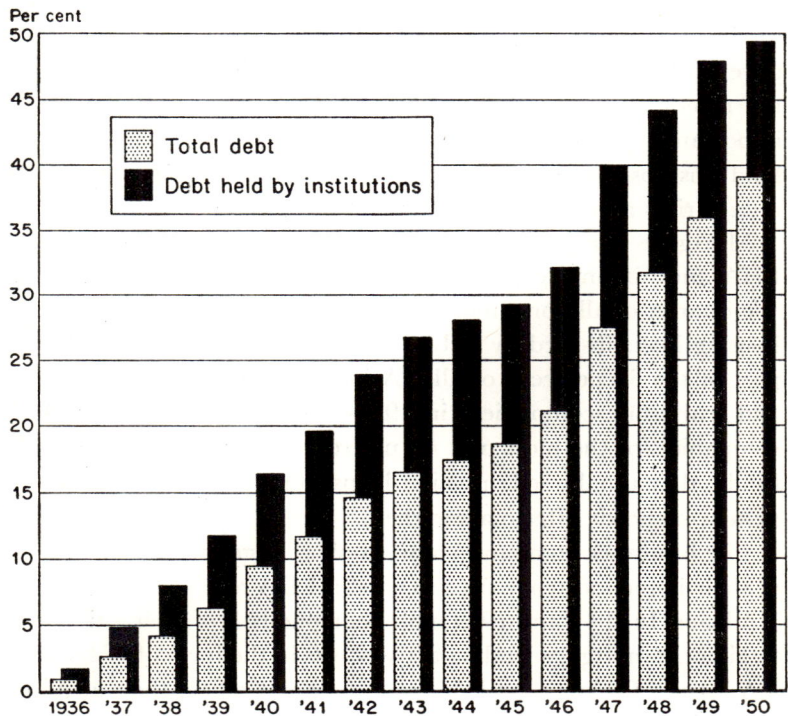

Source: Table 4, Column 10 for total and Column 11 for institutional debt.

As shown in Table 5, FHA and VA loans accounted for 38 to 53 per cent of the annual total amounts of home loans made by commercial banks from 1948 to 1950. The impact of government programs on the position of commercial banks in this field is reflected in the increasing share of home loans made by banks in total home mortgage lending activity — 23 per cent in 1946-1950 as against 14 per cent in 1926-1930 — and in the increasing proportion of their residential mortgage holdings to the total residential mortgage debt — 18 per cent in 1950 as against 10 in 1930 and 9 in 1920.[9]

The stimulation of residential mortgage loan investments by commercial banks is probably one of the outstanding recent changes in the history of mortgage finance as well as of banking. Even before 1935, residential mortgage lending was by no means foreign to commercial banks, in spite of legal limitations.[10] But government insurance of loans has been an important factor in the recent emergence of commercial banks as one of the most important types of residential lenders, and the banks are likely to hold this position with the aid of government arrangements that reduce risks and facilitate shiftability of mortgages.

Mortgage companies have played a large role in originating FHA and VA mortgages. Through 1950 they originated almost one-quarter of all home mortgages and almost one-tenth of rental housing loans insured by FHA,[11] and they accounted for a large part of the 30 per cent of all VA loans orginated by "mortgage and real estate companies" in 1948-1950.[12] However, mortgage companies for the most part do not represent primary sources of funds; they usually sell or assign loans to portfolio lenders immediately or shortly after making them.

Life insurance companies have made a large and growing part of their home mortgage investments in FHA and at times also in VA loans. In 1948 and 1949 more than one-half of their estimated total home mortgage lending activity was in the form of FHA and VA loans (Table 5), and this ratio does not reflect their acquisitions of FHA and VA loans from mortgage companies and other loan originators. Mutual savings banks and savings and loan associations have been less active in making government-insured loans, but the investments of savings banks in these loans expanded rapidly from 1948 to 1950.

The principal types of lending institutions show sharp differ-

---

[9] Based on data in the forthcoming monograph.

[10] Cf. Carl F. Behrens, *Commercial Bank Activities in Urban Mortgage Financing* (National Bureau of Economic Research, New York, 1952).

[11] Consolidated data from FHA Annual Reports.

[12] Home Loan Bank Board, *Statistical Summary, 1951*, Table 9.

TABLE 5

FHA-Insured and VA-Guaranteed Home Loans Made by Principal Types of Lenders in Million Dollars and as a Per Cent of Total Home Loans 1948-1950[a]

	COMMERCIAL BANKS		INSURANCE COMPANIES		SAVINGS & LOAN ASSOCIATIONS		MUTUAL SAVINGS BANKS	
	Amount	Per Cent of Total	Amount	Per Cent of Total	Amount	Per Cent of Total	Amount	Per Cent of Total
A FHA-INSURED LOANS[b]								
1948	657	24.9	468	41.3	221	6.1	64	6.5
1949	672	30.1	507	46.4	238	6.5	107	10.8
1950	730	21.3	514	29.5	266	5.1	189	13.5
B VA-GUARANTEED LOANS[c]								
1948	737	28.0	139	12.3	536	15.0	226	23.1
1949	345	15.4	65	5.9	330	9.1	191	19.3
1950	586	17.1	222	12.7	740	14.1	298	21.3
C FHA AND VA LOANS COMBINED								
1948	1,394	52.9	607	53.6	757	21.0	290	29.6
1949	1,017	45.5	572	52.3	568	15.6	298	30.1
1950	1,316	38.4	736	42.2	1,006	19.2	487	34.8

[a] Comparable data for years before 1948 are not available. In the case of FHA, available earlier data (through 1945) refer to gross mortgages accepted for insurance rather than premium paying mortgages, or include firm commitments under Title VI as well as net mortgages. This precludes a comparison with the total home loans made by each type of lender. In the case of VA, no classification of the amount of loans closed by type of lender is available before 1948. Since insurance companies and mutual savings banks are net purchasers of FHA and probably of VA loans, the data in the table do not represent their total acquisitions of such loans but rather those written in their own names. Total acquisitions of nonfarm VA loans by life insurance companies were $366 million in 1948, $131 million in 1949, and $930 million in 1950. Total acquisitions of FHA loans (both on homes and multifamily projects) by the companies were $1,202 million in 1948, $1,350 million in 1949, and $1,542 million in 1950 (Institute of Life Insurance, New York).

[b] Amounts from *Annual Reports*, Housing and Home Finance Agency. Percentages based on total estimated amount of home mortgage loans made by each type of lender in *Estimated Home Mortgage Debt and Lending Activity*, 1950, Home Loan Bank Board.

[c] Amounts from *Statistical Summary, 1951*, Home Loan Bank Board, Table 9. Percentages based on total estimated amount of home mortgage loans made by each type of lender, referred to in footnote b.

ences in holdings of government-insured loans, both on homes and multifamily structures (Chart E and Table 10). In the case of life insurance companies the ratio of outstanding FHA mortgages to their total residential mortgage portfolio rose from 23 per cent in 1940 to 37 per cent in 1944, and the ratio of FHA and VA loans combined to total holdings reached almost 60 per cent in 1950 — the highest ratio for any of the four principal types of mortgage lenders. More than one-half of the residential mortgage portfolio of insured commercial banks on June 30, 1950 was in the form of government-insured loans. Mutual savings banks in the short span of four years, from 1947 to 1950, doubled their ratio of government-insured mortgage loans to total residential holdings, but at the end of the period still held less than 43 per cent of the total in these types of loans. The ratio for insured savings and loan associations during this period has hovered around one-third.

The FHA and VA programs were influential in the growth of total residential holdings of the various types of lenders. While many factors combined to produce the startling growth differentials revealed in Table 6, it must be considered more than a coincidence that the institutions participating most actively in the mortgage insurance and guaranty programs — commercial banks and life insurance companies — show by far the greatest relative increase in residential mortgage holdings. Savings and loan associations rank third, and mutual savings banks experienced a far slower growth of portfolios than any of the other types of institution. The comparatively small increase of noninstitutional holdings probably reflects the historical decline in the importance of noninstitutional lenders, accelerated by the emphasis in FHA and VA programs on institutional sources of funds.

The Government's Role in the Secondary Market

One of the effects of government insurance of residential mortgage loans has been to create a debt instrument that can be shifted more easily from one lender to another. From the lender's point of view, government insurance endows mortgage loans with greater uniformity of quality than has ever been the case before, and it

CHART E
FHA-Insured and VA-Guaranteed Mortgages Held by Principal Types of Lenders as a Per Cent of their Total Residential Mortgage Loans
1950

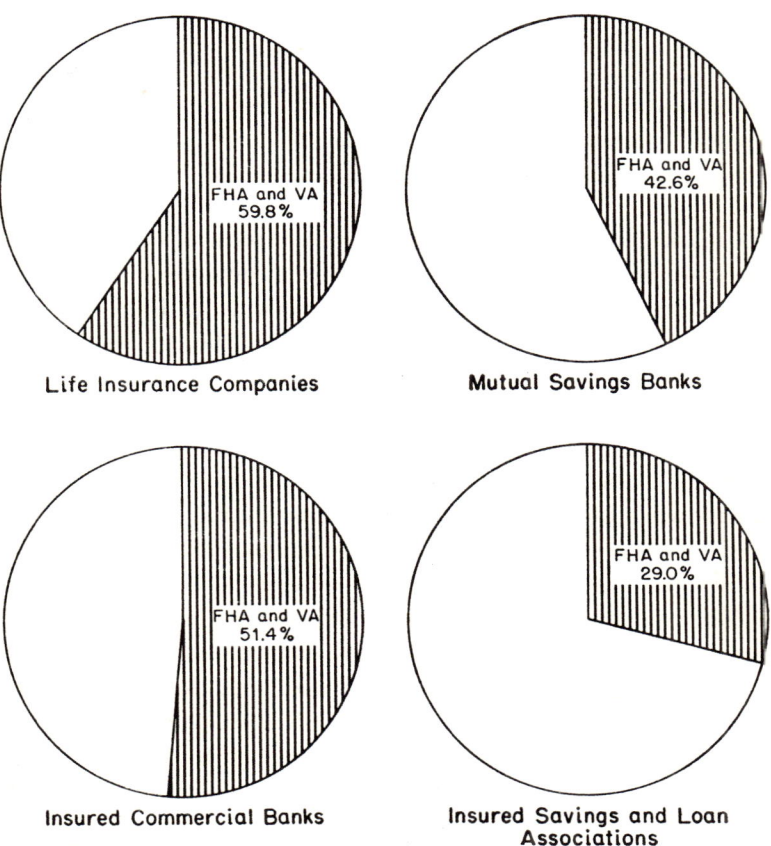

Source: Table 10, last column. Data for commercial banks as of June 30, 1950; for the other types of institutions, as of December 13, 1950.

reduces the necessity for detailed examination that usually accompanies the transfer of loans from one mortgagee to another. As a result, an active "secondary market" for FHA and VA loans has developed, which in turn has widened the geographic scope of

43

TABLE 6

Relative Growth of Residential Mortgage Holdings of Principal Types of Lenders

TYPE OF LENDER	PER CENT INCREASE 1950 OVER	
	1930	1935
Institutional, total	158	193
Noninstitutional, total	3	36
Commercial banks	266	368
Life insurance companies	283	402
Savings and loan associations	112	296
Mutual savings banks	64	84

SOURCE: Based on data in the forthcoming monograph.

the market for mortgage loans and given it some of the characteristics of national capital markets. It has become quite customary, for example, to quote premiums and discounts for FHA and VA loans offered and sought in this market, and the deviations from par are largely determined by general mortgage market conditions rather than by the quality of the underlying security of specific loans.

The Federal National Mortgage Association, a wholly government-owned facility, has played an important role in the development of the secondary market. Its operations at times have had a substantial influence on the volume of construction.

The volume of transfers of FHA home loans among mortgagees is shown in Table 11. Aggregate transfers increased steadily except for the late war and early postwar years, and they exceeded $1 billion each in 1949 and 1950. From 1935 to 1950 the face amount of loans involved in transfers totaled about $7.5 billion. The annual number of home loans transferred from 1946 to 1950 varied between 6 and 13 per cent of the total number of FHA home loans in force. According to preliminary results of the 1950 Survey of Residential Financing by the Bureau of the Census, one-third of the FHA-insured loans and almost one-fourth of the VA-guaranteed loans on owner-occupied houses had been acquired by purchase rather than origination of the mortgage, as against 13 per cent for conventional loans. These figures show a velocity probably unequaled in the history of mortgage finance in this country, except for the refinancing operations of the government-owned Home Owners' Loan Corporation.

In these transfers mortgage companies and savings and loan associations have been consistent net sellers. Insurance companies and mutual savings banks, as well as the Federal National Mortgage Association, have been net purchasers, although the latter's sales exceeded purchases during certain years. Commercial banks as a group have been net purchasers in some years and net sellers in others. Table 12 shows purchases and sales for each of the four principal types of private institutional lenders. While these lenders in the aggregate have been net purchasers of FHA home loans their sales activity has been substantial, the amount of annual sales to annual purchases ranging roughly from 40 to 80 per cent. In other words, there has been an active secondary market among the various types of portfolio lenders, in addition to transfers from loan originators such as mortgage companies to portfolio lenders and federal agencies.[13]

Data on transfers of FHA rental housing mortgages are not available for the entire period, but substantial velocity is indicated for recent years. In 1950 the face amount of loans transferred was more than $518 million, equal to 16 per cent of the face amount of such mortgages outstanding at the end of the year.[14] No transfer figures are published for VA home loans.

The role of the federal agencies in the secondary market for FHA home loans has varied greatly from year to year. During the period 1935-1950 purchases by federal agencies represented almost 12 per cent of all purchases (Table 13).

Federal activity in the "secondary market" increased sharply in the postwar period, primarily in support of the VA home loan program. From 1948 through 1951 the Federal National Mortgage Association (FNMA), now the only agency specifically authorized to buy and sell FHA and VA loans, purchased almost $2.7 billion worth of government-insured loans, about ten times

---

[13] Although there have been substantial transfers of FHA mortgages among different types of portfolio lenders, individual institutions tend to be either net buyers or net sellers.

[14] *Fourth Annual Report,* Housing and Home Finance Agency, 1950, Tables 35 and 36, pp. 289-90.

as much as during the preceding ten years. Of these, more than $2 billion or 80 per cent were VA loans. Sales from 1948 to 1951 totaled $600 million, and less than half of these were VA loans. The mortgage portfolio of FNMA on December 31, 1951 was almost $1.85 billion, of which about 90 per cent were in VA loans (Table 7). The FNMA holdings of VA loans at the end of 1950 represented more than 11 per cent of the estimated total balance of VA loans outstanding.

The overwhelming proportion of VA loans in recent operations of the FNMA illustrates the government's influence on mortgage lending and on the management of the residential mortgage debt in critical situations. Most of the FNMA purchases of VA loans occurred in 1949 and 1950, on the heels of an increase in government bond yields and mortgage interest rates in 1948. As a result of these changes in the mortgage market, the supply of funds for VA loans at 4 per cent threatened to dry up. In fact, the volume of new VA loans dropped from about $3.3 billion in 1947 to less than $1.9 in 1948 and $1.4 in 1949. The purchases by FNMA in 1949 and 1950 combined with an easing of the money market to overcome these difficulties and were partly responsible for the spectacular increase in VA loans to more than $3 billion in 1950. During 1949 and 1950, FNMA purchases of VA loans equaled approximately one-third of all VA home loans made. These were also years of high and increasing volume of residential construction. The FNMA at that time was an instrument for maintaining a fixed interest rate pattern and for continuing a high level of housing construction in the face of changing conditions in the mortgage market.

Much of FNMA's effectiveness during this period was due to the issuance of advance commitments to purchase, which was begun on July 1, 1948 and terminated on March 13, 1950. The commitments enabled mortgage lenders to originate FHA and VA loans with the intention of selling them immediately to FNMA which, under the procedure, was commited to buy. "The commitment program made it possible for the lending institution . . . to arrange the needed financing for construction since the commitment assured a market for the permanent mortgage on the completed

TABLE 7

Operations of the Federal National Mortgage Association
(millions of dollars)

	1938-47	1948	1949	1950	1951	1938-51
Purchases of loans						
FHA	272	187	253	49	74	835
VA	0	11	420	995	603	2,029
Total	272	198	673	1,044	677	2,864
Sales of loans						
FHA	167	0	19	261	28	475
VA	0	0	*	208	83	291
Total	167	0	20	469	111	766
Balance of loans held at end of period						
FHA	4	188	403	169	204	....
VA	0	11	425	1,178	1,646	....
Total	4	199	828	1,347	1,850	....

*Less than $1 million.
SOURCE: Housing and Home Finance Agency, *Housing Statistics*, December 1951, and *Annual Reports*. Because of rounding, the components do not necessarily add up to totals.

house. The procedure was of particular significance in facilitating the flow of credit for housing programs involving FHA-insured mortgages and VA-guaranteed mortgages."[15] Advance commitments issued during these 21 months totaled almost $2.5 billion, of which about $1.5 billion was outstanding at the end of the period. Purchases by FNMA declined substantially in 1951 after advance commitments were discontinued and the anti-inflation program necessitated by the Korean war came into operation.[16]

Another significant aspect of FNMA operations is the restriction of purchases, among other things, to loans with an original principal of not more than $10,000 per unit.[17] This limitation is another means of "channeling" new housing construction into predetermined price classes.

[15] Housing and Home Finance Agency, *Fourth Annual Report*, 1950, p. 74.
[16] Advance commitments up to $200 million were again authorized for defense housing in the Defense Housing and Community Facilities and Services Act of 1951, Public Law 139, Chapter 378, (92 Cong., 1 Sess.) and increased by another $52 million by Public Law 309, enacted April 9, 1952.
[17] Public Law 387, approved October 25, 1949.

There is a real question whether the FNMA has been a secondary market facility or a primary supplier of mortgage funds. Its facilities have been widely used by mortgage loan originators who did not intend to hold loans in their portfolios, and the advance commitment procedure for a time sanctioned the role of FNMA as a primary source of funds. The distinction between primary and secondary credit facilities is, of course, largely a matter of definition. In the mortgage market, the distinction has come to be based on the method of originating mortgages, with the originator defined as a primary source and the first portfolio holder, if he is not identical with the originator, considered a secondary lender. The method of originating mortgage loans, however, depends on the organization of the mortgage market and has little significance for an analysis of the real sources of funds. For the latter, the distinction between portfolio lenders who supply funds and other lenders who act as "feeders" to portfolio lenders is more meaningful. On this criterion, the FNMA has at least at times served as a substantial primary source of mortgage funds.

This interpretation is supported by the fact that the agency, originally designed as a stand-by purchaser of FHA loans from portfolio holders or interim portfolio lenders, has more and more developed into an instrument for the support of new lending activity. In this function, the FNMA operates under specific Congressional authorizations, in contrast to the open market purchases of government bonds by the Federal Reserve Banks. The support of new lending activity in some instances performed special services. Thus the FNMA in recent years purchased new types of FHA-insured loans on defense housing projects, which private institutions were initially reluctant to acquire. It usually was able to sell the loans after a period of "seasoning" to private portfolio lenders. On the whole, however, this pioneering activity has accounted for a relatively small portion of FNMA purchases during the postwar period.

The Federal Home Loan Banks, by advances to member institutions secured for the most part by residential mortgage loans, also provide some secondary credit. Advances outstanding did not exceed $200 million in the late thirties, but increased rapidly during the postwar period and reached almost $816 million at the end of 1950.[18]

Influence on Cost and Terms of Financing

Beginning with the then revolutionary terms on which the Home Owners' Loan Corporation from 1933 to 1936 refinanced $3 billion of the outstanding home mortgage debt,[19] federal programs in the residential mortgage field have persistently sought to reduce contract interest rates, lengthen contract terms to maturity, and increase loan-to-value ratios. The interest rate on HOLC loans, originally 5 per cent, was reduced to $4\frac{1}{2}$ per cent in October 1939. The maximum interest rate on all FHA-insured mortgages was established in 1934 at 5 per cent (exclusive of the mortgage insurance premium), but was reduced by regulation in 1939 to $4\frac{1}{2}$ per cent, and maximum permissible service charges were lowered simultaneously. The maximum interest rate on FHA home loans under Title VI was cut down to 4 per cent in 1946 in conjunction with the veterans emergency housing program. In early 1953 the maximum rate was $4\frac{1}{4}$ per cent for home loans and 4 per cent for loans on rental and cooperative housing projects.

The Servicemen's Readjustment Act in 1944 established a maximum of 4 per cent for home loans guaranteed by the Veterans Administration, and an amendment of 1948 authorizing an increase to $4\frac{1}{2}$ per cent was not used before the spring of 1953 when the maximum interest rate on both VA and FHA home loans was raised to $4\frac{1}{2}$ per cent.

The maximum contract term for FHA home loans, originally 20 years, was extended in 1938 to 25 years for small new houses and now ranges from 25 to 30 years on new home construction, with 40 years allowed on rental and cooperative housing projects. The original maximum term of 20 years for veterans home loans was extended in two steps to 30 years. Similar successive steps

---

[18] *Fourth Annual Report,* Housing and Home Finance Agency, 1950, Table 1, p. 198.

[19] These terms were 5 per cent interest, maximum contract length of 15 years, and maximum loan-to-value ratio of 80 per cent.

reduced the downpayment requirements for FHA-insured mortgages on new construction, and the Servicemen's Readjustment Act eliminated such requirements for veterans home loans.[20]

The effects of these actions on interest rates and other contract terms for residential mortgages, of course, cannot be dissociated from the effects of changes in the entire market for capital funds, particularly the decline of interest rates from the middle thirties to the late forties. It is reasonable to assume that much of the drop in mortgage interest rates would have occurred without the federal aids, in response to competitive forces in the capital market and the easy money policies of the monetary authorities. As a matter of general observation, however, the federal programs seem to have hastened the reduction of contract interest rates on mortgages and the use of more liberal contract terms.

A few data are at hand to illustrate the actual differences in terms between FHA and VA mortgages and conventional loans. The average contract interest rate on a sample of mortgages on 1- to 4-family houses held by 24 leading life insurance companies at the end of 1946 was 4.5 per cent for FHA loans and 4.1 per cent for VA loans, but varied between 4.6 and 4.9 per cent for conventional loans.[21] The comparable figures for a sample of loans held by 170 commercial banks in June 1947 were 4.5 per cent for FHA loans, 4 per cent for VA loans, and 4.8 per cent for conventional mortgages.[22] A sample of similar loans made by 92 savings and loan associations in 1946-1947 showed that practically all of the VA and FHA loans carried contract interest rates of less than 5 per cent, while only 16.3 per cent of the original amount of conven-

[20] Terms for FHA and VA loans were tightened temporarily in the summer of 1950 as part of the anti-inflation policies instituted after the Korean war, and in anticipation of Credit Regulation X for conventional mortgage loans. The restrictions on FHA and VA loans were relaxed in the summer of 1952 when Regulation X was suspended, and the legal maxima were restored in spring 1953.

[21] R. J. Saulnier, *op. cit.*, p. 56. Figures represent averages of current, or last contract, interest rates weighed by amounts outstanding. The maximum interest rate for VA home loans is 4 per cent, and the reported 4.1 per cent is due apparently to erroneous inclusion of service fees or similar charges.

[22] Carl F. Behrens, *op. cit.*, p. 45. Averages are weighted by the outstanding balance of each loan.

tional mortgages fell in this class.[23] A survey of house purchases from October 1950 to March 1951 found that 43 per cent of the loans obtained by veterans had contract interest rates of 4 per cent or less as against 13 per cent of the loans obtained by non-veterans.[24]

Contract interest rates are not, of course, an accurate basis for comparison of cost to borrowers in view of differences in non-interest charges. Nevertheless, it would appear that the average spread between contract rates on FHA and conventional home loans in the postwar period was relatively small. Moreover, from the borrower's point of view, the spread was offset largely by his obligation to pay a mortgage insurance premium of $\frac{1}{2}$ of 1 per cent, even considering the possibility of a rebate of premium payments upon termination of the loan. The average spread between veterans home loans and conventional loans was more substantial, particularly since the borrower on VA guaranteed mortgages was free of any charges comparable to the FHA mortgage insurance premium.

On contract length, the sample of commercial bank loans showed that 58.6 per cent of government-insured mortgages had terms of 15 years or more, as against only 2.4 per cent for noninsured loans.[25] In the sample of mortgages loans made by savings and loan associations, practically all FHA-insured loans and over 60 per cent of the VA-guaranteed loans were for 20 years or more, while only 7 per cent of the conventional loans fell in this group.[26]

While these data are for loans on both new and existing construction, contract terms more favorable to borrowers have been concentrated in the new house field. A sample survey of first mortgages on single-family houses bought October 1950-March 1951 indicates generally lower interest rates and longer maturities for

---

[23] Edward E. Edwards, "Urban Real Estate Financing by Savings and Loan Associations" (National Bureau of Economic Research, Manuscript, 1950), p. III-16. Based on original amounts of loans.

[24] "House Purchases in the Five Months Following the Introduction of Real Estate Credit Regulation," *Federal Reserve Bulletin*, July 1951, Table 13.

[25] Carl F. Behrens, *op. cit.*, p. 44. Percentages refer to amounts outstanding.

[26] Edward E. Edwards, *op. cit.*, p. III-13. Percentages refer to original amounts of loans.

loans on new dwellings than for loans on existing dwellings. About 78 per cent of the mortgages on new houses bought during this period carried interest rates of less than 5 per cent as against 51 per cent of the mortgages on old houses. More than two-thirds of the loans on new houses had maturities of 20 years or more, as against one-third of the loans on old houses.[27] Differences in terms for mortgages on new and existing dwellings would be expected on the basis of risk considerations alone, but some of these differentials are probably due to the greater emphasis in the government programs on new construction (Table 3, column 7).

Much of this information covers only short periods and in some cases is based on small samples. In the absence of more comprehensive data, however, the findings may be accepted as reflecting broadly the contract terms prevailing during recent years.

The information on contract interest rates and contract lengths in combination suggests considerable differences between periodic charges on government-insured and conventional loans per $1,000 of loan. But to the extent that FHA and VA loans usually are for larger percentages of appraised value,[28] the differences per $1,000 of purchase price would be smaller. Moreover, the factors discussed in the section "Widening the Market" need to be considered at this point. The easier financing terms may have served to induce purchasers to buy more expensive houses, particularly in the sellers' market of the early postwar years, as well as to facilitate purchase by families who otherwise could not have afforded to buy.

The nationwide terms for FHA and VA loans have probably made a great contribution toward the narrowing of geographic differentials in residential mortgage interest rates and other contract provisions. By and large, the maximum interest rates have become standard rates under the programs; that is, even in areas of relatively abundant supply of funds few FHA and VA mortgages have been made at rates below the maxima. The uniformity of rates has given added impetus to the long-term forces operating toward a reduction of geographic differentials in interest rates and

[27] "House Purchases in the Five Months Following the Introduction of Real Estate Credit Regulation," *Federal Reserve Bulletin,* July 1951, Table 21.

[28] The aforementioned sources confirm this observation; see also p. 25.

other loan terms.[29] On the other hand, it appears at times to have diminished the flow of funds into new residential construction in certain areas with prevailing higher interest rates, and geographic differentials have taken the form of premiums and discounts on FHA and VA loans.

In summary, the federal credit aids since the middle thirties have probably accelerated the decline in residential mortgage interest rates and the liberalization of other contract terms. Lower interest rates and particularly longer contract terms on FHA and VA loans, compared to conventional mortgages, represent advantages to borrowers under these programs so far as periodic outlays are concerned. Because of the indirect influence of easy credit on prices paid for new as well as existing construction during the war and postwar periods, however, these advantages were at least partially canceled by price effects.

[29] Data on this effect of federal programs in many credit fields will be given in the forthcoming volume by R. J. Saulnier and others on federal lending, loan insurance, and guarantees (National Bureau of Economic Research).

# 4

A Note on the Future of Federal Credit Aids

Whichever of the data presented in the preceding sections are considered, it is clear that roughly half the market for residential construction and mortgage financing of new housing has come to operate directly under the auspices of the federal aid programs. The flow of mortgage funds into residential construction has been increasingly influenced by the terms and other stipulations, prescribed by laws and administrative rulings, under which the FHA and VA will accept mortgages for insurance or guaranty. For about half the total market, the pattern of interest rates, down-payment requirements, and amortization periods, as well as borrowers' credit ratings and location and physical design of new construction, have been subject to governmental as well as private decisions. Market forces operating on the mortgage interest rate can be modified by opening or widening the gates of the Federal National Mortgage Association and using this government agency as a primary source of funds almost equivalent to direct federal loans.

The scope of the government programs is such that political decisions can influence the volume and composition of building activity in an appreciable though as yet not fully determinable measure. This drastic change in the channeling of funds into investment has come about in the brief span of about 15 years and, accentuated by the exigencies of World War II, has reached a peak during the postwar period.

The size alone of the federal programs, both in absolute and relative terms, suggests the extent and intensity of their implications. The full effect of these operations on housing production and the flow of mortgage funds, as well as on the economy as a whole, defies simple measurement. Their share in total residential construction and mortgage lending does not take account of their far-reaching indirect influences on building types in residential construction, land planning in new subdivisions, the structure of the housebuilding industry, the extent of home ownership, general lending practices, sources of funds, terms of conventional mortgages, and other facets of this complex business. Only a few of the implications of the governmental activities are selected for discussion here — those which have a bearing on the future course of capital formation and financing in this field.

An appraisal of the future role of federal credit aids must concern itself with at least three questions:

1. Does the observed increase in scope and intensity of federal aids since 1935 suggest a trend, or is it perhaps more adequately explained as a response to temporary pressures and maladjustments in housing markets?

2. Are there limits to the effectiveness of present means of federal assistance, and if so, what are the alternatives?

3. If the assumption of a trend is warranted, what consequences will arise for the volume and stability of capital formation and financing in this field?

In considering these questions, the investigator shifts from the relatively secure ground of historical analysis to a more treacherous field, where judgment plays a larger role; and his only qualification at this point is perhaps the development, through training and experience, of an attitude that should assure judicious consideration of all relevant factors and minimize if not prevent the injection of his own biases.

A Trend?

Each of the federal credit aids for private residential construction had a special justification when it was established. The mortgage insurance program of the FHA was enacted originally in response to "pump-priming" considerations and the need for improvements in the mortgage system. The principal steps toward more liberal credit terms for FHA-insured loans were taken to meet crises in war housing and to help relieve the postwar housing shortage. The guarantee of veterans home loans was adopted as part of a program to ease the adjustment of ex-servicemen to civilian life. The use of the Federal National Mortgage Association for practically direct government lending operations was authorized as a stop-gap solution when the supply of mortgage funds for FHA and VA loans at fixed interest rates threatened to diminish.[1]

One might thus be led to believe that many if not all of these operations could be withdrawn if their original purposes were served or no major emergencies arose. However, here as in the interpretation of other events, it is necessary to distinguish sharply between the incidents that give rise to political actions and the more deep-seated forces that underlie the actions.

Basically, the development of federal aids for housing, comprising not only the activities analyzed in this paper but also public housing and assistance in urban redevelopment, must be viewed as part of a long-term social change which vests housing conditions, and not only those of the poor and indigent, with broad and probably intensifying public interest. This change seems to reflect basic attitudes of the community-at-large, although its intensity and, therefore, the pace and form of federal programs may vary over time and in different political and economic climates.[2] This broad concept was recognized by Congress in the "Declaration of National Housing Policy," which forms the preamble to the Housing Act of 1949. It is reflected in the organizational assembly of all federal agencies concerned with housing and credit for housing (except the Veterans Administration) in the Housing and Home Finance Agency; and while the organization of federal agencies is subject to change, it is unlikely that the forces pulling in the direction of an over-all federal strategy on housing activities will abate in the long run.

[1] For a more detailed account, see Miles L. Colean, *op. cit.*

[2] It is of interest to note in this connection that the platforms of the Democratic and Republican parties for 1944, 1948, and 1952 do not touch at all upon the FHA mortgage insurance and VA home loan guarantee programs or on the operations of the Federal National Mortgage Association. In contrast, they differ substantially on public housing and slum clearance and redevelopment whenever these items appear.

The use of federal credit aids as tools in a broad program to improve housing conditions is supported by the still broader, widely accepted social objective of maintaining reasonably full employment. It is almost inconceivable that aids to housing production will not be incorporated in programs to combat unemployment if and when the time for such programs comes. In fact, existing aids will most probably be intensified and supplemented under such conditions, or they will be extended beyond their original expiration date. Such a contingency, for example, may affect the termination of the home loan program for veterans of World War II, now scheduled for 1957.

The employment of federal credit aids is supported also by a widely held notion that the housebuilding "industry," however defined, is backward in comparison with other industries meeting essential consumers' needs. In this view, new housing historically has been a luxury product available only to the upper income groups, and government action is necessary to compensate for the apparent inability of the industry to meet the need for houses of good standards within the reach of every family, or the average family, or however the "need" may be defined.[3]

The "trend" suggested by these observations is strengthened by the conviction of strategic groups that continued government aids are indispensable to effective operation of the processes by which new housing is built and marketed. Critical issues during the past few years provide vivid illustrations. One is the termination in 1945 of the wartime Title VI of the National Housing Act,

[3] This viewpoint permeates much of the housing literature of the past 20 years, government reports, and Congressional deliberations. Cf. U. S. Congress, Investigation of Concentration of Economic Power, Temporary National Economic Committee: Monograph No. 8, *Toward More Housing* (76 Cong., 3 Sess.) and *Hearings before the Temporary National Economic Committee* (76 Cong., 1 Sess.), Part 11, Construction Industry, 1940; Charles Abrams, *The Future of Housing* (Harper & Brothers, 1946), Chapters 5, 13; Robert Lasch, *Breaking the Building Blockade* (University of Chicago Press, 1946), pp. 7-10; and numerous statements in *Hearings before the Committee on Banking and Currency on S. 1592* (79 Cong., 1 Sess.); *Housing: Hearings before the Committee on Banking and Currency on S. 287, S. 866, S. 701, S. 801, S. 802, S. 803, and S. 804* (80 Cong., 1 Sess.), *passim*. See also *High Cost of Housing: Report of a Subcommittee of the Joint Committee on Housing* (80 Cong., 2 Sess., House Document No. 647, 1948); and Nathan Straus, *Two Thirds of a Nation* (Alfred A. Knopf, 1952).

with its "firm commitments" to builders and its generous financing terms, and its re-enactment in slightly modified form in 1946 after a short lapse, as part of the veterans emergency housing program.[4] Another is the liberalization in 1950 of financing terms for rental and cooperative housing projects under Title II of this Act when Section 608, designed to encourage rental construction under war and postwar conditions, was allowed to expire.[5] A third is the increase in 1950 of the guaranty for veterans home loans from 50 per cent of the loan amount not exceeding $4,000 to 60 per cent not exceeding $7,500, plus an extension of the maximum maturity from 25 to 30 years[6] — a revision that followed the falling off in the volume of these loans in 1948 and 1949 and one which contributed to the spectacular increase of housing starts in 1950. Still another example is the 1951 liberalization by Congressional action of housing credit restrictions imposed in 1950 under Congressional authority.[7]

In all these instances, consumers' and builders' and sometimes mortgage lending interests combined to produce demands for more potent federal aids when a decline in the volume of building occurred or threatened. The apparent dependence on the federal programs developed under conditions which, on the whole, were favorable to a high level of residential building activity. It will unquestionably be felt more acutely when circumstances are less favorable. Under such circumstances, any diminution of aids would be considered widely to be a calamity, and complete withdrawal would be held to spell disaster — regardless of what the real as distinguished from the anticipated impact of withdrawal may be.

War and postwar dislocations unquestionably accelerated the scope of government activities in this field, but it would seem more reasonable to anticipate a continued and growing role of the federal government than to expect a diminution or withdrawal of aids in the long run. This "trend" will not necessarily apply to the

[4] Public Law 388, Chapter 268, (79 Cong., 2 Sess.).
[5] Public Law 475, Chapter 94, (81 Cong., 2 Sess.).
[6] *Ibid.*
[7] Public Law 139, Chapter 378, (82 Cong., 1 Sess.).

FHA mortgage insurance system or the VA home loan guarantee program as they now stand. The share of FHA financing in new construction may not exceed 30 or 40 per cent unless there is a war or the relative attractiveness of FHA loans is drastically changed, and the importance of VA financing may diminish as distance from World War II increases. In fact, there seem to be narrow limits to the intensification of these aids in the future, as will be pointed out below, and the trend toward a greater role of the federal government in residential construction and its financing may express itself in the use of new financial devices.

Limits to Present Types of Aids

If the assumption of a "trend" is warranted, what are the limits to the use of the present types of aids, and what are the probable alternatives?

This question is perhaps most pertinent if declining employment and incomes are assumed. For it is in such a situation that the demands for increased federal aids will become most pronounced. The record of experience is not instructive on this point since the federal programs so far have operated on a broadly rising market.

Little is known about how the demand for new construction responds to changes in credit terms during the downward phase of a cycle. How much would the demand for new housing be stimulated if, under conditions of falling incomes, terms under a government mortgage insurance program were changed from, say, a 10 per cent minimum downpayment to zero downpayment, a 25-year maximum maturity to 35 years, and 4 per cent interest to $3\frac{1}{2}$ per cent? Arithmetically, this change would produce a monthly mortgage carrying charge (level-payment) of $4.13 per $1,000 of purchase price of a single-family house, as against $4.75 before. The reduction in loan payments would be 13 per cent but the decline in total monthly outlays for housing would be much less, perhaps only 6 to 8 per cent; for real estate tax, maintenance, heating, and other operational expenses would not be affected by the decline in mortgage payments. The complete elimination of downpayment may be a stimulating factor when consumers as well as business firms prefer liquidity. But cash outlays of several hundred dollars would still be required for closing costs, additional landscaping, and other incidental expenses usually associated with house purchase, even in the absence of downpayments; and uncertainty would still discourage the undertaking of fixed commitments.

The extension of maturities will have rapidly diminishing effects on mortgage carrying charges compared to the effects of past actions in this direction. The amount by which monthly level payments are reduced when the maturity of a 4 per cent loan is extended from 30 to 40 years is 59 cents per $1,000 of loan, as against $1.29 for an extension from 20 to 30 years. The per cent reduction is little over 12 per cent compared to 21 per cent.[8]

Moreover, the large supply in a falling market of existing housing at declining prices or rents, often in the nature of distress sales or rentals, would limit the volume of new housing that could be marketed even at greatly liberalized credit terms. An annual production of one million dwelling units, for example, equals little more than 2 per cent of the number of existing nonfarm dwelling units — about 42 million in 1952. If only one-tenth of the existing supply were offered at distress prices or rents[9] the quantity of old dwelling units coming on the market would be four times as large as the volume of new construction — a competing supply which would reduce the marketability of new housing even though the latter may be more attractive both in physical characteristics and in liberal debt-financing.

Limits would also exist in the supply of funds for mortgage loans by private institutions. The insurance of bank deposits and of accounts in savings and loan associations might relieve pressure that would otherwise accentuate the liquidity preference of financial institutions. But whether protection from runs on deposits and mortgage insurance would induce lenders to continue the financ-

---

[8] Cf. Ernest M. Fisher, *Urban Real Estate Markets: Characteristics and Financing* (National Bureau of Economic Research, 1951), pp. 71-2. For a general discussion of the effects of changes of loan terms in instalment financing, see also Avram Kisselgoff, *Factors Affecting the Demand for Consumers' Instalment Sales Credit* (Technical Paper 7, National Bureau of Economic Research, 1952).

[9] Distress prices or rents may be defined as those which reflect the actual or anticipated elimination of equities through foreclosure.

ing of new construction in the face of rising vacancies, defaults, and foreclosures is an open question.

Apart from higher interest rates there is little leeway left for making investments in insured or guaranteed mortgages more attractive under unfavorable business conditions. Further inducements might be covering more or all of the risks still left with the mortgagee (such as the excess of foreclosure costs over the maximum covered by FHA and liberalization of the "waste provisions" under which the mortgagee bears the risk of unusual damage to property after institution of foreclosure proceedings), or in making the interest rate and terms of FHA debentures exchanged for foreclosed properties more attractive.[10] In the case of VA loans, the maximum amounts and percentages of the guaranty could again be raised. The effectiveness of these inducements must be weighed against the conditions that would create caution and reluctance in lending on new construction.

If there are narrow limits to the effectiveness of more intensive use of mortgage insurance programs under conditions of business contraction, demands for "stronger medicine" will undoubtedly develop. The direction of any attempts to meet them can be inferred from scattered examples already on the record. Among these is the direct home loan program of the Veterans Administration, now of small magnitude and on legal maximum terms identical with those of private mortgage lenders making VA loans. Another is the Connecticut program under which the State Housing Authority grants direct mortgage loans at 1½ per cent interest with a maximum maturity of 25 to 30 years. These loans are serviced by mortgage lending institutions at the usual fee of 0.5 per cent. The state funds are obtained by short-term borrowing.[11] A third example is the New York City program of rental housing without cash subsidies, designed for income groups above the admission limits for public housing with cash subsidies.[12] In this case, rentals

---

[10] For an instructive discussion of these points, see *Mortgage Financing*, Hearings before the Senate Committee on Banking and Currency, (82 Cong., 2 Sess.).

[11] Chester Bowles, "The Role of the States," in Nathan Straus, *Two Thirds of a Nation* (Alfred A. Knopf, 1952), pp. 236 ff.

[12] Annual Reports of the New York City Housing Authority, 1949-1951.

are set to meet a debt charge based on low-cost, tax-exempt public financing, as well as operating costs and (reduced) charges in lieu of real estate taxes. Various schemes along similar lines have been enacted in other states. Finally, as was pointed out before, the Federal National Mortgage Association provides an instrument that can be used for primary lending on nonmarket terms even though private lending institutions might originate and service the loans.

If these observations are correct, the boundaries between "private" and "public" residential construction would become less determinate. To date, the term "public housing" has been reserved broadly for the programs under which public capital funds or subsidies are made available for projects owned and managed by public agencies. The record of European housing since World War I is replete with arrangements under which the distinction between private and public housing is difficult if not impossible to maintain. It is at least conceivable that forces at work in this country point in the same direction.

Consequences for Capital Formation and Financing

On the whole, past and projected federal policies in this field may be interpreted as efforts to raise permanently the proportion of total resources devoted to housing construction above the level that would be obtained from the interplay of market forces. To the extent that the efforts succeed, new residential construction will be maintained at a higher volume than would be possible without existing and prospective government aids.

Enough has been said about the uncertainties of consumers' reactions to more liberal credit terms to indicate that the quantitative effects are unpredictable. Moreover, government aid will be only one of many factors conditioning the future course of residential building. No comprehensive appraisal of long-term prospects for capital formation in this field is possible without analysis of all factors which seem relevant according to past performance. Such an analysis will be attempted in the forthcoming monograph. In the meantime, however, it is possible to sketch some of the problems and consequences of governmental efforts to raise the level of residential construction.

One of these problems concerns the interaction between new construction and the market for existing residential facilities. A high volume of new construction offered at financial terms much more advantageous than those for existing residential real estate might aggravate declines in occupancy and prices of old housing. The federal government itself, however, has a great stake in the residential mortgage debt on existing property, represented at the end of 1950 by the contingent liabilities involved in $22 billion of FHA and VA loans outstanding.[13] The government has therefore a substantial fiscal interest in avoiding any decline in prices that may directly or indirectly affect its contingent liabilities. Because the markets for new and old housing are closely interconnected, any drastic revision of financing terms in favor of new construction might involve corresponding changes for loans on existing residential real estate,[14] and possibly a transfer of insured or guaranteed loans from private to public holdings.

There is a question as to the effect of continued or strengthened government support of the housebuilding industry on its productive efficiency. The implied assurance of output may tend to slow down technological change or improved production processes, and may thus retard progress toward lower-priced or better products. It has been alleged, for example, that the government support received by the British housebuilding industry over the past 30 years has operated in this direction.[15] The record in this country, however, is none too clear and has never been adequately analyzed. By accelerating the development of large-scale operative builders, the FHA program may have raised efficiency. Moreover, the industry was not noted for advances in efficiency before the advent of federal aids when fluctuations in output were extreme, and

[13] This amount is the total of such loans outstanding. In the case of VA guaranteed loans, the guaranty itself covers only a portion of the principal, averaging roughly 50 per cent of the total amount of such loans.

[14] Existing houses originally built under FHA inspection are already eligible for loans on terms equal to those for the financing of new construction under FHA.

[15] Anglo-American Council on Productivity, *Productivity Team Report: Building* (London and New York, 1950), p. 4.

implied assurance of more stable production may foster rather than retard progress. Such an assurance will be more effective if the past practice of short-term and last-minute changes in housing legislation is modified. This practice has sometimes created uncertainties no less aggravating to builders and mortgage lenders than the uncertainties of market forces.

The timing of federal aids in any form will assume increasing significance if their influence on the volume of residential construction becomes more pronounced. In the first place, timing will have a bearing on the effectiveness of aids in meeting the objective of a larger, sustained volume of residential construction in price and rental ranges within the reach of a wider segment of the population. Second, the general economic and fiscal implications of federal housing programs will need to be considered.

It is instructive in this connection to examine the record of experience in the timing of government aids to date — a record covering more than 15 years.

A review of this record dampens any expectation that proper timing of federal credit aids might moderate the violence of long swings in residential construction. The policy of expansion of federal credit aids and liberalization of credit terms, inaugurated during the late thirties in a period of low construction volume and low prices and rents for existing residential real estate, was continued and intensified during the postwar years when pressures on all resources and particularly construction resources were great and prices rising or high.

"There has been little recognition in federal policy of the fundamental difference in the effects of liberal credit during periods of substantial underutilization of resources and during periods of full employment or overemployment of resources. During the thirties, of course, it was possible through liberal credit to stimulate the demand for housing without substantial rise in the cost of, and the price for, new dwellings. The large unused resources for construction could be brought back into employment without bidding up wages and materials prices. Moreover, the market for existing houses was a buyers' market in most areas and localities, and the large number of such houses offered for sale at distress or near-distress prices served as a check on prices for new dwellings. When the volume of new construction is limited by materials and labor supply and a sellers' market prevails for existing houses, as was the case from VJ-day to late in 1948, liberal credit is likely to push up costs and prices rather than to increase production, i.e., to be inflationary."[16]

There is evidence that in a sellers' market more generous credit terms were eventually capitalized into higher house prices and larger loan amounts, which diminished the benefits of lower interest rates, longer amortization periods, and lower or no downpayment requirements. Liberalization of credit under these conditions tended to defeat its purpose of helping lower income groups to buy houses.

There may be some question whether the record after World War II represents a fair test of the political and social difficulties that beset a policy designed to bring greater stability to residential construction. The test has been limited to a postwar period in which a severe housing shortage and the problem of providing housing for veterans created unusual pressures. Nevertheless, it may be reasonable to draw this much of an inference: the fact that housing has been increasingly clothed with public interest and that the volume of residential building is subject to strong governmental influences does not of itself assure greater stability. A real conflict may exist between the social objective of economic stability and the social objective of maximum volume of housing construction when there is full employment and general pressure on resources. In such a situation, "housing production cannot be maximized without sacrifice of economic stability," and "economic stability cannot be maintained without sacrifice of maximum housing construction."[17]

Whatever the merits of this analysis as applied to the years fol-

---

[16] Leo Grebler, "Stabilizing Residential Construction — A Review of the Postwar Test," *American Economic Review* XXXIX, No. 5, September 1949, pp. 901-2. On the relationship between credit terms and price levels, see also Ernest M. Fisher, *Urban Real Estate Markets,* pp. 69-90, and "The Role of Credit in the Real Estate Market," address before the 41st Annual Meeting of the American Life Convention in Chicago, October 7-11, 1946.

[17] Leo Grebler, *op. cit.,* p. 906.

lowing World War II, the need for meshing existing and new federal aids to residential construction with general fiscal and economic policy is becoming increasingly apparent. It was recognized in the institution of Regulation X after the outbreak of the Korean hostilities and in accompanying restrictions on FHA and VA mortgage loans. The principle is also embodied in the provision of federal funds for urban redevelopment and of federal contributions for public housing.[18] But the transformation of principle into practical policy always requires statesmanship in the face of social pressures and, more fundamentally, a balancing by the community-at-large of reasonable expectations of long-run benefit against apparent or real short-term advantages. The solution of this problem will in large measure determine whether the government's influence on residential construction will tend toward greater stability in this important sector of the economy.

Finally, a trend toward a larger role of the federal government in the financing of residential construction would loosen if not break the nexus between the savings process and investment in new residential real estate. Historically, the flow of funds into housing construction has been determined by the economic forces affecting the volume of savings and the alternative attractions of different types of investment, that is, new residential construction has competed with all other potential uses of savings. While the insurance or guarantee of residential mortgages has influenced their attractiveness relative to other investment outlets, direct government lending (already foreshadowed in the operations of the Federal National Mortgage Association) would tend to divorce the level of investment in new housing more clearly from the level of savings and the competition of other potential uses of savings. The federal

---

[18] Section 102 (e) of the Housing Act of 1949 stipulates that the annual amount of the federal notes and obligations authorized for loans to local public agencies for urban redevelopment may be increased by specified amounts "upon a determination by the President, after receiving advice from the Council of Economic Advisers as to the general effect of such increase upon the conditions in the building industry and upon the national economy, that such action is in the public interest." Section 304 (a) of the Act contains identical language in regard to the maximum amount of annual contributions which the Public Housing Authority is authorized to contract with local housing authorities. (Public Law 171, 81 Cong.)

government, too, may have to borrow money and may have to accommodate itself to changing conditions in the market for capital funds. But it has means of influencing that market which are beyond the power of private financial institutions. The restraints on federal financing for housing or any other purposes are less direct than those which operate on private financial institutions, and the choice of the use of federal funds for alternative investments is a matter of public decision rather than of relative attractiveness of investment outlets.

In conclusion, it appears that the level and timing of residential construction expenditures during the next few decades will depend more on political decisions than on the market-oriented decisions which were controlling before the thirties. Government interest and activity in this field will attempt to maintain a high volume of capital formation in residential construction, even in the face of declining market demand. The test of the effectiveness of such a policy under adverse conditions is yet to come. While it is true that political decisions can modify the operations of market forces, history is also replete with instances in which economic forces have modified the aspirations of the body politic. The most recent example in the field of government aids to private residential construction was the increase of maximum interest rates on VA and FHA home loans to $4\frac{1}{2}$ per cent in the spring of 1953, which was a belated adjustment to changed conditions in capital markets as well as a reflection of changed monetary policy.

In any event, governmental efforts to maintain a high level of residential building will most likely involve major changes in the institutional arrangements for allocating funds to new building activity. Under the FHA and VA programs the government to date has sought to meet its objectives by incentive, persuasion, and the assumption of risks. In this framework, many of the existing institutional arrangements in the creation and ownership of residential mortgage debt have been preserved. There is a real question whether these arrangements will or can be maintained if the public demand for new financial tools, such as direct lending by government, grows in intensity.

TABLE 8

New Nonfarm Dwelling Units Financed with FHA-Insured and VA-Guaranteed Loans Compared with All Privately Financed New Dwelling Units Started, 1935-1951

	FHA STARTS			VA STARTS[c]	TOTAL PRIVATELY FINANCED STARTS		
	Total (1)	One- to Four-Family Houses[a] (2)	Multifamily Structures[b] (3)	(4)	Total (5)	One- and Two-Family Houses (6)	Multifamily Structures (7)
1935	13,964	13,226	738	...	216,000	190,000	26,000
1936	49,376	48,752	624	...	304,000	252,000	52,000
1937	60,003	56,980	3,023	...	332,000	281,000	51,000
1938	118,741	106,811	11,930	...	399,000	334,000	65,000
1939	158,119	144,657	13,462	...	458,000	392,000	66,000
1940	180,091	176,645	3,446	...	530,000	474,000	56,000
1941	220,387	217,091	3,296	...	620,000	562,000	58,000
1942	165,662	160,204	5,458	...	301,000	270,000	31,000
1943	146,154	126,119	20,035	...	184,000	154,000	30,000
1944	93,259	83,604	9,655	...	139,000	125,000	14,000
1945	41,159	38,897	2,262	6,000	208,000	193,000	15,000
1946	69,033	67,122	1,911	83,000	662,000	614,000	48,000
1947	228,818	178,052	50,766	211,000	846,000	774,000	72,000
1948	291,053	213,443	77,610	102,000	914,000	810,000	104,000
1949	360,538	249,465	111,076	105,000	989,000	827,000	162,000
1950	485,933	327,866	158,064	200,000	1,352,000	1,193,000	159,000
1951	263,523	188,252	75,271	149,000	1,023,000	938,000	85,000
1935-1951	2,945,813	2,397,186	548,627	856,000	9,477,000	8,383,000	1,094,000

Notes to Table 8:

[a] Based on FHA first compliance inspections, excluding a small number of new dwelling units financed under Title I, Class 3 of the National Housing Act.

[b] Includes rental and cooperative housing projects and military housing (Secs. 207, 213, 608, and 803); Sec. 611 projects included under 1- and 4-family houses.

[c] Estimated on basis of first mortgage loans guaranteed by VA prior to June 1950, since then based on VA first compliance inspection.

Source: Housing and Home Finance Agency, *Housing Statistics,* January 1952, p. 38. The comparison between starts under the FHA and VA programs with total starts is only approximate in respect to units for owner-occupancy and rental. In this comparison, one- and two-family houses reported by the Bureau of Labor Statistics are assumed to be built for owner occupancy, and units in three- or more family dwellings (multifamily structures) are assumed to be built for rent. The classification of FHA starts by units in one- to four-family houses and rental projects does not quite match the BLS classification. Likewise, some of the new houses bought on VA guaranteed loans may contain one or more dwelling units for rent. However, the proportion of dwelling units in FHA and VA financed two- to four-family houses (as against single-family houses) has been very small. Finally, definitions of type of structure vary. For example, a group of row houses for rent may be classified by FHA as a multifamily (rental) housing project and by the BLS as single-family houses.

TABLE 9

FHA and VA Loans Made on One- to Four-Family Houses in Million Dollars and as a Per Cent of Total Loans of This Kind 1935-1951

	FHA-INSURED LOANS		VA-GUARANTEED LOANS		FHA AND VA
	Amount	Per Cent of Total	Amount	Per Cent of Total	AS PER CENT OF TOTAL
	(1)	(2)	(3)	(4)	(5)
1935	94	4.2	....	....	4.2
1936	309	13.4	....	....	13.4
1937	424	16.4	....	....	16.4
1938	473	19.4	....	....	19.4
1939	669	23.0	....	....	23.0
1940	736	21.0	....	....	21.0
1941	890	22.6	....	....	22.6
1942	958	28.9	....	....	28.9
1943	762	22.7	....	....	22.7
1944	707	17.7	....	....	17.7
1945	474	9.7	192	3.9	13.6
1946	422	4.2	2,302	23.0	27.2
1947	895	8.0	3,286	29.3	37.3
1948	2,109	18.6	1,881	16.6	35.2
1949	2,198	19.9	1,424	12.9	32.8
1950	2,489	15.5	3,073	19.2	34.7
1951	1,935	....	3,614	....	....

SOURCE, BY COLUMN:

(1) Housing and Home Finance Agency, *Annual Report, 1950,* Table 4, p. 238, and *Housing Statistics,* January 1952, p. 48. Excludes a small amount of home mortgages insured under Title I, Class 3.

(2), (4) Totals estimated by Home Loan Bank Board, "Estimated Home Mortgage Debt and Lending Activity, 1950."

(3) Housing and Home Finance Agency, *Annual Report, 1950,* Table 18, p. 133, and *Housing Statistics,* January 1952, p. 50. The 1945 figure includes small amount of VA loans closed in 1944.

(5) Sum of Cols. 2 and 4.

TABLE 10

FHA and VA Loans Held by Principal Types of Lenders in Million Dollars and as Per Cent of Their Residential Loans Year-Ends, 1940-1950

END OF YEAR	FHA AND VA MORTGAGES	TOTAL RESIDENTIAL MORTGAGES[a]	FHA AND VA AS A PER CENT OF TOTAL
A Life Insurance Companies[b]			
1940	$ 668	$ 2,887	23.1
1941	815	3,235	25.2
1942	1,096	3,625	30.2
1943	1,286	3,835	33.5
1944	1,408	3,819	36.9
1945	1,425	3,632	39.2
1946	1,484	4,021	36.9
1947	2,260	5,005	45.2
1948	3,482	6,754	51.6
1949	4,672	8,232	56.8
1950	6,597	11,035	59.8
B Mutual Savings Banks[c]			
1947	807	3,937	20.5
1948	1,334	4,758	28.0
1949	1,943	5,569	34.9
1950	3,006	7,054	42.6
C Insured Commercial Banks[d]			
1950	4,799	9,344	51.4
D Insured Savings and Loan Associations[e]			
1947	2,025	6,592	30.7
1948	2,326	7,783	29.9
1949	2,658	9,037	29.4
1950	3,242	11,188	29.0

[a] Totals as estimated in the forthcoming monograph.
[b] For FHA and VA mortgages: Institute of Life Insurance, *Life Insurance Fact Books*, except for 1945 and 1946, which include rough estimates for VA loan holdings. FHA holdings were $1,394 million in 1945 and $1,228 million in 1946.
[c] For FHA and VA mortgages: Reports "Mutual Savings Bank Mortgage Loan Activities" of the National Association of Mutual Savings Banks.
[d] Federal Deposit Insurance Corporation, *Report No. 33*. Figures as of June 30.
[e] Home Loan Bank Board, *Statistical Summary*, 1950 and 1951.

TABLE 11

Transfers Among Mortgagees of FHA-Insured Home Loans
1935-1950
(dollar amounts in millions; numbers of loans in thousands)

	FACE AMOUNT OF LOANS TRANSFERRED		NUMBER OF LOANS TRANSFERRED (3)	NUMBER OF LOANS IN FORCE AT YEAR END (4)	COL. 3 AS A % OF COL. 4 (5)
	Total[a] (1)	Excl. of Federal Agencies[b] (2)			
1935-36	65	54	n.a.	....	....
1937	115	93	n.a.	....	....
1938	199	153	n.a.	....	....
1939	309	230	n.a.	....	....
1940	401	343	n.a.	....	....
1941	442	400	n.a.	....	....
1942	492	462	n.a.	....	....
1943	594	480	n.a.	....	....
1944	463	429	n.a.	....	....
1945	478	395	n.a.	....	....
1946	266	244	56	940	6.0
1947	278	276	51	912	5.6
1948	887	784	134	1,088	12.3
1949[c]	1,100	841	157	1,302	12.1
1950[c]	1,421	1,292	202	1,511	13.4

[a] Face amount of loans purchased and sold. Includes resales but excludes inter-federal agency transfers.

[b] Column 1 minus net purchases or sales of federal agencies as shown in Table 13.

[c] Beginning 1949 data include mortgages insured under Sec. 603 pursuant to Sec. 610.

n.a. = not available.

SOURCE: *Annual Reports* of Federal Housing Administration.

TABLE 12

Purchases and Sales of FHA-Insured Home Mortgages by Private Institutional Mortgage Lenders
(millions of dollars)

	COMMERCIAL BANKS		INSURANCE COMPANIES		SAVINGS AND LOAN ASSOCIATIONS		SAVINGS BANKS		TOTAL	
	Purchases	Sales	Purchases	Sales	Purchases	Sales	Purchases	Sales	Purchases	Sales
1938	54	80	64	8	6	16	8	1	132	105
1939	87	114	94	12	7	18	18	0	206	144
1940	123	121	55	22	8	33	34	3	220	169
1941	126	149	198	25	7	30	29	5	360	209
1942	142	168	244	16	5	31	35	6	425	220
1943	194	151	263	25	23	24	40	2	520	202
1944	132	142	187	25	9	30	63	1	391	198
1945	173	125	190	22	14	18	46	4	423	169
1946	121	70	99	20	5	14	21	2	246	106
1947	98	86	133	25	3	21	30	1	294	163
1948	157	253	487	60	3	48	90	3	737	364
1949	86	281	569	80	4	73	145	7	804	541
1950	230	320	757	74	17	64	268	11	1,272	669

SOURCE: *Annual Reports* of Federal Housing Administration. Annual data prior to 1938 are not available.

TABLE 13

Purchases and Sales of FHA Loans
on One- to Four-Family Houses
by Federal Agencies
1935-1950
(amounts in thousands of dollars)

	PURCHASES		SALES	
	Amount	Per Cent of All Purchases[a]	Amount	Per Cent of All Sales[a]
1935-36	$ 10,242	15.8	$ 73	*
1937	28,720	24.9	6,426	5.6
1938	56,447	28.3	10,489	5.3
1939	87,865	28.4	9,002	2.9
1940	63,644	15.9	5,584	1.4
1941	47,184	10.7	4,762	1.1
1942	39,576	8.1	9,842	2.0
1943	41,568	7.0	156,004	26.3
1944	48,339	10.4	13,976	3.0
1945	20,848	4.4	104,256	21.8
1946	910	*	23,095	8.7
1947	179	*	1,914	0.7
1948	104,264	11.8	1,461	*
1949	259,880	23.6	991	*
1950	82,432	5.8	211,591	14.9
Total	$892,098	11.9	$559,466	7.4

[a] Per cent of total purchase and sales by all mortgagees, as shown in column 1 of Table 11.

*Less than 0.5 per cent.

SOURCE: FHA *Annual Reports*. Sales include resales. Federal agencies include the RFC Mortgage Company, Federal National Mortgage Association, Federal Deposit Insurance Corporation, U. S. Housing Corporation.

Other National Bureau Publications

STUDIES IN URBAN MORTGAGE FINANCING (BOOKS)

1. *Urban Mortgage Lending by Life Insurance Companies* (1950)
   R. J. Saulnier — 202 pp., 2.50

2. *The Impact of Government on Real Estate Finance in the United States* (1950)
   Miles L. Colean — 190 pp., 2.50

3. *Urban Real Estate Markets: Characteristics and Financing* (1951)
   Ernest M. Fisher — 208 pp., 3.00

4. *History and Policies of the Home Owners' Loan Corporation* (1951)
   C. Lowell Harriss — 224 pp., 3.00

5. *Commercial Bank Activities in Urban Mortgage Financing* (1952)
   Carl F. Behrens — 152 pp., 2.50

OCCASIONAL PAPERS

3. *Finished Commodities since 1879: Output and Its Composition* (1941)
   William H. Shaw — .25

5. *Railway Freight Traffic in Prosperity and Depression* (1942)
   Thor Hultgren — .25

10. *The Effect of War on Business Financing: Manufacturing and Trade, World War I* (1943)
    C. H. Schmidt and R. A. Young — .50

11. *The Effect of War on Currency and Deposits* (1943)
    Charles R. Whittlesey — .35

12. *Prices in a War Economy: Some Aspects of the Present Price Structure of the United States* (1943)
    Frederick C. Mills — .50

13. *Railroad Travel and the State of Business* (1943)
    Thor Hultgren — .35

14. *The Labor Force in Wartime America* (1944)
    Clarence D. Long — .50

15. *Railway Traffic Expansion and Use of Resources in World War II* (1944)
    Thor Hultgren — .35

17. *National Product, War and Prewar* (1944)
    Simon Kuznets — .50

18. *Production of Industrial Materials in World Wars I and II* (1944)
    Geoffrey H. Moore — .50

19. *Canada's Financial System in War* (1944)
    Benjamin H. Higgins — .50

20. *Nazi War Finance and Banking* (1944)
    Otto Nathan — .50

22	*Bank Liquidity and the War* (1945) Charles R. Whittlesey	.50
23	*Labor Savings in American Industry, 1899-1939* (1945) Solomon Fabricant	.50
24	*Domestic Servants in the United States, 1900-1940* (1946) George J. Stigler	.50
25	*Recent Developments in Dominion-Provincial Fiscal Relations in Canada* (1948) J. A. Maxwell	.50
27	*The Structure of Postwar Prices* (1948) Frederick C. Mills	.75
28	*Lombard Street in War and Reconstruction* (1949) Benjamin H. Higgins	1.00
29	*The Rising Trend of Government Employment* (1949) Solomon Fabricant	.50
30	*Costs and Returns on Farm Mortgage Lending by Life Insurance Companies, 1945-1947* (1949) R. J. Saulnier	1.00
31	*Statistical Indicators of Cyclical Revivals and Recessions* (1950) Geoffrey H. Moore	1.50
32	*Cyclical Diversities in the Fortunes of Industrial Corporations* (1950) Thor Hultgren	.50
33	*Employment and Compensation in Education* (1950) George J. Stigler	1.00
34	*Behavior of Wage Rates during Business Cycles* (1950) Daniel Creamer	1.00
35	*Shares of Upper Income Groups in Income and Savings* (1950) Simon Kuznets	1.00
36	*The Labor Force in War and Transition: Four Countries* (1952) Clarence D. Long	1.00
37	*Trends and Cycles in Corporate Bond Financing* (1952) W. Braddock Hickman	.75
38	*Productivity and Economic Progress* (1952) Frederick C. Mills	.75

TECHNICAL PAPERS

3	*Basic Yields of Corporate Bonds, 1900-1942* (1942) David Durand	.50
4	*Currency Held by the Public, the Banks, and the Treasury, Monthly, December 1917-December 1944* (1947) Anna Jacobson Schwartz and Elma Oliver	.75
5	*Concerning a New Federal Financial Statement* (1947) Morris A. Copeland	1.00
7	*Factors Affecting the Demand for Consumer Instalment Sales Credit* (1952) Avram Kisselgoff	1.50
8	*A Study of Aggregate Consumption Functions* Robert Ferber	(in press)

How to Obtain
National Bureau Publications

The National Bureau of Economic Research is a nonprofit membership corporation organized to make impartial studies in economic science.

Its books are published and distributed (since April 1, 1953) by Princeton University Press; its *Occasional Papers* and *Technical Papers* are published and distributed by the National Bureau itself.

Publications may be obtained either on contributing subscriptions or by purchase.

A contributor of $25 or more a year receives a complimentary copy of each current publication — *books, Occasional Papers, Technical Papers,* and the *Annual Report* — in advance of release to the public. In addition, a contributor is entitled to a one-third discount on all National Bureau publications purchased.

An associate contributor of $5 a year receives complimentary copies of *Occasional Papers, Technical Papers,* and the *Annual Report,* and is entitled to a one-third discount on all publications purchased. Only the following are eligible to become associates: teachers, students, and libraries in recognized educational institutions; members of scientific societies or of private nonprofit research agencies.

A contributor of $2 receives four issues of the *Occasional Paper* or *Technical Paper,* and the *Annual Report.*

Contributions to the National Bureau are deductible in calculating federal income taxes.

NON-CONTRIBUTORS should send orders for *books* to:

> Princeton University Press
> Princeton, New Jersey

NON-CONTRIBUTORS should send orders for *Papers* and requests for the *Annual Report* directly to:

CONTRIBUTORS should send all orders for *books* and *Papers,* and requests for the *Annual Report* directly to:

NATIONAL BUREAU OF ECONOMIC RESEARCH, INC.
1819 Broadway   New York 23, N. Y.